Introduction
to
VAX-11
ARCHITECTURE AND ASSEMBLY LANGUAGE

Thomas S. Frank

Le Moyne College, Syracuse

PRENTICE-HALL, INC., Englewood Cliffs, NJ 07632

Library of Congress Cataloging-in-Publication Data

Frank, Thomas S., (date)
    Introduction to VAX-11 architecture and assembly
language.

    Includes index.
    1. VAX-11 (Computer)—Programming. 2. Computer
architecture. 3. Assembler language (Computer program
language) I. Title.
QA76.8.V37F73   1987   005.2′45   86-21229
ISBN 0-13-498841-8

Editorial/production supervision
    and interior design by Margaret Rizzi
Cover design by 20/20 Services, Inc.
Manufacturing buyer: Ed O'Dougherty

© 1987 by Prentice-Hall, Inc.
A Division of Simon & Schuster
Englewood Cliffs, New Jersey 07632

Printed in the United States of America

10 9 8 7 6 5 4 3 2 1

ISBN 0-13-498841-8   025

PRENTICE-HALL INTERNATIONAL (UK) LIMITED, *London*
PRENTICE-HALL OF AUSTRALIA PTY. LIMITED, *Sydney*
PRENTICE-HALL CANADA INC., *Toronto*
PRENTICE-HALL HISPANOAMERICANA, S.A., *Mexico*
PRENTICE-HALL OF INDIA PRIVATE LIMITED, *New Delhi*
PRENTICE-HALL OF JAPAN, INC., *Tokyo*
PRENTICE-HALL OF SOUTHEAST ASIA PTE. LTD., *Singapore*
EDITORA PRENTICE-HALL DO BRASIL, LTDA., *Rio de Janeiro*

CONTENTS

Preface   *xi*

PART I
**FUNDAMENTALS OF COMPUTER HARDWARE
AND PROGRAMMING**

1   BASIC COMPUTER SYSTEMS   *1*

    1.1   Computers, 1
    1.2   Basic Computer Systems, 2
    1.3   Main Memory, 3
    1.4   Peripheral Devices, 3
    1.5   The Central Processing Unit, 4
    1.6   Buses, 5
    1.7   Closing Comment, 6

2   MAIN MEMORY AND COMPUTER ARITHMETIC   *7*

    2.1   Information, 7
    2.2   Stored Information, 8
    2.3   Computer Storage Devices, 9
    2.4   Memory Units, 11
    2.5   Number Representations, 12
    2.6   A Change in Notation, 16

2.7   Computer Words and Main Memory, 17
2.8   Computer Number Systems and Arithmetic, 18
2.9   Signed Numbers, 20
2.10 Twos-Complement Arithmetic, 27
2.11 The Central Processing Unit Condition Codes, 30
2.12 Exercises, 32

3   LOGIC   *37*

3.1   Statements and Connectives, 37
3.2   Switching Circuits, 42
3.3   Statements Revisited, 44
3.4   Logic Gates, 44
3.5   Some Simple Computer Circuitry, 49
3.6   Exercises, 52

4   MEMORY ADDRESSING AND DATATYPES   *56*

4.1   8-Bit Memory Units (Bytes), 56
4.2   Number Representations, 57
4.3   Memory Addresses, 59
4.4   Some Additional Memory Structures, 61
4.5   Ambiguity of the Addressing Scheme, 63
4.6   Datatypes, 63
4.7   The *Character* Datatype, 64
4.8   Closing Comments, 66
4.9   Exercises, 66

5   INSTRUCTION EXECUTION AND STORED PROGRAM COMPUTERS   *70*

5.1   Introduction, 70
5.2   Operations and Instructions, 71
5.3   Main Memory Accessing, 72
5.4   The Stored Instruction Concept, 73
5.5   The Program Counter and Instruction Execution, 77
5.6   The Instruction Execution Cycle, 82
5.7   Loading Main Memory, 84
5.8   Branching, 84
5.9   Conditional Branching and the Processor Status Register, 90
5.10 A Simple Addition Program, 95
5.11 The General Registers, 97
5.12 Putting the General Registers to Use, 99
5.13 Closing Comment, 101
5.14 Exercises, 102

6   MACHINE LANGUAGE PROGRAMS AND PROGRAM ASSEMBLY   *105*

6.1   Machine Language Programs, 105
6.2   A Sample Program, 106

Contents

6.3   A Mnemonic Language, 116
6.4   The Sample Program Again, Written in Mnemonics, 122
6.5   The Assembly of the Mnemonic Program, 127
6.6   The VAX Assembler, 134
6.7   The Program Entry Mask Word, 142
6.8   Exercises, 145

PART II
BASIC VAX ARCHITECTURE

7   VAX ADDRESSING MODES   *148*

7.1   Operations and Instructions, 148
7.2   Operand Specifiers, 149
7.3   Mode Bytes, 150
7.4   Operand Access Modes: General Register Addressing, 152
7.5   Modes 0, 1, 2, and 3: *Short Literal* Mode, 173
7.6   Operand Access Modes: Program Counter Addressing, 176
7.7   Summary of Addressing Modes, 188
7.8   Exercises, 190

**8   BASIC VAX OPERATIONS
AND ASSEMBLER DIRECTIVES   *195***

8.1   Introduction, 195
8.2   Operand Descriptors, 197
8.3   Data Transfer and Conversion Operations, 200
8.4   Control Transfer Operations, 205
8.5   Arithmetic Operations, 206
8.6   Bit Operations, 214
8.7   Loop-Controlling Operations, 225
8.8   Miscellaneous Operations, 229
8.9   Basic Assembler Directives, 230
8.10   Some Programming Examples, 235
8.11   Exercises, 239

9   SUBROUTINES, STACKS, AND PROCEDURES   *245*

9.1   Introduction to Subroutines, 245
9.2   A First Solution to the "Subroutine Return" Problem, 248
9.3   The Transmission of Arguments to a Subroutine, 251
9.4   Deficiencies of the "Subroutine Return" Scheme, 253
9.5   A Second Solution to the "Subroutine Return" Problem, 261
9.6   Stacks and Their Uses, 274
9.7   The Hardware Stack and Jump-to-Subroutine Operations, 281
9.8   Some Other Stack Operations, 286
9.9   Transmitting Arguments in an Argument Table, 288
9.10   Transmitting Arguments on the Stack, 297
9.11   The CALLS and CALLG Operations, 303

9.12 The Nesting of CALLG and CALLS Operations, 314
9.13 CALLG and CALLS Programming Examples, 317
9.14 Terminology, Conventions, and Closing Comments, 326
9.15 Exercises, 328

10 EXTERNAL SYMBOLS, LOADING, RELOCATION, AND LINKING *336*

10.1 Introduction, 336
10.2 Externally Defined Symbols and the .EXTERNAL Directive, 340
10.3 Object Module Loading and Relocation, 341
10.4 The Resolution of External References, 347
10.5 The VAX Linker and Object Module Linking, 352
10.6 The Structure of VAX Object Files, 354
10.7 Position-Independent Code and Program Relocation, 355
10.8 Exercises, 356

PART III
**EXTENSIONS OF THE VAX ARCHITECTURE
AND ASSEMBLER**

11 EXCEPTIONS AND CONDITION HANDLING *359*

11.1 Errors, 359
11.2 Traps and Faults, 360
11.3 Exception Handling, 361
11.4 User-Written Exception Handlers, 363
11.5 Exception Handlers for Mainline Programs, 369
11.6 Multiple Exception Handlers, 370
11.7 Default Exception Handlers, 372
11.8 Further Comments on Exception Handling, 372
11.9 Exercises, 373

12 FLOATING-POINT DATATYPES *375*

12.1 Introduction, 375
12.2 Fixed-Point Data, 375
12.3 Floating-Point Data, 377
12.4 A Representation Scheme for Floating-Point Numbers, 380
12.5 The Floating-Point Number Zero, 389
12.6 Floating-Point Ranges and Precision, 390
12.7 Truncation Versus Rounding, 390
12.8 Closing Comments, 397
12.9 VAX Floating-Point Representations, 398
12.10 Floating-Point Directives, 401
12.11 Floating-Point Operations, 401
12.12 Addressing Mode Considerations, 402
12.13 Exercises, 404

13   NUMERICAL STRING DATATYPES   407

13.1   Strings of Digits, 407
13.2   Leading Separate Numeric Strings, 408
13.3   Trailing Numeric Strings, 410
13.4   Packed Decimal Strings, 412
13.5   Conversions Between Datatypes, 415
13.6   Arithmetic Operations on Packed Decimal Strings, 418
13.7   A Programming Example, 420
13.8   Closing Comments, 420
13.9   Exercises, 422

14   CHARACTER STRINGS   426

14.1   Character Strings, 426
14.2   Basic Character String Operations, 427
14.3   Character Strings and Translation Tables, 435
14.4   Exercises, 441

15   VARIABLE-LENGTH BIT FIELDS   445

15.1   A Binary-to-Hexadecimal Conversion Algorithm, 445
15.2   Variable-Length Bit Fields, 447
15.3   Variable-Length Bit Field Operations, 449
15.4   A Bit Field Programming Example, 454
15.5   Exercises, 457

16   LINKED LISTS AND QUEUES   460

16.1   Linked Lists, 460
16.2   Basic Operations on Linked Lists, 465
16.3   Linked Lists with Header Entries, 467
16.4   The Management of Available Storage in Linked Lists, 471
16.5   Bidirectional Linked Lists, 475
16.6   The VAX Operations INSQUE and REMQUE, 477
16.7   Circular Lists and Queues, 479
16.8   Exercises, 480

17   PROGRAM SECTIONS   485

17.1   Program Modularization, 485
17.2   Program Sections, 486
17.3   The Management of Program Sections by the Linker, 490
17.4   Program Section Attributes, 492
17.5   The Global Nature of Program Section Names, 495
17.6   The FORTRAN "COMMON" Statement, 502
17.7   Exercises, 503

Contents

**18   MACROINSTRUCTIONS
        AND CONDITIONAL ASSEMBLIES   505**

18.1   Subroutines Revisited, 505
18.2   Macroinstructions, 506
18.3   The VAX Macroinstruction Assembler, 507
18.4   Passing Arguments to a Macroinstruction, 513
18.5   Elided Arguments, Default Values,
        and Keyword Arguments, 520
18.6   The Concatenation of Arguments, 523
18.7   Local Labels, 528
18.8   Automatically Generated Local Labels, 532
18.9   Repeat Blocks, 537
18.10   Conditional Assemblies: Immediate Conditionals, 545
18.11   Conditional Assemblies: Conditionals
        and Subconditionals, 553
18.12   The Directive .MEXIT, 558
18.13   Closing Comments, 560
18.14   Exercises, 562

APPENDICES

A   THE VAX INSTRUCTION SET   571

A.1   Operand Descriptors, 571
A.2   Notation, 573
A.3   The VAX Instruction Set in Mnemonic Order, 574
A.4   The VAX Instruction Set in Operation Code Order, 620

B   VAX-11 ASSEMBLER CONVENTIONS   623

B.1   Introduction, 623
B.2   The VAX Character, 623
B.3   Special Characters, 623
B.4   Source Statement Format, 624
B.5   Symbols, 625
B.6   Numbers, 626
B.7   The Location Counter, 626
B.8   The Unary Operator, Circumflex (^), 626
B.9   The Continuation Symbol, Hyphen (-), 628
B.10   The Repeat Count Symbol, [...], 628
B.11   The Arithmetic Shift Operator, Commercial-At (@), 629
B.12   The Logical Operators AND (&), OR (!),
        and EXCLUSIVE-OR (\), 629
B.13   Assembler Directives, 630
B.14   Assembly Time Errors, 632

C   TABLE OF ASCII CODES   635

D   **THE INPUT/OUTPUT MACROINSTRUCTIONS**   *637*

D.1   Introduction, 637
D.2   Basic Character Output Macroinstructions, 638
D.3   Character and Character String Input Macroinstructions, 640
D.4   Numerical Output Macroinstructions, 641
D.5   Numerical Input Macroinstructions, 643
D.6   Implementation of the Macroinstructions, 645
D.7   Floating-Point Input and Output, 656

E   **SOLUTIONS TO SELECTED EXERCISES**   *659*

Index   *673*

Contents

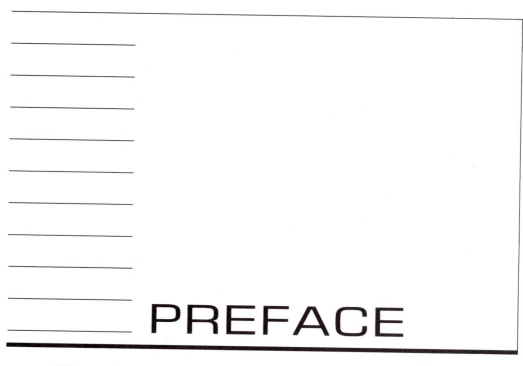

PREFACE

This text is intended for use in a one-semester course in the fundamentals of computer hardware, architecture and programming, as viewed by the assembly language programmer. The conscientious student who completes this material will have a basic understanding of the components that make up a computer system and how they relate to one another, as well as a knowledge of the machine instructions used by such systems to manipulate data. In addition, the student will have developed some proficiency in assembly language programming and will be in an excellent position quickly to progress in those areas of computer science which require some depth of understanding of machine concepts, including microprocessing, system programming and computer architecture.

The prerequisites for an understanding of the text material are quite modest. In particular, no background in electronics is assumed, since the development of gates and circuits in the early chapters is self-contained. Indeed, hardware is discussed more at a *concepts* rather than an *electronics* level; thus, for example, while the logic diagram for the 4-bit full adder is discussed in some detail, it is done in an attempt to remove some of the mystery of how computers can do arithmetic electronically; it is the *concept* of electronic addition that henceforth plays the principal role, not the gates that form that unit, how it is integrated into the ALU, or the ways in which data is routed to it from processor registers. In a similar fashion, destructive reading of memory and the need for memory refreshing are mentioned, but the details of how these are dealt with are intentionally omitted, for to do otherwise would distract from the main focus of the text and would require more background than we choose to assume. Such details are more properly left to courses in computer architecture or digital electronics, once the student understands *what* the problems are, *how* they arise and *why* they need to be addressed.

We do assume that the student has had some prior experience with programming, preferably in a high-level language. For while programming at a *machine* or *assembly language* level is discussed in much detail, the general programming concepts of problem analysis and algorithm design are assumed to be familiar ground. In like fashion, the structure and style that lead to readable and easily maintained programs are taught more through example than precept. The student without some minimal background in these concepts would be at a decided disadvantage.

Finally, we deem the most important attribute that a student can bring to any course dealing with the present topics to be *perseverance*. Many of the concepts themselves are nontrivial, and the programming at this level can be quite frustrating, even for the experienced practitioner. An ability to cope with and learn from persistent errors will pay huge dividends in the long term.

By almost any standards, the VAX has a highly complex architecture, a fact which makes it perhaps not the ideal machine for the student's first encounter with computers at this level. For this reason much attention has been paid to the *organization* of the text, with many of the esoterica of the system initially stripped away in order that the basic machine might more easily be studied. Specifically, Part 1 deals with a number of introductory topics which are for the most part machine-independent. These include concepts of basic hardware, arithmetic, number systems, logic and circuitry, memory addressing, and datatypes. The stored-program computer is also introduced here, along with registers, address pointers, computer operations and instructions and elementary programming concepts. This part concludes with a detailed look at a small but complete program, how it is fashioned "by hand" from the VAX operations into executable code, and finally how the VAX assembler takes over most of the tasks by the translation of user-defined mnemonics.

Part 2 deals with basic VAX architecture concepts, including addressing modes and the fundamental arithmetical, logical and bit-manipulating operations. A vast amount of detail is included here, a fact for which we make no apologies. The concepts are difficult upon first encounter, and the student who understands them only in a fuzzy fashion will surely experience frustrating disappointment in his or her programming efforts. [For example, the student who does not understand just *when* in the execution cycle of an autoincremented instruction the incrementing takes place will scarcely be able to make sense of an instruction such as **CMPW (R2)+,(R2)+**.] The final topic of Part 2 concerns subroutines, the rather complex CALL operations (the first operations the student encounters which are in a sense nonstandard, VAX-specific operations), and external symbols and program module linking.

Finally, Part 3 of the text deals with those features that go to distinguish the VAX from other computers. The remaining datatypes are introduced here (floating point, numeric string, character string, and variable length bit field). Other concepts include error (condition) handling, macroinstructions, conditional assemblies, and program sections. We recognize that the VAX has an architecture which is so rich that it is unlikely that all of its features can normally be investigated in the period of a single semester, and yet Parts 1 and 2 are inadequate to fill a semester's course. For this reason each chapter of Part 3 has been designed to depend at most on the material of Parts 1 and 2, and in particular to be independent of the other chapters of Part 3. The instructor may thus select from these topics those which best suit his or her specific interests or needs. In addition, these chapters contain many illustrative examples and a level of detail in the exposition designed to make them suitable for self-study by any student conversant with the material of Parts 1 and 2.

As much care has been taken with the *development* of the material as with its organization. Insofar as is possible, each new topic is introduced by considering some problem which can be stated in terms already familiar, which is of interest, and the solution to which is accessible with currently available tools. Thus, for example, the subroutine concept is stated as a problem involving the desirability of conserving code, and this problem is dealt with using only known operations. This leads in a natural way to companion "jump-to/return-from" instructions, which in turn lead ultimately to the development of the stack concept. And the need to transmit arguments to subroutines leads further to the "discovery" of the CALL operations.

The book contains over 200 programming examples, in the form of complete programs or program segments, and for all but a few of these, detailed discussions are included in the accompanying text. End-of-chapter exercises are aimed at specific chapter sections, and these are numbered accordingly—$C.S.n$ is the number of the nth exercise pertaining to section S of Chapter C. The exercises range from routine computational problems; to *questions* (which might be called "oral exercises") in which, for example, the student is asked to view a familiar concept in a new light, or to consider the consequences of an apparently trivial change in some development, and which rarely require paper and pencil; to the writing of *segments*: a few lines of code to do a specific task; to the writing, debugging, testing and running of complete programs. Large-scale programming exercises—"term projects"—are not proposed, although some of the examples and other exercises might suggest them. Rather, it is felt that the individual instructor, drawing on his or her own interests, experience, and expertise, can better devise such projects consonant with the students' specific environment.

The appendices make the book particularly useful as a reference. The principal of these describes all but a few of the VAX operations at a level of detail similar to that found in the *VAX Architecture Handbook*. (The EDIT operations, along with POLY, EMOD, and the few operations which require special privileges are not discussed here or elsewhere.) Another appendix describes the VAX assembler conventions (character set, source line formatting, directives, error messages, and so forth). A third consists of a table of ASCII codes, in decimal and hexadecimal formats. About 40 percent of the text's exercises are solved in the final appendix.

Input-to and output-from programs written by the student—and especially those written early on in the course—always pose a problem for the instructor, since these activities are nontrivial at the assembly language level. Traditionally there are two solutions to this problem, the first of which is simply to employ the VAX debugger and insert breakpoints at certain key places in the program. We choose instead the other, equally popular technique, and supply the student (and instructor) with a procedure which contains a number of easily-used routines for input and output. If our offering in this direction is in any way unique, it is for three reasons. First, considering the amount of flexibility and convenience they provide, they are very *short*. (We recognize that an instructor may have to reproduce the source code for these modules.) Second, not all routines in the package need be implemented. Thus if only simple character input/output is all that is required in a particular environment, only those modules need be implemented, rather than the entire package since, as the result of various conditional statements in the modules, the routine "knows" what modules have been included in the package. And finally, the modules have been written in such a way that they appear to the user to correspond, insofar as possible, to the Pascal **read** (. . .), **readln, write** (. . .), and **writeln** procedures. The description of how these routines are used in a program along with completely documented source code is provided in an appendix.

The text does *not* deal in any detail with the various operating system programs which lie at the heart of file construction and management. Thus, although much discussion centers around VAX Macro as an *assembler*, and a chapter is devoted to linking and loading, there is little information provided which deals directly with the specifics of the VMS routines **LINK, EDIT, RMS, DEBUG**, and so forth. It is felt that the individual instructor, who knows the environment and the particular installation within which students will create, assemble, link, and execute their programs, can best supply this material on an *ad hoc* basis. The one exception to this position is found in the chapter on error (condition) handling, the point at which the VAX hardware and operating system software work most closely together.

Finally, a topic which might most naturally be included with material of the sort discussed here but which is absent from the present text is *processor interrupts* and *interrupt handling*. The combinations of bus structures which *might* be on any given VAX is so varied, and the processing is so complex (to say nothing of requiring privileges that virtually necessitate use of a dedicated system) that this topic is better left to separate instruction than to an inadequate exposition here.

The author wishes to acknowledge the support provided by the Le Moyne College Computer Center in the preparation of the manuscript and program listings, and the assistance of those students in CSC 162 who suffered through portions of the text in its draft form and proved to be the book's most insightful critics. And last, the expertise, suggestions, and guidance of Prentice-Hall, its editorial staff, and reviewers, is recognized with gratitude.

Thomas S. Frank

1

BASIC COMPUTER SYSTEMS

1.1 COMPUTERS

In this book we investigate **computers** in general and one in particular, the Digital Equipment Corporation *VAX-11*. We elect not to attempt any precise definition of the term "computer" for a variety of reasons. First, the variety of *kinds* of computers which are available these days is so vast that no single definition can come close to describing all of them. They range from the very specialized machines designed to do a specific job (automobile trip computers, those which control manufacturing processes on production lines, and the computers incorporated into the popular automatic phone dialers are three examples); to the small and inexpensive "personal" or microcomputers; to the midrange general-purpose mini- and superminicomputers (of which the VAX is an example); to the very large and powerful "mainframe" machines. (*Large* and *powerful* are adjectives which are not very well defined, but "large" generally refers to a computer's ability to "store" massive amounts of information, while "powerful" typically means that it can process—do arithmetic on—a large number of data in a very short time.)

A dictionary definition of a computer such as "a person or machine that computes" is far too broad, whereas "an automatic electronic machine that performs arithmetic" is simultaneously too broad and too narrow. For our purposes a more-or-less satisfactory descriptive phrase might be *an electronic, binary, stored-instruction, programmable, sequential, automatic data processor*, but until we understand what each of those words means, and how they are to be understood in this context, we have not advanced the problem very far. Indeed, it is precisely the purpose of much of the first part of this book to describe these terms and their context.

A final difficulty we have in attempting a definition of a computer is that various people view computers in different ways. To the user who programs in a high-level language, a computer is simply a machine that "understands" Pascal or FORTRAN, for example. To the computer engineer, a computer is electronic circuitry that behaves in a certain predictable way. Our view will be somewhere in between these two—we shall investigate the ways in which machines can be designed to "do" arithmetic, for example; and the reader will find references to high-level-language concepts. But for the most part we shall remain in a middle ground, studying the kinds of basic operations that a computer can perform, and the ways in which it performs them.

However we might view a computer, it is above all a *machine*, and in fact in comparison with many of the machines with which we have daily contact—automobiles and television sets, for example—it is relatively simple; the number of different things that a computer can do is quite limited. What gives a computer the *appearance* of complexity is the fact that the limited number of its primitive functions can be combined into an unlimited variety of *sequences* of actions, and this apparent complexity is further reinforced by the machine's *speed*—a few hundred billionths of a second is all that is required to perform each of these functions. But like any machine, to be truly useful a computer's behavior must be *predictable* and *controllable*, and we shall devote much time to an investigation of how the machine's primitive actions can be controlled, and how sequences of these actions can be formed to produce useful results.

1.2 BASIC COMPUTER SYSTEMS

Despite our failure adequately to define a computer, we can at least give a description of what we shall mean by a **basic computer system**. For our purposes, such a system will consist of the following components.

> **Central processing unit,** or **processor**
> **Main memory** or **main store**, or more simply, **memory** or **storage**
> **Peripheral devices**
> **Buses**

In the remainder of this chapter we describe these components and their functions, but only in the most general terms, in order that the reader might have some overview of the total structure of a computing system. In large measure the text is devoted to a study of the block diagram of Figure 1.2.1, what the purposes of the individual components are, and how they relate to one another.

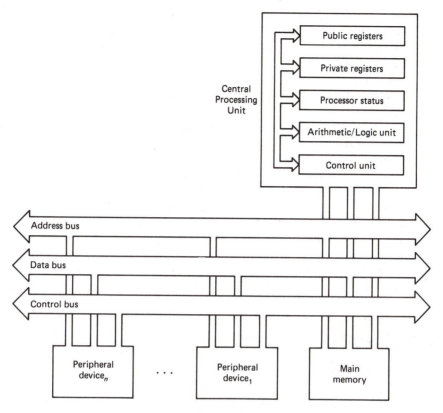

Figure 1.2.1

1.3. MAIN MEMORY

In a typical application, a computer may have to "manage" thousands of pieces of data or information, and those data must be "held" somewhere so as to be available for whatever manipulations are required of them. It is the purpose of the device that we have denoted **main memory** to "store" this information. For example, in order to add four numbers, the four numbers must "reside" in main memory so that they can be accessed by the central processing unit for adding. The result of the addition might be "stored" by the central processing unit back in main memory, possibly for further processing, or perhaps for printing. Main memory is sometimes referred to as **primary storage**.

1.4 PERIPHERAL DEVICES

We mentioned above that a computer system might, for example, calculate the sum of four numbers and store the result in main memory. And while it might be desirable for a machine to be able to do these kinds of arithmetic computations, its utility will be severely limited if the *user* cannot also access main memory in some fashion, so that, for example, the numbers to be added can be specified by placing them in main memory for the central processing unit's use, and in order that the result can be displayed in some fashion from main memory. Thus some device is required that acts as a channel of communication between the computing system and the outside word. A device that performs this function is known as a **communication device**, and it is one of two categories of computer **peripheral devices**.

A peripheral device is one that is connected to the central processing unit, but which is *not* an integral part of the central processing unit itself and is *not* main memory. Probably the most common peripheral device, one with which the reader is probably familiar, is the **computer terminal**, the typewriterlike device that allows the user more-or-less direct communication with the computer system. Others include printers, card readers, graphics displays, and plotters. These are all communications devices. The second category of peripheral devices is made up of the **bulk storage devices**, which provide extensions of main memory on which information can be stored, but normally *not* in a form that is directly usable by the outside world. Magnetic tapes and disks are examples of bulk storage devices, sometimes called **secondary storage devices**.

1.5 THE CENTRAL PROCESSING UNIT

By far the most complex device, and the one that is at the heart of the computing system, is the **central processing unit** (CPU), or more simply, the **processor**. This is where the majority of the activity takes place, and as we see from Figure 1.2.1, it is made up of a number of subunits, which we shall describe individually.

(a) Registers

The central processing unit contains a number of *registers* which, like the elements of main memory, may be used to store information. The distinctions between these register storage units and their main memory counterparts are that the registers are *not* a part of main memory and that data stored in registers are typically there for relatively short periods of time relative to information stored in main memory (although this need not be the case). There are two categories of processor registers, to which we informally give the following names.

Public registers. Public registers are memory units which can store data, and which are accessible to the computer system user. That is, the user can directly access and affect the contents of these storage units in the CPU, for whatever purpose.

Private registers. Private registers are memory units which can store data, but which are *not* accessible to the computer system user. They are for the "private" use of the central processor itself. (As an example, consider the subtraction problem $A - B$. The processor treats this problem in the following way. First, the negative $-B$ of the number B is calculated, and then that result is *added* to the number A. When the negative of B is calculated, it is put in a "processor-private" register, which is then added to A.)

(b) Processor status

The processor status is a collection of "indicators" which give some indication of the *current* state of the central processing unit at any moment. We cannot say much more about processor status at this point, except to give a simple example. Suppose that the processor carries out the subtraction $4 - 7$, as in the example above. Since the result of that subtraction is a negative number, at the completion of this arithmetic operation, one of the indicators in the processor status will show that the last processor operation yielded a *negative* result. In a similar fashion, $7 - 7$ would set the processor status in such a way as to indicate that the last operation yielded a *zero* result.

(c) Arithmetic-Logic Unit

As the name implies, it is in the **arithmetic-logic unit** (ALU) that the arithmetic operations are performed—addition, subtraction, and so on. Some "logical" operations are carried out here as well, and we shall see in Chapter 3 what these are.

(d) Control unit

The **control unit** in the CPU manages the movement of data within the processor. For example, the contents of public or private registers might have to be moved to the arithmetic-logic unit so that the latter unit can perform an arithmetic operation on them. Similarly, data might have to be moved from the processor to main memory for storage, or from main memory to the CPU for some kind of processing (an arithmetic operation, for instance). It is the responsibility of the control unit to manage this movement of data, and to do numerous other tasks as well. Incorporated within the control unit is a **decoder**, which determines just which operation the processor is to carry out at any time.

1.6 BUSES

Implicit in the discussions above is the *moving about* of information within the computing system—data are moved to the processor from memory for some arithmetic operation; the result is moved back to memory; some number, perhaps in a public register, is moved to a peripheral device for printing; and so on. A **bus** is simply a collection of wires that connect the various components of the system, and along which the data, in the form of electric currents, move. As indicated in Figure 1.2.1, a computer system typically has three such buses—sets of wires— the **address bus**, the **data bus**, and the **control bus**. Although we have now *named* them, it will be some time before we are in a position to see the significance of each of these buses.

We should comment that the "bus structure"—the way in which information is moved about—on the VAX is somewhat more complicated than what is described here, and further details are given in subsequent chapters. In the meantime, however, the diagram gives a perfectly accurate *conceptual* view of the VAX.

1.7 CLOSING COMMENT

Given this very sketchy description of computer systems, we do not expect that the reader will have a particularly clear picture of what the purposes of the various units are, how they function, and how they relate to one another. The addition of some of the details (registers, processor status, buses, and so on) has probably done little to enhance understanding. However, Figure 1.2.1 and the surrounding development has given us a start, and the reader is assured that most of the mysteries that we have introduced here will eventually be unveiled.

CHAPTER 2

MAIN MEMORY AND COMPUTER ARITHMETIC

2.1 INFORMATION

We noted in Chapter 1 that computers operate on *information* or *data*, the operations typically taking place within the central processing unit, and that we frequently need to "store" that information somehow for access by the computer system. We shall investigate in detail just how that information is stored and how stored information can be utilized; and in somewhat less depth we shall inquire into the actual devices that are used for such storage—the individual components that make up main memory.

A formal study of "information" is well beyond the scope of the book; the topic in all its details is so complex that entire branches of mathematics, physics, and engineering are devoted to it. One of the reasons for this complexity is the very nature of much of the information with which human beings are constantly bombarded, and which must thus be "processed." Auditory and visual information is more often than not so complex that its analysis is very difficult, if not altogether beyond reach. A half-hour television program or a Tchaikovsky symphony contains millions of pieces of information, and it is remarkable that the human brain has learned to deal with this much data, and apparently with little effort. In addition to meaningful data, we are also frequently confronted with *unwanted* information—**noise**, as it is usually called. Static on an AM radio as the result of a thunderstorm is "information"—it is the radio-frequency information contained in lightning discharges, which also contain visible information (the "flashes" themselves)—but since, relative to the radio broadcast, this information is unwanted, we refer to it as "noise." In driving an automobile a mile or two in city traffic we need to process in a successful fashion an incredible amount of both useful information and noise, yet we seem to be able to do so, frequently "without really thinking about it."

The few examples of information we have given are fairly complex, but we also deal on a daily basis with data that are especially simple. Suppose, for instance, that we enter a room and observe that the overhead light is *on*, or that it is *off*. The state of the light is information, but it is as crude as information can be. While the fixture may have various attributes, such as incandescent or fluorescent, ceiling-mounted or suspended, and so on, the light itself can exist in one and only one of two states—*on* and *off*—and thus from this standpoint the light can convey at any time *one* of only *two* pieces of information. In fact, a good deal of the information that we process is of this *yes-no, on-off, true-false* nature—it is "two-state" information. As information, it is so simple that it scarcely requires any analysis; its significance to us derives from the fact that the data that are processed in a computing system can always ultimately be reduced to information of a two-state nature.

2.2 STORED INFORMATION

The concept of **stored information** is a familiar one; books, audio and video tapes, and films are all examples of stored information. But the primary repository of stored information is the human brain in its function as a *memory device*. It will be useful to our development of computer concepts to examine briefly some of the familiar activities of human memory.

Although the actual psychological, biological and electrochemical mechanisms that come into play when we "remember" things, and then later "recall" them, are not completely understood, we can nonetheless distinguish among various *kinds* of memory. **Long-term memory** consists of events and data that we remember, frequently without conscious effort, for very long periods of time. Especially pleasant and unpleasant experiences seem to be "placed" in long-term memory, and these are apparently quite permanent—as much as we might like to, there seems to be no way to "erase" unpleasant memories. **Short-term memory** seems to hold information that is of little consequence to us, and we remember certain events for relatively short periods of time. For example, although we can probably remember what we had for breakfast this morning, or even yesterday morning, our breakfast of seven years ago today is ordinarily well beyond recall. Between these two types of memory there are gray areas of midrange memory—events or information that we may remember for some time, but not for extended periods.

The type of memory with which we shall concern ourselves is long-term memory in which the data "stored" there are the result of **memorization**—a **conscious effort** to remember. For example, the reader may not recall the details of *how* he or she learned the multiplication table, but certainly remembers the table itself. This information was placed in memory through a specific effort to do precisely that. Experience also shows that when data are memorized, apparently some periodic "refreshing" of that memorization process is required to ensure that the data are permanently "burned into" memory—once memorized, the multiplication table would be easily forgotten were it not for the fact that it is used so frequently.

Memorization of information has three significant aspects. First, the information remembered is **specific** rather than random—we select *particular* facts to be remembered. Second, through some conscious effort we **store** those facts in our memory, although just what goes on in doing so is only imperfectly understood. Third, the stored information can be **retrieved** upon demand. We shall require that computer memories have these features: The information the computer deals with must be *specific*, it must be able to be *stored* or saved somewhere, and it must be able to be *retrieved* when needed.

2.3 COMPUTER STORAGE DEVICES

What we are seeking in the way of a storage device is some sort of physical entity which can "store" information in such a way that the storage process itself, as well as the process required to retrieve that information, is controlled by an electric current. Possibly the conceptually simplest device that has these characteristics is the **capacitor**, which we can think of as a pair of metal plates, separated from one another by a very small distance, as shown in Figure 2.3.1. When a current is placed across the plates (shown in the figure as a 1-volt source—a battery, perhaps), the two plates become oppositely "charged"; one of the plates acquires a surplus of electrons, the other a deficiency of them. We say that the capacitor is in a **charged state**. The interesting property of the capacitor is that even if the voltage source is *removed*, the charge on the plates remains; the capacitor, so to say, "remembers" that it was charged by the battery. If we choose to have the capacitor in its opposite, or **discharged state**, we can easily achieve that by momentarily connecting a wire between the two plates to equalize the charge on the plates. Thus we have a device that can be put in one of two states, and which "remembers" the last state that it was given.

How can we *determine* the state of a capacitor? The answer is quite simple; we need only put a meter (voltmeter) in the circuit with the capacitor, as in Figure 2.3.2. If the capacitor was charged at the time, the needle on the meter will deflect somewhat; if it was discharged, no such deflection will be observed.

We have now discovered one of the devices we were seeking. The capacitor has the properties that (1) it can be put in one of two states (charged or discharged)

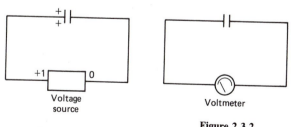

Voltage
source

Voltmeter

Figure 2.3.1

Figure 2.3.2

by the presence or absence of an electric current, and (2) the state can later be determined or "recalled." But observe how primitive the information is; it is of the two-state nature that we mentioned earlier, and in fact any less information would be no information at all. Nonetheless, this is a start toward what we are trying to accomplish—the creation of a device (computer memory) that can store large amounts of fairly complex data.

As a device for the storage of information, the capacitor has two undesirable properties. First, we stated that once a capacitor has been put in a charged state, it remains charged until we discharge it. In fact, a capacitor's charge tends to diminish—to "leak" or "bleed off"—so that after a period of time it may appear to be discharged unless corrective action is taken. What needs to be done is to examine the state of the capacitor from time to time, and if it is in a charged state, to **refresh** the charge (by charging it again) so that it will not be mistaken for a discharged capacitor. Second, when we examine the state of a capacitor, by means of a voltmeter, for example, that act has the effect of *discharging* the capacitor. Thus if a capacitor *were* charged, we would detect that fact but in the process of determining its state, we would have *altered* the state. Of course, since we would then know it was charged, we could recharge it—put it back into its original state. Both of these problems can be dealt with by appropriate engineering.

The capacitor is an example of a **bistable device**, a device that can exist in one of *two* states, and which is *stable* or permanently set in that state until some event changes it. When we set the capacitor to a known state, by charging it or discharging it, we say that we **write** information into the capacitor. When we determine the state of the capacitor (with a meter, or however), we say that we **read** the information held in the capacitor. The phenomenon mentioned in the preceding paragraph, in which the information is possibly *destroyed* when it is read, is referred to as **destructive reading**.

We mention one more bistable device that is suitable as an information storage device and, in fact, is still in use in some computers. This is the **magnetic core**, which consists of a small doughnut-shaped piece of ferromagnetic material, a substance that can be magnetized. The core can be magnetized in one of two directions, clockwise or counterclockwise (see Figure 2.3.3). The core is magnetized in the following way. A wire is put through the hole in the core, and a current is passed through the wire. The direction of the current determines the direction of the magnetiziation. In Figure 2.3.3 we show the current passing through the **write wire** from top to bottom, which results in the core being magnetized in a clockwise direction when viewed from above. If the current had been in the opposite direction, the core would have been magnetized in a counterclockwise direction. Thus the information that is held in a core is the direction of its magnetization, information that can be written into the core by means of an electric current. Once the direction of magnetization has been established by passing a current through the write wire, that current may be removed, and the core will remain magnetized in that direction *indefinitely*. Magnetic cores require *no* refreshing, which is a property that makes them particularly desirable as information storage devices.

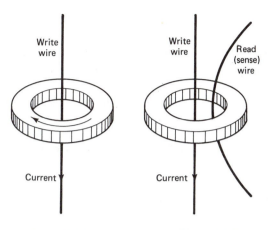

Figure 2.3.3   **Figure 2.3.4**

To read the information held in a core, we pass a current through the write wire *in a fixed direction*. Depending on how the core *was* magnetized, this action will either do nothing, or it will reverse the direction of magnetization in the core. In the latter case, a small magnetic field in the "hole" of the core will *collapse* and rebuild in the opposite direction. We now place an additional wire through the hole in the core, a **read wire** or **sense wire**, as shown in Figure 2.3.4. If the magnetic field in the core's hole does collapse—if the fixed-direction current in the write wire causes a change in the direction of the core's magnetization—a small current will be induced in the read wire. If the core's direction of magnetization does not change, no such current will be induced in the read wire. In this way we can determine—read—the information in the core, although observe that again the reading is destructive; if the information read from the core resulted in its being destroyed, it will have to be rewritten.

In fact, as important as the core is from an historical standpoint, it is used only infrequently nowadays. Most computer memories now are made up of **solid-state** or **semiconductor** devices, which have the behavior of simple switches and which can be written and read far faster than the rather slow cores, since no time is required waiting for a magnetic field to change, and since the reading is not destructive. However, unlike the magnetic core, such devices require that power be constantly applied to them, and this produces special problems with which the engineer must deal.

2.4 MEMORY UNITS

We shall call a single bistable device—capacitor, core, semiconductor, or whatever—a **memory cell**. As we have seen, it has the ability to store a single piece of two-state information. The actual *value* that a memory cell has—charged or discharged, clockwise or counterclockwise, conducting or nonconducting—is of no real consequence to us. In fact, we have not yet even attached any *meaning* to the state of such a device; for example, we might observe that a capacitor is charged and that it therefore "holds" some information, but as yet we have no *interpretation* of that information. Thus for the time being we shall simply refer to the two states of a bistable device as *a* and *b*.

It is difficult to envision a situation in which a single bistable device's information can be very useful, consisting as it does of either *a* or *b* at any given time. The *amount* of information that can be conveyed by the device is simply too small to be useful in most circumstances. But consider now *two* such devices, each of which can take on a value *a* or *b*, and which we think of as *ordered*, in the sense that one of the devices is *first*, or *leftmost*. Then this pair of devices, working as a unit, can take on *four* distinct values:

C_1	C_2	U_2
a	*a*	*aa*
a	*b*	*ab*
b	*a*	*ba*
b	*b*	*bb*

Here we have let C_1 and C_2 denote the values that the two individual cells can take on, and U_2 denote the value that the *pair* of cells, as a unit, takes on. Observe that it is essential that we treat the cells as ordered (C_1 being the *first*), for if they were not, we would be unable to distinguish between the values *ab* and *ba*. If we now combine *three* cells, C_1, C_2, and C_3, into an ordered unit U_3, then U_3 can take on *eight* distinct configurations, each of which is a *triple* of values of the individual cells. Thus a typical value for U_3 would be *abb*, where C_1 takes on the value *a*, C_2 the value *b*, and C_3 also the value *b*.

We shall define a **memory unit** to be an ordered collection of memory cells, denoted by U_n, where *n* is the number of cells in the unit. The reader should have no difficulty establishing that if a memory unit U_n is made up of *n* ordered memory cells, then the *values* that U_n takes on are "strings" of length *n* of the characters *a* and *b*, and that there are 2^n such distinct strings. For example, a value for U_n might be *abbbaaba...bba*.

It is now clear that we can construct memory units that can hold as many different pieces of information as we might want, simply by stringing sufficiently many bistable devices together. But what should such "information" *mean*? That is, how do we *interpret* a string of states such as *abbbaaba...bba*? We shall discover a most useful interpretation after a brief digression to discuss number system representations.

2.5 NUMBER REPRESENTATIONS

When we speak of "the number 2106" we are guilty of an imprecision, or minimally a slopiness that causes us no problems because of certain tacit assumptions to which we all agree. "2106" is *not*, strictly speaking, a number. **Number** is an abstract concept, which may be described as a *property of a set*. For instance, the collection of pages in this book has a numerical attribute, which the reader can determine by looking at the last page. The set of stripes on the United States flag has the numerical characteristic of "thirteenness." "Four" is the attribute we assign to the set of members in a barbershop quartet, as well as to the set of values that can be taken on by a two-celled memory unit. Thus the 2106 in the phrase "the number 2106" might more accurately be described as a *symbolic representation* of the abstract quality of "2106-ness."

If "2106" is not a number but rather a number representation, just what role is played by the individual symbols 2, 1, 0, and 6? A little reflection will reveal that they are simply a shorthand notation for the expression

$$2 \cdot 1000 + 1 \cdot 100 + 0 \cdot 10 + 6 \cdot 1$$

or equivalently,

$$2 \cdot 10^3 + 1 \cdot 10^2 + 0 \cdot 10^1 + 6 \cdot 10^0$$

This last form could as well be written as

$$2 \cdot x^3 + 1 \cdot x^2 + 0 \cdot x^1 + 6 \cdot x^0$$

where we understand that x stands for 10. That is, "2106" is a representation of a **polynomial in x**, where $x = 10$ and where we agree for the sake of economy to write only the coefficients of the polynomial, rather than the entire polynomial itself. Notice, however, that the coefficients are written *positionally* and that care must be taken to include those terms which have a zero coefficient—there is a difference between 2106 and 216.

In the polynomial above, why should x be *ten*? This unquestionably stems from the fact that we have 10 fingers, and our counting scheme,

$$0, 1, 2, 3, 4, 5, 6, 7, 8, 9, 10, 11, 12, 13, \ldots$$

is based on the fact that from the beginning (and, in fact, even today), fingers were a convenient *set* of "things" to use for "matching." For when we say that a collection (of pennies, automobiles, marbles, and so on) contains "five" things, we mean that there is a correspondence between that set and the collection of fingers on one hand. If we each had four fingers on each hand rather than five, we would undoubtedly count

$$0, 1, 2, 3, 4, 5, 6, 7, 10, 11, 12, 13, \ldots$$

But now what does the symbol "10" mean? It simply means "one complete collection of things (fingers) plus no additional things." In a similar fashion, "11" means "one complete collection of things plus one additional thing." Thus in a normal (ten-fingered) environment, "10" is the number of pennies in a dime, whereas in an eight-fingered society, "10" is the number of tones in the diatonic scale.

The symbol x in the polynomial expression above is called the **base of the number representation system**. Thus "the number 2106" is formally "the representation of the quality of 2106-ness, written in the base ten number representation system." The fact that x may have different values, combined with our choice of identical symbols "1, 2, 3, ..." regardless of the value of x, can bring about a certain amount of confusion. For simply stating that "2106 is a number" is inadequate, since it also requires that the base of the number system be known, or that it *be understood*. (In our daily dealings with numbers, of course, the base is understood to be *ten*.) To be precise, we should say "the number whose representation in the base ten number system is 2106," although we rarely do this. But mention of the base is essential if any ambiguity is possible, and we can do this by writing

$$2106 \text{ (base 10)}$$

or more simply

$$2106_{10}$$

The reader should verify that $2106_8 = 1094_{10}$ and that $2106_{10} = 4072_8$. (The first equality results from an evaluation, in the base-10 system, of the expression $2 \cdot 8^3 + 1 \cdot 8^2 + 0 \cdot 8^1 + 6 \cdot 8^0$. The second is left as an exercise.)

We have examined briefly the representation of numbers in a base-8 system, and some other bases are investigated below and in the exercises. The reader is already intimately familiar with base-10 representations. Observe that in base 8, and in representations in which the base is *smaller* than *ten*, we already have at hand the "symbols" $0, 1, 2, \ldots$ which we can adopt to represent the number system elements (symbols that correspond to "collections of fingers," for example). But what if the base is *larger* than *ten*? As a concrete example, consider a number system with base *twelve*. We can use the symbols $0, 1, 2, \ldots, 9$ to represent *some* of the number system elements, but we need two additional symbols. Could we use "10" and "11"? No, for "10" means "the base of the system itself" (which in this example is *twelve*), and "11" means "the number system base plus *one*." Thus we shall have to invent two new symbols, and we simply use A and B for these purposes. Hence in base *twelve* we count

$$0, 1, 2, 3, 4, 5, 6, 7, 8, 9, \text{A}, \text{B}, 10, 11, \ldots$$

Again we leave as an exercise the verification that $2106_{12} = 3606_{10}$ and that $2106_{10} = 1276_{12}$.

In addition to the familiar **decimal** (base-10) number representation system, two others will be of special significance to us throughout the text. One of these is the **hexadecimal** representation system, whose base is *sixteen*. Just as in the case of base *twelve*, here we shall evidently have to create *six* new symbols, and we choose A, B, C, D, E, and F, where A is the successor of 9 (that is, *ten*), B is the successor of A (*eleven*), ..., and F is the successor of E (*fifteen*); the names in parentheses are the usual names, in the *decimal* system, by which we know these numbers. Counting in hexadecimal proceeds as follows:

$$0, 1, 2, \ldots, 8, 9, \text{A}, \text{B}, \text{C}, \text{D}, \text{E}, \text{F}, 10, 11, \ldots, 19, 1\text{A}, \ldots$$

$$1\text{F}, 20, 21, \ldots, 9\text{E}, 9\text{F}, \text{A0}, \text{A1}, \ldots, \text{FD}, \text{FE}, \text{FF}, 100, 101, \ldots$$

How is arithmetic performed in the hexadecimal system, or any other number representation system, for that matter? The answer is, the same way in which the reader has always performed arithmetic in *decimal*. That is, the algorithms for addition, subtraction, square roots, and so on, are *independent of the number base*; the procedures for "carries and borrows," for example, which the reader learned in grade school are as valid in hexadecimal (base 16) or octal (base 8) as they are in base 10. Thus aside from gaining familiarity with systems other than decimal, there is nothing new to learn in performing arithmetic operations. Figure 2.5.1 shows examples of addition, subtraction, and multiplication in which the same problem is solved in decimal, octal, and hexadecimal. The reader is invited to verify not only that the arithmetic is correct, but also that the procedures involved are the same regardless of the base, and that in each case the same pair of numbers is represented, in different bases.

It should be clear that there is no "largest" base upon which to build a number representation system, for the base can be as large as we wish, provided that we are willing to create perhaps many new and unfamiliar "number symbols." In base 35, for example, we need 35 symbols to represent the number system elements, and even if we take advantage of the familiar 0, 1, ..., 9, we still have to invent 25 symbols to represent the other elements. In fact, once the base exceeds *twenty* or so, the situation becomes so unwieldy as to be impractical. But if there is no largest base, there is a smallest, namely *two*. In the **binary number representation system**—base 2—there are only two symbols required, which we take to be 0 and 1, and the counting scheme is

$$0, 1, 10, 11, 100, 101, 110, 111, 1000, 1001, 1010, \ldots$$

Note that "10" is "one times the base, plus zero," which is *two*; that "101" is "one times the base squared, plus zero times the base, plus one," which is *five*; and so on. All the arithmetic operations in base 2 are especially easy, since there are

FIGURE 2.5.1

(a)	$\begin{array}{r} 45662_{10} \\ +\ 7722_{10} \\ \hline 53384_{10} \end{array}$	$\begin{array}{r} 131136_8 \\ +\ 17052_8 \\ \hline 150210_8 \end{array}$	$\begin{array}{r} B25E_{16} \\ +\ 1E2A_{16} \\ \hline D088_{16} \end{array}$
(b)	$\begin{array}{r} 45662_{10} \\ -\ 7722_{10} \\ \hline 37940_{10} \end{array}$	$\begin{array}{r} 131136_8 \\ -\ 17052_8 \\ \hline 112064_8 \end{array}$	$\begin{array}{r} B25E_{16} \\ -\ 1E2A_{16} \\ \hline 9434_{16} \end{array}$
(c)	$\begin{array}{r} 678_{10} \\ \times\ 75_{10} \\ \hline 3390_{10} \\ 4746_{10} \\ \hline 50850_{10} \end{array}$	$\begin{array}{r} 1246_8 \\ \times\ 113_8 \\ \hline 3762_8 \\ 1246_8 \\ 1246_8 \\ \hline 143242_8 \end{array}$	$\begin{array}{r} 2A6_{16} \\ \times\ 4B_{16} \\ \hline 1D22_{16} \\ A98_{16} \\ \hline C6A2_{16} \end{array}$

only two symbols with which to deal. (Interestingly, this is the one base in which multiplication is the most trivial operation, since it reduces to multiplications by 0 or by 1.)

The reader may have observed in some of our examples that the larger the base, the fewer "digits" are required to represent a given number, and this is generally true. For example, the three-digit hexadecimal number $E4A_{16}$ requires four digits in decimal: 3658_{10}, and also four in octal: 7112_8. But in binary, the representation of this number requires *twelve* digits: 111001001010_2. Thus from the standpoint of compactness of representation, the larger bases seem to be most practical, whereas simplicity of arithmetic favors the smaller bases.

We have stated that hexadecimal and binary representations will be of particular importance to us. The significance of the hexadecimal representations is described in Chapter 4, and we shall put the binary number system to use immediately. In the meantime, the reader is also assured that we have not abandoned the decimal number representation system, and in fact we shall use it whenever possible, in those cases in which some other representation is not dictated by the environment. But once again we caution that unless the number system base is implicitly known or assumed, some care will have to be taken to make it explicit.

2.6 A CHANGE IN NOTATION

In Section 2.4 we discovered that the "values" taken on by memory units could be represented as collections of states of bistable devices, which we could write as a string of *a*'s and *b*'s, thus:

$$abbbaaba \ldots bba$$

and we left that section with the question: What is the *meaning* of such a string of states? We can now give one possible response to that question if we simply change the notation. If instead of letting the states of a bistable device be denoted by *a* and *b*, we use the symbols 1 and 0, respectively, the string above becomes

$$10001101 \ldots 001$$

And *if* we *interpret* this string of 1s and 0s to be the binary representation of a *number*, then we have imposed on the memory unit a *numerical interpretation*. For example, if a memory unit U_3 is made up of three capacitors C_1, C_2, and C_3, if we represent a charged capacitor by "1" and a discharged capacitor by "0", and if C_1 and C_3 are charged while C_2 is discharged, the memory unit can be *described* by the string "101". If we *interpret* this string of 1s and 0s as the binary representation of a number, we could say that the current state of the memory unit "represents the number 5."

The reader is cautioned against thinking that memory units have suddenly been endowed with the ability to "hold numbers." It is our *representation* of the *states* of the cells that make up a memory unit, as 1s and 0s, that leads us to *interpret* those states as a binary number representation. If they "hold" anything, memory units "hold" memory cell states. Throughout the remainder of the book we shall make statements such as "the contents of this memory unit is the number 27" and "that memory unit holds 132." What is meant, of course, is "when the cell states of this memory unit are described in terms of 1s and 0s, and the resulting states interpreted as a binary number representation, the decimal form of the binary number so represented is 27." An insistence on such an extreme level of formalism would only hamper the development, and therefore we have no hesitation in making imprecise statements such as those above. But the reader would be well advised to keep the truth of the matter in mind, for on occasion it is precisely the formal description that will be the most meaningful.

2.7 COMPUTER WORDS AND MAIN MEMORY

We mentioned earlier that a memory unit is made up of so-and-so many memory cells, and that the more cells that were in a unit, the more distinct pieces of information that unit could represent. By now the reader has probably surmised that these memory units are going to be used as the basic building blocks of *main memory*, the computer system device that will be used to hold information to be used by the central processing unit. But now the question of main memory *organization* arises. If memory units are used to make up main memory, and if a memory unit is itself made up of memory cells (cores, semiconductors, or whatever), how is the number of cells in a unit to be determined? To answer this we must recognize some constraints on memory organization. First, we must be aware that main memory does not consist of a *single* memory unit (which could then "store" only a single number). Rather, main memories typically are made up of hundreds of thousands or millions of such memory units. If each such unit consists of a very large number of cells, thereby allowing for the storage of a large number of large numbers, then the sheer cost of main memory may be prohibitive. Second, whatever decision is made regarding the number of cells in each unit, engineering considerations dictate that each memory unit consist of the *same number* of cells. Thus the decisions surrounding the number of cells in each unit, and the total number of such units, will almost always involve some trade-off. But we must also be practical about the matter. Memory units consisting of two cells each— no matter how many of them there might be—are simply too small to be of significance. They can hold only the (binary) numbers 00, 01, 10, and 11 (0 to 3 in decimal), and these units will not hold enough distinct numbers to be useful. Even eight-celled units can hold only numbers in the range 0 to 255, which is quite limited by most standards. (Many of the popular personal and microcomputers have memories whose units consist of eight cells, and for some purposes this small number range may be adequate. But even so, in these machines the processing of significant data may require a great deal of effort; fortunately, the computer vendor usually supplies the programming to manage "large" numbers, so the system user rarely needs to get involved with these details.)

Throughout the remainder of this chapter and into the next we shall deal with memory units made up of four memory cells each. We realize that such units are so small that they cannot hold realistically significant information, yet for our

x	y	z	w

x, y, z, w = 0 or 1   **Figure 2.7.1**

present purposes they will be large enough to develop the concepts we wish to investigate. The cells that make up a memory unit are called **bits**, a contraction of the term "binary digits." On a temporary basis, we shall refer to a memory unit made up of four cells or bits as a **4-bit word**, since the term *word* has been in use in computer systems almost from the beginning to signify the basic unit of information that is held in main memory. (This is a term we shall redefine in Chapter 4 to correspond to current usage on the VAX-11, the machine of principal interest to us.) So that we can easily reference the bits in a word, we introduce the bit numbering scheme shown in Figure 2.7.1. Notice that the *position* of each bit, 3 down to 0, corresponds to the power of 2 which that bit represents. That is, the numerical *value* of the word in Figure 2.7.1 is

$$x \cdot 2^3 + y \cdot 2^2 + z \cdot 2^1 + w \cdot 2^0$$

The bit in bit position 3 is called the **high-order bit** or **most-significant bit**; the bit in position 0 is called the **low-order bit** or **least-significant bit**.

Despite the fact that the bit numbering system described above seems quite natural, there is nothing that dictates that it must be used. Some computer system manufacturers use the opposite designations, with bit position 0 being the leftmost, and bit position 3 the rightmost, although then the bit position itself does not indicate the power of 2 which corresponds to that bit.

2.8 COMPUTER NUMBER SYSTEMS AND ARITHMETIC

At this point we need to make some assumptions about the capabilities of the central processing unit (CPU). While we shall gain some insights into the processes that go on in the CPU's arithmetic unit in Chapter 3, for the time being we assume that the computer has the capability of *incrementing*—adding 1 to—the contents of any of its main memory words; the incrementing will have the effect on the word's contents of adding to it the binary number 0001. Suppose we start with a word whose contents is 0000. When this is incremented, the result is 0000 + 0001 = 0001. (In decimal, 0 + 1 = 1.) If the word is incremented again, the result is 0001 + 0001 = 0010 (decimal 2). Another increment yields 0011, another gives 0100, and so on. Eventually, the contents of the word will be 1110, and a further increment yields 1110 + 0001 = 1111. (In decimal, 14 + 1 = 15.) But what happens when the contents of this word is incremented again? The resulting sum is

$$1111 + 0001 = 10000$$

and we recognize a problem here. The sum 15 + 1 = 16 requires *five* bits for its representation, but the word which is being incremented, and hence holds the result, is only *four* bits long. What happens to the high-order bit (1) of the result?

In the process of doing the addition, the arithmetic unit simply *discards* this bit, since it cannot fit it into the 4-bit result. That is, this bit is *lost*, and thus the result is

$$1111 + 0001 = (1)0000 = 0000$$

We are now faced with the rather disquieting equation: $15 + 1 = 0$. From the arithmetic standpoint, this is nonsense *if the number system is infinite.* But we already knew that 4-bit words could not hold arbitrarily large numbers; with some prior thought we should have anticipated this problem. The number system simply "wraps around" on itself—is *circular*—as shown in Figure 2.8.1 [shown in binary in part (a), in decimal in part (b)].

Could the problem of this 1 being "carried out of" the 4-bit word have been eliminated if we had considered instead, say, a 5-bit word? Not really, for in that case, while 10000 *can* be held in the word, the analogous problem will arise when we increment the word whose contents is 11111 (decimal 31). Analogous to the 4-bit case, we have

$$11111 + 00001 = (1)00000 = 00000$$

and although this unpleasant phenomenon may have been postponed, it has not been eliminated. It should be clear that the number of bits which make up a computer word has nothing to do with the fact that the word's number system is circular, although it will of course influence just *where* the "discontinuity" in the number system will occur.

If we now assume that the processor's arithmetic unit contains appropriate circuitry to perform *additions* (rather than just increments) of 4-bit words, then by now we might expect that not all will be well with some of these additions, for the phenomenon that we just uncovered when incrementing words—a carry out of the high-order bit, yielding an arithmetically incorrect result—will probably occur during additions as well. Indeed,

$$1001 + 0101 = 1110 \qquad (9 + 5 = 14)$$

is correct, but

$$1101 + 0101 = (1)0010 = 0010 \qquad (13 + 5 = 2)$$

is not. In the first case, no carry out of the high-order bit occurred, but such a carry *did* occur in the second. Evidently, this carry out of the high-order bit is of

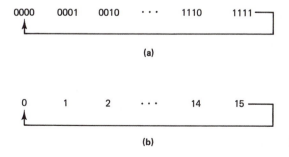

(a)

(b)

Figure 2.8.1

significance to the correctness of processor arithmetic, and we shall have more to say about it later in this chapter.

The reader may with some justification be disappointed with a computing system that sometimes produces arithmetically correct results, and at other times does not. But it is easy to track down the cause of the problem. First, the fault does *not* lie with the central processing unit's addition or incrementing circuitry. If the word size is 4 bits (cells), and if an addition yields a 5-bit result, some one bit *must* be lost in the process. The difficulty lies with the *finiteness* of computer words, combined with our *interpretation* of the contents of words as *numbers* and the consequent circularity of the number system, together with our preconceived notion of what the sum of two numbers should be. In brief, this is a *fact* of computing, and it is one that we shall have to learn not only to live with, but also to be on the lookout for and to cope with as best we can. Once again we caution that the phenomenon is *not* related to the small size (4 bits) of the words presently under consideration, although that size did cause the problem to show up rather quickly. Later we shall deal with structures that are 128 bits long, structures that can "hold" gigantic numbers, yet the "carry out of the high-order bit" problem is with us as surely as in the 4-bit case.

Even if we assume appropriate electronic circuitry to perform *subtraction*, that operation causes some special problems which prompt us to postpone a detailed discussion of it. To see what the difficulty is, consider the subtraction problem

$$1010 - 0100 = 0110 \qquad (10 - 4 = 6)$$

This result is, of course, correct, but notice that to perform the subtraction, a "borrow from bit 3" was required to do the subtraction at bit 2. But consider now

$$0011 - 0101 = ??10 \qquad (3 - 5 = ?)$$

No problems occur at bits 0 and 1, but a "borrow" is required at bit 2, and there is nothing to borrow from—there is no "1" in the next-higher-order bit of the minuend. What is needed here is a slightly different approach to the operation of subtraction.

2.9 SIGNED NUMBERS

One of the deficiencies of the computer number system as it has been devised so far is that it does not provide for *negative* numbers, and this would be a severe limitation for most applications. Thus in this section we will search for a "reasonable" way to implement **signed numbers** (positive and negative, as well as zero), reasonable both from the standpoint of user convenience and from the point of view of the effort that is required of the central processing unit in manipulating them arithmetically. (As yet we have not examined how the central processor performs arithmetic, so it is difficult to assess the "effort" that must be expended by the CPU to do a task. However, it is generally true that if a procedure appears complex *to us*, it is probably complex for the processor.)

We must understand that in introducing negative numbers we mean more than simply changing our current number system, 0 to 15, to a new system in which the range is 0 to -15; this would accomplish little, if anything. Rather, we need to deal with both positive and negative numbers, and in so doing we will be placing even more narrow constraints on the ranges of numbers. For if we have 16 possible numbers (bit configurations) that can be held in a 4-bit word, it seems reasonable to make approximately half of them negative and the other half positive. Thus the ranges of numbers we can deal with will be something like 0 to $+7$ and -8 to -1, for example. How can we indicate that a number is positive, or that it is negative? More properly, what bit configurations will we recognize as having one sign or the other? We are going to use the high-order bit, bit 3, for this purpose, and we adopt the following convention. If the high-order bit of a word is *on* (or *1*, or *set*), we will interpret the number as being *negative*. If the high-order bit of a word is *off* (or *0* or *clear*), we will interpret the number as being *positive*. We realize that we have left the number zero out of consideration here, but that will be dealt with as we look at some particular implementations.

The conceptually simplest scheme for the implementation of both positive and negative numbers is the **sign-magnitude** representation, in which the high-order bit (bit 3) acts as the **sign bit** as described above, and the remaining 3 bits of the word define the **magnitude** of the number. For example, the bit configuration

$$1 \quad 0 \; 1 \; 1$$

represents the signed number -3, since the *sign* bit—bit 3—is *on*, and the remaining bits—2, 1, and 0—represent the *magnitude*, the binary number 3. In a similar fashion,

$$0 \quad 1 \; 0 \; 1 = +5$$

Observe the ease with which a number is *negated*; we need only change the state of the sign bit. All in all, this seems to be a most convenient signed number system, at least from *our* point of view.

Before we become too enamored of this system, we should note that there are some problems which a little thought will reveal. For example, the number zero is clearly represented by the bit configuration 0000. But what of 1000? The magnitude of this number, 000, is zero, and the sign is *negative*. Is this zero, or is it not? Should we refer to this as -0? Although *we* can circumvent fairly easily the annoyance of having two distinct representations of the number zero, it turns out that the problem is somewhat more critical for the central processing unit. However, rather than pursue a repair of the "multiple versions of zero" problem, we look into the question of addition, where even more severe difficulties present themselves. In dealing with sign-magnitude numbers, addition must be reduced to some special cases. That is, unlike the uniform process for adding the "unsigned" numbers of the preceding section, in which the operation was simply the bit-by-bit addition of binary numbers, for sign-magnitude numbers we must consider whether the signs of the two numbers are the same or are different. The following is an algorithm for the addition of sign-magnitude numbers.

1. If the two numbers to be added have the same sign, add the magnitudes of the two numbers (bits 2, 1, and 0), with any carries out of bit 2 being *lost*; then set bit 3 of the result to the (common) sign bit of the two numbers.

2. If the two numbers have opposite sign, subtract the *smaller magnitude* from the *larger magnitude* (irrespective of sign); then set bit 3 of the result to be the same as the sign bit of the number with the larger magnitude.

As some simple applications of the algorithm, consider

$$0101 + 0010 = 0111 \quad [+5 + (+2) = +7]$$

and

$$1011 + 1001 = 1100 \quad [-3 + (-1) = -4]$$

These are applications of step 1 of the algorithm above, as is

$$0110 + 0101 = 0(1)011 = 0011 \quad [+6 + (+5) = +3]$$

but notice that here there was a (lost) carry out of bit 2 of the result, and in fact the "answer" is incorrect. [Here and in what follows we shall indicate a "1" bit which is lost as the result of a carry by enclosing it in parentheses: (1).] As an example of step 2 of the algorithm, consider

$$0011 + 1101 = 1 \quad (101 - 011) = 1 \quad 010$$
$$= 1010 \quad [+3 + (-5) = -2]$$

Now that we know how to add two sign-magnitude numbers, even if the process is not particularly "clean," we observe that subtraction is no problem whatever. To subtract B from A we need only negate B and add the result to A; and we have already commented that negation is an especially simple process. Thus

$$A - B = A + (-B)$$

If the reader is somewhat disturbed that the addition of two sign-magnitude numbers must be dealt with in cases, and that there are two distinct representations of zero, he will understand why computers do not frequently implement this number system. It is certainly possible to deal with this technique in processor circuitry, although it is scarcely a trivial matter, since it requires that the circuitry do comparisons and make some decisions as to what operations are to be performed, all of which tends to extend the time required to perform these arithmetic operations. But complications aside, there is another feature which argues against this scheme. In Section 2.8 we introduced an **unsigned number system**, in which the 4 bits of a word were devoted to its numerical value, without regard to sign. Unsigned numbers can be useful in many applications, yet the sign-magnitude system which we have just introduced is *not* compatible with these unsigned numbers. For if the contents of a 4-bit word is interpreted as an unsigned number, then of course all 4 bits contribute to the *value* of the number, and in particular, bit 3 is simply another numerical bit—it represents the decimal number 8. When two such 4-bit unsigned words are added, the bits in bit position 3 are added just as are all the other bit positions. But when a 4-bit word is given its sign-magnitude interpretation, bit 3 is *not* a part of the numerical value of the word; the word is in fact *split* into its sign bit (bit 3) and its magnitude bits (bits 2, 1, and 0). We have already observed that bit 3 does not even enter into the addition; rather, its values in the two words are later used to determine how bit 3 of the result should be set. It is this fact that makes sign-magnitude addition incompatible with unsigned, 4-bit addition.

To deal with this incompatibility of number systems we must do one of three things. First, we can simply discard the unsigned system altogether, thereby losing its value in certain circumstances. Second, we can maintain *two* systems, both signed and unsigned, but then we will also have to maintain two distinct sets of arithmetic operations—signed addition and unsigned addition, for example, are *not* performed in the same way. The third alternative is to associate with each unsigned number its corresponding *signed, positive* counterpart; that is, the bit configuration *0yzw* can be considered *either* as the *positive* number *0yzw or* as the *unsigned* number *0yzw*. In this case, addition of signed and unsigned numbers are compatible operations, but notice that the range of an unsigned number has been halved because of the requirement that its high-order bit be 0. In short, the problems here are sufficiently severe that we will not attempt to implement this system.

The next signed number system that we consider is the **ones-complement** representation, a term that requires some explanation. In the one's-complement system, the high-order bit is again interpreted as the sign bit, a 0 representing a positive number, with 1 representing a negative number. The positive numbers (sign bit = 0) have the same values as in the sign-magnitude system. Rather than explain exactly what number is represented by a particular bit configuration with sign bit = 1, we describe how to *negate* any number. If $xyzw$ is a bit configuration, then the **ones-complement** of $xyzw$ is $x'y'z'w'$, where each primed bit has as its value the *opposite* of the corresponding unprimed bit. For example, if $x = 0$, then $x' = 1$, and if $x = 1$, then $x' = 0$. x' is called the **ones-complement** of x, since x' is obtained from x by subtracing the value x from 1: $x' = 1 - 0 = 1$ (if $x = 0$) and $x' = 1 - 1 = 0$ (if $x = 1$). For example, the one's complement of the bit configuration 1011 is 0100, and that of 0011 is 1100. We now define the *negative* of a 4-bit number to be its one's complement. Notice among other things that the one's complement changes the sign bit (bit 3), as we would expect. The following table shows the one's-complement negatives of the positive 4-bit numbers.

Decimal	Binary	Negative	Decimal
+0	0000	1111	−0
+1	0001	1110	−1
+2	0010	1101	−2
+3	0011	1100	−3
+4	0100	1011	−4
+5	0101	1010	−5
+6	0110	1001	−6
+7	0111	1000	−7

Notice that we are once more plagued by the two different versions of zero, "±0" as they are usually denoted. Lest the reader attach no particular importance to this fact, we note that one of the conditions that the *processor can detect* is that the last operation it performed resulted in zero. This "zero detection" on the part of the processor is quite important in many applications, and it is going to be a more complicated procedure for the processor if zero comes in two different forms.

As we see from the table, the negative numbers appear in a far less pleasing form, from *our* point of view, than in the sign-magnitude case. For if we look at a bit configuration such as 0101, we observe that it is positive, ignore the sign bit (0), and announce that the value is 5. But for 1101, we cannot use the same process. We recognize that the number is negative, since the sign bit is set, but unlike the sign-magnitude case, in which the remaining bits 101 are evaluated to 5, in the ones-complement case we must mentally *recomplement* these bits to get 010, and then finally announce that the number's value is −2.

We saw that one of the disadvantages of the sign-magnitude number system was that it *failed* conveniently to deal with *unsigned* numbers. In the ones-complement system that incompatibility simply disappears (almost), since the sign bit is no longer treated as a "separate unit" as it was in the sign-magnitude case. Let us see what will happen if we agree to add two ones-complement 4-bit numbers as we added *un*signed numbers—pure 4-bit binary addition. (In the following equations we show the decimal equivalents of both the ones-complement interpretation and the unsigned interpretation.)

(a) $0101 + 0001 = 0110$ $[+5 + (+1) = +6; 5 + 1 = 6]$

(b) $0101 + 0110 = 1011$ $[+5 + (+6) = -4; 5 + 6 = 11]$

(c) $1010 + 0100 = 1110$ $[-5 + (+4) = -1; 10 + 4 = 14]$

(d) $1010 + 0110 = (1)0000 = 0000$ $[-5 + (+6) = +0; 10 + 6 = 0]$

(e) $1010 + 0101 = 1111$ $[-5 + (+5) = -0; 10 + 5 = 15]$

(f) $1010 + 1100 = (1)0110 = 0110$ $[-5 + (-3) = +6; 10 + 12 = 6]$

In example (a), both signed and unsigned addition are correct. But in example (b), we see that while unsigned addition is correct, the signed case has failed, and the reason is fairly clear; a carry occurred from bit 2 into bit 3, thereby bringing about a change of sign. In example (c), the result is correct in both the signed and unsigned cases, but observe that here *no* carries occurred. In example (d), the result is incorrect in the unsigned case, because of a carry out of bit 3, a phenomenon we have already discussed. In the signed case, the result is not quite correct—it should be +1 rather than +0—but this can actually be repaired with an appropriate adjustment (see Exercise 2.9.6). Note that a carry also occurred *into* bit 3. In equation (e), the result is again correct in either the signed or unsigned case, but we see that in the ones-complement interpretation, 1111 must be taken to be 0 (more precisely, −0). Observe again that no carry, either into or out of bit 3, took place. Finally, in (f), a carry out of bit 3 occurred, no carry into bit 3 occurred, and the addition has gone badly in both the signed and unsigned interpretations.

There are several conclusions that can be drawn from these examples. First, the addition is compatible with the unsigned operation that was introduced earlier. In the ones-complement case, some of the additions are correct, some are incorrect, and one is "almost" correct. But what is of principal significance is that evidently the correctness or incorrectness of the results in either interpretation seems to hinge upon *carries* into and out of bit 3—the sign bit. The reader is asked in some of the exercises to determine the conditions under which results are arithmetically correct, and to make appropriate adjustments when results are "almost" correct. We decline to pursue the matter further here, since the ones-complement number representation system is only infrequently used in modern computers, having yielded to a system in which a number of the problems we have encountered simply do not arise and thus which is the easiest (and hence fastest) for the central processing unit to manage.

Although we did not make a great fuss over it, we commented on the undesirability of a dual representation of the number 0 which occurred in both the sign-magnitude and ones-complement systems. We shall now attempt to eliminate that problem, and in the process we shall discover a truly useful signed number system, one that is most convenient for the processor, if not the human user. To determine what caused this dual representation, we look at the representations of the number -1 in each of the two signed number systems. In the sign-magnitude case, -1 is represented as 1001. If we *add* $+1$ (0001) to this, our addition algorithm can actually yield *either* 0000 *or* 1000. In the ones-complement case, $-1 = 1110$, and adding $+1$ (0001) to this yields 1111, the bit configuration we referred to as -0. Let us return for the moment to Figure 2.8.1(a), which describes the *circularity* of the unsigned 4-bit number system, and ask the following question: If these sixteen 4-bit words are to be interpreted as representing *signed* numbers, what should be taken as the signed number -1? Recalling that Figure 2.8.1(a) displays among other things the *order* of the numbers, each number being its predecessor *plus one*, it is reasonable to say that -1 should be the predecessor of 0. But we see that the predecessor of 0 is the bit configuration 1111, due to the fact that the number system wraps around on itself. In the unsigned interpretation, 1111 is the bit configuration we have taken as decimal 15, but let us pursue this approach by letting 1111 represent the *signed* number -1 and see what results.

We wish to maintain one of the features of signed numbers that has already been introduced, namely that bit 3 shall be used as a sign bit, 0 meaning a positive number (or zero), 1 meaning a negative number. Note that assigning the value -1 to the configuration 1111 is compatible with that objective. Thus whatever this number system looks like, it evidently will contain eight negative numbers (1111 1110 ... 1000), seven positive numbers (0001 0010 ... 0111), and zero (0000). Once again we shall determine the value of a negative number by describing instead how a number is *negated*. If the arithmetic of this new system is to be compatible with our usual notions of integer arithmetic, then the following equations must hold. Let k be *any* number (bit configuration) in the system, and observe that

$$-k = 0 - k$$
$$= (1 - 1) - k$$
$$= 1 + (-1) - k$$
$$= [(-1) - k] + 1$$

The significance of the expression

$$(-1) - k$$

lies in the fact that $-1 = 1111$; hence the subtraction of the bit configuration k from this number will never require any "borrowing," and in fact as the reader can easily verify, the result of this subtraction is simply the *ones-complement of k*. The expression

$$[(-1) - k] + 1 = [\text{ones complement of } k] + 1$$

is called the **twos-complement** of k. As we see, the twos-complement of a number is calculated by taking its ones-complement (by simply reversing all its bits), and then adding 1 to the result. The resulting number system is shown in the following table, where "negative" now means "twos-complement."

Decimal	Binary	Negative	Decimal
0	0000	0000	0
+1	0001	1111	−1
+2	0010	1110	−2
+3	0011	1101	−3
+4	0100	1100	−4
+5	0101	1011	−5
+6	0110	1010	−6
+7	0111	1001	−7
.	....	1000	−8

There are a number of observations that we can make from an examination of this table. First, note that $-0 = 0$, as is easily verified by finding the twos-complement of the configuration 0000. Thus in this system, 0 has a *unique* representation, and that was one of our goals. Next, we see that the *form* of the negative numbers is really quite unpleasant, as far as *we* are concerned, for to determine what number a negative configuration represents (one in which the sign bit is on), we must actually go through the twos-complement of the number to change its sign, a process that is more difficult than in the ones-complement case, and a problem that simply did not exist in the sign-magnitude representation. But we shall see that although this number scheme may be more difficult for *us* to interpret, the apparent complexity is more than compensated for by a vastly increased *simplicity* for the central processing unit. It is this simplicity that motivates the use of twos-complement number systems on the VAX-11, and in fact, on most

Main Memory and Computer Arithmetic   Chap. 2

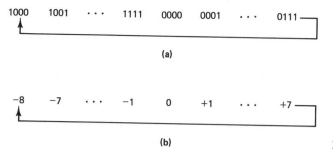

(a)

(b)

Figure 2.9.1

modern-day computing systems. Finally, note the last line of the table. We have introduced a number, -8, which has no positive counterpart. In fact, if we calculate the negative (twos-complement) of -8, we find that it equals -8 itself; that is, $-(-8) = -8$. The fact that we now have *two* bit configurations—0000 and 1000—which are their own negatives turns out to be far more a curiosity than a problem, although there is one case that we shall see later in which -8 needs to be given some special attention. The sudden appearance of this number -8 results from the fact that now there is *no* second representation of 0.

Figure 2.9.1 is analogous to Figure 2.8.1 and shows the structure of the twos-complement number system for 4-bit words. Notice that the "discontinuity" in the number scheme, which in the unsigned case occurs between 15 and 0, now appears between $+7$ and -8.

Before moving on to some twos-complement arithmetic we comment on the term itself—*twos*-complement. The term derives from the fact that for any number k of the number system, the negative $-k$ can be calculated by subtracting k's bit configuration from $10000 = 2^4$, although of course this number is *not* itself in the number system. For example, the negative of $1011 = -5$ is calculated as

$$-1011 = 10000 - 1011 = 0101$$

In particular, note that

$$-0000 = 10000 - 0000 = 10000$$

which, in a *four*-bit word representation, is truncated to 0000; and

$$-1000 = 10000 - 1000 = 1000$$

that is, $-(-8) = -8$.

2.10 TWOS-COMPLEMENT ARITHMETIC

Consider the following 4-bit word addition problem:

$$0101 + 0001 = 0110$$

If the words are considered as unsigned numbers, the addition is correct: $5 + 1 = 6$. If, instead, they are interpreted as signed, twos-complement numbers, the addition is also correct: $+5 + (+1) = +6$. But now consider

$$0101 + 0110 = 1011$$

As unsigned addition, this is $5 + 6 = 11$, which is correct. But treated as the sum of signed numbers it is $+5 + (+6) = -5$, which, of course, is incorrect. What has gone wrong in this case is evidently a result of the fact that there was a carry *into* bit 3; and since bit 3 is interpreted as the sign bit in twos-complement arithmetic, a sign change has resulted.

The addition

$$1010 + 0100 = 1110$$

is correct in either the unsigned interpretation ($10 + 4 = 14$) or the signed interpretation $[-6 + (+4) = -2]$. Observe that in this case there was *no* carry into the high-order bit.

Consider next the addition

$$1010 + 0110 = (1)0000 = 0000$$

In the unsigned interpretation, this is $10 + 6 = 0$, which is not correct. In its signed interpretation, the addition is $-6 + (+6) = 0$, and this result is correct. But something interesting has occurred here. There *was* a carry *into* the sign bit, yet unlike the preceding example, the arithmetic is correct. But notice that, unlike the preceding case, there has also been a carry *out of* the sign bit.

Finally, consider

$$1010 + 1100 = (1)0110 = 0110$$

As unsigned addition, this is $10 + 12 = 6$. As signed arithmetic, it is $-6 + (-4) = +6$. Both of these are incorrect, and we note that whereas there was a carry out of bit 3, there was no carry into bit 3.

It should be clear that the correctness or incorrectness of addition, in both the unsigned and twos-complement signed interpretations, is closely related to which carries, into and out of the high-order bit of the word, did or did not occur. In fact, we have the following general results, which the reader is asked to establish as an exercise.

> **Unsigned addition** is correct if and only if *no* carry out of the high-order bit of the sum occurred.
>
> **Signed (twos-complement) addition** is correct if and only if either (1) neither a carry *into* nor a carry *out of* the high-order bit of the sum occurred; or (2) *both* a carry *into* and *out of* the high-order bit of the sum occurred. (Equivalently, signed addition is *incorrect* if and only if precisely *one* carry, into or out of the high-order bit of the sum, occurred.)

Subtraction can be dealt with quite easily, for we take $A - B$ to be the same as $A + (-B)$, where $-B$ is the twos-complement of B, *regardless* of whether the numbers are interpreted as signed or unsigned. Consider the following examples.

(As before, the decimal equivalents for the signed and unsigned interpretations are shown in brackets.)

$$(a)\ 0110 - 0011 = 0110 + 1101 = (1)0011 = 0011$$
$$[+6 - (+3) = +3; 6 - 3 = 3]$$

$$(b)\ 0011 - 0110 = 0011 + 1010 = 1101$$
$$[+3 - (+6) = -3; 3 - 6 = 13]$$

$$(c)\ 1011 - 0100 = 1011 + 1100 = (1)0111 = 0111$$
$$[-5 - (+4) = +7; 11 - 4 = 7]$$

$$(d)\ 0100 - 1011 = 0100 + 0101 = 1001$$
$$[+4 - (-5) = -7; 4 - 11 = 7]$$

The reader can verify that signed subtraction is correct in case (a), where both carries into and out of bit 3 occur, and in case (b), where neither of these carries occur. Signed subtraction is incorrect in (c) and (d), where exactly one of these carries takes place. Thus based on this evidence, the correctness and incorrectness of signed subtraction appear to follow the rules for signed addition. In the unsigned case, however, exactly the opposite seems to be the case. Carries *out of* bit 3 occur in examples (a) and (c), cases in which the subtraction is *correct*. In examples (b) and (d), where no such carry out of the high-order bit occurs, the unsigned subtraction yields arithmetically incorrect results. In fact, as the reader is asked to verify, this is precisely the case.

> Subtraction $(A - B)$ in a twos-complement number system is converted to the addition of the minuend (A) and the twos-complement $(-B)$ of the subtrahend. The carries into and out of the high-order bit of the sum determine the arithmetic correctness and incorrectness of the subtraction, as follows:
>
> **Unsigned subtraction** is correct if and only if a carry out of the high-order bit of the sum occurred.
>
> **Signed (twos-complement) subtraction** is correct if and only if either (1) neither a carry *into* nor a carry *out of* the high-order bit of the sum occurred; or (2) *both* a carry *into* and *out of* the high-order bit of the sum occurred. (Equivalently, signed subtraction is *incorrect* if and only if precisely *one* carry, into or out of the high-order bit of the sum, occurred.)

There is one case which, although appearing to be an exception to these rules, in fact is not, with the proper interpretation. Consider the subtraction

$$1100 - 1000 = 1100 + 1000 = (1)0100 = 0100$$
$$[-4 - (-8) = +4; 12 - 8 = 4]$$

We note that there is a carry out of bit 3, and that the unsigned subtraction is correct, as expected. But there appears to be no carry *into* bit 3, and thus we would expect signed subtraction to be *incorrect*, yet it is not. In fact, there *is* a carry into bit 3—it occurred when 1000 was twos-complemented, for the twos-complement of 1000 is 0111 + 1 = 1000, with a carry out of bit 2. Thus the number 1000 needs to be treated with a bit more care than other twos-complement numbers; but note also that this is the *only* number for which this apparent contradiction occurs. (But see also Exercise 2.10.4.)

We commented earlier that processes that appear *to us* to be complex are also likely to be complex for the central processor, and therefore considerations of efficiency and speed dictate that they be avoided. The twos-complement number system may *appear* to be complex, mainly because the negative numbers are in a form that is not particularly convenient for us readily to recognize. But from the processor's standpoint, we have devised an especially simple scheme, for both addition and subtraction are *uniform* processes, which are independent of the signs of the numbers and of whether *we* interpret those numbers as signed or unsigned. That is, the processor never needs to "know" what our interpretations are, and thus there is no costly decision making on the part of the CPU in performing the arithmetic. It is for this reason that most computers, including the VAX, employ twos-complement arithmetic when dealing with the arithmetic of words.

2.11 THE CENTRAL PROCESSING UNIT CONDITION CODES

Just because we know how the central processing unit performs additions and subtractions, and thus we can anticipate the correctness and incorrectness of the results, does not mean that our problems are over. For in the course of performing a collection of computations it is by no means unusual that the processor will be dealing with data whose values *we do not know*. Indeed, if we knew all the "answers," there would be no need for the computer in the first place. Thus typically, a task begins with data that are known to us, many computations take place within the CPU, and the purpose of the computations is to produce the end result we were seeking. But it is certainly conceivable that some of these intermediate calculations will result in numbers that are arithmetically incorrect, as we have seen. The situation is going to be chaotic at worst, and unreliable at best, unless *we* can somehow determine that something has gone amiss and perhaps can take corrective action.

Within the central processing unit are four "indicators" which give us much information about what occurred as a result of the *last* operation carried out by the processor. In fact, these indicators are part of the register which in Figure 1.2.1 is labeled "processor status." Each time the CPU completes an arithmetic operation, it sets these four indicators in a particular way, depending on what the operation was and what took place in the course of performing it. We can think of these indicators as 1-bit "miniwords," each of which can take on only the values 0 or 1. If an indicator is given the value 1, we say that the processor **sets** the indicator; if it is given the value 0, the processor is said to **clear** the indicator. The indicators and how the processor sets and clears them are described below.

The **negative indicator**, abbreviated N, is *set* if the result of the last operation was *negative* (that is, resulted in bit 3 being set); otherwise, N is *cleared*.

The **zero indicator**, abbreviated Z, is *set* if the result of the last operation was *zero* (that is, resulted in a word all of whose bits were 0); otherwise, Z is *cleared*.

The **overflow indicator** is abbreviated V (not O, so that there is no confusion between the letter O and the numeral 0). The term "overflow" refers to an overflow of the twos-complement signed number system—a result that caused a carry *out of* bit 2. Thus V is typically *set* if a carry out of bit 2 and into bit 3 occurred; if no such carry occurred, V is typically *cleared*.

The **carry indicator**, abbreviated C, is associated with carries *out of* bit 3. C is normally *set* if a carry out of bit 3 occurred and is *cleared* otherwise.

These four indicators are collectively referred to as the **processor condition codes**, and their importance lies in the fact that at the end of an arithmetic computation we can examine them, and based on their values, we can gain much information about what took place as a result of the calculation. Of particular importance to us at present is that by examining the condition codes immediately following an addition or subtraction, we can determine the correctness of the result. And while it is not yet clear just exactly *how* we are to examine these codes, we can rest assured that any problems that might arise as the result of some arithmetic operation will not have gone unnoticed by the processor.

In the descriptions above of how the processor deals with the condition codes, we have been a little vague, having used words such as "typically" and "normally." This has been intentional, for in fact it is *not* the case that the processor *always* sets C whenever a carry out of bit 3 occurs, for example. To see why this is so, suppose for the moment that the processor behaved in a completely slavish fashion, *always* setting C on carries out of bit 3, and *always* setting V on carries into bit 3. Consider now the addition (which we interpret as signed)

$$1010 + 0111 = 0001 \quad [-6 + (+7) = +1]$$

Since both carries into and out of bit 3 took place, both V and C should be set. But now if we wish to determine the correctness of this addition, we examine V and note that it is *set*. What does this tell us? Nothing, until we examine C as well. (Noting that C is also set indicates that the signed addition is correct.) Thus in order to gain the required information from the condition codes, it has been necessary for us to examine *two* indicators.

In fact, we simply cannot give hard-and-fast rules as to how the processor sets and clears its condition codes, for its behavior relative to these indicators depends not only on the *result* of the operation being performed (addition, subtraction, increment, or whatever), but also on *the operation itself*—its behavior relative to addition and subtraction, for example, is *different*. We shall describe here how the processor treats the condition codes upon twos-complement addition and subtraction; its behavior relative to any *other* operation is dependent on that operation and will be described at the appropriate time.

At the completion of the operation of **addition**, the central processor sets its condition codes as follows.

N is *set* if the result of the addition is negative (bit 3 is on); **N** is *cleared* otherwise.

Z is *set* if the result of the addition is zero (all 4 bits are 0); **Z** is *cleared* otherwise.

V is *set* if a twos-complement overflow occurred, that is, if the resulting signed number could not be held in bits 2, 1, and 0. More precisely, **V** is *set* if precisely one carry, into or out of bit 3, occurred; **V** is cleared otherwise.

C is *set* if a carry out of bit 3 occurred as a result of the addition; **C** is cleared otherwise.

At the completion of the operation of **subtraction**, the central processor sets its condition codes as follows.

N is *set* if the result of the subtraction is negative (bit 3 is on); **N** is *cleared* otherwise.

Z is *set* if the result of the subtraction is zero (all 4 bits are 0); **Z** is *cleared* otherwise.

V is *set* if a twos-complement overflow occurred, that is, if the resulting signed number could not be held in bits 2, 1, and 0. More precisely, **V** is *set* if precisely one carry, into or out of bit 3, occurred; **V** is cleared otherwise.

C is *set* if a carry out of bit 3 did *not* occur as a result of the subtraction; **C** is cleared otherwise.

The reader should take the time to examine these actions in detail and to observe that the processor has set the codes, and in particular V and C, in such a way as to give the user the maximum useful information. Specifically, the state of the V indicator tells us precisely the correctness or incorrectness of signed addition or subtraction. The state of the C indicator gives us complete information about the correctness or incorrectness of unsigned addition and subtraction. In particular, notice that C is set in exactly opposite ways for addition and subtraction, and these correspond to the rules for unsigned addition and subtraction which we had derived in the preceding section. In summary, a signed addition or subtraction is *correct* if and only if, upon completion of the operation, V is *clear*; and an unsigned addition or subtraction is *correct* if and only if, upon completion of the operation, C is *clear*.

2.12 EXERCISES

2.4.1. Show that a memory unit made up of n ordered memory cells can take on 2^n distinct configurations. (Something along the lines of the Principle of Mathematical Induction is required for a formal proof of this result.)

2.5.1. Verify that $2106_8 = 1094_{10}$ and that $2106_{10} = 4072_8$.

2.5.2. Convert each of the following number representations to a representation in the base specified.

(a) $421_5 = ?_2$ (b) $1221_4 = ?_8$ (c) $1011101_2 = ?_6$

(d) $1011_2 = ?_6$ (e) $1011_6 = ?_2$ (f) $1212_3 = ?_{10}$

(g) $1212_{10} = ?_3$ (h) $11_5 = ?_7$ (i) $11_7 = ?_5$

2.5.3. Convert each of the following decimal numbers to its binary representation.

(a) 27   (b) 101   (c) 64   (d) 63   (e) 127

(f) 1023   (g) 2047   (h) 2048

2.5.4. Convert each of the following binary numbers to its decimal representation.

(a) 101   (b) 11101   (c) 100000   (d) 11111

(e) 1000001   (f) 11100011   (g) 11111111

2.5.5. Convert each of the decimal numbers in Exercise 2.5.3 to its hexadecimal (base-16) representation.

2.5.6. Convert each of the binary numbers in Exercise 2.5.4 to its hexadecimal (base-16) representation.

2.5.7. Convert each of the following hexadecimal numbers to its binary representation.

(a) A2E   (b) 1101   (c) 1D00   (d) 10FF

(e) FFF   (f) 1FFF   (g) ABC   (h) 15

2.5.8. Convert each of the hexadecimal numbers in Exercise 2.5.7 to its decimal representation.

2.5.9. Perform the indicated operations in the bases specified, and check the computations by converting to the base-10 representation.

(a) $172_8 + 633_8$ (b) $142_{16} + 2A4_{16}$

(c) $101110_2 + 11101_2$ (d) $101110_2 - 11101_2$

(e) $2A7_{16} - 1FA_{16}$ (f) $10110_2 \cdot 1101_2$

(g) $1D4_{16} \cdot C2_{16}$ (h) $2A7_{12} + 12B_{12}$

2.5.10. If, in the decimal representation system, 125.32 means

$$1 \cdot 10^2 + 2 \cdot 10^1 + 5 \cdot 10^0 + 3 \cdot 10^{-1} + 2 \cdot 10^{-2}$$

then

(a) What is meant by $1A4.3D_{16}$?

(b) What is the value of the quotient $831_{16}/24_{16}$?

2.5.11. It is fairly obvious that the "digits" required to represent a given number generally increases as the base of the number representation system decreases. Show that the number of digits required for a number's representation in base n may be as many as k times as large as that required for the number's representation in base n^k.

2.7.1. Determine the largest number that can be held in a 8-bit, 12-bit, 16-bit, 24-bit, and 32-bit word.

2.7.2. Show in general that if a memory word contains n bits, the largest number which that word can contain is $2^n - 1$.

2.8.1. We define the **complement of a bit** to be the bit's reverse state—the complement of 0 is 1, and the complement of 1 is 0. Show that a 4-bit word can be *incremented* by complementing bit 0; if the result is 0, we complement bit 1; if the result is 0, we complement bit 2; if the result is 0, we complement bit 3. More succinctly, beginning at bit 0, we complement bits until the result of the last complement is a 1.

2.8.2. Evaluate the sums of the following 4-bit words, and state the corresponding results in decimal.

(a) $1001 + 0011$ (b) $0111 + 0110$ (c) $1101 + 0110$
(d) $1111 + 1111$ (e) $0001 + 1111$ (f) $1001 + 0111$

2.8.3. Prove that the sum of two 4-bit words is arithmetically correct if and only if the sum resulted in *no* carry out of bit 3.

2.8.4. Evaluate, or attempt to evaluate, the following 4-bit subtractions, and state the corresponding results in decimal.
(a) $1001 - 0011$ (b) $0111 - 0110$ (c) $1101 - 0110$
(d) $1111 - 1111$ (e) $0110 - 1001$ (f) $0111 - 1011$

2.9.1. Perform the additions and subtractions of the following 4-bit numbers, interpreted as *sign-magnitude* numbers, and state the corresponding results in decimal.
(a) $1011 + 1011$ (b) $0110 + 0011$ (c) $1000 + 0101$
(d) $1011 - 1100$ (e) $1000 - 0101$ (f) $0101 - 1000$
(g) $0101 - 0000$ (h) $0000 - 0101$ (i) $1000 - 0000$

2.9.2. (a) Prove that the sum of two sign-magnitude numbers having the *same* sign will be arithmetically correct if and only if the addition results in *no* carry out of bit 2 of the sum.
(b) Prove that the sum of two sign-magnitude numbers having *opposite* signs will *always* be arithmetically correct.
(c) Prove that the *difference* of two sign-magnitude numbers having the *same* sign will *always* be arithmetically correct.
(d) State and prove a result concerning the arithmetic correctness of the difference of two sign-magnitude numbers having *opposite* signs.

2.9.3. Find the ones-complement of each of the following 4-bit words.
(a) 1101   (b) 0110   (c) 1111   (d) 0000   (e) 1010

2.9.4. State the decimal value of each of the 4-bit words in Exercise 2.9.3, interpreted as ones-complement numbers.

2.9.5. Prove that the sum of two ones-complement *positive* numbers is arithmetically correct if and only if there occurs *no* carry out of bit 2. (Take "sum" to mean ordinary 4-bit binary addition.)

2.9.6. We have seen that in some circumstances, applying 4-bit addition to words interpreted as ones-complement numbers results in correct results (see Exercise 2.9.5, for example), whereas in others the results are quite incorrect. In a few cases, the results are "almost" arithmetically correct. For example,

$$1011 + 0111 = (1)0010 \qquad [-4 + (+7) = +2]$$

should yield $+3$ as a result. The problem centers on the carry out of bit 3, and this situation can be salvaged if we redefine what is meant by **ones-complement addition**. Specifically, define the sum of two ones-complement 4-bit words to be the 4-bit binary sum *plus the carry* (0 or 1) *out of bit 3*. The example above then becomes

$$1011 + 0111 = 0010 + (1) = 0011 \qquad [-4 + (+7) = +3]$$

Determine conditions, in terms of carries into and out of bit 3, under which the addition of two ones-complement numbers will be arithmetically correct.

2.9.7. How does the definition of ones-complement addition, as stated in Exercise 2.9.6, affect the addition of two 4-bit words which are interpreted as *unsigned*? That is, is this new definition of addition compatible with the standard 4-bit binary addition we have been using for unsigned numbers?

2.9.8. Define the **difference** of two ones-complement numbers A and B to be $A - B = A + (-B)$, where the addition is the ones-complement addition defined in Exercise 2.9.6, and $-B$ is the ones-complement of B. Determine the conditions under which ones-complement subtraction is correct.

2.9.9. Using the definitions of Exercises 2.9.6 and 2.9.8, evaluate each of the following ones-complement sums and differences, and in each case state whether the result is correct. If a result is incorrect, state *why* it is incorrect.

    (a) $0101 + 0011$ **(b)** $1011 + 1100$ **(c)** $1011 + 0010$
    (d) $0101 - 0011$ **(e)** $1011 - 1100$ **(f)** $1010 - 0000$
    (g) $1010 - 1000$ **(h)** $1010 - 1111$ **(i)** $1010 + 1111$

2.10.1. Find the twos-complement of each of the 4-bit words in Exercise 2.9.3.

2.10.2. Prove that the only twos-complement numbers which equal their own (twos-complement) negatives are 0 and -8.

2.10.3. Perform the indicated operations on the following pairs of 4-bit words, with their twos-complement interpretation. In each case state the result; whether a carry into and/or out of bit 3 occurred; and whether the result is correct or incorrect when the word contents are interpreted as unsigned and signed numbers. Then verify that the correctness or incorrectness is compatible with the results stated in Section 2.10.

    (a) $0101 + 0011$ **(b)** $1010 + 1010$ **(c)** $1101 - 0011$
    (d) $1010 + 0011$ **(e)** $1110 - 1000$ **(f)** $0011 - 1010$
    (g) $1010 + 0000$ **(h)** $1010 - 0000$ **(i)** $0110 - 0000$

2.10.4. It was stated that when the number $-8 = 1000$ is twos-complemented, a carry *into* bit 3 occurs, and this accounts for the correctness of certain subtractions which our general rules would otherwise indicate should be incorrect. Although -8 may be the only number for which what appears to be an *obvious* contradiction needs to be explained, it is not the only number in which a carry occurs upon negation. In fact, consider

$$1100 - 0000 = 1100 + 0000 = 1100$$

$$[-4 - 0 = -4; 12 - 0 = 12]$$

The result is correct in both the signed and unsigned interpretations, yet it should be *incorrect*, at least in the unsigned case, for there appears to be no carry *out of* bit 3. But show in fact that *both* carries, into and out of bit 3, occurred when 0000 was twos-complemented, and thus the correctness in this case is compatible with the general results established in Section 2.10.

2.10.5. Show that if 4-bit words are interpreted as *signed, twos-complement* numbers, the addition of two such *positive* numbers will be correct if and only if no carry into bit 3 occurred.

2.10.6. Show that if 4-bit words are interpreted as *signed, twos-complement* numbers, the addition of two such *negative* numbers will be correct if and only if a carry into bit 3 occurred. (Notice that a carry *out of* bit 3 will always occur in this case.)

2.10.7. Show that if 4-bit words are interpreted as *signed, twos-complement* numbers, the addition of a *positive* number and a *negative* number will *always* be correct, and that a carry *into* the sign bit occurs if and only if a carry *out of* the sign bit also occurs.

2.10.8. Show that the *difference* of two *unsigned* 4-bit numbers will be arithmetically correct if and only if, upon addition of the twos-complement of the subtrahend, a carry out of the high-order bit occurs. Show that this condition is equivalent to the saying that in the subtraction at bit 3, no "borrow" was required.

2.10.9. Establish the results stated in Section 2.10 for the correctness of *signed* (twos-complement) subtraction.

2.11.1. Repeat Exercise 2.10.3 and determine the state of the condition codes N, Z, V, and C after the arithmetic operation.

CHAPTER

3 LOGIC

3.1 STATEMENTS AND CONNECTIVES

We consider the principal task of a computer to be the processing of data, and the familiar arithmetic operations of addition, subtraction, multiplication, and division come most naturally to mind as the kinds of processing that are done. In Chapter 2 we explicitly assumed that the central processing unit was capable of performing some of these operations on 4-bit words. But even the operation of addition— an operation that we tend to think of as fairly "primitive" relative to, say, the extraction of square roots and the evaluation of trigonometric functions—is quite high on the scale of complexity when compared with some other operations performed by the computer's circuitry. It is one of the goals of this chapter to discover the basic "building blocks" that are combined to form the more complex functions of the central processing unit. Our approach is of some historical interest, and the reader may be surprised to learn that much of today's computing derives from the *logic of statements*.

We are going to be concerned here with the concept of "statement," which we can think of as an English sentence with a special property. Consider the following three sentences: "Watch your weight!", "What time is it?", and "Today is Tuesday." We recognize each of these as satisfying some set of grammatical rules which makes them sentences, yet they differ in a *secondary* characteristic of interest. The last of these is the only one of the three for which it is *meaningful* to ask the question: Is the sentence *true* or *false*? Truth and falsity are concepts that simply do not apply to the first two of the sentences. As to "Today is Tuesday," we might assign "true" or "false" to this as a *value*, depending on the day of the week. That is, the value is dependent on circumstances beyond the meaning of the sentence itself. In contrast, some sentences are *always* true ("The square of a nonzero real number is positive"), while some are always false ("The Cubs will win the American League pennant this year").

We informally define a **statement** to be a declarative English sentence to which we can meaningfully assign one and only one of the **truth values, true** or **false**. Thus "Today is Tuesday" is a statement, whereas "Watch your weight!" is not, because in the latter case no *meaning* can be attached to the truth or falsity of such a sentence. Lest the reader think that any declarative sentence will automatically satisfy our definition, consider the classic example: "This sentence is false." If we attempt to assign to this "statement" the value *true*, the statement asserts its own *falsity*. Conversely, to say that the statement is *false* leads to the conclusion that it is *not false*—that it is *true*. Thus it is not possible to assign a *unique*—one and only one—truth value to this sentence, and consequently it will *not* be included among the statements. Notice that the definition of "statement" insists only that a unique truth value *can* be assigned to a sentence, but it says nothing about *how* such an assignment is to be made. In fact, we do not *care* what the truth value of a sentence is, only that it has one, and only one. Indeed, we shall shortly abandon all interest in the *content* of statements and concentrate our attention on the *structure* of statements.

When we speak or write in English, we rarely do so in simple sentences of the "subject-verb-object" type. Rather, for variety and efficiency, and for the transmission of exact meaning, we combine simple statements into more complex structures with special-purpose words, called **connectives**, used precisely to "connect" simple statements. Examples of these are AND, OR, BUT, IF...THEN, UNLESS, and so on. We shall center our investigation of connectives on just a few of these, and even at that our approach will be quite unsophisticated; a formal study of **statement logic** would do little to enhance our understanding of computing, and a more informal development will move us along quickly to our ultimate goal: the construction of computer circuitry to perform simple but important **logical operations**.

A **compound statement** is a statement constructed by joining two statements with a connective. Observe that this definition states explicitly that a compound statement is itself a *statement*—that is, the compound statement can be assigned a truth value in a unique fashion. For example, if p and q are statements (each capable of assuming one of the values *true* and *false*), then p AND q also has that property. Now we have observed that the *method* of assigning truth values to statements is left unspecified, and thus values can be assigned to p AND q any way we might choose. But common English usage not only implies that the value of a compound statement depends in some fashion on the values of the simple statements that compose it, but also dictates the value of the compound statement once the values of the simple statements are specified. To gain some direction as to how values should be assigned to p AND q for given values of p and q, consider the example p: "Today is Tuesday" and q: "It is raining." Our ordinary interpretation of "Today is Tuesday AND it is raining" would lead us to assign the value *true* to this compound statement on any rainy Tuesday, but on clear days,

FIGURE 3.1.1

p	q	p AND q
True	True	True
True	False	False
False	True	False
False	False	False

FIGURE 3.1.2

p	q	p OR q
True	True	True
True	False	True
False	True	True
False	False	False

or days other than Tuesday, we would assign this the value *false*. Thus English usage appears to assign the value *true* to a **conjunction**—a statement formed by joining statements with the connective AND—*only* in the case that *both* simple statements are *true*, the compound statement having the value *false* otherwise. With this guidance we can give a *definition* of the connective AND, as shown in Figure 3.1.1. Notice that the table allows for all possible combinations of assignments for the individual statements p and q and that, as we had inferred from English usage, the conjunction p AND q is true only when both p and q are *true*.

Another common connective is OR, and with the groundwork laid above, we can treat it in a more cursory fashion. If the reader uses again the sample statements given above and considers "Today is Tuesday OR it is raining," he or she will doubtless conclude that the only case in which this **disjunction**—the compound statement formed by the connective OR—will be *false* is that in which both p and q are *false* (for example, on a sunny Thursday). Thus we claim that the definition of Figure 3.1.2 is compatible with the common usage of the connective OR.

We have a second interpretation of OR which is used frequently in conversation and which can lead to misunderstandings, since we have no distinctive *word* for it. This is the *exclusive* use of the word OR, in which the context or some other suggestion such as verbal emphasis or intonation *excludes* the first line of the table in Figure 3.1.2. As a simple example, consider "This weekend I am flying to Philadelphia OR Seattle." What is implied here is the rarely appended phrase "but not both," and it is this phrase that distinguishes OR from EXCLUSIVE-OR, whose **truth table** (table of truth values) is given in Figure 3.1.3. Notice that it coincides with the table for OR except in the case in which both p and q are *true*.

There are many other connectives which are used in written and verbal communication, but the three we have already discussed are sufficient for our present purposes; indeed, we have even gone further here than was really required. How-

FIGURE 3.1.3

p	q	p EXCLUSIVE-OR q
True	True	False
True	False	True
False	True	True
False	False	False

FIGURE 3.1.4

p	NOT p
True	False
False	True

ever, we do need one more concept from English, one that is not a connective, but rather a **modifier**—it does not *connect* simple statements, it *modifies* the value of a single statement. The modifier is NOT, and its truth table is shown in Figure 3.1.4. As is seen, it simply reverses the value of a statement, a concept not unlike the ones-complementing of a bit value.

Figure 3.1.5 summarizes the definitions we have constructed of the connectives and the modifier NOT, in which we have made the following *notational* changes. In the definition of conjunction, we have replaced the connective AND by "·" (although simple juxtaposition of the statement labels is equally satisfactory). Thus $p \cdot q$ (or simply pq) denotes p AND q. In a similar fashion, OR is replaced by "+," EXCLUSIVE-OR by "$\oplus$," and NOT by the prime ('). These changes are made in the interest of economy of expression of these terms, and the symbolic representations we have chosen correspond to current notational usage in **Boolean algebra**, the study of the logical structure of statements. Finally, *true* and *false* have been replaced by the symbols 1 and 0, respectively. The reader is cautioned against reading too much into the results of Figure 3.1.5; · (or juxtaposition), +, and ' *look like* multiplication, addition, and ones-complementing, and in fact the tables themselves almost appear to be tables for the arithmetic of these operations. But the appearance results only from notational sleight-of-hand, as a review of the *source* of these definitions will reveal.

Statements may be more complex than the simple $p \cdot q$ or $p + q$ we have studied so far. As an example, consider the compound statement $(p \cdot q)'$. To determine the value of this statement for given values of the individual statements p and q, we need only treat $p \cdot q$ first, and then invert (NOT) the result, as shown

FIGURE 3.1.5

AND				OR		
p	q	$p \cdot q$		p	q	$p + q$
1	1	1		1	1	1
1	0	0		1	0	1
0	1	0		0	1	1
0	0	0		0	0	0
(a)				**(b)**		

EXCLUSIVE-OR				NOT	
p	q	$p \oplus q$		p	p'
1	1	0		1	0
1	0	1		0	1
0	1	1			
0	0	0		**(d)**	
(c)					

FIGURE 3.1.6

p	q	$p \cdot q$	$(p \cdot q)'$
1	1	1	0
1	0	0	1
0	1	0	1
0	0	0	1

FIGURE 3.1.7

p	q	p'	q'	$p' + q'$
1	1	0	0	0
1	0	0	1	1
0	1	1	0	1
0	0	1	1	1

in Figure 3.1.6. In a similar fashion, $p' + q'$ is dealt with as shown in Figure 3.1.7.

These last two examples have the interesting property that for given values of the individual statements p and q, each compound statement has exactly the *same* truth value, as a glance at the last columns of the tables of Figures 3.1.6 and 3.1.7 shows. When two statements S_1 and S_2 made up (by means of connectives and the modifier NOT) of simple statements p, q, r, ..., always have the same truth values for each assignment of values to p, q, r, ..., the two statements are said to be **equivalent**, and we write $S_1 = S_2$. Thus our result above could be written: $(pq)' = p' + q'$.

As one final example, we show in Figure 3.1.8 that $p \oplus q = (p + q)(pq)'$. This example suggests what we had in mind when we stated that in introducing the connectives AND, OR, and EXCLUSIVE-OR, we had even gone further than was necessary. We see now that EXCLUSIVE-OR can be written in terms of AND, OR, and NOT, and thus we would not have had to include it in our list of connectives. · But EXCLUSIVE-OR will be seen later to have some rather important uses, and thus we shall maintain it as a separate connective. (In fact, as the reader is asked to show in the exercises, AND can be written in terms of OR and NOT, and thus all of our statement logic could if desired be reduced to these two primitive constructions.)

We conclude this section with some facts about the logical connectives and modifier which are easily verified, and which will be of use in the simplification of expressions. In the equations of Figure 3.1.9, which we shall refer to as the **Boolean relations**, a statement shown as "0" is a statement that can *only* take on the value *false*. An example of such a statement is $p \cdot p'$, where p is any simple statement. In a similar fashion, a statement shown as "1" is one that *always* takes on the value *true* (for example, $p + p'$).

FIGURE 3.1.8

p	q	$p \oplus q$
1	1	0
1	0	1
0	1	1
0	0	0

(a)

p	q	$p + q$	$p \cdot q$	$(p \cdot q)'$	$(p + q) \cdot (p \cdot q)'$
1	1	1	1	0	0
1	0	1	0	1	1
0	1	1	0	1	1
0	0	0	0	1	0

AND

(b)

FIGURE 3.1.9

(a) $p + q = q + p$	(a') $p \cdot q = q \cdot p$
(b) $p + (q + r) = (p + q) + r$	(b') $p \cdot (q \cdot r) = (p \cdot q) \cdot r$
(c) $0 + p = p$	(c') $1 \cdot p = p$
(d) $1 + p = 1$	(d') $0 \cdot p = 0$
(e) $p + p' = 1$	(e') $p \cdot p' = 0$
(f) $p \cdot (q + r) = p \cdot q + p \cdot r$	(f') $p + q \cdot r = (p + q) \cdot (p + r)$
(g) $(p + q)' = p' \cdot q'$	(g') $(p \cdot q)' = p' + q'$
(h) $p + p = p$	(h') $p \cdot p = p$
(i) $(p')' = p$	

3.2 SWITCHING CIRCUITS

A **switch** is a device in an electric circuit that can exist in one of two states, **closed** and **open**. In its closed state, the switch allows current to flow in the circuit; in its open state, it prevents the flow of current. Figure 3.2.1 shows the usual diagrams for a switch in these states. In subsequent diagrams we shall normally show switches in their open states, since in their closed positions they are difficult to distinguish from straight-through wires, and we shall rely on the context to determine their states.

The simplest circuit containing a switch is shown in Figure 3.2.2, in which we have added a *voltage source* (assumed to be 1 volt) and a voltmeter, as a means of determining the switch's state or, otherwise interpreted, the **output** of the circuit. It should be clear that if the switch is *closed*, a current will flow in the circuit and the output of the circuit (the reading on the meter) will be 1. If the switch is *open*, the output will be 0. These results are summarized in Figure 3.2.3(a). Since the output of the circuit is directly related to the switch position, we make a slight shift in notation; a *closed* switch will be said to have the **switch value** 1, and an *open* switch the value 0. This notational change is reflected in Figure 3.2.3(b).

A circuit containing a single switch is almost too simple to be of interest, so we move on to more complex situations. Figure 3.2.4(a) shows a circuit containing

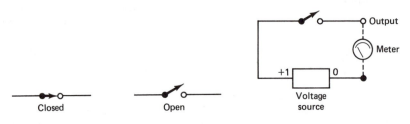

Closed	Open	Voltage source
Figure 3.2.1		**Figure 3.2.2**

Logic   Chap. 3

Switch	Output
Closed	1
Open	0

(a)

Switch	Output
1	1
0	0

(b)

Figure 3.2.3

two switches **in series**. Figure 3.2.4(b) shows the table of output values corresponding to various settings of the switches A and B, and note that since A and B can be set in either of their positions independently of one another, there are *four* possible combinations of switch settings. Since completing (closing) the circuit requires that *both* switches A and B be closed, we see that only the first line of the table yields an output of 1.

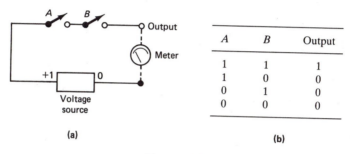

(a)

A	B	Output
1	1	1
1	0	0
0	1	0
0	0	0

(b)

Figure 3.2.4

Figure 3.2.5(a) shows the only other circuit that contains two switches, this time **in parallel**. The reader should have no difficulty in verifying that the table of Figure 3.2.5(b) correctly describes the output of the circuit for the four possible switch settings. We have not bothered to show the voltmeter in this figure, nor shall we in subsequent figures; rather, we assume that the output can be measured in some way or other.

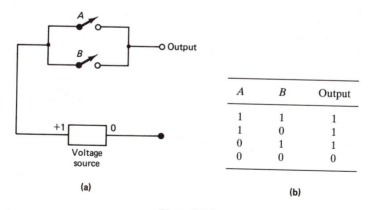

(a)

A	B	Output
1	1	1
1	0	1
0	1	1
0	0	0

(b)

Figure 3.2.5

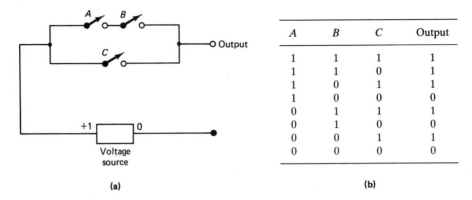

A	B	C	Output
1	1	1	1
1	1	0	1
1	0	1	1
1	0	0	0
0	1	1	1
0	1	0	0
0	0	1	1 .
0	0	0	0

(a)   (b)

Figure 3.2.6

Although these are the only circuits containing two switches, circuits can be made more complex by including more switches. We show one such example in Figure 3.2.6 and leave it to the reader to verify the correctness of the output table. Notice that here there are *eight* distinct switch settings that must be considered.

3.3 STATEMENTS REVISITED

The reader has doubtless observed a similarity between some of the tables constructed in Section 3.1 for *statements* and in Section 3.2 for *switching circuits*. In fact, except for the *names* of the elements, and the *interpretations* of the 0 and 1 entries, there is no difference between Figures 3.1.5(a) and 3.2.4(b), and between Figures 3.1.5(b) and 3.2.5(b). Thus a series switching circuit can be considered to be a *physical representation* of the logical connective AND, where we interpret a *closed* switch as representing the value *true*, and an *open* switch the value *false*. In a similar fashion, a parallel switching circuit and the connective OR are simply different representations of the same abstract concept. And the switching circuit of Figure 3.2.6 has as its corresponding logical statement $AB + C$.

We have not introduced switching circuits that correspond to the connective EXCLUSIVE-OR or the modifier NOT, since these are not easily represented by the type of simple switches we have been considering. These are dealt with in the following section. Also in the next section we develop some consequences of this dual representation. Meanwhile we see that with the proper interpretations, a logical statement can be represented *physically* by a switching circuit; and by the same token, a switching circuit can be represented *logically* by a statement.

3.4 LOGIC GATES

The switches of Section 3.3, shown there as the manually actuated type, will not quite do for our purposes, for what we are seeking is a switch that can be set to its open or closed state by means of the presence or absence of an *electric current*,

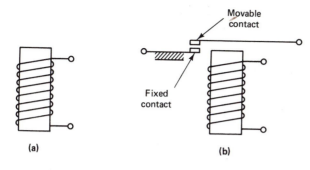

Movable
contact

Fixed
contact

(a)   (b)   Figure 3.4.1

much as a memory cell is set to one of its states. Such switches are easily constructed, however. Consider an iron rod with a wire wound around it, as in Figure
3.4.1(a). Such an arrangement is called an **electromagnet**. When a current is
passed through the wire, the iron rod becomes magnetized, and we can take advantage of this fact to construct a current-activated switch. The embellished electromagnet shown in Figure 3.4.1(b) is called a **relay**. Note that we have included
two contacts, one of which is *fixed*, the other attached to the end of a thin piece
of spring steel and thus *movable*. When a current flows through the wire, the iron
rod becomes a magnet and attracts the spring steel, closing the contacts. When
the current is removed, the spring steel returns to its original position, thereby
opening the contacts. Thus the contacts take the place of our simple switch, and
the state of the contacts—closed or open—is controlled by the presence or absence,
respectively, of a current in the electromagnet. We shall now use relays to rebuild
the switching circuits of Section 3.3, which represent the logical connectives AND
and OR.

Before investigating the details of the relay circuit of Figure 3.4.3, we need
to interpret what is meant when two wires are shown as *crossing* in the figure.
Figure 3.4.2 indicates the difference between two wires which are *not* connected
at their apparent point of intersection, and those which *are* to be interpreted as
connected.

We can now deal with the circuit of Figure 3.4.3. (The dashed lines that
surround most of the circuit will be explained momentarily.) In that figure the
lines labeled A and B are called *inputs* to the switching circuit. If A is at 0 volts,
no current is flowing in the leftmost relay, and hence switch S_A is *open*. On the
other hand, if A is at 1 volt, a current does flow through that relay, and the contacts
of switch S_A are *closed*. Switch S_B is similarly controlled by 0 or 1 volt at input
B. It is not difficult to verify that the output of the circuit will be 1 if and only if
both inputs A and B are at 1 volt. Thus this circuit represents the ANDing of A
and B. We leave it to the reader to verify that Figure 3.4.4 represents A OR B.

At this point our interest focuses only on the *existence* of circuits whose outputs
are the ANDing or ORing of their inputs, not precisely *how* they are constructed.

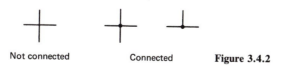

Not connected   Connected   Figure 3.4.2

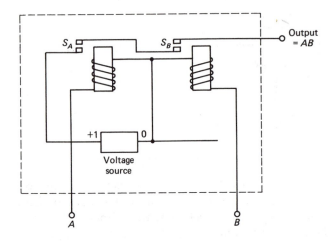

Output = AB

Figure 3.4.3

In our examples we have used relays, since they are conceptually simple devices. But relays have not been used for these purposes since the very early days of computing, having been replaced by a variety of semiconductor devices. No matter—what is important to us is that there *are* such circuits. In fact, for the circuits of Figures 3.4.3 and 3.4.4 we shall reduce everything except the inputs and output—that is, everything within the dashed lines—to a "black box," which is simply a *function* whose output depends in some well-defined way on its inputs. Of course, we know that these circuits also require some voltage source, but we suppress the explicit diagramming of it and simply assume that it is present. In Figure 3.4.5 we show the usual symbols associated with the black boxes for AND and OR circuits, circuits that are called **gates**.

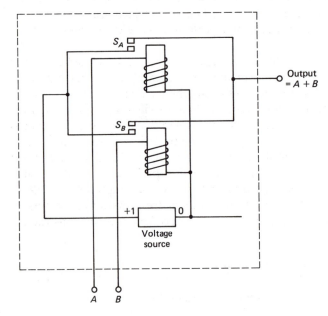

Output = A + B

Figure 3.4.4

Figure 3.4.5

We can also use a relay to construct a physical representation of the logical modifier NOT, although we need to rearrange the relay switch contacts so that they are *normally closed* (see Figure 3.4.6). In this case the contacts are *closed* in the *absence* of a current (that is, when the input A is 0 volts), and they are *open* in the *presence* of a current (when A is at 1 volt). Again we reduce this circuit to a black box called a NOT gate or **inverter**, shown in Figure 3.4.7.

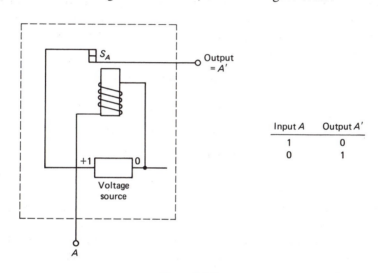

Input A	Output A'
1	0
0	1

Figure 3.4.6

We can finally deal with the connective whose importance has been asserted but for which we have yet to produce a corresponding circuit. Using the relation $p \oplus q = (p + q) \cdot (p \cdot q)'$ we can represent EXCLUSIVE-OR by the combination of gates shown in Figure 3.4.8, as the reader should verify. The circuit symbol for an EXCLUSIVE-OR gate is shown in Figure 3.4.9. Henceforth, in the interest of economy and compatibility with some VAX terminology, we shall use XOR as an abbreviation for EXCLUSIVE-OR.

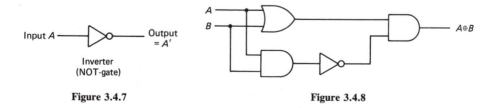

Figure 3.4.7

Figure 3.4.8

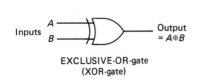

Inputs A / B

Output = A⊕B

EXCLUSIVE-OR-gate
(XOR-gate)

Figure 3.4.9

$AB' + BA'$

Figure 3.4.10

We can now put the Boolean relations of Figure 3.1.9 to use for the purposes of circuit simplification. We give two examples here, and more will be found in the exercises. Consider first the circuit of Figure 3.4.10. The corresponding *logical* statement is $AB' + BA'$, since the circuit consists of the ORing of two gate outputs, each of which is the ANDing of one of the inputs with the NOT of the other. This logical expression can be simplified in the following way (the letters in parentheses corresponding to the Boolean relations of Section 3.1, which are employed at each step):

$$AB' + BA' = (0 + AB') + (BA' + 0) \qquad \text{(c)}$$
$$= (AA' + AB') + (BA' + BB') \qquad \text{(e')}$$
$$= A(A' + B') + B(A' + B') \qquad \text{(f)}$$
$$= (A + B)(A' + B') \qquad \text{(f)}$$
$$= (A + B)(AB)' \qquad \text{(g)}$$

But this last expression is the same as $A \oplus B$, the XOR of A and B. Thus the circuit of Figure 3.4.10 is equivalent to that of Figure 3.4.8.

Next consider the circuit of Figure 3.4.11. The corresponding statement form is $((A + B')' + B')'$, as can readily be verified. Again we simplify this logical expression.

$$((A + B')' + B')' = (A'(B')' + B')' \qquad \text{(g)}$$
$$= (A'B + B')' \qquad \text{(i)}$$
$$= (A'B)'(B')' \qquad \text{(g)}$$
$$= (A'B)'B \qquad \text{(i)}$$
$$= ((A')' + B')B \qquad \text{(g')}$$
$$= (A + B')B \qquad \text{(i)}$$
$$= AB + B'B \qquad \text{(f)}$$
$$= AB + 0 \qquad \text{(e')}$$
$$= AB \qquad \text{(c)}$$

That is, the circuit of Figure 3.4.11 can be reduced to a simple AND gate.

Logic   Chap. 3

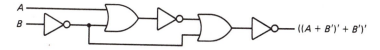

Figure 3.4.11

3.5 SOME SIMPLE COMPUTER CIRCUITRY

We stated that one of the principal goals of this chapter is to discover the basic building blocks which the central processing unit could use to perform the useful tasks of which computers should be capable. In fact, we have discovered them— they are the *gates* of Section 3.4. In this section we shall see a few examples of how these simple gates can be combined into more complex circuits that enable the CPU to "do" arithmetic.

Let us investigate one of the most primitive of arithmetic operations, the addition of two single bits, say x and y. Since each of x and y can assume only the values 1 and 0, we can enumerate the possible values that the sum of these two bits can take on, and these are shown in Figure 3.5.1(a). Comparing this result with that of Figure 3.1.5(c), we see that the sum of x and y is simply their EXCLUSIVE-OR. Now one of the phenomena associated with addition to which we paid much attention in Chapter 2 was a *carry out* of a bit, and this also occurs here, even though we are dealing only with a single bit. Figure 3.5.1(b) enumerates the carry condition for each combination of values for x and y, and it is clear that the carry is nothing but the AND of x and y.

With these results we can now draw a circuit that represents the sum of the single bits x and y and also the carry C that is generated. The circuit is shown in Figure 3.5.2. It is called a **half-adder**, a circuit that turns out not to be particularly useful as a unit itself, but rather as a subunit of more sophisticated circuits. If we think of this little circuit as generating the sum of the ith bits of a 4-bit word, then as we have seen, it will perform the addition of these two bits, generating the sum and also the carry into the next-higher-order bit. The reason for the adjective "half" is that the circuit does *not* take into account any carry *into* this bit position from the *preceding* (next-lower-order) bit.

We shall shortly see that two half-adders can be combined to produce a circuit that *does* take the preceding carry into account and thus is more useful for the construction of a word addition circuit. In the meantime we shall use half-adders

FIGURE 3.5.1

x	y	Sum of x and y = $x \oplus y$
1	1	0
1	0	1
0	1	1
0	0	0

(a)

x	y	Carry = $x \cdot y$
1	1	1
1	0	0
0	1	0
0	0	0

(b)

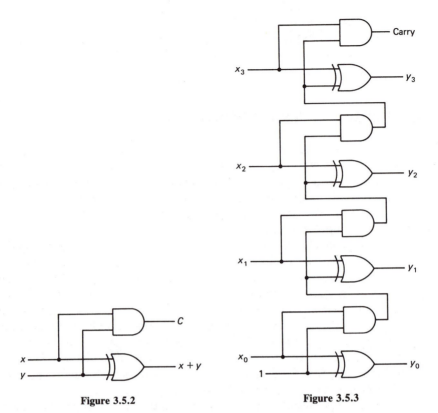

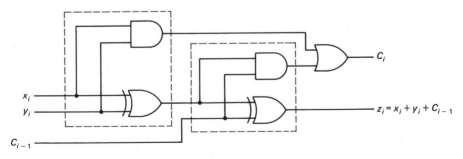

Figure 3.5.2

Figure 3.5.3

to construct a circuit to *increment*—add 1 to—a 4-bit word, a circuit whose existence was assumed in Chapter 2. Figure 3.5.3 is such an incrementing circuit, which represents the 4-bit word arithmetic operation $y_3y_2y_1y_0 = x_3x_2x_1x_0 + 1$. Notice that at the bit 0 level, we have used a *fixed* value of 1 as input to the first XOR gate, which of course represents the number being added. At each subsequent level, one of the inputs is the carry from the preceding bit. Finally, observe that the carry out of bit 3 is *not* used, but we have included it as a part of the bit 3 half-adder.

Figure 3.5.4 is the circuit called a **full adder**. It consists of two half-adders (shown enclosed in dashed lines), the leftmost of which adds the two inputs x_i and

Figure 3.5.4

y_i, and the rightmost adds in the carry C_{i-1} from the *preceding* bit level. We leave to the reader the verification that the OR of the two half-adder carries is the correct carry C_i *out* of this bit, into the next-higher bit level. As opposed to the half-adder, the full adder *does* account for the preceding carry, and we observe that it has *three* inputs.

We can finally deal with 4-bit word addition. An appropriate circuit is shown in Figure 3.5.5, made up for the most part of full adders, as we might expect. We leave most of the analysis to the reader. We do note, however, that at the bit 0 level we have used a half-adder, since there is no preceding (next-lower-order) bit and hence no carry *into* bit 0 with which we have to be concerned. We have also appended a little circuitry at bit 3—*carry* and *overflow* outputs, each of which will be 1 or 0, and which behave according to the way in which the CPU sets the carry (C) and overflow (V) indicators upon addition, as described in Chapter 2. This suggests how the processor can keep track of its "status"—what took place as the result of the last CPU operation.

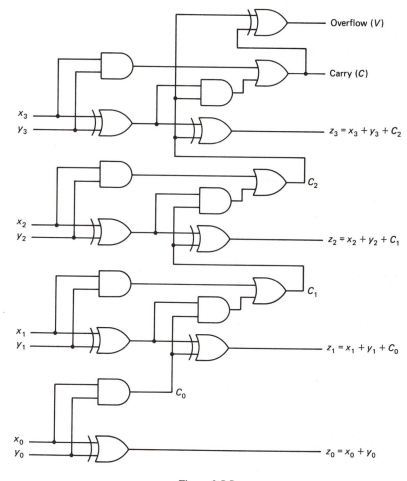

Figure 3.5.5

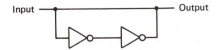

Figure 3.5.6

The last circuit we examine is *not* one that does arithmetic at all, but rather is one that can act as a *memory cell* (Figure 3.5.6). It is called a **coupled inverter latch**, a term which comes from the fact that two inverters are coupled together, and the circuit has the capability of *latching* or *capturing* data that are input to it. To see how it works, suppose that the input is set to 1. Then that 1 acts as an input to the left inverter, whose output is then 0. This 0 then acts as an input to the right inverter, which consequently produces 1 as an output. Now if the original input 1 is *removed*, the latch will remain in this state, since each inverter is being given an appropriate input. (There is a certain amount of "tail-chasing" going on here.) Thus the output will be maintained at 1, even after the input is removed. In a similar fashion, if a 0 input is presented to the circuit, the output will be 0, even after the input is removed. But these actions are precisely what is required of a memory cell, and we now have a concrete example of such a cell which is more up-to-date than the capacitors and cores that we discussed earlier.

We do not choose to push these ideas of computer circuitry beyond the few examples already given, for by now we have made our point—it is possible, by the use of these fundamental gates as building blocks, to design circuitry that will perform arithmetic operations. Nor do we wish to leave the reader with the impression that this is all there is to it, for there are many complexities that must be dealt with to achieve the proper functioning of the central processing unit; but these are primarily of an engineering nature, and discussion of the details would lead us away from our main objective, namely, a study of what computers do and, in general terms, how they do it. However, what we have done so far does justify a claim made early on, namely that computers are relatively simple devices, since their processing amounts to a large extent to the rather fundamental manipulation of 1s and 0s, as we have just seen. Finally, we do not claim that the VAX, or any other computer, for that matter, contains circuitry *identical* to that shown in these examples. Those circuits do perform as advertised, but most processors contain units more primitive than these, which are then used in *combination* with one another to produce the desired results.

3.6 EXERCISES

3.1.1. Define, by means of a table of truth values, each of the following connectives.
 (a) BUT   **(b)** UNLESS   **(c)** IF...THEN

3.1.2. Use truth tables to establish each of the Boolean relations of Figure 3.1.9.

3.1.3. Show that the connective AND can be written in terms of OR and NOT. [*Suggestion:* Take advantage of the Boolean relations of Figure 3.1.9, especially those labeled (g') and (i).]

3.1.4. Use the Boolean relations to show that $(p + r) \cdot (p + r') = p$.

3.1.5. Show that the logical statement $((p' + q) \cdot p)' + q$ always has the value *true*, regardless of the values of p and q.

3.1.6. Define the connective IMPLIES, whose symbol is →, by the table of Figure 3.6.1.

    (a) Show that $p→q = (p·q')' = p' + q$.

    (b) Show that the statement $(p·(p→q))→q$ is always *true*, regardless of the values of p and q.

    (c) Each of the connectives AND, OR, and EXCLUSIVE-OR is *commutative*; that is, $p\,C\,q = q\,C\,p$ for any statements p and q for each such connective C. Show that IMPLIES is *not* commutative.

FIGURE 3.6.1

p	q	$p→q$
1	1	1
1	0	0
0	1	1
0	0	1

3.4.1. (a) Show that if one of the inputs to an OR gate is 0, the output of the OR gate is simply the other input.

    (b) Show that if one of the inputs to an AND gate is 1, the output of the AND gate is simply the other input.

    (c) Show that if one of the inputs to an XOR gate is 0, the output of the XOR gate is simply the other input.

    (d) Show that if one of the inputs to an XOR gate is 1, the XOR gate acts as an *inverter* relative to the other input.

3.4.2. Show that the output of the circuit of Figure 3.6.2 is *always* 1, regardless of the inputs A and B:

    (a) By finding the output for all possible combinations of inputs.

    (b) By comparing this circuit with the result of Exercise 3.1.5.

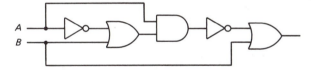

Figure 3.6.2

3.4.3. Write the logical expression equivalent to the circuit of Figure 3.6.3(a). Then use the Boolean relations of Section 3.1 to reduce this expression to one that is equivalent to the circuit of Figure 3.6.3(b).

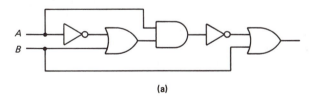

(a)

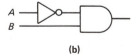

(b)

Figure 3.6.3

3.4.4. As in Exercise 3.4.3, reduce the circuit of Figure 3.6.4 to a corresponding simpler circuit.

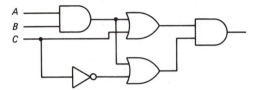

Figure 3.6.4

3.4.5. Define the connective NOR by: p NOR q = NOT(p OR q). Figure 3.6.5 shows the symbol for a NOR gate and the corresponding table of values of this gate.

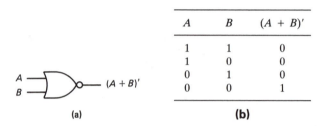

A	B	$(A + B)'$
1	1	0
1	0	0
0	1	0
0	0	1

(a)   **(b)**

Figure 3.6.5

(a) Show that the NOR gate of Figure 3.6.6(a) is wired in such a way that it acts as an *inverter* (NOT gate).

(b) Show that the circuit of Figure 3.6.6(b) has as its output the OR of its inputs A and B.

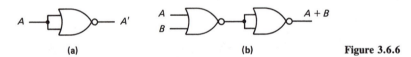

(a)   (b)   **Figure 3.6.6**

(c) Using only NOR gates, construct a circuit that is equivalent to an AND gate.

(d) Using only NOR gates, construct a circuit that is equivalent to an XOR gate. (This exercise establishes that all the connectives, together with NOT, and hence all the gates, can be constructed from this single primitive concept, NOR.)

3.4.6. Define the connective NAND by: p NAND q = NOT(p AND q). In a fashion analogous to that of Exercise 3.4.5, show that all the connectives and NOT, and hence all the logic gates, can be written as various combinations of NAND.

3.5.1. Design a circuit to *decrement* a 4-bit word. [*Suggestion:* At each bit level, one of the inputs to an XOR gate is some combination of the output from the preceding (next-lower-order) gate and one of the inputs to that preceding gate.]

3.5.2. By an analysis similar to that which led to the tables of Figure 3.5.1 and the circuit of Figure 3.5.2, show that the full adder of Figure 3.5.4 adds two bits together with the carry from the preceding bit, and also that it generates the sum and carry out of that bit position.

3.5.3. The effect of the circuit of Figure 3.6.7 has an arithmetic interpretation when $x_3x_2x_1x_0$ and $y_3y_2y_1y_0$ are interpreted as 4-bit words. What is it? What meaning, if any, can be attached to the output of the topmost OR gate (labeled "?" in the figure)?

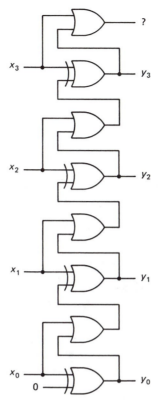

Figure 3.6.7

3.5.4. The circuit in Figure 3.6.8 is called an **RS flip-flop** and, like that of Figure 3.5.6, acts as a **latch**. It differs from the coupled inverter latch in that the input to the flip-flop is never *removed*—it is always either 0 or 1.

(a) Show that if S is set to 0 and R is set to 1, then Q will have the value 1. (Q', which is the complement of Q, will then have the value 0.)

(b) With the state as described in part (a) (that is, with S set to 0 and R set to 1), show that if S is reset to 1 (and if R is left unchanged), then the outputs Q and Q' are unaffected.

(c) With the state as described in part (b), show that if R is now set to 0, then Q's value will change to 0 (and the value of Q' will reset to 1).

(d) Finally, show that resetting R to 1 will leave the outputs Q and Q' unaffected.

(e) Determine the outputs Q and Q' if *both* S and R are set simultaneously to 0. What will be the outputs Q and Q' if S and R are reset simultaneously from their 0 values to a value of 1?

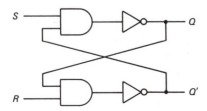

Figure 3.6.8

CHAPTER 4

MEMORY ADDRESSING AND DATATYPES

4.1 8-BIT MEMORY UNITS (BYTES)

We observed in Chapter 2 that the 4-bit words which were introduced there were simply too small to be of any practical use—little realistic processing can be done when one is limited to a number system that ranges from 0 to 15 (unsigned) or -8 to $+7$ (signed). Yet those 4-bit words have served us well throughout Chapters 2 and 3. Their limited size, far from being a hindrance, has allowed us to examine them in detail, to look at all possible cases of various phenomena, and through these examinations to discover several concepts of significance about computer memory and hardware: signed and unsigned number systems, various complementing schemes, overflow and carry conditions, and a glimpse into the electronic circuitry required for the processor to carry out the many types of operations of which a modern computer should be capable. Thus although we are about to embark on an examination of some larger structures that make for more realistic computing, the reader should be aware that relative to the concepts we have already uncovered, there is nothing new to learn.

The first expanded memory unit we shall investigate is the **byte**, which consists of 8 memory bits. Analogous to the 4-bit case, we number the bits of a byte 0 through 7, with bit 0 being the **least-significant bit** (representing 2^0) and bit 7 the **most-significant bit** (representing 2^7). Clearly, the bit configurations of a byte can range from 00000000 to 11111111, and if we interpret these as *unsigned* binary numbers, the range of such numbers is 0 to 255, as is easily verified. On the other hand, if these eight 1s and 0s are to represent a *signed* binary number, with bit 7 serving as the twos-complement sign bit, the range of numbers is -128 to $+127$.

What hardware is required to implement, say, the addition of two 8-bit bytes? The answer is that we need only add to the 4-bit adder of Section 3.5 four more copies of the full adder shown in Figure 3.5.4. How can we determine the correctness of the (signed or unsigned) addition of two bytes? We do so exactly as in the case of 4-bit words, by examining the carries into and out of the high-order bit (which is now bit 7 rather than bit 3). And to assist us in this task, the processor sets the V and C indicators in precisely the same fashion as before: If a carry out of bit 7 occurred, C is set, otherwise it is cleared; and if exactly one carry into or out of bit 7 occurred, V is set, else V is cleared. In brief, each 4-bit concept has its exact analog in the 8-bit case.

4.2 NUMBER REPRESENTATIONS

When we dealt with 4-bit words, we had no particular difficulty in grasping the meaning of a four-digit string of 1s and 0s such as 1101, and even its verbalization

"one-one-oh-one"

was easily understood. In moving to an 8-bit byte, however, a problem begins to reveal itself, namely, that the number of binary digits is growing large enough to become a little cumbersome. Even if a written representation such as 11000110 presents no special problems, the verbalization

"one-one-oh-oh-oh-one-one-oh"

is beginning to become somewhat difficult to comprehend. What is sought is a scheme to compress the notation in such a way that fewer digits are required to represent a byte's contents than the eight that are needed for its binary representation. (The reader who is not convinced that some relief is required here need only consider what would be required for the binary representation of a 16-bit or 32-bit structure. In fact, we shall ultimately consider 128-bit structures, and by then the binary representation will have become completely unmanageable.) Suppose that we take this binary number 11000110 and divide it into four groups of 2 bits each, thus:

1 1   0 0   0 1   1 0

Then since each group consists of 2 bits, each group in itself can take on any of the values 00, 01, 10, and 11 or, in decimal, 0, 1, 2, and 3. Since these are precisely the digits used in a base-4 number system, we can interpret each group of 2 bits as the representation of a single base-4 digit, and thus we can rewrite the binary number as

1 1   0 0   0 1   1 0
3   0   1   2

That is, we claim that $11000110_2 = 3012_4$. (The reader is asked in the exercises to justify these and some other number system restructurings.) This is certainly the direction of progress, for we have managed to reduce the number of digits required for an 8-bit number representation from 8 to 4, simply by changing the base of the number system in which the bits are represented.

We see that if we attempt to extend this process one step further, by grouping the bits *three* at a time, we uncover a small unpleasantness:

$$1\ 1\ \ 0\ 0\ 0\ \ 1\ 1\ 0$$

namely, the 8-bit byte does not divide nicely into groups of 3 bits each; the two high-order bits do not have a third companion as the other two groups have. Nonetheless, we can complete the process by noting that each group can take on values from 000 to 111 (in decimal, 0 to 7) and can thus be interpreted as a base-8 (octal) digit. In this particular case, then, we have

$$1\ 1\ \ 0\ 0\ 0\ \ 1\ 1\ 0$$
$$3\quad\ \ 0\quad\ \ 6$$

or $11000110_2 = 306_8$. We have now managed to eliminate one more digit from the representation, although here we do have a special case: the leading digit will always be in the range 0 to 3, whereas the remaining digits can take on values from 0 to 7.

We make one more attempt at compressing an 8-bit number's representation, this time taking groups of 4 bits each:

$$1\ 1\ 0\ 0\ \ 0\ 1\ 1\ 0$$

Since each of these groups can take on values between 0000 and 1111 inclusive (in decimal, 0 to 15), each can be represented by a digit in the base-16 (hexadecimal) number system, which we investigated briefly in Chapter 2. Thus

$$1\ 1\ 0\ 0\ \ 0\ 1\ 1\ 0$$
$$C\qquad\ \ 6$$

is this number's hexadecimal representation, since $110001101_2 = C6_{16}$.

There is little point in going any further with this scheme, for dividing this 8-bit number into groups of 5 bits each will yield no progress as far as a further reduction in the number of digits in the number's representation is concerned, and such a grouping would require that we work in a base-32 number system, in which we would have to invent 22 new "digits." In fact, the reader might argue that going to 4-bit groups and consequently having to deal with a number system (hexadecimal) in which six unfamiliar digit symbols are required was perhaps going one step too far. Although that argument might be defensible on the grounds of familiarity, we shall see as we begin to develop additional concepts of memory structures, and especially as we investigate the *operations* that the processor performs, that for the VAX the most "natural" number representation is hexadecimal. For other computers hexadecimal might not do as well as, say, octal, and so for those we would doubtless choose base 8 as the "natural" number system. What matters here is that we are choosing a representation that is most convenient *for us*, and nothing that we do in this regard alters the fact that the contents of an 8-

bit byte is a sequence of eight 1s and 0s (or, even more accurately, is a sequence of states of eight bistable devices).

Before closing this discussion we need to deal with a small problem that is going to be with us throughout the remainder of the book. In spite of the fact that hexadecimal is for many purposes the preferred number system for the VAX, we shall still rely heavily on decimal (base-10) numbers. But, then, what are we going to mean when we write, for example, "the number 319"? Does this mean the *decimal* number 319, or does it mean the *hexadecimal* number 319 = 793_{10}? (Note that for "the number A4D" there can be no confusion, since A and D are not decimal digits.) We could rely on the context to guide us, and in fact when there can be no doubt about the base of the number system in use at the time, we shall do this. More usually, however, we shall write decimal numbers as we have been writing them (without any special notation), and hexadecimal numbers will be denoted explicitly by preceding them with the symbol ^X (circumflex-X); thus ^X319 will mean 319_{16} = 793. (Notice that we have used no special symbol preceding or following the "793" since, by our convention, this will be taken to be decimal.) As an extension of this notation, we will occasionally use the symbol ^B to denote a binary number. Hence if 101 is to mean "one hundred and one," it will be written as 101. But if it is the binary representation of the number 5, we shall either *state* that it is a binary representation, or we shall write it as 101_2 or ^B101.

4.3 MEMORY ADDRESSES

We have not bothered with a detailed account of what happens when an 8-bit byte is incremented, or when 2 bytes are added since, as we noted above, the situation is entirely analogous to the 4-bit case. But a question that may have occurred to the reader, and in fact as early as Chapter 2, is the following. When we speak of "incrementing a byte" or of "adding 2 bytes," just *which* byte is to be incremented, or *which* 2 bytes are to be added? VAX memories typically consist of *millions* of bytes, and thus somehow the processor is going to have to be notified of which byte is to be incremented, or of which bytes are to be added. A byte identification scheme is easily achieved simply by associating with each byte a unique *number*, called the **address of the byte**. (The word "address" is a most appropriate one, for in many regards these numbers act just as do the house numbers for houses on the same street. They are used to identify a specific byte in memory, just as house numbers are used to identify a specific residence, and they may also be used to indicate when one byte is "uptown" or "downtown" from another byte, which bytes are adjacent—"next door"—and so on. Like house numbers, byte addresses are *unsigned*; it would make no sense to speak of the *negative* of a byte address any more than the negative of a house number is a meaningful concept. Unlike most house numbers, however, there are no gaps in the byte addressing scheme.)

The addresses associated with bytes are simply consecutive numbers, beginning with 0 and extending to the address of the last byte in main memory. Just

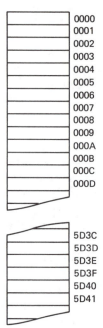

0000
0001
0002
0003
0004
0005
0006
0007
0008
0009
000A
000B
000C
000D

5D3C
5D3D
5D3E
5D3F
5D40
5D41

Figure 4.3.1

what this last address is depends on our interpretation of the word "last." A VAX memory address is any number that can be held in 32 binary digits, and thus there are 2^{32} possible addresses, extending from 0 to $2^{32} - 1$. In this sense, then, $2^{32} - 1 = 4,294,967,295$ is the "last" byte address. On the other hand, the last *valid* address is the address of the last *physical* byte that actually exists in main memory, and this in turn depends on the particular VAX installation—not all VAX systems, even those which are otherwise identical need to have the same amount of memory. (Two million bytes is a good average figure to keep in mind, but some systems are smaller. Systems with 4 million bytes of memory are not atypical, and many are even larger.)

Figure 4.3.1 is a diagram of main memory in which we have indicated the addresses of the individual bytes. There are two things to observe about the addresses as we have written them. First, they are evidently given in hexadecimal, even though we have not used the ^X notation introduced above. The reason for this is that we shall consistently specify addresses as hexadecimal numbers, never decimal, and thus provided that we know a number is an address, the ^X would be redundant. (Here is a case in which the context specifies the number system representation.) Second, we have given these addresses as *four* hexadecimal digits. If, as stated above, a byte address can be any number that can be held in 32 binary digits, we should require *eight* hexadecimal digits for the representation. We have used this particular abbreviation because in most of our examples we shall restrict ourselves to relatively small addresses, in the range from 0 to a few thousand or so, and thus we have suppressed the leading four digits, which will almost always be zeros, simply to avoid cluttering up the discussions and examples with these unnecessary 0s. If, in some circumstances, we need to consider relatively large addresses, we can always include the necessary additional leading hexadecimal digits.

4.4 SOME ADDITIONAL MEMORY STRUCTURES

Having examined 8-bit bytes in some detail, and in particular having devised an identification (addressing) scheme for them, we move on to other structures. For although the numbers (0 to 255, or -128 to $+127$) that can be held in a byte might be adequate for some purposes, in general they are still too small to be of practical use in real-world situations. Thus we create still larger structures, but we do so with much less fanfare—the 4-bit word and 8-bite byte concepts which we already know will carry over to these new structures with only the obvious modifications, so there is little need to rehash increments and additions, carries and overflows, and so on. The reader can verify an understanding of these new ideas by investigating some of the exercises at the end of the chapter.

The first memory structure we consider is the 16-bit **double-byte**. It consists of *two contiguous* bytes, where by "contiguous" we mean adjacent in the sense of the addressing scheme. Thus the 2 bytes in a double-byte *must* have addresses which are consecutive numbers. The bits in a double-byte are numbered from 0 (the least-significant bit) to 15 (the most-significant bit). Bits 15 to 8 in the double-byte occupy the bits of the higher-addressed byte (called the **high-order byte**), with bits 7 to 0 of the double-byte being the bits of the lower-addressed byte (the **low-order byte**). If the contents of the double-byte is interpreted as a *signed* number, bit 15 acts as the twos-complement sign bit. The address of a double-byte is the same as the address of its low-order byte.

In truth, the term "double-byte" is almost never used. Rather, this 16-bit structure is referred to as a **memory word**, a term that comes into conflict with the use of this term in Chapter 2, where we called the structures investigated there "4-bit words." That earlier use of the term was strictly temporary, as we noted at the time, and in fact a 4-bit structure—a **half-byte**—usually goes unnamed, in part because it is so small as not to be terribly useful *in most circumstances*, and partly because it is not directly *addressable*, as a byte is. When it is named, it is usually called a **nibble**. (This term seems to have crept into the literature several years ago, where its original spelling was "nybble," presumably to correspond with "byte." However, that spelling seems to have fallen out of favor of late.) The diagrams of a memory word, with both its unsigned and signed interpretations, are given in Figure 4.4.1, where A is simply a *symbol* that stands for the *numerical address* of the low-order byte (and hence also of the word), and consequently A + 1 must be the symbolic address of the high-order byte. Observe that the range of numbers that can be held in a word is 0 to $2^{16} - 1$ (0 to 65535) unsigned, or -2^{15} to $+2^{15} - 1$ (-32768 to $+32767$) signed.

The next larger memory structure to be considered is the **longword**, consisting of four consecutive bytes. (The terms **double-word** and **quad-byte** would be equally acceptable.) Its bits are numbered 0 (least-significant) to 31 (most-significant), and its address is the same as the address of its lowest-addressed byte. Bit 31 acts

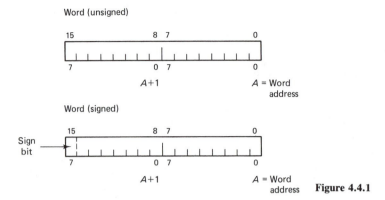

Word (unsigned)

Word (signed)

Sign
bit

Figure 4.4.1

as the twos-complement sign bit *if* the longword is interpreted as the representation of a signed number (see Figure 4.4.2). A longword can hold numbers in the range 0 to $2^{32} - 1$ (0 to 4,294,967,295) unsigned, or -2^{31} to $+2^{31} - 1$ ($-2,147,483,648$ to $+2,147,483,647$) signed. For reasons that will be made clear later, the longword is the most frequently used of all the VAX numerical memory structures. In the meantime, note that the longword is the smallest structure that can hold an *address*.

Even though a longword can hold relatively large numbers, in cases where even larger numbers are involved, two further numerical structures are available. However, we should note that not all of the arithmetic operations which the VAX performs on bytes, words, and longwords (for example, *increment* and *add*) are implemented for these expanded structures.

A **quadword** consists of eight consecutive bytes (four consecutive words), with bit numbers ranging from 0 to 63. Bit 63 acts as the sign bit in the signed interpretation. The range of numbers that can be held in a quadword are 0 to $2^{64} - 1$ unsigned, or -2^{63} to $+2^{63} - 1$ signed. The address of a quadword is the same as the address of its lowest-addressed byte.

The final structure we discuss here, and one that we shall not frequently use, is the **octaword**, consisting of 16 consecutive bytes. Its bits are numbered 0 to 127, with bit 127 being the sign bit for signed numbers. The range of numbers that can be held in an octaword is 0 to $2^{128} - 1$ unsigned, or -2^{127} to $+2^{127} - 1$ signed. As with the other structures, the address of an octaword is the address of its lowest-addressed byte.

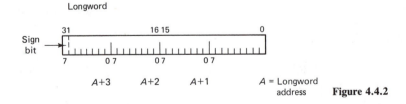

Longword

Sign
bit

Figure 4.4.2

Memory Addressing and Datatypes   Chap. 4

4.5 AMBIGUITY OF THE ADDRESSING SCHEME

In the preceding sections we have introduced a number of new memory structures, but along with them we have *not* created any additional addressing schemes—means to indicate just *where* in main memory a particular word or quadword is—relying on the address of the lowest-addressed byte of the structure to act as the address of the entire structure. The reader may be troubled by an inherent ambiguity here; a phrase such as "the structure whose address is 00001F2C" is ambiguous unless we explicitly state just *which* type of structure we have in mind. If the intended structure is a *quadword*, for example, it consists of the bytes whose addresses are 00001F2C through 00001F33, whereas the corresponding *word* would be composed of the two bytes with addresses 00001F2C and 00001F2D.

In Section 4.3 we introduced the concept of address precisely to eliminate ambiguity, so that an instruction such as "increment a byte" could distinguish among all the bytes in main memory just which one byte we wanted incremented. But that ambiguity seems to have reappeared, for it is clear that an instruction such as "increment the contents of the structure whose address is C243" cannot properly be dealt with by the processor *unless* it knows what that structure is. In fact, there is no such instruction as "increment the structure whose address is ..."; rather, there are *three distinct* instructions: "increment the *byte* whose address is ..."; "increment the *word* whose address is ..."; and "increment the *longword* whose address is ...". Thus it is the instructions themselves, not the addressing scheme, which eliminates the ambiguity. (Incidentally, these three are the only increment operations which are available. As noted in Section 4.4, the VAX does *not* have instructions to increment quadwords or octawords. This is not to say that these two structures *cannot* be incremented, only that there is no *single* instruction to do so. A quadword, for example, *can* be incremented, but the increment involves treating separately the high-order and low-order longwords that make up the quadword.)

4.6 DATATYPES

In this chapter we have introduced five different memory structures—byte, word, longword, quadword, and octaword—and to each of these we have assigned two distinct interpretations: the contents of each structure may be considered as a signed integer or as an unsigned integer. Thus we now have 10 distinct "types" of data with which we can deal, and it is this notion that we wish to describe somewhat more formally.

A **datatype** is a contiguous collection of bits, together with a **context** for that collection, that is, an **interpretation** of what those bits mean and how they are operated on. We also require that the processor have (hardware) instructions to operate on those bits in a way that is consistent with the interpretation or context. For example, a 16-bit word which we interpret as a signed integer is a datatype, since it consists of a collection of bits along with a context. As we know, there are hardware instructions which can operate on these signed numbers. We have already assured the reader of the possibility of incrementing such a word, and there are many other operations that can be performed on this dataype: *negate, clear* (set to 0), *add, subtract, multiply, complement,* and so on.

It may seem somewhat surprising that we have described a datatype as consisting of contiguous *bits* rather than one or more contiguous *bytes*, since all the datatypes we know so far do consist of so-and-so-many bytes. The reason for this is that some datatypes do *not* consist of full bytes, but rather are made up of contiguous bits which may be "buried" within bytes, for example. However, it will be some time before we see examples of these.

4.3 THE *CHARACTER* DATATYPE

The datatypes we have examined so far are all *numerical*, in the sense that our *interpretation* of the contents of a byte, word, or whatever has involved the *value* of the sequence of 1s and 0s which is the structure's contents as a binary *number*. But other interpretations are possible; for example, the contents of a word might be interpreted simply as a **bit configuration**—a sequence of sixteen 1s and 0s, but without regard to the fact that that sequence also has a numerical value. In this section we examine one such type, based on a byte structure, but distinct from the "unsigned or signed 8-bit integer" contexts that we have investigated at some length.

The processing of numerical data is certainly an important part of a computer's capabilities, and the early computers were designed to do just that exclusively— to find the numerical solutions of systems of differential equations, for example. But with the exception of some rather special-purpose machines, most modern general-purpose computers (and the VAX is one of these) spend substantial amounts of time in the manipulation of *characters*. The creation and maintenance of mailing lists, and the currently popular activity known as *word processing*, are just two examples of applications in which the data to be processed are oriented toward *text*—strings of *characters*—rather than numbers.

Now a character **Q**, for example, cannot be stored *as is* in main memory, for by now we know that the only "things" that can be stored are sequences of 1s and 0s, however we might interpret those sequences. Thus if we need to "store" a character, we shall have to **encode** it somehow into a collection of bits, which may then be stored (in a byte or word, for example). Just what scheme we use to convert characters to bit configurations is of little consequence, provided that we adhere to one constraint and a few practical guidelines. The constraint is the following. However a character is converted to a collection of bits, the conversion must be done in such a way that no two distinct characters are converted to the *same* bit configuration. For example, if **Q** and $ were *both* converted to the configuration 11010, there would be no problem in doing the encoding, but now we would have no way to look at this stored collection of bits and **decode** it— determine the character it was meant to represent, a **Q** or a $. Thus the encoding scheme must not assign two characters to the same bit configuration. In the mathematician's terminology, the assignment must be determined by an *invertible*, or *one-to-one* function.

In selecting the codes to be assigned to the various alphabetic, numerical, and **special characters** ($, %, +, and so on), we first observe that even if we encode all the lower- and uppercase alphabetic characters (52 in all), the numerical characters 0...9, and the special characters mentioned above, we have only 100 or so such encodings to deal with. Since there seems to be no compelling reason to use larger bit configurations for these codes than are actually needed, we will be able to fit any code comfortably into an 8-bit byte. Thus we can assign the code 00 to the first character (whatever that might be), 01 to the next, 02 to the third, 03 to the fourth, and so. (The numbers here are shown as the hexadecimal representations of the encoded bytes). Provided that we adhere to the constraint of uniqueness discussed above, there is no *theoretical* reason why we cannot assign codes at random. However, there are two *practical* considerations to be borne in mind. The first of these involves the scheme's potential *usefulness*. For example, if we assign to the character A the code 41 (65, in decimal), it may make sense to assign to B the code 42 (66), to C the code 43 (67), and so on. For if we do so, it will be possible to detect that the letter A *alphabetically precedes* the letter C, since the code for A is *numerically less than* the code for C. That is, although we did not start out to assign *numbers* to the characters, but rather *bit configurations* to them, we find some useful consequences of *interpreting* those configurations as numbers, provided that we assign the codes in some rational fashion. For similar reasons we would probably want to assign codes to the lowercase alphabetic characters a...z and to the numerals 0...9 in this same sort of increasing order. However, it is not clear just where the special characters such as %, $, [, and so on, would fit into this scheme, since there seems to be no natural "alphabetic" ordering among these.

The second practical consideration concerns *standardization*. If we devise a coding scheme for characters, then even though it may serve our purposes very well, it will be useless or at least inconvenient if we need to communicate with another computer installation which uses a *different* coding scheme. Thus a universally standardized code is quite desirable, and as a result, over the years the hundreds of different schemes that have been used at one time or another have been reduced to just a handful. The most frequently used code today in the United States is **ASCII code**, which stands for *American Standard Code for Information Interchange*, and a list of ASCII codes is given in Appendix C. The reader might find it useful to spend a few minutes examining that table, drawing whatever conclusions are to be found there. Among these should be the fact that 128 distinct characters are converted to ASCII code (although some of these, such as BEL and DELETE, are not "printing" characters), and that each code is represented in 7 bits and thus can be held in a single byte.

This rather lengthy development leads us to the principal topic of this section. A byte is of **character type** if its contents is interpreted as the 7-bit ASCII code for a character. The VAX has operations that perform various functions on this datatype (more properly, on *strings* of characters—consecutive bytes containing

ASCII-coded characters), although it will be some time before we are in a position to understand them. Notice that a byte which contains a character code is *not*, strictly speaking, interpreted as containing a numerical value—character-encoded bytes have a different context from numerical-valued bytes—but if we choose to reinterpret a byte's contents as being a number, and then use that number to determine alphabetic precedence of characters, or to generate a character's alphabetic successor by incrementing the byte, for example, we are of course free to do so.

4.8 CLOSING COMMENTS

Some of the features that define a computer's **architecture** are its *instruction set*, the memory structures which are addressable and the *addressing scheme* itself, and the *datatypes* which are implemented by the hardware. Some machines, principally the earlier and smaller microprocessors, are **byte-oriented** in the sense that the 8-bit byte is the smallest addressable memory structure. But many of these machines implement *only* the simple numerical-valued byte datatype, and this restriction can be a nuisance in a programming environment in which fairly large numbers must be manipulated. Other computers, including some predecessors of the VAX, are byte-oriented but also implement 16-bit word datatypes. One early but successful (although mostly experimental) microcomputer was even *nibble*-oriented. The VAX, which, as we know, is byte-addressable, has a very rich architecture, in the sense that it has an extensive collection of useful datatypes and a powerful set of instructions to operate on them. We have seen the integer-valued and character types in this chapter; as useful and important as these are, they are only a sampling of the types available on this machine.

4.9 EXERCISES

4.1.1. State what decimal number each of the following 8-bit bytes represents if the byte's contents is taken (1) as an *unsigned* integer, and (2) as a *signed* integer.
    (a) 10110001   **(b)** 00011011   **(c)** 11111111   **(d)** 01101101

4.1.2. Find the 8-bit binary (byte) representation of each of the following signed decimal numbers.
    (a) 37 **(b)** -37 **(c)** -125 **(d)** -127 **(e)** 127 **(f)** -128
    (g) 0   **(h)** -1 **(i)** -64 **(j)** -63

4.1.3. For each of the bytes whose contents is shown below, state the ones-complement and twos-complement.
    (a) 10110001   **(b)** 00011011   **(c)** 11111111   **(d)** 01101101

4.1.4. Perform the indicated arithmetic on the bytes shown below. In each case state the arithmetic result; which if any carries into or out of the high-order bit (bit 7) occurred; the status of the Carry and Overflow indicators after the operation; and whether the result is correct when the bytes are considered as (1) unsigned numbers, and (2) signed numbers.

(a) 10011101	**(b)** 00111011	**(c)** 11111111
+01100101	+10110110	−00110110
(d) 01101110	**(e)** 11101111	**(f)** 00000000
−11011111	+00010000	−10000000

4.2.1. Convert each of the following 8-bit binary numbers to its base-4 representation.
   (a) 11010110   **(b)** 00001010   **(c)** 00000000   **(d)** 11111111
   (e) 00011011   **(f)** 11100100

4.2.2. Convert each of the following base-4 numbers to its equivalent 8-bit binary representation.
   (a) 2301   **(b)** 0123   **(c)** 0000   **(d)** 3333

4.2.3. Convert each of the following 8-bit binary numbers to its hexadecimal representation.
   (a) 11010110   **(b)** 00001010   **(c)** 00000000   **(d)** 11111111
   (e) 00011011   **(f)** 11100100

4.2.4. Convert each of the following hexadecimal numbers to its equivalent 8-bit binary representation.
   (a) FA   **(b)** 05   **(c)** 8A   **(d)** 7F   **(e)** FF   **(f)** AA

4.2.5. For each of the bytes whose contents is shown below in hexadecimal, state (in hexadecimal) its ones-complement and its twos-complement.
   (a) FA   **(b)** 10   **(c)** 7F   **(d)** FF   **(e)** 00   **(f)** 80

4.2.6. Perform the indicated arithmetic on the following bytes, given in their hexadecimal representations. In each case state the arithmetic result; which if any carries into or out of the high-order bit (bit 7) occurred; the status of the Carry and Overflow indicators after the operation; and whether the result is correct when the bytes are considered as (1) unsigned numbers, and (2) signed numbers.

(a) FE	**(b)** 2D	**(c)** 80	**(d)** FF	**(e)** 6E
+65	−08	−80	+36	−80

4.2.7. Show that the conversion of an 8-bit byte from its binary representation to its base-4 representation, as described in Section 4.2, is legitimate by proving that

$$\sum_{i=0}^{7} a_i \cdot 2^i = \sum_{j=0}^{3} \left[\sum_{k=0}^{1} a_{2j+k} \cdot 2^k \right] 4^j$$

where each a_i = 0 or 1.

4.2.8. Show that the conversion of an 8-bit byte from its binary representation to its hexadecimal representation, as described in Section 4.2, is legitimate by proving that

$$\sum_{i=0}^{7} a_i \cdot 2^i = \sum_{j=0}^{1} \left[\sum_{k=0}^{3} a_{4j+k} \cdot 2^k \right] 16^j$$

where each a_i = 0 or 1.

4.4.1. For each of the words whose contents is shown below in hexadecimal, state (in hexadecimal) its ones-complement and its twos-complement.
   (a) 2AF9   **(b)** FFFF   **(c)** A6E6   **(d)** 8000   **(e)** 0000

4.4.2. For each of the longwords whose contents is shown below in hexadecimal, state (in hexadecimal) its ones-complement and its twos-complement.
   (a) FFFFF2FO   **(b)** A70500AB   **(c)** 00000000   **(d)** 80000000

4.4.3. For each of the quadwords whose contents is shown below in hexadecimal, state (in hexadecimal) its ones-complement and its twos-complement.
   (a) 123456789ABCDEF0   **(b)** FFFFFFFFFFFFFFFF
   (c) 0000000000000000   **(d)** 8000000000000000

4.4.4 Perform the indicated arithmetic on the following words, given in their hexadecimal representations. In each case state the arithmetic result; which if any carries into or out of the high-order bit (bit 15) occurred; the status of the Carry and Overflow indicators after the operation; and whether the result is correct when the words are considered as (1) unsigned numbers, and (2) signed numbers.

(a)	2F33	**(b)**	8C72	**(c)**	FEF2	**(d)**	A701
	+7049		+7049		−A26D		−C04F

4.4.5. Perform the indicated arithmetic on the following longwords, given in their hexadecimal representations. In each case state the arithmetic result; which if any carries into or out of the high-order bit (bit 31) occurred; the status of the Carry and Overflow indicators after the operation; and whether the result is correct when the longwords are considered as (1) unsigned numbers, and (2) signed numbers.

(a)	2F23A6AB	**(b)**	80F2660A	**(c)**	000320F5
	+D842F046		−F2A4ABC6		−80000000
(d)	80000000	**(e)**	1F22A04D	**(f)**	F205F206
	−80000000		+D3204000		+0DF48077

4.4.6. Perform the indicated arithmetic on the following quadwords, given in their hexadecimal representations. In each case state the arithmetic result; which if any carries into or out of the high-order bit (bit 63) occurred; the status of the Carry and Overflow indicators after the operation; and whether the result is correct when the quadwords are considered as (1) unsigned numbers, and (2) signed numbers.

(a)	A20023A5686012DC	**(b)**	0002001A3055DOCE
	+684D0965A02DCAB1		−8644AO2949CDO202
(c)	8000000000000000	**(d)**	A60945EDA81F2209
	−8000000000000000		+FFFFFFFFFFFFFFFF

4.4.7. For each of the words whose address and contents are given below, state the addresses of the two bytes that make up the word, and the contents of each of those bytes. [We use the notation "c(...)" to denote "the contents of...."]

(a) c(04F2) = A469 **(b)** c(A702) = 0233 **(c)** c(0001) = 8001

4.4.8. For each of the longwords whose address and contents are given below, state the addresses of the four bytes that make up the word, and the contents of each of those bytes. [We use the notation "c(...)" to denote "the contents of...."]

(a) c(120A) = A677094E **(b)** c(0003) = 80008081
(c) c(OFFE) = 1772A094 **(d)** c(FFFD) = 0544A5DC

4.4.9. For each of the quadwords whose address and contents are given below, state the addresses of the eight bytes that make up the word, and the contents of each of those bytes. [We use the notation "c(...)" to denote "the contents of...."]

(a) c(FFF9) = 92884AC264D10003
(b) c(0001) = AAF2096D104AB233

4.5.1. It was stated in Section 4.5 that there are three distinct VAX operations to increment a byte, word, and longword. Are all three of these really necessary? That is, since the incrementing of the contents of any of these three structures amounts to adding the number 1 to it, is this not equivalent to adding 1 to—incrementing—the *low-order* byte of the structure? To see that this is *not* the case, consider what happens when the *byte* containing FF, the *word* containing xxFF, and the *longword* containing xxxxxxFF are incremented (where the x's mean "don't care"). But is the argument correct in all *other* cases?

4.5.2. When the contents of the word 147F is incremented, the result is 1480. When just the *low-order byte* of that word (7F) is incremented, the result is again 1480. But show that the results of these two operations are not *identical*.

4.5.3. It was stated in Section 4.5 that there is no VAX operation to increment the contents of a quadword. Show, however, that if the quadword is divided into two longwords, it is possible to increment the contents of the quadword by incrementing the contents of one or both of its component longwords (although this cannot be done in a single step).

4.5.4. Using an argument similar to that of Exercise 4.5.3, show how two quadwords might be added, even though there is no VAX "add quadwords" operation. Derive a similar result for octawords.

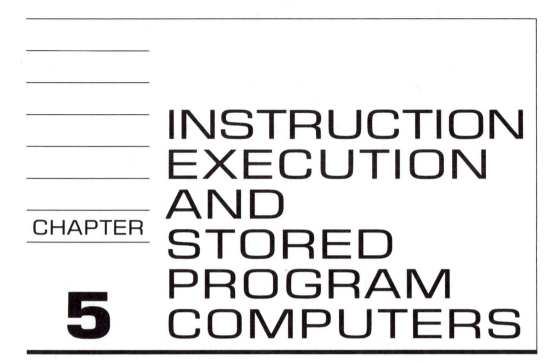

CHAPTER 5

INSTRUCTION EXECUTION AND STORED PROGRAM COMPUTERS

5.1 INTRODUCTION

In the preceding chapters we have presented an overview of computer systems, and we have investigated in varying degrees of detail how main memory is constructed, how it is organized into various structures (bytes, longwords, and so on), what interpretations, numerical and otherwise, can be imposed on these structures, and how the processor electronically performs certain operations. In so doing, however, we have implicitly raised more questions than we have answered, among which are the following.

1. What is a computer *operation*?
2. What operations can the central processing unit perform?
3. What is a computer *instruction*, and how does it differ from an *operation*? (We have been careful not to use these words interchangeably.)
4. How does the processor *access main memory* (which it must be able to do in order, for example, to add the contents of two words).
5. How do *we* inform the processor of which instructions we want it to perform?
6. What does an instruction "look like" to the processor?

This chapter, and indeed much of the remainder of the book, is devoted to responding to these questions, although the reader is advised that completely satisfactory answers cannot be given in a sentence or two—much background material is required before a significant depth of understanding of many of these concepts can be acquired.

5.2 OPERATIONS AND INSTRUCTIONS

We must necessarily be somewhat vague about just what a computer operation is at this point, but for the time being we can take the following as a working definition. A computer **operation** is any of the arithmetic or logical actions that takes place electronically within the central processing unit. Thus, as investigated in Chapter 3, *incrementing, addition, twos-complementing* (negating), *decrementing*, and so on, are operations. The adjectives "arithmetic" and "logical" in this context are perhaps a bit more narrow than what we wish to convey, for although they imply such activities as subtraction and the bit-by-bit ANDing of bytes or words, there are many important processor operations which are not, strictly speaking, the results of these familiar arithmetic constructions. These include, for instance, the shifting left by one position of all the bits of a longword, and the examination of the processor's condition codes.

We noted in Chapter 4 that specifying an operation to be performed is normally by no means sufficient information for the processor to take any action, for we must also indicate *on what* the operation is to be performed, a concept that led us to the creation of memory addresses. This is what will distinguish between an *operation* and an *instruction*. A computer **instruction** is a computer operation, together with any required **operands**—information (frequently in the form of memory addresses) which is required in order that the processor be able to take some arithmetic or logical action. For example, "add" is an *operation*, but it is not an *instruction*, since it gives no indication of what is to be added. On the other hand, "add the contents of the longword whose address is 0000204F to the contents of the longword whose address is 0000A204, and place the result in the longword whose address is 00003AB2" *is* an instruction, for it consists of an *operation*—add—together with three *operands*—three longwords whose addresses are specified.

Just what operations is the central processor capable of performing? As one might expect, this depends on what **logic** (circuitry) has been designed into the CPU, and this varies from machine to machine. Most general-purpose computers can perform the usual arithmetic operations, although some of the smaller microcomputers do *not* have the logic necessary for division, or even multiplication, operations that must then be accomplished by means of *programming*—sequences of those operations which *are* available. The VAX has a very extensive set of operations, and these are described in detail in Appendix A. However, it would be premature to launch into an investigation of these at this time, since much preparatory groundwork needs to be laid before many of these operations will even be meaningful.

5.3 MAIN MEMORY ACCESSING

In the course of executing (performing) an instruction, the processor may need to obtain the contents of a memory location (byte, word, longword, or whatever), for instruction operands are frequently the contents of main memory locations. Outlined below are some of the steps that must be taken for a *memory access*. There are a few details involved here which we have not included, but they are primarily of an engineering nature, and an examination of them would not enhance our understanding of the principal concepts. A **memory access** consists of the following actions.

1. The processor places the **address** of the location to be accessed on the **address bus** (see Figure 1.2.1).
2. The processor then transmits, on the **control bus**, a signal called a **read signal**.
3. Main memory responds to the read signal by examining the address on the address bus and placing the contents of the specified location on the **data bus**.
4. Main memory then signals the processor that it has obtained the desired data by sending another signal back to the processor on the control bus.
5. The processor reads the requested location contents from the data bus.

We have used the word "location" here without being particularly specific about just what was meant by that term. In fact, we intend to remain somewhat vague about the meaning, saying simply that a **location** is a memory byte, word, longword, quadword, or octaword, without specifying precisely which. In brief, "location" is a convenient catch-all term to be used when we do not really care just *what* memory structure is involved.

The reader may be somewhat puzzled, then, that we have spoken above of main memory placing the contents of a specified *location* on the data bus, because it would appear that if the location is a byte, then memory would place *eight* bits on the data bus, whereas if the location is a word, *sixteen* bits would have to be placed on the data bus. In fact, data are always transmitted from memory to the central processing unit in *thirty-two*-bit packages—longwords—even if fewer bits were actually requested. (The processor, after all, does not *have* to use all the data available to it.) The situation is even more complicated, for not any consecutive 32 bits can be transmitted. To understand how data move from memory to the CPU, we need to expand some of our main memory concepts.

We stated in Chapter 4 that a byte consists of 8 bits, and that a byte has an address. In a similar fashion, a word and longword consist of 16 and 32 bits, respectively, and each of these structures has as its address the (byte) address of its low-order byte. Now on some machines (including a predecessor of the VAX), a byte can have any address whatever, but a *word*—a package of two consecutively addressed bytes—must have an *even* address; that is, the address of the low-order byte of a word must be even. For these machines we say that words must be **aligned on even address boundaries**. For the VAX, however, *any* address, even or otherwise, will do as the address of *any* structure, no matter its size. Thus a number such as 000012A7 could be the address of a byte, a word, a longword, or whatever. Despite this fact, even on the VAX there are **natural address boundaries for words and longwords**, namely those addresses which are *multiples of 2 and 4*, respectively. Thus while 000012A7 and 00004A38 are both *possible* longword addresses, only the latter is a *natural* longword address. In what sense do we use the term "natural"? It is used in relation to memory accesses, for the truth of the matter is that when memory is accessed, main memory places on the data bus the contents of a longword *which is aligned on an address that is a multiple of 4*. But if this is the case, how can the processor obtain the contents of the *word* whose address is 000012A7, and thus consists of the two *bytes* having addresses 000012A7 and 000012A8, for this word crosses a natural longword boundary? The answer is that the processor must do *two* memory accesses, once to get the contents of the longword whose address is 000012A4 and a second time to get the contents of the longword whose address is 000012A8. The processor must then "assemble" the contents of the desired word from this superfluity of information.

It may strike the reader as somewhat inefficient to place words and longwords in memory in such a way that multiple memory accesses are required to read their contents. This is quite true, and in many cases it may be desirable or even necessary to take special pains to ensure that words and longwords are actually aligned on word and longword "boundaries." On the other hand, the memory structure of the VAX is very efficient in that no bytes ever need to be "wasted" simply to achieve some proper word or longword alignment. Once again, there are trade-offs in efficiency involved here—the most economical use of main memory against high speed of memory access.

But the loss of efficiency that results from misalignment is the only "hidden cost" paid in accessing main memory. In particular, the actual *position* in physical memory—whether at low or high addresses—is immaterial; the processor can access any longword in main memory as easily as any other. For this reason memory is referred to as **random access memory (RAM)**.

5.4 THE STORED INSTRUCTION CONCEPT

While we have had much to say about what the central processing unit can do, and even to some extent how it carries out its operations electronically, we have still not addressed the question of how we can instruct the processor to execute a *particular* one of its operations or, of even greater importance, an entire *sequence* of operations. For unless the machine can be instructed as to which of its operations it is to perform, and in what order it is to perform them, it will be of little use as a "computing machine." We can gain some insights into how computers are controlled by examining the ubiquitous electronic **calculator**.

Electronic calculators are computerlike in that they can add, subtract, multiply, and divide, and many of them can do considerably more than that. Further, most calculators have a small memory which can be used to hold one or two numbers. In addition, they have an input device (the keypad) and an output device (the LED or LCD display panel). In fact, with a couple of exceptions, Figure 1.2.1 is a reasonably accurate block diagram of a modern electronic calculator. Now a computer has vastly more memory than a calculator (several million bytes as opposed to storage locations for one or two numbers in the calculator); its input and output devices are far more sophisticated, consisting of terminals, disks, printers, tape units, and so on; calculators do not have the large supply of registers available to the computer user; and the bus structures in a calculator are very simple compared to the high level of complexity of the corresponding computer devices. But these differences are more of *degree* than of *substance*; an electronic calculator is capable of many of the same actions that a computing system can take, and it executes these operations at roughly the same high speed as does the computer's processor. Yet we do *not* think of the computer as simply a big calculator—there *is* a difference of substance between these two machines.

Consider the following trivial problem as executed on a calculator: 2 + 5 = ? The problem is solved by performing, in sequence, the following steps.

1. Press the key marked CLEAR.
2. Press the key marked 2.
3. Press the + key.
4. Press the 5 key.
5. Press the = key.
6. Read the display.

Now we do not really care about the result, and in fact we will not even investigate just what is going on inside the calculator when these commands are issued to it, although by now we are actually in a good position to make some educated conjectures in this direction. Rather our interest lies in *how* the calculator obtains the information it needs in order to know what operations are to be performed and on what numbers it is to perform them. That is, what is the *source* of the commands to the calculator? The answer, of course, is that this information is transmitted to the calculator by means of the keys on the keypad, and these in turn are controlled by our finger, together with certain coordinating eye and brain functions. Now what takes place when the CLEAR key is pressed, as in step 1? The calculator presumably clears some internal registers, as well as the display, and it does this in a millionth of a second or so. What does the calculator do then? The answer is, it can do nothing *until* it is issued another command, for instance the request to store the number 2 in some register, as issued in step 2. This action is performed, in a millionth of a second, say, and then once again the calculator must *wait* (interminably, at least compared with calculator speeds) until the *next* command is given.

In sum, a calculator is an extremely slow device as far as the completion of its *total* task is concerned, even though the individual steps that make up that task can be performed very rapidly. The source of the problem is easily identified. When the calculator has completed a particular operation, it has no way of *de-*

manding from us the *next* operation; it must simply wait until we are disposed to press another key. The reason for this is that the *sequence* of commands that the calculator must ultimately carry out is not "packaged" in any form that makes it accessible to the calculator. The sequence is in our heads, and *we* access each command in the sequence and then transfer it to the calculator with our finger, an exceedingly slow "input device." This leads us to the distinction between a calculator and a computer: When a computer completes the execution of an instruction, it can immediately access (somehow) the *next* operation it is to perform; a calculator must depend for its next command on some *outside intervention*; it *cannot* immediately access its next instruction *on demand*. This description implies two things about a computer. First, once started, a computer is an "automatic calculating machine," in that it can execute a command, access the *next* command and execute it, and so on, without further outside intervention. And second, the sequence of operations to be carried out by the computer must be thought out ahead of time. It is this prescribed sequence of instructions that we refer to as a **computer program**.

To see just how a sequence of instructions can be made available to a computer so that the processor, upon completion of an operation, can demand the *next* instruction (and thus *keep the instruction execution process going*), we look at a scheme that was employed early in the development of computers. Figure 5.4.1 shows a short length of **paper tape**. Holes are punched in the tape in various patterns, each pattern running across the short dimension of the tape (shown in the figure as top to bottom). Such a pattern is called a **tape frame**, and tapes typically are punched with approximately 10 frames per longitudinal inch. The individual punch positions in each frame are called **channels**, so the tape shown in the figure evidently has six channels (although five- and eight-channel tapes are the more usual). When such a tape is put in a device called a **paper tape reader** and the reader is activated, the holes and nonholes in the tape can be "read" by the reader as a pattern. For example, the frame outlined in Figure 5.4.1 might be "read" (top to bottom) as the sequence

hole-hole-nohole-hole-hole-hole

or perhaps more simply as

1 1 0 1 1 1

Let us suppose that a particular set of punches (that is, a frame of tape) represents a computer *operation* in some *encoded form*, or represents information about an

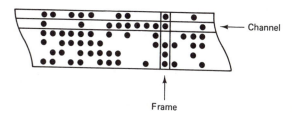

Frame

Figure 5.4.1

operand for some instruction. Now if the processor—perhaps in its control unit—contains circuitry that (1) can *start the tape reader* and *access the next coded frame*, and (2) can *decode* the punches in that frame and interpret them as a processor operation or instruction operand, then we have a **computer** as described above. For the tape can be prepunched with the codes for the instructions (operators and operands) that we want executed, the tape can be started, and the computer then "keeps itself going," presumably until the reader runs out of tape or the control unit reads an explicit command to "halt" this automatic mode of operation.

Although we have now given an example of a system that we think of as a true computer, it is still terribly inefficient. To see why, consider a computer whose processor can execute 10,000 instructions per second. (This is quite slow; modern machines execute several million instructions per second.) Suppose this computer has a paper tape reader that is capable of reading 1000 frames per second. (This is almost unrealistically fast—over 8 feet per second, at 10 frames per inch.) Finally, assume that on the average, an instruction (operator and operands) requires two frames. Thus the processor can access 500 instructions per second from the tape. But since it can *execute* 10,000 instructions per second, a little arithmetic reveals that the processor is *idle 95% of the time*! That is, the processor is waiting to get its next instruction almost all of the time and executing instructions almost none of the time. (In fact, since in this example we have consistently erred on the conservative side, the inefficiency is actually much more extreme.)

To improve efficiency, a most ingenious step was taken, which resulted in a technique that is the cornerstone of the architecture of today's general-purpose computers. Rather than require that the processor access encoded commands from a *mechanical* (and thus slow) device which is external to the computing system itself, we place these instruction codes *in the computer's main memory*. Now when an operation needs to be accessed, it is accessed directly from main memory; the advantage of this scheme is that data can be accessed from main memory at processor speeds—a million or so per second. It is the fact that memory accesses are purely *electronic* actions, which require no *mechanical* activities, that provides the impressive speed of execution of computers in which the instructions are *stored* in main memory. It can be argued that if the processor can execute an instruction in, say, one millionth of a second, and if it can also obtain that instruction from memory in one millionth of a second, then it is still waiting half the time. But even granting that this is true, we see a dramatic improvement over the earlier situation. In fact, modern processors are designed in such a way that even this amount of inefficiency is reduced substantially; processors are engineered so that they can quite literally be doing a number of things at once. For example, one segment of the processor may be completing the execution of the current instruction while another is accessing memory for the next encoded instruction. Thus the processor can be kept busy performing useful tasks almost all the time (although there is still a certain small amount of waiting time).

For the record, then, we define a **stored instruction computer** to be one in which the commands to the processor are stored in the computer's main memory, in some coded form. This concept leads to a number of interesting questions, which we can dispose of quite easily in the following three sections.

1. When the processor is ready to access main memory for an instruction, how does it know *where* in memory to look for it?
2. If an instruction resides in main memory in coded form, and if data also reside in main memory, how can the processor distinguish between the two?
3. How can we ensure that prior to the beginning of execution, the desired instruction codes are located in the proper memory locations?

5.5 THE PROGRAM COUNTER AND INSTRUCTION EXECUTION

Recall that in Section 1.5 we briefly introduced the concept of **processor registers**, which we claimed to be units in which information can be stored. We can now be much more specific about what these units are, and in particular we shall restrict our attention to the *public* registers—those registers which are accessible to the computer user. A public register is nothing more than a 32-bit longword which differs from the familiar 32-bit longwords in main memory in three principal ways. First, and for our purposes the least important, processor registers are physically constructed in such a way that they are extremely high-speed devices, able to change their states far faster than main memory units. (But since, as opposed to main memory longwords, we need only a few processor registers, cost is not a serious concern.) Second, the processor registers do *not* reside in main memory and thus they do *not* have *addresses*. (We shall see that they can still be referenced, but this is done in a way different from the way in which memory locations are referenced.) Third, while registers can behave much like memory locations, in that data can be stored in them, the contents of two registers can be added, and so on, they have some special functions that are *not* shared by main memory longwords.

Since a public register is a 32-bit structure, it can hold a main memory address. But note that saying that a register "contains an address" is a matter of *interpretation*—a register contains 32 bits, each of which is 1 or 0, and if we choose to say that they represent the address of a main memory location, so be it; but we could with equal validity say that those 32 bits represent the value (in binary) of a signed integer, or an unsigned integer, or four ASCII-coded characters. In any event, we shall have to exercise some care in being explicit about how we interpret the contents of a register, just as, for example, we needed to specify that a main memory byte contained a signed number, unsigned number, or character code. Now if the contents of a public register is interpreted as the address of a memory location, we say that the register **points at the contents** of that location. For example, suppose that the memory *word* whose address is 00002F3C contains the (hexadecimal) number 1042, and that the contents of register R is 00002F3C. Then R *points at* the number 1042. (Once again we have used the somewhat vague word "location" here, with its attendant lack of specificity and need for clarification, either explicitly or by means of the context. For we could as well say, in the example above, that R points at the *byte* 42, since R's contents can also be interpreted to be the address of a byte location.)

Since we will need to make a distinction between a register and its contents, and between memory units and their contents, we introduce the following notation: c(...) is read "the **contents** of...." For instance, the example of the preceding paragraph could more simply have been stated: If c(R) = 00002F3C is interpreted as a *word* address, and if c(00002F3C) = 1042, then R *points at* the number 1042.

We can now deal with the question: If computer instructions are stored in main memory (as some encoded configurations of bits), how can the processor know where in memory to look for the next instruction it is to execute? The answer is that one of the public registers, called the **program counter** (abbreviated **PC**), always *point at* the *next* instruction code. Thus when the processor has completed its current instruction and is ready to begin execution of the next operation, it obtains the contents of the program counter, which it then uses as the *address* of its next encoded instruction. We shall shortly look into some further details of this action (which we refer to as an **instruction fetch**), but in the meantime we note that the concept of a register—the PC—pointing at the next instruction leads to three obvious questions. First, we say that the PC points at an instruction code, and that the processor then accesses this code from main memory. But just what is the PC pointing at? Is it a word, byte, longword? (Knowing an address does not imply anything about the *size* of the structure having that address.) The answer is that all the operation codes on the VAX are *single bytes*. (This is not quite true; there are a few exceptional cases which are two bytes long, but these can be dealt with later. For the time being the reader can safely assume that operation codes are always 8 bits long.) Thus when the processor is ready to begin execution of an instruction, it obtains an address from the program counter and then accesses the *byte* of main memory having that address.

The second question involving instruction execution concerns instruction *operands*. We have stated on several occasions that an instruction consists of an *operation* (*add*, *increment*, or whatever), *together with* some further information concerning its *operands*, which indicates to the processor *on what structures* the operation is to be performed. After obtaining from memory the code for an operation, how does the processor know where to find the instruction's operands? This is quite simple, for information about the operands of an instruction *immediately follows* the operation code in main memory. Thus if the processor can locate the operator code (its address is the contents of the program counter), it can also find the operands that "belong to" that operator.

A third question arises naturally as a result of this instruction fetch concept. If the PC points at the code for an operation, and if the processor accesses that code and executes the corresponding instruction, what does the processor do upon completion of that instruction execution? We have implied (correctly) that it *repeats* this "fetch an operation code and execute the instruction" cycle. But will it not simply fetch the *same* operation code? Nothing we have said so far has indicated that c(PC) has changed, and if it has not, then it still points at the same operator. It is clear that unless some provision is made for *changing* the contents of the program counter somehow in this process, the same instruction will simply be executed over and over, indefinitely. In fact, each time the program counter is accessed to obtain the address of an operator, c(PC) is *incremented by one*. And each time the program counter is used to obtain information about an operand (which information may be a byte, word, 32-bit address, and so on), c(PC) is *incremented by the number of bytes occupied by that operand information.*

The time has come to examine a concrete example of instruction execution, which reveals a few further complications that cannot be treated completely at this time. In Figure 5.5.1 we show a segment of main memory, namely those locations with addresses from 0000D828 through 0000D831 (which we have chosen arbitrarily). The column labeled "address" shows the numerical addresses of the memory locations in question, and there are two things to note about these addresses. First, we have listed only the last four (hexadecimal) digits of the address, the first four being assumed to be zero. (This is consistent with the convention we adopted in Chapter 4.) Second, the addresses listed are not those of *all* the consecutive bytes between 0000D828 and 0000D831. Rather, we have listed only the address of the low-order byte of whatever structure resides at that address, and we note that in one case (at 0000D82A) the structure is a *word*, and in another (0000D82D) it is a *longword*. In all other cases the locations' contents are *bytes*. (When we say that a particular "structure"—byte, word, or whatever—resides at a memory location, we mean that in the sense of memory *as viewed by the processor* in the course of instruction execution. This concept will become clear as we look at the details of how the processor treats this specific instruction.) The column labeled "contents" represents the numerical contents of each of the memory locations whose addresses are given. Finally, the remarks in the column labeled "comment" will be explained as we examine this example in detail.

We suppose that when the processor has completed its current instruction, the program counter contains the number (address) 0000D828. Thus the PC is pointing at the byte A0, as indicated in the figure. The processor accesses this byte and increments the contents of the program counter by one, so that c(PC) is now 0000D829. This 8-bit byte A0 is passed to the decoding circuitry, and the code is found to represent the operation: *Add* two *words*, and place the sum in the location occupied by the *second* of those two words. (In a high-level language such as FORTRAN or Pascal, this instruction would be written as B = A + B or B := A + B, respectively.) Now that the processor knows that it is to perform a word addition, it must of course know *which* words to add. In fact, the particular addition instruction represented here is the following: Add the (hexadecimal) *num-*

FIGURE 5.5.1

	Contents	Address	Comment
PC →	A0	D828	Operation code for "add two 16-bit words"
	8F	D829	⟨Mode byte⟩
	270F	D82A	VALUE of first word to be added
	9F	D82C	⟨Mode byte⟩
	0000DC24	D82D	ADDRESS of second word to be added
	—	D831	⟨Next operation code⟩

ber 270F to the *contents* of the word whose address is 0000DC24 and place the result back in the word whose address is 0000DC24. Thus in this case the *operands* for the addition operation are the *number* 207F and the *contents* of 0000DC24, and we shall see that all of this required operand information is in main memory, immediately following the code A0 for the word-addition operator itself.

The processor needs to access the first operand, and as it did with the operator code itself, it does so by obtaining an address from the program counter. Recall that because of the processor's fetch of the operation code A0, c(PC) has already been moved up to 0000D829. But what is the PC now pointing at (that is, what is in location 0000D829)? It is the byte 8F, referred to in the comment on that line as a "mode byte," a term that requires quite a bit of explanation. Before offering it, however, we note that in the course of the processor's accessing of this mode byte, the contents of the program counter is once again advanced by 1, so that now c(PC) = 0000D82A.

We know that this particular instruction adds two *words*, and thus those operand words must be accessible to the processor. But the question of interest here is: In what *form* are the words being made available to the processor? For example, a word might be presented directly, by placing its actual *value* in memory as an operand following the operator code. (This is the case here for the first operand.) Or the word's *address* might be used as the necessary operand information, which would mean that the processor would have to do another memory access to get the word itself. Or we might indicate that the word consists of the 16 low-order bits of some public register, or perhaps that some public register contains the *address* of the word—that is, that some register is *pointing at* the operand. In brief, there are a number of ways in which we might tell the processor how it can access the word operand. It is the purpose of the **mode byte** to inform the processor of this "mode of access" to the operand. In the particular case in hand, in which the mode byte is 8F, these 8 bits tell the processor that *the program counter is currently pointing at* the operand word. Now since currently c(PC) = 0000D82A, the processor knows that this address is the address of the first of the word summands. Thus this word—270F—is accessed as the first operand, and the program counter is again incremented, but this time *by 2*, since the processor has fetched from memory a *2-byte word*. Thus by now, c(PC) = 0000D82C.

To obtain the second of the two operands, the processor again fetches a single byte, which it takes to be a mode byte, and in the process advances the contents of the program counter by 1 (to correspond to the single byte that was fetched). It gets the byte 9F, which is interpreted as meaning that the program counter is currently pointing at the *address* of the (word) operand. Since c(PC) = 0000D82D, the processor fetches the (32-bit = 4-byte) address from location 0000D82D and advances the PC contents by 4 (to account for the 4-byte address). Thus by now c(PC) = 0000D831, the processor has the address 0000DC24, it accesses c(0000DC24) as the second word summand, adds the first (270F) to it, and finally puts the sum back into the *word* whose address is 0000DC24. This completes the execution of the *add* instruction, and the processor is ready to begin execution of the next instruction—at 0000D831—currently pointed at by the program counter.

There are a great many details that we have had to examine here, and perhaps they have contributed to obscuring what is actually a relatively straightforward process. It will help if we introduce the term **operand specifier**, by which we mean a *mode byte*, together with any further information required by the processor to determine the *location* of the instruction operand. For example, the first operand in the example above—the number 270F—is determined by the mode byte 8F and the *word* 270F, the mode byte telling the processor that the program counter is pointing at the operand itself. Thus the three bytes

270F   8F

(which are read right to left in order of increasing addresses) form this operand's "operand specifier." Using this informal notion, we offer a second version of Figure 5.5.1 (Figure 5.5.2), in which the bytes in each operand specifier have been gathered together on a single line. Thus the execution of this *add* instruction can be described more compactly as follows. The processor fetches the operation code byte pointed at by the PC, and increments c(PC) by 1. On the basis of the operation code, the decoder informs the processor that the instruction has two operands, each of which is a *word*. The processor fetches the first operand specifier to determine the location of the first operand, and adjusts the contents of the PC by as many bytes as there are in that specifier. It then fetches the second operand specifier to determine the location of the second operand, and again adjusts c(PC) appropriately. Since the processor now knows where to locate the two operands, and consequently can obtain those two operands, it can complete execution of the *add* instruction.

We leave this section with two comments. Not much has been said about the mode bytes which have been used by the processor to determine the locations of operands. These are somewhat complicated affairs, and they contribute to a large extent to the "architecture" of the VAX and to the power of this particular processor. Chapter 7 is devoted exclusively to a close examination of these mode bytes. In the meantime we shall continue to use them, offering the necessary explanations of their meanings, until we are in a better position to launch upon a detailed investigation of them and their implications. The second comment involves the three questions that closed Section 5.4. We have now responded to the first two of these. For we have seen that the processor "knows where in

FIGURE 5.5.2

	Contents	Address	Comment
PC →	A0	D828	Operation code for "add two 16-bit words"
	270F 8F	D829	First "operand specifier"
	0000DC24 9F	D82C	Second "operand specifier"
	—	D831	⟨Next operation code⟩

memory" to look for an operation code by examining the address in the program counter. As to the question of "how the processor distinguishes between data and instruction" since each reside in main memory as bit configurations, we know now that the processor *cannot* distinguish between them. But, in fact, it *need* not be able to, for it is clear that *any* memory structure will be interpreted as an operation code or operand specifier *if* it is pointed at by the PC. Since we know how the PC contents is affected by instruction execution (incremented by various values depending on the structure accessed), we need only take care that instruction codes and data are kept separated in main memory so that the program counter will never "point at" any byte (or word, longword, and so on) which *we* intend to be *data*.

5.6 THE INSTRUCTION EXECUTION CYCLE

We summarize here some of the results of Section 5.5, and go into a bit more of the detail of what occurs during instruction execution, for these actions lie at the heart of the activities of the entire computing system. We have used the term "fetch" a number of times, and we shall be more explicit about its use. When the processor obtains the contents of a memory location *pointed at by the program counter*, and at the same time the program counter is *incremented by the number of bytes accessed* by the processor, we say that the processor has **fetched** the contents of the location. There are three important notions associated with this concept. First, we have again used the term "location," which might contain a byte, longword, quadword, or whatever, a term left intentionally vague since, as we have seen, the processor may fetch different types of structures in the course of instruction execution. Second, the term "fetch" is used *only* when the location accessed is *pointed at by the PC*. (Thus not every memory access is a fetch.) Finally, upon a fetch the contents of the program counter is *incremented*—by 1 if the fetched structure was a byte, by 2 if it was a word, and so on.

One of the consequences of a fetch is the incrementing of c(PC) by the processor. How does the processor know by how much to increment the PC contents? This is equivalent to asking: How does the processor know the *size* of the structure it is to fetch? The answer lies in part with the operation code, which informs the processor of the size (structure) of the various operands. For instance, in the principal example of Section 5.5, the operation code A0 informed the processor that it was to add two *words*, and thus the size of each of the operands is *two* bytes. In addition, further information may be provided by the mode byte, for as we saw, the processor may interpret the mode byte as specifying that the *address*—a *four*-byte structure—of an operand is being pointed at by the PC.

Because of the fact that the VAX has several different *classes* of instructions, which we shall ultimately examine in detail, we cannot give a *single* description of what occurs during the execution of an instruction. However, we describe below the process for a large group of instructions, namely, those in which the operands are determined by "operand specifiers"—mode bytes possibly followed by operand values or addresses.

When VAX instructions are executed, the processor performs the following activities, referred to as the *instruction execution cycle.*

1. The processor fetches the instruction operation code byte, and in the process it increments c(PC) by 1. [There are a few instructions whose operation code requires 2 bytes. In these cases the first of the two bytes is either FD or FF, and these act as a signal to the processor that an *additional* fetch of the second operation code byte is required, together with an additional incrementing by 1 of c(PC).]

2. The processor fetches the mode byte and increments c(PC) by 1.

3. Based on the bit configuration in the mode byte, it may be necessary for the processor to fetch further information about the operand. (In some cases the mode byte itself completely specifies the operand, so no further fetches are required.) The contents of the program counter is incremented by the number of bytes fetched. This completes the accessing of the operand information.

4. If there are further instruction operands, the processor repeats steps 2 and 3. Otherwise, go to step 5.

5. The processor performs the specified operation on the operands obtained in steps 2 and 3.

It is clear that the key to the execution cycle, and equally to the processor's ability to execute the *next* instruction—to "keep execution going"—is the interpretation of the program counter's contents as an address, and the processor's action of incrementing the program counter contents by an appropriate amount on each fetch.

One of the questions with which we have not dealt is just how the processor accesses the memory locations which contain the information required for instruction execution, that is, the locations whose addresses are in the program counter. We discussed memory accessing in Section 5.3, and of course that is what takes place when the processor needs instruction information from main memory. We also noted there that memory accesses are always in 32-bit packages. In fact, when the processor accesses memory for the purpose of obtaining instruction information (operation codes or mode bytes, for example, as opposed, say, to operand values) it does so in *eight*-byte packages. Thus eight bytes at a time are brought into a processor area known as the *instruction buffer*, and it is from this buffer that the required instruction information is read by the processor. We mentioned earlier that modern processors are designed so that they can perform some operations *simultaneously*, to improve efficiency. The filling of this instruction buffer is a case in point; the processor can access memory to refill the instruction buffer at the same time that the current instruction is completing its execution.

5.7 LOADING MAIN MEMORY

We finally deal with the third question posed at the end of Section 5.4: How we can ensure that the proper operator codes, mode bytes, and operand information actually exist in specific locations in main memory, so that the instructions we want performed will be fetched and executed by the processor.

Some older computers were manufactured with a set of switches that the user could employ in loading main memory. These switches formed what was usually called a *front panel*, a device that was directly connected to the processor and to main memory. It was thus possible for the user to set 32 switches, bit by bit, to some address and thus, by depressing another switch, to *select* that address. The switches were then reset to a *value*, and yet another switch would then *deposit* the switches' (32-bit) value in the previously selected address. In this straightforward (albeit extremely tedious) fashion, as much of memory could be loaded with specific contents as was desired. Provision was also made for the setting of the public registers. Since the program counter is one of these, the PC could be set to the value corresponding to the address of the first instruction's operation code, and thus when control was given over to the processor (by depressing a START switch), program execution would begin.

In later models the front panel is replaced by the **console terminal**, the specific terminal more or less directly connected to the processor. The console terminal can be used in much the same way as the "bit switches" on the front panel, to examine and load main memory, set the values in registers, start the processor, and so on, but in a more convenient way. But even at that, the console terminal is rarely used in this way, and never by the ordinary user, for the loading of memory in this byte-by-byte fashion is far too lengthy a process to be practical. The user who wishes to load main memory with the codes for the instructions of some program takes advantage of sophisticated **loader software**, programs that are provided specifically for this purpose. Exactly how these programs work is fairly complicated and well outside the scope of the book, although we shall briefly discuss these and a few others which collectively make up the **system software** in later chapters. In the meantime the reader is assured of the *possibility*—via bit switches, or the console terminal, or whatever other means—of ensuring that specific bit configurations are in specific locations in main memory.

5.8 BRANCHING

In Section 5.6 we described in some detail the instruction execution cycle, one of the features of which is the incrementing (by appropriate amounts) of the contents of the program counter. Implicit in that feature is the fact that the program counter's contents *increases* through main memory, going from lower addresses to higher addresses, and from this we conclude that when the processor has completed an instruction, it looks for the operation code for the *next* instruction in the *next* memory byte. Thus execution of instructions evidently proceeds *linearly* through main memory.

Now the reader's prior experience with computer programs undoubtedly reveals that not all algorithms proceed in this linear or sequential fashion; in fact, very few of them do, for it is more customary that for various reasons the program is to cease executing at one point and to resume execution elsewhere. The very nature of the *solution* of the problem at hand frequently dictates this "branching" or "jumping" from one place in the algorithm to another. (Indeed, even the description of the instruction execution cycle of Section 5.6, which is an *algorithm*— a *procedure* that describes what the processor must do to execute an instruction— has such a branch in it. At step 4 in that algorithm we stated that "*If* there are further instruction operands," *then* the procedure is to *branch* back to step 2.)

Given the way in which execution takes place—serially through increasing memory addresses—how can we achieve a "branch" of this sort? That is, how can the *program*—the prescribed set of instructions that the processor is to execute—indicate that the processor is *not* to fetch the next operation code from the byte immediately following its current instruction location, but rather that it is to fetch an operation code from elsewhere in memory? Since the processor *always* fetches whatever the program counter is pointing at, it is clear that a **branch** or **jump** can be achieved if the processor executes an instruction which explicitly *alters the contents of the program counter*. As a concrete example of such a construction, consider the few lines of instruction codes of Figure 5.8.1. We assume that upon completion of the last instruction, c(PC) = 0000128C, so that the program counter is pointing at the operation code byte D6. This byte is fetched, together with the mode byte (55), and the instruction is decoded as "increment the contents of one of the processor's public registers." Because of the incrementing of c(PC) on each

FIGURE 5.8.1

	Contents	Address	Comment
	.	.	
	.	.	
PC →	D6	128C	Increment (by 1) the contents of one of
	55	128D	the public registers
	17	128E	Put the number ˆX000020A4
	9F	128F	into the
	000020A4	1290	program counter
	D7	1294	Decrement (by 1) the contents
	58	1295	of another of the public registers
		.	
		.	
	A0	20A4	Add the two WORDS whose addresses
	9F	20A5	are
	000020C6	20A6	000020C6
	9F	20AA	and
	000020C8	20AB	000020C8
	—	20AF	(Next operation code)
		.	
		.	

of these two fetches, by now c(PC) = 0000128E. The register increment instruction is executed, and the processor is ready to execute the next instruction. The byte being pointed at by the PC, namely 17, is fetched, the mode byte (9F) is fetched, and the PC contents has been advanced to 00001290. The operation code and mode bytes are decoded by the processor as the following instruction: Put the 32-bit number (address), *currently* pointed at by the program counter, *into the program counter*. The number being pointed at by the program counter (000020A4) is *fetched*, and the program counter contents is incremented *by 4* (since a four-byte structure was fetched), so that now c(PC) = 00001294. Now that the processor has all the information required to process this instruction, it executes it. But what happens upon execution? As stated above, the number 000020A4 is put in the *program counter*. Having completed execution of this instruction, the processor is now ready to begin execution of the next instruction, and as usual it fetches the operation code byte being pointed at by the program counter. But the program counter is no longer pointing at the "decrement a public register" instruction at location 00001294, since the *last* instruction *altered* c(PC). Rather, the program counter is pointing at the byte A0 at 000020A4, the operation code byte for an addition instruction, which is fetched, c(PC) is incremented by 1, and so on. (This addition instruction is similar to that of the example of Section 5.5, although the first operand is given by its address rather than by its value.) Thus we see that it is possible by program instructions explicitly to modify the contents of the program counter, and as a result processor execution can be transferred from one location in main memory to another.

There is one other way in which the contents of the program counter can be modified (as opposed to putting some number directly into it, as above), and that involves *adding* to c(PC) some number, positive or negative. It should be clear that if an instruction has the effect of adding a *positive* number to c(PC), execution of the *next* instruction will take place at some *higher* addressed memory location, whereas if a *negative* number is added to c(PC), the next instruction to be executed will be at a *lower* addressed memory location. The VAX has an instruction that adds a *signed* (positive or negative) *byte* to the contents of the program counter, and we shall investigate it in some detail. Now there is some question about just what is to be meant by the sum of a signed 8-bit byte and the 32-bit contents of the program counter, for these two structures are not compatible as far as their numerical contexts are concerned. What goes on internally in the processor to accommodate this addition is the following. The 8-bit byte is **sign extended** to a 32-bit longword (within a private processor register), and the resulting longword is then added to c(PC), with the result replacing c(PC). By "sign extended" we mean that the high-order bit of the byte—the byte's *sign bit*—is *replicated* into bits 8 up through 31 of the longword. We give two examples. When the byte ˆX5B = ˆB01011011 is sign extended, the sign bit (0, in this case) is used as the value for bits 8 through 31 of the sign-extended longword; that is, the byte

$$\text{ˆX5B} = \text{ˆB01011011}$$

Instruction Execution and Stored Program Computers   Chap. 5

is sign extended to the longword

$$\text{^X0000005B} = \text{^B00000000000000000000000001011011}$$

Notice that the *byte* ^X5B has the same *numerical* value as the longword ^X0000005B, that is, (decimal) 91. In a similar fashion, the byte

$$\text{^XA7} = \text{^B10100111}$$

is sign extended to the longword

$$\text{^XFFFFFFA7} = \text{^B11111111111111111111111110100111}$$

since in this case the sign bit of the byte is 1. Again, both the byte and the longword have the same *numerical* value, (decimal) -89.

We shall consider two examples of this type of branch instruction, in which a signed byte value is added to c(PC), with the result replacing the current program counter contents. The number added to c(PC) is called a **program counter displacement** since it *displaces* the PC—the pointer to the next instruction to be executed. The code for this branch operation is (hexadecimal) 11, and this code is immediately followed by the displacement byte itself; as we have already noted, the processor then sign extends this displacement byte and adds it to c(PC). But note that execution of this instruction does *not* follow the procedure as described in Section 5.6. Instead, when the processor fetches the operation code 11, it realizes that the instruction is a branch instruction and that the PC is currently pointing at the byte displacement rather than at a *mode* byte. This is then fetched, sign extended, and added to the program counter contents.

In Figure 5.8.2 we assume that the program counter has the contents 000012BC. The operation code D6 and mode byte 55 for the "increment public register contents" instruction are fetched and executed, upon completion of which we have c(PC) = 000012BE. The processor then fetches c(000012BE) = 11, and the program counter contents advances to 000012BF. Since the processor recognizes this code as a branch operator, it does another fetch to get the program counter displacement, 6F, and again c(PC) advances, this time to 000012C0. The byte displacement 6F is sign extended to 0000006F, and this is added to the current contents of the program counter, 000012C0. The result is 0000132F, and this is the *new* contents of the program counter. Since the branch instruction is now complete, the processor again begins the instruction execution cycle, by doing a fetch. What is fetched? It is the byte pointed at by the program counter, that is, A0, the operation code for the *add* instruction. Thus again we have managed to skip forward in memory, but observe that the *way* in which the program counter contents was changed here is essentially different from that of Figure 5.8.1. Notice also that when the sign-extended displacement was added to c(PC), it was added to the *current* program counter contents, 000012C0, the program counter value *after* the displacement byte had been fetched.

FIGURE 5.8.2

	Contents	Address	Comment
	.		
	.		
PC →	D6	12BC	Increment (by 1) the contents
	55	12BD	of one of the public registers
	11	12BE	Add the sign-extended byte ˆX6F to
	6F	12BF	c(PC) and replace c(PC) by the sum
	D7	12C0	Decrement (by 1) the contents
	58	12C1	of another of the public registers
	.		
	.		
	A0	132F	Add the WORDS whose addresses
	9F	1330	are
	000020C6	1331	000020C6
	9F	1335	and
	000020C8	1336	000020C8
	—	133A	⟨next operation code⟩
	.		
	.		

We offer one more example, in which the PC displacement is *negative*, so that the branch takes place back into lower addressed memory locations. In Figure 5.8.3 we assume that c(PC) = 0000132F when the processor completes its current instruction. Again we encounter an "increment a public register" instruction; the code (D6) and mode byte (55) are fetched and the register increment is executed, leaving c(PC) = 00001331. The next operation code, 11, is fetched, and the processor recognizes a "branch with byte displacement" instruction. The displacement, 89, is fetched, c(PC) is advanced to 00001333, and the fetched displacement is sign extended. But observe that in the displacement byte 89, the sign bit is *on*, so the sign-extended value is FFFFFF89. This number is added to the current contents of the program counter, 00001333, and the result, 000012BC, is put back into the program counter. This completes execution of the branch instruction, and the processor then fetches the next operation code byte, *pointed at by the PC*, the byte A0 at 000012BC. This is another *add* operation, and the processor proceeds as we have seen several times before.

The reader may be somewhat concerned that if a byte is taken as a *signed* displacement of c(PC), then only relatively small displacements are possible, for as signed numbers, bytes can only take on values in the (decimal) range −128 to +127, a range that does not provide for branching very far from the program counter's current position. This is quite correct, although actual programming experience has shown that such branches are very frequently quite "local," within a few dozen or so bytes of the current PC. However, provision is made for extended branching, and in fact we saw one such in the example of Figure 5.8.1, in which *any* address can be *put directly into* the program counter to achieve the branch. That construction will be referred to as a *jump*, to distinguish it from the more local type of **branch** we have just discussed. In addition to the "jump-anywhere" instruction of Figure 5.8.1 and the "branch-locally" instructions of Figures 5.8.2 and 5.8.3, there is also an intermediate range type of branch, which like the "branch with byte displacement" adds a (positive or negative) number to the program counter contents. This is the "branch with word displacement" instruction, which uses a 16-bit word as a program counter displacement, rather than an 8-bit byte. We offer one simple example in Figure 5.8.4, without extensive comment, leaving to the reader an investigation of the effects of the instruction on c(PC). We note only that the operation code for this instruction is 31, and that a 16-bit word is sign extended to a 32-bit longword by replicating, into bits 16 to 31, the high-order (sign) bit of the word.

Why should the processor implement these two somewhat limited "branch" instructions, with either byte or word displacement, when the "jump" instruction can move the PC to *anywhere* in memory? The answer lies in the fact that the "jump" instruction always requires 6 bytes for its code, whereas the "branch with byte or word displacement" requires 2 or 3 bytes, respectively. Since by the nature of algorithms (programs) this branching is a rather frequent activity, substantial amounts of main memory can be saved by using the shorter, more "local" branches in place of "jump" where possible.

FIGURE 5.8.3

	Contents	Address	Comment
		.	
		.	
	A0	12BC	Add the WORDS whose addresses
	9F	12BD	are
	000020C6	12BE	000020C6
	9F	12C2	and
	000020C8	12C3	000020C8
	—	12C7	⟨next operation code⟩
		.	
		.	
PC →	D6	132F	Increment (by 1) the contents
	55	1330	of one of the public registers
	11	1331	Add the sign-extended byte ˆX89 to
	89	1332	c(PC) and replace c(PC) by the sum
	D7	1333	Decrement (by 1) the contents
	58	1334	of another of the public registers
		.	

FIGURE 5.8.4

	Contents	Address	Comment
		.	
		.	
	A0	12BC	Add the WORDS whose addresses
	9F	12BD	are
	000020C6	12BE	000020C6
	9F	12C2	and
	000020C8	12C3	000020C8
	—	12C7	⟨next operation code⟩
		.	
		.	
PC →	D6	6488	Increment (by 1) the contents
	55	6489	of one of the public registers
	31	648A	Add the sign-extended word ˆXAE2F to
	AE2F	648B	c(PC) and replace c(PC) by the sum
	D7	648D	Decrement (by 1) the contents
	58	648E	of another of the public registers
		.	
		.	

5.9 CONDITIONAL BRANCHING AND THE PROCESSOR STATUS REGISTER

Consider the simple task of finding the sum of the positive integers between 1 and 10, inclusive. Shown below is a complete program to calculate this sum and then HALT—the result is *not* printed. The program is written in the BASIC programming language, although it would have approximately the same appearance in many other high-level languages.

```
10  SUM = 0
20  COUNTER = 10
30  SUM = SUM + COUNTER
40  COUNTER = COUNTER − 1
50  IF COUNTER > 0 THEN GOTO 30
60  STOP
70  END
```

The logic of the algorithm is perfectly straightforward, with the possible exception of the fact that the sum of the integers is accumulated from 10 down to 1, rather than from 1 up to 10. The BASIC statement of interest to us is that found at line 50. This is a **conditional** statement, for it tells the processor to do something (GOTO 30) *provided that* some condition is *true* (namely, COUNTER > 0); otherwise, the statement in the THEN clause is to be ignored, and control resumes at line 60, where the processor is to STOP.

The reader is doubtless aware of the importance of these **conditional branches** (IF...THEN GOTO...) and the fact that they are employed far more frequently than the **unconditional branches** (GOTO...) in everyday programming tasks. In fact, one of the most common high-level language constructions is the loop (FOR...NEXT in BASIC, DO in FORTRAN, WHILE...DO and REPEAT...UNTIL in Pascal, and so on), and these statements are nothing other than thinly disguised conditional branch constructions, implemented for the programmer's convenience rather than out of sheer necessity.

The branch and jump instructions of the preceding sections are, of course, unconditional. But the VAX also implements an extensive group of *conditional* branch instructions. Before investigating one of these in detail, we introduce a convenient notation and then treat somewhat more formally than earlier the concept of *processor status*. A collection of contiguous bits, as a substructure of a larger structure (byte, word, longword, and so on) is denoted by specifying the substructure's highest and lowest ordered bit numbers, separated by a colon. For example, the bits between bits 12 and 5, inclusive, of a word (or longword or quadword or octaword) is denoted by 12:5. In a similar fashion, the low-order byte of a longword can be denoted by the bits 7:0, while the high-order byte can be referred to as bits 31:24.

In Section 2.11 we discussed the *processor status*, and in particular our concern at that time was with the *condition codes* and how they were set or cleared as a result of various arithmetic instructions. It is an appropriate time to look in more detail at the central processor register which we have referred to as the **processor status register**, although the term **processor status longword** (abbreviated **PSL**) is the more customary term. A diagram of this register is shown in Figure 5.9.1. The low-order word of this register, bits 15:0, is called the **processor status word (PSW)**. (The high-order word of the PSL—bits 31:16—will not be discussed here. Most of those bits have significance, but not to the everyday use to which the programmer will put the computer.) Bits 15:8 (the high-order byte) of the PSW are labeled "MBZ," which stands for *Must Be Zero*; these bits are unused, and no attempt should be made to set any of them to 1. The next four bits, 7:4, are the **trap enable flags**, and the significance of some of them is discussed in Chapter 6, but for the moment we decline even to name them. In fact, our interest centers on bits 3:0, for these are the **condition codes**—N, Z, V, and C—which were introduced in Section 2.11. As was mentioned there, these bits are set or cleared by the processor at the conclusion of most of its operations, to indicate the *effect*

Processor Status Longword (PSL)

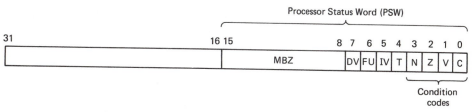

Figure 5.9.1

of the operation. For example, if an operation has resulted in a negative number [for instance, the addition $3 + (-14)$], the N-bit will be *set* (to 1), and the Z-bit will be *cleared* (to 0). If an operation resulted in zero, the Z-bit will be set. We have already discussed in some detail the setting and clearing of V and C, at least in the cases of addition and subtraction. Most of the operators affect these bits in some way, and these effects are stated explicitly as part of the descriptions of each of the operators described in Appendix A.

Our interest in the condition codes of the processor status word derives from the fact that the VAX's **conditional branch instructions** execute branches based on the status of these condition codes. All the conditional branches are structurally identical to the "branch with byte displacement" operator which we investigated in Section 5.8, in that they add a sign extended byte displacement to c(PC), *except* that the branch takes place *on the condition* that one or more of the condition codes in the PSW is set (or cleared) in a particular way. For example, if the current processor operation yields a *positive* result, we can conclude that $N = 0$ *and* $Z = 0$—the result was neither negative nor zero (and thus must be positive). Another way of putting this is that the operation yielded a positive result if, and only if, upon completion of the instruction, we have $N + Z = 0$ (where "$+$" is the Boolean OR operator). One of VAX conditional branches, which we shall informally call "branch if positive," has operation code (hexadecimal) 14, and executes as follows. The operator code is followed in main memory by a byte, which the processor interprets as a signed program counter displacement. When the "branch if positive" operator code (14) and the displacement byte are fetched (during which actions c(PC) is incremented by 2), the processor checks the status of the condition code bits N and Z. If *both* are zero, the displacement byte is sign extended to a 32-bit longword displacement and added to the contents of the program counter, just as before. But if *either* N *or* Z is 1, the processor simply fetches the *next* operation code. That is, in the latter case the processor in effect *ignores* the "branch if positive" instruction. (Compare this action with that of line 50 of the BASIC program that opened this section:

IF COUNTER > 0 THEN GOTO 30

If the result of the preceding instruction—decrement COUNTER—was positive, control is transferred to line 30. Otherwise, what happens? In effect, nothing—execution simply continues at the *next* instruction.)

As an example of "branch if positive," consider the instruction of Figure 5.9.2. Assuming that the program counter contains the value 0000302A, the operation code 14 will be fetched by the processor, the PC contents will be advanced to 0000302B, and the operation will be interpreted as the conditional "branch if positive." The displacement byte B2 is fetched, and by now c(PC) = 0000302C. The processor now checks the condition codes N and Z. If either is *set* (to 1), the processor terminates execution of the current instruction and begins another instruction execution cycle, by fetching the contents of the operation code at 0000302C; that is, in this case the processor "ignores" the branch instruction. However, if both N *and* Z are 0, the displacement byte B2 is sign extended to the 32-bit value

FIGURE 5.9.2

	Contents	Address	Comment
		.	
		.	
		.	
PC →	14	302A	Branch-if-positive with
	B2	302B	byte displacement = B2
			(= decimal −78)
	—	302C	⟨Next operation code⟩

FFFFFFB2, added to the current PC contents (0000302C), and the PC then has the value 00002FDE. It is from this location that the next operation is fetched—that is, instruction execution has branched to 00002FDE.

As a second example of this same conditional branch instruction, we offer in Figure 5.9.3 a complete program, which in fact is the program shown at the beginning of this section (to add the first 10 positive integers), but this time written in the machine's own "native" language—called a **machine language program**. Since the numbers we will have to deal with are quite small, we have chosen *word* structures to hold them (although, in fact, even bytes would do, since none of the results ever exceeds the −128 to +127 range that can be held in 8 bits). Thus the word at 00002000 is given the value 0 (this is where the SUM will be accumulated), and the word at 00002002 has the vaue 10 (the COUNTER). The actual program instructions begin at 00003000. These particular choices of memory locations in which we have loaded data and instructions are completely arbitrary, since the processor can access any memory location as easily as any other. The only constraints under which we *must* operate are (1) the codes for the instructions must be in *sequential* memory locations (because of the combined actions of the

FIGURE 5.9.3

	Contents	Address	Comment
	0000	2000	SUM accumulated here (initially 0)
	000A	2002	COUNTER (initially 10)
		.	
		.	
		.	
PC →	A0	3000	Add the WORD whose address is
	9F	3001	00002002 (COUNTER) to the
	00002002	3002	WORD whose address is 00002000
	9F	3006	(SUM) and put the result back
	00002000	3007	in the WORD at 00002000
	B7	300B	Decrement (by 1) the WORD
	9F	300C	whose address is 00002002
	00002002	300D	(that is, decrement COUNTER)
	14	3011	IF the result is GREATER THAN 0,
	ED	3012	branch back to location 00003000
	00	3013	otherwise, HALT the processor

processor and the program counter), and (2) the two data words must be kept out of the mainstream of program instruction. Aside from adhering to these two conditions, the data and instruction codes could be placed anywhere in main memory.

Having loaded main memory as shown, we now set the program counter value to 00003000 and start the processor. The code A0 is fetched and decoded as the "add two words" instruction we have seen several times before. By the time the mode bytes and word addresses have been fetched and the program counter contents has been advanced to 0000300B, the processor knows that it is to add the contents of 00002002 (the COUNTER) to the contents of 00002000 (the SUM), and place the result back in location 00002000. This instruction is executed, and since (decimal) 10 is added to 0, c(00002000) is now 10. The next operation code, B7, is fetched and interpreted as a "word decrement (by 1)." The mode byte 9F indicates that the program counter (whose contents by now is 0000300D) is pointing at the *address* of the word to be decremented. This address is fetched [and c(PC) is incremented to 00003011], and the processor decrements the contents of the word at 00002002—the COUNTER—which then has the value 9. Next, the "branch if positive" operation code, 14, is fetched, as is the byte displacement, ED. The processor examines the condition codes N and Z and finds them *both clear*. This is a result of the fact that when c(00002002) was decremented (to 9), the result was *neither* negative *nor* zero. Consequently, the branch *is* executed, as follows. The displacement is sign extended to FFFFFFED, and this value is added to the *current* program counter contents, 00003013. The result, 00003000, is put back into the program counter. Thus the next operation fetched is at 00003000, the "add two words" instruction. This time, the COUNTER (9) is added to the SUM (10) and the result stored back in SUM. Again the COUNTER is decremented (to 8), the N and Z bits are tested and found to be clear, and another branch returns control to the *add* instruction. This looping process continues, until finally c(00002002), that is, COUNTER, has the value 1. After 1 is added to the SUM, this counter is decremented *to zero*, and at this point the PSW Z bit is turned *on*. Now when the "branch if positive" instruction is fetched and the processor tests the N and Z bits, it finds the Z bit is set and thus does *not* execute the branch; rather, the processor begins a new fetch-and-execute cycle. The byte fetched is 00 at 00003013, the code for the "halt the processor" instruction, and the processor stops. At this point c(00002000) = 55 (the SUM), c(00002002) = 0 (the COUNTER), and c(PC) = 00003014.

If this little program has a deficiency, it is that once the desired sum has been calculated, the processor simply HALTs, and we have made no provision for the program to *announce* the result. (We did not make any such provision in the BASIC version of this program either, although it would have been easy enough to replace line 60 with

60   PRINT SUM

so that we could see the result.) The reason for this is that input to and output from a machine language program are fairly complicated processes, and in these early stages of program development we choose not to clutter our discussion with these distracting details. We provide these capabilities in Chapter 6 after we have a somewhat more firm understanding of processor action, instruction execution, and just how one *creates* a program in the machine's native language.

5.10 A SIMPLE ADDITION PROGRAM

In this section we write a program to add 8 numbers, and we assume that at least some of them are sufficiently large that they require a longword structure to hold them. Since the VAX has no provision to add the contents of structures of mixed context, *all* the numbers will be stored in longwords. Further, the longwords that hold the numbers will be in *contiguous* memory locations, for reasons that will become clear shortly. Now it would be simple enough to write 8 "add longword" instructions to accumulate the sum, but this is patently inelegant and would be unreasonable if, instead of 8 numbers, we had to add 800 numbers. Thus we seek a more sophisticated approach to the problem. A program to do this task is shown in Figure 5.10.1, and again we have chosen some addresses more or less arbitrarily. Observe that the numbers themselves are loaded at 00001000, a longword zero has been established at 00001020 to accumulate the SUM of the numbers, and a byte containing the number 8 is at 00001024, which acts as a COUNTER as we go through a loop of instructions, adding one of the numbers each time through. As indicated, execution begins with the instruction at 00001200.

The instruction at 00001200 is straightforward; it is "add two longwords and place the sum back in the second of the two longwords." This is virtually identical to the *add* instructions we have already seen, except that in the earlier cases we added *word* contents. In fact, comparison of the instruction at 00001200 with, for example, the instruction at address 00003000 in Figure 5.9.3, reveals that the only difference (other than the two addresses) is in the operation code itself—A0 for "add words" and C0 for "add longwords." This instruction adds c(00001000) (the first number) to c(00001020) (the SUM) and puts the result back in 00001020. Thus we have accumulated the first number in 00001020, and we now want to add the next of the numbers to SUM, provided that there *is* a next number. To determine if there is we decrement the COUNTER and see if it is still positive. The instruction at 0000120B is "decrement (by 1) the contents of the byte at 00001024," and this is followed by a conditional branch instruction. However, this is *not* "branch if positive"—rather, it is "branch if zero;" that is, the branch will take place *if* the PSW condition code Z bit is set. In this case it is not, since we have just decremented the COUNTER from 8 to 7. Thus the branch is ignored. At this point we need to add another number, but it will not do simply to branch back to location 00001200, where we already have an *add* instruction. For this would simply add the contents of 00001000 *again*, and instead we want to add the *next* number, the contents of 00001004. But the "add two longwords" instruction at 00001200 *can* be reused, *provided* that we modify the address portion of that instruction prior to its reuse.

Since by now c(PC) = 00001213, the operation code C0 is fetched. Once again this is an "add two longwords" operator, and the mode byte 8F at 00001214

FIGURE 5.10.1

	Contents	Address	Comment
			The numbers to be added. In decimal:
	000007C8	1000	1992
	0000007F	1004	127
	0003CBC4	1008	248772
	FFFFFE6C	100C	−404
	000C9FC3	1010	827331
	0000000E	1014	14
	FFFFFC17	1018	−1001
	00000057	101C	87
	00000000	1020	SUM accumulated here (initialized to 0)
	08	1024	The COUNTER (initialized to 8)
PC →	C0	1200	Add the LONGWORD
	9F	1201	at
	00001000	1202	00001000 (later modified)
	9F	1206	to the LONGWORD at
	00001020	1207	00001020 (the SUM)
	97	120B	Decrement (by 1) the contents of
	9F	120C	the BYTE at
	00001024	120D	00001024 (the COUNTER)
	13	1211	The "branch if equal to 0
	0D	1212	to 00001220" instruction
	C0	1213	Add the LONGWORD whose value
	8F	1214	is
	00000004	1215	4
	9F	1219	to the LONGWORD at
	00001202	121A	00001202
	11	121E	"branch with byte displacement
	E0	121F	to 00001200" instruction
	00	1220	HALT the processor

indicates that the program counter is currently pointing at the number to be added, 00000004. (Compare this situation with the "add two words" instruction of Figure 5.5.1.) Thus the first operand is the number 4, and the second is decoded as the longword whose address is 00001202; the 4 is added to the contents of that longword—00001000—and the result (00001004) is put back into 00001202. We now return to location 00001200 with the "branch with byte displacement" instruction at 0000121E and reexecute the longword *add* instruction. But this time that instruction has the effect of adding the longword contents of 00001004—the *second* number—to the contents of 00001020 (SUM).

This same process is continued; the COUNTER is decremented, and if it is not zero, 4 is added to the address portion of the longword *add* instruction at 00001200, and that instruction is then executed another time. In this way the sum of the eight numbers is accumulated at 00001020 (SUM) until COUNTER is decremented to 0. Then the conditional "branch if zero" at 00001211 *is* executed, the program counter contents is reset to 00001220, the operation code (00) there is fetched, and the processor HALTs.

There are a number of observations that need to be made before leaving this example. First, we have written a program that actually *modifies one of its own instructions* in the course of execution. This may strike the reader as somewhat bizarre especially in terms of high-level languages such as COBOL or Pascal, where such modifications are simply not possible. But notice that what has happened here is that we have added the number 4 to the contents of a memory location. That the location happened to hold an *instruction component* is of no consequence to the processor, and as we know, it has no way of discerning that fact anyway. We do not claim that such instruction modification is desirable, only that in this case it has achieved the needed result. In fact, programs that modify their own instructions are generally very difficult to follow from the standpoint of the logic of their algorithms, and they are prone to errors that can be extremely elusive. In Section 5.12 we shall rewrite this task in a way that requires none of this modification, and in fact streamlines the present offering in a number of other ways.

Second, it should now be clear why we insisted that the numbers to be added resided in *contiguous* longwords. If, instead, they had been scattered randomly around main memory, the scheme of adjusting the address portion of the longword *add* instruction would never have succeeded.

Finally, we note that again we have no provision for announcing the result. But even further, we have made no provision for the possibility of an *overflow* occurring when the numbers were added, and thus the possibility of an incorrect sum. As it turns out, there is no such problem with these particular numbers, but it is easy to conceive of a collection of numbers whose (signed) sum could not fit in 31 bits. Thus some overflow would occur, the result would be arithmetically incorrect, and yet we would not be aware of that. Such overflow can be detected (there is a conditional branch instruction which branches if the PSW V-bit is set), but we have not included the necessary programming here.

5.11 THE GENERAL REGISTERS

We noted in Chapter 1 that the central processing unit contains a number of registers, some of which are "public" in the sense that they are available for use by the computer user, whereas others are "private" to the processor itself. One of the public registers is the processor status longword, although in practice we use only the low-order word (PSW) of that register. In addition, there are 16 "general" registers for the programmer's use (sometimes referred to as "general-purpose" registers, athough this is something of a misnomer). We name these R0, R1, ..., R15, and they are displayed in Figure 5.11.1. Observe that the first six of these are labeled "restricted use," a term that requires some explanation. The term is actually far stronger than we intend, for there is no reason why the programmer cannot use these registers for whatever purpose might be appropriate *in most cases*; the only caution that must be given is that there are a few VAX instructions which use some or all of these registers *implicitly*. That is, in the course of executing these instructions, the contents of these registers may be altered

FIGURE 5.11.1

```
R0  ⎫
R1  ⎪
R2  ⎬  Restricted
R3  ⎪  use
R4  ⎪
R5  ⎭

R6  ⎫
R7  ⎪
R8  ⎬  Unrestricted
R9  ⎪  use
R10 ⎪
R11 ⎭

R12 ⎫
R13 ⎬  Special
R14 ⎪  purpose
R15 ⎭
```

even though the registers do not appear explicitly to enter into the operation. But it will be some time before we encounter any of these instructions, and they are not frequently used in most everyday programming anyway, so in the meantime the reader should feel free to use R0 through R5 for whatever purpose.

R6 through R11 are, as labeled, for "unrestricted use," since they are affected only by instructions which explicitly reference them.

R12 through R15 are "special-purpose" registers and thus are generally *not* used by the programmer except in rather specific ways. We cannot say much more about these four registers at this point (they are discussed in detail in Chapter 9), except to say that R15 is, in fact, the *program counter*. It should be obvious that because of its central role in instruction execution, the program counter is "special purpose" indeed.

The registers, being 32-bit longwords, can be used for any purpose to which we might put a 32-bit memory longword. In fact, the low-order 16 bits of a register behave like a memory word, while its low-order 8 bits act as a memory byte. Thus register contents can be added to other register contents, as longwords, words, or bytes; register contents can be incremented, decremented, and so on. Their behavior relative to carries, overflows, setting of the condition codes, and so on, is identical to that of their main memory counterparts. Registers can function as accumulators and counters, so that the *memory locations* which acted as the SUM and COUNTER of the programs of Figures 5.9.3 and 5.10.1 could have been replaced by, say, R4 and R10. The advantages of the use of a register over a memory location is twofold. First, a register is a high-speed device, and thus the processing of register contents takes place more rapidly than that of a memory location. Second, since registers are an integral part of the central processing unit, the processor does not need to do a memory access to obtain the contents of a register. Both of these can be of significance when a vast amount of processing needs to be done—a few **milliseconds** (thousandths of a second) or **microseconds** (millionths of a second) saved may have little impact *until* such savings accumulate perhaps millions of times.

One of the most significant features of the general registers, and one that makes them more than just "high-speed" memory longwords, is that since they are 32-bit structures, they can hold *addresses*. Just as was the case with the program counter, when a general register contains a 32-bit longword that *we interpret* as the address of some location, we say that the register **points at** the contents of that location. We shall see in the next and subsequent sections the power of this concept.

We have already noted that registers, being CPU-resident, do *not* have addresses as do main memory locations, and this leads to the following question. If we need to perform an operation on the contents of a memory location, we so inform the processor by explicitly stating the numerical *address* of the location; but if we wish to operate on some *register*, say R3, in some fashion (perhaps increment its contents, or add its contents to another register or memory location), how do we notify the processor of that fact? The answer is that the needed register information is in the *mode byte(s)* of the instruction. Although the complete details of this concept will be deferred until Chapter 7, we shall at least deal briefly with them in specific cases in the next section.

5.12 PUTTING THE GENERAL REGISTERS TO USE

In this section we take advantage of the general registers to rewrite in a far more pleasing and efficient way the addition program of Figure 5.10, in such a way that the address modification of that program is no longer required. In Figure 5.12.1 we proceed as in the earlier version, with the following exceptions. The location in which the SUM is to be accumulated is now Register 4 rather than a memory longword, and the COUNTER is located in Register 3 rather than a memory byte. Notice that whereas we can specify an initial value for a memory location (the SUM was given the initial value 0, and the COUNTER the initial value 8), when dealing with *registers* we must set their values by explicit *programming instructions*. Thus the instruction at 00001200 has the effect of putting the number 8 into R3 (the COUNTER), while the instruction at location 00001207 *clears* (sets to 0) the contents of R4 (the SUM). In particular, let us examine the action of the instruction at 00001200 which puts the number 8 into R3. The operation code byte currently pointed at by the program counter, D0, is decoded as "*move* (or *copy*) a longword from one location to another." Now that the processor knows that a longword is to be moved, it must determine the **source** ("from where") and **destination** ("to where") of the move. The source is the first operand, so the processor fetches the mode byte from location 00001201, namely 8F. We have seen this mode a couple of times before, and it is interpreted by the processor to mean that the program counter is currently *pointing at* the source operand. Since the current program counter contents is 00001202, the first or source operand is evidently the longword 00000008. The source operand is fetched, and the program counter contents is moved up to 00001206. (Before moving on to the destination operand, it is worth noting that the *mode byte* for the source operand is 8F, and F in decimal is 15—the register number of the program counter. This is no accident, for the low-order 4 bits of the mode typically specify the register involved in locating the operand. Note that in this case it was indeed R15—the PC—that was used in locating the operand, 00000008.) Now the destination operand is determined, and the processor fetches the mode byte 53, moving c(PC) up to 00001207. The mode 53 states that the destination is actually R3. Thus the effect of this instruction is to move the number 8 into R3, as indicated in the comment.

The next instruction to be executed is at 00001207, with operation code D4. The processor interprets this as meaning "clear (set to 0) the longword whose location is given by the operand." Thus the processor fetches the mode byte 54, and as in the preceding instruction, it decodes 54 to mean that the operand is in fact R4, and thus the contents of R4 is cleared to 0.

The instruction at 00001209 is another "move a longword from source to

FIGURE 5.12.1

	Contents	Address	Comment
			The numbers to be added. In decimal:
	000007C8	1000	1992
	0000007F	1004	127
	0003CBC4	1008	248772
	FFFFFE6C	100C	−404
	000C9FC3	1010	827331
	0000000E	1014	14
	FFFFFC17	1018	−1001
	00000057	101C	87
PC →	D0	1200	Put the number 8 in
	8F	1201	Register 3
	00000008	1202	to act as the
	53	1206	COUNTER
	D4	1207	Clear (to 0) Register 4
	54	1208	to accumulate the SUM
	D0	1209	Put the address
	8F	120A	00001000 of the first
	00001000	120B	of the numbers in Register 6
	56	120F	to act as a POINTER
	C0	1210	Add the longword pointed at by
	86	1211	Register 6 to contents of
	54	1212	Register 4 and increment c(Register 6) by 4
	D7	1213	Decrement (by 1) contents of
	53	1214	Register 3 (the COUNTER)
	14	1215	"branch if positive to
	F9	1216	00001210" instruction
	00	1217	HALT the processor

destination operands," and we leave it to the reader to verify that the longword 00001000 is moved to R6. The significance of this "move" is that 00001000 is the *address* of the first of the data numbers.

The heart of the program is in the instruction at 00001210. We have seen the operation code byte C0 before, which is decoded as a longword *add*, so we concentrate on the operands—what is to be added to what. The mode byte 86 is interpreted as follows. The first operand for the *add* is the longword *pointed at* by R6. Now since currently c(R6) = 00001000, this means that the first operand is c(00001000), namely 000007C8 (or decimal 1992)—the first of the data numbers. But this mode byte 86 specifies even more. It indicates to the processor that once c(R6) has been used as the address of the operand, c(R6) is to be *incremented by 4*—by *4*, since the add instruction is a *longword* (= 4 byte) instruction. It is important to observe two things. First, the incrementing of the register contents takes place *after* the contents of the register has been used as the operand address. Second, the incrementing of the register contents is done *by the processor*, as a result of the processor's interpretation of the *mode byte 86 itself*—there is no user-written "add 4 to c(R6)" instruction here. The second operand for the longword *add* instruction is Register 4 itself, so the net result of the instruction is to add the number 000007C8 to c(R4) = 00000000, to obtain c(R4) = 000007C8. Note that by now we have c(R6) = 00001004, and c(PC) = 00001213.

The next two instructions decrement the contents of R3 (to 7) and branch-if-positive to 00001210. Since the result of the last instruction [the "decrement c(R3)"] is positive, the branch takes place and execution resumes at 00001210.

The *add* instruction at 00001210 executes again, and since now c(R6) = 00001004, c(00001004) is added to c(R4), and c(R6) is again incremented by 4, so that now R6 points at the *third* data number. The process should be fairly clear by now. Each time through this loop of program instructions, another data number is added to c(R4) and the "pointer," R6, is moved up to the next number. c(R3) keeps track of how many times this loop is executed, finally exiting from the loop with the HALT instruction at 00001217.

Observe that this version of the "add 8 numbers" program also relies on the fact that the numbers are in consecutive memory locations, and for essentially the same reason as before. Here R6, the *pointer* to the data, "steps through" these locations, one after another, on each pass through the loop. This action, which is a feature of the *add* instruction itself, has greatly simplified the *structure* of the program, for it has eliminated the necessity for the program itself to modify the address portion of one of its instructions. This example has given the reader a glimpse at the power not only of the register concept, but also of the *addressing modes* available on the VAX. These extensive modes (there are 16 of them) are pivotal in defining the *architectural structure* of this particular machine.

5.13 CLOSING COMMENT

In Chapter 1 we informally defined a computer to be *an electronic, binary, stored-instruction, programmable, sequential, automatic data processor*. None of those terms had much if any meaning at that time, but by now the reader should understand all of them and recognize that they are descriptive of the kinds of machines we have been studying. In particular, we know that a computer is an *electronic* device, in that the circuitry that performs its basic operations is made up of components that react in various ways to electric currents; its number system is based on the *binary* (base-2) number representation; its *instructions* are *stored* in encoded form in its own memory; it is *programmable* in the sense that the set of instructions the processor carries out is predetermined by the user; the processing of information is *sequential*—one discrete instruction after another (although some instruction components do overlap, and this "parallelism" is becoming more pronounced as each new model is unveiled); it is *automatic* in that the processor's "fetch-execute" cycle keeps the processor going automatically; and it *processes data* in the broad sense, going far beyond the basic arithmetic operations on numerical information.

5.14 EXERCISES

5.1.1. If each frame of a five-channel paper tape holds an operation code for a particular computer, and if the paper tape reader will not tolerate a frame with *no* holes punched at all, show that this machine can implement 31 distinct operations. But show also that this number can easily be raised to 61 by the following scheme. *One* of the 31 punch combinations is interpreted by the processor as meaning "the operation is of a *secondary* class of operations, and its code will be found in the *next* tape frame." (This scheme can clearly be extended even further, but only at the expense of additional tape reads.)

5.5.1. In Figure 5.5.1 we saw that the operation code for "add two words" is (hexadecimal) A0. In Section 5.10 we shall see that the operation code for "add two *longwords*" is C0. The code for "add two *bytes*" is 80. By expanding each of these codes to its 8-bit binary form, make some conjectures about how the decoding circuitry can examine these bit configurations and extract some operand information from them. Are these conjectures consistent with the fact that "increment byte" has code 96, "increment word" has code B6, and "increment longword" has code D6?

5.8.1. For each of the bytes or words given below in hexadecimal, determine the corresponding sign extended longword.
   (a) 24   **(b)** 84   **(c)** F4   **(d)** 002A
   (e) 009A   **(f)** 9207   **(g)** 00   **(h)** FFFF

5.8.2. Suppose that each of the following "branch with byte displacement" instructions is located at 0000B2D7. Determine the "target address" of each such branch, that is, the address in memory to which control will be transferred by the instruction. [More simply asked: What will be c(PC) *after* execution of the instruction?]
   (a) 11   **(b)** 11   **(c)** 11   **(d)** 11
       2A   7F   80   F2
   (e) 11   **(f)** 11   **(g)** 11   **(h)** 11
       FE   00   02   FC

5.8.3. The same as in Exercise 5.8.2, for each of the following "branch with word displacement" instructions. Assume again that the first byte of the instruction is located at 0000B2D7.

(a)	31	(b)	31	(c)	31	(d)	31
	012A		FFF8		120A		0000
(e)	31	(f)	31	(g)	31	(h)	31
	FFFD		0002		8000		7FFF

5.8.4. Assume that a "branch to TARGET" instruction is to be located at 0000709D, where TARGET is a symbolic name for some memory location. Write the 2 or 3 bytes of code for a "branch with byte displacement to TARGET" instruction (code = 11) or "branch with word displacement to TARGET" instruction (code = 31) for each of the values of TARGET given below, under the following conditions. If TARGET can be reached with a *byte* displacement, use a "branch with byte displacement" instruction; otherwise, use a "branch with word displacement" instruction. If TARGET cannot be reached with a word displacement, state that TARGET is "out of range."

- (a) 00007124
- (b) 00007088
- (c) 0000C177
- (d) 00001059
- (e) 0000709F
- (f) 0000F279
- (g) 0000709D
- (h) 0000709B
- (i) 00000000

5.9.1. For each of the TARGET addresses given below, construct a "branch if positive" instruction (code = 14) at location 000014A7, if possible. (If not possible, state that TARGET is "out of range.")

- (a) 000014B2
- (b) 00000704
- (c) 00001444
- (d) 000014A7
- (e) 000014A9
- (f) 000014A2

5.9.2. Suppose we wish to locate a "branch if *not* zero" instruction (operation code = 12) at 00001E4F, but that the location to which we want to branch (conditionally) is 00002857, which is too far to reach with a byte displacement. That is, there is no byte we can place at 00001E50 to achieve the branch:

$$
\begin{array}{lll}
12 & 1E4F & \text{"branch if not zero} \\
?? & 1E50 & \quad\text{to 00002857"}
\end{array}
$$

However, show that the same effect can be achieved by the sequence

$$
\begin{array}{lll}
13 & 1E4F & \text{"branch if } zero \\
03 & 1E50 & \quad\text{to 00001E54"} \\
31 & 1E51 & \text{"branch with } word \text{ displace-} \\
0A03 & 1E52 & \quad\text{ment to 00002857"}
\end{array}
$$

Thus, although the conditional branches are somewhat restricted in that they only branch rather locally, the range of the branch can easily be extended by combining a "branch with word displacement" or even a "jump" instruction with the *complementary* conditional branch instruction.

5.9.3. We informally named the conditional branch instruction that adds a sign-extended byte displacement to c(PC) *if* N + Z = 0, "branch if positive." In a similar fashion, devise informal "names" for instructions that generate branches on each of the following conditions.

- (a) Z = 0
- (b) N = 0
- (c) Z = 1
- (d) N = 1
- (e) N + Z = 0
- (f) N + Z = 1
- (g) C = 1
- (h) C = 0
- (i) C + Z = 1
- (j) C + Z = 0
- (k) V = 1
- (l) V = 0

FIGURE 5.14.1

Contents	Address	Comment
	.	
	.	
	.	
B7	6244	"decrement (by 1) the
9F	6245	contents of the WORD
00001466	6246	at 00001466" instruction
12	624A	"branch if nonzero to
F8	624B	00006244" instruction
00	624C	HALT the processor
	.	
	.	

5.10.1. Consider the program segment shown in Figure 5.14.1. How many times will the "branch" instruction be executed (whether the branch actually takes place or is ignored) if initially c(00001466) is 7? Is 1? If the initial contents of 00001466 is 0 or negative, will this sequence of instructions *ever* HALT, or will it execute indefinitely? Explain.

5.10.2. Show that the logical flow of the instructions of the program of Figure 5.10.1 can be tidied up a bit if the algorithm is rewritten as follows.

> Add longword at 00001000 to longword at 00001020;
> Add longword 00000004 to c(00001202);
> Decrement byte at 00001024;
> Branch if positive to 00001200,
>   else HALT.

Rewrite that program, complete with addresses, address contents, and comments, based on this modified algorithm. (Assume that the data, SUM, and COUNTER are in the locations shown, and that the first longword *add* instruction is located at 00001200, as in Figure 5.10.1.)

5.12.1. Calculate the (decimal) number of bytes required for the instruction codes (not data) for the two programs of Figures 5.10.1 and 5.12.1. (This suggests that the use of registers for data and pointers not only improves performance and adds flexibility in the ways in which operands are specified, but can result in substantial savings in the main memory occupied by a program.)

5.12.2. When the program of Figure 5.10.1 is loaded into memory at the addresses shown, the program counter is set to 00001200, and the processor STARTed, the sum of the eight numbers is calculated and the processor HALTs at 00001220 [with c(PC) = 00001221]. Suppose that the program is then *reexecuted* simply by resetting the program counter to 00001200 and restarting the processor. Show that the program will *not* execute as it did the first time. Explain exactly what *will* happen during the second execution.

In contradistinction to this situation, show that if the program of Figure 5.12.1 is reexecuted in an analogous fashion, the second execution *will* be identical to the first. (These examples illustrate the consequences that may be paid when programs modify their own instructions and fail to initialize various memory locations prior to their use.) How could the program of Figure 5.10.1 be modified so that it *can* be reexecuted?

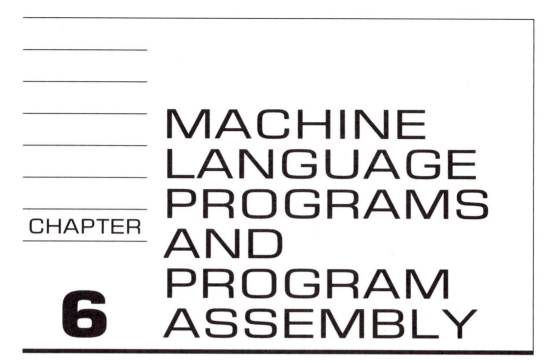

MACHINE LANGUAGE PROGRAMS AND PROGRAM ASSEMBLY

CHAPTER

6

6.1 MACHINE LANGUAGE PROGRAMS

In Chapter 5 we presented three examples—Figures 5.9.3, 5.10.1, and 5.12.1—of "programs," although we never precisely defined that term. In a high-level language—FORTRAN, BASIC, Pascal, or whatever—a formal definition can be quite complex. At the machine level it is a bit easier to describe what we mean by a *program*. If, for these purposes, we define an *instruction* to be any byte or collection of bytes (or words or longwords) in main memory which is ultimately pointed at by the program counter, and if all other bytes in main memory are termed *data*, then we can define a **machine language program** to be a collection of data and instructions in main memory which, upon execution (that is, upon setting the contents of the PC and STARTing the processor), will ultimately cause the processor to HALT. Observe that the three sample programs have this last property, and in those examples it is fairly easy to determine which bytes are data and which are operation codes or instruction components. We would probably also want to insist that the effect of execution—the results of the processor's actions—is *meaningful* or *useful*, but these are such vague terms that we shall not attempt to expand further upon this description. Suffice it to say that all the sample programs we shall deal with will be meaningful and will solve some stated problem.

Experience with high-level languages indicates that when we solve a problem by means of the writing of a computer program, we go through a number of phases in achieving the solution. The first of these is to ensure that we fully understand the problem, what data are available to us, and what results are to be generated.

Next, we develop a basic approach to the task, perhaps deciding that although several methods will do the job, a particular one is most appealing on the grounds of familiarity, expediency, or efficiency. We then make a formal attack on the problem, developing an algorithm, or formal procedure, to solve the problem. It is at this stage that the computer language, and perhaps even machine considerations, are introduced, for if we decide that ultimately the program will be written in, say, FORTRAN 77, then the features and constraints of that language will to some extent influence the procedures we develop. Finally, the algorithm is transcribed into the particular computer language and executed. This last step is ordinarily not particularly difficult and is in some sense an anticlimax; the real action is in the development of the algorithm itself.

When writing programs in the machine's own "native" language, these steps also apply. But in this case, the last step—the transcription of an algorithm into a sequence of machine instructions—may well be anticlimactic, but it is also a very difficult, time-consuming, and demanding task, which is prone to more numerous and obscure errors than are encountered in high-level languages. The sample programs we have shown so far contain no errors *as presented*. But what the reader has not yet seen is the process of the *creation* of these programs—their actual byte-by-byte development—in which errors did occur and were ultimately located and removed. In this chapter we go through the details of this creation process for a reasonably simple but important problem.

6.2 A SAMPLE PROGRAM

Consider the task of finding the largest of a collection of numbers, an activity that arises in a wide variety of applications. The problem is not very difficult, nor is the logic of the algorithm required to solve it particularly intricate, but it illustrates many of the features of programming at the machine level that we wish to investigate. There are a number of algorithmic approaches we might take to program a solution, but perhaps the one that comes most naturally to mind is the following. Suppose that the numbers in question are

$$12, \ -17, \ 43, \ 0, \ 93, \ -4, \ 82, \ 41$$

Of course, this collection is so small that we can easily scan it and announce the result—93 is the largest of these numbers. But a more formal approach might proceed as follows. Let the first number (12) be the largest. In fact, if we are to scan the numbers left to right, then since 12 is the first number we see, it *is* the largest of all we have seen so far—perhaps "temporary maximum" would be a more appropriate term. We now look at the next number in line, -17. If this is *larger* that the current temporary maximum, we *replace* the temporary maximum with this number. Otherwise (which is the case here), we simply move on to the next number. This next number, 43, *is* larger than the current temporary maximum (12), so we replace the temporary maximum with 43 and move on to the next number, 0, and so on, until we have completed the list. The temporary maximum, which in this case is 93 (having replaced 43 on the fourth comparison), is now *the* maximum of the collection.

We shall now write this algorithm somewhat more formally, including several of the details that are required for its transcription into a programming language.

1. **Set a COUNTER equal to 1 less than the number of numbers.** The COUNTER will act to control the number of comparisons that are made, and the number of comparisons is always 1 less than the number of numbers.

2. **Set TEMPMAX equal to the first number.** The first number *is* initially the temporary maximum.

3. **Get the *next* data number and call it NUM.** We shall go through the numbers, one at a time, in each case referring to the current number as NUM.

4. **If NUM is less than or equal to TEMPMAX, go to step 6.** Compare the current number with the temporary maximum. If it is not larger, skip the next step.

5. **Set TEMPMAX equal to NUM.** Replace the present value of TEMPMAX with the current larger number NUM.

6. **Reduce COUNTER by 1.** Decrement the counter to see if there are further numbers in the list to compare with TEMPMAX.

7. **If COUNTER is still greater than zero, go to step 3.** If there are still more numbers in the list, get the next one, compare it with TEMPMAX, and so on.

8. **HALT the processor.** The procedure is complete, since all of the numbers have been compared. The largest of the numbers is in the location we have referred to as TEMPMAX.

We are now ready to cast this algorithm into machine language, and some decisions need to be made regarding just *where* various values (TEMPMAX, COUNTER, and so on) will be held, where the data numbers themselves will be stored, and so on. For the sake of definiteness we assume that we have eight numbers that we must deal with, that they are small enough that they can be held in individual *bytes*, and that they are interpreted as *unsigned* numbers. Although we shall see that these assumptions *do* have an influence on the precise form of certain constructions within the final program, they have no *substantive* effect on the overall construction of the program. The resulting machine language program would be almost identical if, for example, we were finding the largest of 74 signed longwords.

It is clear from Chapter 5 that the use of registers for the holding of certain data can vastly simplify the programming instructions, so we shall use them whenever possible and reasonable. Now the eight pieces of data with which we must deal are probably too large a collection to put in individual registers, and in fact to have the data themselves in registers would be terribly inconvenient; thus the data will be placed somewhere in memory, a matter we shall deal with momentarily. But suppose that we use, say, R6 to hold (number of data)-1—the COUNTER— which in this case is the number 7. We shall also use a register, R8, to serve the purpose of TEMPMAX. Finally, since we shall have to move through the data numbers one at a time, it will be most convenient to establish them in consecutive memory locations and use a register—R4—to "point at" them. The choice of these particular general-purpose registers for these tasks is, of course, quite arbitrary.

Having made certain decisions about which programming elements are to be in which registers and memory locations, we reproduce the algorithm in this "machine" setting; this will yield further insights into just what programming instructions will be required when we come to the last stage of program construction, the actual writing of the instructions themselves. (The steps shown below are numbered to correspond approximately to those of the "English language" algorithm described above.)

1. **Put the number 7 in R6.** This sets the COUNTER to 1 less than the number of numbers.

1a. **Put the *address* of the first number (byte) in R4.** This sets a pointer to the first data number.

2. **Put the first data number in R8.** The low-order byte of R8 acts as TEMP-MAX, and it is initialized with the first data number. If this "put" has the property that when the byte whose address is in R4 is put in R8, c(R4) is incremented by 1, then R4 will be pointing at the *second* data number, in preparation for the first comparison. Compare this "automatic incrementing" of register contents with the *add* instruction of Figure 5.12.1.

3. **R4 is correctly pointing at the *next* data number.** This is the number referred to above as NUM, and the fact that R4 is correctly pointing at it results from the automatic incrementing of the register contents from step 2 and, later, from step 4.

4. **Compare the contents of the byte pointed at by R4 with the contents of the low-order byte of R8.** That is, compare the size of NUM with that of TEMP-MAX. If this instruction also increments the contents of R4 by 1, then R4 will automatically be pointing at the *next* data number, so that no further adjustments will be required when we return to this step for the next comparison.

4a. **If the number that *was* pointed at by R4 is no larger than c(R8), go to step 6.** If TEMPMAX should *not* be replaced, skip step 5.

5. **Put the number (byte) that *was* pointed at by R4 into R8.** That is, replace the contents of the low-order byte of R8—TEMPMAX—with the last number compared. But there is a problem here, since the pointer R4 has already advanced *beyond* the data number in question. This problem will be dealt with when we come to the details of program instruction generation.

6. **Decrement c(R6) by 1.** This decrements the COUNTER.

7. **If the result of the subtraction in step 6 is greater than zero, branch back to step 4.** There will be a conditional "branch if greater than zero" construction here, to continue the comparisons if further data numbers remain.

Machine Language Programs and Program Assembly   Chap. 6

8. **HALT the processor.** If no further data numbers remain, HALT the processor—the maximum of the numbers is in the low-order byte of R8.

We are now ready to begin the actual generation of encoded instructions in main memory, but we must first decide on just *where* in memory the instructions and data are to reside. Let us agree that since memory is random access and thus any location is as satisfactory as any other, we will begin at location 00000000. Recall that the algorithm (steps 2 and 4) depends on the eight data numbers occupying *consecutive* bytes, so we shall agree that these bytes will immediately follow the programming instructions themselves in main memory. Now the first instruction we must create is "put the number 7 in R6;" this is step 1 of the algorithm. This construction has already been used, for example in Figure 5.12.1, so it is not difficult to generate its code. But before doing so, we should ask ourselves just how we are to know *what* the various codes and mode bytes are, and in fact what possible operators are available for the machine at hand. The answers to these questions must be supplied by the computer manufacturer, in the form of tables of operations; their codes; what precisely those operations do and the effects they have on condition codes, for example; the effects of various "usage modes" of the operations; and so on. Thus, in fact, in this case we must *look up* the code for "put an absolute number, in the form of a longword, into R6." We find that the code for "put a longword" is D0, the mode byte in this case is 8F, and the reference to R6 is accomplished by the coded byte 56. Thus the instruction, which begins at location 00000000 and extends through 00000006, has the form shown in Figure 6.2.1.

Step 1a requires that we "put a longword (the *address* of the first data byte) into R4," and this construction is identical with the instruction that we just generated. However, there is a problem here, for we do not *know* what this longword (address) is. That is, at this early stage of code development it is not possible to anticipate just where in memory the data bytes will begin. We have encountered a **forward reference** which it is not possible for us to resolve *at this time*. Of course, eventually we will come to the end of the program instructions themselves, and at that time we will know just where the data begins. But in the meantime the best we can do is to realize that a 4-byte longword address *should* be put in memory here, so we simply leave room for it, make a notation on our listing that the reference must later be completed, and move on to the next instruction (Figure 6.2.2). Observe that we have been careful properly to advance the memory addresses at which the instruction components are located (allowing 4 bytes for the unknown address), since knowing the precise address at which various constructions

FIGURE 6.2.1

Contents	Address	Comment
D0	0000	Code for "put a longword"
8F	0001	(mode byte)
00000007	0002	The number to be "put"
56	0006	into R6 (COUNTER)

FIGURE 6.2.2

Contents	Address	Comment
D0	0000	
8F	0001	
00000007	0002	
56	0006	
D0	0007	Code for "put a longword"
8F	0008	⟨mode byte⟩
————	0009	The unknown "address of the first data byte," to be put into R4 (data pointer)
54	000D	

are loaded is absolutely essential to the proper construction of various instructions and to the execution of the ultimate program.

Step 2 calls for putting the first data number into the low-order byte of R8, to initialize the value of the temporary maximum. That is, we must "copy" the contents of the byte currently being pointed at by R4 into R8, and at the same time it is desirable that c(R4) be *automatically incremented* by 1, so that R4 will then point at the *second* data number. (In this case, the increment should be by 1 since the data are in the form of individual bytes. Had we been dealing with word or longword data, we would want the contents of the pointer—R4—to be incremented by 2 or 4, respectively.) There is such a "copy byte" instruction, and an appropriate choice of mode byte will also ensure that c(R4) will be incremented by 1 *after* c(R4) has been used as the address of the byte to be copied. The "copy byte" operator has code 90, the required mode byte is 84, and in this case the "destination" of the copy—R8—is signified by the single byte 58 (once again, the "8" part of it denoting R8). This instruction is shown in its completed form in Figure 6.2.3.

FIGURE 6.2.3

Contents	Address	Comment
D0	0000	
8F	0001	
00000007	0002	
56	0006	
D0	0007	
8F	0008	
————	0009	
54	000D	
90	000E	"copy" the byte (first data number)
84	000F	pointed at by R4 (data pointer)
58	0010	into R8 (TEMPMAX) and increment c(R4) by 1

Step 3 in the algorithm requires no code generation, it being more an observation, and indeed we have noted that at this point *upon execution* (although we are certainly far from the execution of these instructions), R4 will be pointing at the *next* data byte.

Step 4 requires that we *compare* two bytes, namely the byte being pointed at by R4 and the low-order byte of R8 (TEMPMAX), and we need to investigate just what such a comparison involves. When we compare two numbers, say 5 and 7, we are inclined to say "5 is smaller than 7" or "7 is larger than 5." But the VAX has no way *directly* to indicate "smaller than" or "larger than." However, we can rephrase the statement "5 is smaller than 7" as "5 − 7 is smaller than 0—is *negative*," and the VAX *does* have a means of telling us that a number—the *difference* between 5 and 7—is negative: it sets the condition code N-bit. In fact, the VAX "compare" operator does just exactly this. When two numbers (of compatible size) are compared:

Compare A with B

the processor calculates the difference

$$A - B$$

and sets the condition codes accordingly, just as it does on *any* subtraction. In fact, the only difference between the processor's action upon a subtraction and a compare is that when a compare is done, neither of the operands' values (A and B) is affected; only the condition codes are set according to the result of the subtraction. It is also important to observe the *order* in which the subtraction takes place: $A - B$, not $B - A$.

We can now complete the code generation for the action of step 4. The "compare bytes" operator has code 91, the mode byte 84 will specify the byte pointed at by R4 and will also yield an automatic incrementing of c(R4) by 1 after its contents has been used as the address of one of the bytes to be compared, and finally, the mode byte 58 specifies the other operand of the compare instruction, R8. This instruction is shown in Figure 6.2.4, where we note that the construction is in the form

Compare (byte pointed at by R4) with (low-order byte of R8)

not the other way around, so that the condition codes are set according to the result of the subtraction

(byte pointed at by R4) − (low-order byte of R8)

a matter that will be crucial for the next instruction.

Step 4a requires that if the result of the comparison revealed that NUM (the byte pointed at by R4) was less than or equal to TEMPMAX (the low-order byte of R8), a step should be *skipped*. We recognize a conditional branch instruction here, and there are two questions with which we need to deal. First, on just *what* condition (in terms of the PSW's condition codes) should the branch take place; and second, to *where* should control be passed if, in fact, the branch does take place? As to the first question, recall that we are dealing with *unsigned* numbers,

FIGURE 6.2.4

Contents	Address	Comments
D0	0000	
8F	0001	
00000007	0002	
56	0006	
D0	0007	
8F	0008	
————	0009	
54	000D	
90	000E	
84	000F	
58	0010	
91	0011	"compare" the byte being
84	0012	pointed at by R4
58	0013	(NUM) with the con-
		tents of the low-order
		byte of R8 (TEMP-
		MAX), set the condition
		codes accordingly and
		increment c(R4) by 1

and that one number (TEMPMAX) has been subtracted from another number (NUM) as a result of the comparison instruction. Thus we need to ask the conditions under which A − B will result in a number that is less than or equal to 0 when A and B are treated as unsigned numbers. Now if the two numbers are *equal*, the subtraction will set the Z-bit, so one of the conditions on which we want the branch to occur is: Z = 1. On the other hand, if A is *less than* B (in the unsigned sense), the subtraction A − B will result in an *incorrect* unsigned result; and we already know that this occurs if and only if the PSW's C-bit is set. Thus the condition that determines whether the branch takes place is: "branch *if* C = 1 *or* Z = 1." The VAX has such a conditional branch instruction, and its operation code is 1B.

The location to which this branch is to take place (if the conditions dictate that it is to occur at all) is more difficult to determine. For this is another forward reference, and it is not possible at this point to predict exactly the address of the instruction that should be executed if NUM is less than or equal to TEMPMAX. However, we do know that the "target" of the branch instruction will be specified by a single byte, a program counter displacement. Thus we shall simply have to leave an unspecified byte at location 00000015, to be filled in later, as shown in Figure 6.2.5.

If the conditional branch of step 4a (locations 00000014–00000015) does *not* take place, it is because NUM is greater than TEMPMAX, and thus TEMPMAX should be replaced by NUM. Unfortunately, R4 no longer points at the number which was compared at 00000011–00000013, since c(R4) was automatically incremented by 1 as a result of the *form* of the "compare" instruction itself. However, it is easy enough to adjust c(R4) back by 1, with a "decrement c(R4) by 1" instruction, as shown in Figure 6.2.6.

FIGURE 6.2.5

Contents	Address	Comment
D0	0000	
8F	0001	
00000007	0002	
56	0006	
D0	0007	
8F	0008	
————	0009	
54	000D	
90	000E	
84	000F	
58	0010	
91	0011	
84	0012	
58	0013	
1B	0014	Branch IF C-bit OR Z-bit is set
—	0015	(to somewhere)

Now that R4 is again pointing at the byte that is to replace the temporary maximum (the low-order byte of R8), we can "copy" that byte into R8, and at the same time we can adjust c(R4) up by 1, so that again it points at the next number to be compared. This instruction is shown in Figure 6.2.7, and again we comment that the "automatic incrementing" of c(R4) by 1 takes place *after* c(R4) is used as the address of the byte to be copied to R8. This instruction corresponds to step 5 of the algorithm.

FIGURE 6.2.6

Contents	Address	Comment
D0	0000	
8F	0001	
00000007	0002	
56	0006	
D0	0007	
8F	0008	
————	0009	
54	000D	
90	000E	
84	000F	
58	0010	
91	0011	
84	0012	
58	0013	
1B	0014	
—	0015	
D7	0016	"Decrement (by 1)" the contents
54	0017	of R4 (data pointer)

FIGURE 6.2.7

Contents	Address	Comment
D0	0000	
8F	0001	
00000007	0002	
56	0006	
DO	0007	
8F	0008	
————	0009	
54	000D	
90	000E	
84	000F	
58	0010	
91	0011	
84	0012	
58	0013	
1B	0014	
—	0015	
D7	0016	
54	0017	
90	0018	"copy" the byte pointed at by
84	0019	R4 (data pointer) to the low-order
58	001A	of R8 (TEMPMAX), and increment
		c(R4) by 1 ("undoes" the decrement
		instruction at 00000016–00000017)

Having dealt with the current data number (and recalling that R4 is already pointing at the *next* data number), we should decrement c(R6) (the COUNTER) to determine if there are further numbers to compare against TEMPMAX. The appropriate "decrement c(R6) by 1" instruction is shown in Figure 6.2.8, which is step 6 of the algorithm.

Step 7 directs us to branch back to step 4 *if* the result of the preceding decrement was greater than zero. Again we recognize a conditional branch, "branch if greater than zero," an instruction we have already encountered (see, for example, Figure 5.12.1). What should the "target location" of this branch be? Evidently, we wish to return for another comparison (step 4), and the "compare bytes" instruction is located at 00000011. We must thus calculate the program counter displacement, and to do so we must recognize that *upon execution* of the conditional branch instruction, and *after* the operation code byte and displacement byte have been fetched by the processor, the PC will have the value 0000001F. A trivial calculation determines that the appropriate PC displacement is $-0E$ bytes, and thus the displacement byte is F2, as shown in Figure 6.2.9.

All that now remains to complete the program is to insert the "halt" instruction of step 8 at 0000001F, and then to put in the 8 data bytes, beginning at 00000020 (Figure 6.2.10).

There are still two matters that need to be tidied up, namely the bytes of the program that we were initially unable to complete because of forward references.

FIGURE 6.2.8

Contents	Address	Comment
D0	0000	
8F	0001	
00000007	0002	
56	0006	
D0	0007	
8F	0008	
————	0009	
54	000D	
90	000E	
84	000F	
58	0010	
91	0011	
84	0012	
58	0013	
1B	0014	
—	0015	
D7	0016	
54	0017	
90	0018	
84	0019	
58	001A	
D7	001B	"decrement (by 1)" contents
56	001C	of R6 (COUNTER)

The first of these, the (then unknown) address of the first data byte at 00000009–0000000C, we now know to be 00000020. The second is a program counter displacement, the second byte of the conditional branch at 00000014. It should be clear that if that branch *does* take place—that is, if TEMPMAX is *not* to be replaced—control should be transferred to the "decrement COUNTER" instruction at 0000001B. Since by the time the displacement byte has been fetched, c(PC) will be 00000016, the correct byte displacement is evidently 05 (= 0000001B – 00000016).

The completed program, with all comments, is shown in Figure 6.2.11, and if the operation and operand codes, together with the data bytes, are loaded into main memory beginning at location 00000000, the program counter set to 00000000, and the processor started, the program will presumably execute properly, halting with c(PC) = 00000020 and with the number E9 in the low-order byte of R8. In so doing we had best hope that there are no errors, especially of a logical nature. For even a trivial mistake may require the insertion or deletion of a byte or two of instruction code for its repair, and such changes may very well alter some of the addresses of the program components. Such address changes can affect instructions which involve those addresses, either directly or as program counter displacements. Thus even apparently superficial changes may have far-reaching effects that can require major rewriting of the program's code.

FIGURE 6.2.9

Contents	Address	Comment
D0	0000	
8F	0001	
00000007	0002	
56	0006	
D0	0007	
8F	0008	
————	0009	
54	000D	
90	000E	
84	000F	
58	0010	
91	0011	
84	0012	
58	0013	
1B	0014	
—	0015	
D7	0016	
54	0017	
90	0018	
84	0019	
58	001A	
D7	001B	
56	001C	
14	001D	"branch if greater than zero"
F2	001E	(that is, if N = 0 AND Z = 0) to location 00000011—the "compare bytes" instruction

6.3 A MNEMONIC LANGUAGE

In generating the sample program of Section 6.2 we have gone into a great deal of detail—looking up operation codes and mode bytes, determining addresses, calculating displacements, and so on—but it should be clear that all of this detail was necessary to the determination of the code that ultimately must reside in memory for the processor to perform this particular task. The reader might well wonder if the construction of machine language programs is really as difficult as we have made it out to be, and the answer is "Yes"; in fact, it is usually much, much *worse*. For the program we have been dealing with here is very short and logically simple; imagine the complexity involved in writing a machine language program that consists perhaps of thousands of instructions.

An analysis of the task of program construction reveals that the chief cause of the complexity is not that the individual tasks that must be done are particularly difficult, but that a number of activities must take place *simultaneously*: the looking up (in a table, say) of operation codes and mode bytes; the maintaining of a "memory location counter" so that we can keep track of the current location at which each instruction will ultimately be loaded, and the adjustment of that counter

FIGURE 6.2.10

Contents	Address	Comment
D0	0000	
8F	0001	
00000007	0002	
56	0006	
D0	0007	
8F	0008	
————	0009	
54	000D	
90	000E	
84	000F	
58	0010	
91	0011	
84	0012	
58	0013	
1B	0014	
——	0015	
D7	0016	
54	0017	
90	0018	
84	0019	
58	001A	
D7	001B	
56	001C	
14	001D	
F2	001E	
00	001F	"halt" the processor
72	0020	The
4F	0021	eight
D1	0022	(unsigned)
03	0023	8-bit
D7	0024	numbers
AE	0025	whose
E9	0026	maximum
7A	0027	is to be found

by an appropriate number of bytes each time a new instruction component is generated; the determination of those addresses which are used as operands, some of which may be forward references and thus cannot immediately be determined; the calculation of program counter displacements; and throughout all of these details, maintaining a sense of the *logic flow* of the underlying algorithm. Indeed, it is this last feature that causes the most frequent problems, for it is easy to become so involved with purely computational details that one forgets just what instruction is being generated and just what its function is relative to the total task. The fact that instructions are *encoded* into numerical representations adds to the problem. For example, in the program of Figure 6.2.11, when the "branch if greater than zero" instruction at location 0000001D was generated, we might know from the logic of the algorithm that we were to branch back to the "compare bytes" instruction (at 00000011), but without the comments that were written down alongside

FIGURE 6.2.11

Contents	Address	Comment
D0	0000	Code for "put a longword"
8F	0001	⟨mode byte⟩
00000007	0002	the number to be "put"
56	0006	into R6 (COUNTER)
D0	0007	Code for "put a longword"
8F	0008	⟨mode byte⟩
00000020	0009	the "address of the
		first data byte," to be put
54	000D	into R4 (data pointer)
90	000E	"copy" the byte (first data number)
84	000F	pointed at by R4 (data pointer)
58	0010	into R8 (TEMPMAX), and
		increment c(R4) by 1
91	0011	"compare" the byte being pointed at
84	0012	by R4 (NUM) with the contents of
58	0013	the low-order byte of R8 (TEMPMAX),
		set the condition codes accordingly,
		and increment c(R4) by 1
1B	0014	Branch IF C-bit OR Z-bit is set
05	0015	to location 0000001B the
		"decrement COUNTER" instruction)
D7	0016	"decrement (by 1)" the contents
54	0017	of R4 (data pointer)
90	0018	"copy" the byte pointed at by
84	0019	R4 (data pointer) to the low-order
58	001A	of R8 (TEMPMAX), and increment
		c(R4) by 1 ("undoes" the decrement
		instruction at 00000016–00000017)
D7	001B	"decrement (by 1)" contents
56	001C	of R6 (COUNTER)
14	001D	"branch if greater than zero"
		(that is, if N = 0 AND Z = 0)
F2	001E	to location 00000011—the
		"compare bytes" instruction
00	001F	"halt" the processor
72	0020	The
4F	0021	eight
D1	0022	(unsigned)
03	0023	8-bit
D7	0024	numbers
AE	0025	whose
E9	0026	maximum
7A	0027	is to be found

the machine code, it is unlikely that we would have been able easily to locate that instruction in the morass of numerical codes we had already generated, without a great deal of backtracking and further table lookups; unless we were extremely practiced in writing programs at this level, we would probably not know offhand that we should be looking for a "91" byte in the program.

Although we cannot eliminate any of the steps that we have gone through to generate this program (they are all clearly necessary), we can at least simplify the process by not trying to do too much at any one time. That is, we will *separate* the processes of the writing of the instructions and the generation of the numeric codes that are the machine language program, in the following way. We have already noted two features of our attempts so far that contribute to the complexity of program generation: the fact that instructions are in *numerical* form, which numbers must be looked up in some table or reference manual, and that once these encoded instructions have been written down, they are frequently no longer recognizable as particular instructions. The problem, of course, stems from the fact that it is unnatural for us to think of a comparison as a "91"—we think of it as "compare." Similarly, we think of "branch if positive with some PC displacement" as "go to some specific location if N = 0 and Z = 0," not as "14." Most machine language programmers make up abbreviations which are more readily understood by them—"miniwords" or, as they are more usually called, **mnemonics** (from the Greek, mnēmonikos, "to remember")—to stand for the machine instructions.

For example, we might use the mnemonic CMP to stand for "compare." (COM or COMP might seem more natural, but we may want to reserve either of these for a representation of "ones-complement.") Now when we compare two numbers, those numbers might be in the form of *bytes* (as in the program of this chapter), or *words* or *longwords*, and as we have already noted, these generate strictly different instructions. Thus to indicate which instruction we are using—that is, which type of data structures are being compared—let us agree to create three separate mnemonics: CMPB, CMPW, and CMPL. In a similar fashion, INCB, INCW, and INCL might stand for the codes for the three forms of the "increment by 1" instruction, and DECB, DECW, and DECL for the "decrement by 1" instructions. A natural mnemonic for the conditional branch instruction "branch if greater than zero" or "branch if positive" might be BGTZ or BPOS, although the standard VAX mnemonic for this instruction is BGTR—"*Branch if GreaTeR* (than zero)"—and thus this is the "miniword" we shall use for this instruction. It is a bit more difficult to concoct a natural mnemonic for the conditional branch at location 00000014 of Figure 6.2.11—"branch if C-bit or Z-bit is set." Since the sense of that branch is that the branch is to take place if the first of two unsigned numbers if *less than or equal* to the second, and since a "compare" amounts to a subtraction of the second number from the first, we shall use BLEQU— "*Branch if Less than or EQual* (to zero), *Unsigned.*" Although we have used a number of other instructions, for the most part the mnemonics that we will invent for them are sufficiently suggestive that little or no explanation will be required. (A complete list, with full descriptions of the instructions, is provided in Appendix A.) One instruction, however, does deserve mention, and that is the "copy" instruction which we have used on several occasions. COPY or COP might be most natural, and since bytes, words, longwords, and so on, can be copied from one place to another, mnemonics such as COPB, COPW, and COPL would seem to fit these purposes well. The standard VAX mnemonic for this instruction, however, is MOV—"move"—a term which *could* be interpreted as meaning that information is being moved *from* some **source** *to* some **destination,** and thus that information no longer exists at the source of the MOV. This, of course, is not the case, since data can never really be "destroyed," only overwritten. We shall use MOV (more precisely, MOVB, MOVW, MOVL, and so on) to conform to VAX standards, but the reader should be aware that MOVing a piece of data does not destroy it at the location from which it was moved—rather, it moves a *copy* of this datum.

Having invented "miniwords" for each of the machine operations, we are still not in a position to write a "program" in terms of these mnemonics, for we need to establish some conventions about how instruction operands will be denoted. In some of the instructions we have already written, we have seen that general-purpose registers are sometimes used as operands. For these we have already introduced the informal notation R0, R1, ..., and there seems no reason not to continue the use of those designations. But recall (Figure 6.2.11) that the registers were used in a variety of ways (modes). For example, in one case register R6, the COUNTER, was the operand itself, being given the value 7 initially, and then decremented by 1 each time through a programming loop. But R4, the data pointer, was never used in this direct way, except for the one occasion on which its contents was decremented. Rather, the operand of several instructions was the byte whose *address* was *in* R4, and furthermore, those instructions also auto-matically incremented c(R4). We need to devise a designation that indicates just *how* the register is being used. Suppose that we adopt the following notations. If a register is used *directly* (as R6 and R8 were in the program of Section 6.2), we shall simply use the register designation itself, namely R6 or R8 or whatever. For example, to indicate the instruction that decrements the contents of R6 by 1, we would write

DECL   R6

In a similar fashion, the mnemonic statement

MOVW   R5,R11

will mean that the low-order word of R5 is to be copied into the low-order word of R11.

To deal with the concept of a register being not the operand itself, but rather holding the *address* of the operand (that is, pointing at the operand), we shall use the parenthesis notation (Rn) for the operand. [This is to some extent consistent with our notation c(Rn) to denote not the register, but rather its contents.] For example,

MOVW   (R5),R11

will mean that the (16-bit) word whose address is in R5 is to be copied into the low-order 16 bits of R11. Finally, to indicate that the contents of a register is to be used as the address of an operand, and that subsequent to this the contents of the register is to be automatically incremented, we elect to use the notation (Rn) + .

Thus

$$\text{MOVW} \quad (R5)+,R11$$

means that the (16-bit) word whose address is in R5 is to be copied into the low-order word of R11, and that c(R5) is then to be incremented *by 2*. [The reason for the incrementing by 2 is that MOVW is a *word*-type operation, and thus c(R5) is adjusted upward by 2, corresponding to the two bytes occupied by a word. MOVB would adjust c(R5) by 1, and MOVL would adjust c(R5) by 4.] Thus the compare instruction, which lies at the heart of the "find maximum" program, would be written as

$$\text{CMPB} \quad (R4)+,R8$$

—that is, compare the byte (NUM) whose address is in R4 (the data pointer) with the low-order byte of R8 (TEMPMAX), and adjust c(R4) up by 1.

An instruction operand need not be a register or the location whose address is in a register. If an operand is the contents of a main memory location, then the numerical address of that location will serve to specify the operand. We denote such an operand simply by its address; for example,

$$\text{INCW} \quad 125$$

will mean "increment (by 1) the contents of the memory word whose address is 00000125," while

$$\text{CLRL} \quad 42CA$$

means "*CLeaR* (set to zero) the contents of the *L*ongword whose address is 000042CA." In a similar fashion,

$$\text{BGTR} \quad 11$$

is notation for a branch to 00000011, provided that both the N and Z bits of the PSW's condition codes are clear.

The first instruction of the sample program of this chapter is

Put (move) the number 7 into R6, to act as a COUNTER

Because of the notation we have just introduced, it will *not* do to write this construction in mnemonics as

$$\text{MOVL} \quad 7,R6$$

since this would be interpreted as "move the contents of the longword whose address is 7, into R6," and this is certainly not what is intended. We need to devise a new notation to indicate this particular construction, and since what we want to accomplish is to operate on a *number* (that is, an absolute number as opposed to the contents of a numerical address), we choose to use the "number sign" (#) to denote this. Thus

$$\text{MOVL} \quad \#7,R6$$

will mean "move the absolute number 7, as a longword, into R6." (Notice that the mnemonically stated instruction

$$\text{MOVB} \quad \#7,R6$$

would be interpreted by us as "move the absolute number 7, as an 8-bit byte, into R6—that is, into the low-order byte of R6, leaving bits 31:8 of R6 unaffected.")

We are finally in a position to begin writing programs in terms of mnemonics. There are some other constructions for which we will ultimately need to invent symbolic notation, but the conventions we have established so far will be sufficient to rewrite the principal example of this chapter in mnemonic form. Before doing so, however, we comment that the mnemonics and other notations we have devised so far are by no means God given. If a particular user prefers ZER to CLR ("zero" to "clear") or COP to MOV, so be it—programmer convenience is the key word here. We have selected mnemonics that adhere to established standards for the VAX-11, and doing so will, as in the case of standardized character coding, ensure interinstallation communication.

6.4 THE SAMPLE PROGRAM AGAIN, WRITTEN IN MNEMONICS

One of the first questions with which we dealt in writing the machine language version of the program to find the largest of eight numbers was: Where in main memory should the program's code be loaded? The question is not inconsequential, for some of the instructions within the program rely on memory addresses for their operands, and these addresses are in turn determined by the program's initial, or **load address.** (Recall that we chose to begin at 00000000, that being as good a location as any.) When writing in instruction mnemonics, we shall not concern ourselves with just where in memory the instructions are. This is one of the details that we want to suppress for the time being, to simplify the task of writing the program as a reflection of the *logical algorithm*. Thus we are ready to begin generating mnemonics, and since the first instruction puts the number 7 in R6 (see Figure 6.2.11, for example), we write

$$\text{MOVL} \quad \#7,R6$$

The next instruction specifies that the *address* of the first data byte is to be put in R4, to be used as a data pointer. But here again the forward reference is a problem for we do not know what that address is, and in fact for two reasons. First, we have not yet come to the data portion of the program. But second, even if we *had* already encountered the data, we would not know their numerical address, for as we noted above, the maintaining of any kind of location counter is one of the tasks with which we are not dealing at this stage. Thus although we know that the first data byte will ultimately have such a numerical address, we simply do not know what it is at this point. Whatever it is, suppose we simply give it a **symbolic name,** say DATA. (It is important to understand that DATA is the name we have assigned to the *address* of the memory location that contains the first data byte; it is not the first data byte itself. In fact, Figure 6.2.11 reveals that DATA is simply another name for the number 00000020.) Since the number DATA is to be put into R4, we can write

MOVL   #DATA,R4

Observe that a MOV *Long* was used here, since DATA is just the name of a numerical address, and addresses are always 32 bits long.

The next step in the algorithm is to put the first data byte (currently pointed at by R4) in R8 as the temporary maximum and to increment c(R4) by 1 in the process. This is achieved with the mnemonic instruction

MOVB   (R4)+,R8

Next we compare the byte pointed at by R4 with the low-order byte of R8 (TEMPMAX), and again automatically increment c(R4) by 1:

CMPB   (R4)+,R8

If the resulting subtraction of the unsigned bytes is less than or equal to zero, we want to branch to somewhere, but again the "somewhere" is a forward reference, so we will simply call the address of that memory location NEXT, thus:

BGEQU   NEXT

Now what is to be done if the result of the compare CMPB indicates that the number NUM (pointed at by R4) was *greater than* c(R8)—TEMPMAX? Then TEMPMAX should be replaced by NUM and, as we learned in Section 6.2 while generating the machine code for this program, the pointer R4 had already been advanced beyond the number compared. Thus we must back R4 up by 1 so that it again points at the preceding number, put that number (byte) in TEMPMAX (R8), and readjust R4 up by 1 again. In mnemonic form these instructions are

DECL   R4
MOVB   (R4)+,R8

Having compared the current number with TEMPMAX, and either replaced TEMPMAX or not, we now need to decrement R6 (COUNTER) by 1 and, if it is still positive, branch back to do the next compare. The instruction is written as

DECL   R6

but before inserting this instruction in the mnemonic program and moving on to the conditional branch, we need to recognize that this DECL instruction will be loaded at the memory location (whatever it might be) whose numerical address we have already named NEXT, used above in the BLEQU instruction, and we should make some note of the fact that *this* is the location named NEXT. We do this by placing the name NEXT *in front of* the instruction, and following that name with a colon (:) to separate it from the DECL instruction, thus:

NEXT: DECL   R6

The name-colon combination is called a **label**, and it simply indicates that we have assigned the name NEXT to the address of this particular memory location (whatever it turns out to be).

Our "program" as written so far is shown in Figure 6.4.1, where we have assigned a "Line number" to each line of instruction for easier reference. Comments are also included as an indispensable aid in understanding the logic of the algorithm.

Now if the result of decrementing the counter was greater than zero, we must reexecute the "compare" instruction of the next number against TEMPMAX. That is, we are to return to the instruction

CMPB   (R4)+,R8

This is easily achieved if we place a label, say TEST:, on that compare instruction

FIGURE 6.4.1

Line	Label	Mnemonic		Comments
1		MOVL	#7,R6	⟨Data count −1⟩ in R6 (= COUNTER)
2		MOVL	#DATA,R4	R4 is pointer to DATA
3		MOVB	(R4)+,R8	Put first number in R8 (= TEMPMAX)
4		CMPB	(R4)+,R8	Compare current byte (NUM) with TEMPMAX
5		BLEQU	NEXT	Skip if not bigger than TEMPMAX
6		DECL	R4	else back pointer up 1 byte,
7		MOVB	(R4)+,R8	replace TEMPMAX, and readjust data pointer
8	NEXT:	DECL	R6	Decrement COUNTER

and then include the instruction

BGTR   TEST

after the instruction that decremented the COUNTER. But if there are no more numbers to compare, we simply HALT, a mnemonic that stands for "instruct the processor to *cease* its fetch-execute activities." Finally, we can include the eight data bytes, in eight consecutive memory bytes, but there are a few details we need to address here. First, we must remember that the address of the first of these bytes has already been referred to as DATA, so we must be sure to place that label on the first byte generated. But how are we to indicate that a certain byte is to hold a *data number*, as opposed to an instruction code? It will not do simply to write down a number in the midst of the "program" instructions, such as

```
NEXT:  DECL  R6
       BGTR  TEST
       HALT
DATA:  114
```

for two reasons. First, by appearance alone (that is, without an explicit context) we have no way of knowing whether this number 114 is intended to be held as a byte, word, longword, octaword, or whatever. Thus we need some means of being specific about the *structure* of the number. We do this by preceding the number itself with the "mnemonic" .BYTE, thus:

```
DATA:  .BYTE  114
```

It is important to note that .BYTE is not an *instruction* mnemonic, since no code generation will ever be required here. Rather, for the moment we shall informally refer to it as a **numerical context indicator**; others might be .WORD and .LONG-WORD (although we shall shorten this to .LONG for the sake of economy of expression). Notice that further to distinguish these constructions from instruction mnemonics, we have prefixed them with a dot, or period(.).

The second problem involved with these numerical data involves their *representation*. In what *base* are we to interpret the number 114? It could be either decimal or hexadecimal, and without some agreement as to what the **standard** or **default number system base** is, such a number is ambiguous. (Notice that one other number has already appeared in these mnemonics, namely the "7" in the first instruction, but of course in this case the representation is nonambiguous, regardless of our interpretation of number base.) Since the decimal representation is the one with which we are the most comfortable, let us agree that unless explicitly indicated otherwise, numbers are to be interpreted as being written in the decimal number system representation. In the particular program at hand, however, we are going to represent the numbers in hexadecimal, since we already have their hexadecimal representations from the program of Figure 6.2.11. Thus, instead of

DATA: .BYTE 114

we shall use the "^X" notation (Section 4.2) to indicate hexadecimal:

DATA: .BYTE ^X72

The completed "program" is shown in Figure 6.4.2.

Just what have we accomplished here? If the reader interprets "program" to mean machine code that can be loaded into memory and executed, we have done nothing in the way of advancing a solution to the problem of program construction, since not a single byte of executable code has been generated. On the other hand, what we *have* written has been done with relative ease, and the resulting collection of mnemonics is a readable, almost-English *representation* of what the machine language program *should* look like. We have accomplished this simplicity of "program" writing by means of ignoring many of the addressing and computational details that were required during our first attempt at this task in Section 6.2. It is true that the machine code must still be generated, and that task will be addressed in the next section. In the meantime the reader should note that because of the readability of our current product we have some confidence that it is logically correct, and provided that we do a careful job of translating these mnemonics into machine code, the resulting machine language program should execute as desired.

FIGURE 6.4.2

Line	Label	Mnemonic		Comment
1		MOVL	#7,R6	⟨data count −1⟩ in R6 (= COUNTER)
2		MOVL	#DATA,R4	R4 is pointer to DATA
3		MOVB	(R4)+,R8	Put first number in R8 (= TEMPMAX)
4	TEST:	CMPB	(R4)+,R8	Compare current byte (NUM) with TEMPMAX
5		BLEQU	NEXT	Skip if not bigger than TEMPMAX
6		DECL	R4	else back pointer up 1 byte,
7		MOVB	(R4)+,R8	replace TEMPMAX, and read-just data pointer
8	NEXT:	DECL	R6	Decrement COUNTER
9		BGTR	TEST	and test next byte if positive
10		HALT		else HALT the processor
11	DATA:	.BYTE	^X72	The
12		.BYTE	^X4F	eight
13		.BYTE	^XD1	(unsigned)
14		.BYTE	^X03	8-bit
15		.BYTE	^XD7	numbers
16		.BYTE	^XAE	whose
17		.BYTE	^XE9	maximum
18		.BYTE	^X7A	is to be found

6.5 THE ASSEMBLY OF THE MNEMONIC PROGRAM

The process of translating a collection of mnemonics into a machine language program is called **mnemonic program assembly**, and the mnemonic "program" itself is frequently referred to as an **assembly language program**. Thus our task at this point is to assemble the "program" of Figure 6.4.2. The only real decision that has to be made before we begin the translation process has to do with where in memory we shall assume that the machine language program will ultimately be loaded. As before, we shall choose location 00000000, although any other address would do as well.

The first instruction to assemble is

$$\text{MOVL} \quad \#7,\text{R6}$$

We determine that the code for MOVL—"move a longword"—is D0, and thus this byte is placed at location 00000000. The "number sign" (#) indicates that the source of the MOV is an absolute number, and the mode byte corresponding to this construction is 8F, which is put at 00000001, the next 4 bytes to be occupied by the longword form of the number itself. Thus 00000007 goes at 00000002–00000005. Finally, since R6 is the destination of this MOV, we find that the register (6) is referred to in "mode 5," so that the next byte, at 00000006, should be 56. We would then move on to the next instruction, which in fact we decline to do; we have been through this process before, in Section 6.2, in all its detail.

Notice that in assembling the MOVL instruction above, we needed to look up the machine code for that operation, determine mode bytes, keep track of some kind of address or location counter (to know to which address each instruction component is to be assigned), and so on, and each of the remaining instructions will require the same level of detail. But the one consideration with which we did *not* have to deal was *why* this particular instruction was being assembled at all. That is, we had to concern ourselves only with what the instruction *was*, not with what it *did*; the logic of the surrounding program can be, and most properly should be, ignored, our efforts being focused on the computational details. Indeed, this was the principal purpose in our devising the mnemonic language in the first place, to separate the logical program design from the computational assembly process. But if this is the case, why are we doing this assembly step at all? To be sure, it must be done in order to obtain the machine code to load into memory and execute, but could we not as well hire a clerk to deal with this task? The answer is "Yes," and it will be most instructive to investigate just what information the clerk must have and just what he must be able to do in order to assemble instruction mnemonics.

Clearly, the clerk must have some kind of table which contains the mnemonics we have devised, together with the machine code for those mnemonics. He must also know the conventions we have established concerning register names, addressing modes—Rn, (Rn) and (Rn)+, for example—and other operand types, and he will have to know how many operands each operation takes as well as the permitted types of those operands (since not all types of operands are valid for all operations). He will need to have specific information concerning various data structures (bytes, words, and so on). Finally, of course, he will need to be able to do the simple arithmetic required for program counter displacements, as occur for example in the assembly of conditional and unconditional branch instructions. But also of significance (at least to our understanding of the process) is what the clerk does *not* need to know. Specifically, he does not need to know what a CLRW operation does, only that its machine code is B4. In fact, he need know nothing of what a particular program does or is intended to do, or even to have any idea of what in general a "program" is. In brief, it is not required that he have any idea of what he is doing or what his end product will be used for; his job is strictly clerical. In particular, our clerk is not a *critic*, and thus he can make no judgments concerning the soundness of the *logical* structure of our mnemonic programs. We shall see at the close of this section that we can certainly present the clerk with mnemonic constructions which he will recognize as being invalid, but *logical* errors—using INCB when we intended INCW, or leaving out a crucial instruction, for example—will pass his scrutiny undetected.

For the sake of having a concrete example to which to refer in the following discussion, we offer the mnemonic program of Figure 6.5.1, which might be a copy of a typical program sheet that we would pass to the clerk for assembly. Notice that we have included comments here, even though they would be meaningless to

1		MOVL	#7,R6	;⟨data count −1⟩ in R6
2				; (= COUNTER)
3		MOVL	#DATA,R4	;R4 is pointer to DATA
4		MOVB	(R4)+,R8	;Put 1st number in R8
5				; (= TEMPMAX)
6	TEST:	CMPB	(R4)+,R8	;Compare current byte (NUM)
7				; with TEMPMAX
8		BLEQU	NEXT	;Skip if not bigger than TEMPMAX
9		DECL	R4	; else back pointer up 1 byte,
10		MOVB	(R4)+,R8	; replace TEMPMAX, and readjust
11				; data pointer
12	NEXT:	DECL	R6	;Decrement COUNTER
13		BGTR	TEST	; and test next byte if positive
14		HALT		; else HALT the processor
15				;
16	DATA:	.BYTE	^X72	;The
17		.BYTE	^X4F	; eight
18		.BYTE	^XD1	; (unsigned)
19		.BYTE	^X03	; 8-bit
20		.BYTE	^XD7	; numbers
21		.BYTE	^XAE	; whose
22		.BYTE	^XE9	; maximum
23		.BYTE	^X7A	; is to be found

Figure 6.5.1

the clerk. To avoid any possible confusion on the clerk's part, we have preceded each comments with a semicolon (;), one of our established conventions being that the clerk is to ignore anything to the right of and including any semicolon found in a line of mnemonics. Note also that we have numbered each line of mnemonics; this is purely for the purposes of the current discussion, to improve our references to various instructions; ordinarily, this would not be done.

When the clerk approaches the assembly process, he must decide what the **assembly load address** is to be, that is, the address at which the first byte of the program will ultimately be loaded *for execution*. (Once again we remind the reader that we are far from the program execution phase here; at this point mnemonics are being translated into machine instructions, and this translation process has nothing to do with instruction execution. However, the addresses at which instructions and data are *assumed* to be loaded can have an effect on those and other program instructions.) In the absence of any specific information from the programmer, the clerk will use a *default* assembly load address, which is almost always taken to be the first available memory address, 00000000.

Since the clerk will always need to know at which address an instruction is assumed to be located, he will keep track of this by setting a counter, the **assembler location assignment counter**, or **location counter**, for short, to this beginning address 00000000, and each time a byte, word, longword, and so on, is generated, he will adjust this location counter by the appropriate amount—1, 2, 4 or whatever—so that the counter will always be pointing at the address of the instruction component currently being assembled. Now the clerk realizes that there are likely some symbols within the mnemonic program which were defined by the programmer (such as TEST, NEXT, and DATA in the sample program), so rather than begin the translation process immediately, he proceeds as follows. The program is scanned, instruction by instruction, for these user-defined symbols. In so doing, of course, the clerk must maintain his location counter so that symbol *values* can be recorded. This process for the sample program will be the following. The first line of mnemonics is examined, and no user-defined symbols are found. Thus the location counter is advanced by the proper amount (7, in this case, so that its value is now 00000007) and the next line is examined. Line 2 happens to be exclusively a comment, so the clerk moves to line 3. Here he *does* find a symbol, namely DATA. This symbol is entered into a **symbol table**, together with its *value*. However, at this point the clerk does not know the value of this symbol (it not yet having been encountered as a *label*), and thus the symbol table entry for DATA will be something like

DATA   ********

the asterisks indicating that the value is *unknown*. The next symbol encountered is TEST at line 6. But notice that in this case, the symbol's value *is* known, since the symbol has been used as a *label*. Its value is simply assigned the current value of the clerk's location counter, which is 00000011, and the symbol table entry will be

TEST   00000011

At line 8 the symbol NEXT is encountered, and since it is not yet in the table it is inserted with an "unknown" value:

$$\text{NEXT} \quad *******$$

The symbol NEXT is encountered again at line 12, this time as a *label*, having value 0000001B (since that is the current contents of the location counter). Searching the symbol table for NEXT, the clerk finds that an entry has already been made but that the *value* is unknown. Thus he can now replace the unknown value (********) with the known value (0000001B), so that at this point the symbol table has the following appearance:

DATA	********
TEST	00000011
NEXT	0000001B

At the next line (13), the symbol TEST is encountered again, but a search of the symbol table reveals that it has already been entered, and the reference at line 13 is *not* a "value-assigning" reference. Finally, DATA is found as a label at line 16, and thus DATA's unknown value can be replaced in the symbol table by the current location counter, 00000020. Since this is the last symbol reference, the symbol table is complete and contains the entries

DATA	00000020
TEST	00000011
NEXT	0000001B

Now that the values of all symbols are known to him, the clerk can make a second pass on the mnemonic program, this time doing the actual instruction translation, confident that there will no longer be the unknown forward references that caused us so much trouble earlier. Since we have already been through the details of that process, we shall not repeat them here. When the clerk completes his task, he will return the sheet of Figure 6.5.1 to us, with the machine code and addresses filled in (Figure 6.5.2).

As we have already mentioned, the clerk cannot be expected to criticize the *logic* of any program he assembles, since there is no reason to believe that he knows what the underlying algorithm is, or in fact even realizes that he is "assembling a computer program." Thus it is possible for the programmer to commit monstrous errors in program design without any complaints from the assembling clerk. But certain errors *will* be detected, and we shall mention a few of them here. The first and most obvious error that might be committed is the submission to the clerk of a line of program that contains an unrecognized mnemonic. For example, if the standard "data transfer" mnemonic is MOV, a line such as

$$\text{COPL} \quad \text{R2,R9}$$

will not be able to be translated by the clerk, and he will report an error message

D0	0000	1		MOVL	#7,R6	;⟨data count −1⟩ in R6
8F	0001					
00000007	0002					
56	0006					
	0007	2				; (= COUNTER)
D0	0007	3		MOVL	#DATA,R4	;R4 is pointer to DATA
8F	0008					
00000020	0009					
54	000D					
90	000E	4		MOVB	(R4)+,R8	;Put first number in R8
84	000F					
58	0010					
	0011	5				; (= TEMPMAX)
91	0011	6	TEST:	CMPB	(R4)+,R8	;Compare current byte (NUM)
84	0012					
58	0013					
	0014	7				; with TEMPMAX
1B	0014	8		BLEQU	NEXT	;Skip if not bigger than TEMPMAX
05	0015					
D7	0016	9		DECL	R4	; else back pointer up 1 byte,
54	0017					
90	0018	10		MOVB	(R4)+,R8	; replace TEMPMAX, and readjust
84	0019					
58	001A					
	001B	11				; data pointer
D7	001B	12	NEXT:	DECL	R6	;Decrement COUNTER
56	001C					
14	001D	13		BGTR	TEST	; and test next byte if positive
F2	001E					
00	001F	14		HALT		; else HALT the processor
	0020	15				;
72	0020	16	DATA:	.BYTE	^X72	;The
4F	0021	17		.BYTE	^X4F	; eight
D1	0022	18		.BYTE	^XD1	; (unsigned)
03	0023	19		.BYTE	^X03	; 8-bit
D7	0024	20		.BYTE	^XD7	; numbers
AE	0025	21		.BYTE	^XAE	; whose
E9	0026	22		.BYTE	^XE9	; maximum
7A	0027	23		.BYTE	^X7A	; is to be found

Figure 6.5.2

Sec. 6.5   The Assembly of the Mnemonic Program

of some sort, such as

?Unrecognized symbol

since he does not find COP in his table of instruction mnemonics, and its *position* in the line, namely *first*, precludes the possibility that COP is a user-defined symbol which stands for a numerical address.

Next, consider the statement

.BYTE   307

The clerk will take .BYTE to be a numerical context indicator, so that he is to generate a *byte* in the program containing a certain number. But the number 307, which is taken to be in its decimal representation, will not *fit* in an 8-bit byte. Again, some appropriate error message should be given to us to indicate that the clerk found the specified task to be impossible.

A fairly common programmer error, which generally results from careless-ness, is the failure to define a symbol. Suppose that in constructing the mnemonic program of Figure 6.5.1 we had neglected to place the label DATA: on the first of the data bytes. Then at the end of the clerk's first pass through the program, the symbol table would be

DATA   ********
TEST   00000011
NEXT   0000001B

Upon encountering the second instruction (line 3) on the *second* pass, the clerk would find a reference to DATA and would search the symbol table for this entry. What he would find is

DATA   ********

that is, that DATA had *no* definition, and thus it would not be possible for him to complete the assembly of this instruction. Again, some message such as

?Undefined symbol

would inform us of the problem.

Finally, suppose that we had inadvertently placed the *same* label on *two* statements. For example, suppose as shown that we had labeled line 12 of Figure 6.5.2 with NEXT:, but that we had also used the same label at line 6 (where the figure shows the label TEST:). As described above, this would result in the symbol TEST being undefined when it was referenced at line 13. But our concern here is with the dual definition of NEXT. When, on the first pass, the clerk encounters NEXT: at line 6, he enters it in the symbol table as

NEXT   00000011

Later, at line 12, he again encounters the symbol NEXT, with the definition 0000001B. As with any other symbol, the clerk scans the symbol table to see if the entry NEXT is currently present, and he finds that it *is*. Now this situation will be acceptable *provided* that the present occurrence of NEXT is a *reference* and not a definition, *or* the occurrence of NEXT *is* a definition but the entry in the table reveals that the symbol has *not yet been defined*, that is, that the symbol's entry is ********. But in this instance neither of these is the case; NEXT is already defined (its table entry being 00000011), and here we have a *new* definition of it, 0000001B. The clerk cannot cope with this situation, so he indicates that he has encountered a

?Multiple definition of label

and in fact replaces its current definition in the table with the new definition, 0000001B. But now a problem is also going to occur on the *second* pass through the mnemonic program. For when the first reference to NEXT occurs at line 6 (as a label), the clerk will find that the value of this symbol *should* be 00000011, since that is the current value of the location counter on this second pass, yet the symbol table shows that its value is given as 0000001B. Somehow (and of course we know how) between the first and second passes the value NEXT has *changed*— "has gotten out of phase." Thus in addition to the "multiple definition" message, the clerk will also report the message

?Symbol out of phase

What we have illustrated here are simply a few of the errors that might occur in writing mnemonic programs and the untenable positions in which they leave the clerk. They are four of the most common errors, and several others are described in Appendix B. How should the clerk react to a programmer error? We have already stated that he should indicate that he has encountered some construction with which he cannot deal, but should he abandon the assembly at this point, or should he forge ahead, even knowing that the program will require repair and that he will have to reassemble it later? From the clerk's standpoint, abandonment might seem to be the more prudent course of action. But from the programmer's point of view, it makes far more sense for the clerk to continue the translation process and thus to detect all the errors at one time, so that as many repairs as possible can be made in one "debugging" session. Thus we shall direct the clerk to assemble the entire program, even if errors are detected prior to the end of the program.

Now even if the clerk detects no errors in *form* in the program, and thus he can return the sheet of Figure 6.5.2 to us with all mnemonics assembled, we have no assurance that the machine language program will execute as desired, since there may be errors of logic within the program design. But even putting that question aside, there is one more misstep we might make here which will prevent proper execution. We noted that in beginning the assembly process, the clerk assumed the *default* assembly load address of 00000000, and the mnemonics were translated on the assumption that the program would be loaded for execution at that address. Suppose that upon receiving the assembled program from him, we had decided for whatever reason to load this code at 0000204C instead. If we do so, the program will *not* execute properly. The problem lies at line 3 of the mnemonic program, specifically at assembled location 00000009 of Figure 6.5.2, where there is a reference to DATA. The clerk determined that based on a load address of 00000000, the value of DATA would be 00000020. But if the program is **relocated** to 0000204C, then, in fact, the first data byte will be loaded at 0000206C, and if we do not change the value at location 00000009 (which will now actually be 00002055), the references to DATA will be to some unknown bytes in low memory (at 00000020), *not* to the data bytes in the program. The problem occurs since the value of the symbol DATA is **sensitive to program relocation**, and in order to move the program away from its assumed load address, references to the *values* of any such **relocation sensitive** symbols must be repaired prior to execution. In the program at hand, this happens to be the only such reference that contains the actual value of the symbol, but in general programs may contain many such references. On the other hand, observe, for example, that in line 8 there is a reference to the symbol NEXT, namely

BLEQU   NEXT

and that NEXT is certainly relocation sensitive. But in this case the assembled instruction contains *not* the *address* (value) NEXT, but rather the *displacement* to NEXT. And this displacement will be 5 bytes, *regardless* of what the actual load address is. Thus although the symbol NEXT might be sensitive to relocation, this particular instruction is *independent* of its location in main memory. Such a construction is called **position independent**.

6.6 THE *VAX* ASSEMBLER

Given that the assembly process is primarily clerical in nature, one might wonder about the possibility of writing a *program* to do the translating that we or our clerk has done heretofore. Such a program would have to do table lookups to determine mnemonics employed in a user's program, but this should be possible, since "matching" a mnemonic with a table entry amounts to comparing strings of characters, which can be reduced to a sequence of CMPBs. Building and managing a symbol table should also be possible, since again the entries consist of strings of characters and 32-bit numerical values. Any required displacement calculations amount simply to SUBtractions. In brief, such a program would likely be sizable and nontrivial, but it is possible to write a program that will emulate the activities of the clerk. Such a program is called an **assembler**, and assemblers are typically supplied by the computer manufacturer as an aid in program development. An assembler is supplied by Digital Equipment Corporation for use on the VAX (that is, an assembler that translates mnemonics into VAX machine code), which goes by the name MACRO since it is a **macroassembler**, a term that is explained in detail in

Chapter 18. The advantages of replacing the clerk with a program to do mnemonic program assemblies should be obvious; the assembler will perform consistently without error (which is too much to ask of even the most conscientious clerk), and assemblies will be returned to us in a matter of seconds, rather than hours or even days, thereby allowing us to make the best possible use of program development and "debugging" time.

Before looking at the details of the activities of the VAX assembler (which differ conceptually only trivially from those of the clerk), it will be useful to establish some terminology and to have a look at the *environment* within which our programs will be assembled and executed. The mnemonic program submitted to the assembler for translation is called the **source program**. The result of the assembly— the collection of machine-executable instruction codes—is called the **object program**. Most modern computing systems rely on *magnetic disks* for the storage of data, and it is on such disks that our source programs will reside, as **files** of ASCII-coded characters. The assembler will produce another disk file, consisting of the object program, which is a collection of numerical rather than character data. For this reason the source and object programs are frequently called the **source file** and **object file**. In addition to generating an object file, the assembler can be instructed to produce a **listing file** (similar to that of Figure 6.5.2), which might be directed to the user's terminal, or to a disk file, or perhaps to a high-speed printing device.

The source program of Figure 6.5.1, which we presented to the clerk for assembly, will almost do for submission to the VAX assembler, but a few changes are required, and a few additional concepts need to be introduced to take into account the environment under which the object program will ultimately be executed. (At the risk of repetition, we remind the reader that program assembly is *not* program execution.) We must be aware that unlike the early computers, today's systems are highly structured and complex in the way in which they process user programs. The economics of computing has dictated that systems be easy to use, and thus a great deal of **system software** (programming) has been developed to assist users in the creation, modification, deletion, and execution of files. The VAX assembler itself is one of these programs, and the reader is also probably already familiar with a *text editor* of some sort. All of these pieces of system software form what is collectively known as the **operating system**, and two of its primary purposes are to supply the programmer with **system utilities** (programs) to increase his or her efficiency and productivity, and also to act as a "watchdog" on the system, to ensure that no user does anything to disrupt the total environment's efficiency for any other user. For despite whatever impressions we may have given, in most VAX systems the user does *not* have complete control of the processor at any time, even when executing programs written at the machine level; there are some services the software can provide even as our programs are executing, and there are even cases in which the operating system will intervene to "trap" the execution of an instruction if such execution could be "damaging" to the system environment. We shall give an example of this self-protective feature later in this section.

An acceptable version of the program of Figure 6.5.1 is shown in Figure 6.6.1, in which we have marked the features of special interest, and the assembler's listing file is given in Figure 6.6.2. The program of Figure 6.6.1 is identical to that of Figure 6.5.1 as far as being a machine equivalent of the algorithm of Section 6.2. The principal differences have to do with *additions* to the earlier version, some of which are included to enhance the program, others being forced on us by the assembler or the operating system. (The lettered paragraph headings below correspond to the instructions marked in Figures 6.6.1 and 6.6.2.)

(A) The "program entry mask word"

This word, which we see from Figure 6.6.1 has contents 0000 and is termed "Program 'entry mask'," involves concepts of sufficient complexity that we devote the next section to them. In the meantime the reader is advised that every program must have such an "entry mask" word at the location at which execution is to begin. Some related comments will be found in paragraph (f) below.

Ⓐ	START:	.WORD	0	;Program 'entry mask'
Ⓑ		MOVL	#7,R6	;⟨data count −1⟩ in R6
				; (= COUNTER)
Ⓒ		MOVL	#DATA,R4	;R4 is pointer to DATA
		MOVB	(R4) + ,R8	;Put 1st number in R8
				; (= TEMPMAX)
	TEST:	CMPB	(R4) + ,R8	;Compare current byte (NUM)
				; with TEMPMAX
		BLEQU	NEXT	;Skip if not bigger than TEMPMAX
		DECL	R4	; else back pointer up 1 byte,
		MOVB	(R4) + ,R8	; replace TEMPMAX, and readjust
				; data pointer
	NEXT:	DECL	R6	;Decrement COUNTER
		BGTR	TEST	; and test next byte if positive
Ⓓ		$O.1H	R8	; else print maximum,
		$O.NL		; generate a 'new line'
Ⓔ		$EXIT		; and exit to operating system
				;
	DATA:	.BYTE	^X72	;The
		.BYTE	^X4F	; eight
		.BYTE	^XD1	; (unsigned)
		.BYTE	^X03	; 8-bit
		.BYTE	^XD7	; numbers
		.BYTE	^XAE	; whose
		.BYTE	^XE9	; maximum
		.BYTE	^X7A	; is to be found
				;
Ⓕ		.END	START	;Begin execution at 'START'

Figure 6.6.1

```
Ⓐ    0000  0000  1 START: .WORD   0        ;Program 'entry mask'
     D0    0002  2         MOVL    #7,R6    ;<data count -1> in R6
Ⓑ    07    0003
     56    0004
           0005  3                          ;  (= COUNTER)
     D0    0005  4         MOVL    #DATA,R4 ;R4 is pointer to DATA
     8F    0006
Ⓒ 00000047' 0007
     54    000B
     90    000C  5         MOVB    (R4)+,R8 ;Put 1st number in R8
     84    000D
     58    000E
           000F  6                          ;  (= TEMPMAX)
     91    000F  7 TEST:   CMPB    (R4)+,R8 ;Compare current byte (NUM)
     84    0010
     58    0011
           0012  8                          ;  with TEMPMAX
     1B    0012  9         BLEQU   NEXT     ;Skip if not bigger than TEMPMAX
     05    0013
     D7    0014 10         DECL    R4       ;  else back pointer up 1 byte,
     54    0015
     90    0016 11         MOVB    (R4)+,R8 ;  replace TEMPMAX, and readjust
     84    0017
     58    0018
           0019 12                          ;  data pointer
     D7    0019 13 NEXT:   DECL    R6       ;Decrement COUNTER
     56    001A
     14    001B 14         BGTR    TEST     ;  and test next byte if positive
     F2    001C
Ⓓ         001D 15         $O.1H   R8       ;  else print maximum,
           002F 16         $O.NL            ;  generate a 'new line'
Ⓔ         003B 17         $EXIT            ;  and exit to operating system
           0047 18                          ;
     72    0047 19 DATA:   .BYTE   ^X72     ;The
     4F    0048 20         .BYTE   ^X4F     ;  eight
     D1    0049 21         .BYTE   ^XD1     ;  (unsigned)
     03    004A 22         .BYTE   ^X03     ;  8-bit
     D7    004B 23         .BYTE   ^XD7     ;  numbers
     AE    004C 24         .BYTE   ^XAE     ;  whose
     E9    004D 25         .BYTE   ^XE9     ;  maximum
     7A    004E 26         .BYTE   ^X7A     ;  is to be found
           004F 27                          ;
Ⓕ         004F 28         .END    START    ;Begin execution at 'START'
```

Figure 6.6.2

(B) The "short literal" construction

There is nothing peculiar about the line marked B in the source program (Figure
6.6.1). Rather, Figure 6.6.2 shows that the VAX assembler has generated code
which is *different* from that constructed by our clerk. What we expect to see is
D0 (MOVL), followed by the mode byte 8F, followed by the longword itself,
namely 00000007. What we find, however, is D0 followed by 07. What has

happened here is that the assembler "realized" that the absolute number to be moved, namely 7, was small enough to fit in just a few bits. Thus it has generated what is called a **short literal** construction, in which a byte is formed consisting partly of *mode bits*, and partly of *data bits*. This construction is discussed in detail in Chapter 7; in the meantime we observe that the assembler has managed to save 4 bytes of code by employing this device. We should also note that there are ways of *forcing* the assembler to generate the expected (but less efficient) longword construction.

(C) The relocation-sensitive address DATA

Again, there is nothing peculiar about the line of source instruction marked C, and in fact the assembler has generated the code we expected, the longword 00000047 representing the value (address) DATA. But we wish to bring to the reader's attention the apostrophe (') which the assembler has attached to this longword. This is the assembler's indicator that the reference is to a relocation-sensitive construction, and thus if the program is moved away from the presumed load address 00000000, this word will require repair before the program can be executed successfully. As we have already noted, this is the only occurrence of this phenomenon in this particular program

(D) $O.1H and $O.NL — program output "instructions"

The reader may already have observed a severe deficiency in all the programs we have written so far, constructed either as machine language or mnemonic programs. None of them "announces the result" in any way. The principal sample program of this chapter, for example, leaves the maximum of the eight numbers in R8 and then simply HALTs. There is no way for *us* to determine the result, short of directly examining the contents of R8 (which, under normal circumstances, we cannot do). Although input to and output from the computing system is essential to meaningful programming, these tasks are rather complex at this level, far more involved than we are in a position to handle at this stage in the development of our knowledge of the VAX. To facilitate these activities, we have supplied input and output **macroinstructions**—collections of ordinary VAX instructions which are "packaged" under a specific *name*. One of these is **$O.1H**, consisting of a half dozen or so instructions, which are named "$O.1H" as a *package*, and we note that those instructions are *not* listed on the object program listing, although we see from the addresses that they evidently require (decimal) 18 bytes of memory. The effect of this "instruction" (perhaps "command" is a better term),

$$\text{\$O.1H} \quad \text{R8}$$

is to *O*utput the *1* byte, in its *H*exadecimal format, which is contained in R8, that number being printed on the user's terminal. (To output all *4* bytes of R8 in their *decimal* format, we would use the macroinstruction **$O.4D** instead.) There is nothing sacred about the dollar sign character ($), since it is as valid a VAX assembler character as any other; we have used it for all of the various macroinstructions simply to emphasize the fact that these macroinstructions are something a bit different; they are *not* processor instruction mnemonics, nor are they assembler directives. (See paragraph (F) below.)

Now one of the features of the output macroinstructions is that having printed on the terminal the requested number of bytes in the specified format, they do *not* return the terminal's cursor or printhead to the left margin. The purpose of the macroinstruction **$O.NL** is to generate a "*New Line*," a carriage return followed by a line feed.

(The reader will find all the details of the keyboard input and terminal output macroinstructions in Appendix D, although some of those details require material from Chapter 8 for a complete understanding.)

(E) $EXIT—return control to the operating system

Each of our programs to date, upon completion of its task, simply HALTs. HALT, as a processor operation, means quite literally that—instruct the processor to *cease* its fetch-execute cycles. But in most VAX systems, the processor is being *shared* by many users simultaneously, and if one user HALTs the processor, then it is unavailable to all other users. Thus HALT is one of the operations that the operating system, working closely with the processor, will not permit *any* user to execute; if a user attempts to HALT the processor, the operating system will abort execution of the offending program with a warning message. What is needed, then, when a user has completed program execution is some orderly way to terminate execution of that program and return control to the operating system. The macroinstruction **$EXIT** serves this purpose and should be used in place of HALT in user programs.

(F) The .END directive

The clerk whom we employed briefly in this chapter was able to detect the end of a mnemonic program simply by observing that he had run out of mnemonics. The VAX assembler can only detect an end-of-file condition on the source file, and this may not correspond exactly to the end of the source program. Thus we use the symbol ".END" to notify the assembler that it has come to the end of the source program. .END is an **assembler directive**, the symbolic form of a "message" to the assembler to provide a service *other than* the translation of mnemonics. We have already seen two directives, .BYTE and .WORD, which direct the assembler to generate a byte or word containing a specific number, in memory at its current location counter value. We shall see numerous other of these assembler directives in the course of our programming; they are easily distinguished from operation mnemonics, since they begin with a period, or dot (.).

In the program of Figures 6.6.1 and 6.6.2 the .END directive also contains an *address*—START. This is the address at which we intend execution to begin, and the reader may find it puzzling that the assembler would have the least interest in this **transfer address** or **start address**, especially in view of the fact that we have mentioned on several occasions that *assembly time* is not the same as *execution time* (or *run time*). Although it is true that the assembler does not execute programs, it will nonetheless make a note of this "transfer address," the location at which execution is ultimately to begin, as separate informational material in the object file, so that once the program *is* loaded for execution, the system utility program responsible for program execution will be able to reference this address. (The details of this process are given in Chapter 10.)

Now it would appear that if START is specified by the programmer as the location where execution is to begin, and if we have placed the "program entry mask word" at that location—a word whose contents is 0000—then when execution takes place, this word (0000), rather than the MOVL instruction, will be the first thing "executed." In fact, as explained in further detail in the next section, the system utility responsible for executing the program *expects* this word to be here and begins execution *two bytes down* from this location.

There are two final comments about the transfer address which, although trivial, should be made to dispel any false inferences that the reader might be tempted to make. First, there is nothing about the particular choice of the label START that has anything to do with "start" addresses. Programs can have any start address—BEGIN, CAT, or even START+6 or CAT-^2E will do as well—as long as the address is the location at which execution is to begin. (But recall that the transfer address *must* contain the program entry mask word.) Second, assembly language programs need not "start" at the first physical byte of the program. All of our examples so far do, but unlike a high-level language program, which typically *does* begin at its first executable instruction, assembly language programs may be begun anywhere within the section of main memory occupied by the program. For example, if we had chosen to place the data bytes of the program of Figure 6.6.1 at the *beginning* of the program rather than at the end, the program's transfer address (START) would be location 00000008 instead of 00000000.

We conclude this section by revealing the whole truth about the appearance of VAX assembler program listings. In fact, the components that make up each instruction are *not* listed in a vertical fashion as we have shown them, each with its corresponding memory address. Rather, the various bytes, words, and so on, that make up an individual machine instruction are listed *horizontally*, the individual bytes being read right to left in order of increasing addresses. For example, the first executable instruction of the current program,

MOVL   #7,R6

we have shown in Figure 6.6.2 as

```
D0   0002    MOVL   #7,R6
07   0003
56   0004
     0005    ⟨next instruction⟩
```

whereas in fact this is listed by the assembler as

$$56 \quad 07 \quad D0 \quad 0002 \qquad \text{MOVL} \quad \#7, R6$$
$$0005 \qquad \langle \text{next instruction} \rangle$$

Figure 6.6.3 shows an actual assembler listing of the source program of Figure 6.6.1 (although even here we have deleted some extraneous material). Because of the fact that the assembler lists instruction codes horizontally, the listing is so wide that we have found it necessary to remove the comments to accommodate page width.

Notice that the assembler has printed a listing of the symbol table, in alphabetic order of the symbols, together with their values. The symbol R printed after each value is simply a notation which indicates that that value is relocation sensitive.

There is one final mystery here, which will have to remain such for the time

```
<date and time> VAX-11 Macro V03-00                        Page   1

                        0000  0000    1 START:  .WORD    0
              56   07   D0    0002    2          MOVL    #7,R6
        54  00000047'8F     D0    0005    3          MOVL    #DATA,R4
              58   84   90    000C    4          MOVB    (R4)+,R8
              58   84   91    000F    5 TEST:   CMPB    (R4)+,R8
              05   1B         0012    6          BLEQU   NEXT
              54   D7         0014    7          DECL    R4
              58   84   90    0016    8          MOVB    (R4)+,R8
              56   D7         0019    9 NEXT:   DECL    R6
              F2   14         001B   10          BGTR    TEST
                             001D   11          $0.1H   R8
                             002F   12          $0.NL
                             003B   13          $EXIT
                             0047   14          ;
              72             0047   15 DATA:   .BYTE   ^X72
              4F             0048   16          .BYTE   ^X4F
              D1             0049   17          .BYTE   ^XD1
              03             004A   18          .BYTE   ^X03
              D7             004B   19          .BYTE   ^XD7
              AE             004C   20          .BYTE   ^XAE
              E9             004D   21          .BYTE   ^XE9
              7A             004E   22          .BYTE   ^X7A
                             004F   23          ;
                             004F   24          .END    START


        Symbol table

        ...$              *******  X
        DATA             00000047 R
        NEXT             00000019 R
        START            00000000 R
        TEST             0000000F R
```

Figure 6.6.3

being. There is a symbol ...$ included in the symbol table which we did *not* define within the program; its value is evidently undefined (********); and it is annotated X. ...$ is, in fact, a symbol that is *referenced* by each of the macroinstructions $O.1H, $O.NL, and $EXIT, but not *defined* by any of them. It is a symbol which is **external** (X) to this programming module. These concepts are developed in detail in Chapter 10. In the meantime the reader should expect to see ...$ appearing in the symbol table of any program that invokes any of the input and output macroinstructions.

6.7 THE PROGRAM ENTRY MASK WORD

In Chapter 2 we discussed at some length the conditions under which certain operations will yield arithmetically correct results, and how incorrect results can be detected (see in particular Section 2.11). One of the concepts of special importance was that of "integer overflow," in which an addition or subtraction of signed integers yielded a result that could not be held in the given structure (byte, word, and so on) as a *signed* integer, and we found that this phenomenon could be detected by noting that the V-bit in the processor status word was set after execution of the instruction in question. Now in some programming environments we might very well anticipate that such overflows could occur, and we may even provide tests at critical points to detect such overflows—tests in the form of conditional branches which sample the V-bit and deal in some appropriate fashion with these overflows, should they occur. But in other programs, such overflows may be completely unexpected and would be a result of errors, either in the programming itself or in the data being processed. In this event we would probably not provide programming to test for these unanticipated problems. However, in these cases we can still detect such errors by taking advantage of *operating system services* which will, upon detection of an integer overflow, abort execution and inform us of the problem via an appropriate error message. To inform the processor that this service is requested, we need to *set* (turn *on*) bit 5 of the PSW. Referring to Figure 5.9.1, we see that this bit is labeled IV—Integer o*V*erflow—and if it is *set* at the time an integer overflow occurs during execution, the operating system will intervene as described above. If it is *clear*, no such operating system action will take place, the overflow simply being allowed to occur. (The other **trap enable flags** "DV" and "FU"—Decimal o*V*erflow and *F*loating *U*nderflow—which correspond to bits 7 and 6 of the PSW, refer to numerical structures and contexts which we will investigate in later chapters, and the response of the operating system to these flags will be discussed at that time.)

Now if we want system intervention to take place on integer overflows, we must ensure that bit 5 of the PSW is set when the program is executing. This is easy enough to do, for there is a processor operation that can be used to manipulate the bits of the PSW. On the other hand, the VAX provides a means of setting this bit, and also setting or clearing bit 7—"DV"—which is far easier, namely, by specifying a particular **program entry mask word**. (A byte, word, or longword whose *bit configuration*—sequence of 1s and 0s—rather than *value* is used to determine some conditions or affect some other structure in a particular way is frequently referred to as a **mask** or **template**.) In the case at hand our attention focuses on the 1s in the entry mask word, and in particular if bit 15 of this mask word is *set*, then bit 7 (DV) of the PSW will be set; if bit 14 of this word is *set*, bit 5 (IV) of the PSW will be set. Thus if we wish to enable system intervention in the event of an integer overflow, the program entry mask word should be

.WORD ^X4000   or   .WORD ^B0100000000000000

Enabling "decimal overflow" intervention could be accomplished with

.WORD ^X8000   or   .WORD ^B1000000000000000

and both could be achieved with

.WORD ^XC000   or   .WORD ^B1100000000000000

(The other bits in the mask word have significance in some settings, but since they have no direct bearing on *program execution*—the topic of interest here—we postpone a discussion of them until they are needed in Chapter 9.)

Since the program entry mask word seems to be some sort of reference word rather than anything *executable*, we need to pause for a moment to see exactly how and when this word is used. We have already indicated that user programs do not execute in total isolation from the surrounding operating system, and in fact the operating system plays a role immediately upon program execution. For when a program is "run"—when execution is begun—the operating system is notified of the transfer address, which as we know is the address in main memory to which the program counter is to be set to begin execution. However, the operating system does not set the program counter to this address and immediately pass control to the user program. Rather, it uses this address to obtain the *program entry mask word*, then it sets the "DV" and "IV" flags in the PSW according to bits 15 and 14 of this word, and finally it passes control to the user program at the transfer address *plus two* (to account for the 2 bytes that make up the mask word). Thus we see that the operating system intervenes initially, at the beginning of program execution, to provide a service for us, and it is now clear that because of this operating system action, every program *must* contain such an entry mask word—the failure to include it will result not only in some unpredictable PSW bits, but also in execution beginning two bytes *beyond* the intended "start" address.

Finally, then, we see why we have inserted in the program of Figure 6.6.1 the line marked A:

START: .WORD 0

for this is the program entry mask word which indicates that we specifically wish *no* system services relative to integer overflow (or decimal overflow). Indeed, such system intervention in the case of this program could be disastrous, for we are dealing with *unsigned* numbers here and thus integer *overflows* can occur but are of no real significance (although integer *carries* might be).

We conclude this discussion of mask words with two peripheral topics. First, the programmer need not construct the mask word directly, by calculating which bits should be on and which should be off and then generating the appropriate 16-bit word for that bit configuration. Rather, the assembler will construct the word for us, in a more convenient fashion, if we indicate to it that it is to do so. Specifically, the **mask word context indicator** is the symbol ^M ("circumflex-M") followed by key symbols, separated by commas, and enclosed in angle brackets: ⟨...⟩. The key symbols of present concern to us are DV and IV—decimal overflow and integer overflow, respectively— and thus to generate a mask word to enable system intervention in the event of integer overflows we can write

$$.WORD \quad \text{^M⟨IV⟩}$$

instead of the more obscure

$$.WORD \quad \text{^X4000}$$

In a similar fashion,

$$.WORD \quad \text{^M⟨DV⟩}$$

will enable decimal overflow "trapping," while

$$.WORD \quad \text{^M⟨DV,IV⟩} \quad \text{or} \quad .WORD \quad \text{^M⟨IV,DV⟩}$$

will enable both. Thus in the program of Figure 6.6.1 we could have written

$$\text{START:} \quad .WORD \quad \text{^M⟨ ⟩}$$

(the "⟨ ⟩" indicating that *no* mask bits are to be set) and since this is more explicit than the .WORD 0 that was used in the program, we consider it to be the construction of choice and shall employ it henceforth except in special circumstances.

There is a second possible construction that we could have used here, based on another assembler directive. The directive is .ENTRY, and it declares a program (or other module) **entry point**. The format of the .ENTRY directive is

$$.ENTRY \quad label, mask$$

and its effect is the same as

$$label: \quad .WORD \quad mask$$

Thus the first line of the program of Figure 6.6.1 could have been

$$.ENTRY \ START,0 \quad \text{or} \quad .ENTRY \ START,\text{^M⟨ ⟩}$$

We have declined to take advantage of this construction, and we will consistently do so in the future, for one reason. The .ENTRY construction tends to "bury" the label (START, in this case), so that it is difficult to find when we scan the program listing—the label does not stand out in the left margin the way a normally formed label does. (.ENTRY has one further effect that we are not presently in a position to discuss, but it is of no consequence to us in any event.)

6.8 EXERCISES

6.2.1. In constructing the program of Section 6.2, one of the problems that was encountered was the *forward reference* to the address of the first data byte (Figure 6.2.2). Show that this problem could have been eliminated by loading the data bytes *first*—into locations 00000000 to 00000007. Another forward reference was encountered in the conditional branch instruction that followed the "compare" (Figure 6.2.5). How, if at all, could the logic of the algorithm have been rearranged to eliminate that problem?

6.2.2. In the program of Section 6.2 the automatic incrementing of c(R4) (the data pointer) was a useful device until it came time to replace the contents of R8 (TEMPMAX), and then we found that the pointer had already been advanced too far. We managed to cope with the problem, but suppose that instead we had referenced the byte pointed at by R4 *without* automatic incrementing of c(R4). Without attempting to generate any machine code, explain what modifications would be required to accommodate this approach.

6.2.3. In Figure 6.2.4 we compared the byte pointed at by R4 (NUM) with the low-order byte of R8 (TEMPMAX). If the compare had been constructed in the reverse order—"compare the low-order byte of R8 with the byte pointed at by R4"—what consequences would this have for the conditional branch instruction that follows? In particular, without attempting to generate any machine code, determine the *conditions* under which the branch should take place.

6.2.4. Without attempting to generate any machine code, explain what modifications would be required to the program of Figure 6.2.11 if:
   (a) The *minimum* of 8 unsigned bytes is to be found.
   (b) The maximum of 8 *signed* bytes is to be found.
   (c) The maximum of 8 *unsigned words* is to be found.

6.3.1. Devise mnemonics for each of the following VAX operators, and determine the numbers and types of operands they should have. Then check these against those given in Appendix A. (A little searching will probably be required here, and Appendix A contains some details and notations with which the reader is not yet familiar.)
   (a) **Add** longword A and B, and put the result in longword C.
   (b) **Add** words A and B, and put the result back in word B.
   (c) **Subtract** word A from word B, and put the result in word C.
   (d) **Subtract** longword A from longword B, and put the result back in longword B.
   (e) **Branch** if the PSW's C-bit is *clear*.
   (f) **Branch** if the PSW's C-bit is *set*.
   (g) **Branch** if the PSW's Z-bit is *clear*.
   (h) **Branch** if the PSW's Z-bit is *set*.
   (i) **Branch** if the PSW's N-bit is *clear*.
   (j) **Branch** if the PSW's N-bit is *set*.
   (k) **Negate** (twos-complement) byte A and put the result in byte B.

(l) Complement (ones-complement) longword A and put the result in longword B.

(m) Calculate byte A EXCLUSIVE-OR byte B, and put the result in byte C.

(n) Calculate word A OR word B, and put the result back in word B.

6.3.2. We know that

$$\text{MOVL} \quad \hat{}\text{X2F7,R9}$$

means "move (copy) the longword whose address is 000002F7 to R9," that

$$\text{MOVL} \quad \text{R9,}\hat{}\text{X2F7}$$

means "move (copy) the longword contents of R9 to the longword whose address is 000002F7," and that

$$\text{MOVL} \quad \#\hat{}\text{X2F7,R9}$$

means "move (copy) the absolute longword number ˆX000002F7 to R9." What, if anything, would be the meaning of

$$\text{MOVL} \quad \text{R9,}\#\hat{}\text{X2F7}$$

6.3.3. We have devised the notation (Rn)+ for the automatic incrementing, which we have found in our programs so far to be quite useful. The VAX also has an "addressing mode," which automatically *decrements* the contents of a register (by an amount consistent with the size of the structure involved in the instruction), but in this case the decrementing takes place *prior to* the register's use as a pointer to data. Devise an appropriate symbolic notation for this register use.

6.4.1. In the mnemonic program of Figure 6.4.2 we have the construction

$$\text{BLEQU NEXT}$$
$$\cdot \ \cdot \ \cdot \ \cdot \ \cdot \ \cdot$$
$$\text{NEXT:} \quad \text{DECL R6}$$

The reader may find this reminiscent of the BASIC statements

$$100 \quad \text{IF X} < \, = 0 \text{ THEN GOTO 200}$$
$$\cdot \ \cdot \ \cdot \ \cdot \ \cdot \ \cdot \ \cdot \ \cdot \ \cdot \ \cdot$$
$$200 \quad \text{K} = \text{K} - 1$$

or the FORTRAN statements

$$\text{IF (X .LE. 0) GOTO 960}$$
$$\cdot \ \cdot \ \cdot \ \cdot \ \cdot \ \cdot \ \cdot \ \cdot \ \cdot \ \cdot$$
$$960 \quad \text{COUNT} = \text{COUNT} - 1$$

How does the symbolic address NEXT relate to the BASIC line number 200 and the FORTRAN statement identifier 960?

6.5.1. We saw that if a symbol is referenced in a mnemonic program, but if that symbol is never defined there, the clerk will be unable to complete certain constructions and will announce the error with an appropriate message. Will any problems be caused by a symbol that is *defined* within a mnemonic program but never *referenced* in it?

6.5.2. What would have been the consequences, for the clerk and for our ultimate program execution, if we had inadvertently neglected to include the HALT instruction in the program of Figure 6.5.1.?

6.5.3. How might the clerk respond to

.BYTE   307

Should he generate a byte? If so, what should he place in it?

6.6.1. How can the assembler (or the clerk) determine which symbols and which constructions are sensitive to program relocation?

VAX ADDRESSING MODES

7.1 OPERATIONS AND INSTRUCTIONS

In Chapter 5 we noted the distinction between an *operation* and an *instruction*. Specifically, an **operation** is an arithmetic or logical *activity*, the performance for which the central processing unit contains electronic circuitry. Thus *add, subtract, branch, halt,* and so on, are operations, and in fact we have seen some sample electronics for *increment* (Figure 3.5.3) and *add* (Figure 3.5.5). We have already observed that each of these operations is *encoded*, in main memory, into an 8-bit byte (although a handful require 2 bytes), and for execution, this byte must be *decoded* by circuitry within the central processing unit.

Now most operations perform actions on *data structures* of some sort. (A very few operations do not—HALT is an example—but we shall not be concerned with them in the present discussion.) That data structure might be a byte, word, or longword, for example, and it might reside in main memory or in a register. Whatever the structure on which the operation operates, and wherever it may reside, that structure is called an operation **operand**. For instance, at line 1 of Figure 6.5.2 we MOVed the longword 7 to R6. The *number* 7 is an operand, and it resides in main memory (at locations 00000002 to 00000005, in that example), and the 32-bit longword that is the *contents* of register 6 is another operand, this time residing in a register.

We can now define as before an **instruction** to be an *operation* together with its *operands*. At the mnemonic level, for example.

MOVL

is an *operation*, whereas

$$MOVL \quad \#7,R6$$

is an *instruction*.

7.2 OPERAND SPECIFIERS

In Chapter 5, when we first introduced the notion of instruction, we devised the concept of "operand specifier" in an attempt to simplify what were at that time some fairly complex ideas (see Section 5.5, in particular, Figure 5.5.2). We can now deal with that notion on a more formal basis and define an **operand specifier** to be a collection of bytes that are used by the processor to determine the *location* of the *structure* to be used as an instruction operand. A few examples from the program of Figure 6.5.2 will clarify this notion.

One of the simplest operand specifiers consists of a single byte, and an example is found at line 9 of that program:

$$DECL \quad R4$$

We see that it has been assembled as the 2 bytes (read right to left in order of increasing addresses)

$$54 \quad D7$$

The first of these (D7) is the code for the "decrement longword" operation, and the second (54) is the operand specifier. It informs the processor that the operand—the structure to be incremented—is the longword contents of R4.

As a slightly more involved example, which requires two operands, consider the instruction at line 4:

$$MOVB \quad (R4)+,R8$$

which assembles as

$$58 \quad 84 \quad 90$$

where 90 is the operation code for MOVB. Now the first, or *source*, operand specifier is 84, and it says something about register 4. In particular it indicates that the data structure (in this case, byte) which is to be moved is *not* in R4, but rather is the byte whose *address* is the 32-bit longword in R4. Thus in this case, the operand is *memory* resident, although it has been specified by referencing, in a somewhat indirect way, a *register*. [As we discussed in some detail at the time, this instruction also has the effect of incrementing c(R4) by 1; this so-called "side effect" was critical to that program, but we shall not be concerned with it in the present discussion.] The *destination* operand specifier is 58, and this specifies that the destination of the MOVB is the low-order byte of R8.

Finally, consider the instruction at line 3:

MOVL #DATA,R4

The code generated for this instruction is

54 00 00 00 20 8F DO

where DO is the code for the MOVL operation. The byte 8*F* informs the processor that the program counter (register 15—"F") is *pointing at* the longword to be moved. And the longword currently pointed at by the PC is 00000020. Thus the five bytes

00 00 00 20 8F

form the operand specifier, and it specifies that the operand is the longword 00000020 (which, in the program of Figure 6.5.2, is the address of the first data number). The last byte of the instruction, 54, specifies that the destination of the move is the longword contents of R4.

By now the reader may have inferred that the *first* (or *only*) byte of an operand specifier has something to do with a general register (R6, R4, and R15 = PC in the examples above), and for the most part this is quite correct. There are instructions for which the operand specifier does not reference a register (the branch instructions are examples), but for the vast majority of instructions, the leading byte of the operand specifier makes reference to one of the general registers.

7.3 MODE BYTES

When the first byte of an operand specifier references a general register, that byte will be called a **mode byte**, also referred to as an **access mode byte**, since it informs the processor of the way (*mode*) in which an operand is to be located (*accessed*). (There is one type of "mode byte" which is an exception to this definition, but it is easily dealt with in Section 7.5.) Each mode byte has the form shown in Figure 7.3.1, where the **mode bits** are 7:4, and thus can take on the values 0 to 15 (0 to F), and the **register bits** are 3:0, and hence can also take on the values 0 to 15. Thus *any* of the registers may enter into a mode byte, and in fact **mode-register byte** might be a more appropriate term. When the decoder accesses a mode byte, it examines the register bits to determine the register referenced. Since the reg-

Figure 7.3.1

isters are processor-resident, the register's contents is immediately available for the decoder's use. An examination of the mode bits then tells the decoder *how* that register's contents is to be used.

Before investigating the processor's interpretation of the 16 possible mode bits, we need to clear up one potential point of confusion. We stated above that *most*, but not all, operations take operands that begin with mode-register bytes. But if this is the case, how can the decoder tell whether to interpret the *next* byte (that is, the byte following the operation code byte) as a mode byte or not? The answer is that the operation code byte itself contains the information that the operand specifier is or is not of the form "mode byte, followed (possibly) by further operand information." We shall see that if the operand specifier *does* contain a mode byte, then that mode byte, together with information contained in the operation code, determine for the processor the *number* of remaining bytes (if any) which make up that operand specifier.

Finally, we note that general registers can be used as operands in *quadword* instructions, and since a quadword is a 64-bit structure and a register is only 32 bits long, there is some question as to what an instruction such as

CLRQ Rn

might mean. In these cases a quadword is formed of the register, acting as bits 31:0 of the quadword, and the *next-higher-numbered register*, acting as bits 63:32 of the quadword. The two registers are said to be **concatenated**, and we denote this structure by R[n + 1]'R[n], the apostrophe being used to indicate concatenation, and the brackets simply as grouping symbols. (In the case of specific registers, the brackets would not normally be used—for example, R7'R6 rather than R[7]'R[6].) Figure 7.3.2(a) diagrams this register concatenation. In a similar fashion, an *octaword* instruction (such as CLRO) which references a register as an operand will operate on the register concatenated with the next three higher-numbered registers, as shown in Figure 7.3.2(b). Two words of caution are needed here. First, if the concatenation of registers requires that a register *beyond* R15 be involved, the result of the operation will be unpredictable. Second, not all VAX systems contain the circuitry to implement octaword instructions. On those systems any attempt to *execute* an octaword instruction, such as MOVO, will result in a "reserved instruction" fault, although such instructions will *assemble* properly.

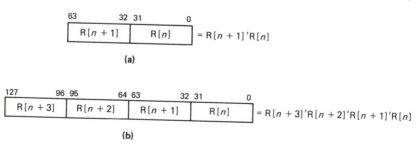

Figure 7.3.2

7.4 OPERAND ACCESS MODES: GENERAL REGISTER ADDRESSING

In our investigation of addressing modes, or operand access modes, we will look at a number of examples, programming segments that illustrate each of these modes. However, we shall *not* use R15—the program counter—as the general register in any of the illustrative examples. The reason for this is *not* that R15's behavior relative to these modes is peculiar; in fact, it behaves just as the other general registers do. Rather, R15 plays the special role of the program counter, and thus an examination of its behavior requires a bit more care. Section 7.6 is devoted to an investigation of this behavior.

We shall look at the various possible modes, not in the obvious, numerical order—0, 1, . . . , 15—but rather in order of increasing complexity.

(a) Mode 5

Name	Register
Assembler symbol	Rn
Description	The contents of the register Rn, as a byte, word, or longword, is the operand. If the data structure specified by the instruction is a quadword or octaword, the operand is the (64-bit) contents of $R[n+1]'R[n]$ or the (128-bit) contents of $R[n+3]'R[n+2]'R[n+1]'R[n]$, respectively.
Machine code example	The instruction

DECL   R9

will be assembled as

D7   operation code for "decrement longword"
59   mode byte (mode = 5, register = 9)

and upon execution will decrement the (longword) contents of R9.

We have already seen several examples of this addressing mode; see, for example, lines 2, 10, and 13 of Figure 6.6.2. This is the most straightforward of all the modes, and it is typically employed when the register is used as a counter or accumulator. The one caution we should issue is that when a register is used in mode 5 with an instruction that is *not* in longword form, then some substructure of the register is the operand, and we need to know the action of the operation on that substructure. In particular, byte instructions will address only bits 7:0 of the register, and word instructions will address bits 15:0. For example,

CLRB   R3

will clear bits 7:0 of R3, but bits 31:8 will be *unaffected*. In a similar fashion, if $c(R9) = 2C457AD4$ and $c(R11) = FF28B259$, the instruction

MOVW   R9,11

will result in c(R9) = 2C457AD4 (unchanged) and c(R11) = FF287AD4. These actions, which are frequently most desirable, can also be an area of potential error. For example, if R6 is to be used as a counter, we mght be tempted to use

$$\text{MOVB} \quad \#7,R6$$

since 7 is small enough to fit in a single byte. But then we must understand that the contents of R6, as a 32-bit structure, is *not* 7—rather, its low-order byte contains the number 7, but we may know nothing of bits 31:8. It is now clear that subsequent *longword* or *word* operations on R6 may well produce results that we did not intend. (There is a type of "move byte" operation which *does* preserve the value of the number moved, even if the number was in byte or word form; this is discussed in Chapter 8.)

(b) Mode 6

Name	Register deferred
Assembler symbol	(Rn)
Description	The contents of the register is the 32-bit *address* of the operand.
Machine code example	The instruction

$$\text{CLRW} \quad (R7)$$

will be assembled as

B4	operation code for "clear word"
67	mode byte(mode = 6, register = 7)

and upon execution will clear the word whose address is in R7.

In mode 6 the register does not contain the operand, as in mode 5, but rather it *points at* the operand—contains the operand's address. That is, the operand reference is *deferred* one level. (This addressing mode is sometimes called **indirect addressing**, since the operand address is not given directly, but rather *indirectly*, by means of the register contents.) For example, if c(R5) = 000001A4, and if the longword at 000001A4 is 20D38B2C, then

$$\text{CLRB} \quad (R5)$$

will clear the contents of the byte at 000001A4, so that the longword at 000001A4 will now be 20D38B00, while

$$\text{CLRW} \quad (R5)$$

will clear the contents of both bytes at 000001A4 and 000001A5.

Register deferred mode is frequently used when the address of a structure needs to be *calculated*. As a simple example of this, suppose that we have a table of (contiguous) *words* in main memory, which we interpret as an *array* of numbers, and suppose we agree that the *index*—position in the array—will begin at the number 0. That is, the first number in the array has *index 0*, the second has *index 1*, and so on. We wish to write a program segment that allows us to enter, on the keyboard, the index number of an array entry, and which then prints the value of that entry. The segment of Figure 7.4.1 will accomplish this. Although it is quite simple, there are two features that are new and thus require some explanation. The first line of the program segment,

INDEX: .BLKL 1

contains the assembler directive .BLKL (*BLocK of Longwords*), which is similar to the directive .LONG, introduced earlier. However, whereas .LONG requests that the assembler generate a longword having a *specific* value, here we are asking the assembler simply to *set aside* one 4-byte block of memory at this point in the object program, but *without* assigning any particular value to those 4 bytes. The second new feature involves the macroinstruction

$I.4D INDEX

```
;-----------------------------------------------------------;
; Segment to locate and print a table entry, based on       ;
; the entry's index (position) in the table.                ;
;-----------------------------------------------------------;
        .
        .
INDEX:  .BLKL   1                       ;Entry's index (position)
        .
        .
TABLE:  .WORD   1293                    ;The table of word values
        .WORD   -174
        .WORD   1984
        .WORD   0
        .WORD   32105
        .WORD   -16553
        .
        .
        $I.4D   INDEX                   ;Read the index into longword
        MOVL    INDEX,R4               ; and put it in R4
        ADDL    R4,R4                  ;Double the index (since each
                                       ; entry requires 2 bytes)
        ADDL    #TABLE,R4              ;Add the TABLE address
        $O.2D   (R4)                   ;Print the TABLE entry
                                       ; -- R4 now points at it --
        $O.NL                          ; and generate a "new line"
        .
        .
```

Figure 7.4.1

which requests *I*nput (from the keyboard) of a *4*-byte structure (longword), assumed to be in *D*ecimal format, the number so obtained to be placed in the longword labeled INDEX. The input macroinstructions (Appendix D) cannot read keyboard input directly into a register, and that accounts for the next instruction, which moves the number just read into R4. The index is now doubled by means of the ADDL instruction, since this index is the "offset" from the beginning of the table, and each of the table entries requires two bytes. The *address* of the first (that is, index = 0) table entry is now added to c(R4) (the

ADDL   #TABLE,R4

instruction), so we now have R4 *pointing at* the desired table entry—c(R4) is the entry's address. The entry is now printed using

$0.2D   (R4)

Observe that we have *O*utput the *2*-byte structure (word) in *D*ecimal format, whose address is *in* R4. (If we had output the *contents* of R4, that is, if we had used the macroinstruction

$0.4D   R4   or $0.4H   R4

we would have printed the entry's *address* rather than its value.) The reader is encouraged to assign some arbitrary address to TABLE, and hence to each of the TABLE entries, and follow the segment's execution when, say, 3 is read into INDEX.

(c) Mode 8

Name	Autoincrement
Assembler symbol	(Rn)+
Description	The contents of the register is the 32-bit *address* of the operand. Once the operand address has been obtained from the register, the contents of the register is incremented, by 1, 2, 4, 8, or 16, according to whether the operation that references it is a byte, word, longword, quadword, or octaword operation, respectively.
Machine code example	The instruction

INCL   (R10)+

will be assembled as

D6   operation code for "increment longword"
8A   mode byte (mode = 8, register = 10)

and upon execution will increment (by 1) the contents of the longword whose address is in R10, and will increment the contents of R10 by 4.

The autoincrementing of the register contents is called an **instruction side effect**. In general, a **side effect** is some action taken as a result of execution of the instruction which is *not* a direct effect of the operation on the operand or operands. Thus in mode 8, the register contents itself is not the operand (it contains the address of the operand), yet the register contents itself *is* affected by the operation. We shall see a few other examples of side effects later, in fact some in which registers are affected *even though* they are not explicitly mentioned in the instruction. (Since the condition codes N, Z, V, and C are usually affected by instructions, these condition code changes are also, strictly speaking, "side effects," although they are not usually referred to as such.)

We have already encountered several examples of this mode (Figures 5.12.1 and 6.6.2, for instance), and we have seen that its principal use is not only to use the register as a *pointer* to data (as in mode 6), but also to enable that register to "step through memory," that is, easily to process data which are in *consecutive* memory locations. Indeed, this is precisely how this mode has been used in previous examples, and it is how the mode is almost always employed. Although we may already be familiar with its use, there is one matter that must be addressed, and that involves *timing*—just *when* in the course of instruction execution the register's contents is automatically incremented.

When a register is used in mode 8, its contents is accessed by the processor to determine the main memory address of the instruction operand. *At that time*, as soon as its contents has been accessed, the register's contents is updated (by 1, 2, ...), *not* after instruction execution has gone to completion. To see why knowing this is important, consider the instruction

$$\text{CMPB} \quad (\text{R2}) + , (\text{R2})$$

The machine code for this instruction is

91	operation code for "compare byte"
82	mode byte (mode = 8, register = 2)
62	mode byte (mode = 6, register = 2)

Suppose for the sake of definiteness that c(R2) = 000010A5 prior to execution of this instruction. After the operation code 91 has been fetched, the PC will be pointing at the mode byte 82. c(R2) = 000010A5 is obtained by the processor as the address of the first operand and saved in a private register. *At this time* c(R2) is autoincremented to 000010A6. By now the PC is pointing at the mode byte 62, which is fetched by the processor. Because of the mode and register bits, c(R2) = 000010A6 is used as the address of the second byte operand [but note that mode 6 does *not* update c(R2)]. Thus the effect of the instruction is to compare a byte with the byte that immediately succeeds it in main memory. It should be clear that if the autoincrementing took place *after* obtaining both operand addresses, this instruction would compare a byte with itself.

As an example of this important concept, we offer a little program (Figure 7.4.2) that simply counts the number of bytes in an array which are larger than

```
;-----------------------------------------------------------------;
; Calculate the number of bytes in an array of positive ;
; bytes which exceed their immediate successors, using  ;
; an autoincremented data pointer.  (Array ends in a    ;
; 0-byte.)                                              ;
;-----------------------------------------------------------------;

DATA:    .BYTE   24,102,4,10,122,57,64,32,4,0

START:   .WORD   ^M<>            ;(Program entry mask word)
         CLRL    R1              ;Clear counter
         MOVL    #DATA,R2        ;Set data pointer
TEST:    CMPB    (R2)+,(R2)      ;Compare byte with next byte
         BLEQ    TEST            ;Do next if doesn't exceed successor
         TSTB    (R2)            ;Was nonpositive no. just compared?
         BLEQ    PRINT           ;Yes -- print result
         INCL    R1              ;No -- add 1 to counter
         BRB     TEST            ;  and test next pair of bytes

PRINT:   $O.4D   R1              ;Print the counter value
         $O.NL                   ;  and generate a "new line"
         $EXIT                   ;Return to operating system

         .END    START
```

Figure 7.4.2

their immediate successors. We assume that all the bytes in question are *positive*, and thus rather than actually count the number of bytes to be compared, we have followed the bytes in question with a 0 byte, and the program has been designed to stop comparing when it encounters a nonpositive byte in the array of bytes. Notice that 0 is *not* to be considered one of the data entries in the array, so in fact there are 4 bytes that exceed their immediate successors: 102, 122, 64, and 32. The heart of the program is the CMPB instruction at TEST, and it is precisely what was discussed above. The only new feature of the program is the instruction

$$ \text{TSTB} \quad (\text{R2}) $$

which *TeST*s the *B*yte whose address is in R2. The effect of the test is simply to set the condition codes N and Z, according to the value of the structure being tested; the structure itself is unaffected. (What is being checked here is to see if the second operand of the CMPB instruction is nonpositive—the end-of-array indicator.)

We offer one final example of autoincrement mode, which is a variation of the array program segment of Figure 7.4.1 (see Figure 7.4.3). We assume that a block of 36 words, the first of which is labeled ARRAY, is established in main memory, and we suppose that some specific data words have been put in that block. Now the programmer, rather than viewing this block as a *linear* array as in the program segment of Figure 7.4.1, instead considers these 36 numbers to be a *two-dimensional* structure, consisting of six rows of six entries each; that is, the array is a 6 by 6 *matrix*. The program segment of Figure 7.4.3 prints the 36 words in

```
;-------------------------------------------------------;
; Segment to print a 6-by-6 array of words, using an    ;
; autoincremented array pointer.                        ;
;-------------------------------------------------------;
        .
        .
ARRAY:  .BLKW   36                  ;Array of 36 words
        .
        .
        MOVL    #6,R4               ;Set number of rows
        MOVL    #ARRAY,R6           ;Put array address in R6
LOOP1:  MOVL    #6,R5               ;Set number of columns
LOOP2:  $0.2D   (R6)+               ;Print a row entry
        DECL    R5                  ;  and decrement column counter
        BGTR    LOOP2               ;Print next entry if more
                                    ;  in current row
        $0.NL                       ;  else generate "new line"
        DECL    R4                  ;Decrement row counter
        BGTR    LOOP1               ;  and process next row
                                    ;  if more rows in ARRAY
        .
        .
```

Figure 7.4.3

this matrix form, that is, in the form most natural from the programmer's point of view. The reader should have little difficulty in following the logic of the algorithm, consisting of two *nested* loops, the inner loop (LOOP2:) processing the entries in a given row, and the outer loop (LOOP1:) running through the rows themselves. The instruction of present interest to us, of course, is

$$\$0.2D \quad (R6)+$$

the autoincrementing being by 2 since $0.2D processes *word* data, thus moving the pointer R6 thorugh the 36 array entries.

(d) Mode 7

Name	Autodecrement
Assembler symbol	-(Rn)
Description	The contents of the register is decremented, by 1, 2, 4, 8, or 16, according to whether the operation which references it is a byte, word, longword, quadword, or octaword operation, respectively. The (new) contents of the register is *then* used as the address of the operand.
Machine code example	The instruction

$$\text{INCL} \quad -(R10)$$

will be assembled as

D6	operation code for "increment longword"
7A	mode byte (mode = 7, register = 10)

and upon execution will first decrement the contents of R10 by 4, and then increment (by 1) the contents of the longword whose address is currently in R10.

This mode differs from mode 8 (autoincrement) in two respects. First, of course, the contents of the register is decremented rather than incremented. But also, the register contents adjustment takes place *prior to* its use as an operand address, whereas in autoincrement mode, the adjustment takes place *subsequent* to the register contents' use as an address. We sometimes reinforce this important difference by referring to *post*autoincrement and *pre*autodecrement modes. Indeed, the assembler symbolism even emphasizes this, for in the autoincrement case, the "plus sign" *follows* the register notation, while in autodecrement mode, the "minus sign" *precedes* the register designator.

It is clear that both modes have substantially the same uses, with autodecrement mode providing for a pointer (register) to *back up* through a sequence of memory locations. We offer one simple example, a program in which a collection of signed longwords is added. The programming is quite straightforward, but there are a couple of items of interest in Figure 7.4.4. First, we have made no provision to test for integer overflow within the program. Thus we have *enabled* integer overflow trapping by the operating system, for even though we have not bothered to deal with it ourselves (perhaps with a BVS instruction—Branch on

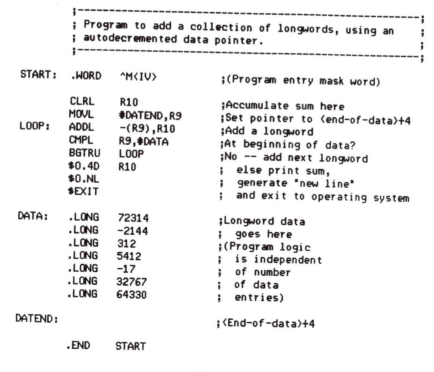

```
;--------------------------------------------------------;
; Program to add a collection of longwords, using an     ;
; autodecremented data pointer.                          ;
;--------------------------------------------------------;

START:  .WORD   ^M<IV>          ;(Program entry mask word)

        CLRL    R10             ;Accumulate sum here
        MOVL    #DATEND,R9      ;Set pointer to <end-of-data>+4
LOOP:   ADDL    -(R9),R10       ;Add a longword
        CMPL    R9,#DATA        ;At beginning of data?
        BGTRU   LOOP            ;No -- add next longword
        $0.4D   R10             ; else print sum,
        $0.NL                   ; generate "new line"
        $EXIT                   ; and exit to operating system

DATA:   .LONG   72314           ;Longword data
        .LONG   -2144           ; goes here
        .LONG   312             ;(Program logic
        .LONG   5412            ; is independent
        .LONG   -17             ; of number
        .LONG   32767           ; of data
        .LONG   64330           ; entries)

DATEND:                         ;<End-of-data>+4

        .END    START
```

Figure 7.4.4

oVerflow *Set*—following the ADDL instruction), in the event that an overflow does occur, we would at least like to know about it. This trap enable is reflected in the "program entry mask word" at START. Second, we have initialized the pointer (R9) to the first longword *beyond* the end of the data longwords. This is because the first autodecrement will back up the pointer to the last data number *prior to* execution of the ADDL instruction. (The reader may find the line labeled DATEND: a bit peculiar, inasmuch as it contains no mnemonics. But a little reflection will reveal that the assembler will simply assign to DATEND the current location counter, and since no code is generated, it will *not* adjust its location counter; it will simply move on to the next line of source program.) Next, observe that there is no "counting" going on here; the "add" loop simply ends when R9 contains the *address* DATA, for by the time c(R9) is equal to the number DATA, the longword at DATA has already been accumulated. Finally, note that the "branch if greater than" instruction following that compare is *unsigned*—BGTRU— since *addresses* are always treated as unsigned numbers.

(e) Mode 9

Name	Autoincrement deferred
Assembler symbol	@(Rn)+
Description	The contents of the register is accessed and used as the (32-bit) address of a memory location *longword*, M. The (32-bit) contents of M is the *address* of the operand. Then the contents of the register is incremented by 4.
Machine code example	The instruction

$$\text{INCB} \quad @(R8)+$$

will be assembled as

96	operation code for "increment byte"
98	mode byte (mode = 9, register = 8)

and upon execution will increment the byte whose address is in the memory location (longword) whose address is in R8. After this address has been calculated, c(R8) will be incremented by 4.

This mode is clearly more complex than those we have seen so far, for the operand is "doubly deferred" (or at a "second level of indirectness," as is sometimes said). The *address* of the operand is *not* c(Rn), but rather is c(c(Rn)). A concrete example will help to clarify the action of this double deferment. Suppose that c(R8) = 000042A8, c(000042A8) = 0020B4A3, and the *byte* whose address is 0020B4A3 has the value 82. Then the instruction

$$\text{INCB} \quad @(R8)+$$

has the following effects (Figure 7.4.5).

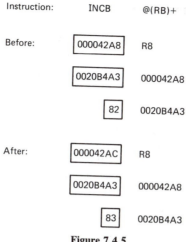

Instruction: INCB   @(RB)+

Before:

000042A8   R8

0020B4A3   000042A8

82   0020B4A3

After:

000042AC   R8

0020B4A3   000042A8

83   0020B4A3

Figure 7.4.5

1. The contents of R8 (000042A8) is used as the address of a memory location.
2. The contents of that memory location (whose address is 000042A8), namely 0020B4A3, is the *address* of the operand, namely, the byte to be incremented.
3. The contents of register 8 is incremented *by 4*, to 000042AC.
4. The byte operand (the 82 at 0020B4A3) is incremented.

To be honest, autoincrement deferred mode is not in constant use in everyday programming, for the register, rather than pointing at the data to be manipulated, points at the *addresses* of those data, and this environment does not frequently arise in a natural way. Thus we must reach a bit for a meaningful example, but the sample program segment offered in Figure 7.4.7, in addition to providing an example of mode 9 register addressing, also introduces another interesting concept. We define a **character string** (or more simply, a **string**) to be a collection of consecutive bytes, each of which contains the ASCII code for a character, the last (highest addressed) of which contains the value 0, the "character" we call NUL (see Appendix C). This character NUL is not usually thought of as being one of the characters in the string, but is rather treated as a **terminator character**. Figure

FIGURE 7.4.6

Contents	Address	Character
56	2049	V
41	204A	A
58	204B	X
2D	204C	-
31	204D	1
31	204E	1
00	204F	NUL

7.4.6 shows how the string of characters

would appear in memory.

Now the reason that a terminating character, of some other scheme, is required is that strings of characters are frequently and naturally of arbitrary length, as opposed to all being of the same fixed length. If *all* strings were, say, exactly nine characters long, there would be no need for the terminator—every string could simply be allocated 9 bytes for its characters. Thus the terminator allows us to create strings of any length and still to know when we have come to the end of a string. This variable-length concept causes special problems when it comes to the storage of strings in main memory, and the subsequent accessing of those strings. In storing a collection of *words*, for example, it is easy to allocate precisely *two* bytes for each of them, and in fact if these are allocated in *consecutive* pairs of memory bytes, we can use autoincrement or autodecrement mode to move easily from one word to the next. Clearly, this simple structure will not carry over to a collection of strings, for they will likely be "spread around" main memory in a rather unstructured way. But *any* string may be located or identified by its *address*—more properly, by the address of its first byte. And addresses *are* uniform structures, since they are all 4 bytes in length. Thus even if a collection of strings cannot be put in consecutive memory locations in a uniform and structured way, their *addresses* can, and this is the approach we take in Figure 7.4.7.

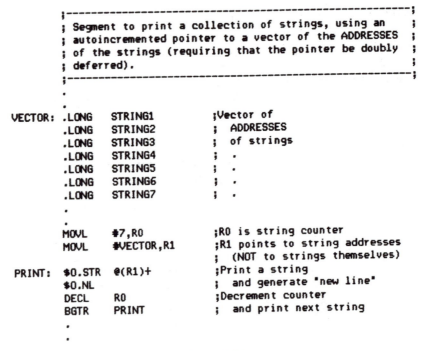

```
;-------------------------------------------------------------;
; Segment to print a collection of strings, using an          ;
; autoincremented pointer to a vector of the ADDRESSES        ;
; of the strings (requiring that the pointer be doubly        ;
; deferred).                                                  ;
;-------------------------------------------------------------;
        .
        .
        .
VECTOR: .LONG   STRING1         ;Vector of
        .LONG   STRING2         ;  ADDRESSES
        .LONG   STRING3         ;  of strings
        .LONG   STRING4         ;  .
        .LONG   STRING5         ;  .
        .LONG   STRING6         ;  .
        .LONG   STRING7         ;  .
        .
        .
        MOVL    #7,R0           ;R0 is string counter
        MOVL    #VECTOR,R1      ;R1 points to string addresses
                                ;  (NOT to strings themselves)
PRINT:  $O.STR  @(R1)+          ;Print a string
        $O.NL                   ;  and generate "new line"
        DECL    R0              ;Decrement counter
        BGTR    PRINT           ;  and print next string
        .
        .
```

Figure 7.4.7

162   VAX Addressing Modes   Chap. 7

For the sake of definiteness we deal with seven strings, which are located (somewhere) in memory. Their *addresses*, STRING1, STRING2, ..., STRING7, are placed in seven *consecutive* longwords, the first of which is labeled VECTOR. The only object of this program segment is to print the strings, using the macroinstruction $0.STR. This macroinstruction requires an *address*, which it takes to be the address of the first string character. $0.STR then prints characters until it encounters the terminating NUL. As with the other output macroinstructions, $0.STR does not end its printing with a carriage return and line feed, so we supply those characters with $0.NL. The feature of interest is that the addresses of the strings are given to $0.STR by means of R1, which is doubly deferred. [For example, c(R1) = VECTOR; c(c(R1)) = STRING1.] The autoincrementing by 4 will ensure that once a string address has been accessed, R1 will then point at the next string address.

The reason for the side effect of this addressing mode—incrementing the register contents by 4, uniformly, regardless of the size of the structure affected by the operation—should now be clear. For the register is evidently pointing at an *address*, and it will point at the *next* address only if it is incremented by 4.

(f) Modes 10, 12, and 14

Name	Displacement
Assembler symbol	D(Rn)
Description	The number D is called the **register displacement**. In mode 10, D is given as a *byte*, and upon execution is sign extended to a longword; in mode 12, D is given as a *word*, and upon execution is sign extended to a longword; in mode 14, D is given as a *longword*. The number D (sign extended to a longword in modes 10 and 12) and the contents of the register Rn are added to form the address of the operand. The contents of the register is unaffected.
Machine code example	The instruction

$$\text{CLRW} \quad 9(\text{R4})$$

will be assembled as

B4	operation code for "clear word"
A4	mode byte (mode = 10, register = 4)
09	displacement D = 9

Upon execution, the number 9 (the displacement) will be sign extended to 00000009 and then added to c(R4). The resulting sum is the address of the word to be cleared. The contents of R4 is unaffected.

Displacement mode affords us the opportunity of "displacing" or "offsetting" the contents of a register *without* affecting that register's contents as the autoincrement and autodecrement modes do. We shall see numerous applications of this mode thoughout the remainder of the text, especially in Chapter 9. In the meantime we offer one simple example, which tidies up a minor annoyance that has been with us for some time. In the principal program of Chapter 6, in which the largest of a collection of unsigned numbers (bytes) was calculated, we correctly and naturally used autoincrement mode to direct a pointer register through the array of numbers. But a problem occurred when we needed to replace the "temporary maximum" because the data number just compared was larger than it—we had already moved the pointer *beyond* the number just compared, and some provision had to be made to back up the pointer, replace the temporary maximum, and then again advance the pointer. Referring to Figure 6.6.2, we find that these adjustments took place at lines 10 and 11, where c(R4) was decremented, and the temporary maximum (R8) was then replaced with an autoincremented MOVB. But with an appropriate displacement mode MOVB, this R4 adjustment is unnecessary, since c(R4) can be *offset* by −1 in order to "reach back to" the number just compared. Figure 7.4.8 shows the few lines of instructions that could be used to replace those of Figure 6.6.2. Notice that the revision not only requires one fewer instruction, but also that it is *clearer* what is taking place—the pointer is being displaced by one data number (byte, in this case), rather than the more obscure "decrement/autoincrement" combination.

As in the example above, we often think of the register that enters into a displacement mode instruction as containing some kind of "base address" which is then adjusted by the displacement. For example, suppose that DATA is the symbolic address 000016E9 and that the number DATA has been put in R7 with, say,

$$MOVL \quad \#DATA,R7$$

Then the instruction

$$ADDW \quad 13(R7),R2$$

will add the contents of the word whose address is 000016F6 [= 0D + c(R7) = 0D + DATA = 0000000D + 000016E9] to the low-order word of R2. The

```
91   000F  7  TEST:  CMPB   (R4)+,R8      ;Compare current byte (NUM)
84   0010
58   0011
     0012  8                              ;  with TEMPMAX
1B   0012  9         BLEQU  NEXT          ;Skip if not bigger than TEMPMAX
04   0013
90   0014 10         MOVB   -1(R4),R8     ;  else replace TEMPMAX
A4   0015
FF   0016
58   0017
D7   0018 11 NEXT:   DECL   R6            ;Decrement COUNTER
56   0019
```

Figure 7

instruction will be assembled as

A0	operation code for "add words"
A7	mode byte (mode = 10, register = 7)
0D	displacement byte
52	mode byte (mode = 5, register = 2)

But another way to view this instruction, which is a different construction but which has the same effect *upon execution*, is the following. We put the number 13 in R7:

$$\text{MOVL} \quad \#13,\text{R7}$$

and then execute the instruction

$$\text{ADDW} \quad \text{DATA(R7),R2}$$

This instruction will add the contents of the word whose address is 000016F6 (= DATA + c(R7) = 000016E9 + 0000000D) to the low-order word of R2, and it will be assembled as

A0	operation code for "add words"
C7	mode byte (mode = 12, register = 7)
16E9	displacement word
52	mode byte (mode = 5, register = 2)

Thus although these are different constructions, there is no substantive difference in their *effects*; any differences really come down to our *interpretations* of register contents and displacements.

An interesting thing has occurred in the assembly of the second version of this ADDW instruction. The assembler has generated a *word* displacement (16E9), and has used mode 12 (C), even though we think of the displacement as a 32-bit *address* (DATA). In fact, in all the preceding examples, the assembler has generated a *byte* displacement and used mode *10* (A). To understand what has taken place in these examples, we need to know how the assembler views such an instruction. When the assembler treats a displacement mode instruction, it will use the *smallest* structure, and generate the corresponding mode, which is large enough to hold the specified displacement. In all but the last example, the displacements (9, −1, and 13) have been small enough to be held in a single byte, and thus the assembler has generated a mode 10 instruction and a byte displacement. In the last example, a word was required to hold the displacement (16E9) and thus it has generated a mode 12 instruction.

Now it is possible that on the assembler's first pass through a program, it will encounter a displacement mode instruction in which the displacement is not known *at that time*. For example, the segment of Figure 7.4.9 shows a construction involving the symbolic value DATA, which is defined *subsequent* to its use. The

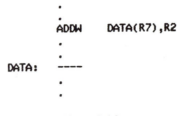

Figure 7.4.9

assembler deals with this as follows. Since it does not yet know the value of the displacement and thus cannot make a judgment as to whether to use a byte, word, or longword displacement, it *assumes* a *word* displacement, and thus it leaves a word in the object code at this point. This word is ultimately filled in on the second pass, as shown in Figure 7.4.10.

This action of the assembler, using a word as the *default* displacement on the first pass if the displacement is not yet known, can have two types of undesirable consequences. First, it may happen that the unknown displacement is not small enough to fit in a 16-bit word. An example is shown in Figure 7.4.11, where the value of the symbol ADDR is 0001290A. On the first pass, since the assembler has not yet encountered the definition of ADDR, it leaves a *word* (at 00000206) to be filled in later, when the value of ADDR presumably will be known, and builds a mode 12 construction. When this construction is again encountered on the *second* pass, the assembler now knows that ADDR = 0001290A, but it cannot fit this into the word that has been set aside for it. Further, the assembler cannot "change its mind" about the displacement size at this point, since much of its subsequent assembly has relied on the location counter values used on the first pass, and these values are determined in part by the fact that a *word* resides at 00000206. Thus the assembler simply *truncates* the value of ADDR, and we see that it has constructed the word 290A at 00000206. Even though we see that this is incorrect, and thus that the object program cannot execute properly, the assembler has given no indication that anything has gone wrong. In fact, it will not be until we study some of the concepts from Chapter 10, in which more details of actual program execution are unveiled, that we will be in a position to understand precisely the consequences of this assembler behavior. In any event, we are aware that not all has gone well here.

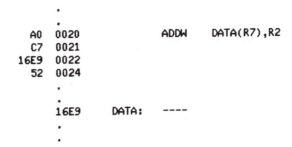

Figure 7.4.10

```
        D4   00000204                   CLRL     ADDR(R6)
        C6   00000205
      290A   00000206
             .
             .
        0001290A         ADDR:  ----
             .
             .
```

Figure 7.4.11

The second problem, which is far less catastrophic than the first, is illustrated by the program segment of Figure 7.4.12. The displacement here is the *difference* PRINT-LOOP, and since neither is defined at the time the assembler reaches this instruction on the first pass, once again it sets aside a word displacement. Now in this case it turns out that the labels LOOP and PRINT are relatively close together, and in fact PRINT-LOOP = (hexadecimal) 23, a displacement small enough to fit in a single byte. Thus it would have been more economical if the assembler had used a mode 10 construction with a byte displacement.

Both of these problems can be eliminated by imposing our will on the assembler, rather than letting it use its best judgment, relative to the matter of displacement sizes. The byte, word, or longword structure is *forced* by preceding the displacement with one of the symbols B (byte), W (word), or L (longword), followed by the circumflex (^). Thus

B^D(Rn)   forces the assembler to use a byte displacement D
W^D(Rn)   forces the assembler to use a word displacement D
L^D(Rn)   forces the assembler to use a longword displacement D

(Observe that the symbols are *followed* by the circumflex, not preceded by it as in the radix and mask indicators ^X, ^B, ^M, etc.) We use these constructions to solve the two problems of Figures 7.4.11 and 7.4.12. The appropriate revisions are shown in Figures 7.4.13 and 7.4.14, respectively.

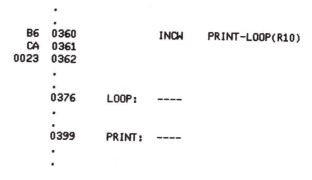

```
        B6   0360                   INCW     PRINT-LOOP(R10)
        CA   0361
      0023   0362
             .
             .
             0376         LOOP:  ----
             .
             0399         PRINT: ----
             .
             .
```

Figure 7.4.12

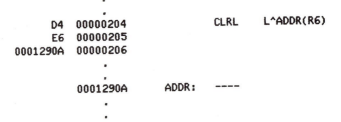

```
        .
        .
    D4  00000204              CLRL      L^ADDR(R6)
    E6  00000205
0001290A  00000206
        .
        .
0001290A          ADDR:   ----
        .
        .
```

Figure 7.4.13

```
        .
        .
    B6  0360                  INCW      B^PRINT-LOOP(R10)
    AA  0361
    23  0362
        .
        .
0375       LOOP:   ----
        .
        .
0398       PRINT:  ----
        .
        .
```

Figure 7.4.14

(g) Modes 11, 13, and 15

Name	Displacement deferred
Assembler symbol	@D(Rn)
Description	The number D is called the **register displacement**. In mode 11, D is given as a *byte*, and upon execution is sign extended to a longword; in mode 13, D is given as a *word*, and upon execution is sign extended to a longword; in mode 15, D is given as a *longword*. The number D (sign extended to a longword in modes 11 and 13) and the contents of the register Rn are added to form the address of a *longword* M. The contents of the longword M is the *address* of the operand. The contents of the register is unaffected.
Machine code example	The instruction

CLRW   @9(R4)

will be assembled as

B4	operation code for "clear word"
B4	mode byte (mode = 11, register = 4)
09	displacement D = 9

Upon execution, the number 9 (the displacement) will be sign extended to 00000009 and then added to c(R4). The resulting sum is the address of a longword, whose contents is the address of the word to be cleared. The contents of R4 is unaffected.

We recognize these modes as additionally deferred versions of the corresponding modes 10, 12, and 14, and they bear conceptually the same relationship to them as @(Rn)+ does to (Rn)+. The statements that were made above concerning the sizes of the displacements generated by the assembler all hold here, and in particular specific displacement sizes can be forced:

@B^D(Rn)	forces the assembler to use a byte displacement D
@W^D(Rn)	forces the assembler to use a word displacement D
@L^D(Rn)	forces the assembler to use a longword displacement D

As with mode 9 (autoincrement deferred), the displacement deferred mode is not used with great frequency in day-to-day programming. We do offer one example in which it is precisely what is needed, and without it some rather more awkward programming would be required. The example also introduces the interesting concept of "dispatch table."

Suppose that in the course of an algorithm we need to branch to one of a collection of segments of instructions, say, SEG1, SEG2, SEG3, ..., the specific segment to be executed dependent on some current circumstances. In particular, we shall assume that at the time the decision is to be made concerning which segment is to be executed, the appropriate segment *number* (1, 2, 3, ...) is in R3. We want to use this value in R3 to "dispatch" to the appropriate segment. In Figure 7.4.15 we have constructed a "dispatch table" of the *addresses* of the segments, and although we have only included three such segments here, it will be evident that there is no real limitation on the number of such instruction segments. The idea of Figure 7.4.15 is to use c(R3) as an offset, to jump *through* the table to the appropriate segment (although in fact the table address DSPTCH will ultimately be used as the offset, or displacement). Now the address of SEGment *1* is $0 [= 0 \cdot 4 = (1-1) \cdot 4]$ bytes from DSPTCH—the beginning of the dispatch table— the address of SEGment *2* is $4 [= 1 \cdot 4 = (2-1) \cdot 4]$ bytes from DSPTCH, and the address of SEGment *3* is $8 [= 2 \cdot 4 = (3-1) \cdot 4]$ bytes from DSPTCH. Thus to find the byte offset from DSPTCH to the desired SEGment address, we must decrement c(R3) by 1 and then multiply the result by 4. (The "multiply by 4" has been treated as two ADDLs, although there are more efficient ways to do this.) Once the correct byte offset has been placed in R3, the instruction

JMP   @DSPTCH(R3)

will add that number to the number (address) DSPTCH, and the result will be used as the *address* of a 32-bit longword which contains the *address* of the operand, the address to which to jump.

```
              .
              .
              .
DSPTCH: .LONG    SEG1                ;Addresses of the
        .LONG    SEG2                ;  programming segments
        .LONG    SEG3                ;   to be "jumped to"
              .
              .
                                     ;SEGment number (1, 2 or 3)
                                     ;  in R3
        DECL     R3                  ;Convert SEGment number to
                                     ;  position array DSPTCH
        ADDL     R3,R3               ;  (by decrementing and
        ADDL     R3,R3               ;  multiplying by 4)
        JMP      @DSPTCH(R3)         ;Jump THROUGH the table
                                     ;   to the requested SEGment
              .
              .
SEG1:   <1st SEG1 instruction>
              .
SEG2:   <1st SEG2 instruction>
              .
SEG3:   <1st SEG3 instruction>
              .
              .
```

Figure 7.4.15

(h) Mode 4

Name   Index

Assembler symbol Base[Rn]

Description   **Base** is any operand specifier which determines the address of a *main memory* location, called the **base address**. The contents of the register Rn, the **index register**, is multiplied by 1, 2, 4, 8, or 16, according to whether the operation that references it is a byte, word, longword, quadword, or octaword operation, respectively. This product is added to the base address, and the result is the address of the operand. The contents of Rn is unaffected by the operation.

Machine code example The instruction

$$\text{INCW} \quad 4(R2)[R7]$$

will be assembled as

B6	operation code for "increment word"
47	mode byte (mode = 4, register = 7)
A2	mode byte (mode = 10, register = 2)
04	byte displacement

Upon execution, the base address will be calculated as follows: The byte displacement (04) will be sign extended to a longword (00000004) and added to c(R2). To this base address is added *twice* the contents of R7 (twice, since the operation is a *word* operation), and the result is used as the address of the operand.

Any of the addressing modes we have discussed so far will do to determine the base address, *except* register mode (mode 5), since this mode does *not* specify a main memory address—it specifies a register.

If an index mode instruction uses Rn as the index register, and the base address is specified by the *same* register Rn in *autoincrement*, *autodecrement*, or *autoincrement deferred* mode, the results will be unpredictable. Thus constructions such as

$$\text{DECB} \quad @(R4)+[R4]$$

should be avoided. However, this is no real hardship, for it is difficult even to contrive examples in which such a construction might be useful. Even a valid instruction such as

$$\text{MOVL} \quad 2(R7)[R7],R5$$

would be useful only in the most bizarre of circumstances.

Index mode is somewhat reminiscent of displacement mode, in that some base address is "displaced" by some number. There are two significant differences, however. First, the base address in index mode may be calculated in an extensive variety of ways, since most addressing modes will produce valid base addresses. Second, the "displacement" (or "offset")—the contents of the index register—is *adjusted* by a factor that is compatible with the datatype context of the operation.

Index mode is implemented by the processor to provide the machine language programmer with a means of managing, in a relatively easy fashion, what in high-level languages are sometimes called **subscripted variables** or **arrays**, in which storage is allocated for an array of variables, all under the same name, and individual variables are referenced by *subscripting* the array name. As a concrete example, consider the following instructions from a FORTRAN program:

$$\text{INTEGER}*4 \text{ LIST}(12)$$

.
.
.

$$\text{LIST}(7) \quad = 69872$$

.
.
.

The statement INTEGER*4 establishes 12 longwords (which in FORTRAN are 4-byte integers) in main memory and labels the first of these LIST. Individual entries in this array of longwords are specified by the name of the array, LIST, followed by the *subscript*, enclosed in parentheses, the subscripting assumed to begin at 1. Thus LIST(7) refers to the seventh longword in the array. At the machine level, this array could be established with

LIST: .BLKL   12

where .BLKL stands for "a *BLocK* of *Longwords*," in this case of length 12. The FORTRAN statement above which puts a value in LIST(7) could be achieved at the machine level by the sequence

```
MOVL   #LIST,R4
MOVL   #6,R8
MOVL   #69872,(R4)[R8]
```

The first instruction puts the address LIST in R4, to be used in the index mode instruction as the base address. The second instruction establishes the value of the index register, R8. (There is a slight annoyance here. In FORTRAN, the subscripting always starts at *1* unless otherwise specified, and thus the first entry in the array is *at* LIST; that is, it is offset from the beginning of the array by 0. This is the reason for putting 6 in R8 rather than 7; the FORTRAN *subscript* will always be one more than the machine level *index*.) Finally, the destination of the MOVL instruction is calculated as follows: The base address is the address (number) in R4, namely LIST. The contents of R8, namely 6, is multiplied by 4, since the operation is a *long*word MOVe. The result, 24, is added to the base address, and consequently the destination of the MOVL is the longword whose address is LIST+24—what we think of as the seventh array entry.

As a more familiar example of indexing through an array, consider again the array of 36 words of Figure 7.4.3, in which a 6 by 6 array is printed. Figure 7.4.16 offers another version, in which an index (R10) is initialized at 0 and then is incremented by 1 within the inner loop. Note that in this version, the base address is c(R6), namely ARRAY, as in the earlier version. But here this base is unchanged throughout the loop, whereas before c(R6) was autoincremented to the end of the array. (We do not claim a preference for either version. In one case the ARRAY pointer steps through the array; in the other case it remains fixed, and an index moves through the array as an offset from the base address. The relative desirability of each of these will depend on the total program environment.)

Thus we see that the principal desirable effect of index mode is to allow us to refer to an entry in an array of numbers of some datatype without having to adjust a pointer (index) to account for the number of bytes in that datatype. This adjustment must be done, but here the task is taken over by the processor.

Because of the large variety of base address modes it is not practical to give examples of all possible versions of index mode. But we shall examine one more in detail, for it will clarify an area of potential confusion. Suppose that c(R1) = 00001A4D, c(00001A52) = 0000407E, and c(R9) = 0000001B. We want to de-

```
;-------------------------------------------------------------;
; Segment to print a 6-by-6 array of words, using a           ;
; register in index mode.  (Compare with Figure 7.4.3.)       ;
;-------------------------------------------------------------;
        .
        .
ARRAY:  .BLKW   36                      ;Array of 36 words

        .
        MOVL    #6,R4                   ;Set number of rows
        MOVL    #ARRAY,R6               ;Put array address in R6
        CLRL    R10                     ;Set index to 0
LOOP1:  MOVL    #6,R5                   ;Set number of columns
LOOP2:  $0.2D   (R6)[R10]               ;Print a row entry,
        INCL    R10                     ;  increment index (by one)
        DECL    R5                      ;  and decrement column counter
        BGTR    LOOP2                   ;Print next entry if more
                                        ;  in current row
        $0.NL                           ;  else generate "new line"
        DECL    R4                      ;Decrement row counter
        BGTR    LOOP1                   ;  and process next row
                                        ;  if more rows in ARRAY
        .
        .
```

Figure 7.4.16

termine the address of the (longword) operand of the instruction

$$\text{DECL} \quad @5(\text{R1})[\text{R9}]$$

That address is calculated as follows.   The contents of R1 (00001A4D) is displaced by 5 (00000005), to obtain 00001A4D + 00000005 = 00001A52.   We next find the contents of 00001A52, namely 0000407E.   It is to *this* address that 4 times c(R9) is added—the addition results in 0000407E + 0000006C = 000040EA.   It is this number that is the address of the longword operand, the 32-bit number to be decremented.   The question that can arise here is: Just *when* is the adjusted index added to the various addresses that entered into calculation of the base address?   The answer, as we have seen, is that the adjusted index is added only *after* the calculation of the base address *has gone to completion.*

Finally, we comment that the base address of an index mode instruction cannot itself be determined by an index mode construction.   Thus an instruction such as

$$\text{CLRW} \quad (\text{R2}) + [\text{R4}][\text{R6}]$$

where (R2)+[R4] is intended to determine the base address, is not valid.

7.5 MODES 0, 1, 2, AND 3: *SHORT LITERAL* MODE

We have now dealt with all addressing modes except 0, 1, 2, and 3, and these are treated in this section.   But, in fact, these modes are *not* general register addressing modes, since they reference no register at all as did the modes of the preceding section. Thus they are something of exceptional cases, implemented for programming economy. Indeed, "they" are really a *single* addressing mode, if the term "mode" even applies here.

One of the most frequent uses for registers is as *counters*, perhaps to control the number of times a loop is executed; and when a register is used as a counter it must first be *initialized* to some value, a value that experience shows is typically in a rather limited range of positive numbers. Thus we often execute instructions such as

MOVL #7,R6

Now this instruction assembles as

56 00000007 8F D0

which requires 7 bytes of code. In a similar fashion we frequently add to or subtract from register contents relatively small numbers, and again an instruction such as

SUBL #3,R9

requires 7 bytes:

59 00000003 8F C2

Of course, it is essential that these operations be *longword* operations if the *numerical* integrity of the value of the 32-bit register contents is to be maintained. The **short literal mode** is implemented to reduce the amount of storage for such instructions to *3* bytes of code, a saving that can be substantial in a large program.

The layout of the short literal "mode" byte is shown in Figure 7.5.1. As we see, bits 7 and 6 are both zero, and thus if the processor interprets this byte as a mode byte, it will see the mode bits as 0000, 0001, 0010, or 0011 (depending on bits 5:4), that is, it will see a mode of 0, 1, 2, or 3. It will then interpret bits 5:0 as a **literal number**, *without a sign bit* (and thus in the range 0 to 63, positive or unsigned), and this literal number will be used as the *operand* for the instruction. (Observe that bits 5:4 are serving double duty; they are the two low-order bits of the mode and the two high-order bits of the literal number.) Thus if

MOVL #7,R6

is assembled as a short literal instruction, its code will be

56 07 D0

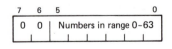

Figure 7.5.1

the "07" representing the byte

$$0\ 0\ 0\ 0\quad 0\ 1\ 1\ 1$$

which, as a mode byte, has "mode" 0. In a similar fashion,

$$ADDL\quad \#39,R6$$

would be assembled as

$$56\quad 27\quad C0$$

the "27" representing the byte

$$0\ 0\ 1\ 0\quad 0\ 1\ 1\ 1$$

which is a "mode" 2 construction. In fact, we saw this construction in Figure 6.6.2, where we commented on the fact that a "short literal" construction had been used by the assembler.

When does the assembler use this mode? The answer is, it uses it whenever an absolute or "literal" positive number (signified by the number sign, #) is specified, *and* whenever that number is small enough to fit in the 6 bits 5:0 of the mode byte. Now we have already commented on the fact that in some cases the assembler may not yet *know* the value of a number (if, for example, it is expressed in terms of symbols that are forward references), and in those cases it "plays it safe" and allocates space for a number of the appropriate size. Consider, for example, the program segment of Figure 7.5.2. When the MOVL instruction is encountered on the first pass, neither DATA nor PRINT is defined, and thus the assembler leaves a 4-byte longword at 000003A4 to accommodate the number to be MOVed. On the second pass, once DATA and PRINT have known values, that number (13) is filled in at this location. Now the programmer may be able to foresee that, in fact, DATA and PRINT are going to be relatively close to one another and that a short literal construction would do. In this event the programmer can *force* the assembler to generate a short literal construction by preceding the number (to be

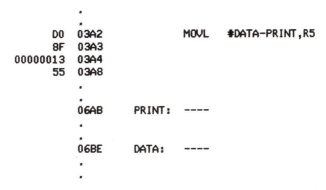

Figure 7.5.2

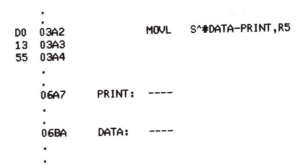

```
   .
   .
DO 03A2              MOVL    S^#DATA-PRINT,R5
13 03A3
55 03A4
   .
   .
   06A7    PRINT:    ----
   .
   .
   06BA    DATA:     ----
   .
   .
```

Figure 7.5.3

MOVed, or whatever) by the symbols S^. This is shown in Figure 7.5.3, and as we see, the assembler has successfully built a short literal construction.

Although the ability to force short literals can achieve savings in encoded bytes, it must be used with some care. For example, in Figure 7.5.4 we show a case in which the programmer has forced a short literal construction, but because of a miscalculation, or because additional code was added at a later time between PRINT and DATA, the difference DATA-PRINT is *not* in the range 0 to 63. In fact, in this case DATA-PRINT = 1A3, and as we see, the assembler has simply *truncated* this down to A3 when it was forced to build the short literal construction. But the situation is even more serious than the assembler's inability to construct the correct short literal. Upon execution, the byte A3 will not even be decoded by the processor as a literal at all—it will be treated as a *displacement* mode construction (mode 10, register 3), and it is clear that we will lose complete control of the program if we attempt to execute it in its present form.

7.6 OPERAND ACCESS MODES: PROGRAM COUNTER ADDRESSING

We stated in Section 7.4 that no use would be made at that time of register 15, since although its behavior relative to those modes was not different from that of the other registers, its special role as the *program counter*, and in particular the

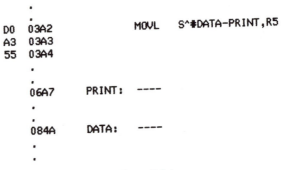

```
   .
   .
DO 03A2              MOVL    S^#DATA-PRINT,R5
A3 03A3
55 03A4
   .
   .
   06A7    PRINT:    ----
   .
   .
   084A    DATA:     ----
   .
   .
```

Figure 7.5.4

fact that its contents is *incremented* when the processor does *fetches* of instruction components, requires that a treatment of its behavior take some extra care. In fact, because of the way in which the processor has been designed, some of the addressing modes we have already discussed for the general registers are not even valid for R15. In particular, modes 0, 1, 2, and 3 (short literals, which are not even register modes at all); mode 4 (index mode—the program counter may not be used as an index register); mode 5 (direct register mode); mode 6 (register deferred mode); and mode 7 (autodecrement mode) are *not valid* for R15, the program counter.

The remaining addressing modes, 8 through 15, *are* valid for R15, although at first thought it is difficult to imagine how they might be used. In fact, our first example (Figure 7.6.1) shows that although a mode 8 instruction which references the PC yields a well-defined effect, the action of the processor in this mode and for this register seems to be so extraordinary as to be all but useless. Consider the instruction

$$\text{CLRW} \quad (\text{PC})+$$

a mode 8 (autoincrement) word instruction that references the PC. This instruction will assemble as shown in Figure 7.6.1, where we have chosen addresses arbitrarily, just for the sake of definiteness. Assuming that c(PC) = 00000B27, the operation code byte B4 will be fetched, and c(PC) will be moved up to 00000B28. Since CLRW requires a mode byte, the byte 8F will be fetched, and again c(PC) will be updated to 00000B29. This mode byte indicates that the register (R15) is *pointing at* (contains the address of) the operand word. But c(PC) = 00000B29, and thus the word at this address is the operand, the word to be cleared. In addition, mode 8 implies the autoincrement side effect, and thus c(PC) is incremented *by 2* (since CLRW is a *word* operation), so now c(PC) = 00000B2B. Thus the word operand is cleared, the CLRW instruction has gone to completion, and the processor is ready to execute the next instruction, with the program counter at 00000B2B, as shown in Figure 7.6.2.

It is unlikely that we would ever want to execute such an instruction, for the clearing of a word that is *directly in the stream of instruction codes* seems useless at best. But what is peculiar here, and a feature of which we may be able to take advantage, is the fact that the *operand itself* is an *instruction component*; in all of our earlier examples, the operand was in a register or a memory location pointed

FIGURE 7.6.1

	Contents	Address	Comment
PC →	B4	0B27	Operation code for "clear word"
	8F	0B28	Mode byte (mode = 8, register = 15) "autoincrement PC" mode
	----	0B29	2-byte word in instruction stream, contents initially unknown
	--	0B2B	Next byte in instruction stream

FIGURE 7.6.2

	Contents	Address	Comment
	B4	0B27	Operation code for "clear word"
	8F	0B28	Mode byte (mode = 8, register = 15) "autoincrement PC" mode
	0000	0B29	2-byte word in instruction stream, contents initially unknown, replaced by 0000 upon execution
PC →	--	0B2B	Next byte in instruction stream

at by a register, the register in turn being an instruction component. The reason this has happened is that the operand was pointed at by the program counter R15, and the program counter by its nature points at instruction components.

Consider the task of adding the (longword) number 12 to the contents of, say, R4. We could of course put a 12 in R6, for example, and then execute

ADDL   R6,R4

but instead, let us attempt to place the number 12 directly into the instruction stream as a numerical operand. Consider the sequence

ADDL   (PC)+,R4
.LONG   12

The assembled version is shown in Figure 7.6.3 (the addresses again chosen arbitrarily), and we shall see that upon execution, things do not go quite as planned. The ADDL code C0 is fetched, c(PC) is moved up to 000017D5, and the processor sees that the operation requires fetching of a mode byte. Thus the byte 8F is fetched and c(PC) is incremented to 000017D6. This mode byte specifies the *source* operand of the ADDL, and it states that the register (R15) is pointing at the longword operand. But R15 is pointing at the longword 00000C54 in locations 000017D6 to 000017D9. Since mode 8 specifies autoincrementing, c(PC) is moved up to 000017DA (the incrementing by 4, since the operation is a longword operation). Thus the source operand is the number 00000C54 (which we did not intend), and the program counter should now be pointing at the mode byte specifier

FIGURE 7.6.3

	Contents	Address	Comment
PC →	C0	17D4	Operation code for "add two longwords"
	8F	17D5	Mode byte (mode = 8, register = 15) "autoincrement PC" mode
	54	17D6	Mode byte (mode = 5, register = 4)
	0000000C	17D7	".LONG 12"—the longword to be added to c(R4)
	--	17DB	Next byte in instruction stream

of the destination operand. Unfortunately, the PC is now pointing at 00 at 000017DA, which the processor will interpret as a short literal, a mode that is meaningless in this environment.

It is clear that the situation has come apart upon execution, and it is also clear just why. The mode byte 54, which was generated by the assembler *before* the longword 0000000C, should be placed *after* it. Although there is no mnemonic that we currently have at our disposal which will generate such a construction, we can build up these bytes ourselves with .BYTE and .LONG constructions:

.BYTE	C0	operation code for ADDL
.BYTE	8F	mode byte, PC autoincrement
.LONG	0000000C	the absolute longword number 12
.BYTE	54	mode byte, R5, register mode

Notice that the assembler will have no translating to do here; it will simply place these bytes and longwords in memory as requested. The "assembled" version is shown in Figure 7.6.4, and a brief analysis will reveal that this sequence *does* have the desired effect. For the byte C0 is fetched and decoded as ADDL. The mode byte 8F is fetched, and c(PC) is moved up to 000017D6. As before, this is a PC autoincrement mode, and thus the first (source) operand is pointed at by the PC. This time, as desired, the operand is the absolute number 0000000C. The autoincrementing moves c(PC) to 000017DA, where 54 is fetched as the destination operand specifier, namely R4. Thus the effect of the sequence of instruction components is to add the longword number 12 to the contents of R4, precisely what we had intended to do.

Any enthusiasm we might have for the ability to place numerical operands directly into the instruction stream must be tempered a bit by the awkwardness of the construction, for it requires that we look up operation codes and mode bytes. It was precisely to eliminate these details that we created the assembler mnemonics in the first place. On the other hand, it should be easy enough to get the assembler to create these constructions, provided we inform it that this is what we want done. This is done with the number sign (#) construction preceding the numerical value of the operand. Thus if the last example had been written mnemonically as

ADDL   #12,R4

the assembler would generate the code shown in Figure 7.6.4.

FIGURE 7.6.4

	Contents	Address	Comment
PC →	C0	17D4	Operation code for "add two longwords"
	8F	17D5	Mode byte (mode = 8, register = 15) "autoincrement PC" mode
	0000000C	17D6	".LONG 12"—the longword to be added to c(R4)
	54	17DA	Mode byte (mode = 5, register = 4)
	--	17DB	Next byte in instruction stream

What we have done here will come as no surprise to the reader, for we have been using this construction for some time. If there is anything new here it is the *explanation* of how the processor deals with this construction upon execution. For the record we state formally the symbolism and name associated with this mode.

(a) Mode 8, program counter addressing

Name	Immediate
Assembler symbol	#N
Description	The number N, as a byte, word, longword, quadword, or octaword (the structure depending on the context of the operation) is the operand.
Machine code example	The instruction

$$\text{CMPB} \quad \#13,(\text{R0})$$

will be assembled as

91	operation code for "compare byte"
8F	mode byte (mode = 8, register = 15)
0D	immediate operand (= 13)
60	mode byte (mode = 6, register = 0)

Upon execution, the byte whose address is in R0 will be subtracted from the number (byte) 0D, and the condition codes N and Z will be set according to the result of the subtraction.

We have already seen that some immediate mode constructions will be treated by the assembler as short literal constructions (see Section 7.5 in particular). Just as it was possible to *force* a short literal construction even though the assembler might not be inclined to use it, it is also possible to force an immediate mode construction, even in those cases where the assembler would default to a short literal. The symbol for a **forced immediate mode** construction is I^, preceding the operand. For example,

$$\text{MOVW} \quad \text{I}^\wedge \#7,\text{R3}$$

will force the assembler to generate the code

B0	operation code for "move word"
8F	mode byte (mode = 8, register = 15)
0007	immediate operand (= 7)
53	mode byte (mode = 5, register = 3)

rather than the short literal construction

B0	operation code for "move word"
07	short literal "mode" byte (operand = 7)
53	mode byte (mode = 5, register = 3)

FIGURE 7.6.5

	Contents	Address	Comment
PC →	B6	E418	Operation code for "increment word"
	43	E419	Mode byte (mode = 4, register = 3)
	8F	E41A	Mode byte (mode = 8, register = 15)
	0042	E41B	Immediate operand (= 42)
	--	E41D	Next byte in instruction stream

Immediate mode may *validly* be used to construct the base address of an index mode instruction; however, it is rarely used to do so. For the base address then becomes the *address*, in the instruction stream, of the immediate operand and has nothing to do with the *value* of that operand. For example, suppose that c(R3) = 7 and we execute the instruction

$$INCW \quad \#^{\wedge}X42[R3]$$

the assembled code for which is shown in Figure 7.6.5. The operation code byte is fetched, and the next byte (43) indicates an index mode instruction, with c(R3) acting as the index. The next mode byte, 8F, specifies that R15, the program counter, *contains the operand address*. But at this point, c(PC) = 0000E41B, so *this* becomes the instruction's base address. It is to *this* address that twice c(R3), namely 0000000E, is added. Thus the operand, the word to be incremented, is the word whose address is 0000E429. Thus, in effect, we have specified the operand by a *program counter offset* in this case, and although this *concept* may be useful, we shall see that there are far easier and more straightforward ways of generating it.

With the insights gained above, we can deal with program counter addressing mode 9—autoincrement deferred—in a more cursory fashion. Thus consider the construction shown in Figure 7.6.6. After the ADDL operation code C0 has been fetched, the mode byte 9F is fetched and c(PC) is moved up to 000040A6. Mode 9 is interpreted as follows: The register (R15 = PC) contains the address of a longword (000040A6) whose longword contents (0001C094) is the *address* of the operand. Thus the source operand for this ADDL instruction is c(0001C094). Since c(PC) has been incremented by 4 (always, in mode 9), the processor fetches

FIGURE 7.6.6

	Contents	Address	Comment
PC →	C0	40A4	Operation code for "add two longwords"
	9F	40A5	Mode byte (mode = 9, register = 15) "autoincrement deferred PC" mode
	0001C094	40A6	This longword is the address of the source operand
	54	40AA	Mode byte (mode = 5, register = 4)
	--	40AB	Next byte in instruction stream

54 as the mode byte specifier of the destination operand. Thus the effect of the instruction is to add to c(R4) the contents of the longword whose address is 0001C094. Since we presently have no symbolism which will indicate to the assembler that we want it to generate this construction, we devise one; we shall use the symbols @#, followed by the address of the operand, to indicate that the assembler is to construct a mode 9 program counter mode byte, followed by the (32-bit) address. (@# seems a reasonable symbol, since it is the *deferred* version of *immediate* mode.)

(b) Mode 9, program counter addressing

Name   Absolute

Assembler symbol   @#A

Description   The number A is the address of the operand.

Machine code example   The instruction

$$\text{CMPB} \quad @\#\hat{}X2047,(R0)$$

will be assembled as

91	operation code for "compare byte"
9F	mode byte (mode = 9, register = 15)
00002047	address of the source operand
60	mode byte (mode = 6, register = 0)

Upon execution, the byte whose address is in R0 will be subtracted from the number (byte) whose address is 00002047, and the condition codes N and Z will be set according to the result of the subtraction.

(In practice, of course, an instruction such as

$$\text{CMPB} \quad @\#\hat{}X2047,(R0)$$

would rarely be used, since the address would normally be given symbolically; thus

$$\text{CMPB} \quad @\#CHAR,(R0)$$

where CHAR = 00002047.)

Absolute mode may be used to determine the base address of an index mode instruction, and it is frequently used to do so. For example,

$$\text{TSTL} \quad @\#ARRAY[R10]$$

tests the longword whose address is ARRAY plus 4 times c(R10).

The displacement modes (10, 12, and 14) are also valid for the program counter, and in fact these are among the most frequently used of all addressing modes. Let us consider an INCW instruction in which the operand is specified as

FIGURE 7.6.7

	Contents	Address	Comment
PC →	B6	4E18	Operation code for "increment word"
	AF	4E19	Mode byte (mode = 10, register = 15)
	72	4E1A	Displacement byte
	--	4E1B	Next byte in instruction stream

being mode 10, R15 (see Figure 7.6.7). After the operation code byte B6 has been fetched, the processor fetches the mode byte AF, and the program counter is now pointing at a *byte* displacement, 72. At this time c(PC) = 00004E1A, and because of the mode (10), the processor must do an additional fetch, to obtain the displacement, which is known to be a single byte. The 72 is fetched, and now we have c(PC) = 00004E1B. The displacement is sign extended to a longword (00000072) and added to the register. But in this case the register that specifies the operand is the program counter. Thus 00000072 is added to the *current* contents of the program counter, namely 00004E1B, to get the *address* of the operand, 00004E8D. Thus the word whose address is 00004E8D is incremented.

What has gone on here is quite straightforward, and if the displacement were specified as a word or longword (modes 12 or 14), the situation would be no more complex. But consider now what is required on the part of the programmer to *construct* such a sequence of code. In particular, suppose that we desire to generate a PC displacement mode MOVL instruction at location 00000109, in which the longword to be moved has address 00009662, and the destination of the MOVL is R1 (see Figure 7.6.8). The code for MOVL is D0, which will evidently reside at 00000109. The next byte (at 0000010A) will denote PC displacement mode, but in order to determine which of the three possible modes to use, we must make some judgment as to the *size* of the structure needed to hold the displacement itself. Since the instruction (and hence the contents of the program counter) is at approximately 00000100, and since the source operand is at 00009662, we see that the displacement is about 9500 or so. Now we might be tempted to conclude that since 9500 will fit in a *word*, a word displacement would do here, using mode CF. However, we must be aware that as a word, a number in the neighborhood of 9500 is *negative*, and upon execution such a displacement would be sign extended to

FIGURE 7.6.8

	Contents	Address	Comment
PC →	D0	0109	Operation code for "move longword"
	EF	010A	Mode byte (mode = 14, register = 15)
	--------	010B	Longword displacement to 00009662
	51	010F	Mode byte (mode = 5, register = 1)
		.	
		.	
	--------	9662	Longword source operand for MOVL

FFFF9500, say. This is certainly not what is intended, since we need to make a reference *forward*, not backward into memory. Thus a longword displacement is required here, so we place the mode byte EF (mode = 14, register = 15) at 0000010A. The displacement longword itself will occupy addresses 0000010B through 0000010E. Finally, the mode byte for the destination, namely 51, will be at 0000010F. (The present situation is shown in Figure 7.6.8.) Finally, to calculate the displacement longword we must anticipate the execution of this instruction. By the time the displacement has been fetched, c(PC) = 0000010F, and thus the desired displacement is 00009662 − 0000010F = 00009553.

Once again it is clear that although this addressing mode *can* be used with the program counter, it is equally clear that we would never use it, for the computational details will infringe upon the logical development of the program structure. However, we should be able to "teach" the assembler to do these computations on demand, provided only that it knows that such a mode is to be used. (We have seen that no information was required in the example above that was not available to the assembler.) We indicate to the assembler that PC displacement mode is to be used, and thus that it is to do the necessary displacement calculations, by specifying the operand address *without* any "punctuation"—#, or @#, or whatever—such as

$$\text{MOVL} \quad \text{˄X9662,R1}$$

or more likely as

$$\text{MOVL} \quad \text{NUMBER,R1}$$

where NUMBER is the symbolic name for the address 00009662.

(c) Modes 10, 12, and 14, program counter addressing

Name	Relative
Assembler symbol	A
Description	The number A is the address of the operand. The assembler calculates the difference between the current c(PC) and A and uses it as a byte, word, or longword displacement in a PC displacement mode operand specifier.
Machine code example	The instruction

$$\text{CMPB} \quad \text{˄X2047,(R0)}$$

will be assembled as

91	operation code for "compare byte"
mF	mode byte (mode = m, register = 15, where m = 10, 12, or 14 according as the displacement is a byte, word, or longword)

VAX Addressing Modes   Chap. 7

dd byte, word, or longword displacement
60   mode byte (mode = 6, register = 0)

Upon execution, the byte whose address is in R0 will be subtracted from the number (byte) whose address is the current PC contents plus the displacement dd (possibly sign extended) and the condition codes N and Z will be set according to the result of the subtraction.

It will come as no surprise that the assembler, in calculating the displacement, will use the smallest structure (byte, word, longword) that can properly hold the displacement. As in the case of general register modes 10, 12, and 14, a specific displacement structure can be *forced* with B^, W^, or L^:

BˆA   forces the assembler to use a byte displacement to A
WˆA   forces the assembler to use a word displacement to A
LˆA   forces the assembler to use a longword displacement to A

In the event that the operand address of a program counter relative instruction is not known on the first pass (for example, is a forward reference), the assembler will allocate a *longword*—4 bytes—for it, to be filled in on the second pass, when presumably the operand address will be known. (The programmer who knows enough about the values of these "unknown" symbols, and thus about the eventual displacement that will have to be calculated, can force this longword allocation down to a word or byte, using the constructions described immediately above.) But as the program segment of Figure 7.6.9 shows, the assembler does something rather peculiar here. The reference to DATA1 has been handled correctly, the assembler having calculated a word displacement of FCF8. But in the case of the reference to DATA2, instead of calculating the correct displacement on the second pass (which in the example should be 00000100), it has placed the *value* 00000542

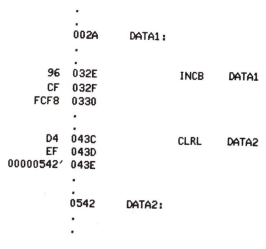

```
              .
              .
        002A     DATA1:
              .
              .
   96   032E              INCB    DATA1
   CF   032F
 FCF8   0330
              .
              .
   D4   043C              CLRL    DATA2
   EF   043D
00000542´ 043E
              .
              .
        0542     DATA2:
              .
              .
```

Figure 7.6.9

of DATA2 in this longword, yet the mode byte (EF) indicates that it has treated it as a program counter *relative* instruction and not a program counter *absolute* instruction. We see that this cannot possibly be correct, and unfortunately we are not presently in a position to clear away all the questions that arise here. At this point the best we can say is that this situation will always arise when the assembler must deal with a symbol that is unknown on the first pass; that by the time the program is *executed*, the correct displacement will have been filled in here (somehow); and that more will be said about the matter in Chapter 10.

Program counter relative expressions can and frequently are used as the base address in index mode instructions. For example,

$$\text{MOVW} \quad \text{ARRAY[R2],ARRAY} + 2\text{[R2]}$$

copies the value of some ARRAY entry into its immediate successor.

We now have two different ways in which the contents of a memory location can be specified by its address: program counter absolute mode and program counter relative mode. Thus either of the instructions

$$\text{TSTW} \quad @\#\text{ADDR} \quad \text{or} \quad \text{TSTW} \quad \text{ADDR}$$

will test the word whose address is ADDR (and set the condition codes N and Z accordingly). In absolute mode the address itself is the operand specifier, whereas in relative mode the operand specifier is the PC displacement to the location. We realize that a bit more effort is required of the assembler and the processor in relative mode, since some trivial arithmetic is required to deal with the displacement. But to the programmer, either mode specifies the operand, and thus the use of one or the other is a toss-up. However, note that in absolute mode, the actual operand *address* appears in the assembled code, and thus this component of the instruction is *sensitive to relocation*, whereas in relative mode, only the PC *displacement* is used in the instruction, and this displacement is *not* sensitive to relocation. Thus relative mode instructions may be relocated with impunity; they are *position independent*. We commented briefly on this concept in Section 6.5; we have more to say about the desirability of position-independent code in Chapter 10.

Modes 11, 13, and 15 are simply deferred versions of modes 10, 12, and 14, so the reader should have little difficulty foreseeing how operand addresses are calculated. In particular, we use the symbol @ to defer the operand one additional step, as in

$$\text{CLRB} \quad @\text{DATA}$$

where the longword at DATA is used as the *address* of the byte to be cleared. But note that in a construction such as @DATA, what the assembler generates is the displacement to DATA, *not* the displacement to the longword whose contents is DATA. That is, the additional deferment takes place *upon execution*, after the address of the longword labeled DATA has been calculated. Thus we see from

```
00000110  0000    VECTOR:  .LONG   BYTE1    ;Array
00000111  0004             .LONG   BYTE2    ;  of byte
00000112  0008             .LONG   BYTE3    ;  addresses
          .
          .
      27  0110    BYTE1:   .BYTE   ^X27
      12  0111    BYTE2:   .BYTE   ^X12
      D7  0112    BYTE3:   .BYTE   -^X29
          .
          .
      97  0335             DECB    @VECTOR+4  ;Decrement c(BYTE2)
      DF  0336
    FCCB  0337
          .
          .
```

Figure 7.6.10

the example of Figure 7.6.10 that the instruction

$$\text{DECB} \quad @\text{VECTOR}+4$$

has been assembled as a *word* displacement (FCCB), hence mode DF, instruction, and the displacement is to VECTOR + 4, *not* to BYTE2 (which is the address *in* VECTOR + 4).

(d) Modes 11, 13, and 15, program counter addressing

Name   Relative deferred

Assembler symbol   @A

Description   The number A is the address of a longword whose contents is the address of the operand. The assembler calculates the difference between the current c(PC) and A and uses it as a byte, word, or longword displacement in a PC displacement deferred mode operand specifier.

Machine code example   The instruction

$$\text{CMPB} \quad @\text{\^{}X2047},(\text{R0})$$

will be assembled as

91	operation code for "compare byte"
mF	mode byte (mode = m, register = 15, where m = 11, 13, or 15 according as the displacement is a byte, word, or longword)
dd	byte, word, or longword displacement
60	mode byte (mode = 6, register = 0)

Upon execution, the byte whose address is in R0 will be subtracted from the number (byte) whose address is in the longword whose address is the current PC contents plus the displacement *dd* (possibly sign extended), and the condition codes N and Z will be set according to the result of the subtraction.

Most of the comments that we have made about program counter relative mode apply equally to program counter relative deferred mode. In particular, byte, word, or longword displacements may be forced with the constructions

@B^A   forces the assembler to use a byte displacement to A
@W^A   forces the assembler to use a word displacement to A
@L^A   forces the assembler to use a longword displacement to A

The peculiar construction generated in the case of an unknown (or forward) reference in which the assembler places the *value* of the symbol rather than the *displacement to* the symbol in the displacement longword, occurs in this mode as well.

Relative deferred mode may be used to generate the base address of an index mode instruction, but some care needs to be exercised here. Consider again the program segment of Figure 7.4.7, in which an array labeled VECTOR contains the addresses of a collection of character strings. Assuming that c(R0) = 3, we might think that the instruction

$$\text{MOVB} \quad @\text{VECTOR}[\text{R0}],\text{R1}$$

would put the first character of the fourth (*not* the third) string, STRING4, into R1. In fact, it puts the *fourth* character of the *first* string into R1, and to see why we must examine the action of the index mode instruction. Recalling that the base address is always calculated to completion *before* it is indexed, we see that the address of the base operand is c(c(VECTOR)), that is, c(STRING1). It is this operand address that is moved up by 3, and thus @VECTOR[R0] contains the address of the fourth byte of STRING1. If what we really want is the first byte of STRING4, we must use a more complex construction. The two instructions

$$\text{MOVL} \quad \text{VECTOR}[\text{R0}],\text{R2}$$
$$\text{MOVB} \quad (\text{R2}),\text{R1}$$

will put the first byte of STRING4 in R1. Notice that the longword indexing of VECTOR (not @VECTOR) has moved us down to STRING4, where we then select the first character.

7.7 SUMMARY OF ADDRESSING MODES

The table of Figure 7.7.1 gives a very brief but compact summary of the general register and program counter addressing modes. The columns show the mode number (in decimal); the symbol for the mode that is recognized by the VAX

FIGURE 7.7.1

Mode	Symbol	Name	Operand	Index base?
		General register addressing		
0–3	S^#N	Short literal	N	
4	b[Rn]	Index	c(b + s·c(Rn))	No
5	Rn	Register	c(Rn)	No
6	(Rn)	Register deferred	c(c(Rn))	No
7	–(Rn)	Autodecrement	{Rn ← c(Rn) – s} c(c(Rn))	Yes
8	(Rn)+	Autoincrement	c(c(Rn)) {Rn ← c(Rn) + s}	?
9	@(Rn)+	Autoincrement deferred	c(c(c(Rn))) {Rn ← c(Rn) + 4}	?
10	B^D(Rn)	Byte displacement	c(c(Rn) + e(D))	?
11	@B^D(Rn)	Byte displacement deferred	c(c(c(Rn) + e(D)))	Yes
12	W^D(Rn)	Word displacement	c(c(Rn) + e(D))	Yes
13	@W^D(Rn)	Word displacement deferred	c(c(c(Rn) + e(D)))	Yes
14	L^D(Rn)	Longword displacement	c(c(Rn) + D)	Yes
15	@L^D(Rn)	Longword displacement deferred	c(c(c(Rn) + D))	Yes
		Program counter addressing		
8	I^#N	Immediate	N	Yes
9	@#A	Absolute	c(A)	Yes
10	B^A	Byte relative	c(A) = c(c(PC) + e(D))	Yes
11	@B^A	Byte relative deferred	c(c(A)) = c(c(c(PC) + e(D)))	Yes
12	W^A	Word relative	c(A) = c(c(PC) + e(D))	Yes
13	@W^A	Word relative deferred	c(c(A)) = c(c(c(PC) + e(D)))	Yes
14	L^A	Longword relative	c(A) = c(c(PC) + D)	Yes
15	@L^A	Longword relative deferred	c(c(A)) = c(c(c(PC) + D))	Yes

Notes:

N	Absolute (literal number)
c(...)	"contents of ..."
b	Index mode base address
s	Operand size, dependent on operation context: s = 1, 2, 4, 8, or 16 according as the operation is a byte, word, longword, quadword, or octaword operation
{...}	Indicates operation side effect
Rn ← ...	"Rn is assigned the value ..."
?	Yes, provided that Rn is not the index register
e(D)	Value of displacement byte or word, sign extended to a longword
A	Memory address

assembler; the mode name; the operand determined by the mode (*not* the operand's location); and whether or not the mode may be used to determine the base address of an index mode instruction.

7.8 EXERCISES

7.4.1. Each of the sequences of machine codes shown below represents a MOVB (90), MOVW (B0), or MOVL (D0) instruction. Assume that prior to the execution of each of these instructions, we have

c(R3) = 0020406A	c(00000208)	= 104327E5
c(R4) = 00000208	c(0000020C)	= 00030EF4
c(R5) = 00000002	c(00030EF4)	= 1072A5A6
	c(00204066)	= 00030EF4
	c(0020406A)	= 0000020A

State what register or memory contents is modified by each of these instructions, and write the instruction's mnemonic form.

(a)	D0	**(b)**	D0	**(c)**	B0	**(d)**	90
	53		54		53		54
	54		53		54		53
(e)	B0	**(f)**	D0	**(g)**	90	**(h)**	D0
	53		84		A4		93
	64		53		02		54
					83		
(i)	B0	**(j)**	D0	**(k)**	B0	**(l)**	D0
	A3		B4		73		A3
	02		04		54		FC
	C4		53		54		
	0004						
(m)	D0	**(n)**	90	**(o)**	90	**(p)**	D0
	D3		E5		A3		C5
	FFFC		0020406A		02		0208
	54		84		84		A3
							00
(q)	90	**(r)**	B0	**(s)**	90	**(t)**	D0
	53		45		45		45
	45		64		93		A4
	64		63		54		FC
							53
(u)	90						
	45						
	B3						
	FC						
	45						
	64						

7.4.2. We have not defined the symbol @(Rn), but show (by submitting such a construction to the VAX assembler) that the assembler will treat this as @0(Rn). In particular, state what machine code the assembler will generate for the instruction

$$\text{CLRW} \quad @(R2)$$

and tell what effect this instruction will have.

7.4.3. The instruction

$$\text{CLRQ} \quad R1$$

will clear (set to zero) the contents of both R1 and R2. State what the instruction

$$\text{MOVQ} \quad R1,R2$$

will do.

7.4.4. Given that the machine codes for MOVB, MOVW, and MOVL are 90, B0, and D0, respectively, and assuming that initially we have

$$
\begin{array}{ll}
c(R0) = 00000001 & c(0002047F) = 0004A2A4 \\
c(R6) = 0002047F & c(0004A2A4) = 1204389B \\
c(R9) = 010A4028 & c(010A4028) = 0EF0137D
\end{array}
$$

write instructions that will have the following effects on the contents of registers or memory locations. (*Note:* The instructions may not be unique.) In each case specify both the mnemonic and machine code form of the instruction.

(a) c(R9)   = 0002047F   (b) c(R9)   = 010A407F
(c) c(R0)   = 00000028   (d) c(R6)   = 000204A4
(e) c(R6)   = 00020413   (f) c(R9)   = 010A389B
(g) c(R9)   = 010A0438   (h) c(010A4028) = 0EF0139B
(i) c(0004A2A4) = 0EF0389B   (j) c(0002047F) = 00F013A4

7.4.5. Show that the decrementing of c(R3) in Figure 7.4.15 is not required if the JMP instruction of that program segment is changed to

$$\text{JMP} \quad @\text{DSPTCH-4(R3)}$$

7.4.6. Rewrite the programming segment of Figure 7.4.15 *without* the use of a displacement deferred mode instruction.

7.4.7. Clearing the low-order word of a register is done with one instruction:

$$\text{CLRW} \quad Rn$$

How can the *high*-order word of a register be cleared (without affecting the low-order word)?

7.4.8. Explain how the low- and high-order words of a register might be *interchanged*.

7.4.9. What is the difference (if any) between the instructions

$$\text{CMPW} \quad (R3)+,(R3) \quad \text{and} \quad \text{CMPW} \quad (R3),2(R3)$$

7.4.10. Show that the program segment of Figure 7.8.1 has the same effect as the segment of Figure 7.4.16.

```
;-----------------------------------------------------------;
; Segment to print a 6-by-6 array of words, using a         ;
; register in index mode.  (Compare with Figure 7.4.16.)    ;
;-----------------------------------------------------------;
                .
                .
ARRAY:  .BLKW    36                  ;Array of 36 words
                .
                .

        MOVL     #ARRAY+<2*36>,R6    ;Put address of
                                     ;  <end of ARRAY>+2 in R6
        MOVL     #-36,R10            ;Set index to -36
LOOP1:  MOVL     #6,R5               ;Set number of columns
LOOP2:  $0.2D    (R6)[R10]           ;Print a row entry,
        INCL     R10                 ;  increment index (by one)
        BEQL     DONE                ;Exit loop if index = 0
        DECL     R5                  ;  else decrement column counter
        BGTR     LOOP2               ;Print next entry if more
                                     ;  in current row
        $0.NL                        ;  else generate "new line"
        BRB      LOOP1               ;  and process next row
DONE:
                .
                .
```

Figure 7.8.1

7.5.1. State what effects the instruction

$$\text{TSTL} \quad (R4)+$$

has. How does this differ from

$$\text{ADDL} \quad \#4,R4$$

What are the effects of

$$\text{TSTx} \quad (R4)+$$

where x = B or W? (This example illustrates an easy way, and one that uses fewer bytes than ADDx, of adding 2 or 4 to the contents of a register.)

7.6.1. Given that the machine code for INCW is B6, and that the first byte of each of the following instructions is at 00001047, state or describe the address of the word which upon execution will be incremented. Assume that c(R5) = 0000002A. In each case, write the mnemonic form of the instruction.

(a)	B6	(b)	B6	(c)	B6	(d)	B6
	AF		BF		AF		CF
	38		38		FF		00FF
(e)	B6	(f)	B6	(g)	B6	(h)	B6
	45		45		45		BF
	AF		DF		BF		00
	38		0038		FF		

7.6.2. What is the difference (if any) between the instructions

$$\text{MOVB} \quad \#5,\text{R3} \quad \text{and} \quad \text{MOVB} \quad \text{S}\hat{}\#5,\text{R3}$$

7.6.3. Explain how the assembler will treat the two instructions

$$\text{MOVL} \quad \#5,\text{R2} \quad \text{and} \quad \text{MOVL} \quad \#-5,\text{R2}$$

7.6.4. What is the difference (if any) between the instructions

$$\text{MOVB} \quad \text{ARRAY[R2],R3} \quad \text{and} \quad \text{MOVB} \quad \text{ARRAY(R2),R3}$$

7.6.5. What is the difference (if any) between the instructions

$$\text{MOVB} \quad @\text{ARRAY[R2],R3} \quad \text{and} \quad \text{MOVB} \quad @\text{ARRAY(R2),R3}$$

7.6.6. Show how, in the program segment of Figure 7.4.1, the manipulation of c(R4) could have been eliminated by the use of the index mode instruction

$$\$0.2D \quad \text{TABLE[R4]}$$

7.6.7. Show that, in the segment of Figure 7.4.3, the outer loop could have been controlled by the statements

$$\text{CMPL} \quad \text{R6,\#ARRAY} + \langle 2*36 \rangle$$
$$\text{BNEQ} \quad \text{LOOP1}$$

rather than being controlled by the counter c(R4). (The expression 2*36 is valid; the angle brackets are used as grouping symbols here, and they are required, since arithmetic operations are performed by the assembler in a left-to-right order, without regard to any hierarchy of the arithmetic operators.)

7.6.8. In the program segment of Figure 7.6.5, why did the assembler not generate a short literal construction for the immediate operand (hexadecimal) 42?

7.6.9. Refer to the program segment of Figure 7.6.9 and
(a) Verify that the displacement word FCF8 to DATA1 is correct.
(b) Verify that the displacement to DATA2 *should* be 00000100, as was stated in the text.

7.6.10. In program counter relative deferred mode, the assembler calculates the displacement to a longword whose contents is the operand address. Why does it not calculate the displacement to the operand itself?

7.6.11. In the example at the end of Section 7.6, we had

$$\text{MOVL} \quad \text{VECTOR[R0],R2}$$
$$\text{MOVB} \quad \text{(R2),R1}$$

Explain why we could, or could not, have used

$$\text{MOVL} \quad \text{VECTOR[R0],R1}$$
$$\text{MOVB} \quad \text{(R1),R1}$$

7.6.12. In Chapter 6 we saw that forward references required that the assembler make two passes through the mnemonic program, the first pass to assign values to the symbols, and the second pass to complete the actual translation. This two-pass construction is not a problem, for the source program typically resides on some high-speed bulk storage device, such as a disk, and thus the accessing of the source file twice is a reasonably rapid affair. However, in the early history of assemblers, such bulk storage devices did not exist, and most systems were card oriented. The following steps were required to assemble a mnemonic program.

1. A deck of cards (consisting perhaps of 1000 or more cards) containing the machine code for the assembler itself was loaded into main memory by means of a card reader.
2. The programmer's source (mnemonic) statements, on cards, were then loaded into the card reader.
3. The assembler (now memory resident) made its first pass on the programmer's card deck.
4. Finally, the programmer's source deck was reloaded so that the assembler could make its second pass.

To reduce the time and effort required to assemble a program, much thought was devoted to the concept of a *one*-pass assembler, one that could produce executable code in a single pass, despite forward references. How might it be possible to design such an assembler? (All the equipment necessary to answer this question is currently at hand, but the solution is far from trivial.)

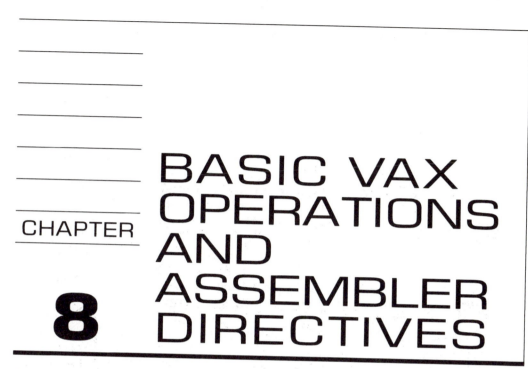

BASIC VAX OPERATIONS AND ASSEMBLER DIRECTIVES

CHAPTER

8

8.1 INTRODUCTION

In the preceding chapters we have introduced a number of VAX operations—MOV, TST, CMP, BNEQ, ADD—on an as-needed basis, and the time has come to make a more organized and formal study of the operations that are implemented by this processor. We shall restrict our discussion for the most part to integer type operations, that is, those operations which manipulate bytes, words, and longwords considered to contain (signed or unsigned) integer data. The VAX also supports a variety of other types, including character (which we have already introduced), strings, packed decimal, and floating point. These and other types and their operations, together with a few "exotic" operations, are discussed in detail in Part III. The full details of all the VAX operations, including their effects on registers and condition codes, are given in Appendix A.

Now there is more to specifying an operation than merely defining what effect it has; for we must also know on what type of data it can operate. As a familiar example of this, consider the "branch with byte displacement" operation introduced in Section 5.8, to which we assigned the mnemonic BRB. An instruction such as

BRB   LOOP

is perfectly meaningful, for the assembler need only calculate the distance from its current location counter to the value LOOP, and assuming that this distance is in the range −128 to +127, insert the byte displacement in the instruction stream after the operation code 11. Thus in this case the only operand that makes sense is the displacement to some *memory* location. In contradistinction to this, consider the mnemonic

BRB   R9

There seems to be no way to assign any meaning to this construction. Now we might argue that if c(R4) = LOOP, an instruction such as

BRB   (R4)

is perfectly meaningful. Although this may be meaningful to *us*, it cannot be so to the assembler, since because of the structure of the instruction itself, the assembler must calculate a *displacement*; and of course the assembler has no knowledge of the contents of R4, which in fact has no well-defined value *at assembly time*. Thus in describing an operation, we must state not only what effect that operation has, but also the form or forms that may be taken by its operands.

As a second and even more illuminating example, consider the operation JMP—*Ju*MP. This operation was also introduced in Section 5.8, where we stated that JMP could transfer control to *any* location in main memory, as opposed to the somewhat restricted BRB and BRW ("*BR*anch with *W*ord displacement"). Thus

JMP   SEGMENT

is a meaningful instruction, and it will be assembled as

17   operation code for "jump"
EF   mode byte (mode = 14, register = 15)
————   longword displacement to SEGMENT

Its effect upon execution is to put the number SEGMENT into the program counter. But unlike BRB or BRW, the equivalent construction

JMP   (R4)

is valid. Similarly,

JMP   @(R8)   and   JMP   @ADDR(R10)

are also valid constructions. Thus in describing this operation, we must specify that the operand is an *address* (the "target" of the jump), and that that address can be specified in a variety of ways. [In the three examples immediately above, those addresses are c(R4), c(c(R8)), and c(ADDR + c(R10)), respectively.] Notice that

JMP

is not a valid construction, since R7 is *not* the address of a memory location, even though its *contents*—referred to by (R7)—may be.

This operation has another interesting feature. When we write the instruction

$$\text{CLRB} \quad (\text{R1})+$$

we expect, upon execution, that c(R1) will be incremented *by 1*, since CLRB is a *byte* operation. Similarly, we anticipate, correctly, that

$$\text{ADDL} \quad (\text{R2})+,(\text{R6})+$$

will autoincrement both c(R2) and c(R6) by 4 when this instruction is executed. But consider the instruction

$$\text{JMP} \quad (\text{R8})+$$

The instruction is valid, and the "target" address will be c(R8), as discussed above. But what effect will the autoincrement have? Unlike CLRB and ADDL, JMP has no *natural* "datatype context" that can act as a guide in answering this question. In fact, JMP has *byte* context, and therefore c(R8) will be incremented by 1. But again, this is information that is required for a complete description of this operation.

8.2 OPERAND DESCRIPTORS

The examples of Section 8.1 illustrate the need for a careful and complete description of the operands on which an operation works, and in this section we describe a notational scheme which presents that information in a very compact way. With some minor variations, the notation used here corresponds to that devised by the Digital Equipment Corporation and described in the *VAX Architecture Handbook*.

The purpose of an operand specifier is to describe *how* an operand is to be accessed, and what the *context* of that operand is. Thus we discovered above that the JMP operation requires that its operand specify an *address*, and that the operand has *byte* context, an important piece of information when considering side effects. To supply this information, we use an **operand descriptor**, a string of characters consisting of three components, namely

$$\langle name\rangle.\langle access\ type\rangle\langle datatype\ context\rangle$$

(where the angle brackets are used here as grouping symbols and are not actually used for a specific descriptor). The three components and their possible values are as follows.

(a) name

The *name* component of a descriptor is quite informal; it is simply any word or abbreviation that is descriptive of the sort of operand involved. Thus names such as *src* ("source"), *dest* ("destination"), *loc* ("location"), *pos* ("position"), and so on, are used to give some indication as to the significance of the operand.

(b) access type

The *access type* component of a descriptor can take on a number of possible values, since as we know, some operands must specify addresses, while others can specify the contents of a memory location or a register, or even a literal number. A branch instruction operand must be a (byte or word) program counter displacement. The possible access type descriptors are the following.

> *r* **read-only.** The operand is a structure (byte, word, etc., depending on the operation's context) whose location is specified by any general register or program counter addressing mode. The operand is read by the processor, but is not written by it.
>
> *w* **written-only.** The operand is a structure (byte, word, etc., depending on the operation's context) whose location is specified by any addressing mode *except* 0, 1, 2, or 3 (short literal) or program counter mode 8 (immediate). The operand is written by the processor, but is not read by it.
>
> *m* **modified.** The operand is a structure (byte, word, etc., depending on the operation's context) whose location is specified by any addressing mode *except* 0, 1, 2, or 3 (short literal) or program counter mode 8 (immediate). The operand is read by the processor, and it *may* be modified and its new value written back to its location.
>
> *b* **branch displacement.** There is no operand reference. Rather, the operand is a program counter displacement, whose size is determined by the operation's context, and whose value is sign extended to a longword upon execution.
>
> *a* **address access.** The operand is the *address* of a structure (byte, word, etc., depending on the operation's context). The operand may be specified by any addressing mode *except* 0, 1, 2, 3 (short literal); general register mode 5 (register); and program counter mode 8 (immediate). Regardless of the operation's context, the operand is always a longword (since it is an address). The context of the address calculation is determined by the operation's context.
>
> *v* **variable bit field.** The operand is one of the following.
>
> > 1. The *address* of a structure (byte, word, etc., depending on the operation's context). The operand may be specified by any addressing mode *except* 0, 1, 2, 3 (short literal); general register mode 5 (register); and program counter mode 8 (immediate). Regardless of the operation's context, the operand is always a longword (since it is an address). The context of the address calculation is determined by the operation's context.
> >
> > 2. The contents of a register, the operand being specified by a general

register mode 5 construction—Rn. The operand is the contents of Rn, or of R[n + 1]'R[n].

(c) datatype context

The *datatype context* component of the descriptor specifies the operation's context and is used to determine side effects, to calculate addresses, and to determine the factor by which register contents are multiplied in index mode instructions. The possible datatype descriptors are the following.

b   byte

w   word

l   longword

q   quadword

o   octaword

x   datatype of the first (or only) operand specified by the operation

y   datatype of the second operand specified by the operation

Some examples are certainly in order here, and for the moment we restrict ourselves to descriptors for a few of the operations with which we are already familiar. The large number of possible combinations of access types and datatype contexts precludes our giving examples of all of these, but by the time we have examined the various operations and operation classes of this chapter, we will have seen instances of most of them.

The operation MOVL has operand descriptor *src.rl,dest.wl*, since the source operand (*src*) is read-only (*r*) and has longword context (*l*), and the destination operand (*dest*) is written-only (*w*) and also has longword context (*l*). Similarly, CLRB has descriptor *dest.wb*, since the operation's destination operand (which is its only operand) is written-only and has byte context. We could now go on to describe the operands for CLRW and CLRL, but it is easier to specify the operand for *all* the CLR operations by *dest.wx*, where *x* is *b,w,* or *l*, according as the operation is CLRB, CLRW, or CLRL.

We describe the operands for ADDL by *add.rl,sum.ml*, and our choice of *names* perhaps requires some explanation. The first operand is named *add,* since it is an *addend* (one of the numbers to be added). That operand is read-only and of longword context. The second operand is also an addend, of course, but recall that in addition it specifies the location where the *sum* is written. It is for this reason that we have named it as we have; and it is of *modify* access type, since it is read by the processor, the first operand is added to it, and the second operand is then *written.* It, too, is of longword datatype context.

CMP (B, W, or L) has operand descriptor *src1.rx,src2.rx*. Notice here that both operands are read-only, since CMP affects neither operand. The conditional branches (BNEQ, for instance) have operand descriptors that might be written as *disp.bb*, where *disp* stands for "displacement." For although *we* might write the operand mnemonically as an address, in fact the assembler generates a *displacement* as the operand component of the branch instruction. And that operand is of *branch* access type and of *byte* datatype. Finally, we can deal with JMP, one of the operations that led us to these descriptors. Its operand can be described by *dest.ab*, for the destination, or "target address" of a jump instruction must be determined by an *address*; and as we have already noted, JMP is of byte context.

8.3 DATA TRANSFER AND CONVERSION OPERATIONS

The VAX implements a variety of operations that move data from one place to another, in some instances converting the datatype of the data in the process. Two additional classes of transfer operations are deferred to Section 8.5, since they more naturally fall into the category of "arithmetic operations," even though they also perform data transfers.

In the descriptions that follow, the symbols x and y are used to represent the first and second operation operands, respectively. The machine code for each operation is shown in parentheses immediately following the operation's mnemonic.

(a) MOVx   MOVe data

There are five forms of the MOVx operation. These are

MOVB (90)   MOVW (B0)   MOVL (D0)   MOVQ (7D)   MOVO (7DFD)

The operand descriptor for MOVx is

$$src.rx, dest.wx$$

As we see, the first or "source" operand is read-only; the second or "destination" operand is written-only. The context of both operands is $x = b, w, l, q,$ or o (although again we caution that not all VAX systems will support octaword operations). Since MOV in various forms has been used throughout the preceding chapters, we offer no further examples here.

(b) MOVAx   *MOVe Address to longword*

There are five forms of the MOVAx operation. They are

MOVAB (9E)   MOVAW (3E)   MOVAL (DE)
MOVAQ (7E)   MOVAO (7EFD)

The operand descriptor for MOVAx is

$$src.ax, dest.wl$$

where $x = b, w, l, q,$ or o. This is the first time we have encountered these operations or anything like them. Their effect is to move the *address* specified by the first operand to the second (longword) operand. Note that the source operand must be of "address access" type, and its context is the same as the context of the operation itself. The destination of the MOVAx is a longword (since a 32-bit address is being moved), and it is written-only.

We have already moved addresses without the benefit of these operations. For example, at line 4 of the program of Figure 6.6.2 we used the instruction

$$\text{MOVL} \quad \text{\#DATA,R4}$$

which had the effect of putting the longword number (address) DATA (00000047) into R4, exactly the result we wanted to achieve. Using the "move address" instruction, this could have been written as

$$\text{MOVAB} \quad \text{DATA,R4}$$

and there are a number of consequences of this construction. First, we note that this could be written equivalently as

$$\text{MOVAB} \quad \text{@\#DATA,R4}$$

and these two versions would be assembled as shown in Figure 8.3.1. (Observe again the apparently "incorrect" program counter displacement in the first of these.) Now recall that in the program of Figure 6.6.2, DATA is intended to be the address of the first of a collection of *bytes*. The operation MOVAB makes this fact far more clear than does the MOVL instruction that we used there, since MOVL gives no hint as to the structure of the underlying data whose address is being manipulated.

But the consequences of MOVAx go far beyond the mere enhancement of program clarity. To see why, consider the following situation. Suppose that we have five contiguous *words* in main memory, the first of which is labeled NUM, and that we have a block of five longwords, the first labeled ADDR. The task we want to accomplish is to put the *address* of the first word in ADDR, the *address* of the second word in ADDR+4, the *address* of the next in ADDR+8, and so on. Finally, suppose that the number NUM is in R0 and that the number ADDR is in R1. Figure 8.3.2 shows a program segment that will do. NUM and ADDR are put in R0 and R1, respectively (using appropriate MOVAx instructions), and on the first pass through the loop the instruction at LOOP, namely

$$\text{MOVAW} \quad (\text{R0})+,(\text{R1})+$$

```
        9E   0005   MOVAB   DATA,R4              9E   0005   MOVAB   @#DATA,R4
        EF   0006                                9F   0006
00000047'  0007                          00000047'  0007
        54   000B                                54   000B
```

Figure 8.3.1

```
NUM:      .WORD    1204
          .WORD    -27753
          .WORD    903
          .WORD    10799
          .WORD    17
NUMEND:
             .
             .
ADDR:     .BLKL    5
             .
             .
          MOVAW    NUM,R0
          MOVAL    ADDR,R1
LOOP:     MOVAW    (R0)+,(R1)+
          CMPL     R0,#NUMEND
          BLSSU    LOOP
             .
             .
```

Figure 8.3.2

will move the *address* contained in R0, namely NUM, to the *longword* whose address ADDR is in R1. In the course of execution of this instruction, c(R0) is autoincremented *by 2* and thus now contains NUM+2, the address of the *second* word; and c(R1) is autoincremented *by 4*, so c(R1) is now ADDR+4. These effects are exactly what is needed for this task.

(c) MOVZxy   *MOVe data with Zero extend*

The three forms of this type of MOV operation are

$$\text{MOVZBW (9B)} \qquad \text{MOVZBL (9A)} \qquad \text{MOVZWL (3C)}$$

and their operand descriptor is

$$src.rx,dest.wy$$

The effect of these operations is to move data of one type (size) to another type, in such a way that the *unsigned* value of the data being moved is preserved. This is achieved by the "zero extend" feature of the operations—unused bits in the destination operand are replaced with 0s. We have already noted, for example, that when the low-order *byte* of a register is MOVed to another register, it is only the low-order byte of the destination that is affected. For example, if c(R4) = 10F42B23 and c(R8) = 012A4075, then after execution of

$$\text{MOVB   R4,R8}$$

we will have c(R8) = 012A4023. On the other hand, after

$$\text{MOVZBL   R4,R8}$$

we will have c(R8) = 00000023. The significance of this result is that the byte has been extended to a longword in such a way that its unsigned value—namely, (decimal) 35—has been preserved, a feature not shared with MOVB. But note that

MOVZBW   R4,R8

will give c(R8) = 012A0023, which preserves the value of the low-order byte of R4 only into the low-order *word* of R8. In a similar fashion, if c(R2) = 00B76A42 and c(R7) = A452EFD1, then

MOVZWL   R2,R7

will result in c(R7) = 00006A42.

Notice that MOVZxy preserves the *unsigned* value of the source operand, not the signed value. As an example, suppose that the byte whose address is NUM contains the number F7. As a byte, and interpreted as a *signed* number, this has value (decimal) -9. After execution of

MOVZBL   NUM,R3

R3 will contain 000000F7, which as a signed longword has value $+247$, not -9.

Finally, observe from the operand descriptor the *contexts* of the source and destination operands. These contexts agree with the sizes of the operands, a most desirable effect when it comes to register autoincrementing and autodecrementing side effects, as well as to index mode instructions.

(d) CVTxy   *ConVerT* data with sign extend or truncation

There are six forms of the "convert" opertion,

CVTBW (99)	CVTBL (98)	CVTWL (32)
CVTWB (33)	CVTLB (F6)	CVTLW (F7)

In each case the operand descriptor is of the form

src.rx,dest.wy

The effect of the operations is the following. The source operand is transferred to the destination. If the source operand is a *smaller* structure than the destination operand (CVTBW, CVTBL, and CVTWL), the excess bits in the destination operand are replaced with the higher-order (sign) bit of the source operand. (This is the sign extend feature.) If the source operand is a *larger* structure than the destination operand (CVTWB, CVTLB, and CVTLW), the excess high-order bits in the source operand are not transferred. (This is the truncation feature.)

When the source operand is a smaller structure than the destination operand, CVTxy is the sign-preserving equivalent of MOVZxy. For instance, if NUM is the address of the byte whose contents is ^X23, then after execution of

CVTBL   NUM,R7

we will have c(R7) = 00000023. But if c(NUM) =9A, this instruction will result in c(R7) = FFFFFF9A, and now the contents of NUM (as a signed byte) and the contents of R7 (as a signed longword) are both decimal −102. Thus CVTBW, CVTBL, and CVTWL preserve the *signed* value of the data being moved.

When the source operand is a larger structure than the destination operand, CVTxy does *not* necessarily preserve the signed value of the source. Consider, for example, c(R1) = FFFFFF7B. The signed value of this register's contents is −133 (in decimal). The instruction

CVTLW   R1,DATA

will result in the (word) contents of DATA being FF7B, which as a signed word also has the value −133. But

CVTLB   R1,DATA

results in the *byte* contents of DATA being 7B (because of the truncation), whose decimal value is +123, not −133.

Finally, we observe that register side effects will be as expected, since each operand has its own context. For example,

CVTLW   (R2)+,−(R6)

will autoincrement c(R2) by 4 and autodecrement c(R6) by 2.

Most of these data transfer operations are unnecessary, in the sense that it is *possible* to achieve their effects with a more limited collection of operations. But they afford the programmer a great deal of power and ease when transferring data from one location to another, and when converting one datatype to another. Finally, we comment that there is no reason why the source and destination operands in any of these instructions need to be *different*. In fact, it may well be desirable for them to be the same. Thus, whereas an instruction such as

MOVB   R3,R3

is well defined but really does nothing of interest,

CVTBL   R3,R3   and   MOVZBL   R3,R3

have the effect of extending the low-order byte of R3 to all 32 bits of R3, in the first case in a signed fashion, and in the second in an unsigned way.

8.4 CONTROL TRANSFER OPERATIONS

A "control transfer operation" is one whose execution affects the contents of the program counter, and thus "transfers processor control" to some location in main memory other than the location following the current instruction. These include, for example, BRB, JMP, and BLSSU. Since most of these instructions have already been discussed in some detail, we shall do little here except to enumerate them. There are a few conditional branch instructions which are mentioned but not discussed in the present section; these are dealt with in Section 8.6.

(a) Unconditional transfer operations

There are three unconditional transfer operations,

$$\text{BRB (11)} \qquad \text{BRW (31)} \qquad \text{JMP (17)}$$

BRB **BR**anch with **B**yte displacement has operand descriptor

$$disp.bb$$

the operation code being followed in the instruction stream by a branch displacement of type *byte*.
BRW **BR**anch with **W**ord displacement has operand descriptor

$$disp.bw$$

the operation code being followed in the instruction stream by a branch displacement of type *word*.
JMP **J**u**MP** has operand descriptor

$$dest.ab$$

Thus the operand is of "address access" type—an *address* specifier—and the context of the operation is *byte*.

(b) Conditiontal transfer operations

The conditional transfer operations, their mnemonics, machine codes, and the conditions on which they branch, are given in Figure 8.4.1. The operand descriptor for the conditional branches is

$$disp.bb$$

FIGURE 8.4.1

Conditional Branch Operations

Operation	Code	Name	Branch condition
BBC	E1	Branch on *Bit Clear*	(See Section 8.6)
BBCC	E5	Branch on *Bit Clear and Clear*	(See Section 8.6)
BBCS	E3	Branch on *Bit Clear and Set*	(See Section 8.6)
BBS	E0	Branch on *Bit Set*	(See Section 8.6)
BBSC	E4	Branch on *Bit Set and Clear*	(See Section 8.6)
BBSS	E2	Branch on *Bit Set and Set*	(See Section 8.6)
BCC	1E	Branch on *Carry Clear*	$C = 0$
BCS	1F	Branch on *Carry Set*	$C = 1$
BEQL	13	Branch on *EQuaL* to zero (signed)	$Z = 1$
BEQLU	13	Branch on *EQuaL* to zero (*Unsigned*)	$Z = 1$
BGEQ	18	Branch on *Greater* than or *EQual* to zero (signed)	$N = 0$
BGEQU	1E	Branch on *Greater* than or *EQual* to zero (*Unsigned*)	$C = 0$
BGTR	14	Branch on *GreaTeR* than zero (signed)	$(N=0)$ AND $(Z=0)$
BGTRU	1A	Branch on *GreaTeR* than zero (*Unsigned*)	$(C=0)$ AND $(Z=0)$
BLBC	E9	Branch on *Low Bit Clear*	(See Section 8.6)
BLBS	E8	Branch on *Low Bit Set*	(See Section 8.6)
BLEQ	15	Branch on *Less* than or *EQual* to zero (signed)	$(N=1)$ OR $(Z=1)$
BLEQU	1B	Branch on *Less* than or *EQual* to zero (*Unsigned*)	$(C=1)$ OR $(Z=1)$
BLSS	19	Branch on *LeSS* than zero (signed)	$N = 1$
BLSSU	1F	Branch on *LeSS* than zero (*Unsigned*)	$C = 1$
BNEQ	12	Branch on *Not EQual* to zero (signed)	$Z = 0$
BNEQU	12	Branch on *Not EQual* to zero (*Unsigned*)	$Z = 0$
BVC	1C	Branch on *oVerflow Clear*	$V = 0$
BVS	1D	Branch on *oVerflow Set*	$V = 1$

8.5 ARITHMETIC OPERATIONS

We have already seen a number of arithmetic operations, including ADDx, CLRx, INCx, and DECx. In this section we look at these in more detail, especially those with which we have not yet dealt, such as the multiply and divide operations. In fact, we shall see that even the familiar ADDx and SUBx are more extensive operations than the reader has been led to believe.

(a) Addxn   ADD operands

There are six addition operations with which we shall concerned, namely those formed by letting x have the values B, W, and L, and letting n take on the values 2 and 3.

$$\text{ADDB} = \text{ADDB2 (80)} \quad \text{ADDW} = \text{ADDW2 (A0)} \quad \text{ADDL} = \text{ADDL2 (C0)}$$

$$\text{ADDB3 (81)} \quad \text{ADDW3 (A1)} \quad \text{ADDL3 (C1)}$$

In their two-operand form (ADDB2, ADDW2, and ADDL2), the operand descriptor is

$$add.rx,sum.mx$$

In their three-operand form (ADDB3, ADDW3, and ADDL3), the operand descriptor is

$$add1.rx,add2.rx,sum.wx$$

In the two-operand form, the first operand (*add*) is added to the second (*sum*), and the result replaces the second operand. In the three-operand form, the first operand (*add1*) is added to the second operand (*add2*) and the result is written into the third operand (*sum*). In either case, all operands have the same datatype context.

We have investigated the addition instructions in such depth—their effects, and the significance of carries and overflows—that it would serve no purpose to repeat those conclusions here. The only matter which does deserve comment is that this is the first time we have seen ADD in its *three*-operand form. (The reader has probably inferred, correctly, that if the "2" or "3" is missing, the assembler assumes the two-operand version, ADDx2.) The reason we have not introduced it earlier is that we quite simply have not needed it, as a review of our programs and program segments to date will reveal. Indeed, since ADD is frequently used to *accumulate* sums, ADDx2 is possibly the more frequently used of the two versions. But the three-operand version can also be quite useful, when it is desired that neither of the two numbers being added be changed. For the record we give one example.

$$\text{ADDW3} \quad \text{DATA-7,(R1)+,ARRAY[R3]}$$

will add c(DATA-7) to c(c(R1)) [and autoincrement c(R1) by 2], the sum being put in the memory word whose address is

$$\text{ARRAY} + 2 \cdot \text{c(R3)}$$

(b) SUBxn   *SUB*tract operands

There are six subtraction operations, namely

$$\text{SUBB} = \text{SUBB2 (82)} \quad \text{SUBW} = \text{SUBW2 (A2)} \quad \text{SUBL} = \text{SUBL2 (C2)}$$
$$\text{SUBB3 (83)} \quad \text{SUBW3 (A3)} \quad \text{SUBL3 (C3)}$$

In their two-operand form (SUBB2, SUBW2, and SUBL2), the operand descriptor is

$$sub.rx, diff.mx$$

In their three-operand form (SUBB3, SUBW3, and SUBL3), the operand descriptor is

$$sub.rx, min.rx, diff.wx$$

In the two-operand form, the first operand (subtrahend) is subtracted from the second, and the difference replaces the second operand. In the three-operand form, the first operand (subtrahend) is subtracted from the second operand (minuend) and the difference is written into the third operand. In either case, all operands have the same datatype context.

As with ADDx, if the subtract operation is used without explicit mention of the number of operands (two or three), the two-operand form is assumed by the assembler.

(c) CLRx   *CLeaR* operand

The *clear* operation may be used with all datatype contexts. Specifically,

CLRB (94)   CLRW (B4)   CLRL (D4)   CLRQ (7C)   CLRO (7CFD)

have operand descriptor given by

$$dest.wx$$

Their effect is to *clear* (set to zero) the operand.

(d) INCx   *INC*rement operand

The *increment* operation is valid for $x = b$, w, and l:

INCB (96)   INCW (B6)   INCL (D6)

The operand descriptor is

$$src.mx$$

since the source operand is *modified*—has 1 added to it—and the result is then written back to that operand.

(e) DECx   *DEC*rement operand

The *decrement* operation is valid for $x = b$, w, and l:

$$\text{DECB (97)} \quad \text{DECW (B7)} \quad \text{DECL (D7)}$$

The operand descriptor is

$$src.mx$$

since the source operand is *modified*—has 1 subtracted from it—and the result is then written back to that operand.

(f) MULxn   *MUL*tiply operands

There are six versions of the *multiply* operation,

$$\text{MULB} = \text{MULB2 (84)} \quad \text{MULW} = \text{MULW2 (A4)} \quad \text{MULL} = \text{MULL2 (C4)}$$
$$\text{MULB3 (85)} \qquad\qquad \text{MULW3 (A5)} \qquad\qquad \text{MULL3 (C5)}$$

In their two-operand form (MULB2, MULW2, and MULL2), the operand descriptor is

$$fact.rx,prod.mx$$

The effect of the operation is the multiplication of the first operand (one of the *factors* in the product) by the second operand (also a factor), the resulting *product* replacing the second operand, which explains why the second operand is of *modify* access type. In the three-operand form (MULB3, MULW3, and MULL3), the operand descriptor is

$$fact1.rx,fact2.rx,prod.wx$$

In this version the first two operands (factors) are multiplied, the product replacing the third operand.

Special care needs to be exercised when multiplying two numbers. For in general, when the n-bit numbers are multiplied, the resulting product will be $2 \cdot n$ bits long. Yet we see that no provision is made by MUL for the product to be a double-length structure—the product is of the same datatype as the factors. For example, if FACT1 and FACT2 are two (memory) bytes which contain the numbers $55 = {}^{\wedge}X37 = {}^{\wedge}B00110111$ and $98 = {}^{\wedge}X62 = {}^{\wedge}B01100010$, respectively, when the instruction

$$\text{MULB3   FACT1,FACT2,PROD}$$

is executed, then the contents of the *byte* labeled PROD will be

$$\text{^B}(00010101)\ 00001110 = \text{^X}(15)0E = \text{^X}0E$$

As we see, the high-order bits of the product are *lost*, and the result left in PROD is arithmetically incorrect.

In this particular case the problem is easily dealt with. For if we simply extend FACT1 and FACT2 to *word* length (perhaps using the CVTBW operation), and if PROD is taken to be a *word*, then FACT1 will contain $55 = \text{^X}0037 = \text{^B}0000000000110111$, FACT2 will contain $98 = \text{^X}0062 = \text{^B}0000000001100010$, and the result of

$$\text{MULW3}\quad \text{FACT1,FACT2,PROD}$$

will be

$$5390 = \text{^X}150E = \text{^B}0001010100001110$$

which *is* correct. In a similar fashion, if the factors to be multiplied are sufficiently large that they need to be held in 16-bit words, extending them to longwords and executing a MULL2 or MULL3 instruction will ensure that carries out of the product longword will not occur. However, this same device cannot be used for the multiplication of numbers of such a size which requires that they be stored in longwords; these cannot be extended to quadwords, since there are no MULQ2 or MULQ3 operations. This problem will nonetheless be dealt with shortly.

Finally, we note that if the multiplication of two structures results in a product that cannot be held in a structure of the same size (because of carries into or out of the high-order bit), the processor will set the PSW V-bit. Thus incorrect results can at least be detected and perhaps dealt with. However, MULxn *clears* the PSW C-bit, *regardless* of whether a carry out of the high-order bit might have occurred. Therefore, the V-bit can be used to determine the correctness of *signed* multiplication, but *unsigned* multiplication has no such convenient indicator. Some suggestions for detecting an incorrect unsigned product are given in the exercises.

(g) EMUL   *Extended MULtiply operation*

The operation EMUL has code 7A and requires *four* operands, whose descriptor is

$$\textit{fact1.rl,fact2,rl,add.rl,prod.wq}$$

The effect of EMUL is the following. The first operand (*fact1*) is multiplied by the second operand (*fact2*) and the result is *double-length*—that is, is saved temporarily as a *quadword*. The third operand (*add*) is sign extended to a quadword and added to the product of the first two operands. This result is then written to the fourth operand (*prod*).

This operation deals with a problem mentioned above, namely, the possibility of overflows occurring when two longwords are multiplied. This special operation, unlike the more simple MULxn, *does* allow for a double-length product, thereby precluding the possibility of overflows. This is the significant difference between EMUL and MULL3. But there is another difference, and at first sight it is peculiar. We are referring of course to the third operand, *add*, which is added into the product of the first two operands. It is difficult to imagine circumstances in which we might want to use this feature, although we shall see one useful case in Section 8.10. More will be said about it when we discuss extended *division* in paragraph (i) below. In the meantime, the reader should be aware that this operand can effectively be "ignored" if it is given the value #0—a literal zero—so that its addition to the product has no effect.

(h) DIVxn   *DIV*ide operands

There are six versions of the *divide* operation,

DIVB = DIVB2 (86)   DIVW = DIVW2 (A6)   DIVL = DIVL2 (C6)
         DIVB3 (87)   DIVW3 (A7)   DIVL3 (C7)

In their two-operand form (DIVB2, DIVW2, and DIVL2), the operand descriptor is

$$divsr.rx, quot.mx$$

The effect of the operation is the division of the second operand by the first, the resulting *quotient* replacing the second operand, which explains why the second operand is of *modify* access type. In the three-operand form (DIVB3, DIVW3, and DIVL3), the operand descriptor is

$$divsr.rx, dvdnd.rx, quot.wx$$

In this version the second operand (the dividend) is divided by the first operand (the divisor), and the resulting quotient replaces the third operand.

Division is performed in such a way that the remainder (which is *lost* in the process) has the same sign as the dividend. Thus the resulting quotient is always *truncated toward 0*. For example, $7/2 = +3$ (with remainder $+1$); $7/(-2) = -3$ (with a remainder $+1$); $(-7)/2 = -3$ (with remainder -1); and $(-7)/(-2) = +3$ (with remainder -1).

Notice that once again the two or three operands that enter into these operations are all of the same datatype. But in the case of division, this does not cause the potential problem that existed for multiplication, since when one n-bit number is divided by another, the result will still fit in n bits. (There is one exception to this: The largest *negative* number—for example, ^X80 as a byte or ^X8000 as a word—when divided by -1 will result in an integer overflow, and the V-bit of the PSW will be set.) In fact, in many cases a $2 \cdot n$-bit structure can

```
;Divisor in R0, dividend in R1, quotient put in R2
;
DIVW3    R0,R1,R2          ;Perform the division
MULW3    R0,R2,R3          ;Multiply divisor by quotient
SUBW3    R3,R1,R3          ; and subtract result from dividend
                          ;Remainder is in R3
```

Figure 8.5.1

successfully be divided by an *n*-bit structure without the division resulting in an overflow.

If the reader is concerned that the remainder is lost in the course of a division, we supply in Figure 8.5.1 a little segment of code which recaptures the remainder in the case of *word* division. But observe that DIVW2 *cannot* be used here, since that operation destroys the dividend.

(i) EDIV   *Extended DIVision operation*

EDIV has operation code 7B and requires *four* operands, whose descriptor is

$$divsr.rl, dvdnd.rq, quot.wl, rem.wl$$

The effect of EDIV is the following. The second operand (*dvdnd*), as a *quadword*, is divided by the first operand (*divsr*), as a *longword*. The results are a longword quotient (*quot*) and a longword remainder (*rem*).

This operation speaks to two of the comments mentioned above. First, it allows for the dividend being a double-length structure relative to the divisor, although in providing this facility we reintroduce the possibility of overflows. Second, EDIV does *not* lose the remainder—it is captured in the fourth (longword) operand. As with DIVxn, the remainder has the same sign as the dividend (*dvdnd*) operand.

Finally, we offer some justification for a peculiarity of EMUL, namely, the "extra" operand *add.rl* in that operation. EDIV in effect performs the following operation:

$$\langle dvdnd \rangle / \langle divsr \rangle = \langle quot \rangle + \langle rem \rangle / \langle divsr \rangle$$

But this is equivalent to

$$\langle divsr \rangle * \langle quot \rangle + \langle rem \rangle = \langle dvdnd \rangle$$

and this is *precisely* the effect of EMUL, even down to the *sizes* of the operands. Thus in this sense EMUL and EDIV are truly inverse operations.

(j) MNEGx   *Move NEGated data*

MNEG has three forms,

MNEGB (8E)   MNEGW (AE)   MNEGL (CE)

each of which has two operands with descriptor

$$src.rx,dest.wx$$

The effect of MNEGx is to *negate* (that is, twos-complement) the first (source) operand and to write the result to the second (destination) operand. The first operand is unaffected by the operation.

There is little to say about this operation, except to comment that we frequently want to negate a number "where it stands," that is, without moving it somewhere else. In this case, we can simply make the destination operand the same as the source; for example,

MNEGW   R2,R2

will negate the low-order word of R2 (without affecting the high-order word of R2).

(k) MCOMx   *Move COMplemented data*

The operation MCOM has three forms,

MCOMB (92)   MCOMW (B2)   MCOML (D2)

each of which has two operands with descriptor

$$src.rx,dest.wx$$

The effect of MCOMx is to *complement* (that is, ones-complement) the first (source) operand and to write the result to the second (destination) operand. The first operand is unaffected by the operation.

As with MNEGx, MCOMx may be used to complement a number without moving the complemented result, by specifying the destination operand to be the same as the source operand.

(1) ADWC   *ADd operands With Carry*

The machine code for ADWC is D8, and its operand descriptor is

$$add.rl,sum.ml$$

The effect of ADWC is to add the first operand (*add*) to the second operand (*sum*), then to add to that result the current contents (0 or 1) of the *carry* bit C, and to place the result back in the second operand.

This operation is implemented for the purpose of performing certain **double-precision** operations. As an example, assume that QUAD1 and QUAD2 are the symbolic addresses of two quadwords, and suppose we wish to *add* c(QUAD1) to c(QUAD2). Now the VAX does not implement a quadword add (ADDQ), but we can achieve the same effect by adding the two quadwords one longword at a time. In particular, the sequence of instructions

$$\text{ADDL} \quad \text{QUAD1,QUAD2}$$
$$\text{ADWC} \quad \text{QUAD1}+4,\text{QUAD2}+4$$

will do the desired double-precision addition. The first of these adds the low-order longwords of the two quadwords, the addition possibly resulting in a carry which should then carry into the high-order longword of the result. That carry (which may be 0) is taken into account by the ADWC operation, which not only adds the high-order longwords of the quadwords, but also adds in any carry that may have occurred as a result of the first addition.

(m) SBWC *SuBtract operands With Carry*

The machine code for SBWC is D9, and its operand descriptor is

$$sub.rl,diff.ml$$

The effect of SBWC is to subtract the first operand (the subtrahend *sub*) from the second operand (*diff*), then to subtract from that result the current contents (0 or 1) of the *carry* bit C, and to place the result back in the second operand. As with ADWC, SBWC is implemented for the purpose of extended precision arithmetic, the details of which are left to the exercises.

8.6 BIT OPERATIONS

One of the tasks that can be done at a machine level with considerably more ease than in most high-level languages is the manipulation of the individual *bits* of a data structure. A bit of a word, for example, can be examined to see whether it is a 0 or 1; various bits of a byte can be set or cleared; structures can be ANDed and ORed; the bits of a longword can be shifted right or left; and so on. In this section we describe the bit operations implemented by the VAX processor.

(a) BISxn *BIt Set*

The operation BIS has six forms,

BISB = BISB2 (88)	BISW = BISW2 (A8)	BISL = BISL2 (C8)
BISB3 (89)	BISW3 (A9)	BISL3 (C9)

In their two-operand form, their operand descriptor is

$$mask.rx,dest.mx$$

The effect of the operation is to perform a logical OR of the corresponding bits of the first operand (the *mask* operand) and the second operand (*dest*), the result replacing the second operand. (The logical OR of two bits is defined by: 1 + 1 = 1; 1 + 0 = 1; 0 + 1 = 1; 0 + 0 = 0.) In their three-operand form, their operand descriptor is

mask.rx,src.rx,dest.wx

The effect of the operation is to perform a logical OR of the corresponding bits of the first operand (the *mask* operand) and the second operand (the *src* operand), the result replacing the third operand (*dest*). (We have used the word "mask" here in the same sense as in Section 6.7, where the term was used in describing "program entry mask words.")

The effect of BISxn can be stated as follows. Any bit in the mask which is *on* will result in that same bit in the destination being turned *on*. Bits in the mask which are *off* leave the corresponding bits in the destination unaffected.

As a simple example, we note that the *OR* of the two bytes 10110001 and 00111010 is 10111011. As an application, suppose that we want to "turn on" bits 12, 5, 4, and 0 of the low-order word of R2. We can do this simply with the instruction

BISW2   #ˆB0001000000110001,R2   or   BISW   #ˆX1031,R2

Similarly, if the byte whose address is NUMBR contains an 8-bit number between 0 and 9, we can generate the ASCII code for the corresponding numerical character and place that code in the byte labeled ACODE with the instruction

BISB3   #ˆX30,NUMBR,ACODE

(b) BICxn   *BIt Clear*

The operation BIC has six forms,

BICB = BICB2 (8A)   BICW = BICW2 (AA)   BICL = BICL2 (CA)
        BICB3 (8B)   BICW3 (AB)   BICL3 (CB)

In their two-operand form, their operand descriptor is

mask.rx,dest.mx

The effect of the operation is to perform a logical AND of the corresponding bits of the *ones-complement* of the first operand (the *mask* operand) and the bits of the second operand (*dest*), the result replacing the second operand. (The logical AND of two bits is defined by: $1 \cdot 1 = 1$; $1 \cdot 0 = 0$; $0 \cdot 1 = 0$; $0 \cdot 0 = 0$.) In the three-operand form, their operand descriptor is

$$mask.rx,src.rx,dest.wx$$

The effect of the operation is to perform a logical AND of the corresponding bits of the *ones-complement* of the first operand (the *mask* operand) and the bits of the second operand (the *src* operand), the result replacing the third operand (*dest*).

It is important to understand that the *first* operand is *complemented* before the ANDing takes place. Thus, if we let the symbol ' represent ones-complement, the action of BICx2 can be described by ⟨*mask*⟩' AND ⟨*dest*⟩, and that of BICx3 by ⟨*mask*⟩' AND ⟨*src*⟩. Note that in the case of BISxn, the operation is *commutative* with respect to the two operands, since A OR B is the same as B OR A (where A and B are structures of the same type). But in the case of BICxn, A' AND B is *not* the same as B' AND A, and thus BISxn is *not* a commutative operation. Another way of describing BICx2 is to say that the operation *turns off* any bit in the destination operand which is *on* in the mask operand. BICx3 may be described by saying that the second (source) operand is first copied to the destination operand, and then any bit that is *on* in the mask operand is turned *off* in the destination operand. In both cases, bits that are *off* in the mask operand leave the corresponding bits in the destination operand unaffected.

As an example, suppose that we have

$$c(R0) = F02755E2 = \text{^B}1111000000100111010101011111100010$$
$$c(R2) = 592A71B4 = \text{^B}01011001001010100111000110110100$$

Then

$$c(R0)' = F02755E2' = 0FD8AA1D$$
$$= \text{^B}00001111110110001010101000011101$$

so the instruction

$$\text{BICL3} \quad \text{R0,R2,R7}$$

will result in

$$c(R7) = 09082014 = \text{^B}00001001000010000010000000010100$$

with c(R0) and c(R2) unaffected.

As a second example, suppose we want to ensure that the high-order word of the longword whose address is DATA consists of 0s. The instruction CLRW

DATA + 2 would do, of course, but consider instead

$$\text{BICL} \quad \#\char"5E XFFFF0000,DATA$$

The significance of this construction is that it can be used to clear the high-order word of a *register*, a word that is *not* addressable as DATA + 2 is; for example,

$$\text{BICL} \quad \#\char"5E XFFFF0000,R10$$

(c) XORxn   eXclusive-OR

The operation XOR has six forms,

XORB = XORB2 (8C)   XORW = XORW2 (AC)   XORL = XORL2 (CC)
     XORB3 (8D)   XORW3 (AD)   XORL3 (CD)

In their two-operand form, their operand descriptor is

$$mask.rx,dest.mx$$

The effect of the operation is to perform a logical EXCLUSIVE-OR of the corresponding bits of the first operand (the *mask* operand) and the second operand (*dest*), the result replacing the second operand. (The logical EXCLUSIVE-OR of two bits is defined by: $1 \oplus 1 = 0; 1 \oplus 0 = 1; 0 \oplus 1 = 1; 0 \oplus 0 = 0$.) In their three-operand form, their operand descriptor is

$$mask.rx,src.rx,dest.wx$$

The effect of the operation is to perform a logical EXCLUSIVE-OR of the corresponding bits of the first operand (the *mask* operand) and the second operand (the *src* operand), the result replacing the third operand (*dest*).

 As an example, suppose that $c(R3) = 000012A4$, the word whose address is 000012A4 contains C525, and $c(R6) = B62A59E8$. Then the instruction

$$\text{XORW2} \quad (R3)+,R6$$

results in the EXCLUSIVE-ORing of the words

$$c(000012A4) = \char"5E B \qquad\qquad 1100010100100101$$
$$c(R6) = \char"5E B1011011000101010010101100111101000$$

so that upon execution, we will have

$$c(R6) = B62A9CCD = \char"5E B1011011000101010101001110011001101$$

(d) BISPSW   *BIt Set PSW*
BICPSW   *BIt Clear PSW*

The operation codes for these instructions are

$$\text{BISPSW (B8)} \qquad \text{BICPSW (B9)}$$

and their operand descriptor is

mask.rw

The effect of BISPSW is to *set* any bit in the PSW for which the corresponding bit in the mask is *on*. The effect of BICPSW is to *clear* any bit in the PSW for which the corresponding bit in the mask is *on*. In either operation, bits that are *off* in the mask leave the corresponding bits in the PSW unaffected. Despite the fact that the context of the mask is *word* (*w*), the assembler generates a *byte* mask; thus only bits 7:0 of the PSW can be affected by BICPSW and BISPSW.

These operations allow for the setting or clearing of the condition codes (bits 3:0) of the PSW, although it is by no means clear at this time why we might want to do so. Similarly, the "trap enable" bits (7:4) can also be set or cleared, although this would normally be done at the "program entry mask word," where it can be done more conveniently. We shall see an example in Chapter 9 in which it is useful to manipulate these bits, but in fact this is rarely done. For now we have included these operations here simply because they are bit-manipulating operations.

(e) ASHx   *Arithmetic SHift*

There are two forms of the *arithmetic shift* operation,

$$\text{ASHL (78)} \qquad \text{ASHQ (79)}$$

and each has the operand descriptor

count.rb,src.rx,dest.wx

The effects of ASHL and ASHQ are to *shift* the bits of the *src* operand a number of places left or right, according to the contents of the *count* operand, and place the resulting shifted structure in the *dest* operand.

To see what takes place during the "shift," consider the effect of a "left shift by 1" as shown in Figure 8.6.1(a). The high-order bit of the structure (longword or quadword) is shifted out and lost; the next-lower-order bit is shifted into the high-order bit; ...; bit 2 is shifted into bit 3; bit 1 is shifted into bit 2; bit 0 is shifted into bit 1; and finally, a 0 is shifted into the vacated bit 0. On a "right shift by 1" [Figure 8.6.1(b)], bit 0 is shifted out and lost; bit 1 is shifted into bit 0; ...; the high-order bit is shifted into the next-lower-order bit; and finally, the high-order bit is *replicated*—is copied into itself. (This last action does *not* correspond

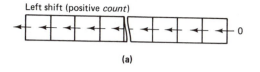

(a)

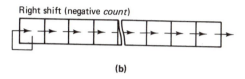

(b)

Figure 8.6.1

to the equivalent action at bit 0 on a left shift; that is, the high-order bit is *not* filled in with a 0.)

As an example, consider the longword ˆX9A248B73, whose value in binary is

ˆB10011010000100100100010110110011

The result of a left shift on this longword is

ˆB00110100001001001000101101110011 0 = ˆX344916E6

The effect of a right shift is

ˆB11001101000100100100010110111001 = ˆXCD1245B9

A *repeated* shift is simply a right or left shift by 1 repeated a number of times. Thus a "left shift by 5" is a left shift, followed by a left shift of the result, and so on, five times. If the value of the *count* operand is *positive*, the shift is a *left* shift repeated *count* times; if the value of *count* is *negative*, the shift is a *right* shift repeated −*count* times. Suppose, for example, that c(R6) = ˆX729A42ED. Then the instruction

ASHL   #5,R6,R1

will result in c(R1) = ˆX53485DA0, as the reader should verify. Similarly,

ASHL   #−3,R6,R1

will yield c(R1) = ˆX0E53485D.

It should be clear that if a longword (quadword) is shifted *left* 32 (64) times or more, the resulting longword (quadword) will be filled with 0s. If a longword (quadword) is shifted *right* 31 (63) times or more, the resulting longword (quadword) will be filled with 1s or 0s, according to whether the high-order bit of the *src* operated is 1 or 0, respectively.

If a register Rn is operated on by ASHQ, the 64-bit quadword that is shifted is $R[n+1]'R[n]$, the concatenation of $R[n+1]$ with $R[n]$.

The two examples of ASHx we have given so far specify the *count* operand as a literal—#5 and #−3—although there is no reason why this operand cannot be specified as a register or memory location contents. Thus

$$\text{ASHQ} \quad (R4)+,\text{DATA},\text{DATA}$$

will shift the quadword contents of DATA right or left according to the contents of the *byte* whose address is in R4, c(R4) will be autoincremented *by 1*, and the resulting shifted quadword will be put back in the quadword at DATA. The reason for the shift count being taken as the contents of the *byte* pointed at by R4 and for c(R4) being incremented by 1 is that the operand *count* has a *byte* datatype context.

One of the consequences of the left and right shift operations is that they perform multiplications and divisions by powers of 2. To see this, suppose that

$$c(R3) = 9 = \text{^B0000000000000000000000000001001}$$

and we execute

$$\text{ASHL} \quad \#3,R3,R3$$

The resulting contents of R3 will be

$$c(R3) = 72 = \text{^B0000000000000000000000001001000}$$

which is $9 \cdot 8 = 9 \cdot 2^3$. In a similar fashion, a right shift of c(R3) by 2 will result in $c(R3) = 9.2^{-2} = 9/2^2 = 9/4 = 2$, the remainder (1) having been shifted out and lost. Because of the fact that the sign bit is replicated on right shifts, these shifts properly preserve the signed values when numbers are divided by powers of 2.

When ASHx is used to perform signed multiplication by a power of 2, there is one potential problem which deserves mention. Consider a longword that contains the number ^X59332AD4, shifted left by 2. As we see, the original number is positive, and the resulting shifted longword is also positive, namely ^X64CCAB50. This *should* be $4 = 2^2$ times the original value, but it is not. The problem is that in the course of the shifting, there has been an *overflow* into the high-order bit. For the *first* left shift by 1 resulted in ^XB26655AB, which we see is *negative*. The second shift reset the high-order bit back to 0. But this situation has not gone unnoticed by the processor, for if in the course of shifting a longword or quadword *left* by some shift count, the high-order bit ever takes on a value different from the high-order bit of the *src* operand, the PSW V-bit will be set.

We can now use this instruction to clean up the program segment of Figure 7.4.15. Recall that is was necessary to multiply the contents of R3 by 4, and at that time we dealt with the multiplication by means of a construction which at best was inelegant:

$$ADDL \quad R3,R3$$

$$ADDL \quad R3,R3$$

It is now clear that we could use

$$MULL \quad \#4,R3$$

or the even more efficient (from a processor standpoint)

$$ASHL \quad \#2,R3,R3$$

(f) ROTL   *ROTate Longword*

The operation ROTL has code 9C and operand descriptor

$$count.rb, scr.rl, dest.wl$$

The effect of ROTL is to *rotate* the longword source (*src*) by the number of bits specified by the *count* operand, left if the count value is positive and right if it is negative, and to place the resulting rotated longword in the destination operand (*dest*).

A left rotate by 1 is shown in Figure 8.6.2(a). Each bit is replaced by the next-lower-order bit; the high-order bit (bit 31) is shifted out of the longword and replaces the vacated bit 0. A left rotate by *n* simply repeats this action *n* times. In a similar fashion, a right rotate by 1 is shown in Figure 8.6.2(b). Each bit is replaced by the next-higher-order bit; the low-order bit (bit 0) is shifted out of the longword and replaces the vacated bit 31. A right rotate by *n* simply repeats this action *n* times.

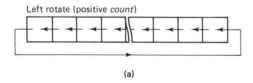

(a)

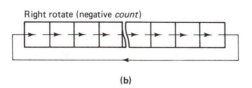

(b)

Figure 8.6.2

(g) BITx *Bit Test operand*

The operation codes for these instructions are

$$\text{BITB (93)} \qquad \text{BITW (B3)} \qquad \text{BITL (D3)}$$

and their operand descriptor is

$$mask.rx,src.rx$$

The effect is to calculate the bit-by-bit ANDing of the first (*mask*) and second (*src*) operands and then to set the condition codes N and Z according to the result. Both operands are unaffected (are read-only).

As an example, suppose that

$$c(R9) = {}^{\wedge}X804A731D = {}^{\wedge}B10000000010010100111001100011101$$

and that DATA is the address of a *word*:

$$c(DATA) = {}^{\wedge}XB2A5 = {}^{\wedge}B1011001010100101$$

The result of ANDing the low-order word of R9 and the word at DATA is

$${}^{\wedge}X3205 = {}^{\wedge}B0011001000000101$$

Since this number is neither negative nor zero, the result of the instruction

$$\text{BITW} \quad \text{R9,DATA}$$

would be to clear both N and Z.

As an application of this instruction, suppose we wish to know whether bit 4 of the byte whose address is ADDR is set or clear. The instruction

$$\text{BITB} \quad \#{}^{\wedge}\text{B00010000,ADDR}$$

will AND with c(ADDR) the byte that has only bit 4 set; if the result of this instruction is *zero*, then evidently c(ADDR) has bit 4 clear; if the result is nonzero, bit 4 of c(ADDR) must be set. It should be clear that BITx can be used to test any collection of bits of a structure to see if they are *all* clear, or if *at least one* of them is set.

(h) BLBC *Branch on Low-order Bit Clear*
BLBS *Branch on Low-order Bit Set*

The operation codes for these instructions are

$$\text{BLBC (E9)} \qquad \text{BLBS (EB)}$$

and their operand descriptor is

$$src.rl,disp.bb$$

The effect of the instruction is to branch if the low-order bit of the source longword (*src*) is *clear* (BLBC) or *set* (BLBS), in either case the target of the branch being calculated by sign extending the displacement (*disp*) operand and adding the result to the current contents of the program counter (as in any conditional branch). Notice that the source operand has *longword* context, even though only its low-order bit (bit 0) is tested.

In fact, there is nothing in this instruction that we cannot easily accomplish with operations already at hand. For if we take SOURCE to be the address of the longword whose low-order bit is to be tested and TARGET to be the branch target address, then the instruction

BLBS   SOURCE,TARGET

could as well be achieved with the instructions

BITL   #1,SOURCE
BNEQ TARGET

BLBC and BLBS are included in the set of processor operations since, in some applications, the low-order bit of a byte, word, or whatever can have much significance and thus frequently needs to be tested.

(i) BBC   **Branch on *Bit* Clear**
BBS   **Branch on *Bit* Set**
BBCC   **Branch on *Bit* Clear and Clear**
BBCS   **Branch on *Bit* Clear and Set**
BBSC   **Branch on *Bit* Set and Clear**
BBSS   **Branch on *Bit* Set and Set**

The machine codes for these operations are

BBC (E1)   BBS (E0)
BBCC (E5)   BBCS (E3)
BBSC (E4)   BBSS (E2)

and each has the operand descriptor

$$pos.rl,base.vb,disp.bb$$

Each operation tests the bit specified by the base address operand (*base*) and the position operand (*pos*). For BBC, BBCC, and BBCS, the specified branch occurs if the tested bit is clear; for BBS, BBSC, and BBSS, the specified branch occurs if the tested bit is set. In the case of BBCC and BBSC, the tested bit is *cleared*, regardless of whether or not the branch takes place. In the case of BBCS and BBSS, the tested bit is *set*, regardless of whether or not the branch takes place.

Basically, all six of these operations test a particular bit (somewhere) and then take some action based on the state of that bit—cleared or set. The operations are especially interesting to us inasmuch as they are the first we have seen in which one of the operands has access type *v—base.vb.*—the "variable bit field" access type. It is this operand, together with the "position" operand, that specifies the location of the bit to be tested, and some explanations are required here. Now a bit in main memory can be specified by saying that it is a particular bit of some addressed structure (for example, bit 57 of a given quadword), *or* by stating that it is so and so many bits *above* or *below* some "base address" (toward higher or lower addresses). By **base address** in this context we mean the address of a *byte*, and bits in main memory are identified by their *position* relative to bit 0 of this byte. For example, bit 6 of this byte is identified as being "6 bits *up* from" bit 0 of this byte. Bit 6 of the *preceding* byte is identified as being "2 bits *down* from" bit 0 of this byte. Figure 8.6.3 shows the identification scheme, relative to the byte whose address is given symbolically as A. For example, bit 4 of the byte whose address is A + 2 could be identified by the base address A and the bit position 20, while bit 2 of the byte whose address is A − 3 can be identified by the base address A and bit position − 22.

"Variable bit field" access type also permits a register to serve as the base address, in which case the operands are a position and a register, and thus the bit being tested (and possibly set or cleared) is some bit of a register, described by its position from bit 0 of that register. In the case of a register base address, however, the condition

$$0 \le pos \le 31$$

is imposed on the permissible range of values that may be taken on by *pos*.

It is unlikely that the reader has gained much appreciation for the power of these bit-manipulating operations from this brief discussion; some of them may appear intrinsically interesting but of little practical use, while others must seem fairly bizarre, causing one to wonder why efforts would ever be expended to

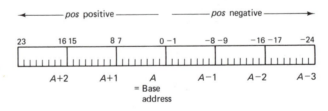

Figure 8.6.3

implement them in the hardware. To the user who has programmed in high-level languages this is a natural reaction, for such programmers tend to think of bytes and words as indivisible entities, each holding a *number* of some sort, or perhaps an ASCII-coded character. But the practiced machine language programmer, who is more accustomed to assigning meanings to the individual bits of a byte or word, can recognize the inherent power of these operations.

We offer one brief example as small justification for this claim. Consider an array of 24 longwords, *some* of which may be occupied by data of some sort. Unlike the arrays we have dealt with so far, in which the data were *static*, the array in question is *dynamic*, in the sense that items may be added to it, and other items may be removed from it. The only requirement is that no more than 24 data items will be in the array at any one time. Because of the dynamic nature of the array, we are going to have to keep track of which positions are occupied at any given time, and which are free. For when an item is to be added, we must be able to find an unoccupied position for it; and when an item is removed, we must note that its position is now free and thus can be used for any new datum that is to be inserted. We can easily keep track of occupied and unoccupied locations with the following scheme. We set aside 24 bits (3 bytes) in such a way that each bit corresponds to one of the longwords in the array, perhaps the lowest order of these bits representing the first longword, and the highest-order bit representing the last, or 24th, longword. Now we agree that if a bit has the value 1, the corresponding longword in the array is occupied; if it is 0, the array entry is unoccupied. This collection of bits is sometimes called a **bit map** or **allocation map** for the array, and it should be evident to the reader that some of the bit-manipulating operations we have introduced here can be quite useful. For example, if a new entry is to be put in the array, the bit map must be searched for the first 0 bit, which signifies a corresponding unused location in the array, which can then be used for the new item. And of course, that bit must now be set to 1, to indicate that the array location is no longer unoccupied. This suggests a possible use for the operation BBCS. Some suggestions for such programming examples are given in the exercises.

8.7 LOOP-CONTROLLING OPERATIONS

Many of our sample programs and program segments have involved *loops*, collections of instructions which are executed repeatedly. This iteration of execution has frequently been controlled by some register, whose contents has been initialized at some value and then decremented and tested each time through the loop. Figure 8.7.1 shows two typical examples of loops which are of the sort we have used several times. Since this activity is so commonly used in programs solving a wide variety of problems, the VAX hardware implements two control operations which emulate precisely the "loop-terminating" sequences of Figure 8.7.1.

```
              .
              .
              .
              MOVL    #N,Rn                          MOVL    #N,Rn
LOOP:         ----                       LOOP:       ----
              .                                      .
              .                                      .
              DECL    Rn                             DECL    Rn
              BGTR    LOOP                           BGEQ    LOOP
              .                                      .
              .                                      .
```

Figure 8.7.1

(a) SOBGTR *Subtract One and Branch if GreaTeR
than zero*
    SOBGEQ *Subtract One and Branch if Greater
than or EQual to zero*

The operation codes for these instructions are

$$\text{SOBGTR (F5)} \qquad \text{SOBGEQ (F4)}$$

and their operand descriptor is

$$index \cdot ml, disp \cdot bb$$

The effect of the operations is to subtract one from the first operand (the longword *index*). If the resulting value is positive (for SOBGTR) or nonnegative (for SOBGEQ), the displacement operand (*disp*) is sign extended to a longword and added to c(PC).

Notice that the *index* operand is a longword; although that longword is frequently the contents of a register, it need not be; any longword will do as a loop controlling "index." Note also that the index is decremented by 1 *first* and then tested to see if it is positive (SOBGTR) or nonnegative (SOBGEQ). Finally, observe that since the displacement is of byte type, SOBGTR and SOBGEQ can be used to control loops that are no longer than about 128 bytes.

We offer just one example of SOBGEQ, since these operations will be used frequently throughout the remainder of the book. In the program segment of Figure 8.7.2 we wish to count the number of bits in R5 which are *set*; we initialize c(R0) to 31, to act as a "bit position" pointer, taking on the values from 31 down to 0; and the number of "set" bits in R5 will be counted in the low-order byte of R1. The reader should have no difficulty in following the logic of this little segment, but special note should be taken of the use of the operation BBC.

As useful as the SOB-type loops are, it is more customary in practice, in high-level languages, for the loop-controlling index to *increment* through its set of values.

```
;--------------------------------------------------------;
; Segment to count the bits in R5 which are SET (= 1).   ;
; The loop is controlled with an SOBGEQ instruction.     ;
;--------------------------------------------------------;
        .
        .
        .
        CLRB    R1              ;Clear "set bit" counter
        MOVL    #31,R0          ;Set "position" to high-order bit
LOOP:   BBC     R0,R5,NOTSET    ;Test bit and branch if clear
        INCB    R1              ;  else increment counter
NOTSET: SOBGEQ  R0,LOOP         ;Decrement "bit position"
                                ;  and test next position if
                                ;  "bit position" nonnegative
        .
        .
        .
```

Figure 8.7.2

For example, in BASIC we frequently see FOR...NEXT loops such as

$$120 \quad \text{FOR I} = 1 \text{ TO N}$$

$$\ldots\ldots$$

$$200 \quad \text{NEXT I}$$

The corresponding construction in Pascal might look something like

$$\text{for index} := 1 \text{ to N do}$$
$$\text{begin}$$
$$\ldots\ldots\ldots$$
$$\text{end;}$$

The VAX also implements loops of this type, in which the number 1 is *added to* the index, although in this case we must include an "upper limit" as an operand ("N" in the high-level examples above); this was not needed in the SOB-type instructions, since the *lower* limit there was *assumed* to be 0.

(b) AOBLSS   ***Add One and Branch if LeSS than limit***

      AOBLEQ   ***Add One and Branch if Less than or EQual to limit***

The operation codes for these instructions are

$$\text{AOBLSS (F2)} \qquad \text{AOBLEQ (F3)}$$

and their operand descriptor is

$$limit \cdot rl, index \cdot ml, disp \cdot bb$$

```
;-----------------------------------------------------------;
; Segment to count the bits in R5 which are SET (= 1).      ;
; The loop is controlled with an AOBLEQ instruction.        ;
;-----------------------------------------------------------;
        .
        .
        .
        CLRQ    R0              ;Clear "bit position" index (R0)
                                ; and "bit counter" (R1)
LOOP:   BBC     R0,R5,NOTSET    ;Test bit and branch if clear
        INCB    R1              ; else increment counter
NOTSET: AOBLEQ  #31,R0,LOOP     ;Increment "bit position"
                                ; and test next position if
                                ; "bit position" < 32
        .
        .
        .
```

Figure 8.7.3

The effect of the operations is to add 1 to the index operand (the longword *index*). If the resulting value is less than (for AOBLSS) or less than or equal to (for AOBLEQ) the value of the longword operand *limit*, then the displacement operand (*disp*) is sign extended to a longword and added to c(PC).

The program segment of Figure 8.7.3 is the equivalent of that of Figure 8.7.2, using AOBLEQ and allowing the "bit position" register to increase from 0 to 31, rather than to decrease from 31 down to 0.

The last loop-controlling operations we examine are not used as frequently as AOB and SOB, but they are nonetheless very useful. They implement, at the machine level, the equivalents of the BASIC constructions

120   FOR I = 1 TO N STEP K   and   120   FOR I = N TO 1 STEP −K
. . . .
200   NEXT I   200   NEXT I

in which the so-called "step size" is not +1.

(c) ACBx   *Add Compare and Branch*

The operation codes for the three ACB operations are

ACBB (9D)   ACBW (3D)   ACBL (F1)

and their operand descriptor is

limit.rx,add.rx,index.mx,disp.bw

The effects of these operations are as follows. The value of the operand *add* is added to the operand *index*. If *add* is non~~ ive, and if the computed value of

```
;-------------------------------------------------------------;
; Segment to count the bits in R5 which are SET (= 1)         ;
; and are in EVEN bit positions (0, 2, 4, ..., 30).           ;
; The loop is controlled with an ACB instruction.             ;
;-------------------------------------------------------------;
        .
        .
        .
        CLRQ    R0                  ;Clear "bit position" index (R0)
                                    ;  and "bit counter" (R1)
LOOP:   BBC     R0,R5,NOTSET        ;Test bit and branch if clear
        INCB    R1                  ;  else increment counter
NOTSET: ACBB    #30,#2,R0,LOOP      ;Increment "bit position" by 2
                                    ;  and test next position if
                                    ;  "bit position" < 32
        .
        .
        .
```

Figure 8.7.4

index is less than or equal to the value of the operand *limit*, then the operand *disp* is sign extended to a longword and added to c(PC). If *add* is negative, and if the computed value of *index* is greater than or equal to the value of the operand *limit*, then the operand *disp* is sign extended to a longword and added to c(PC).

Notice that the datatype context symbol x refers to the operands that enter into the arithmetic and the compare; the displacement operand *disp* has *word* context.

As an example of the use of ACB, we modify the program segment of Figure 8.7.3 to determine the number of set bits in R5 which are in *even* bit positions— 0, 2, 4, ..., 30 (see Figure 8.7.4). Note that despite the fact that we have cleared the longword contents of registers 0 and 1 (with CLRQ), we use only the low-order bytes of those registers (ACBB), since the numbers we are dealing with are in the range 1 to 31.

8.8 MISCELLANEOUS OPERATIONS

(a) CMPx   *CoMPare operands*

The *compare* operations have machine codes

$$\text{CMPB (91)} \qquad \text{CMPW (B1)} \qquad \text{CMPL (D1)}$$

and operand descriptor

$$src1.rx, src2.rx$$

The effect of the operations is to subtract the second operand (*src2*) from the first operand (*src1*) and to set the condition codes N and Z according to the result of the subtraction. Neither operand is affected. (Observe that the subtraction in CMP is in the *opposite* order from the subtraction in the SUB operation.)

(b) HALT   HALT the processor

HALT has operation code 00; it has *no* operands; and its effect is to halt the processor, that is, to force the processor to cease its fetch-execute cycles. Under ordinary circumstances, the operating system will not permit execution of HALT.

(c) NOP   *No OPeration*

NOP has operation code 01 and has *no* operands. It has no effect upon execution, except that it does require that the processor perform an instruction execution cycle. The principal use of NOP is in program debugging, in which, for example, an instruction can be temporarily "removed" from the executable program in memory by overlaying its code with NOPs.

(d) TSTx   *TeST operand*

The TST operations have machine code

$$\text{TSTB (95)} \qquad \text{TSTW (B5)} \qquad \text{TSTL (D5)}$$

and operand descriptor

$$src.rx$$

The effect of the operation is to examine the operand and set the condition codes N and Z accordingly.

8.9 BASIC ASSEMBLER DIRECTIVES

Most of the directives listed below have already been encountered in programming examples, and these are given by way of summary. A few are new, and some assembler directives are not included here. These are given in Appendix B.

Recall that an assembler directive is a "command" to the assembler to perform some service *other than* the translation of a machine instruction mnemonic (for example, .BLKB), or it is a "notification" to the assembler of some occurrence (for example, .END).

In the descriptions that follow, the expression ⟨*datatype list*⟩ shall mean a *list* of elements of the specified *datatype*, separated by commas.

(a) .ADDRESS   *ADDRESS storage directive*

The .ADDRESS directive has the format

$$.ADDRESS \quad address\ list$$

where each address in the *address list* is a longword. The assembler will generate a collection of longwords containing the specified addresses, in the order given.

From the programmer's standpoint there is no difference between .ADDRESS and .LONG, except that the use of the former makes more clear what is stored at these locations.

(b) .ASCII   ASCII string storage directive
.ASCIC   ASCII string storage directive,
Counted
.ASCIZ   ASCII string storage directive,
Zero terminated

The format of the .ASCIx directives is

.ASCIx   */character list/*

The slash or stroke (/) is used as a **string delimiter**; however, *any* printing character may be used as a delimiter *except* the left angle bracket (⟨), the equal sign (=), and the semicolon (;). The assembler takes the following action upon encountering a .ASCIx directive. It takes the first (nonblank, nontab) character as a delimiter. It then generates bytes containing the ASCII code for the characters in the string, one character to a byte, until it encounters the *next* occurrence of the delimiter. Code generation ceases at that point.

.ASCII causes character generation exactly as described above. For example, consider the directive

.ASCII   /Made in USA/

The assembler will generate the following bytes (read right to left in order of increasing addresses):

41 53 55 20 6E 69 20 65 64 61 4D
A   S   U   b̷   n   i   b̷   e   d   a   M

(the character b̷ is used to represent a "blank" or "space" character).

The directive .ASCIC causes generation of the same bytes as .ASCII, except that the bytes are *preceded* by a single byte containing the count of characters in the string. For example,

.ASCIC   #Made in USA#

will cause the assembler to generate

41 53 55 20 6E 69 20 65 64 61 4D 0B

the character count (decimal 11) being the first byte of storage.

```
              .
              .
              .
     $O.STR  PROMPT              ;Send "prompt"
     $I.1D   COUNT               ;  and get counter
              .
              .
     $O.STR  ERROR               ;Send error message
     $O.NL                       ;  and generate "new line"
              .
              .
PROMPT: .ASCIZ  /Input count (as a decimal byte)/
ERROR:  .ASCIZ  /ERROR! -- Integer overflow/
              .
              .
```

Figure 8.9.1

The directive .ASCIZ causes the assembler to generate the same set of bytes as .ASCII, except that this collection is *followed* by a byte containing the number 0. Thus

.ASCIZ   tMade in USAt

will cause generation of the bytes

00   41   53   55   20   6E   69   20   65   64   61   4D

The significance of this directive is that the macroinstruction **$0.STR** (see Appendix D) assumes that the string it is to print ends in a 0 byte. That is, **$0.STR** begins printing characters at the specified address and terminates printing when it encounters a 0 byte. This can be useful for the generation of "input prompts" and various messages in user programs, as shown in Figure 8.9.1. It should further be noted that the macroinstruction **$I.STR,** which *inputs* strings of characters, accepts characters from the keyboard (up to the terminating carriage return) and creates the corresponding bytes in memory, followed by a 0 byte. Thus strings input via **$I.STR** appear exactly as if they had been generated by .ASCIZ.

(c) .BLKB   reserve a *BLocK* of *Bytes*
   .BLKW   reserve a *BLocK* of *Words*
   .BLKL   reserve a *BLocK* of *Longwords*
   .BLKQ   reserve a *BLocK* of *Quadwords*
   .BLKO   reserve a *BLocK* of *Octawords*

The format of the ·BLKx directives is

.BLKx   n

where *n* is the *number* of structures of the specified type to be reserved. This directive causes the assembler to advance its location counter by $k \cdot n$, where k is 1, 2, 4, 8, 16 according as x is B, W, L, Q, or O.

(d) .BYTE   BYTE storage directive

The format of the .BYTE directive is

.BYTE   *byte list*

and it causes the assembler to generate consecutive bytes containing the numbers specified in the *byte list*. For example,

.BYTE   7,23,ˆX4A,12

causes generation of the bytes (shown right to left, in order of increasing addresses)

0C4A 17 07

in consecutive memory bytes.

(e) .END   source program *END* directive

The format of the .END directive is

.END   *transfer address*

where the *transfer address* is the location in the program at which execution will begin.   .END causes the assembler to terminate its examination of the source program on the first pass, and consequently any mnemonics or directives that are located physically *beyond* this directive will not be assembled.

(f) .ENTRY   program *ENTRY* point directive

The directive .ENTRY has the format

.ENTRY   *label,mask*

where *label* is a symbolic name for .ENTRY's location, and *mask* is a "program entry mask word" (see Section 6.7).   From the programmer's standpoint, the effect of this directive is the same as that of

label: .WORD   *mask*

(g) .LONG   *LONG*word storage directive

The format of the .LONG directive is

.LONG   longword list

and it causes the assembler to generate consecutive longwords containing the numbers specified in the *longword list*.

(h) .OCTA   *OCTA*word storage directive

The format of the .OCTA directive is

.OCTA   *octaword list*

and it causes the assembler to generate consecutive octawords containing the numbers specified in the *octaword list*.

(i) .QUAD   *QUAD*word storage directive

The format of the .QUAD directive is

.QUAD   *quadword list*

and it causes the assembler to generate consecutive quadwords containing the numbers in the *quadword list*.

(j) .TITLE   *TITLE* directive

The format of the .TITLE directive is

.TITLE   *program-name comment*

where *program-name* is any string of characters (except spaces and tabs) not exceeding 31 characters in length, and *comment* is any string (including spaces and tabs) not exceeding 40 characters in length. The assembler prints the *program-name* and *comment* at the top of each page of program listing. Thus .TITLE may be used for program identification purposes. If a program is not TITLEd, the assembler uses the default title ".MAIN.".

(k) .WORD   *WORD* storage directive

The format of the .WORD directive is

.WORD   *word list*

and it causes the assembler to generate consecutive words containing the numbers specified in the *word list*.

8.10 SOME PROGRAMMING EXAMPLES

In this section we offer a few programs and program segments which illustrate the uses of many of the operations that have been discussed in this chapter. For the most part we leave the details to the reader, giving only a few explanations of what the purpose of the programming is, and perhaps commenting on some of the more obscure points.

The first program (Figure 8.10.1) evaluates the polynomial

$$1 \cdot x^4 - 2 \cdot x^3 + 4 \cdot x^2 + 6$$

for any value of x which is input to the program. The computation is done in a straightforward way, namely, by evaluating the various powers of the given value of x, multiplying them by their coefficients, and adding the results. The multiplications are done as *word* products, to avoid the danger of integer overflows.

The second version of the polynomial evaluation program (Figure 8.10.2) is an improvement over the first, since the polynomial is rewritten as

$$6 + x(0 + x(4 + x(-2 + x(1))))$$

and this form precludes the necessity for ever having directly to calculate the powers

```
;-----------------------------------------------------------;
; Program to evaluate 4th degree polynomial -- Version 1 ;
;-----------------------------------------------------------;

COEFF:  .BYTE   1,-2,4,0,6      ;Polynomial coefficients
                                ;  (high-order to low-order)
ENDCO:  .BLKB   1               ;End-of-coefficients
                                ;  (value of x read here)

POLY1:  .WORD   ^M<>            ;(program entry mask word)
        $I.1D   ENDCO           ;Read byte into ENDCO
        CVTBW   ENDCO,R0        ;  and convert to word
        MOVAB   ENDCO,R10       ;Put coefficient-end address in R10
        MOVW    #1,R9           ;0th power of x in R9
        CVTBW   -(R10),R11      ;Initialize polynomial value to
                                ;  coefficient of 0th power of x

LOOP:   CMPL    R10,#COEFF      ;Done highest power yet?
        BEQLU   DONE            ;Yes -- print result and exit
        MULW2   R0,R9           ;No -- calculate next higher power
        CVTBW   -(R10),R8       ;Conv. next higher coefficient to word
        MULW2   R9,R8           ;  and multiply by power of x
        ADDW2   R8,R11          ;Accum. product in polynomial value
        BRB     LOOP            ;  and go for next power of x

DONE:   $0.2D   R11             ;Print polynomial value
        $EXIT                   ;  and exit to operating system

        .END    POLY1
```

Figure 8.10.1

```
;----------------------------------------------------------------;
; Program to evaluate 4th degree polynomial -- Version 2 ;
;----------------------------------------------------------------;

COEFF:  .BYTE   1,-2,4,0,6      ;Polynomial coefficients
                                ;  (high-order to low-order)
ENDCO:  .BLKB   1               ;End-of-coefficients
                                ;  (value of x read here)

POLY2:  .WORD   ^M<IV>          ;(program entry mask word --
                                ;  trap integer overflows)
        $I.1D   ENDCO           ;Read byte into ENDCO
        CVTBW   ENDCO,R0        ;  and convert to word
        MOVAB   COEFF,R10       ;Put coefficient address in R10
        CLRW    R11             ;Initialize polynomial value to 0

LOOP:   CVTBW   (R10)+,R8       ;Get next coeff. and conv. to word
        ADDW2   R8,R11          ;Add to polynomial value
        CMPL    R10,#ENDCO      ;Last coefficient?
        BEQLU   DONE            ;Yes -- print and exit
        MULW2   R0,R11          ;No -- multiply by x
        BRB     LOOP            ;  and process next coefficient

DONE:   $O.2D   R11             ;Print polynomial value
        $EXIT                   ;  and exit to operating system

        .END    POLY2
```

Figure 8.10.2

of *x*. Notice that in this version we have enabled the operating system's "integer overflow trapping" feature, so that we will be notified in the event that the value of *x* that we input results in polynomial values too large to be held in a single word.

The final version of the polynomial evaluation program (Figure 8.10.3) uses the same algorithm as the preceding version, but it takes advantage of the EMUL operation, since the computations involved in the algorithm amount to a multiplication followed by an addition—precisely the action of EMUL. Observe, however, that all values (*x* and the coefficients) have had to be converted to longwords to accommodate the datatype context of EMUL.

The programming segment of Figure 8.10.4 finds the *position* of the highest-order bit of c(R2) which is *set*. [Thus if c(R2) = $^X3079A2A4$, this is bit position 29.] The scheme is to rotate the high-order bit down to the low-order bit and then test the low-order bit to see if it is *not* set (BLBC). The TSTL instruction deals with the case that c(R2) = 0 and therefore has *no* bits set. Once the highest-order set bit is found, a further rotation of R2 restores c(R2) to its original value.

At the close of Section 8.6 we discussed a possible application of the bit-manipulating operations, in which bits in an "allocation map" needed to be turned on and off. Suppose that this allocation map comprises the 24 low-order bits of a longword whose address is labeled MAP, and we wish to turn on or off the bit whose *position* is in R0. For example, the contents of R0 might be 17, and we may wish to set bit number 17 = $^X11$ of MAP. It will *not* do to execute

BISL   R0,MAP,MAP

Basic VAX Operations and Assembler Directives   Chap. 8

```
;-------------------------------------------------------------;
; Program to evaluate 4th degree polynomial -- Version 3 ;
;-------------------------------------------------------------;

COEFF:   .LONG   1,-2,4,0,6         ;Polynomial coefficients
                                    ;  (high-order to low-order)
ENDCO:   .BLKB   1                  ;End-of-coefficients
                                    ;  (value of x read here)

POLY3:   .WORD   ^M<>               ;(program entry mask word)
         $I.1D   ENDCO              ;Read byte into ENDCO
         CVTBL   ENDCO,R0           ;  and convert to longword
         MOVAL   COEFF,R10          ;Put coefficient address in R10
         MOVL    (R10)+,R8          ;Initialize polynomial value to
                                    ;  high-order coefficient

LOOP:    CMPL    R10,#ENDCO         ;Last coefficient?
         BEQLU   DONE               ;Yes -- print and exit
         EMUL    R0,R8,(R10)+,R8    ;Multiply previous result by x
                                    ;  and add in next coefficient
         BRB     LOOP               ;Go process next coefficient

DONE:    $0.2D   R8                 ;Print polynomial value
         $EXIT                      ;  and exit to operating system

         .END    POLY3
```

Figure 8.10.3

for in fact this will set bits 0 and 4 of that longword. But the two instructions of Figure 8.10.5 will set the appropriate bit in R4, which can then be used with a BISL or BICL operation to set or clear bit 17 of the longword at MAP.

As a final example, consider the problem of *examining* the contents of a byte. By this we mean that we wish to print, on the terminal, the hexadecimal repre-

```
;-------------------------------------------------------------;
; Segment to locate the highest-order bit of R2 which ;
; is SET (= 1). ;
;-------------------------------------------------------------;

         .
         .
         TSTL    R2                 ;See if all bits are 0
         BEQL    NOBITS             ;Yes -- no set bits in longword
         MOVB    #32,R0             ;Set "bit position" indicator
TEST:    ROTL    #1,R2,R2           ;Rotate high-order bit down
                                    ;  to bit position 0
         DECB    R0                 ;  and decrement bit indicator
         BLBC    R2,TEST            ;Bit is clear -- examine next bit
         ROTL    R0,R2,R2           ;Restore original longword
         .
         .
NOBITS:                             ;Handle longword with no set bits
         .
         .
```

Figure 8.10.4

```
        .
        .
        .
      MOVL    #1,R4              ;Set bit 0 of R4
      ASHL    R0,R4,R4          ;Move "1" up to
                                ;  desired position
        .
        .
        .
```

Figure 8.10.5

sentation of the byte. Now the contents of a byte is not its own hexadecimal representation; in fact, if we consider for example the byte whose contents is ^B10110101, we must convert this bit configuration into *two* ASCII-coded bytes, namely, the ASCII codes for the characters "B" and "5":

high-order nibble = 1011 = ASCII "B" = ^B01000011 = ^X42
low-order nibble = 0101 = ASCII "5" = ^B00110101 = ^X35

In the program segment of Figure 8.10.6 we assume that the byte to be printed is the low-order byte of R6, that the two ASCII-coded bytes that represent this byte are to be put in CODES and CODES + 1, and that the contents of the three high-order bytes of R6 are of no consequence and can thus be destroyed. The idea of the programming is to isolate each nibble and then convert it to ASCII code. Thus the first ROTL instruction moves the high-order nibble of the byte in question

```
        ;-----------------------------------------------------;
        ; Segment to convert the contents of a byte to its    ;
        ; representation as two ASCII-coded characters.       ;
        ;-----------------------------------------------------;
        .
        .
CODES:  .BLKB   2                 ;ASCII codes for high-order
                                  ;  and low-order nibbles
                                  ;  of low-order byte of R6

        .
        .
        ROTL    #-4,R6,R6         ;Bring high nibble to low 4 bits
        BICB    #^XF0,R6          ;  and mask out bits 7:4
        BISB    #^A/0/,R6         ;Convert to ASCII
        CMPB    R6,#^X39          ;Greater than ASCII "9"?
        BLEQ    STOREHI           ;No -- ASCII code OK as is
        ADDB    #7,R6             ;  else convert to range "A...F"
STOREHI: MOVB   R6,CODES          ;Store high-order nibble
        ROTL    #4,R6,R6          ;Bring low nibble back to bits 3:0
        BICB    #^XF0,R6          ;  and mask out bits 7:4
        BISB    #^A/0/,R6         ;Convert to ASCII
        CMPB    R6,#^X39          ;Greater than ASCII "9"?
        BLEQ    STORELO           ;No -- ASCII code OK as is
        ADDB    #7,R6             ;  else convert to range "A...F"
STORELO: MOVB   R6,CODES+1        ;Store low-order nibble
        .
        .
```

Figure 8.10.6

Basic VAX Operations and Assembler Directives   Chap. 8

down to bits 3:1 (and the low-order nibble up to bits 31:28), bits 7:4 are then zeroed, and the resulting byte is converted to ASCII code. The second ROTL brings the low-order nibble back to bits 3:0, where the same conversion sequence again takes place. The remaining details, including the actual conversion to ASCII-coded bytes, are left to the reader. We mention here for later reference that there are easier ways to treat this task, and that the *duplication* of the instructions to convert to ASCII can ultimately be done away with.

There is one new feature introduced here, namely the construction ^A/.../. The "^A" stands for "ASCII code for "; the slashes (/) are used as delimiters, as in the .ASCIx directives; and the construction generates the ASCII code for the character between the delimiting slashes. Thus in this case,

$$^A/0/$$

represents the byte whose contents is the ASCII code for the character 0. Consequently, the instruction

$$BISB \quad \#^A/0/,R6$$

is equivalent to

$$BISB \quad \#^X30,R6$$

that is, bits 5:4 of c(R6) are set, so that the contents of the low-order byte of R6 will be the ASCII code for the numerical character represented by the nibble in question. There is no difference in the code generated by the assembler, only an improvement in readability.

If the ^A/.../ construction is used in a *word* (or *longword*) context, then 2 (or 4) bytes will be generated. In these cases, if fewer than two (four) characters are enclosed within the delimiters, *leading* NUL characters (ASCII code 0) are supplied by the assembler.

8.11 EXERCISES

8.2.1. Devise operand descriptors for each of the following familiar operations.
    (a) TSTB   **(b)** TSTL   **(c)** DECW
    (d) BRB   **(e)** BRW   **(f)** SUBx (x = B, W, or L)

8.3.1. How would the program segment of Figure 8.3.2 have to be written if, with c(R0) = NUM, we had used a MOVL instead of MOVAW to transfer the addresses to the block at ADDR?

8.3.2. Suppose that c(R3) = 2A74809D and c(R4) = 0281B47C. Write an instruction that will result in:
    (a) c(R4) = 0000009D   **(b)** c(R4) = 0281009D
    (c) c(R4) = FFFF809D   **(d)** c(R4) = 0000809D
    (e) c(R3) = 0000809D   **(f)** c(R3) = 2A74007C
    (g) c(R3) = 2A74807C   **(h)** c(R4) = FFFFB47C

8.4.1. Verify that the conditional branch operations of Figure 8.4.1 branch on *appropriate* conditions. (For example, BGEQU branches if C = 0; verify that this is the condition that prevails when an operation on unsigned data yields a nonnegative result.)

8.5.1. (a) What is the difference (if any) between the instructions

$$\text{ADDL2 R1,(R2)} \quad \text{and} \quad \text{ADDL3 R1,(R2),(R2)}$$

(b) What is the difference (if any) between the instructions

$$\text{ADDL2 R1,(R2)+} \quad \text{and} \quad \text{ADDL3 R1,(R2)+,(R2)}$$

8.5.2. Let FACT1 and FACT2 be the addresses of two *bytes,* and consider the instruction

$$\text{MULB2 FACT1,FACT2}$$

For each of the contents of FACT1 and FACT2 shown below in decimal, state the resulting contents of FACT2 in decimal.

(a) c(FACT1) = 74   (b) c(FACT1) = 74   (c) c(FACT1) = 18
    c(FACT2) = 12   c(FACT2) = −1   c(FACT2) = −9

8.5.3. If the contents of two bytes, say A and B, are considered as *unsigned* numbers, and if c(A) = ˆX17 and c(B) = ˆX0B, then

$$\text{MULB3 A,B,C}$$

will result in c(C) = ˆXFD. This is correct as an unsigned product, even though the processor has *set* the V-bit. But now suppose that c(A) = ˆX17 and c(B) = ˆXFB. The resulting c(C) is ˆX8D, which is incorrect as an unsigned product, and in this case the V-bit was *not* set. What has gone wrong with this second unsigned multiplication? Why was the V-bit not set? How can this incorrectness of unsigned multiplication be detected?

8.5.4. What is the actual value of ˆX80/ˆXFF? (This is the largest negative integer byte divided by the byte −1.)

8.5.5. Find the quotients and remainders upon division of the following *words* (given in hexadecimal).

(a) 004F/002A   (b) 002A/004F   (c) 1028/0730
(d) 1028/101A   (e) 82AB/407C   (f) C0A4/B935

8.5.6. What is the difference (if any) between the constructions

$$\text{MNEGL R2,R2} \quad \text{and} \quad \begin{array}{l}\text{MCOML R2,R2}\\ \text{INCL R2}\end{array}$$

8.5.7. Let OCTA1 and OCTA2 be the addresses of two octawords. Write a sequence of instructions that will add the octaword contents of OCTA1 and OCTA2 and put the result in OCTA2.

8.5.8. Let QUAD1 and QUAD2 be the addresses of two quadwords. Write a sequence of instructions that will add the quadword contents of QUAD1 and QUAD2 and put the result in a third quadword at QUAD3.

8.5.9. Let QUAD1 and QUAD2 be the addresses of two quadwords. Write a sequence of instructions that will subtract the quadword contents of QUAD1 from QUAD2 and put the result in QUAD2.

8.5.10. Let QUAD1 and QUAD2 be the addresses of two quadwords. Write a sequence of instructions that will subtract the quadword contents of QUAD1 from QUAD2 and put the result in a third quadword at QUAD3.

8.5.11. Let QUAD be the address of a quadword. Write a sequence of instructions that will *increment* the quadword contents of QUAD. (This sequence will then substitute for the "missing" INCQ operation.)

8.6.1. Write one or two BIS or BIC instructions that will change the contents of R5 from F3074A2B to:

(a) F2272727   **(b)** 2223AAA9   **(c)** F78F6B3B

8.6.2. Explain why

$$\text{BISB3} \quad \#^{\hat{}}\text{X30,NUMBR,ACODE}$$

puts the ASCII code for the number in NUMBR into ACODE, provided that c(NUMBR) is between 0 and 9, inclusive.

8.6.3. Explain why

$$\text{BICx} \quad \text{A,B}$$

turns *off* any bit in B whose corresponding bit in A is *on*, and that bits in A which are *off* leave the corresponding bits in B *unaffected*. (*Suggestion:* 1 *AND* b = b, and 0 *AND* b = 0, for any bit b = 0 or 1.)

8.6.4. Using only BIS and BIC operations, write a sequence of instructions that will put the contents of the high-order word of R10 into the high-order word of R6, leaving the low-order word of R6 unaffected, and which uses no other registers or memory locations. It is permitted to alter c(R10) in the process.

8.6.5. Show that MOVx can be considered a special case of BICx and BISx in that

$$\text{MOVx} \quad \text{A,B}$$

has the same result as

$$\text{BICx} \quad \# -1,B$$
$$\text{BISx} \quad \text{A,B}$$

8.6.6. Show that MOVZxy can be written in terms of BIC and BIS instructions.

8.6.7. Can the CVT operations be written in terms of BIC and BIS? If so, how?

8.6.8. What is the effect of the following sequence of instructions?

$$\text{XORL} \quad \text{R1,R2}$$
$$\text{XORL} \quad \text{R2,R1}$$
$$\text{XORL} \quad \text{R1,R2}$$

8.6.9. Explain why right shifts divide *signed* numbers by powers of 2 correctly.

8.6.10. In addition to the "arithmetic shift right" operation as described in the text, some processors (but not the VAX) implement a "logical shift right" operation, in which the high-order bit, rather than being replicated as in ASHL, is replaced with 0. Show that "logical shift right" will always perform an arithmetically correct "divide by 2" on unsigned numbers. What effect will it have on *signed* numbers?

8.6.11. Write a single instruction that will exchange the high- and low-order words of a register.

8.6.12. Write a program that inputs a longword, uses ROTL and BLBC (or BLBS) to count the number of 1s in the longword, and then outputs that result.

8.6.13. Repeat Exercise 8.6.12, except that now the number is input as a *word*. (*Suggestion:* The easiest way out is to convert the input word to a longword using MOVZWL and then to use the program of Exercise 8.6.12, virtually without change. But is there a more efficient way to treat this problem?)

8.6.14. Show that BLBC and BLBS can be used to see if a number is *even* or *odd*.

8.6.15. For each of the following *base address* and *position* specifiers, identify the address of the byte in which the specified bit resides, and the bit position (0 to 7) the bit has in that byte. (For example, if *base address* = 00204079 and *position* = 9, the specified bit is bit 1 of the byte whose address is 0020407A.)
   (a) Base address = 0094AC4D, position = 125
   (b) Base address = 00000A2B, position = −184
   (c) Base address = 0094AC4D, position = 1227

8.7.1. How many times will the instructions between LOOP and ENDLOOP be executed in the segments of Figure 8.11.1?

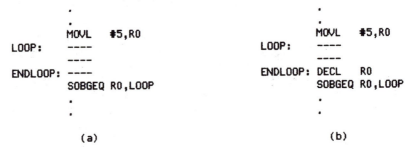

Figure 8.11.1

8.7.2. How many times will be instructions between LOOP and ENDLOOP be executed in the segments of Figure 8.11.2?

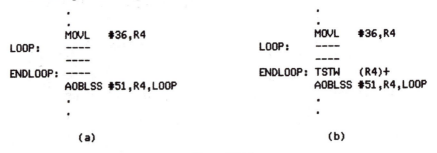

Figure 8.11.2

8.7.3. Explain why the loops in the program segments of Figure 8.11.3 will or will not execute forever.

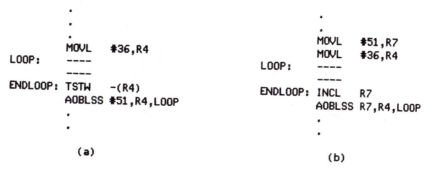

Figure 8.11.3

8.7.4. Show that

$$ACBL \quad \#0,\#-1,index,disp$$

is essentially equivalent to

$$SOBGEQ \quad index,disp$$

(But there is a difference. What is it?)

8.7.5. Show that

$$ACBL \quad limit,\#1,index,disp$$

is essentially equivalent to

$$AOBLEQ \quad limit,index,disp$$

8.7.6. Consider the programming segment

$$029A \quad LOOP: \quad \cdot$$

$$0427 \qquad\qquad SOBGTR \; R7,LOOP$$

Explain what is wrong with this construction, and state at least two ways in which it can be modified so that it will execute as intended.

8.10.1. (a) Referring to the example at the end of Section 8.6, consider a longword whose address is MAP, in which the 24 low-order bits form the allocation map for the array of 24 longwords. Write a program segment to locate the position of the lowest-order bit in MAP which is currently a 0, and simultaneously to reset that bit to 1. The position of this bit is to be left in the low-order byte of R5.

(b) Write a program segment to clear the *n*th bit of MAP $(0 \leqslant n \leqslant 23)$, where *n* is the contents of the byte labeled INDEX (see Figure 8.10.5).

8.10.2. One of the activities to which much computer time is devoted is that of **sorting** numerical or alphabetic data. Write a program to implement an **exchange sort,** or **bubble sort,** as it is frequently called. The technique is as follows. Assume that we have a collection of, say, longwords in an array of contiguous memory, and suppose we wish to sort these into increasing order. We examine the first *pair* of longwords to see if they are in the correct order—that is, if the first is less than or equal to the second. If they are *not*, we *exchange* them and move on to the next pair of numbers; if they are, we leave them alone and move on to the next pair of numbers. (By "next pair" we mean that if the first compare compares numbers 1 and 2, the next compare examines numbers 2 and 3, then 3 and 4, etc.) By the time we have examined all pairs in the array, the *largest* number will have been moved to the end—"bubbled to the top." (Why?) However, this first pass through the numbers has not yet sorted them completely, so we make another pass, identical to the first, *except* that we need not examine the last pair of numbers. (Why not?) When sufficiently many such passes have been made, the numbers will be in increasing order. The task implies the use of some kind of SOB or AOB construction, along with a "compare" such as

$$\text{CMPL} \quad (R0)+,(R0)$$

8.10.3. Another type of sort, which is conceptually simpler but in fact is more difficult to implement at a machine level, is the **selection sort,** which for the increasing case works as follows. We find the smallest number in the array and *exchange* it with the *first* number. We then find the smallest of the *remaining* numbers, and exchange it with the *second* number in the array; and so on. Implement a selection sort for an array of unsigned bytes.

8.10.4. State how it can be determined if a longword contains a power of 2—that is, if precisely *one* bit in the longword is *on*—without resorting to a loop of some sort which examines each bit of the longword. (The solution is almost trivial; discovering the solution is not.)

8.10.5. We define *n*-factorial = *n*! to be

$$n \cdot (n - 1) \cdot (n - 2) \cdots 3 \cdot 2 \cdot 1$$

that is, the product of the numbers from *n* down to 1. Write a program that accepts a *word* value for *n* from the keyboard, and calculates and prints *n*! as a *longword*.

8.10.6. **(a)** Write a program that converts the contents of an unsigned byte NUM to its ASCII decimal representation, with leading zeros. That is, generate three bytes whose contents are the ASCII codes for numbers in the range 000 to 255 which represent the contents of NUM.

(b) Repeat part (a), but generate leading blanks instead of leading zeros.

8.10.7. Let the memory byte labeled NUMBER contain a number between 0 and 99. Write a program that will print the message

The number *xx* is the decimal contents of NUMBER

where *xx* is in the range "ƀ0" to "99" (where ƀ represents a blank or space character).

CHAPTER 9

SUB-ROUTINES, STACKS, AND PROCEDURES

9.1 INTRODUCTION TO SUBROUTINES

In Chapter 7 we used a small segment of assembly language code as an illustrative example of one of the uses of autoincrementing of registers (Figure 7.4.3). We reproduce that segment in Figure 9.1.1, in which we have made a few minor improvements over the earlier version by taking advantage of some operations and constructions which were not available to us at that time. Recall that the environment of that programming example was the following. We assumed that a block of 36 contiguous words, the first of which was labeled ARRAY, was *interpreted by the programmer* as representing a 6 by 6 *array*, in which the first six numbers in the block were thought of as the first row of the array, the next six numbers as the second row, and so on. The task at hand was to print the 36-number block in such a way that the appearance of the output conveyed the 6 by 6 interpretation. It is easy to verify that the segment of Figure 9.1.1 generates such a display.

Suppose now that the 6 by 6 array with which we are dealing in this example is a fairly dynamic affair, with many changes being made in it throughout the course of program execution. This being the case, we may wish to display the array, not just once, but perhaps many times—once after each change in its entries, for example—so that we might keep track of the array's appearance as execution proceeds. As simple as these seven lines of instructions might be, we would not want to reproduce them each time the array is to be printed. To avoid this repetition, we consider the following scheme. The few instructions needed to print the array are included in our program, but are placed out of the mainstream of

```
;----------------------------------------------------;
; Segment to print a 6-by-6 array of words.          ;
;----------------------------------------------------;
        .
        .
        MOVL     #6,R4          ;Set number of rows
        MOVAW    ARRAY,R6       ;Put array address in R6
LOOP1:  MOVL     #6,R5          ;Set number of columns
LOOP2:  $0.2D    (R6)+          ;Print a row entry
        SOBGTR   R5,LOOP2       ;Print next row entry
        $0.NL                   ;  else generate "new line"
        SOBGTR   R4,LOOP1       ;Reset column counter and
                                ;  print next row
                                ;  else done printing array
        .
        .
```

Figure 9.1.1

the other programming instructions. Now whenever we want to print the contents of the array, we simply hand control over to this small segment of code. For example, if we label the first of these instructions with the symbol PRINT (Figure 9.1.2), then

JMP   PRINT

will transfer control to this little routine. But after these few instructions have completed execution, what is to happen? Somehow we must get back (perhaps with another JMP instruction), but back to *where*? The answer, of course, is that we want to *resume* execution at the instruction immediately following the JMP PRINT instruction that gave control to PRINT in the first place. Since we will be passing control to this segment of code from many *different* places in the main portion of the program, it is clear that we cannot resume execution by means of a JMP instruction that references a *fixed* location. As a concrete example, suppose as shown in Figure 9.1.3 that we jump to PRINT at location 00000F2C in

```
;----------------------------------------------------;
; Segment to print a 6-by-6 array of words.          ;
;----------------------------------------------------;
        .
        .
PRINT:  MOVL     #6,R4          ;Set number of rows
        MOVAW    ARRAY,R6       ;Put array address in R6
LOOP1:  MOVL     #6,R5          ;Set number of columns
LOOP2:  $0.2D    (R6)+          ;Print a row entry
        SOBGTR   R5,LOOP2       ;Print next row entry
        $0.NL                   ;  else generate "new line"
        SOBGTR   R4,LOOP1       ;Reset column counter and
                                ;  print next row
                                ;  else done printing array
        .
        .
```

Figure 9.1.2

the program, and then later, at location 0000272A, we also jump to PRINT. Notice the last "instruction" of the segment of code beginning at PRINT—RETURN. In fact, there is no such VAX operation. Rather, we have put this word here to represent what we *want* to have happen when the 36 entries in the array have been printed; we want control of the processor to be RETURNed to the instruction immediately following the JMP instruction, in the main portion of the program, which gave control to this printing routine, *regardless* of where that JMP instruction might be. Thus when the first JMP is executed at 0F2C, and control is passed to the instructions beginning at PRINT, we want RETURN in effect to execute

$$\text{JMP} \quad \text{^X0F32}$$

When the second JMP at 272A causes a jump to PRINT, we want RETURN to have the effect of

$$\text{JMP} \quad \text{^X2730}$$

Thus RETURN should be some sort of JMP instruction, but with a "variable" destination address. If, with the VAX operations we currently have at hand, we can devise an appropriate RETURN "instruction," we will have achieved what we

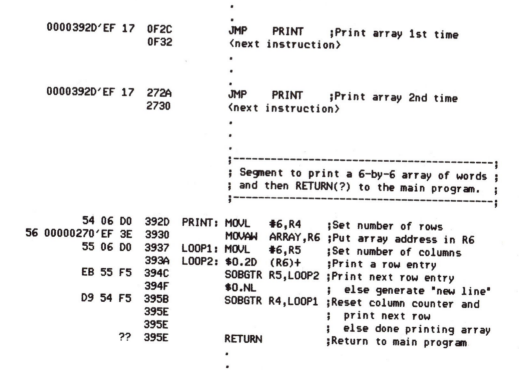

```
                              .
                              .
   0000392D'EF 17   0F2C      JMP     PRINT     ;Print array 1st time
                   0F32       <next instruction>
                              .
                              .
   0000392D'EF 17   272A      JMP     PRINT     ;Print array 2nd time
                   2730       <next instruction>
                              .
                              .
                              .
                   ;------------------------------------------;
                   ; Segment to print a 6-by-6 array of words ;
                   ; and then RETURN(?) to the main program.  ;
                   ;------------------------------------------;
        54 06 D0    392D  PRINT: MOVL  #6,R4       ;Set number of rows
  56 00000270'EF 3E 3930         MOVAW ARRAY,R6    ;Put array address in R6
        55 06 D0    3937  LOOP1: MOVL  #6,R5       ;Set number of columns
                    393A  LOOP2: $0.2D (R6)+       ;Print a row entry
        EB 55 F5    394C         SOBGTR R5,LOOP2   ;Print next row entry
                    394F         $0.NL             ; else generate "new line"
        D9 54 F5    395B         SOBGTR R4,LOOP1   ;Reset column counter and
                    395E                           ; print next row
                    395E                           ; else done printing array
             ??     395E         RETURN            ;Return to main program
                              .
                              .
```

Figure 9.1.3

set out to do. We will have the capability of jumping to the array printing routine from *anywhere* in the program, which in turn will relinquish control in such a way that execution of the main program will resume at the instruction immediately following that jump instruction.

Although we have used the term "routine" several times, we choose not to attempt a precise definition of it. Rather we say informally that a **routine** is a collection of instructions (and possibly data) that is written to do a specific task. Thus the seven instructions of Figure 9.1.1 which print the 6 by 6 array can rightfully be referred to as a "routine." But we can be a little more explicit about the companion term "subroutine." A **subroutine** is a collection of instructions and data, written to do a specific task, to which control is passed from another location in the surrounding program with some sort of "jump" construction, and which provides an instruction or instructions to return control to the location immediately following that jump construction. We say that the instruction that executes the jump to the subroutine **calls** or **invokes** the subroutine, and the program segment containing the jump is sometimes referred to as the **subroutine caller** or **calling program**. The location in the subroutine to which control is passed by means of the jump is called the **subroutine entry point**.

9.2 A FIRST SOLUTION TO THE "SUBROUTINE RETURN" PROBLEM

A little reflection on the situation described in Figure 9.1.3 reveals that whatever the "statement" RETURN is, it must return control back to location 00000F32 in one case, and to 00002730 in the other. That is, the **return address**—the location to which control is to be returned at the conclusion of subroutine execution— is dependent on the value of the program counter *prior to* execution of the JMP instruction in each case. This is clear, for it is c(PC) that determines where these JMPs are, and consequently the locations to which we want to return. On the other hand, it is precisely the function of each such JMP instruction to *destroy* the current PC contents (and, of course, to replace it with the destination address PRINT). Thus if we have any hope of returning back to "where we were," then prior to executing any of these JMP instructions, we must somehow *save* the current c(PC). A register seems a likely place to do so, and thus we might be tempted to execute

```
MOVL   PC,R8
JMP    PRINT
```

where we have chosen R8 as the location in which to save the program counter contents, although almost any other register, or even a memory longword, would do as well. Then the instruction that we have been referring to as RETURN could simply be

```
MOVL   R8,PC
```

Subroutines, Stacks, and Procedures   Chap. 9

thereby restoring the PC's original contents. Actually, the PC contents saved in R8 is the address of the JMP instruction itself—for example, 00000F2C in Figure 9.1.3—*not* that of the next instruction, so that without a small adjustment (which would be easy enough to make), the scheme will not quite work. We do not pursue this technique, however, for a more compelling reason—recall that direct register mode addressing (mode 5) is *invalid* for register 15, the program counter.

Although we were not successful in saving the current c(PC) by the method outlined above, at least now we understand what must be done. The solution is fairly simple, if not aesthetically pleasing. If we place a label on the instruction following the JMP instruction, then the PC value we need to save in order to achieve the return is precisely the value of this symbol, and thus the return address can be saved (again choosing R8) with the instruction

MOVAB   label, R8

Although the original PC cannot be restored directly from R8 with a MOVL instruction, the instruction

JMP   (R8)

has precisely the same effect. Figure 9.2.1 illustrates this technique, where the subroutine is named SUBR and whose code is not shown here. We can now return to the example of Figure 9.1.3 and show (Figure 9.2.2) that the problem posed there is completely solved.

The reader may find the labeling of the instruction immediately following each "jump to subroutine" construction somewhat artificial and even annoying. But with the scheme as we have devised it here—a scheme which, by the way, does perform as advertised—there is no alternative. Considering what has been accomplished, this is surely a small price to pay; the introduction of the subroutine concept adds tremendously to the flexibility in the way programs may be constructed.

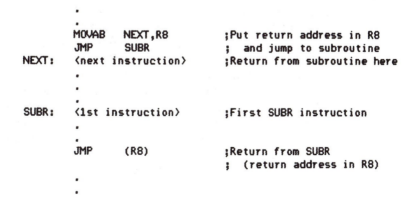

Figure 9.2.1

```
              .
              .
              MOVAB    NEXT,R8            ;Put return address in R8
              JMP      PRINT             ; and jump to PRINT
     NEXT:    <next instruction>         ;Return from PRINT here
              .
              .
              .
              MOVAB    NEXT1,R8          ;Put return address in R8
              JMP      PRINT             ; and jump to PRINT
     NEXT1:   <next instruction>         ;Return from PRINT here
              .
              .

              ;--------------------------------------------------;
              ; Subroutine to print a 6-by-6 array of words and  ;
              ; then to RETURN to the main program.              ;
              ;--------------------------------------------------;

     PRINT:   MOVL     #6,R4             ;Set number of rows
              MOVAW    ARRAY,R6          ;Put array address in R6
     LOOP1:   MOVL     #6,R5             ;Set number of columns
     LOOP2:   $0.2D    (R6)+             ;Print a row entry
              SOBGTR   R5,LOOP2          ;Print next row entry
              $0.NL                      ; else generate "new line"
              SOBGTR   R4,LOOP1          ;Reset column counter and
                                         ; print next row,
                                         ; else done printing array
              JMP      (R8)              ;Resume "mainline" execution
                                         ; (return address in R8)
              .
              .
```

Figure 9.2.2

Before leaving this discussion we note two facts which are quite obvious from the listings of the program segments we have been investigating, but which can nonetheless be a source of many programming errors. First, we have been using R8 to hold the return address, and we stated that that particular choice was quite arbitrary. But once we made this decision, and once the instructions making up the subroutine at PRINT have been written, then at that point we *must* use R8 to save the return address each time PRINT is called, since the RETURN statement in PRINT *assumes* that the return address is in R8. Second, since R8 holds the return address, the subroutine must take care not to execute any instructions that *alter* c(R8). Third, the subroutine at PRINT clearly uses registers 4, 5, and 6, in addition to R8. We must be aware of this register use whenever we call PRINT, for if any of these four registers is currently in use by the main portion of the program, their contents will be destroyed in the process of printing the array, and this could have serious consequences for other processing. Again, this statement is fairly obvious, but a lack of caution here can lead to less obvious errors. The danger lies in the fact that once the code for the routine at PRINT has been written, using R4, R5, and R6, it is easy to forget about the details of that programming segment and simply rely on PRINT to do its job each time it is called. Although it is evident that R8 is being used (since its use is explicit in the subroutine call itself), the use of the other three registers is somewhat more hidden. The best we can offer here is the *caveat* that applies to all programming at this machine level: Attention must be paid to all of the details, for there is no margin for error.

9.3 THE TRANSMISSION OF ARGUMENTS TO A SUBROUTINE

To continue with the example of Sections 9.1 and 9.2, consider a program in which *two* arrays are under consideration: say, ARRAY, which as before we interpret to be a 6 by 6 array of 16-bit words, and ARRAY1, which we think of as 9 by 5. We assume that we will want to print each of these several times during the course of execution. The subroutine PRINT as defined above will display the contents of ARRAY just as before, but it cannot be used to print ARRAY1. Of course, we could write another subroutine, PRINT1 perhaps, to deal with the other array, but that seems to be a brute-force approach to the problem. And if a program had dozens of arrays to be printed, the writing of dozens of subroutines is simply impractical. It is also unnecessary, for a glance at the subroutine PRINT (see Figure 9.2.2, for example) reveals that the reason it can display only the entries in ARRAY is that the values that define ARRAY—the word address (ARRAY), the number of rows (6), and the number of columns (6)—are set *within the subroutine itself*. Let us rewrite PRINT in such a way that it assumes that whenever it is called, R4, R5, and R6 have *already* been set by the calling routine to the number of rows, number of columns, and array address, respectively. The modified version of the subroutine is shown in Figure 9.3.1, which is essentially the earlier version with the register-setting instructions removed. (Notice, however, the use of R7 as a loop-controlling register, into which is copied the number of columns.) Now whenever we want to print *any* array we need only set up the array address (in R6), the row count (in R4), and the column count (in R5) *in the calling segment* of the program, then put the return address in R8 as before, and finally JMP to the routine. Observe that in this version, the use of R4, R5, and

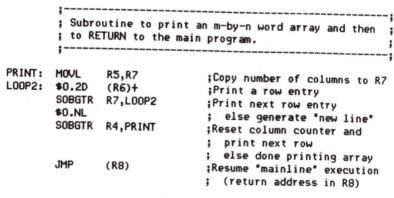

```
;-----------------------------------------------------;
; Subroutine to print an m-by-n word array and then   ;
; to RETURN to the main program.                      ;
;-----------------------------------------------------;

PRINT:  MOVL    R5,R7           ;Copy number of columns to R7
LOOP2:  $0.2D   (R6)+           ;Print a row entry
        SOBGTR  R7,LOOP2        ;Print next row entry
        $0.NL                   ; else generate "new line"
        SOBGTR  R4,PRINT        ;Reset column counter and
                                ; print next row
                                ; else done printing array
        JMP     (R8)            ;Resume "mainline" execution
                                ; (return address in R8)
```

Figure 9.3.1

R6 is far more explicit than before, and thus the chance for error has been reduced accordingly. But the danger has not been removed completely, for now R7 is a "hidden" register. Figure 9.3.2 shows this final version of PRINT, called twice to print the entries in two different arrays.

The chief difference between the two versions of PRINT is that the first always operates on a *fixed* set of data—array address, number of rows, number of columns—whereas the second operates on a *variable* set of data, which is determined by the calling program prior to jumping to the subroutine. Although a little more source code is required in the second case (since the contents of R4, R5, and R6 must be set *each* time PRINT is called), this version is clearly far more versatile than the first. In fact, most subroutines act on data that have been preset

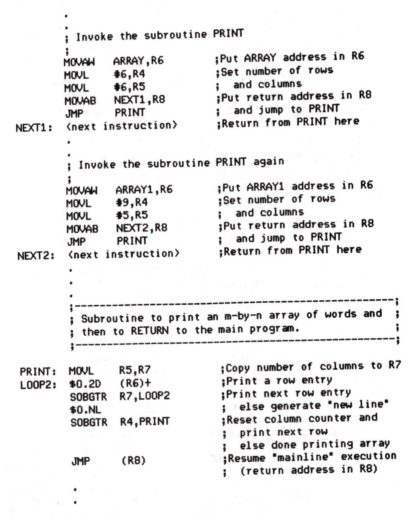

```
        .
        .
        .
    ; Invoke the subroutine PRINT
    ;
        MOVAW   ARRAY,R6        ;Put ARRAY address in R6
        MOVL    #6,R4           ;Set number of rows
        MOVL    #6,R5           ;  and columns
        MOVAB   NEXT1,R8        ;Put return address in R8
        JMP     PRINT           ;  and jump to PRINT
NEXT1:  <next instruction>      ;Return from PRINT here
        .

    ; Invoke the subroutine PRINT again
    ;
        MOVAW   ARRAY1,R6       ;Put ARRAY1 address in R6
        MOVL    #9,R4           ;Set number of rows
        MOVL    #5,R5           ;  and columns
        MOVAB   NEXT2,R8        ;Put return address in R8
        JMP     PRINT           ;  and jump to PRINT
NEXT2:  <next instruction>      ;Return from PRINT here
        .

        .
        .
    ;----------------------------------------------------;
    ; Subroutine to print an m-by-n array of words and   ;
    ; then to RETURN to the main program.                ;
    ;----------------------------------------------------;

PRINT:  MOVL    R5,R7           ;Copy number of columns to R7
LOOP2:  $O.2D   (R6)+           ;Print a row entry
        SOBGTR  R7,LOOP2        ;Print next row entry
        $O.NL                   ;  else generate "new line"
        SOBGTR  R4,PRINT        ;Reset column counter and
                                ;  print next row
                                ;  else done printing array
        JMP     (R8)            ;Resume "mainline" execution
                                ;  (return address in R8)
        .
        .
```

Figure 9.3.2

in this way by the calling program, rather than always operating on the same data each time they are called.

When a calling routine preestablishes data to be used by a subroutine as in the example above, those data are referred to as **arguments** or **parameters** for the subroutine, and the calling routine is said to **transmit** or **pass arguments** to the subroutine. In this specific example, the arguments transmitted to the subroutine PRINT are the array address, and the row and column counts. Notice that in this case the arguments are transmitted via three registers (R6, R4, and R5, respectively), but we shall see in the remainder of this chapter other ways in which information can be passed to a subroutine prior to its being invoked.

9.4 DEFICIENCIES OF THE "SUBROUTINE RETURN" SCHEME

The subroutine return technique that we have developed—putting the return address in, say, R8, jumping to the subroutine, and then returning with

$$\text{JMP} \quad (\text{R8})$$

works well and is not terribly complicated. But it has some deficiencies, and we shall see what these are as we attempt to expand our uses of subroutines in some slightly more complicated programming environments than what we have examined so far. As one of the sample subroutines to be used for illustrative purposes, we choose one that solves a problem with which we have already dealt, namely that of finding the largest of a collection of unsigned bytes (see, for example, the program of Figure 6.6.2). There are a number of ways in which we can provide such a subroutine with the information it needs to find an array maximum; we choose here to pass to it in R1 the address of the first byte in the (assumed contiguous) array and in R2 the number of bytes in the array. The subroutine will return the value of the largest byte in R0.

Figure 9.4.1 shows a sample subroutine, whose entry point we have named MAX, which behaves as described above. Its instructions are straightforward and by now familiar and thus should require no explanation. Observe that the subroutine returns via R8 (the assumption thus being that the calling routine has placed the return program counter value in that register). The programming segment of Figure 9.4.2 shows a typical call to MAX.

In Figure 9.4.3 we present a slight modification of MAX, which we name MAXADR, to which we pass the same information as before—the first-byte address in R1 and the byte count in R2—but which returns in R0 *not* the largest (unsigned) byte in the array, but rather the *address* of that byte. [Note that knowing *where* the largest byte is implies that we can determine the largest byte itself with an indirect reference to R0—(R0)—but that the reverse is *not* true; knowing *what* the largest byte is, as in the subroutine MAX, does not tell us *where* that byte is.] We make these changes for two reasons. First, MAXADR illustrates

```
;--------------------------------------------------------------;
; Subroutine to return in R0 the largest of an array of        ;
; unsigned bytes.  The main program passes to the sub-         ;
; routine the beginning array address in R1 and the            ;
; number of bytes in the array in R2.                          ;
;--------------------------------------------------------------;

MAX:     MOVB    (R1)+,R0        ;Make first number TEMPMAX for now
         BRB     LOOPND          ;Skip around to decrement counter
LOOP:    CMPB    (R1)+,R0        ;Is current number > TEMPMAX?
         BLEQU   LOOPND          ;No -- do not replace TEMPMAX
         MOVB    -1(R1),R0       ;Replace TEMPMAX with larger number
LOOPND:  SOBGTR  R2,LOOP         ;Check next number (if more to do)
         JMP     (R8)            ;Return to caller
```

Figure 9.4.1

another fashion in which a subroutine might return information to a calling program—by *address* rather than by *value*—and second, we are going to employ MAXADR immediately to solve another problem.

We noted in Exercise 8.10.2 that a common computational activity is the *sorting* of numerical data into some specified order. We shall take advantage of the subroutine MAXADR to sort a collection of (unsigned) bytes into *increasing order*; to be more specific, we shall take an array of bytes and rearrange them in such a way that the first is less than or equal to the second, the second is less than

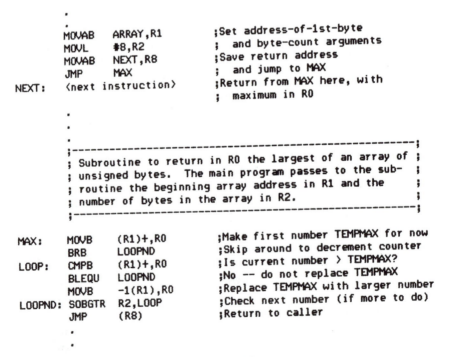

```
         .
         .
         MOVAB    ARRAY,R1       ;Set address-of-1st-byte
         MOVL     #8,R2          ; and byte-count arguments
         MOVAB    NEXT,R8        ;Save return address
         JMP      MAX            ; and jump to MAX
NEXT:    <next instruction>      ;Return from MAX here, with
                                 ; maximum in R0
         .
         .
         .

;--------------------------------------------------------------;
; Subroutine to return in R0 the largest of an array of        ;
; unsigned bytes.  The main program passes to the sub-         ;
; routine the beginning array address in R1 and the            ;
; number of bytes in the array in R2.                          ;
;--------------------------------------------------------------;

MAX:     MOVB    (R1)+,R0        ;Make first number TEMPMAX for now
         BRB     LOOPND          ;Skip around to decrement counter
LOOP:    CMPB    (R1)+,R0        ;Is current number > TEMPMAX?
         BLEQU   LOOPND          ;No -- do not replace TEMPMAX
         MOVB    -1(R1),R0       ;Replace TEMPMAX with larger number
LOOPND:  SOBGTR  R2,LOOP         ;Check next number (if more to do)
         JMP     (R8)            ;Return to caller
         .
         .
```

Figure 9.4.2

Subroutines, Stacks, and Procedures   Chap. 9

```
;----------------------------------------------------------;
; Subroutine to return in R0 the ADDRESS of the largest    ;
; of an array of unsigned bytes.  The main program         ;
; passes to the subroutine the beginning array address     ;
; in R1 and the number of bytes in the array in R2.        ;
;----------------------------------------------------------;

MAXADR: MOVAB    (R1)+,R0        ;Make address of first number
                                 ; TEMPMAX_ADDR for now
        BRB      LOOPND          ;Skip around to decrement counter
LOOP:   CMPB     (R1)+,(R0)      ;Current number > c(TEMPMAX_ADDR)?
        BLEQU    LOOPND          ;No -- do not replace TEMPMAX_ADDR
        MOVAB    -1(R1),R0       ;Replace TEMPMAX_ADDR with address
                                 ; of the larger number
LOOPND: SOBGTR   R2,LOOP         ;Check next number (if more to do)
        JMP      (R8)            ;Return to caller
```

Figure 9.4.3

or equal to the third, and so on. The technique we shall use is conceptually quite easy (although other methods may actually be easier to implement). We examine the entire list for the *largest* byte value. Having located it, we *exchange* that byte with the *last* byte in the list. [See Figure 9.4.4(a), where we have named the array BYTE_ARRY.] The effect, of course, is to do a rearrangement of the bytes so that the largest is at the bottom, and the finding of the largest can be accomplished by the subroutine MAXADR. Note that MAXADR returns the *address* of the largest, and this is precisely what is needed; it would not suffice simply to know the *value* of the largest (as returned by MAX), since the information would not tell us *where* to make the exchange. We now consider the *sublist* of the original array consisting of all the array entries except the *last*, and we simply apply the procedure to this sublist—we find the largest entry in the sublist and exchange the last entry *of the sublist* with it, as shown in Figure 9.4.4(b). Application of the process as many times as there are entries in the original array will result in a sorted

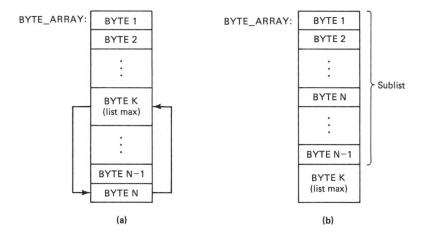

Figure 9.4.4

list, as desired. (Actually, the procedure need only be applied $N - 1$ times. Why?)

In Figure 9.4.5 we show a subroutine with entry point SORT which is intended to implement the algorithm we have just described, and there are a few things the reader should note. First, SORT uses R3 and R4 to make copies of the array address and the byte count, since these are values that are destroyed on each pass through one of SORT's loops; these two registers are somewhat "hidden" from the programmer's view and thus are a potential source of error. Second, the three instructions at XCHNG do the exchanging of the largest entry in the sublist with the last entry in the sublist. Those instructions use R1 as a temporary location to hold one of the values to be exchanged, since by the time the largest has been found, R1's contents is no longer of any value. Observe the use of indexed instructions here; they are exactly what is needed, but since we have used them only infrequently, the reader may need to take some care in examining them and the current contents of the registers involved to verify that these instructions do the desired byte exchange. Finally, SORT as written cannot possibly be successful. For although the calling program can invoke SORT by saving its return address in R8, when SORT invokes MAXADR, *also* saving *its* return address in this same register, the return address back to the *mainline* portion of the program is *lost*. Thus although SORT does in fact sort the list into increasing order, it will be unable to return to its caller. (What *will* happen when SORT attempts to execute its return statement?) The problem can be solved by saving the return address that SORT uses in some register other than R8 (and also different from R0, R1, R2, R3, and R4). We choose R9 for this purpose, and the program segment of Figure 9.4.6 shows a main program that successfully calls SORT to rearrange 8 bytes of ARRAY into increasing order.

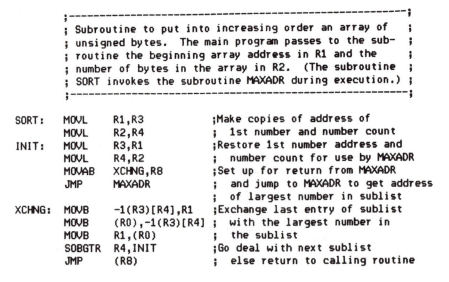

```
;-------------------------------------------------------------;
; Subroutine to put into increasing order an array of         ;
; unsigned bytes.  The main program passes to the sub-        ;
; routine the beginning array address in R1 and the           ;
; number of bytes in the array in R2.  (The subroutine        ;
; SORT invokes the subroutine MAXADR during execution.)       ;
;-------------------------------------------------------------;

SORT:   MOVL    R1,R3           ;Make copies of address of
        MOVL    R2,R4           ; 1st number and number count
INIT:   MOVL    R3,R1           ;Restore 1st number address and
        MOVL    R4,R2           ; number count for use by MAXADR
        MOVAB   XCHNG,R8        ;Set up for return from MAXADR
        JMP     MAXADR          ; and jump to MAXADR to get address
                                ; of largest number in sublist
XCHNG:  MOVB    -1(R3)[R4],R1   ;Exchange last entry of sublist
        MOVB    (R0),-1(R3)[R4] ; with the largest number in
        MOVB    R1,(R0)         ; the sublist
        SOBGTR  R4,INIT         ;Go deal with next sublist
        JMP     (R8)            ; else return to calling routine
```

Figure 9.4.5

Subroutines, Stacks, and Procedures   Chap. 9

```
                    .
                    .
            MOVAB    ARRAY,R1        ;Put ARRAY address in R1
            MOVL     #8,R2           ; and number count in R2
            MOVAB    NEXT,R9         ;Set up return address
            JMP      SORT            ; and go sort the array
   NEXT:    <next instruction>       ;Return from SORT here
                    .
                    .
                    .

;--------------------------------------------------------------;
; Subroutine to put into increasing order an array of          ;
; unsigned bytes.  The main program passes to the sub-         ;
; routine the beginning array address in R1 and the            ;
; number of bytes in the array in R2.  (The subroutine         ;
; SORT invokes the subroutine MAXADR during execution.)        ;
;--------------------------------------------------------------;

SORT:    MOVL    R1,R3           ;Make copies of address of
         MOVL    R2,R4           ; 1st number and number count
INIT:    MOVL    R3,R1           ;Restore 1st number address and
         MOVL    R4,R2           ; number count for use by MAXADR
         MOVAB   XCHNG,R8        ;Set up for return from MAXADR
         JMP     MAXADR          ; and jump to MAXADR to get address
                                 ; of largest number in sublist
XCHNG:   MOVB    -1(R3)[R4],R1   ;Exchange last entry of sublist
         MOVB    (R0),-1(R3)[R4] ; with the largest number in
         MOVB    R1,(R0)         ; the sublist
         SOBGTR  R4,INIT         ;Go deal with next sublist
         JMP     (R9)            ; else return to calling routine
                 .
                 .
                 .

;--------------------------------------------------------------;
; Subroutine to return in R0 the ADDRESS of the largest        ;
; of an array of unsigned bytes.  The main program             ;
; passes to the subroutine the beginning array address         ;
; in R1 and the number of bytes in the array in R2.            ;
;--------------------------------------------------------------;

MAXADR:  MOVAB   (R1)+,R0        ;Make address of first number
                                 ; TEMPMAX_ADDR for now
         BRB     LOOPND          ;Skip around to decrement counter
LOOP:    CMPB    (R1)+,(R0)      ;Current number > c(TEMPMAX_ADDR)?
         BLEQU   LOOPND          ;No -- do not replace TEMPMAX_ADDR
         MOVAB   -1(R1),R0       ;Replace TEMPMAX_ADDR with address
                                 ; of the larger number
LOOPND:  SOBGTR  R2,LOOP         ;Check next number (if more to do)
         JMP     (R8)            ;Return to caller
                 .
                 .
```

Figure 9.4.6

The problem that arose here results from a **nested subroutine call**—one subroutine, in the course of its execution, invoking another subroutine. We have managed to deal with it by changing the "return address register," but by now the reader may be disturbed by a couple of things. First, we may not always have sufficiently many registers to hold return addresses if much nesting goes on within a program, or if the nesting becomes very "deep"—subroutine A calls subroutine B, which in turn calls subroutine C, which calls subroutine D, and so on. Second, we may end up using so many general-purpose registers just to hold return addresses that there will be none left over for the usual register uses—counters, accumulators, pointers, and so on. But as serious as these problems might be, we show in the next two examples that even using different registers to hold the return addresses for subroutines that call other subroutines may not suffice to deal with a dilemma that quite simply has no solution by our present techniques.

Consider two subroutines, with entry points SUBR1 and SUBR2, which assume that the return addresses to their calling routines are saved in R10 and R11, respectively. Thus SUBR1 will return with the instruction

$$\text{JMP} \quad (\text{R10})$$

and SUBR2 with the instruction

$$\text{JMP} \quad (\text{R11})$$

Now for the same reason that the scheme of Figure 9.4.6 succeeded, if a main routine calls SUBR1 (saving its PC in R10), and SUBR1 calls SUBR2 (saving its PC in R11), and *then* SUBR2 executes a RETURN statement, *followed by* SUBR1's execution of a RETURN, control will be properly returned to the main routine. This situation is diagrammed in Figure 9.4.7, where we have used the following informal terminology. The "statement"

$$\text{CALL} \quad \text{SUBR1}\langle 10 \rangle$$

is shorthand for the sequence

```
          MOVAB    label,R10
          JMP      SUBR
label:    ⟨next instruction⟩
```

and the "statement"

$$\text{RETURN} \quad \langle 10 \rangle$$

means the same as

$$\text{JMP} \quad (\text{R10})$$

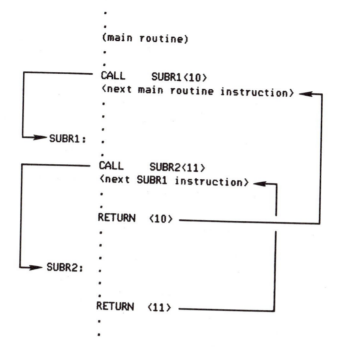

```
                    .
                    .
                    (main routine)
                    .
                    .
        ┌────────  CALL     SUBR1<10>
        │          <next main routine instruction> ◄──────┐
        │             .                                    │
        │             .                                    │
        │             .                                    │
        └─►SUBR1:  .                                        │
                      .                                     │
        ┌────────  CALL     SUBR2<11>                       │
        │          <next SUBR1 instruction> ◄──┐            │
        │             .                        │            │
        │             .                        │            │
        │          RETURN   <10> ──────────────┼────────────┘
        │             .                        │
        │             .                        │
        │             .                        │
        └─►SUBR2:  .                            │
                      .                         │
                      .                         │
                   RETURN   <11> ───────────────┘
                      .
                      .
```

Figure 9.4.7

with analogous interpretations for R11. That is, CALL and RETURN are simply mnemonics for the "call subroutine" and "return from subroutine" constructions we have already discovered.

But consider now what will happen if the main routine calls SUBR1, which in turn calls SUBR2. But this time, prior to executing its RETURN, *SUBR2 calls SUBR1* (see Figure 9.4.8). Then SUBR2 will put its return address in R10 (which is necessary, since SUBR1 does returns via R10), and this step *overlays* the current contents of R10, which was the *main routine* return address. We have here a situation similar to what we encountered earlier in this section, in which both SORT and MAXADR used the same register to save the return address, and then SORT called MAXADR. In the earlier case we were able to salvage the situation by changing SORT's "return address register" to R9, but here there is *nothing* that can be done to avoid the loss of a return address; we must simply dismiss this "A calls B calls A" construction as invalid. Subroutines that call one another are sometimes referred to as **reciprocal** or **complementary routines** (or **coroutines**, for short). We shall see some concrete examples later in the chapter, as well as in the exercises.

As a final example of a subroutine call that leads to an irreparable disaster, consider a subroutine, say the subroutine SUBR1 of the preceding examples, which *calls itself*. Such a subroutine is called **recursive** and a diagram is provided in Figure 9.4.9. The reader should have no difficulty in showing that the main routine return address is lost as soon as SUBR1 invokes itself.

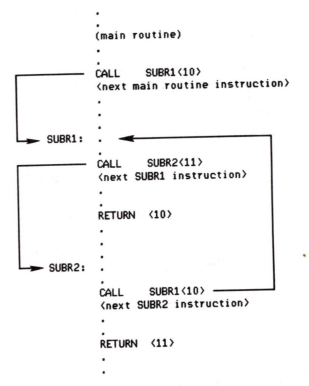

Figure 9.4.8

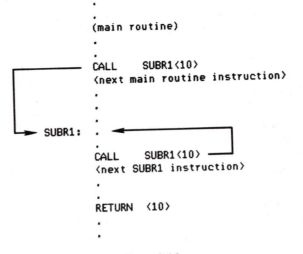

Figure 9.4.9

9.5 A SECOND SOLUTION TO THE "SUBROUTINE RETURN" PROBLEM

In Section 9.4 we noted two principal deficiencies of the "jump to subroutine/ return from subroutine" scheme as we had developed it. One of these involved the tying up of registers, to hold return addresses, thus making those registers unavailable for more general use. The other, and far more serious and substantive, was that the technique did not allow for certain programming constructions that can arise in a natural way in the solutions of problems—the scheme simply comes apart if we attempt recursion, for example. In this section we solve the first of these problems (it is the simpler of the two), and in turn we will be led to a most ingenious solution to the second.

To avoid the use of a register to save the return address when jumping to a subroutine, consider the effect of simply storing the return address in a *fixed memory location* (longword). Of course, we could not use the *same* fixed location for *all* subroutines, because then not even the simple subroutine nesting with which we have already been successful would be possible. But suppose, instead, that we somehow associate *with each subroutine* a longword whose precise function is to hold the return address for those routines which call that subroutine. To see how this scheme might work, consider the following version of the subroutine MAX of Figure 9.4.1. Notice that at the entry point MAX1 (Figure 9.5.1) is *not* MAX1's first executable instruction, but rather a 4-byte = 1-longword block of storage. It is here that the calling routine's return address is going to be saved. Observe also how MAX1 returns to the calling program:

$$\text{JMP} \quad @\text{MAX1}$$

Since the longword labeled MAX1 contains the caller's return address, this deferred instruction will put that return address in the program counter, thus achieving the

```
;--------------------------------------------------------------
; Subroutine to return in R0 the largest of an array of
; unsigned bytes.  The main program passes to the sub-
; routine the beginning array address in R1 and the
; number of bytes in the array in R2.
;--------------------------------------------------------------

MAX1:    .BLKL    1              ;Return address goes here
MAX:     MOVB     (R1)+,R0       ;Make first number TEMPMAX for now
         BRB      LOOPND         ;Skip around to decrement counter
LOOP:    CMPB     (R1)+,R0       ;Is current number > TEMPMAX?
         BLEQU    LOOPND         ;No -- do not replace TEMPMAX
         MOVB     -1(R1),R0      ;Replace TEMPMAX with larger number
LOOPND:  SOBGTR   R2,LOOP        ;Check next number (if more to do)
         JMP      @MAX1          ;Return to caller
```

Figure 9.5.1

return. In Figure 9.5.2 we show a segment in which a mainline program calls MAX1 (compare this listing with that of Figure 9.4.2). Notice that the calling program has put its return address, not in R8, but rather in the longword at MAX1. Then, instead of JMPing to MAX1, the routine now JMPs to MAX1 + 4, the address of MAX1's first executable instruction.

The device we have described here does work, and it has the advantage over the earlier scheme that it does *not* require the use of a register to hold the return address. Thus this technique allows for the writing of as many subroutines in a program as we might wish, without any concern for register use. The reader should verify, perhaps by rewriting the segment of Figure 9.4.6, that no problems will be encountered with subroutine nesting, *provided* that no two subroutines successively call one another, and no subroutine calls itself. That is, we have eliminated the first deficiency mentioned at the beginning of this section, but not the second. (Incidentally, what we have described here is more than a theoretical contrivance— this technique was quite popular in the early development of minicomputers.)

Let us reconsider the diagram of Figure 9.4.8, in which two subroutines called one another. The new version is shown in Figure 9.5.3, in which we have rewritten the CALL and RETURN "statements" to conform to our newly invented "jump to subroutine" technique. An analysis of just why this scheme does *not* work will be most illuminating. When the main routine calls SUBR1, it puts *its* return

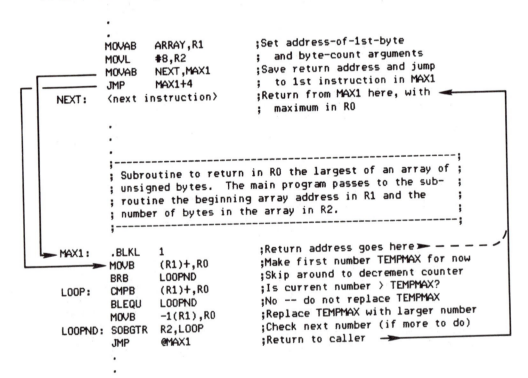

```
        MOVAB   ARRAY,R1        ;Set address-of-1st-byte
        MOVL    #8,R2           ;  and byte-count arguments
        MOVAB   NEXT,MAX1       ;Save return address and jump
        JMP     MAX1+4          ;  to 1st instruction in MAX1
NEXT:   <next instruction>      ;Return from MAX1 here, with
                                ;  maximum in R0
                    .
                    .
                    .
        ;--------------------------------------------------------;
        ; Subroutine to return in R0 the largest of an array of ;
        ; unsigned bytes.  The main program passes to the sub-  ;
        ; routine the beginning array address in R1 and the     ;
        ; number of bytes in the array in R2.                   ;
        ;--------------------------------------------------------;

MAX1:   .BLKL   1               ;Return address goes here
        MOVB    (R1)+,R0        ;Make first number TEMPMAX for now
        BRB     LOOPND          ;Skip around to decrement counter
LOOP:   CMPB    (R1)+,R0        ;Is current number > TEMPMAX?
        BLEQU   LOOPND          ;No -- do not replace TEMPMAX
        MOVB    -1(R1),R0       ;Replace TEMPMAX with larger number
LOOPND: SOBGTR  R2,LOOP         ;Check next number (if more to do)
        JMP     @MAX1           ;Return to caller
                    .
                    .
```

Figure 9.5.2

Subroutines, Stacks, and Procedures   Chap. 9

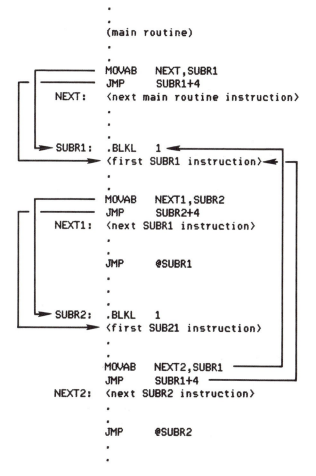

```
                    .
                    .
             (main routine)
                    .
                    .
             MOVAB    NEXT,SUBR1
             JMP      SUBR1+4
     NEXT:   <next main routine instruction>
                    .
                    .
                    .
   SUBR1:    .BLKL    1
             <first SUBR1 instruction>
                    .
                    .
             MOVAB    NEXT1,SUBR2
             JMP      SUBR2+4
    NEXT1:   <next SUBR1 instruction>
                    .
                    .
             JMP      @SUBR1
                    .
                    .
                    .
   SUBR2:    .BLKL    1
             <first SUB21 instruction>
                    .
                    .
             MOVAB    NEXT2,SUBR1
             JMP      SUBR1+4
    NEXT2:   <next SUBR2 instruction>
                    .
                    .
             JMP      @SUBR2
                    .
                    .
```

Figure 9.5.3

address in the longword at SUBR1. When SUBR1 calls SUBR2, it put *its* return address in the longword at SUBR2. All is well until SUBR2 calls SUBR1. For the "jump to subroutine" technique dictates that SUBR2 should put its return address in the longword at SUBR1, but this longword is *already occupied*—it contains the return address back to the main routine. And herein lies the dilemma—we need to save a return address, yet we have no place to save it which will not result in the destruction of essential information.

There appears to be no hope of somehow patching this scheme in a trivial way to avoid the problem we have encountered, yet the use of *memory locations* for the storage of return addresses is most appealing, for reasons of conservation of registers. The heart of the problem lies in the fact that associated with each subroutine is a *single* longword to be used for the storage of return addresses, and under certain circumstances we may have *several* return addresses, each associated with the same subroutine, that need to be saved *simultaneously*, so we shall focus our attention on a solution to that difficulty. Rather than assign to each subroutine a longword to hold return addresses (which we chose to make the first longword of the subroutine), suppose that we simply create an entire block of longwords, somewhere in memory, whose sole purpose shall be to hold return addresses—*any* return addresses needed by *any* subroutine in the program. Now when we need to jump to any subroutine, we store the return address somewhere in this block of storage. When a subroutine is ready to return to its caller, it retrieves the appropriate return address and puts it in the program counter.

Two questions arise immediately. First, when a return address needs to be saved, how are we to know where to save it? That is, how can the calling routine know which longwords in the block of longwords are free and which are currently holding return addresses? Second, when the "appropriate" return address is said to be placed in the program counter to achieve the subroutine return, how can the subroutine know which one this is—which longword in this block of longwords is the one whose contents is the return address for that subroutine call? The first question is relatively easy to deal with. For the sake of a concrete example, suppose we set aside a block of, say, 100 longwords to be used for the saving of return addresses. (As we shall see, this would allow for many more subroutine calls than we would reasonably expect in most programming environments, so this amount of storage will almost always be adequate.) Assume that in a particular program, this block extends from location 00001F24 to 000020B0 inclusive. Now when return addresses need to be saved, the first is put in the last block entry (at 000020B0), the next is placed in the next-to-last entry (at 000020AC), and so on, working from the bottom of the block up toward the top. (Notice that this means we are adding return addresses starting at higher-addressed locations and moving toward lower-addressed locations.) Figure 9.5.4 diagrams this scheme.

The matter of keeping track of which longwords in the block are free and which are in use at any time is easily managed. (As shown in Figure 9.5.4, evidently three longwords are in use, while the other 97 are free.) According to the way we have devised the method of storing return addresses in the block, each new return address gets stacked up on top of the preceding ones. If we let a register, say R6, "point at"—contain the address of—the *last* entry that was put in the block, we will always know that the memory longword whose address is immediately above c(R6)—that is, the longword whose address is c(R6) − 4—is the next available (free) location in the block (see Figure 9.5.5). Suppose now that another return address needs to be put in the block of longwords. (Relative to our concrete example, this would be the "4th return address.") If we assume that that return address has the value NEXT, the instruction

$$\text{MOVAB} \quad \text{NEXT}, -(\text{R6})$$

will have the two necessary effects, namely, c(R6) will *first* be decremented *by 4*, so that it is now pointing at the longword immediately above the last address that was put in the block, and *then* the address NEXT will be placed in the location

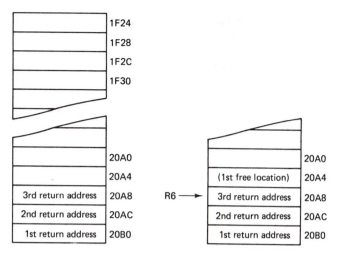

Figure 9.5.4   Figure 9.5.5

pointed at by R6. Figure 9.5.6 diagrams this activity, at the conclusion of which we once again have R6 pointing at the last entry that was put in the block.

Once the block of 100 longwords has been established, but before any return addresses have been placed in it, how should the pointer register R6 be initialized? R6 should be given the value that is the address of the longword immediately *following* the block (namely, 000020B4), so that when the first return address is put in the block, the *preautodecrementing*—(R6)—will *first* decrement c(R6) to 000020B0, and *then* the return address will be put in that location, 000020B0, as desired. Thus in this particular example, R6 can be initialized with the instruction

MOVL   #^X20B4,R6

or if the first (lowest addressed) longword of the block is labeled, say, BLOCK,

MOVAL   BLOCK+⟨4*100⟩,R6

Now that we have seen how return addresses can be saved in this block of longwords in such a way that no new return address will overlay any already-saved address,

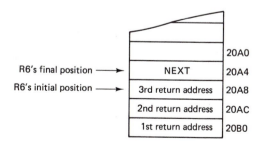

Figure 9.5.6

we deal with the question: How can a subroutine determine *which* of the saved return addresses to use for return back to the routine that called it? A simple example will give us some direction, and we choose the programming segment of Figure 9.5.2 as an illustration. That figure contains the "save return address" instructions

$$\begin{aligned} &\text{MOVAB} \quad \text{NEXT,MAX1} \\ &\text{JMP} \qquad \text{MAX1}+4 \\ \text{NEXT:} \quad &\langle \text{next instruction} \rangle \end{aligned}$$

and these must now be changed to

$$\begin{aligned} &\text{MOVAB} \quad \text{NEXT}, -(\text{R6}) \\ &\text{JMP} \qquad \text{MAX1} \\ \text{NEXT:} \quad &\langle \text{next instruction} \rangle \end{aligned}$$

If we assume that at the time these instructions are encountered there are no return addresses in the block devoted to saving return addresses, then *before* executing these instructions, the block will appear as in Figure 9.5.7, and *after* executing them, the appearance of this block will be as shown in Figure 9.5.8. Once we have JMPed to MAX1, and executed the instructions there, how are we to *return*? Evidently the return address is being "pointed at" by R6, that is, the return address is in memory location 000020B0, and c(R6) = 000020B0. Thus we need to execute the instruction

$$\text{JMP} \quad @0(\text{R6})$$

to put this return address back in the program counter. However, we need also to be aware that we are now *finished* with that return address (NEXT), and thus we should *remove* it from the block of return addresses. This can be done if, instead, we return with the instruction

$$\text{JMP} \quad @(\text{R6})+$$

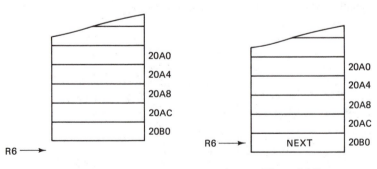

Figure 9.5.7   Figure 9.5.8

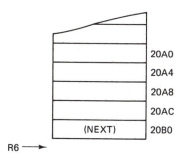

Figure 9.5.9

which will not only put NEXT in the program counter, but will also advance c(R6) to 000020B4. Thus upon completion of the return, the block memory that holds return addresses will again appear as in Figure 9.5.7. Of course, the value NEXT is still physically in location 000020B0, but since the "return address pointer" R6 is *below* that location, we no longer interpret it as one of the saved return addresses. In fact, in this case there are once again no saved addresses (see Figure 9.5.9). Figure 9.5.10 shows the modification of Figure 9.5.2 which implements this technique.

For additional insight into this "save return address/restore return address" technique, consider again the program segment of Figure 9.4.4, in which a main routine called the subroutine SORT, which in turn called the subroutine MAXADR.

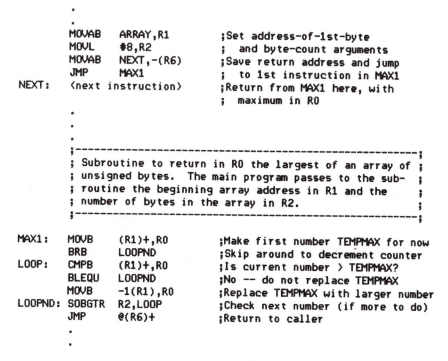

Figure 9.5.10

```
        .
        .
        MOVAB   ARRAY,R1           ;Put ARRAY address in R1
        MOVL    #8,R2             ;  and number count in R2
        MOVAB   NEXT,-(R6)        ;Set up return address
        JMP     SORT             ;  and go sort the array
NEXT:   <next instruction>       ;Return from SORT here
        .
        .
        .

        ;----------------------------------------------------------;
        ; Subroutine to put into increasing order an array of      ;
        ; unsigned bytes.  The main program passes to the sub-     ;
        ; routine the beginning array address in R1 and the        ;
        ; number of bytes in the array in R2.  (The subroutine     ;
        ; SORT invokes the subroutine MAXADR during execution.)    ;
        ;----------------------------------------------------------;

SORT:   MOVL    R1,R3            ;Make copies of address of
        MOVL    R2,R4            ;  1st number and number count
INIT:   MOVL    R3,R1            ;Restore 1st number address and
        MOVL    R4,R2            ;  number count for use by MAXADR
        MOVAB   XCHNG,-(R6)      ;Set up for return from MAXADR
        JMP     MAXADR           ;  and jump to MAXADR to get address
                                 ;  of largest number in sublist
XCHNG:  MOVB    -1(R3)[R4],R1    ;Exchange last entry of sublist
        MOVB    (R0),-1(R3)[R4]  ;  with the largest number in
        MOVB    R1,(R0)          ;  the sublist
        SOBGTR  R4,INIT          ;Go deal with next sublist
        JMP     @(R6)+           ;  else return to calling routine
        .
        .
        .

        ;----------------------------------------------------------;
        ; Subroutine to return in R0 the ADDRESS of the largest    ;
        ; of an array of unsigned bytes.  The main program         ;
        ; passes to the subroutine the beginning array address     ;
        ; in R1 and the number of bytes in the array in R2.        ;
        ;----------------------------------------------------------;

MAXADR: MOVAB   (R1)+,R0         ;Make address of first number
                                 ;  TEMPMAX_ADDR for now
        BRB     LOOPND           ;Skip around to decrement counter
LOOP:   CMPB    (R1)+,(R0)       ;Current number > c(TEMPMAX_ADDR)?
        BLEQU   LOOPND           ;No -- do not replace TEMPMAX_ADDR
        MOVAB   -1(R1),R0        ;Replace TEMPMAX_ADDR with address
                                 ;  of the larger number
LOOPND: SOBGTR  R2,LOOP          ;Check next number (if more to do)
        JMP     @(R6)+           ;Return to caller
        .
        .
```

Figure 9.5.11

This is an example of subroutine call *nesting*, and it will be instructive to follow the condition of the block of return addresses and its pointer, R6. Figure 9.5.11 shows this segment rewritten to correspond to our latest subroutine "jump to/return from" scheme.

We again assume that at the time the main routine is ready to execute its jump to SORT, no return addresses are saved in the block of return address storage, so its appearance is as shown in Figure 9.5.7. When the instruction

JMP   SORT

is executed, that block of storage will contain the return address NEXT, as given in Figure 9.5.12. Now execution picks up at SORT, which after a few instructions puts *its* return address XCHNG in the block of storage and transfers control to MAXADR. The "return address storage" block and its pointer now appear as shown in Figure 9.5.13.

The subroutine MAXADR now executes, and when it is ready to return (after the SOBGTR loop is completed), what return address should it use? Of course we want it to return to the instruction immediately following the jump to MAXADR in the SORT routine; that is, we wish to return to XCHNG. But note that this is precisely the return address currently pointed at by R6 (Figure 9.5.13). Thus since the *last* jump-to-subroutine that was executed (from SORT to MAXADR) saved its return address *on top of* any other return addresses in the block of storage, the *next* return-from-subroutine that is executed should use this last address as its return address, and this is exactly the address to which the return address pointer is pointing. Thus the instruction

JMP   @(R6)+

puts XCHNG in the program counter and *adds 4 to* c(R6), execution resumes at XCHNG, and the block of storage now looks as shown in Figure 9.5.14.

We see that this sequence of instructions—save the return address XCHNG, jump to MAXADR, execute the instructions of MAXADR, restore the return address XCHNG—occurs again in SORT (and, in fact, occurs six more times). But notice that each time XCHNG is saved, the memory longword at 000020AC keeps getting used over again since, as we see from Figure 9.5.14, when MAXADR

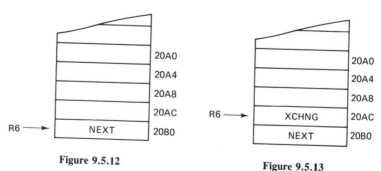

Figure 9.5.12   Figure 9.5.13

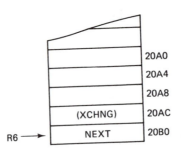

R6 →

Figure 9.5.14

returns, XCHNG is "removed from the block of storage," so to say. Observe, however, that NEXT remains in the block. Finally, SORT is ready to restore a return address (at the JMP instruction following its SOBGTR). What return address will be used here? The answer is, whatever address R6 is pointing to, and as we see from Figure 9.5.14, this is NEXT. Thus we have successfully returned to the main routine that called SORT in the first place.

What is it that makes this scheme work? That is, why is the correct return address always available? The answer lies in part in the fact that the *logic* of the situation dictates that the address to be used for a subroutine return be the address of the instruction immediately following the *last* JMP to that subroutine. Successful implementation of that logic derives from the way we have used the pointer R6 to point at the locations in the block of storage where new return addresses will go (when a subroutine is called), and where subroutines will obtain addresses for returns. It is this **last-in/first-out** structure that has been given to this contiguous block of longwords that makes the scheme work exactly as we want it to—the *last* address that is put *in* the block is the *first* address taken *out* when a subroutine return executes.

Although the reader may find this particular structure and the CALL/RE-TURN scheme which it implements interesting, he or she may remain unimpressed, inasmuch as the other techniques we introduced earlier could handle subroutine nesting with no difficulty. But this latest scheme is distinctly different, for we shall now show that in addition to managing the *nesting* of subroutine calls, it also handles *recursion* in a remarkably automatic fashion. To this end, we construct a recursive subroutine the purpose of which is to calculate *n*! (*factorial n*), where *n* is a nonnegative integer. Recall the definition of **factorial *n*:**

$$n! = \begin{cases} 0 & \text{if } n \leq 1 \\ n \cdot (n-1)! & \text{if } n > 1 \end{cases}$$

As we see, the definition itself is recursive. For example, 3! depends for its definition on $(3 - 1)! = 2!$, which in turn depends on $(2 - 1)! = 1! = 1$. Thus $3! = 3 \cdot (3 - 1)! = 3 \cdot 2! = 3 \cdot 2 \cdot (2 - 1)! = 3 \cdot 2 \cdot 1! = 3 \cdot 2 \cdot 1 = 6$.

We shall follow through the execution of the program of Figure 9.5.15 in some detail, paying particular attention to the state of the saved return addresses and the pointer R6, as the main routine calls the subroutine FACT, and then as FACT calls *itself*. Note that a block (BLOCK) of 100 longwords has been established for the purpose of holding return addresses, and that the first executable

Subroutines, Stacks, and Procedures   Chap. 9

```
;----------------------------------------------------------------;
; Use subroutine FACT to calculate 3! (factorial 3).            ;
;----------------------------------------------------------------;

BLOCK:  .BLKL   100             ;Block for saving
                                ;  return addresses

START:  .WORD   ^M<>            ;Program start address
        MOVAL   BLOCK+400,R6    ;Initialize "return address"
                                ;  pointer at <end of BLOCK>
                                ;  + <1 longword>
        MOVL    #3,R4           ;Number n whose factorial
                                ;  n! is to be found
        MOVL    #1,R5           ;(Needed by routine FACT)
        MOVAB   NEXT,-(R6)      ;Save return address in BLOCK
        JMP     FACT            ;  and jump to subroutine
NEXT:   $0.4D   R5              ;Print n!
        $EXIT                   ;  and exit

;----------------------------------------------------------------;
; Subroutine FACT returns n! in R5.  The calling pro-           ;
; gram passes to FACT the value of n in R4.                     ;
;----------------------------------------------------------------;

FACT:   TSTL    R4              ;Has R4 been decremented to 0?
        BEQL    FACT.6          ;Yes -- begin sequence of returns
        MULL    R4,R5           ;  else accumulate product and
        DECL    R4              ;  decrement c(R4) for next pass
        MOVAB   FACT.6,-(R6)    ;Save return address
        JMP     FACT            ;  and call this routine again
FACT.6: JMP     @(R6)+          ;Return from subroutine

        .END    START           ;Begin execution at START
```

Figure 9.5.15

instruction of the program sets the "saved return address" pointer R6 to the long-word immediately *following* this block. Next, a 3 is put in R4, for we are going to calculate 3!. (This is admittedly not much of a challenge—the answer is 6—but it is large enough to see how the return addresses behave, and it is small enough to avoid a lot of extraneous detail that would only serve to obscure the situation.) The next instruction puts the number 1 in R5. This is needed by the subroutine FACT itself, and it would be far more pleasing to let that register be set within the subroutine. However, measures would then have to be taken to *avoid* resetting it when FACT was called recursively (although this can, in fact, be done), and thus this compromise is used to eliminate some additional, possibly confusing, detail.

The next two instructions jump to the subroutine FACT, from the mainline routine, and at this time we shall begin closely monitoring the status of the return addresses in BLOCK and the pointer, R6. The various stages are shown in Figure 9.5.16, where we show only the last few longwords in the block. Initially, there are no return addresses in BLOCK, which is reflected by the position of R6 in

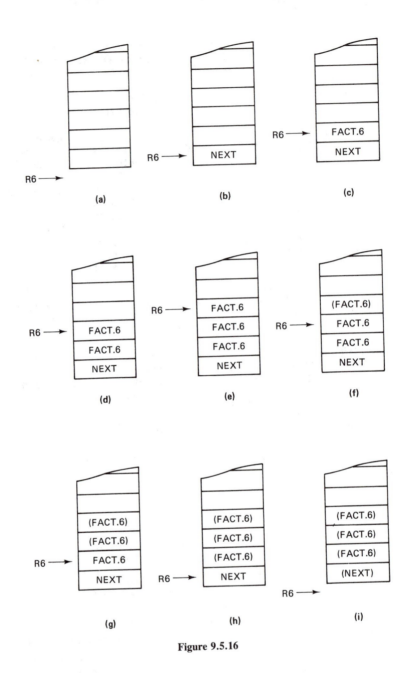

Figure 9.5.16

Figure 9.5.16(a). Figure 9.5.16(b) shows the condition of BLOCK after the return address NEXT has been saved. Execution in the subroutine FACT now begins, and the test (TSTL) reveals that c(R4) = 3; thus the BEQL is *not* executed; instead, c(R5) = 1 is multiplied by c(R4) = 3, and the result (3) is left in R5. c(R4) is then decremented, to 2, and FACT is again jumped to. The return address FACT.6 is saved, as shown in Figure 9.5.16(c), and the routine is reentered at FACT.

Subroutines, Stacks, and Procedures   Chap. 9

Again $c(R4) = 2$ is tested and found to be nonzero, so $c(R5)$ is multiplied by $c(R4)$, giving $c(R5) = 6$, and $c(R4)$ is decremented to 1. FACT is jumped to once again, with the return address FACT.6 once more put in BLOCK [Figure 9.5.16(d)]. Since $c(R4) = 1$ is still nonzero, $c(R5)$ is multiplied by $c(R4)$, $c(R4)$ is decremented to 0, and FACT is jumped to once again, with the return address FACT.6 being put still another time in BLOCK, as shown in Figure 9.5.16(e). But this time, when the TSTL instruction at FACT is executed, $c(R4)$ *is* zero. Consequently, the BEQL transfers control to FACT.6. The effect of the instruction

$$\text{JMP} \quad @(R6)+$$

at FACT.6 is to put the address pointed at by R6 into the program counter and add 4 to $c(R6)$. Since R6 points at the address FACT.6, this value is put in the program counter and BLOCK now appears as shown in Figure 9.5.16(f). But notice that placing FACT.6 in the program counter transfers control right back to FACT.6, where the sequence of events described immediately above takes place *again* [see Figure 9.5.16(g)]. Once more $c(PC) = $ FACT.6, so the "subroutine return" statement is executed again, we have the status of BLOCK as shown in Figure 9.5.16(h), and the program counter is again at FACT.6. But *this time*, when

$$\text{JMP} \quad @(R6)+$$

is executed, the value NEXT is placed in the program counter, BLOCK is back to its initial (empty) state as given in Figure 9.5.16(i), and control is finally returned to the main routine at NEXT. Here the contents of R5, namely $6 = 3!$, is printed, and the program exits.

We have been so involved with the details of saving return addresses in BLOCK and later restoring them that perhaps the reader has lost sight of the objective of this example, which was to show that *multiple* return addresses for the *same* subroutine could be saved *simultaneously*, and that the last-in/first-out structure which we have imposed on BLOCK via the use of R6 would properly maintain the order in which those return addresses were added and in which they were removed. Some care was required in writing the routine FACT so that its return addresses would "unravel" from BLOCK properly. (One of the exercises gives an example of another version of FACT which appears to be logically correct but which, when called recursively, does not handle the successive "returns" properly.) But observe that once the logic has been correctly designed, the successive saving of return addresses, and then later the restoring of those addresses, has been quite automatically handled by the *structure itself.*

We commented earlier in this section that 100 longwords set aside for the saving of return addresses would almost always be adequate for these purposes, and by now we see why that is. For once a return address is put in this block, it does not remain there forever, tying up that longword. Rather, that return address is in the block only until it is used to return from a subroutine, at which time it is "removed" from the block, and the longword is free to be used by another return address that needs to be saved. Thus the area that holds these addresses is a rather dynamic affair, growing and shrinking as subroutines are called and as they execute "return" statements. In the factorial *n* example above, we have sufficient room for the initial call to FACT, together with 99 recursive calls of FACT to itself. (This is an extreme and unrealistic case—calculating 99! results in a number so gigantic that it could scarcely be held in R5. Even 10! is already greater than 3 million.) In most day-to-day programming, a 100-longword block for the storage of return addresses would be excessive; perhaps a dozen or so would do. In other environments, 100 may be inadequate. It is up to the programmer to understand the problem at hand well enough to make a realistic judgment regarding an appropriate size for this "saved return address" block.

9.6 STACKS AND THEIR USES

The block of "return address" storage (BLOCK, in the last example), together with a pointer (R6), form a structure known as a **stack**. Before we give a formal description of this structure, we make a couple of comments about what we have done so far. First, it should be clear that although the pointer R6 was the key to the management of saved and restored return addresses, it should be equally clear that the fact that we used register 6 had nothing to do with the results; any register would have done as well except, of course, R15 = PC. However, the reader will recall that we stated in Chapter 7 that some few hardware operations, none of which we have yet encountered, make use of some or all of R0 to R5; these registers are subject to "hidden" side effects. Thus we may conceivably be on somewhat dangerous ground if we choose one of these as a pointer in place of R6. And it should also be clear that once we have assigned R6 (or some other register) to this task, we must take care not to alter c(R6) *except* by those instructions that actually place return addresses in the block, or remove them from the block to achieve subroutine returns. The reader will recognize a trade-off here. In the first "subroutine return" scheme we devised, return addresses were held in registers, and this technique could easily have used up more registers than we were willing or able to devote to that purpose. In the second scheme, return addresses were stored in the leading longword of the subroutine itself, so *no* registers were required. In our latest and final solution to the "subroutine return" problem, *one* register is used for the management of *all* subroutines, and further, many earlier problems have simply disappeared. The devoting of a single register to this task, thereby making it unavailable for more general uses, seems a small price to pay for what has been accomplished.

Second, the reader may have been puzzled by the fact that once we had allocated 100 longwords as a block of storage for the saving of return addresses, we put the very first address that needed to be saved in the *last* (highest-addressed) longword. In fact, that block of longwords could as well have been managed in a "top-to-bottom" (lowest address to highest address) fashion. But now the pointer, say R6 again, would have to be initialized at the address of the *first* longword of

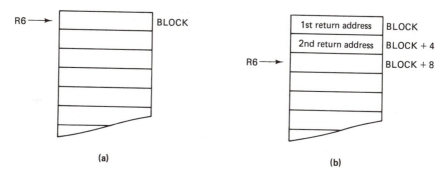

Figure 9.6.1

the block [see Figure 9.6.1(a)]. To add, say, two return addresses we would use the instructions

$$\text{MOVAB} \quad \langle \text{1st return address} \rangle,(R6)+$$
$$\text{MOVAB} \quad \langle \text{2nd return address} \rangle,(R6)+$$

yielding the situation shown in Figure 9.6.1(b). To restore a return address in order to bring about a subroutine return, we might be tempted to use the instruction

$$\text{JMP} \quad @-(R6)$$

which directly corresponds to the earlier $@(R6)+$ mode. But as we know, there *is* no such addressing mode. The best we could do would be to implement some sort of construction as

$$\text{TSTL} \quad -(R6)$$
$$\text{JMP} \quad @(R6)$$

the first instruction doing the necessary adjustment of the pointer by -4, the second instruction doing the actual return to the caller. Thus the scheme is not nearly as tidy as what we have already invented, and in fact we have two other objections. The first is purely visual. We tend to think of the appearance of memory locations in such a way that those with lower addresses are physically *above* those with higher addresses, probably influenced by the fact that the assembler uses lower addresses first, and assembler listings show these addresses in a "lower addresses at the top of the page" format. Since we tend to visualize new return addresses as being "stacked *on top of*" earlier saved addresses, it is somewhat more aesthetically pleasing to have the saved return addresses growing *upward* rather than *downward*. Second, notice that in this second scheme, the pointer register does not point at the last-entered address; rather, it points at the *first unused* longword in the block. It is for these reasons that we prefer the technique as originally developed, but the reader should be aware that there is nothing *wrong* with the second scheme. Despite its awkwardnesses, it would serve our purposes just as well.

We are now in a position to describe more formally what we mean by a stack structure. A **stack** consists of

1. A collection of data (possibly of different types) in main memory, called **stack entries**.
2. A **linear ordering** on the stack entries by which the unique **predecessor** and **successor** (if any) of each entry can be determined. One entry, called the **first entry** or **bottom entry**, has no predecessor; another entry, called the **last entry** or **top entry**, has no successor.

We also require that there be two "operations," called **PUSH_STACK** and **POP_STACK**, with the following properties. PUSH_STACK places a new entry in the stack, and the new entry is *always* the successor of the currently *last* entry, this new entry then becoming the new *last* or *top* entry. POP_STACK removes an entry from the stack, *always* removing the currently *last* entry, thus leaving that entry's predecessor (if any) as the new *last* or *top* entry. Thus the addition and removal of stack entries always takes place at the *top* end of the stack. When an entry is put on the stack, we say that that entry is **pushed onto** the stack; and when an entry is removed from the stack, we say that it is **popped off** the stack. A longword that is used to hold the address of the top entry of the stack is called the **stack pointer** for that stack. Because of the actions of the "operations" PUSH_STACK and POP_STACK, which we declare to be the *only* ways in which entries can enter or leave the stack, a stack is referred to as a **last-in/first-out** or **LIFO** structure.

We recognize, of course, that the structure discussed in detail in Section 9.5 is an example of a stack. In particular, we allocated 100 longwords of storage for return addresses, used R6 as a stack pointer, and when an address needed to be saved, we did so with

MOVAB   NEXT, − (R6)

This instruction serves as an example of PUSH_STACK. In a similar fashion, '

JMP   @(R6)+

removes the top entry from the stack and thus acts as POP_STACK. But the reader should be aware that this example is a rather special case of the use of a stack; there is nothing in the description above of a stack which dictates that it be used exclusively for the saving of return addresses for the management of jumps to and returns from subroutines. In fact, we shall see later in this section that a stack is a very general structure that can be used for a variety of purposes.

At the risk of being pedantic, we need to make a few observations about stacks as we have described them. First, the only concrete example of a stack that we have so far began with the allocation of *contiguous* memory for the structure, and the entries were placed in *consecutively addressed* locations. Yet there is no such requirement in the description, only that a stack be a first-in/last-out structure. In truth, stacks are almost always constructed in this fashion, but they need not be; the reader is asked in some of the exercises to consider a few alternative schemes. Next, if as in the example above, some block of memory is preallocated to hold the stack entries, that block is not, strictly speaking, "the stack." Rather, the stack consists only of the entries that have been added to this block with a PUSH_STACK operation and which have not yet been removed with POP_STACK. (This accounts for our earlier remarks, which stated that once a return address had been "removed"—popped off the stack—it was to be thought of as "no longer in the set of return addresses"—no longer in the stack—even though it physically remained in the block of storage.) Any such storage that is preallocated for stack use might be referred to as **stack space** or **stack area**. Finally, it is clear that to manage a collection of data as a stack, we need to keep track of the *last* or *top* entry. The address of that last entry is almost always held in some register, which is then called the stack pointer, as in our principal example. But a register is not *required* for this purpose, and the reader is again referred to the exercises for some examples.

To see how a stack might be used for purposes other than the saving of return addresses, let us return to the programming example of Figure 9.5.11, in which a mainline routine invoked the subroutine SORT, which in turn called MAXADR. The main program, of course, makes explicit use of R1 and R2 (and R6, for the saving of the return address) when it invokes SORT. However, beyond these three registers, the mainline is perhaps not "aware" that R0, R3, and R4, registers of perhaps some consequence to the mainline, will be employed by SORT and MAXADR. Evidently, the mainline routine will have to be very careful about its own register use to avoid disaster, *unless* each subroutine can make *its* register needs *transparent to the routine that calls it*. This can easily be done if the subroutine simply saves each such register prior to its use and later restores the register's original value, when the subroutine no longer needs it. Where might a subroutine save these values? Since it needs "some" storage (where frequently "some" is not terribly well defined), and since the stack being used to save return addresses is readily available storage (which we can for the moment think of as "unlimited"), we choose to have the subroutine *push* these register contents on the R6-stack— the stack whose pointer is R6. In this case an appropriate PUSH_STACK operation is

$$\text{MOVL} \quad \text{Rn}, -(\text{R6})$$

and the corresponding POP_STACK operation, to be executed prior to the subroutine's return to the calling program, is

$$\text{MOVL} \quad (\text{R6})+, \text{Rn}$$

We show the modification of this program segment in Figure 9.6.2.

It will be useful to have a "snapshot" of the R6-stack at an intermediate point in the execution. When the main routine calls SORT, it pushes the address NEXT on the R6-stack and jumps to SORT. The first thing that SORT does is to push

```
             .
             .
             .
         MOVAB    ARRAY,R1        ;Put ARRAY address in R1
         MOVL     #8,R2           ;  and number count in R2
         MOVAB    NEXT,-(R6)      ;Set up return address
         JMP      SORT            ;  and go sort the array
NEXT:    <next instruction>       ;Return from SORT here
             .
             .
             .

         ;------------------------------------------------------;
         ; Subroutine to put into increasing order an array of  ;
         ; unsigned bytes.  The main program passes to the sub- ;
         ; routine the beginning array address in R1 and the    ;
         ; number of bytes in the array in R2.  (The subroutine ;
         ; SORT invokes the subroutine MAXADR during execution.);
         ;------------------------------------------------------;

SORT:    MOVL     R0,-(R6)        ;Save current c(R0),
         MOVL     R3,-(R6)        ;  c(R3) and
         MOVL     R4,-(R6)        ;  c(R4) on R6-stack
         MOVL     R1,R3           ;Make copies of address of
         MOVL     R2,R4           ;  1st number and number count
INIT:    MOVL     R3,R1           ;Restore 1st number address and
         MOVL     R4,R2           ;  number count for use by MAXADR
         MOVAB    XCHNG,-(R6)     ;Set up for return from MAXADR
         JMP      MAXADR          ;  and jump to MAXADR to get address
                                  ;  of largest number in sublist
XCHNG:   MOVB     -1(R3)[R4],R1   ;Exchange last entry of sublist
         MOVB     (R0),-1(R3)[R4] ;  with the largest number in
         MOVB     R1,(R0)         ;  the sublist
         SOBGTR   R4,INIT         ;Go deal with next sublist
         MOVL     (R6)+,R4        ;  else restore R4,
         MOVL     (R6)+,R3        ;  R3 and
         MOVL     (R6)+,R0        ;  R0 from R6-stack
         JMP      @(R6)+          ;Return to calling routine
             .
             .
             .

         ;------------------------------------------------------;
         ; Subroutine to return in R0 the ADDRESS of the largest;
         ; of an array of unsigned bytes.  The main program     ;
         ; passes to the subroutine the beginning array address ;
         ; in R1 and the number of bytes in the array in R2.    ;
         ;------------------------------------------------------;

MAXADR:  MOVAB    (R1)+,R0        ;Make address of first number
                                  ;  TEMPMAX_ADDR for now
         BRB      LOOPND          ;Skip around to decrement counter
LOOP:    CMPB     (R1)+,(R0)      ;Current number > c(TEMPMAX_ADDR)?
         BLEQU    LOOPND          ;No -- do not replace TEMPMAX_ADDR
         MOVAB    -1(R1),R0       ;Replace TEMPMAX_ADDR with address
                                  ;  of the larger number
LOOPND:  SOBGTR   R2,LOOP         ;Check next number (if more to do)
         JMP      @(R6)+          ;Return to caller
             .
             .
```

Figure 9.6.2

c(R0), c(R3), and c(R4), *in that order*, on the stack, and thus at this point the stack has the appearance shown in Figure 9.6.3. Sort now calls MAXADR a number of times, each time pushing its return address XCHNG onto the stack, *on top of* c(R4), with MAXADR popping that address a corresponding number of times, for its returns to SORT. Thus when SORT has completed the rearranging of the mainline's array into increasing order and is ready to return to the mainline, the stack will again appear as in Figure 9.6.3. Note from Figure 9.6.2 that SORT now executes three POP_STACK instructions to restore R0, R3, and R4 to their main routine states. There are two things to note here. First, the register contents need to be restored in the *reverse* of the order in which they were saved, because of the last-in/first-out structure of the stack. If the top of the stack had been popped into R0, then into R3, and finally into R4 (the order in which they were pushed), R0 and R4 would clearly not be restored to their original values (although, through the accident of being in the middle of the set, R3 would). Second, if SORT inadvertently *fails* to restore the register contents, disaster will strike when SORT executes its return:

$$\text{JMP} \quad @(R6)+$$

for what will be put in the program counter is *not* the address NEXT, but rather the contents of R4. Thus control will not be passed back to the main return, and in fact in this case we have no idea where execution will resume. In any event, it is clear that we will have lost control of program execution.

This example shows that the stack which we had initially intended for the saving of return addresses can also be quite useful for the temporary storage of register contents, and of course its uses are not limited to these two purposes. But it also shows that we need to exercise some care when using the stack. Mismanagement and poor bookkeeping practices will probably result in catastrophe (which is no more than carelessness deserves).

There are a couple of other areas of potential stack mismanagement which deserve mention. Notice that in our examples so far we have "stacked" return addresses and register contents, both of which are *longword* structures. There is no reason why we cannot use the stack to save the contents of words, bytes, quadwords, and so on, but as usual we must pay attention to the details. As an

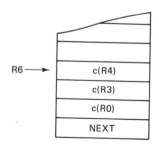

Figure 9.6.3

example of what can go wrong, consider the three instructions

$$\begin{aligned}
&\text{MOVW} \quad \text{WORD1}, -(\text{R6}) \\
&\text{MOVB} \quad \text{BYTE}, -(\text{R6}) \\
&\text{MOVW} \quad \text{WORD2}, -(\text{R6})
\end{aligned}$$

We must understand that on the first "push," c(R6) was predecremented *by 2*, that the MOVB resulted in c(R6) being predecremented *by 1*, and that the last instruction again predecremented c(R6) *by 2*. Thus the R6-stack will have an appearance something like that shown in Figure 9.6.4, where we have assigned some addresses to emphasize just what datatypes are being held in the stack. What would be the consequences of inadvertently restoring these three structures with the instructions

$$\begin{aligned}
&\text{MOVW} \quad (\text{R6})+, \text{WORD2} \\
&\text{MOVW} \quad (\text{R6})+, \text{BYTE} \\
&\text{MOVW} \quad (\text{R6})+, \text{WORD1}
\end{aligned}$$

Notice the error—restoring the contents of BYTE with MOVW rather than a MOVB. c(WORD2) has been properly restored with the contents of 000017F5 and 000017F6, but BYTE *and* BYTE+1 (!) have been given the contents of 000017F7 *and* 000017F8, respectively. Finally, WORD1 gets the contents of 000017F9 and 000017FA, the latter byte not having originally come from the "push" of c(WORD1) at all. Not only have BYTE and WORD1 not been properly restored, if other structures, including possibly return addresses, already existed on the stack, the problems generated here can only cascade farther down the stack and result in perhaps more serious consequences later.

We recognize the cause of this problem again to be a lack of proper book-keeping when dealing with the stack, and some additional care might eliminate them. On the other hand, suppose that a programming environment, perhaps dealing with ASCII-coded characters, requires the stacking and unstacking of numerous *bytes*. Many potential problems of an accounting nature might be eliminated by the creation of a *second* stack (and the attendant use of another general-purpose register as a pointer for it) which will be used exclusively for the pushing and popping of *bytes*.

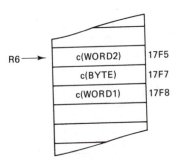

Figure 9.6.4

Subroutines, Stacks, and Procedures   Chap. 9

One final problem requires mention. We seem now to be relying on the stack rather heavily, for saving registers, intermediate results, and so on, in addition to its initial function of saving subroutine call return addresses. The block of 100 longwords with which we began our discussion, and which we earlier concluded was probably far larger than what we would ever use, may now become fairly crowded with various kinds of data. It is certainly possible that we might actually *fill* the stack space with the stack, and if we do, an additional "push" will put the new stack entry in an area that was not intended as stack space, thereby possibly *overlaying* some important data, or perhaps even some part of a program instruction. This phenomenon is called **stack overflow**, and a failure to predict correctly the stack area needs is clearly the cause. As an analogous problem, consider a program with an empty stack that calls a subroutine, the return address being put on the stack. The subroutine then pushes on the same stack the contents of R2. When the subroutine returns, it pops the stack into R2 to restore it, but because of poor programming practice, the programmer also pops the stack into R1. (Of course, it is the *return address* from the caller that goes into R1.) But now what happens on the subroutine's "return" statement? The subroutine gets a "return address" from a longword that is not even in the stack space. This is an instance of **stack underflow**, and its results can obviously be as disastrous as stack overflow.

9.7 THE HARDWARE STACK AND JUMP-TO-SUBROUTINE OPERATIONS

We define **the hardware stack** to be the stack whose pointer is R14, called **the stack pointer**. The VAX assembler recognizes the symbol **SP** as being the same as R14, and henceforth that is the notation we shall use.

There are a number of peculiarities about the immediately preceding brief paragraph that require explanation. First, we have used the word "hardware" in giving a name to this stack, yet as we know, *every* stack should be considered a *hardware stack* inasmuch as stacks typically reside in main memory—a hardware concept. The reason for the use of the term when applied to the SP-stack (the R14-stack) is that some of the *hardware* (processor) *operations* actually use this stack in the course of their execution. Thus just as some operations have as a side effect the modification of some register (autoincrement mode instructions, for example), other operations have as a side effect the modification of SP and the stack to which it is pointing. We have not yet seen any of these operations, but four important ones are discussed later in this section.

Observe the use of the definite article "the" in the phrases "the hardware stack" and "the stack pointer." This is used to emphasize the fact that the SP-stack, because of its use by some processor operations, is in some sense the *principal* stack in any programming environment.

Finally, we comment that whatever other stacks a programmer might *choose* to create in a program, there is *no* choice about the existence of the SP-stack—it *must* exist for certain hardware operations to succeed. But now the reader may be puzzled, in looking back over some of our earlier (successful) programs, that none of these explicitly created this stack, despite our claim that it is necessary. That is quite correct, but the truth of the matter is that at the time that the program was *loaded* into memory for execution, the operating system's loader program actually created the SP-stack with stack area sufficient for most purposes, and it appropriately set SP to point at the first byte beyond that stack space (beyond, in the sense of higher addresses). Could we ourselves have allocated space within a program for the hardware stack area and then properly set the stack pointer, SP? Certainly, although in most programming environments there is little need to do so.

Aside from the fact that the hardware stack always exists and that it is employed by the processor for the processing of some of its instructions, the SP-stack behaves in all respects like the stacks we have already created. It can be used for all the purposes we have already found useful—the saving of return addresses, the temporary storage of register contents, and so on. Thus except in cases of special need, such as in the preceding section, where we suggested the possibility of creating a "byte stack" for the storage of ASCII-coded characters, there is frequently no need to create a stack within a program; if the stack *structure* is required for some purpose or application, we may as well use the hardware stack.

The principal result of this chapter so far concerns the saving of the return address when a routine calls a subroutine. As we have seen, the most useful and automatic technique involves the saving of that address on a stack, and we see now that we may as well use the SP-stack for this purpose. Recall the sequence of instructions required to save the return address and jump to the subroutine:

```
7E   00004030'   EF 9E   4023        MOVAB   NEXT, - (SP)
     000042A3'   EF 17   402A        JMP     SUBR
                         4030  NEXT: ⟨next instruction⟩
```

We have supplied some arbitrary addresses and generated the assembled machine code, since we shall want to look at the details of just exactly how the processor handles this construction upon execution, and we concentrate our attention on the JMP instruction. Having placed the return address NEXT on the stack, the processor is ready to fetch, decode, and execute the JMP instruction, which consists of 6 bytes. The first byte, 17, is the hexadecimal code for JMP, and by the time this has been fetched, $c(PC) = 0000402B$. The next byte (EF) indicates a program counter longword displacement, so the next longword is fetched. Notice that now the program counter contains the number 00004030, which is the value of NEXT. In fact, it is precisely this number (00004030) that was pushed onto the stack by the MOVAB instruction. If we could somehow *modify* the JMP operation so that the processor, *before* actually executing the jump but *after* it had fetched all the operands of the JMP instruction, would push the *current* contents of the PC onto the stack, there would be no need for the MOVAB instruction at all. That is, we need a modified version of JMP which has the following effects:

Subroutines, Stacks, and Procedures   Chap. 9

1. Calculate the JMP destination address.
2. Push the current c(PC) onto the stack.
3. Put the destination address in the PC.

It is this last step, of course, which does the actual jump. But it is step 2, after step 1 has been completed and thus the program counter is already "pointing at" the next instruction, which saves the appropriate return address. Such a modified JMP operation would completely eliminate the need for executing the MOVAB instruction and the necessity for the somewhat artificial labeling (with NEXT, or whatever) of the instruction following the JMP. The VAX processor implements such an operation.

(a) JSB   Jump-to-SuBroutine

The operation JSB has machine code 16 and operand descriptor

$$dest.ab$$

where *dest* is the destination address, given as an address access operand. The effect is to push the current program counter contents onto the hardware stack (as a longword) and to give the PC the destination address *dest*. The condition codes are unaffected by JSB. Note that a side effect of the instruction is the decrementing by 4 of c(SP), to accommodate the longword return address pushed onto the stack.

The effects of JSB are exactly as described as the desired effects of a modified version of JMP:

1. Calculate the destination address, *dest*.
2. Push current c(PC) onto the hardware stack.
3. Replace c(PC) with *dest*.

If we have used JSB to jump to a subroutine, so that the return address is on top of the stack, what instruction or instructions do we need for subroutine return? Just as before, when we were dealing with the R6-stack, we can use

$$JMP \quad @(SP)+$$

However, the VAX supplies an operator that is the companion to JSB.

(b) RSB   Return-from-SuBroutine

RSB has operation code 05. The effect of RSB is to pop the top of the hardware (SP) stack into the program counter. Notice that RSB takes *no* operands, R14 (SP) being implicit in the operator. As a side effect, c(SP) is incremented by 4—the "pop of the stack" into the program counter.

There is little more than can or needs to be said about JSB/RSB. They have the effects of our earlier constructions, but they are easier to use, require fewer bytes of storage to implement, and they eliminate the need for us explicitly to save the return address. For the record, we offer one example here (with many more to come), namely a rewriting of the programming segment of Figure 9.6.2 (see Figure 9.7.1).

Recall that the operator JMP has two closely related "short" versions— unconditional *branches*, actually—BRB and BRW, which, like JMP, transfer control of the processor to some memory location. But unlike JMP, BRB and BRW must be given an actual address operand as the "destination" or "target" of the branch (an address which the *assembler* can calculate, as opposed to an address access operand), and that destination must be within roughly 127 bytes for BRB, and 32,767 bytes for BRW. Thus the range within which branching can be accomplished is somewhat limited, and the way in which the destination is addressed is highly constrained. On the other hand, consistent use of BRB and BRW where possible can result in substantial savings in the amount of storage required in large programs, since these unconditional branches require only 2 or 3 bytes of storage each, whereas JMP may require as many as 6.

In a completely analogous manner, JSB has two "short" versions, described below.

(c) BSBB   Branch to *Su*Broutine with *Byte* displacement

BSBB has operation code 10 and operand descriptor

$$disp.bb$$

where *disp* is the destination address written as a *byte* displacement. Upon execution, the processor sign extends the byte displacement to a longword, which is added to c(PC). The condition codes are unaffected by BSBB. Note that a side effect of the instruction is the decrementing by 4 of c(SP), to accommodate the longword return address pushed onto the stack.

(d) BSBW   Branch to *Su*Broutine with *Word* displacement

BSBW has operation code 30 and operand descriptor

$$disp.bw$$

where *disp* is the destination address written as a *word* displacement. Upon execution, the processor sign extends the word displacement to a longword, which is added to c(PC). The condition codes are unaffected by BSBW. Note that a side effect of the instruction is the decrementing by 4 of c(SP), to accommodate the longword return address pushed onto the stack.

```
              .
              .
        MOVAB    ARRAY,R1          ;Put ARRAY address in R1
        MOVL     #8,R2             ; and number count in R2
        JSB      SORT              ;Go sort the array
        <next instruction>        ;Return from SORT here
              .
              .
              .
;----------------------------------------------------------;
; Subroutine to put into increasing order an array of      ;
; unsigned bytes.  The main program passes to the sub-     ;
; routine the beginning array address in R1 and the        ;
; number of bytes in the array in R2.  (The subroutine     ;
; SORT invokes the subroutine MAXADR during execution.)    ;
;----------------------------------------------------------;

SORT:   MOVL     R0,-(SP)          ;Save current c(R0),
        MOVL     R3,-(SP)          ;  c(R3) and
        MOVL     R4,-(SP)          ;  c(R4) on the hardware stack
        MOVL     R1,R3             ;Make copies of address of
        MOVL     R2,R4             ; 1st number and number count
INIT:   MOVL     R3,R1             ;Restore 1st number address and
        MOVL     R4,R2             ; number count for use by MAXADR
        JSB      MAXADR            ;Jump to MAXADR to get address
                                   ; of largest number in sublist
XCHNG:  MOVB     -1(R3)[R4],R1     ;Exchange last entry of sublist
        MOVB     (R0),-1(R3)[R4]   ; with the largest number in
        MOVB     R1,(R0)           ; the sublist
        SOBGTR   R4,INIT           ;Go deal with next sublist
        MOVL     (SP)+,R4          ; else restore R4,
        MOVL     (SP)+,R3          ; R3 and
        MOVL     (SP)+,R0          ; R0 from the hardware stack
        RSB                        ;Return to calling routine
              .
              .
              .
;----------------------------------------------------------;
; Subroutine to return in R0 the ADDRESS of the largest    ;
; of an array of unsigned bytes.  The main program         ;
; passes to the subroutine the beginning array address     ;
; in R1 and the number of bytes in the array in R2.        ;
;----------------------------------------------------------;

MAXADR: MOVAB    (R1)+,R0          ;Make address of first number
                                   ; TEMPMAX_ADDR for now
        BRB      LOOPND            ;Skip around to decrement counter
LOOP:   CMPB     (R1)+,(R0)        ;Current number > c(TEMPMAX_ADDR)?
        BLEQU    LOOPND            ;No -- do not replace TEMPMAX_ADDR
        MOVAB    -1(R1),R0         ;Replace TEMPMAX_ADDR with address
                                   ; of the larger number
LOOPND: SOBGTR   R2,LOOP           ;Check next number (if more to do)
        RSB                        ;Return to caller
              .
              .
```

Figure 9.7.1

Of course, a subroutine "branched" to with BSBB or BSBW can use RSB for its return statement, just as JSB does.

9.8 SOME OTHER STACK OPERATIONS

In addition to JSB, BSBB, BSBW, and RSB, there is a handful of other operations which make implicit use of the R14-stack, and these are described in this section without much comment. In each case they provide effects that can also be achieved by constructions which are already available; the versions described here are supplied for programmer convenience, for readability (since in some cases the new operation and its mnemonic are more suggestive of the action taken than is the older version), and are typically more economical—they require fewer bytes of code because of the *implicit* reference to SP.

(a) PUSHAx   *PUSH Address onto the stack*

There are five forms of the PUSHA operation,

$$\text{PUSHAB (9F)} \quad \text{PUSHAW (3F)} \quad \text{PUSHAL (DF)}$$
$$\text{PUSHAQ (7F)} \quad \text{PUSHAO (7FFD)}$$

Their operand descriptor is

$$src.ax$$

src is any address access operand. As with MOVAx, the datatype *x* determines the context in which the source operand is treated relative to any source operand side effects (autoincrement, index, etc.). PUSHAx is equivalent to

$$\text{MOVAx} \quad src, -(SP)$$

but requires fewer bytes.

(b) PUSHL   *PUSH Longword onto the stack*

The operation code for PUSHL is DD and its operand descriptor is

$$src.rl$$

where *src* is any longword source. PUSHL is equivalent in effect to

$$\text{MOVL} \quad src, -(SP)$$

but is one byte shorter.

(c) PUSHR   *PUSH Register(s) onto the stack*

The operation code for PUSHR is BB and its operand descriptor is

mask.rw

where *mask* is a 16-bit word whose bit positions 14:0 correspond to register numbers 14 to 0. Bit 15 is ignored. Each register whose *number* corresponds to a set bit in *mask* is pushed onto the stack, with the higher-numbered registers pushed *first* (into higher-addressed memory longwords). c(SP) is decremented by 4, once for each register pushed. PUSHR is equivalent in its principal effect to a sequence of instructions of the form

PUSHL   Rn, − (SP)

(n = 14, 13, ..., 1, 0), but requires far fewer bytes. In addition, PUSHR does not affect the condition codes, whereas PUSHL may alter N and Z.

(d) POPR   *POP Register(s) from the stack*

The operation code for POPR is BA and its operand descriptor is

mask.rw

where *mask* is a 16-bit word whose bit positions 14:0 correspond to the register numbers 14 to 0. Bit 15 is ignored. Each register whose *number* corresponds to a set bit in *mask* is popped off of the stack, with the lower-numbered registers popped *first* (from lower-addressed memory longwords). c(SP) is incremented by 4, once for each register popped. POPR is equivalent in its principal effect to a sequence of instructions of the form

MOVL   (SP)+ ,Rn

(n = 0, 1, ..., 14), but requires far fewer bytes. In addition, POPR does not affect the condition codes, whereas MOVL may alter N and Z.

It is not necessary, in using PUSHR and POPR, for the programmer to create the mask word as a 16-bit word of 1s and 0s. Rather, the assembler can be directed to create the desired word by using the **register mask word** notation ^M, followed by the *names* of the registers, separated by commas, enclosed in angle brackets: ⟨...⟩. For example, the assembler, upon encountering the construction

^M⟨R0,R5,R6,R10,R12⟩

(or for that matter, the construction

$$\hat{}M\langle R5,R0,R10,R12,R6\rangle$$

which it takes to be the same thing) will create the 16-bit mask word

$$\hat{}B0001010001100001 = \hat{}X1461$$

9.9 TRANSMITTING ARGUMENTS IN AN ARGUMENT TABLE

In Section 9.3 we introduced the concept of subroutine arguments and found that they could be transmitted via the general-purpose registers, a technique we have been using ever since, in calls to PRINT, MAX, and SORT, for example. The placing of needed arguments in registers prior to calling a subroutine is a very standard scheme and has the advantage that the arguments are then immediately available to the subroutine. It has the obvious disadvantage that the registers in which the subroutine *expects* to see the arguments *must* be used by the main routine, and it is possible, or even likely, that at the time the main routine needs to call the subroutine, those particular registers may not be available for the purpose of argument transmission. Thus the main routine may first have to save these registers (on the stack, say) and then remember to restore them after the subroutine return. Of course, if the main routine needs to pass a large number of arguments to a subroutine—perhaps a dozen or more—there may simply not be enough registers to satisfy the requirement.

In this section and the next we discuss two argument transmission schemes that have become quite popular, are relatively easy to implement, and have the advantage that although *one* register *is* taken up in this technique, there is no limit to the number of arguments that can be passed to a subroutine. We are going to use R12 for this purpose, and in fact the scheme will prove so useful that henceforth we shall reserve R12 exclusively for this function, thus guaranteeing that it will always be free for argument transmission and not busy with some other duty (such as accumulating, counting, or whatever). A brief review of register use at this time is perhaps appropriate. Of the 16 available registers, R15 is the program counter, so it is not really available for *any* programmer use. We have already devoted R14 = SP to the purpose of being *the* pointer to *the* hardware stack. Now, as we shall see, we will be assigning R12 the exclusive task of assisting in the passing of arguments to subroutines. The net effect will be that of the available registers (not counting R15), two have been removed from the "general purpose" list—R12 and R14. The loss of R14 has been well worth the cost; subroutine calls, nested calls, recursive routines, and coroutines, are now able to be handled in such an automatic fashion that the programmer rarely has to pay too much attention to exactly how return addresses are saved and restored. The loss of R12 will be more than compensated for by the gain in the ease of argument transmission.

Let us review the subroutine MAXADR of Figure 9.7.1, where MAXADR is called by SORT. MAXADR expects to be passed an array address in R1 and

Subroutines, Stacks, and Procedures   Chap. 9

a byte count in R2; it returns the address of the largest array byte in R0. Although R0 will still be used to return this address to the calling routine, we shall now eliminate the need for passing the array address and byte count *in registers*. The key to this scheme is the placing of this address and byte count in two consecutive longwords in memory, as a little *table* of values, and then to have MAXADR reference this table. We do this in the following way. Construct the two-longword table and label the first of these with, say, the symbol TABLE:

TABLE: .LONG   ⟨address of first byte of array⟩
        .LONG   ⟨number of bytes in the array⟩

Now MAXADR must know where to find this table, so prior to invoking MAXADR, we place the table's *address* in some register, and as stated above, we will use R12:

MOVAL   TABLE,R12

MAXADR will now know the table address (in R12) and can thus access the two arguments; they can be referred to as (R12) and 4(R12). Figure 9.9.1 shows a segment of code that implements this technique. Since MAXADR must still step through the bytes in the array, it requires a register for that purpose. As before, we use R1 to point at the array bytes, but observe that we are now careful to save its contents on the stack prior to using it for the array address. A couple of comments are in order here. First, observe that we have used the (preferred) PUSHR instruction at MAXADR, and have directed the assembler to construct the appropriate mask word. The word constructed, of course, will be ^X0002, to correspond to register number 1. Note, however, that we did *not* use the construction

PUSHR   ^M⟨R1⟩   (equivalently, PUSHR   ^X0002)

for upon execution the processor would have used the *contents* of the word whose *address* is ^X00000002 as the mask word, rather than the word ^X0002 itself. Thus the "number sign" (#) is crucial here. Second, we see that the next instruction is

MOVAB   @0(R12),R1

and is intended to put the (byte) array address in R1. Now R12 is currently pointing at that address, and it is a common mistake to use (R12) instead of the doubly deferred construction we have employed here. For (R12), when used as an *address access operand*, specifies the contents of R12 as the address; and the contents of R12 is the address TABLE, not its contents ARRAY. It is for this reason that the register must be deferred a second time.

In contradistinction to earlier versions of MAXADR, we do not bother to put the byte count in a register (R2 was used previously for this purpose). Instead, we let the SOBGTR instruction at LOOPND simply decrement the count, refer-

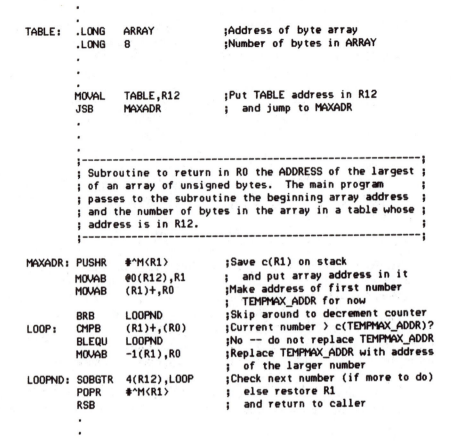

```
                .
                .
                .
TABLE:  .LONG   ARRAY           ;Address of byte array
        .LONG   8               ;Number of bytes in ARRAY
                .
                .
                .
        MOVAL   TABLE,R12       ;Put TABLE address in R12
        JSB     MAXADR          ; and jump to MAXADR
                .
                .
                .
        ;-----------------------------------------------------------;
        ; Subroutine to return in R0 the ADDRESS of the largest ;
        ; of an array of unsigned bytes.  The main program        ;
        ; passes to the subroutine the beginning array address    ;
        ; and the number of bytes in the array in a table whose ;
        ; address is in R12.                                      ;
        ;-----------------------------------------------------------;

MAXADR: PUSHR   #^M<R1>         ;Save c(R1) on stack
        MOVAB   @0(R12),R1      ; and put array address in it
        MOVAB   (R1)+,R0        ;Make address of first number
                                ; TEMPMAX_ADDR for now
        BRB     LOOPND          ;Skip around to decrement counter
LOOP:   CMPB    (R1)+,(R0)      ;Current number > c(TEMPMAX_ADDR)?
        BLEQU   LOOPND          ;No -- do not replace TEMPMAX_ADDR
        MOVAB   -1(R1),R0       ;Replace TEMPMAX_ADDR with address
                                ; of the larger number
LOOPND: SOBGTR  4(R12),LOOP     ;Check next number (if more to do)
        POPR    #^M<R1>         ; else restore R1
        RSB                     ; and return to caller
                .
                .
```

Figure 9.9.1

enced as 4(R12). However, we must now be aware that the second longword in TABLE is actually being decremented, and if that little table is to be used a second time, that second longword will have been decremented to 0 and thus must be repaired. (The first longword—ARRAY—is *not* altered by MAXADR.)

Finally, we note that we could have pointed R12 at the byte count if we had accessed the array address with

$$\text{MOVAB} \quad @(R12)+,R1$$

and then referenced the byte count (in the SOBGTR instruction) as (R12). Thus autoincrement mode—deferred or otherwise—will allow the subroutine to step through an argument list passed to it via a table of this sort. For the record we show this version of the subroutine MAXADR in Figure 9.9.2.

A third possible way for the subroutine to access the table arguments is via *indexing* through the table. For the purposes of the present example, such indexing would be far more complicated than the two more straightforward techniques we

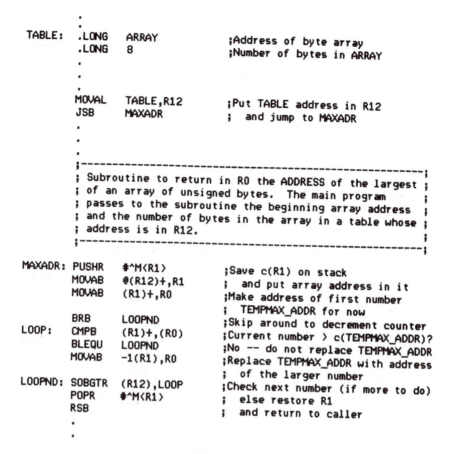

```
TABLE:  .LONG    ARRAY               ;Address of byte array
        .LONG    8                   ;Number of bytes in ARRAY
          .
          .
          .
        MOVAL    TABLE,R12           ;Put TABLE address in R12
        JSB      MAXADR             ;  and jump to MAXADR
          .
          .
          .
;------------------------------------------------------------;
; Subroutine to return in R0 the ADDRESS of the largest      ;
; of an array of unsigned bytes.  The main program           ;
; passes to the subroutine the beginning array address       ;
; and the number of bytes in the array in a table whose      ;
; address is in R12.                                         ;
;------------------------------------------------------------;

MAXADR: PUSHR    #^M<R1>            ;Save c(R1) on stack
        MOVAB    @(R12)+,R1         ;  and put array address in it
        MOVAB    (R1)+,R0           ;Make address of first number
                                    ;  TEMPMAX_ADDR for now
        BRB      LOOPND             ;Skip around to decrement counter
LOOP:   CMPB     (R1)+,(R0)         ;Current number > c(TEMPMAX_ADDR)?
        BLEQU    LOOPND             ;No -- do not replace TEMPMAX_ADDR
        MOVAB    -1(R1),R0          ;Replace TEMPMAX_ADDR with address
                                    ;  of the larger number
LOOPND: SOBGTR   (R12),LOOP         ;Check next number (if more to do)
        POPR     #^M<R1>            ;  else restore R1
        RSB                         ;  and return to caller
          .
          .
```

Figure 9.9.2

have already seen, and thus we decline to pursue it here. However, indexing is a practical method in a wide variety of applications, and we shall use it whenever it gives easiest access to the transmitted arguments.

For the purposes of the next example we shall define a **character string** (or more simply, a **string**) to be a collection of contiguous ASCII-coded bytes, the last of which contains the number 0 (the ASCII "character" NUL; see Appendix C). This NUL character is used to *terminate* the string. Now consider the following task, dealt with frequently by operating system routines. A user types a "command" to be executed, where by that term we mean a *string of characters* which must then be examined—**parsed**—to determine its meaning. Specifically, a system routine may have to determine (perhaps by matching the input string with other strings) just what it is that the user wants done. One of the things that adds to the burden here is the fact that the user may be free to enter strings of characters in lower case and/or uppercase. Many system programs deal with this by converting any lowercase characters to uppercase early in their examination of the strings, thereby reducing somewhat the amount of scanning and number of decisions that must be made. Fortunately, the conversion of lowercase to uppercase is very easy, since the ASCII code for a lowercase character differs from the code for its uppercase counterpart only in that the former code has bit 5 set. For example, the code for 'F' is ^X46 = ^B01000110, whereas the code for 'f' is ^X66 = ^B01100110. Thus the conversion of a lowercase character to uppercase simply involves the suppression of bit 5 in its ASCII code. We shall show an example of a subroutine that does the conversion momentarily (Figure 9.9.3).

When we speak of converting lowercase characters to their uppercase equivalents, we have in mind that the uppercase character would take the place of—be written over—the lowercase byte. But there may be situations in which we must

```
;-----------------------------------------------------------------;
; Subroutine CVT2UC converts character strings to upper-case.     ;
; A string is terminated with a NUL character (ASCII code = 0)    ;
; and is identified by the  address of its first byte.            ;
;                                                                 ;
; CVT2UC will convert each lower-case character of a string and   ;
; overwrite it in the string itself, or it will transfer each     ;
; character to another (destination) string buffer as the        ;
; lower-case characters are converted, leaving the (source)       ;
; string unaffected.                                              ;
;                                                                 ;
; The arguments to CVT2UC are passed in a table of longwords,     ;
; the first of which is the argument count. This is followed      ;
; by the address of the source string and, optionally, by the    ;
; address of a destination buffer. The address of the first      ;
; longword of the table is put in R12 prior to jumping to the     ;
; subroutine.                                                     ;
;-----------------------------------------------------------------;
;

CVT2UC: PUSHR   #^M<R1,R2>      ;Save two pointer registers
        TSTL    (R12)+          ;Ignore argument count for now
        MOVAB   @(R12)+,R1      ;Set pointer to source string
        MOVL    R1,R2           ;  address and copy it to R2
        CMPL    -8(R12),#2      ;See if Argument Count = 2
        BNEQ    CVT.5           ;Isn't 2 -- skip around --
        MOVAB   @0(R12),R2      ;  else reset pointer R2 to
                                ;  destination string address
CVT.5:  CLRB    -(SP)           ;Put a 0-byte on the stack
        CMPB    (R1),#^A/a/     ;Within the range
        BLSS    CVT.6           ;  'a'
        CMPB    (R1),#^A/z/     ;  to
        BGTR    CVT.6           ;  'z'?
        MOVB    #^X20,(SP)      ;Yes -- lower-case -- put byte on
                                ;  stack to adjust to upper-case

CVT.6:  BICB3   (SP)+,(R1)+,-   ;Clear bit (if top-of-stack is
                (R2)+           ;  nonzero) and write to string
        BNEQ    CVT.5           ;Check next character (if not at
                                ;  end-of-string)
        POPR    #^M<R1,R2>      ;Restore pointer registers
        RSB                     ;  and return
```

Figure 9.9.3

not, or choose not to, destroy the original character string in this way. In such cases it is simple enough to write the converted characters to *another* string, so that the original string is preserved. Now, however, we have a slight procedural problem. If we are going to write a subroutine to do the conversion, we will pass to the subroutine the address of the first byte of the string whose characters are to be converted. But if the original string is to be preserved, the subroutine will also have to be given the address of a collection of bytes where the converted string may be placed. That is, in this case the subroutine must know where the *source* string is, and in addition it must know where it can put the *destination* string. The complication, of course, stems from the fact that we need to write a routine with a *variable number* of arguments—in one case, only the address of the source string is passed to the subroutine; in the other, the addresses of the source *and* destination strings need to be passed to the routine. This small dilemma is resolved if we simply agree to pass the argument or arguments in a table as before, but now we pass the *number of arguments* as well, in the *first* longword of the table.

The subroutine CVT2UC of Figure 9.9.3 will convert lowercase to uppercase, and all the necessary information for CVT2UC is found in a table whose address is passed in R12. In particular, the first longword in the table is always either a 1 or a 2, depending on whether one string address or two is passed to the routine. (If one string address is passed, the conversion of that string will go on within that string. If two string addresses are passed—argument count = 2—the string whose address is encountered first is converted, and the converted characters are written to a block of bytes whose beginning address is given as the second argument.) There is nothing special about the assembly code of Figure 9.9.3, except that the reader's attention is drawn to the first few instructions, which determine the number of arguments, and to the mildly interesting use of the BICB3 operator at the line labeled CVT.6. In Figure 9.9.4(a) we see a call to CVT2UC, which employs only the initial string; in the programming segment of Figure 9.9.4(b) is a call in which not only a source string address, but also a destination string address, has been passed to the subroutine. In the latter case the string at STRING1 will not be altered.

This example shows that the construction of an argument table can be useful in the transmission of arguments to a subroutine, and in particular when the number of arguments may be variable. However, there are other ways of managing CVT2UC without resorting to such a table, and we thus offer a final example in which transmission via a table is almost *forced* upon us. The subroutine MAXADR, of which we now have several versions (the latest of which is shown in Figure 9.9.2), relies on the fact that the unsigned bytes, the address of the largest of which it is to return in R0, are in *contiguous* memory locations. But consider now a variation on this problem, in which we need to locate (find the address of) the largest of a collection of unsigned bytes, and we know the address of each byte, but these addresses are *not consecutive*. We will be unable to proceed as before, in which R1 was used as a pointer which stepped through the bytes. However, if we build a table of the byte addresses, include in the table the number of such addresses, and then inform the subroutine of the location of the table, the problem is only a bit more challenging than before. As Figure 9.9.5 shows, the modified version of

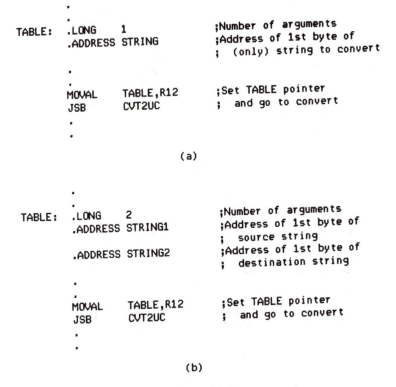

```
              .
              .
   TABLE:  .LONG      1              ;Number of arguments
           .ADDRESS STRING           ;Address of 1st byte of
                                     ;  (only) string to convert

              .
              .
           MOVAL      TABLE,R12       ;Set TABLE pointer
           JSB        CVT2UC          ;  and go to convert
              .
              .
```

(a)

```
              .
              .
   TABLE:  .LONG      2              ;Number of arguments
           .ADDRESS STRING1          ;Address of 1st byte of
                                     ;  source string

           .ADDRESS STRING2          ;Address of 1st byte of
                                     ;  destination string

              .
              .
           MOVAL      TABLE,R12       ;Set TABLE pointer
           JSB        CVT2UC          ;  and go to convert
              .
              .
```

(b)

Figure 9.9.4

MAXADR (called MAXADR_1 here) now uses R1 to step through the *table* of *addresses*, rather than through the array of byte values themselves as was the case before. (Lest the reader feel that the situation is "manufactured," consider the following "minimax" problem. Given a two-dimensional array of unsigned bytes, we *locate* the smallest byte in each row of the array; we then *locate* the largest of these smallest bytes.)

The technique illustrated in these last examples proves to be so useful that we are going to distinguish it with a special *name*.

Subroutine call with general argument list. This technique passes control to a subroutine, and transmits arguments to it, in the following way:

1. The arguments, or their addresses, are placed in a table of consecutive memory locations, the first of which is the *count* of the number of arguments that follow in the table.
2. The address of the table is put in R12, to be used as an **argument pointer**.
3. The subroutine is invoked, with JSB, BSBB, or BSBW.

Once control has been given to the subroutine, it can use R12 to obtain the count of arguments, as well as the arguments themselves.

As to the arguments transmitted to a subroutine, we have seen examples in which the arguments themselves were passed to the subroutine, and some in which the *addresses* of the arguments were transmitted. We have determined through actual programming examples that either scheme is quite manageable, although of course the subroutine must "know" *in advance* what its arguments will look like. There is no reason why the arguments passed to a subroutine cannot be of "mixed" type—some actual values, and some addresses (although this may make the writing of a subroutine with a *variable-length* argument list more difficult).

Does it make any difference just how the arguments get to the subroutine, as long as they are available to the subroutine for whatever is to be done to them? The answer depends on just what the purpose of the subroutine is. In the examples we have seen so far, the only purpose of the subroutine was to *print* an array, *find*

```
          .
          .
          .
TABLE:  .LONG     5                ;Count of byte addresses in table
        .ADDRESS  BYTE_1_VALUE     ;Address of first byte to be tested
        .ADDRESS  BYTE_2_VALUE     ;
        .ADDRESS  BYTE_3_VALUE     ;
        .ADDRESS  BYTE_4_VALUE     ;
        .ADDRESS  BYTE_5_VALUE     ;Address of last byte to be tested
          .
          .
          .
        MOVAL     TABLE,R12        ;Point R12 at table
        JSB       MAXADR_1         ;   and jump to subroutine
          .
          .
;-----------------------------------------------------------;
; Subroutine to return in R0 the ADDRESS of the largest     ;
; of an array of bytes.  The main program passes to the     ;
; subroutine, in R12, the address of a table containing     ;
; the number of byte addresses, followed by an array of     ;
; those byte addresses.                                     ;
;-----------------------------------------------------------;
MAXADR_1:
        PUSHR     #^M<R1,R2>       ;Save two registers
        MOVL      (R12)+,R2        ;Put argument count in R2
        MOVAB     (R12),R1         ;   and point R1 at first address
        MOVAB     @(R1)+,R0        ;Put first byte address in R0
        BRB       LOOPND           ;   and skip around to decrement
                                   ;   the address counter (R2)
LOOP:   CMPB      @(R1)+,(R0)      ;Compare unsigned byte whose
                                   ;   address is next in table with
                                   ;   byte whose address is in R0
        BLEQU     LOOPND           ;Skip if this byte < c(c(R0))
        MOVAB     @-4(R1),R0       ;   else replace current address in R0
LOOPND: SOBGTR    R2,LOOP          ;Check next address (if more to do)
        POPR      #^M<R1,R2>       ;   else restore scratch registers
        RSB                        ;   and return
          .
          .
```

Figure 9.9.5

a maximum, or perhaps *locate* (by address) the maximum of a list of bytes. But suppose we consider a subroutine whose purpose it is to *modify* one or more of the arguments transmitted to it. As a simple, if somewhat contrived illustrative example, suppose that a subroutine, whose entry point is named SWAP, is to test two numbers and if the first is *larger* than the second, it is to exchange these two numbers—replace the first with the second and the second with the first. (This is the principal activity that takes place in a bubble sort, for example; see Exercise 8.10.2.) Now it will do no good for the subroutine simply to know the *values* of the two numbers, although of course it must know those. It must also know *where* in memory the numbers are, so that the contents of those two memory locations can be exchanged, if necessary. Figure 9.9.6 shows this situation, in which the locations NUM1 and NUM2 are the addresses of the numbers to be tested, and as we see, the *contents* of these locations are put in a table. (We have also included in the table the argument count 2, although it is clear in this case that the subroutine already knows that it is dealing with two values. We have done this simply to be consistent with the general subroutine call scheme described above.) We have been unable to complete the writing of the subroutine SWAP. For although SWAP can test the two numbers to determine which is smaller, once it has determined that an exchange may be necessary, what is it to exchange? It will serve no purpose to exchange the numbers *in the table*, and SWAP does *not* know where in memory they reside. On the other hand, if the *addresses* NUM1 and NUM2 of the numbers

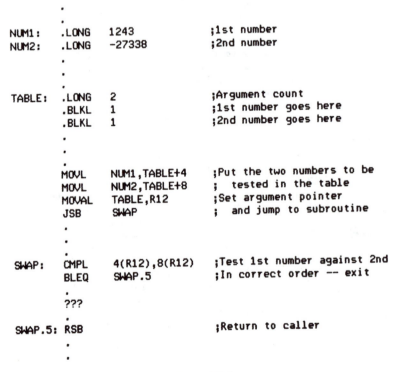

```
        .
        .
NUM1:   .LONG   1243            ;1st number
NUM2:   .LONG   -27338          ;2nd number
        .
        .
        .
TABLE:  .LONG   2               ;Argument count
        .BLKL   1               ;1st number goes here
        .BLKL   1               ;2nd number goes here
        .
        .
        MOVL    NUM1,TABLE+4    ;Put the two numbers to be
        MOVL    NUM2,TABLE+8    ;  tested in the table
        MOVAL   TABLE,R12       ;Set argument pointer
        JSB     SWAP            ;  and jump to subroutine
        .
        .
        .
SWAP:   CMPL    4(R12),8(R12)   ;Test 1st number against 2nd
        BLEQ    SWAP.5          ;In correct order -- exit
        .
        ???
        .
SWAP.5: RSB                     ;Return to caller
        .
        .
```

Figure 9.9.6

Subroutines, Stacks, and Procedures   Chap. 9

```
        .
        .
        .
NUM1:   .LONG   1243              ;1st number
NUM2:   .LONG   -27338            ;2nd number
        .
        .
        .
TABLE:  .LONG   2                 ;Argument count
        .BLKL   1                 ;Address of 1st number here
        .BLKL   1                 ;Address of 2nd number here
        .
        .
        .
        MOVAL   NUM1,TABLE+4      ;Put addresses of the two
        MOVAL   NUM2,TABLE+8      ;  numbers in the table
        MOVAL   TABLE,R12         ;Set argument pointer
        JSB     SWAP              ;  and jump to subroutine
        .
        .
        .
SWAP:   CMPL    @4(R12),@8(R12)   ;Test 1st number against 2nd
        BLEQ    SWAP.5            ;In correct order -- exit
        PUSHL   @4(R12)           ;  else save 1st number,
        MOVL    @8(R12),@4(R12)   ;  replace with 2nd
        MOVL    (SP)+,@8(R12)     ;  and replace 2nd with 1st
SWAP.5: RSB                       ;Return to caller
        .
        .
        .
```

Figure 9.9.7

are known to SWAP (Figure 9.9.7), SWAP *can* exchange these values. Thus we see that in some cases passing the *values* of arguments to a subroutine is appropriate, whereas in others, the addresses of those arguments are required.

When the actual value of an argument is passed to a subroutine, we say that that argument is **transmitted by value**; when the *address* of an argument is passed to a subroutine, we say that that argument is **transmitted by address**, **by name**, or **by reference**.

9.10 TRANSMITTING ARGUMENTS ON THE STACK

We now introduce a second standard technique for the transmission of arguments to a subroutine. It is almost identical to the "subroutine call with general argument list" discussed in the preceding section, and in fact the only difference involves *where* the argument list is placed.

Subroutine call with stacked argument list. This technique passes control to a subroutine, and transmits arguments to it, in the following way:

1. The arguments, or their addresses, are pushed onto the stack. The argument count is then pushed onto the stack.
2. The subroutine is invoked, with JSB, BSBB, or BSBW.

There are now a few little tasks the subroutine must perform initially to make this scheme useful, but before looking at them we note the state of the stack by the time control has been passed to the subroutine (Figure 9.10.1). Notice that we have stacked the arguments in the order "last argument first" so that the list will have the same appearance as the "argument table" of our earlier technique.

If the subroutine is to access the argument list, the mainline must inform it of where the list is. As before, we use R12 to point to the top of the argument list (the argument count), which is now the top of the stack, and this is easily done with the instruction

$$\text{MOVAL} \quad \text{(SP),R12}$$

Now since the subroutine may need to use some general-purpose registers, it will want to save these on the stack, so that by the time the subroutine is ready to begin its actual processing, the stack will be something like that shown in Figure 9.10.2. Observe now what the subroutine "sees." It sees R12 pointing at the top (lowest addressed) of a consecutive collection of locations, with R12 containing the address of the count of the arguments, which arguments immediately follow in memory. That is, this version of the subroutine call sees *precisely* what the last version saw—a "table" of arguments, which this time happens to be a part of the hardware stack. The consequence of this structure is that subroutine processing can proceed *identically*, whether the argument list is passed in a table or on the stack. This coincidence of the two structures greatly enhances the flexibility of subroutine calls that transmit argument lists.

If the writing of subroutines that obtain arguments from a table or from the stack is equally easy, are there any considerations that favor one technique over

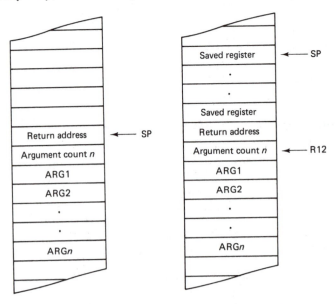

Figure 9.10.1   Figure 9.10.2

the other? This depends on the specific programming environment, but we can make a couple of observations. If arguments are placed on the stack prior to invoking the subroutine, then of course there is no need to build an argument table, and no memory needs to be reserved for the table. On the other hand, an argument table may already exist in a natural way in a particular application. We must also be aware that if large numbers of arguments need to be passed to a subroutine, or if subroutine call nesting becomes quite deep, then the danger of ultimate stack overflow cannot be dismissed.

In Figure 9.10.3 we show a version of Figure 9.9.5 in which the arguments are stacked rather than built into a table, and the reader will note that there are no differences in the routines themselves.

But problems arise when we are ready to return to the calling routine. Of course, we shall first restore the saved registers from the stack, so that now the

```
        .
        .
        PUSHAB   BYTE_5_VALUE      ;Put last byte address on stack
        PUSHAB   BYTE_4_VALUE      ;
        PUSHAB   BYTE_3_VALUE      ;
        PUSHAB   BYTE_2_VALUE      ;
        PUSHAB   BYTE_1_VALUE      ;Put first byte address on stack
        PUSHL    #5                ;Push argument count
        MOVAL    (SP),R12          ;Copy the stack pointer so that
                                   ;  R12 points at argument count
        JSB      MAXADR_1          ;Jump to subroutine
        .

;----------------------------------------------------------------;
; Subroutine to return in R0 the ADDRESS of the largest ;
; of an array of bytes.  The main program passes to the ;
; subroutine, in R12, the address of a table containing ;
; the number of byte addresses, followed by an array of ;
; those byte addresses.                                  ;
;----------------------------------------------------------------;

MAXADR_1:
        PUSHR    #^M<R1,R2>        ;Save two registers
        MOVL     (R12)+,R2         ;Put argument count in R2
        MOVAB    (R12),R1          ;  and point R1 at first address
        MOVAB    @(R1)+,R0         ;Put first byte address in R0
        BRB      LOOPND            ;  and skip around to decrement
                                   ;  the address counter (R2)
LOOP:   CMPB     @(R1)+,(R0)       ;Compare unsigned byte whose
                                   ;  address is next in table with
                                   ;  byte whose address is in R0
        BLEQU    LOOPND            ;Skip if this byte ≤ c(c(R0))
        MOVAB    @-4(R1),R0        ;  else replace current address in R0
LOOPND: SOBGTR   R2,LOOP           ;Check next address (if more to do)
        POPR     #^M<R1,R2>        ;  else restore scratch registers
        RSB                        ;  and return to calling routine??
        .
        .
```

Figure 9.10.3

stack will appear again as in Figure 9.10.1 (although by now R12 will point at the first argument rather than the argument count, as a result of the autoincrement reference to it, but this change is of no consequence). Since the return address is now on top of the stack, we could properly return to the calling routine simply by executing RSB, but observe that the argument count and the arguments themselves would then be *left on the stack*, and this could be disastrous if, for example, the calling routine had something critical on the stack prior to its subroutine call. Thus it appears to be essential that the stack be "cleaned" prior to continuing on with main processing, and for reasons more compelling than a simple devotion to neatness. The question arises: Whose responsibility should stack cleanup be, the caller's or the subroutine's? Either routine *can* do the job, but we suggest that the subroutine is in a better position to do so, since it directly knows the argument count (it is one longword down in the stack from the current SP), and this count is the key to stack cleanup.

What needs to be done here is the following (see Figure 9.10.4). We need to move the calling routine's return address (currently being pointed at by SP) down to the location currently occupied by the last argument (the first argument pushed by the caller), ARGn. Then the stack pointer must be reset to point at this (new) position of the return address. This can be accomplished with four instructions.

$$\text{MOVL} \quad 4(SP),R12$$

puts the argument count itself into R12. (Notice that by now we are through with R12 as a *pointer* to the arguments.) The next instruction

$$\text{MOVL} \quad (SP)+,(SP)[R12]$$

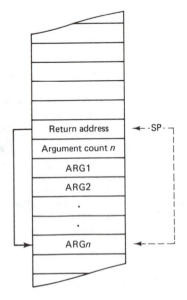

Figure 9.10.4

Subroutines, Stacks, and Procedures   Chap. 9

moves the return address to the position occupied by ARGn, which is overlaid in the process. It is not difficult to follow the sequence of events that takes place in the course of execution of this instruction, and the reader is asked to do the arithmetic necessary to verify that the return address ends up in the desired location. But note that the stack pointer SP is autoincremented as a *source* in the instruction, so that by the time its indexing by c(R12) takes place, SP has already moved up by 4. Finally, we multiply c(R12) (the original argument count) by 4 and add the result to SP:

```
ASHL    #2,R12,R12
ADDL    R12,SP
```

which resets the stack pointer to the return address. An RSB now completes the sequence.

The completed version of the program segment of Figure 9.10.3 is shown in Figure 9.10.5. It is evident that the cleanup relies heavily on the number *n* of arguments, and the fact that those arguments were pushed onto the stack as *long-words*. The indexed construction (SP)[R12], which yields offsets which are multiples of 4, and the multiplication by 4 (in the ASHL instruction) are both oriented toward longword arguments. Thus if *bytes* and/or *words* are to be passed as arguments, they should be stacked with operations such as CVTBL, CVTWL, MOVZBL, MOVZWL, and so on, even if this means leaving a few unused (and hence wasted) bytes on the stack. (Some suggestions for alternative approaches are given in the exercises.) This is not as critical when the argument list is passed through a table, since no longword-dependent stack cleanup is required in that case. However, as a general rule (which can be violated provided that care is taken), we suggest that in either technique, the arguments always be transmitted as longwords.

The reader may well be bothered by the stack manipulations that have gone on here to move the return address, properly readjust the stack pointer, and in the process, to clean the stack of the unwanted arguments. They have evidently brought about the desired result, but we have abused the stack rather severely in so doing, performing operations on it which we had certainly not foreseen and never intended when the stack concept was introduced. If the "rules of the stack game" dictate that entries are pushed and popped *only*, and that SP moves *only* on PUSH_STACK and POP_STACK operations, then we have badly violated those rules. We maintain that the end justifies the means. Much care has been required to ensure that pointers and return addresses are properly set prior to the RSB, but that care has resulted in a usable scheme. (We side with Humpty Dumpty here: "The question is, which is to be master—that's all.")

Despite the fact that these techniques seem quite promising, both subroutine calls—using general (table) and stacked argument lists—suffer from a severe deficiency which has perhaps remained hidden up until now. Neither of these schemes, or a mix of them, can deal properly with *nested* calls. For on each such call, the argument pointer R12 is *reset*, and thus lost to the routine that does the calling, when that routine ultimately regains control of the processor. There are ways,

```
        .
        .
        PUSHAB   BYTE_5_VALUE     ;Put last byte address on stack
        PUSHAB   BYTE_4_VALUE     ;
        PUSHAB   BYTE_3_VALUE     ;
        PUSHAB   BYTE_2_VALUE     ;
        PUSHAB   BYTE_1_VALUE     ;Put first byte address on stack
        PUSHL    #5               ;Push argument count
        MOVAL    (SP),R12         ;Copy the stack pointer so that
                                  ;  R12 points at argument count
        JSB      MAXADR_2         ;Jump to subroutine
        .
        .
        ;-----------------------------------------------------------;
        ; Subroutine to return in R0 the ADDRESS of the largest    ;
        ; of an array of bytes.  The main program passes to the    ;
        ; subroutine, in R12, the address of a table containing    ;
        ; the number of byte addresses, followed by an array of    ;
        ; those byte addresses.                                    ;
        ;-----------------------------------------------------------;

MAXADR_2:
        PUSHR    #^M<R1,R2>       ;Save two registers
        MOVL     (R12)+,R2        ;Put argument count in R2
        MOVAB    (R12),R1         ;  and point R1 at first address
        MOVAB    @(R1)+,R0        ;Put first byte address in R0
        BRB      LOOPND           ;  and skip around to decrement
                                  ;  the address counter (R2)
LOOP:   CMPB     @(R1)+,(R0)      ;Compare unsigned byte whose
                                  ;  address is next in table with
                                  ;  byte whose address is in R0
        BLEQU    LOOPND           ;Skip if this byte ≤ c(c(R0))
        MOVAB    @-4(R1),R0       ;  else replace current address in R0
LOOPND: SOBGTR   R2,LOOP          ;Check next address (if more to do)
        POPR     #^M<R1,R2>       ;  else restore scratch registers


        ; - - - - - - - - - - - - ;
        ; Stack clean-up and return ;
        ; - - - - - - - - - - - - ;

        MOVL     4(SP),R12        ;Put argument count in R12
                                  ;  (R12 is no longer in use)
        MOVL     (SP)+,(SP)[R12]  ;Overlay 1st argument pushed on stack
                                  ;  with calling routine's Return Address
        ASHL     #2,R12,R12       ;Multiply c(R12) by 4 and add to SP
        ADDL     R12,SP           ;  so that it points at Return Address
        RSB                       ;Return (with arguments cleaned
                                  ;  from stack)

        .
        .
```

Figure 9.10.5

with our present knowledge of the VAX operations, in which this problem can be eliminated, and some suggestions will be found in the exercises. However, we elect not to puruse this matter here; we have seen how the argument transmission schemes can be implemented, and in the next section we shall see that much of what we have had to do "manually," so to say, to achieve the desired effects is taken over by the processor itself, *including* the saving of c(R12) each time such a call is executed.

9.11 THE *CALLS* AND *CALLG* OPERATIONS

Just as the hardware, in implementing the operator JSB (or BSBB and BSBW), took over the task of saving the calling routine's return address on the hardware stack, we now investigate two operations that do much of the work required in calling subroutines with both general and stacked argument lists. To this end it would be well to review briefly just what tasks are required in those calls. In the case of a subroutine call with general argument list, it is clear that the placing of the arguments in a table, which is normally headed by the argument count, is the responsibility of the calling program. But recall that the next step was to put the *table address* in R12. This setting of the argument pointer we shall leave to this new operation. Now once control is passed to the subroutine, it is frequently the case that the subroutine needs to save some general-purpose registers for its own use, and this is another task for which we shall impose upon the operation. The third job that needs to be dealt with is the saving of the *current* c(R12). We saw at the end of Section 9.10 that failure to save and restore c(R12) at appropriate times resulted in an inability properly to nest subroutine calls.

The operations that implement these subroutine calls have as their mnemonics CALLG and CALLS, the G and S referring to "general" and "stacked" argument lists. At the present time we are concerned with CALLG, and we must ask: What information does CALLG need to implement the tasks outlined above? Certainly it must know the destination address (the address of the subroutine's entry point), for it will ultimately have to do some kind of JSB-type jump to transfer control to it. It will also have to know the address of the first longword in the table of arguments. But if, in addition, we want the operator to save general-purpose registers for us, how do we pass that information to CALLG? The answer is that we do not inform CALLG *directly* of the registers to be saved; rather, that information is given indirectly, in the subroutine, as a 16-bit *register mask word* at the subroutine entry point. Before going any further, and in particular before giving a formal description of CALLG, it will be helpful to have a concrete example at hand.

Suppose that a subroutine, say SUBR, does a task for which it needs seven arguments, and in the course of its execution requires the use of R1, R3, R4, and R10, which, of course, it should save and later restore. We establish an argument table, such as

$$\text{TABLE:} \quad \text{.LONG} \quad 7$$
$$\text{.LONG} \quad \text{ARG1}$$
$$\text{.LONG} \quad \text{ARG2}$$
$$.$$
$$.$$
$$\text{.LONG} \quad \text{ARG7}$$

The call to SUBR is now given by the instruction

$$\text{CALLG} \quad \text{TABLE,SUBR}$$

The *effect* of the instruction is to save on the stack the current c(R12), to put the address TABLE into R12 (just as if we had written

$$\text{MOVAL} \quad \text{TABLE,R12}$$

as before), and to jump to SUBR, saving the current c(PC) on the stack. Now how is CALLG informed that R1, R3, R4, and R10 are to be saved? The answer lies in the structure of the first word of SUBR. In particular, for this subroutine that first word should have the following appearance:

$$\text{SUBR:} \quad \text{.WORD} \quad \text{^B0000010000011010}$$

This 16-bit word, called the **entry mask word**, is used by CALLG to determine which registers are to be stacked. As we see, the "set" bits are in bit positions 10, 4, 3, and 1, precisely the numbers of the registers to be saved. (There is no need to specify the mask word in this fashion, since we can use the ^M construction to direct the assembler to create this word:

$$\text{SUBR:} \quad \text{.WORD} \quad \text{^M} \langle \text{R1,R3,R4,R10} \rangle$$

See the discussion of mask words following the descriptions of the PUSHR and POPR operators in Section 9.8.) Now since the entry mask occupies the word at SUBR, it is clear that CALLG should *not* produce a jump to SUBR, but rather to SUBR+2.

Notice that the required specifications for CALLG have been divided between the subroutine and its caller in what we claim to be an appropriate fashion. The creation of the argument table, and the reference to that table (in the CALLG instruction), are done by the calling routine, since it is this routine that knows which table of arguments is to be used for a particular call to SUBR. The "table" (mask) of registers to be saved is specified by the subroutine itself rather than by the calling routine, since it is the subroutine that knows which registers *it* uses, and thus needs to save and restore.

(We should point out that the specifying of the symbolic label SUBR at the subroutine's entry point, together with the register mask word that *must* be present there, could have been achieved with a use of the .ENTRY directive:

.ENTRY   SUBR,ˆM⟨R1,R3,R4,R10⟩

as discussed in Section 6.6.   However, we decline to take advantage of this directive, for the same reasons as before—it tends to "hide" the entry point's symbolic name on program listings.)

We have stated that CALLG jumps to SUBR+2, but only after it has saved the contents of R12, PC, and the specified registers on the stack, and it will be useful (but usually not necessary) for us to know just where on the stack those data are stored.   When CALLG executes, it creates a block of storage on the stack, called a **CALL frame**, and a typical such frame is shown in Figure 9.11.1. This is seen to be a relatively complex affair, so we shall examine it, one entry at a time, in some detail.

Working from the bottom up in Figure 9.11.1 (the direction of stack growth), we note that there was a stack of some sort assumed *prior to* the CALLG instruction execution, and that position is marked in the figure.   The next stack "area," denoted "0-3 byte stack alignment block," requires some explanation.   Recall that when the VAX processor accesses memory, it always does so in 32-bit longwords, and the bits accessed are always aligned on longword boundaries.   For example, for the processor to obtain the contents of the memory longword whose address is 00004F24, a single memory access is needed, since that longword is already on a longword (divisible by 4) boundary.   But if the processor needs to access the

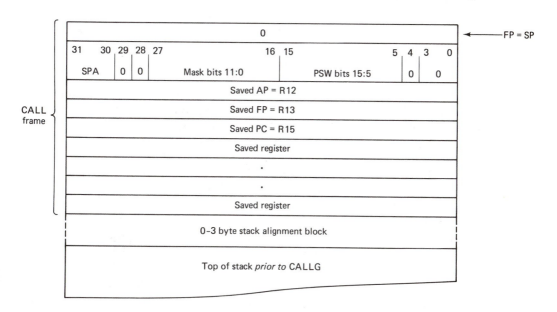

Figure 9.11.1

longword whose address is, say, 00004F61, *two* memory accesses will be required. The processor will need to obtain the contents of 00004F60 *and* of 00004F64, and then build up the 32-bit longword consisting of the bytes whose addresses are 00004F61 to 00004F64. Since a fair number of longwords are going to be pushed onto the stack as a result of CALLG, for the sake of efficiency the processor ensures that the stack pointer SP is aligned on a longword boundary by simply *sweeping off* bits 1:0 of c(SP) and replacing them with two 0s. Notice that this makes c(SP) "smaller"—that is, SP moves "upward," in the direction of normal stack growth, as a result. As an example, if when CALLG is invoked, c(SP) = 3A24A0D6, the removal of the last two bits will give c(SP) = 3A24A0D4, which is now longword aligned. [Of course, if c(SP) had already been longword aligned, two 0s would be removed and replaced by 0s, and thus c(SP) would be unaffected.] The effect of this alignment is to leave a block of unused bytes in the stack, of length 0, 1, 2, or 3 bytes, depending on SP's initial contents. We shall see shortly that the two bits removed from SP's contents are *saved*, so that ultimately c(SP) can be restored to its original condition.

Figure 9.11.1 shows that the registers specified in the mask word at the entry point of the subroutine are now saved on the stack in the order highest-numbered register first, as with the PUSHR operation. Next the current c(PC), which is the caller's return address, is pushed; followed by the contents of R13 (about which we shall have much to say momentarily) and R12. This last step we know to be crucial, for the failure to save R12 across subroutine calls that use R12 for an argument pointer can result later in the inability to access arguments properly. At this point, since c(R12) has been saved, CALLG is free to put the specified argument table address in R12. Notice that R12 is given the alternate mnemonic symbol AP, for **argument pointer**, and R12's use in this regard is so exclusive that henceforth we shall refer to it as AP (rather than R12), and we comment that even the assembler recognizes this new designation for R12. Thus the instruction

MOVAL   TABLE,AP

is acceptable to the assembler, and from a readability standpoint, is even preferred.

The next longword placed in the CALL frame contains a number of bits, the significance of which will not be especially clear until we discuss the "return" operator that "undoes" CALLG. But since it is CALLG that creates this longword, these bits will be discussed at this time. The field in bit positions 31:30, labeled "SPA," contains the two *Stack Pointer Alignment* bits that were swept off c(SP) and replaced by the two 0s. Bit 29 is a 0, because the call was achieved by CALLG. We shall see that CALLS, yet to be discussed, places a 1 in this bit. The next bit, bit 28, is always 0. Bits 27:16 are the low-order 12 bits (bits 11:0) of the entry mask word. (In our specific example, in which SUBR saves R1, R3, R4, and R10, these bits would be 010000011010.) Bits 15:5 contain the high-order 11 bits of the Processor Status Word. Bit 4 corresponds to bit 4 of the PSW, the *trace* bit, and this is set to 0 by CALLG. (We decline to give a reason for this, or even to discuss the trace bit; it will have no effect on our programming in any way.) The remaining three bits, 3:0, are the PSW's condition codes, bits 3:0

(namely, N, Z, V, and C). These are also set to 0 in this CALL frame longword. Thus we see *what* the bits in this longword are, but it is probably not clear *why* they have been saved, or why some of them have been set to 0.

The final (top) longword in the CALL frame has been set to 0. We shall have nothing to say about it at this time, except that it exists and that CALLG gives it the value 0. Although this longword does serve a purpose, we shall postpone further discussion of it until Chapter 11. Notice that R13, also known as FP, has been set to point at the top of the CALL frame. This register is called the **Frame Pointer**, and its purpose is precisely as described—to point to the top of the CALL frame. We shall see the significance of FP when we discuss the operator that achieves "returns" from CALLed subroutines, and in particular in cases in which subroutine calls are *nested*. In the meantime, observe that the stack pointer, SP, as a result of these numerous pushes, is also pointing to the top of the CALL frame.

It is clear that there has been a great deal of processor activity here, but we see that what has been accomplished is just what was needed—the argument pointer AP has been saved and then given as its new value the address of the argument table; the registers to be used by the subroutine have been saved; and control can now be passed to the subroutine at ⟨entry-point⟩ + 2. Thus much of what we had to do "by hand" in Section 9.9 has been taken over by the processor's hardware, which, in fact, has done even more than we had anticipated.

When the subroutine has completed its execution and is ready to return to its calling routine, it is evident that there is much "stack cleaning" that must be done. Whereas before, when we had implemented this subroutine call ourselves, we needed only to remove the saved registers from the stack and execute RSB, now the CALL frame is also going to have to be removed, and a special processor operation, whose mnemonic is RET (*RET*urn from call), takes over this task. We will go through RET's actions one step at a time, to see what it must do and to verify that it has the information available to do it. As the first step in the CALL return scheme, the processor resets the stack pointer to c(FP) + 4 (see Figure 9.11.1). Thus SP is pointing at the word containing the SP Alignment bits, register mask, and so on. This word is *popped* from the stack into a temporary internal (private) CPU register. Registers AP, FP, and PC can now be restored, each with a stack pop, so that SP is now pointing at the last saved general-purpose register. The registers are now restored, in their proper order. RET can do this, since it knows the registers were pushed on the stack highest-number first, and it has a copy of the register mask, bits 11:0, in the temporary register, so that it can determine *which* registers were stacked initially. Next, the stack pointer contents can be put back to its state immediately prior to the CALLG (recall that it had been longword aligned), simply by replacing its two low-order bits with the SPA bits in the temporary register. Now the PSW is restored from the temporary register (bits 15:5), bit 4 is set to 0, and the condition codes, bits 3:0, are taken from bits 3:0 of the temporary register. Finally, instruction execution resumes, and since the return address from the caller has been placed in the PC, control is passed back to the calling routine, as desired.

Now that we have a general idea of what RET does and see that it achieves returns in a way that is consistent with the scheme we had earlier implemented, we need to tidy up a couple of details and make note of a few important consequences of the technique. First, note that when CALLG has completed its execution, the stack pointer is pointing to the top of the CALL frame, and the area above SP is free stack space. Naturally, there is no reason why the subroutine cannot use the stack in any way it may need, just as before. Of course, it will not have to save calling routine register values, for that has been done by CALLG, but it may wish to use the stack for temporary storage, or perhaps for the temporary saving of a register that is serving multiple duty within the subroutine. For the moment we shall informally refer to this stack area as the **subroutine stack space**. Suppose now that when the subroutine is ready to execute RET, there are some data on the stack which the subroutine has pushed into the subroutine stack space but has not yet removed. Does the subroutine have to "clean" its stack area prior to returning? The answer is "no," and a reexamination of the first action of RET reveals why. For RET *resets* SP to c(FP) + 4, and this has the effect of "cleaning" the subroutine stack space. This can be a very useful feature, and we shall have more to say about it in Section 9.12. But observe that one of the consequences of this action of RET is that if in the course of its execution, the subroutine *alters* c(FP), the effect is to lead RET to believe that the CALL frame is somewhere other than where it actually is, and as we see, the return from the call will almost surely result in disaster.

Next, more needs to be said about the way in which the PSW bits are saved, set, and restored, for as we know, their states can have profound effects on programming. We mentioned in Chapter 5, when the PSL and PSW were first discussed, that in addition to the condition codes, the PSW contains some other bits that control the *environment* in which a user program executes. In particular, bits 7:5 of the PSW are labeled DV, FU, and IV, and these stand for Decimal Overflow, Floating Underflow, and Integer Overflow. If, for example, the IV-bit in the PSW is *set* and an integer overflow occurs—that is, an instruction is executed which sets the PSW V-bit—then execution of the user program is aborted and control is passed to the *operating system*, which will typically respond with an appropriate error message. If this bit is *cleared*, no such action takes place, with instruction execution continuing undisturbed. The state of this bit in the PSW can be set in a number of ways. It can be set or cleared directly using the operations BISPSW and BICPSW; or it can be set or cleared when program execution begins, by setting or clearing bit 14 in the *program entry mask word* as discussed in Section 6.7. To date we have normally disabled the integer overflow "trap" by putting a 0 in that word. But now suppose that a program is executing with, say, integer overflow *enabled* (that is, with PSW bit 5 *set*), and there is a call to a subroutine. Suppose we wish the subroutine to execute with integer overflow *disabled*. How can we achieve this in such a way that the setting of this bit will be restored upon the return? The answer lies in bit 14 of the entry point mask word for the subroutine. If this bit is set, IV will be enabled; if it is cleared, IV will be disabled. But whatever its state *within the subroutine*, its state in the calling routine will be restored upon the return, for as we know, RET *restores* bits 15:5 of the PSW. The long and short of it is that the *environment* within which a routine is executing can be altered when control is passed to a subroutine, but that environment will be restored upon subroutine return. (We have said nothing about DV and FU here, nor shall we at this point. The only further comments we make now are that when CALLG is executed, the state within the subroutine of DV is determined by bit 15 of the entry mask word, and FU is cleared.)

Finally, we note that upon entry to a subroutine with CALLG the condition codes are *cleared*, and upon return to the calling routine with RET the condition codes are *restored* from bits 3:0 of the second longword down from the top of the CALL frame. Now those bits in the CALL frame were cleared when that longword was constructed, but that does not necessarily mean that RET will restore them as 0. For there is no reason why the subroutine itself, in the course of its execution, cannot set one or more of those bits. We offer below a sample subroutine which sets one of those bits.

As we have seen in past programming examples, some subroutines operate on and possibly affect the arguments passed to them (the subroutine SWAP of Figure 9.9.7 is an example), whereas others return *values*, such as MAX or MAX-ADR or FACT. (The latter type of subroutine is usually called a *function*, as we have already noted.) There are also subroutines which return a value that is only of a "true-false" or "yes-no" nature, rather than being numerical in character. It is not unreasonable for such a routine to return its value through one of the condition codes, perhaps with 1 meaning "true" and 0 meaning "false." As a simple example, consider a subroutine that merely tests to see if a byte which is passed to it contains the ASCII code for an alphabetic character. Such a subroutine, which we intend to be called via CALLG, is shown in Figure 9.11.2. The calling routine needs only to pass the byte to the subroutine (somehow), and the subroutine returns the desired information back to the caller as follows. If, upon return, the C-bit is *on*, the character in question is alphabetic; if the C-bit is *off*, the character is nonalphabetic. The calling routine, upon return from the subroutine ISALPHA, can then execute a BCC or BCS to direct control to handle the particular situation based on the subroutine's response to the question: Is this character alphabetic? Notice that the C-bit is set by means of the instruction.

BISB   #1,4(FP)

which sets not the *current* C-bit, but rather the C-bit that the PSW *will* have once control is returned to the caller. Observe also the "calling convention," namely that the table whose address is passed in CALLG to ISALPHA contains only the single byte to be tested; thus the table does *not* consist of longwords as our examples to date have, and the table is *not* headed by the argument count (1). Both of these features are in violation of some conventions which we had informally adopted earlier, and this is done for two reasons. First, the situation is so very simple here that we choose not to adhere to the conventions, and in fact doing so would reduce the utility of the routine. Second, it illustrates that the conventions are exactly that—conventions, which we may follow *if we choose*, but which we may abandon in some cases, provided that we are careful about what we do and are aware that we may have to pay some consequences later.

```
;----------------------------------------------------;
; Subroutine ISALPHA -- determines if a byte         ;
; represents the ASCII code for an ALPHABETIC        ;
; character (A...Z or a...z).  Returns with          ;
; C-bit set if alphabetic; C-bit is cleared if       ;
; nonalphabetic.                                     ;
;                                                    ;
; Calling convention:                                ;
;                                                    ;
;           CALLG   addr,ISALPHA                     ;
;                                                    ;
; where 'addr' is the address of the byte to be      ;
; tested.                                            ;
;----------------------------------------------------;

ISALPHA: .WORD   ^M<>            ;Save no registers
         CMPB    (AP),#^A/A/     ;Less than 'A'?
         BLSSU   RETURN          ;Yes -- not alphabetic
         CMPB    (AP),#^A/z/     ;Greater than 'z'?
         BGTRU   RETURN          ;Yes -- not alphabetic
         CMPB    (AP),#^A/Z/     ;Less-or-equal 'Z'?
         BLEQU   SETC            ;Yes -- alphabetic
         CMPB    (AP),#^A/a/     ;Greater-or-equal 'a'?
         BLSSU   RETURN          ;No -- not alphabetic
SETC:    BISB    #1,4(FP)        ;Set C-bit in CALL frame
                                 ; PSW (for return to caller)
RETURN:  RET                     ;Return to caller
```

Figure 9.11.2

We are now in a position to deal completely and yet in a far more cursory fashion with the operator CALLS, which implements subroutine calls in which the argument list is transmitted on the stack. Recall that in Section 9.10 we had stacked the arguments *as longwords*, then stacked the argument count, copied SP into R12 = AP, and finally JSBed to the subroutine. Once in the subroutine, whatever general-purpose registers needed to be saved were pushed onto the stack. We cannot expect CALLS to push the calling routine's argument list on the stack, but we do leave to it the task of pushing the (longword) argument count. Specifically, CALLS is invoked by

$$\text{CALLS} \quad count,dest$$

where *count* is the argument count and *dest* is the destination address—that is, the address of the subroutine entry point. As with CALLG, the *word* at the subroutine entry point is a register save mask word. CALLS builds a CALL frame almost identical to that constructed by CALLG, and again we shall go through it step by step (see Figure 9.11.3). CALLS first pushes the argument count, as specified in the CALLS instruction, onto the stack and copies the current stack pointer contents to a temporary register. SP is now longword aligned as in CALLG; the two low-order bits of c(SP) are removed and replaced by 0s. The registers specified in the entry mask word are then pushed onto the stack, followed by c(PC) (the return address), c(FP), and c(AP). AP can now be given the value of the temporary register, so that AP points at the argument count in the stack. Next, the longword containing SPA, the register save mask bits, PSW bits, and so on, is pushed, and the reader will note that it is identical to its counterpart for CALLG, *except* that bit 29 is set to 1 rather than to 0. Finally, an additional longword whose contents is 0 is pushed, and FP is set to the contents of SP. Thus we see that with a few exceptions, CALLS and CALLG have almost identical behaviors. But in any event, notice that with regard to the setting of AP, both of these CALLS have achieved the same results as our constructions of Sections 9.9 and 9.10.

The RETurn operation for CALLS (whose mnemonic is also RET—in fact, it is simply a second version of the same operation) is a bit more complicated than for CALLG, as we might expect. For not only must RET remove the CALL frame and restore some registers, but to be truly useful to us it should also clean the stack of the *argument list* that was pushed there by the calling routine. RET proceeds in a fashion which is identical to its action for CALLG, up to and including the point at which it "undoes" the SP longword alignment of the CALLS operator, by replacing the two low-order bits of c(SP) with the bits in SPA. At this point, then, SP is pointing at the argument count which was pushed there by CALLS. Now since RET knows that it is returning from a CALLS and not a CALLG (which

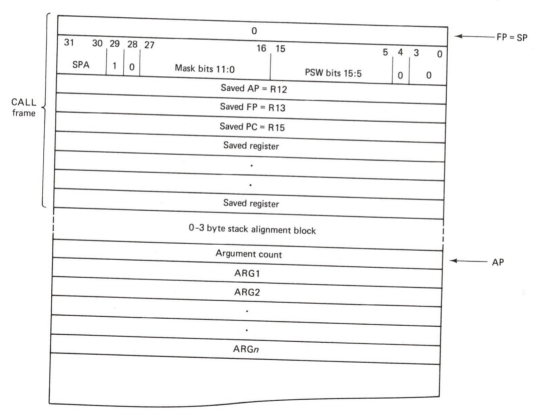

Figure 9.11.3

it determines from bit 29 of the second longword in the CALL frame), it resets c(SP) to "remove" the argument count and argument list. This is done by *popping* a longword off the stack (the argument count), multiplying the popped value by 4, and adding the result to c(SP). Notice that this is precisely the action we took in Section 9.10 to clean the arguments from the stack.

This last action of RET makes it clear that the arguments which are pushed on the stack prior to invoking a subroutine with CALLS *must* be pushed as *longwords*. Consequently, bytes and words which are to be used as arguments should be longword extended, with one of the CVT or MOVZ instructions. It is now evident that one and the same subroutine can be invoked either with CALLG or CALLS, *provided* that in the CALLG case, the argument table is headed by the (longword) count of arguments in the table, and the arguments themselves are longwords. Thus both calls shown in Figure 9.11.4 will produce the same effects for the same subroutine SUBR.

We close this section anticlimactically with formal descriptions of CALLG, CALLS, and RET.

(a) CALLG   CALL subroutine with General argument list

The operation code for CALLG is FA and its operand descriptor is

$$arglist.ab,dest.ab$$

where *arglist* is the address of the subroutine argument list, given as an address access operand, and *dest* is the address of the subroutine entry point, given as an address access operand. Both operands have a *byte* context with regard to operand side effects. The effects of CALLG are as follows.

1. c(SP) is saved in a temporary register *temp*; c(SP) is then longword aligned by replacing bits 1:0 with 0s.

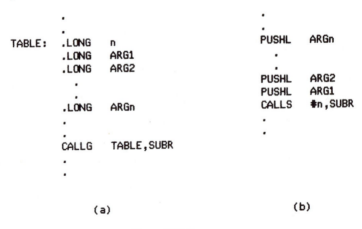

(a)   (b)

Figure 9.11.4

Subroutines, Stacks, and Procedures   Chap. 9

2. c(Rn) is pushed onto the stack for each n for which bit n in the entry mask word is set, for n running from 11 down to 0 (in that order—higher-order registers are pushed first).

3. c(PC), c(FP), and c(AP) are pushed onto the stack, in that order.

4. The condition codes (PSW bits 3:0) are cleared.

5. A longword is pushed onto the stack, containing the following information:

$$\text{bits } 31:30 = \text{bits } 1:0 \text{ of } temp$$
$$\text{bit } 29 \quad = 0$$
$$\text{bit } 28 \quad = 0$$
$$\text{bits } 27:16 = \text{bits } 11:0 \text{ of entry mask word}$$
$$\text{bits } 15:5 \quad = \text{bits } 15:5 \text{ of PSW}$$
$$\text{bits } 4:0 \quad = 0$$

6. A longword containing 0 is pushed onto the stack.

7. c(FP) is replaced by c(SP).

8. c(AP) is replaced by the address *arglist*.

9. Bit 6 of PSW is cleared; bits 7 and 5 of PSW are replaced by bits 15 and 14 of entry mask word, respectively. (Bits 13:12 of entry mask word *must* be 0.)

10. PC is given the value *dest*+2.

(b) CALLS   *CALL* subroutine with Stacked argument list

The operation code for CALLS is FB and its operand descriptor is

$$argcnt.rl, dest.ab$$

where *argcnt* is the longword count of subroutine arguments (which are assumed to be on the stack) and *dest* is the address of the subroutine entry point, given as an address access operand. *dest* has a *byte* context with regard to operand side effects. The effects of CALLS are as follows.

1. The value of *argcnt* is pushed onto the stack.

2. c(SP) is saved in a temporary register *temp*; c(SP) is then longword aligned by replacing bits 1:0 with 0s.

3. c(Rn) is pushed onto the stack for each n for which bit n in the entry mask word is set, for n running from 11 down to 0 (in that order—higher-order registers are pushed first).

4. c(PC), c(FP), and c(AP) are pushed onto the stack, in that order.

5. The condition codes (PSW bits 3:0) are cleared.
6. A longword is pushed onto the stack, containing the following information:

$$bits\ 31:30 = bits\ 1:0\ of\ temp$$

$$bit\ 29 \quad = 1$$

$$bit\ 28 \quad = 0$$

$$bits\ 27:16 = bits\ 11:0\ of\ entry\ mask\ word$$

$$bits\ 15:5 \quad = bits\ 15:5\ of\ PSW$$

$$bits\ 4:0 \quad = 0$$

7. A longword containing 0 is pushed onto the stack.
8. c(FP) is replaced by c(SP).
9. c(AP) is replaced by the contents of *temp*.
10. Bit 6 of PSW is cleared; bits 7 and 5 of PSW are replaced by bits 15 and 14 of entry mask word, respectively. (Bits 13:12 of entry mask word *must* be 0.)
11. PC is given the value *dest* + 2.

(c) RET   *RETurn from CALLG or CALLS subroutine* call

The operation RET has no operands. The effects of the RET operator are:

1. c(SP) is replaced by c(FP) + 4.
2. The top of the stack is popped into a temporary longword register, *temp*.
3. The three longwords on top of the stack are popped into AP, FP, and PC, in that order.
4. Rn is restored by a pop from the stack for each n for which bit n + 16 in *temp* is set, for n running from 0 to 11 (in that order—lower-order registers are popped first).
5. The two low-order bits of c(SP) are replaced by bits 31:30 of *temp*.
6. c(PSW) is replaced by bits 15:0 of *temp*.

If bit 29 of *temp* is 1:

7. The top of the stack is popped into a longword temporary register *temp1*.
8. c(SP) is replaced by c(SP) + 4∗⟨unsigned value of the low-order byte of *temp1*⟩.

9.12 THE NESTING OF *CALLG* AND *CALLS* OPERATIONS

Recall that at the end of Section 9.10 we observed that the technique which we had developed for calling subroutines and passing argument lists to them, either in tables or on the stack, would *fail* if we attempted to nest such calls. It should be evident that that problem has been eliminated with the introduction of CALLS and CALLG, since each of those operators saves c(AP), and it was the failure to do this that was the deficiency of the earlier schemes. Thus we can expect CALLG and CALLS to manage nested calls, and even recursion and "A call B call A" constructions, without error. In fact they do, but it will nonetheless be instructive to look at an example of such nesting. (We leave to the reader an investigation of recursion and coroutines.) Thus we assume that some main routine calls a subroutine, which we refer to as Subroutine1, and at the time of the call, the main routine's stack pointer has some value, which we denote by SP0. We are going to call Subroutine1 with CALLG, although CALLS would produce almost identical results, the differences not being of any substance to our investigation. Now once Subroutine1 has control, it may well use the stack for a variety of purposes, so at some point in the course of Subroutine1's execution, the stack will have the appearance shown in Figure 9.12.1. (SP0, AP0, FP0, and PC0 refer to the values of these registers in the main or calling routine, whereas SP1, AP1, and FP1 are the values of the corresponding registers during Subroutine1 execution. Arglist1 is the address of the argument list passed to Subroutine1 by the main routine's CALLG.) Suppose that at this point Subroutine1 *calls* (with CALLG again) Subroutine2. The resulting stack is shown in Figure 9.12.2, where we assume that Subroutine2 has already begun execution and has also used the stack for some temporary storage. The notation and terminology are analogous to the Subroutine1 situation.

Now when Subroutine2 executes RET, the first action is to replace c(SP2) with c(FP2)+4. Notice that this has the effect of "removing" from the stack any data that Subroutine2 may have left there—even though the stack pointer may

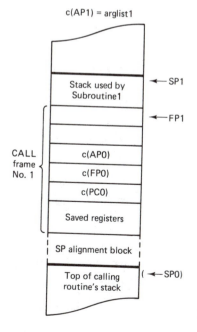

Figure 9.12.1

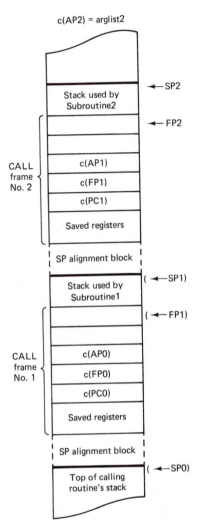

c(AP2) = arglist2

—SP2

Stack used by
Subroutine2

—FP2

CALL
frame
No. 2

c(AP1)

c(FP1)

c(PC1)

Saved registers

SP alignment block

(—SP1)

Stack used by
Subroutine1

(—FP1)

CALL
frame
No. 1

c(AP0)

c(FP0)

c(PC0)

Saved registers

SP alignment block

(—SP0)

Top of calling
routine's stack

Figure 9.12.2

have been changed during the course of Subroutine2's execution, since c(FP2) has not, the stack will be cleaned of any of Subroutine2's leftovers. Since c(FP1) and c(AP1) will be restored by RET, execution will ultimately resume in Subroutine1, with the stack and AP1 exactly as shown in Figure 9.12.1. Finally, perhaps after some further execution, Subroutine1 executes RET, *its* stack is cleaned, registers are restored, and control is returned to the main (calling) routine, with *its* stack in exactly the same condition in which it left it. We see now the importance of saving each Frame Pointer across these subroutine calls, and it is equally evident that no subroutine should do anything to alter its frame pointer or any previous versions of FP. Failure to adhere to this rule will make proper subsequent RETurns impossible.

```
;------------------------------------------------
; Function FACT -- calculate factorial n (n!)
;
; Calling routine pushes n onto the stack as a
; longword and invokes FACT with:
;
;               CALLS   #1,FACT
;
; Result (n!) is returned in R0.
;------------------------------------------------

FACT:    .WORD   ^M<R2>         ;Save c(R2)
         MOVL    4(AP),R2       ;Get argument from stack
         BGTR    FACT.4         ;If arg > 0, skip around
         MOVL    #1,R0          ; else set product to 1
         RET                    ; and begin sequence of
                                ; returns
FACT.4:  DECL    R2             ;Decrement the argument,
         PUSHL   R2             ; push it on the stack
         CALLS   #1,FACT        ; for next call to FACT
         MULL    4(AP),R0       ;Accumulate products in R0
         RET                    ; and do next return
```

Figure 9.13.1

9.13 *CALLG* AND *CALLS* PROGRAMMING EXAMPLES

We devote this section to some programming segments that illustrate the use of CALLG and CALLS in a variety of ways. For the most part we leave to the reader the details of program execution, concentrating the discussion on some of the substantive or unusual features of the constructions.

Figure 9.13.1 shows a version of the factorial n subroutine of Figure 9.5.15, in which FACT is called with CALLS. The main routine stacks the number n whose factorial is to be found and invokes FACT with

CALLS   #1,FACT

Observe that the routine FACT has been slightly rewritten, no longer requiring that the *calling routine* supply the initial value 1, since now the multiplications occur *after* a "return" takes place, rather than *before* the routine is reinvoked. As before, the calls are recursive, and that is the feature of interest here. The reader should construct the CALL frames that are created as the main routine calls FACT, and as FACT calls itself, for a simple case (such as n = 3). It will be evident that as each frame is *removed*, the number 1 (argument count) and the *next higher* multiplier will be on top of the stack.

The routine of Figure 9.13.2 is an implementation of a bubble sort (see Exercise 8.10.2). Two things to note here are that the sort is in *decreasing* order, and the routine sorts *words*, hence the entry point name BUBWD—*BUB*ble sort *W*ords in *D*ecreasing order. The technique is perfectly straightforward, and the only new feature is the use of the **direct assignments**

$$LISTADR = 4$$
$$LISTCNT = 8$$

```
;----------------------------------------------;
; Subroutine BUBWD -- BUBBLE sorts WORDS in    ;
; DECREASING order.  The number of numbers to  ;
; be sorted is pushed on the stack, followed   ;
; by the address of the first of those numbers:;
;                                              ;
;                 PUSHL   <list_count>         ;
;                 PUSHL   <list_address>       ;
;                 CALLS   #2,BUBWD             ;
;                                              ;
; If a table is created consisting of:         ;
;                                              ;
;        TABLE:  .LONG   2                      ;
;                .LONG   <list_address>        ;
;                .LONG   <list_count>          ;
;                                              ;
; then BUBWD can be invoked with:              ;
;                                              ;
;                 CALLG   TABLE,BUBWD          ;
;----------------------------------------------;
```

```
LISTADR = 4      ;Offset from AP of list address
LISTCNT = 8      ;Offset from AP of list count

BUBWD:  .WORD   ^M<R5,R6,R7>    ;Save three registers
        MOVL    LISTADR(AP),R5  ;Get list address
        MOVL    LISTCNT(AP),R6  ; and list count
        DECL    R6              ;Adjust counter for
                                ;  number of passes
BUB.20: MOVL    R6,R7           ;Copy pass counter
                                ;  (= compare counter)
        PUSHL   R5              ;Save list address
BUB.30: CMPW    (R5)+,(R5)      ;Compare two numbers
        BGEQ    BUB.50          ;Skip if in correct order
        MOVW    (R5),-(SP)      ;  else save 2nd word,
        MOVW    -2(R5),(R5)     ;  replace with 1st word
        MOVW    (SP)+,-2(R5)    ;  and replace 1st with 2nd
BUB.50: SOBGTR  R7,BUB.30       ;Compare next pair of words
        MOVL    (SP)+,R5        ;Restore list address
        SOBGTR  R6,BUB.20       ;  and make another pass
        RET                     ;Return when done
```

Figure 9.13.2.

which are simply used as offsets from the AP to locate the list address and the list count, respectively. The sole purpose of these assignments is to clarify the program instructions, since a statement such as

MOVL   LISTADR(AP),R5

is more suggestive of what is being moved to R5 than is

MOVL   4(AP),R5

As indicated in the routine's documentation, BUBWD can be invoked with either CALLS or CALLG, provided that the calling routine takes the appropriate actions prior to calling BUBWD. (This really goes without saying, but perhaps at least once it should be made explicit. This is one of the strong points of the CALLG/CALLS constructions.)

If we wanted to sort a list of 16-bit words in *increasing* order, it is clear that the only change that would have to be made in the segment of Figure 9.13.2 is the replacement of the conditional branch BGEQ by BLEQ. Thus to write a subroutine, called BUBWI, we could simply reproduce all the code shown in that figure, with the exception of the change in this conditional branch. Rather than do so, we write a *single* routine, with *two* entry points, BUBWD and BUBWI, which itself *changes the conditional branch*. That is, this subroutine modifies one of its own instructions, depending on the point at which the routine is entered. This version is shown in Figure 9.13.3, and we must make a couple of comments about it. First, note that the instruction which appears on the listing at the line labeled BUB.40

BRB   BUB.50

is *never* executed, because by the time execution reaches that point, the BRB has been replaced by BGEQ or BLEQ. That is, the appropriate branch instruction has *overlaid* this unconditional branch by program execution itself, at the subroutine entry points. (The BRB instruction was put here to force the assembler to calculate the correct displacement to BUB.50.) Second, our motivation for writing such a self-modifying routine stems from the savings in the writing of source code and the attendant savings in machine code. Finally, we must confess that we are on very shaky ground here. The writing of self-modifying code must be done with extreme care, the environment in which the routine will execute must be taken into account, and despite the fact that we have just done so, we strongly recommend against such eccentricities: these programs are difficult to read, even more difficult to maintain, the chances for error are great, and in certain total program environments they will almost certainly lead to catastrophe. But the example does show what the experienced programmer, who knows just what occurs not only at assembly time but also at *execution* time, can do with the computer system—in brief, we have been unable to resist the temptation.

```
;--------------------------------------------------------;
; Subroutine to bubble-sort word arrays.  Contains TWO   ;
; entry points -- BUBWI and BUBWD -- used when the sort  ;
; is to be in Increasing order or Decreasing order.  At  ;
; each entry point, an appropriate conditional branch    ;
; instruction is written into the location labeled       ;
; 'BUB.40' and thus OVERLAYS the BRB instruction at      ;
; that location to achieve the desired ordering.  See    ;
; Figure 9.13.2 for CALLing and argument transmission    ;
; protocols.                                             ;
;--------------------------------------------------------;

LISTADR = 4       ;Offset from AP of list address
LISTCNT = 8       ;Offset from AP of list count
        ;
BGEQ    = ^X18    ;Binary code for 'BGEQ'
BLEQ    = ^X15    ;Binary code for 'BLEQ'
        ;
BUBWI:  .WORD   ^M<R5,R6,R7>    ;Save three registers
        MOVB    #BLEQ,BUB.40    ;Put 'BLEQ' code in 'BRB' instr.
        BRB     BUB.10          ;Enter main routine
        ;
BUBWD:  .WORD   ^M<R5,R6,R7>    ;Save three registers
        MOVB    #BGEQ,BUB.40    ;Put 'BGEQ' code in 'BRB' instr.

BUB.10: MOVL    LISTADR(AP),R5  ;Get list address
        MOVL    LISTCNT(AP),R6  ;  and list count
        DECL    R6              ;Adjust counter for passes count
BUB.20: MOVL    R6,R7           ;Copy pass count = compare count
        PUSHL   R5              ;Save list address
BUB.30: CMPW    (R5)+,(R5)      ;Compare two numbers
BUB.40: BRB     BUB.50          ;Skip if in correct order
                                ;(NOTE! 'BRB' is replaced
                                ;  with 'BLEQ' or 'BGEQ'
                                ;  at routine entry points)
        MOVW    (R5),-(SP)      ; else save 2nd word,
        MOVW    -2(R5),(R5)     ;  replace with 1st word
        MOVW    (SP)+,-2(R5)    ;  and replace 1st with 2nd
BUB.50: SOBGTR  R7,BUB.30       ;Compare next pair of words
        MOVL    (SP)+,R5        ;Restore list address
        SOBGTR  R6,BUB.20       ;  and make another pass
        RET                     ;Return when done
```

Figure 9.13.3

The routine of Figure 9.13.4 is a modification of that of Figure 9.13.2, in which the "pass count" and "compare count" are maintained on the stack rather than in registers R6 and R7, respectively. Two direct assignments have been added to the routine:

$$PASSCNT = -4$$
$$COMPCNT = -8$$

which are used in the following ways. When the routine BUBWD is called with CALLG or CALLS, a CALL frame is constructed, with FP set to c(SP). Thus

```
;-------------------------------------------------------------;
; Bubble sort an array of words into decreasing order.        ;
; (See Figure 9.13.2 for CALLing and argument transmis-       ;
; sion protocols.)  Uses 'local storage' for the temp-        ;
; orary storage of variable values.                           ;
;-------------------------------------------------------------;

LISTADR = 4         ;Offset from AP of list address
LISTCNT = 8         ;Offset from AP of list count

PASSCNT = -4        ;Offset from FP of pass counter
COMPCNT = -8        ;Offset from FP of compare counter

BUBWD:  .WORD   ^M<R5>              ;Save one register
        MOVAL   COMPCNT(FP),SP      ;Adjust stack pointer to
                                    ;  make room for 'local' storage
        MOVL    LISTADR(AP),R5      ;Get list address
        MOVL    LISTCNT(AP),-
                PASSCNT(FP)         ;Save list count in 'local' storage
        DECL    PASSCNT(FP)         ;Adjust counter for number of passes

BUB.20: MOVL    PASSCNT(FP),-
                COMPCNT(FP)         ;Copy pass counter = compare counter
        PUSHL   R5                  ;Save list address
BUB.30: CMPW    (R5)+,(R5)          ;Compare two numbers
        BGEQ    BUB.50              ;Skip if in correct order
        MOVW    (R5),-(SP)          ;  else save 2nd word,
        MOVW    -2(R5),(R5)         ;  replace with 1st word
        MOVW    (SP)+,-2(R5)        ;  and replace 1st with 2nd

BUB.50: SOBGTR  COMPCNT(FP),-
                BUB.30              ;Compare next pair of words
        MOVL    (SP)+,R5            ;Restore list address
        SOBGTR  PASSCNT(FP),-
                BUB.20              ;  and make another pass
        RET                         ;Return when done
```

Figure 9.13.4

both FP and SP point to the top of the CALL frame. The first executable instruction of the routine:

$$MOVAL \quad COMPCNT(FP),SP$$

has the effect of subtracting 8 (COMPCNT = −8) from c(SP). Thus the stack pointer now points at the longword *two longwords up from* the CALL frame (see Figure 9.13.5.) The longword immediately above the CALL frame will be used for storage of the "pass counter" (formerly R6), and the longword above that for the "compare counter" (formerly R7). We refer to these two longwords collectively as a **local storage area**, the word "local" referring to the fact that this area is *local to* or *private to* BUBWD and is not storage used in any *global* sense—that is, it is not storage available to BUBWD's calling routine, for example. Notice that it was essential to change the stack pointer, for as written, even after these two local longwords were established, the routine still uses the stack for the temporary storage of c(R5). Finally, observe that there is no need for the resetting of the stack pointer when the routine is ready to return, for RET effectively "cleans" these two longwords from the stack when it executes—recall that RET replaces c(SP) with c(FP)+4.

The next subroutine example (Figure 9.13.6) is a variation on the routine ISALPHA of Figure 9.11.2. It is a bit bizarre in some respects, and we include it simply as a further example of what the programmer can do when he or she fully understands the precise actions of CALLG and CALLS. The subroutine LOCALPH is recursive, and its purpose is to *LOC*ate, in a string of characters whose ASCII codes we assume to be in consecutive memory bytes, the *address* of the first *ALPHA*betic character. (Such a routine might be useful in an environment in

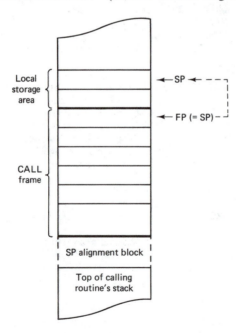

Figure 9.13.5

```
;-----------------------------------------------;
; Subroutine LOCALPH -- finds first alphabetic  ;
; character in a string of ASCII characters.    ;
; Address of first character in string must be  ;
; in R0, and LOCALPH is called with:            ;
;                                               ;
;          CALLG   (R0)+,LOCALPH                 ;
;                                               ;
; Address of first alphabetic character is      ;
; returned in R0.                               ;
;-----------------------------------------------;

LOCALPH: .WORD    ^M<>              ;Save no registers
         CMPB     (AP),#^A/A/       ;Less than 'A'?
         BLSSU    AGAIN             ;Yes -- try again
         CMPB     (AP),#^A/z/       ;Greater than 'z'?
         BGTRU    AGAIN             ;Yes -- try again
         CMPB     (AP),#^A/Z/       ;Less-or-equal 'Z'?
         BLEQU    ALPHA             ;Yes -- found alpha
         CMPB     (AP),#^A/a/       ;Less than 'a'?
         BLSSU    AGAIN             ;Yes -- try again
ALPHA:   DECL     R0                ;Compensate for last
                                    ;  autoincrement
         RET                        ;  and return

AGAIN:   CALLG    (R0)+,LOCALPH     ;Call LOCALPH again
         RET                        ;Start sequence of returns
```

Figure 9.13.6

which strings of characters input from the keyboard must be "parsed" into numbers, letters, special characters, etc.) There is nothing terribly unusual about the logic of the routine except for the way in which it is called. Notice that the calling routine (and consequently LOCALPH, whenever it calls itself) must use CALLG, and the "table address" operand must be R0, *autoincrement mode*. This has the effect of moving R0, as a pointer, along the string of bytes, so that as LOCALPH recursively invokes itself, it will examine each byte in turn to see if it represents an alphabetic character. But this requires that c(R0) be autoincremented *by 1* each time LOCALPH is called; a close examination of the formal description of CALLG will reveal that in fact this is the case. The *arglist* operand is evaluated in a *byte* context and thus will produce byte-type side effects. We leave it to the reader to go through the details of the routine and its recursive calls. The only comment we make is that the byte to be tested is referred to as (AP) rather than 4(AP) since, contrary to our adopted convention, the "table" of arguments that is involved here does *not* begin with an argument count.

Our final example is quite complicated. Early in this chapter we promised the reader an example of "coroutines," subroutines that call one another. It is time to make good on that promise, and we do so in grand style, for not only do the two routines call one another, but each also calls itself recursively. Consider the following task, which is faced by any operating system utility that must communicate directly with a user, through the user's terminal. The program requests a *command string* of some sort and, based on the user's response, must take some appropriate action. The utility has no way of knowing in advance what the user will enter, so it must analyze the string it receives. This is frequently a very demanding task, and to give some assistance, utilities will sometimes "condition" the incoming string prior to attempting an analysis, in the following ways: blanks (spaces) are removed, since these are frequently of no consequence; and lowercase alphabetic characters are converted to uppercase. The utility can now begin scanning the conditioned string—for a particular sequence of uppercase characters, for example.

Shown in Figure 9.13.7 are two subroutines: LC2UC converts lowercase characters to uppercase; and PACK removes blanks (spaces) by moving all the remaining characters in the string one position to the left, thereby "covering up" the blank. We assume that there is some pointer which "points to" successive characters in the string (R4 in LC2UC, and R9 in PACK). LC2UC works in the following way. If the character being pointed at is a space, LC2UC stacks the string pointer and calls PACK. If not, LC2UC converts it to uppercase (if it was lowercase), moves the string pointer up by one character, stacks it, and *calls itself*. PACK does a corresponding thing. If the character being pointed at by the string pointer is not a space, it stacks the pointer and calls LC2UC. If it is a space, it packs the space out (by moving the tail end of the string one byte to the left), stacks the pointer and *calls itself*. We assume that the string of characters ends in a NUL byte (ASCII code 0), and either LC2UC or PACK will terminate its action and begin a sequence of RETurns once it sees this "string terminator."

The routines are initiated in the following way. Let STRING be the address of the first byte of a contiguous collection of ASCII codes, which ends in a ⟨NUL⟩. Then the instructions

```
        PUSHAB   STRING
        CALLS    #1,LC2UC
```

will get the sequence of CALLSs started, and upon return to this calling routine, the string will have been conditioned as described. In fact,

```
        PUSHAB   STRING
        CALLS    #1,PACK
```

will do just as well, since the two routines function, in a sense, "symmetrically."

The only other information the reader needs before investigating these subroutines is the fact that the symbol SPACE is assumed to have the value ^X20, the ASCII code for the "space" or "blank" character. With that we leave it to the reader to uncover the logic of the subroutines (which is the most straightforward part of the total task), to determine what CALL frames are built by which modules, and then to see how these frames begin to unravel when the first RET instruction is encountered. (The situation tends to get quite complicated very rapidly. For a sample string on which to test the routines, we suggest something short and simple, such as "An b̸old b̸ b̸Cat⟨NUL⟩", where the "b̸" characters represent blanks.)

```
        .
        .
        .

;----------------------------------------------------------;
; Procedure LC2UC converts LowerCase characters to         ;
; UpperCase characters.  The argument is the address of    ;
; the beginning of the string whose characters are to be   ;
; converted, which address must be on top of the stack     ;
;----------------------------------------------------------;

LC2UC:  .WORD   ^M<R4>          ;Entry point -- save c(R4)
        MOVL    4(AP),R4        ;Get STRING address from stack
        TSTB    (R4)            ;Pointing at <NUL>?
        BNEQ    LC.10           ;No -- check for 'space'
        RET                     ; else return
LC.10:  CMPB    (R4),#SPACE     ;Pointing at 'space'?
        BNEQ    LC.20           ;No -- check for lower case
        PUSHL   R4              ;Yes -- push address
        CALLS   #1,PACK         ; and go deal with space
        RET                     ;Return
LC.20:  CMPB    (R4),#^A/z/     ;Greater than 'z'?
        BGTRU   LC.40           ;Yes -- not lower case
        CMPB    (R4),#^A/a/     ;Less than 'a'?
        BLSSU   LC.40           ;Yes -- not lower case
        BICB    #^B100000,(R4)  ;Turn off bit to make upper case
LC.40:  INCL    R4              ;Move to next character,
        PUSHL   R4              ; push new address
        CALLS   #1,LC2UC        ; and invoke LC2UC again
        RET                     ;Return

        .
        .

;----------------------------------------------------------;
; Procedure PACK removes space characters from a string.   ;
; The characters of the string are moved up one position   ;
; to overlay the space character.  The address of the      ;
; beginning of the string must be on top of the stack.     ;
;----------------------------------------------------------;

PACK:   .WORD   ^M<R9>          ;Entry point -- save c(R9)
        MOVL    4(AP),R9        ;Get STRING address from stack
        TSTB    (R9)            ;Pointing at <NUL>?
        BNEQ    PACK.10         ;No -- check for 'space'
        RET                     ; else return
PACK.10: CMPB   (R9),#SPACE     ;Pointing at 'space'?
        BEQL    PACK.20         ;Yes -- go pack the string
        PUSHL   R9              ; else save STRING address
        CALLS   #1,LC2UC        ; and invoke LC2UC
        RET                     ;Return
PACK.20: PUSHL  R9              ;Save current STRING address
PACK.30: TSTB   (R9)+           ;Pointing at <NUL>?
        BEQL    PACK.40         ;Yes -- skip to reinvoke PACK
        MOVB    (R9),-1(R9)     ; else move character down in
        BRB     PACK.30         ; STRING and check next character
PACK.40: CALLS  #1,PACK         ;Invoke this routine again
        RET                     ;Return

        .
        .
```

Figure 9.13.7

9.14 TERMINOLOGY, CONVENTIONS, AND CLOSING COMMENTS

We discuss now some terminology and conventions, some of which we have already introduced in an informal way. A **procedure** is a subroutine invoked with CALLG or CALLS. A **standard argument list** transmitted to a procedure consists of a table of consecutive memory longwords, which contain the arguments, the first (lowest addressed) of which is the count of arguments which follow in the table. If the table resides in the hardware stack, the argument list is called a **stacked argument list**; otherwise it is called a **general argument list**. When the *value* of an argument is in the argument list, the argument is said to be **transmitted by value** to the procedure; when its *address* is in the argument list, it is said to be **transmitted by address**, **reference**, or **name**.

The "procedure" terminology derives from the use of the term in certain modern, high-level programming languages which rely heavily on this structure not only for the performance of useful tasks, but also for improving the structural simplicity and readability of these programs. Indeed, a well-written Pascal program, for example, may consist almost exclusively of procedure and function calls, thereby creating a "program" that reads very much like an English-language algorithm. In this way the details of actual individual instruction execution, which can easily obscure the logic flow of a program upon first reading, can successfully be "hidden" while still being available when those details require examination. Although we may not be able to introduce the same degree of structuring at an assembly language level, nonetheless, if, for example, we are assured that the procedure LC2UC converts lowercase alphabetic characters to uppercase, a statement such as

CALLS   #1,LC2UC

in the midst of a sequence of programming instructions will be far less obscuring of the logic flow than if the actual code of which LC2UC consists were placed in the instruction stream at this point. Thus although the degree is distinctly different, the principle is the same—procedures, in addition to conserving code writing and memory, can go far to improve the structural appearance of an assembly language program.

A **function** is a subroutine that returns a *single value* to the calling routine. The subroutine MAX which we devised early in this chapter is an example. According to Digital Equipment Corporation conventions, the value of a function is always returned in R0, or in the register pair R1'R0 (the 64-bit concatenation of R1 with R0). In fact, the convention states that programming should be written so that these two registers are *always* free for the return of function values. As the reader is aware, we have not adhered to this rule, having used R0 and R1 for rather more "permanent" purposes in a number of our examples. But in certain programming environments, especially those in which assembly language routines are written to interface with high-level-language programs or with certain operating system routines, this convention should be adopted, for Digital's language translators (compilers) *expect* it to apply.

The comments made above about the types of arguments passed to procedures, and the methods of their transmission, apply equally to functions, and in particular functions may have arguments that are called by *value*, called by *reference*, or both.

In the "bubble sort" version of Figure 9.13.6 we created two longwords of storage immediately above the CALL frame, which we referred to as "local" storage. As we noted, these longwords, which held the pass counter and compare counter, were available to BUBWD as long as BUBWD was an actively executing module. But when BUBWD executed RETurn, these two longwords were removed from the stack. In addition, if BUBWD had in turn called another subroutine (which, of course, it did not), those two longwords would (normally) not be available to the called routine (but see Exercise 9.14.1). It is in this sense that these longwords are "local" to the routine that has created them. In high-level-language terminology, which we can adopt here for our purposes, this storage (bytes, words, or longwords) is referred to as **local variable** storage.

The act of jumping to a subroutine is sometimes referred to as **subroutine linkage**. In the case of procedure calls, the linkage process has a couple of desirable features—an unlimited number of arguments is easily transmitted to the procedure, and registers needed by the procedure can be saved in an automatic fashion. On the other hand, the reader must have the (correct) impression that such linkages are apt to be slow. There is much activity that takes place upon execution of CALLG or CALLS, and at least as much when RET executes. The longword alignment of the stack pointer improves efficiency somewhat, but nonetheless these are complex, and hence relatively slow, operations. In addition, a great deal of stack space can be taken up when procedures are nested to any depth (consider the routines of Figure 9.13.7). On the other hand, JSB (or BSBB or BSBW) do nothing but stack the current PC contents and execute the jump; these operators are sometimes called **fast linkages**. But of course the transmission of arguments via JSB can be far more inconvenient. Thus the choice between JSB and CALLx involves a trade-off, and we can give no practical guidelines for making a selection. The experienced programmer will be aware of the existence of both, their advantages and disadvantages, and will make a selection designed best to meet current needs.

Based on the emphasis we have placed on recursion and the examples of recursive routines we have offered, the reader is probably under the impression that recursion is a very important concept in programming. In that regard we have not been misleading, for many techniques are best *described* as recursive processes. But we must confess that *in practice* recursively called routines and procedures are not in as widespread use as we may have implied. The reason for this is precisely what is discussed above—recursive procedures execute slowly and may require massive amounts of stack space. Thus although some processes may be described or defined recursively, and *explanatory* algorithms may be written recursively, when the process is actually applied as an executable routine, it is more

```
;-------------------------------------------------;
; Subroutine FACT calculates n! (factorial n)     ;
; by iteration, rather than by recursion.  The    ;
; value of n is transmitted to FACT in R5.        ;
;-------------------------------------------------;

FACT:     MOVL    #1,R0        ;Initialize n! to 1
          TSTL    R5           ;c(R5) nonpositive?
          BLEQ    FACT.6       ;Yes -- exit from routine
FACT.4:   MULL    R5,R0        ; else form next product
          SOBGTR  R5,FACT.4    ;Decrement R5, multiply again
FACT.6:   RSB                  ;Return to calling routine
```

Figure 9.14.1

frequently written as an *iterative* routine. For instance, consider the classic example of a recursive process, factorial n. Factorial n is *defined* recursively (see Section 9.5), and a recursive subroutine (Figure 9.5.15) or procedure (Figure 9.13.1) may be written to *illustrate* the behavior of the FACT function; but in practice it is more likely that for the sake of efficiency, such a routine will be written as an iterative rather than recursive process. Figure 9.14.1 shows an iterative (JSB-type) subroutine which returns factorial n in R0, where n is passed to FACT in R5.

9.15 EXERCISES

9.1.1. Rewrite the segment of Figure 9.1.1 by using R5 as an index in an operand such as ARRAY[R5], and by replacing one of the SOBGTRs by AOBLEQ.

9.2.1. It was noted in Section 9.2 that *if* we could have executed

```
        MOVL   PC,R8
        JMP    PRINT
```

R8 would still not contain quite the correct return address. What adjustments would have to be made to c(R8) prior to executing the JMP instruction? Show how that adjustment could be made in the subroutine, prior to executing

```
        MOVL   R8,PC
```

9.2.2. If, in Figure 9.2.2, the symbol PRINT is "close enough" to the JMP instruction, could JMP be replaced by BRB or BRW? Explain why (or why not) the JMP operator in

```
        JMP    (R8)
```

could be replaced by BRB or BRW, to achieve the return back to the calling routine.

9.2.3. What changes would have to be made in the segment of Figure 9.2.2 if we chose R6 as the register to hold the return address?

9.3.1. What changes would have to be made in the subroutine of Figure 9.2.2 to print a 9 by 5 array?

9.3.2. Rewrite the subroutine PRINT of Figure 9.3.2, and make the appropriate changes in the subroutine "calling" instructions, if the arrays in question are always *square*— *n* by *n*.

9.4.1. Rewrite the subroutine MAX of Figure 9.4.1 so that it returns the *smallest* of an array of unsigned bytes. Call this subroutine MIN.

9.4.2. Write a subroutine with *two* entry points, named MIN and MAX, which returns in R0 either the *MIN*imum or the *MAX*imum of an array of unsigned bytes, depending on which entry point was JMPed to (see Exercise 9.4.1). These subroutines should "share" as much assembly language code as possible.

9.4.3. We noted that the subroutine SORT of Figure 9.4.5 cannot properly return to its calling routine, since the return address in R8 had been corrupted by SORT's calls to MAXADR. State explicitly what *will* happen when SORT executes

JMP   (R8)

9.5.1. Using the "return address saving" technique described at the beginning of Section 9.5, write a complete program to sort the following numbers into increasing order:

12,   −74,   1429,   704,   20928,   −32767,   46224,   0,   121

Model the program after the routines SORT and MAXADR of Figure 9.4.6, with the return address saved in each routine's entry point.

9.5.2. So far we have been transmitting arguments to MAX1 through R1 and R2. But consider the following scheme. The arguments needed by MAX1 are simply placed, in longwords, in the two locations *immediately following* the JMP instruction. This situation is shown in Figure 9.15.1, where the reader will note that NEXT labels the first of the arguments, rather than the next *executable* calling routine instruction. Supply instructions within MAX1 to put the first argument ARG1 in R1 and the second, ARG2, in R2. Then complete the writing of MAX1 (it proceeds pretty much as before) and determine what the RETURN statement should be. How would MAX1's instruction change if NEXT *were* used as a label for the "next instruction" in the calling routine? (This method of transmitting arguments is not as bizarre as it may appear. It is a standard technique for the PDP-11 computer,

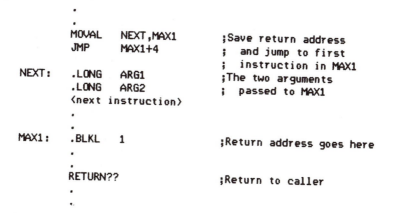

```
        .
        .
        MOVAL   NEXT,MAX1        ;Save return address
        JMP     MAX1+4           ;  and jump to first
                                 ;  instruction in MAX1
NEXT:   .LONG   ARG1             ;The two arguments
        .LONG   ARG2             ;  passed to MAX1
        <next instruction>
        .
        .
MAX1:   .BLKL   1                ;Return address goes here
        .
        .
        RETURN??                 ;Return to caller
        .
        .
```

Figure 9.15.1

one of the VAX-11 progenitors. However, the PDP-11 has an operation, similar to JMP, which behaves in such a way that the accessing of these arguments is a particularly easy task.)

9.5.3. We stated in Section 9.5 that if R6 points at the *last* return address in the block of storage used for return addresses, the instruction

$$\text{MOVAB} \quad \text{NEXT}, -(\text{R6})$$

will *decrement c(R6) by 4*. Why will not MOVA*B* preautodecrement c(R6) by *1*? That is, will not the decrementing of c(R6) be in a *byte* context, so that MOVA*L* will be needed, instead?

9.5.4. We stated that in order to return from a subroutine by using the address "pointed to" by R6 we needed to execute

$$\text{JMP} \quad @(\text{R6})+$$

and *not*

$$\text{JMP} \quad @0(\text{R6})$$

Follow the development of Figures 9.5.11 through 9.5.14 and discuss the consequences of *failing* to autoincrement c(R6) when executing "return" statements.

9.5.5. Show that the version of the factorial function shown in Figure 9.15.2 will *not* execute properly. The problem lies in the logical structure of the "calls" and "returns." What happens to the return addresses in BLOCK as the subroutine executes?

```
BLOCK:   .BLKL   100             ;Block for saving
                                 ; return addresses
         ;
START:   .WORD   ^M<>            ;Program start address
         MOVAL   BLOCK+400,R6    ;Initialize "return address"
                                 ; pointer at <end of BLOCK>
                                 ; + <1 longword>
         MOVL    #3,R4           ;Number n whose factorial
                                 ; n! is to be found
         MOVL    #1,R5           ;(Needed by routine FACT)
         MOVAB   NEXT,-(R6)      ;Save return address in BLOCK
         JMP     FACT            ; and jump to subroutine
NEXT:    $0.4D   R5              ;Print n!
         $EXIT                   ; and exit
         ;
FACT:    MULL    R4,R5           ;Multiply by next factor
         DECL    R4              ; and decrement multiplier
FACT.4:  MOVAB   FACT.6,-(R6)    ;Save return address
         JMP     FACT            ; and re-enter FACT
FACT.6:  DECL    R4              ;Decrement multiplier
         BGTR    FACT.4          ;Reinvoke FACT if still positive
         JMP     @(R6)+          ; else execute "return"
         ;
         .END    START
```

Figure 9.15.2

9.5.6. Figure 9.15.3 shows another version of a program that invokes the factorial subroutine FACT. But notice here that the block of storage BLOCK, which we had originally intended for the exclusive use of return addresses, is also used to save intermediate values of R4. By carefully monitoring the contents of BLOCK and the values in the "pointer" register R6, verify that even though data other than return addresses are placed in this area, the return addresses are in fact being pointed at by R6 when they are needed for subroutine returns. [The programming here has had to be done much more carefully because of the use of BLOCK for the saving of c(R4), and hence the analysis of the contents of BLOCK at any given time is correspondingly more involved.]

```
BLOCK:  .BLKL    100            ;Block for saving
                                ;  return addresses
        ;
START:  .WORD    ^M<>           ;Program start address
        MOVAL    BLOCK+400,R6   ;Initialize "return address"
                                ;  pointer at <end of BLOCK>
                                ;  + <1 longword>
        MOVL     #3,R4          ;Number n whose factorial
                                ;  n! is to be found
        MOVAB    NEXT,-(R6)     ;Save return address in BLOCK
        JMP      FACT           ;  and jump to subroutine
NEXT:   $0.4D    R5             ;Print n!
        $EXIT                   ;  and exit
        ;
FACT:   TSTL     R4             ;Is current c(R4) > 0?
        BGTR     FACT.4         ;Yes -- skip around
        MOVL     #1,R5          ;  else use 1 as product
        JMP      @(R6)+         ;  and begin "returns"
FACT.4: MOVL     R4,-(R6)       ;Save current c(R4) in BLOCK
        DECL     R4             ;  and decrement
        MOVAB    FACT.6,-(R6)   ;Save return address in BLOCK
        JMP      FACT           ;  and invoke FACT again
FACT.6: MULL     (R6)+,R5       ;Multiply by next factor
        JMP      @(R6)+         ;  and execute another "return"
        ;
        .END     START
```

Figure 9.15.3

9.6.1. Suppose that a block of contiguous memory longwords is allocated as stack area, but instead of maintaining this stack's pointer in a *register*, we keep it in a *memory longword*, whose symbolic address is STKPTR. Devise appropriate PUSH_STACK and POP_STACK operations for this situation (but not necessarily as *single* instructions).

9.6.2. Let BLOCK be the address of the first longword in a block of 100 longwords of contiguous storage, to be used as a stack area with stack pointer R6. State how we could detect that the *next* PUSH_STACK operation would result in a stack overflow, and that the *next* POP_STACK operation would result in a stack underflow.

9.6.3. Let BLOCK be the address of the first longword in a block of 100 longwords of contiguous storage, to be used as stack areas for *two* stacks, organized as follows. R10 is given the initial value BLOCK, and R11 is given the initial value BLOCK + 400.

The R10-stack grows *downward*, into higher-addressed memory locations, and the R11-stack grows *upward*, into lower-addressed memory locations.

(a) What is the maximum number of entries that can be in the R10-stack at any time?

(b) What is the maximum number of entries that can be in the R11-stack at any time?

(c) What is the maximum number of entries that can be in both stacks simultaneously?

(d) How can R10-stack and R11-stack *underflows* be detected?

(e) How can R10-stack and R11-stack *overflows* be detected?

9.6.4. Suppose that three longwords are pushed onto the R6-stack by the instructions

```
MOVL   #^X1283AF00, - (R6)
MOVL   #^X4CC426A7, - (R6)
MOVL   #^XEF930482, - (R6)
```

State what the contents of R3, R4, and R5 will be after the following sequences of POP_STACK operations.

(a) MOVL	(R6)+,R3		**(b)** MOVZWL	(R6)+,R3		
MOVZWL	(R6)+,R4		MOVZWL	(R6)+,R4		
MOVL	(R6)+,R5		MOVL	(R6)+,R5		
(c) MOVZWL	(R6)+,R3		**(d)** MOVZWL	(R6)+,R3		
CVTWL	(R6)+,R4		MOVZBL	(R6)+,R4		
MOVZWL	(R6)+,R5		MOVZBL	(R6)+,R5		
(e) CVTBL	(R6)+,R3		**(f)** CVTBL	(R6)+,R3		
MOVL	(R6)+,R4		MOVZWL	(R6)+,R4		
CVTBL	(R6)+,R5		MOVL	(R6)+,R5		

9.6.5. If R6 is used as a stack pointer and we choose to use R6 temporarily for some other purpose, could c(R6) be saved on the R6-stack and later restored?

9.6.6. Consider a stack structured in the following way. Whenever we need to push a longword on the stack, we request *two memory longwords* from a routine GET_STORE, which returns the *address* of the first of a two-longword block of storage in memory. (We are not concerned here with how GET_STORE locates these two currently free longwords, or where they are in memory.) We use the first of these words to contain the item that is to be stacked, and the second of the two longwords holds the *address* of this new entry's *predecessor* in the stack structure. The address of this last pushed entry—the top of the stack—is maintained in another longword, called TOP. Explain what the operations PUSH_STACK and POP_STACK must do to maintain the stack in this particular situation. How can stack *underflow* be detected? (Presumably there is no stack overflow possible, provided that GET_STORE can always honor storage requests.)

9.7.1. Consider the construction

```
MOVAB   SUBR,R7
JSB     (R7)
```

Can JSB be replaced by BSBB or BSBW? Why or why not?

9.7.2. Will the construction

```
MOVAB   SUBR, - (SP)
JSB        @(SP) +
```

successfully jump to SUBR?

9.7.3. Consider the construction

```
MOVL    #ARG, - (SP)
MOVAB   SUBR, - (SP)
JSB        @(SP) +
```

which puts an argument (presumably needed by SUBR) on the stack and then jumps to SUBR. How can SUBR access ARG? When SUBR is ready to return, the argument ARG is on the stack *below* the return address. How can SUBR remove that argument prior to executing RSB?

9.7.4. As a continuation of Exercise 9.7.3, consider the construction

```
MOVAB   SUBR, - (SP)
MOVL    #ARG, - (SP)
JSB        @(SP)
```

Show that this will *not* jump to SUBR. How can the JSB instruction be modified to jump to SUBR? When SUBR is ready to return, how can the stack be cleared of unwanted debris (in particular, ARG)?

9.7.5. Suppose that SUBR = 00004077. State what the contents of R7 will be after execution of

```
MOVAL   SUBR,R7
JSB        (R7) +
```

9.7.6. Consider the following method of transmitting N longword arguments to a subroutine SUBR.

```
        JSB     SUBR
        BRB     NEXT
        .LONG   ARG1

              .
              .

        .LONG   ARGN
NEXT:   ⟨next instruction⟩
```

(a) How can SUBR access ARG1? ARGK for $1 \leq K \leq N$?

(b) How should SUBR return?

(c) Tell how SUBR can determine the number of arguments N that are passed to it, without knowing this number in advance? (It can, and this allows SUBR to be written to accommodate a variable number of arguments.)

9.8.1 What is the hexadecimal representation of the word created by the assembler in response to the construction

(a) ^M⟨R2,R7,R4⟩　　(b) ^M⟨R0,R1,R2,R9,R10,R13⟩

(c) ^M⟨R7,R2,R4⟩　　(d) ^M⟨ ⟩

9.8.2. What are the effects on c(R8) of

(a) PUSHL　　(R8)+　　　　(b) PUSHAB　(R8)+

(c) PUSHAW　@(R8)+　　　(d) PUSHAB　@(R8)+

(e) PUSHAW　−(R8)　　　　(f) PUSHL　　−(R8)

9.9.1. How should the routine of Figure 9.9.1 be changed if MAXADR is to return the location of the maximum of an array of *signed words*? (Assume the appropriate changes in the argument table.)

9.9.2. Consider a collection of longwords in a general argument table, whose first entry is the count of longwords. Write a subroutine that returns in R0 the number of longwords which exceed their immediate successors in the table. (Any registers that are used by the routine should be saved and restored.)

9.9.3. How can we create a table, with a variable number of longword arguments (the first longword of which is the argument count), in such a way that some arguments are passed by value and others are passed by address? The called subroutine must be able to distinguish these two types of variables.

9.9.4. Implement a bubble sort (see Exercise 8.10.2) of a list of numbers, as a subroutine, in which the arguments (address of the first list entry and number of entries) are passed to the subroutine in an argument table.

9.10.1. How should the "return" scheme—in particular, the stack cleanup—be changed if the arguments pushed on the stack are *words* and the argument count is pushed as a *word*?

9.10.2. Consider a collection of longwords pushed on the stack, followed by a (longword) push of the count of those longwords. Write a subroutine that returns in R0 the number of longwords which exceed their immediate successors in the table. (Any registers that are used by the routine should be saved and restored.)

9.10.3. How should the result of Exercise 9.10.2 be changed if "longword" is changed to "byte" throughout?

9.10.4. We saw that nested subroutine calls will not succeed if R12 points at an argument table. How can these techniques be modified to save and restore R12, so that such calls *can* be nested?

9.13.1. Improve the bubble sort BUBWD of Figure 9.13.2 in the following way. It may happen, after just a few passes through the numbers to be sorted, that the technique has already sorted the numbers, and that any further passes would be a waste of time. Rewrite BUBWD to detect that fact. (*Suggestion*: BUBWD can determine that further passes are unnecessary if on some pass it finds that *no* exchanges were required.)

9.13.2. In the sort routine of Figure 9.13.3 the routine modified one of its own instructions. Consider an environment in which two independent programs are *sharing* this sorting routine, and either of the programs may have its execution interrupted at any time (even in the midst of execution of the sorting routine), to allow the other program to continue its execution. Show that in this case the sorting routine will probably fail at least one of the users, and in fact that a *shared* routine should *never* modify its own code.

9.14.1. Suppose that a mainline routine CALLs a procedure PROC1, which creates a "local variable"—a longword entry at $c(FP) - 4$. Now PROC1 CALLs PROC2. Explain how PROC2 can access this longword—PROC1's local variable—provided that PROC2 "knows" that PROC1 has created it.

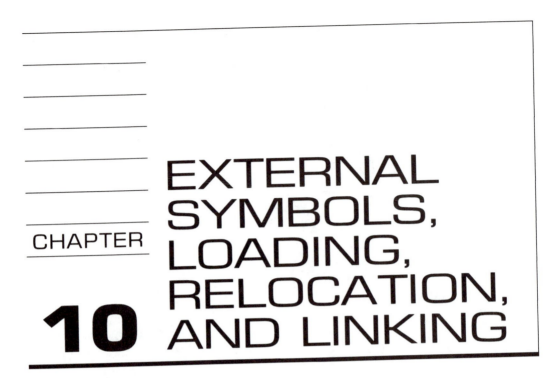

10 EXTERNAL SYMBOLS, LOADING, RELOCATION, AND LINKING

CHAPTER

10.1 INTRODUCTION

The initial example of Chapter 9 involved the printing of the elements of a 36-word array, which we interpreted as a 6 by 6 *matrix* or *two-dimensional array*. Later in that chapter we "improved" the printing routine in such a way that we could pass to it the array name, together with the numbers of rows and columns in the array, thus allowing us to print, in matrix form, the words of *any* array. At that time, the arguments were passed to the routine via general registers; in Figure 10.1.1 we show this same printing routine, which we have renamed MATPRINT, written as a *procedure*. It is quite straightforward and does not differ substantially from its earlier version, with the following exceptions. First, the "entry point mask word" takes care of the saving of any needed registers, to be restored later by means of the RET instruction. Since the argument pointer AP will be pointing at the argument count, the array address and row and column counts are referenced by appropriate offsets from c(AP). Finally, because it is simply a bit more efficient to do so, we have used AOBLSS instructions rather than SOBGTR instructions. In Figure 10.1.1 the routine is called with a CALLS instruction, after the column count, row count, and array address have been pushed on the stack. Figure 10.1.2 shows the same call to MATPRINT, this time using a CALLG instruction. Note that a table has been created containing the same information, and in the same order, that was on the stack in the preceding example.

This subroutine, or procedure, is rather general-purpose, for it can print a two-dimensional array having any address and of any shape (numbers of rows and columns). However, the array *must* consist of *word* entries, as we see from the

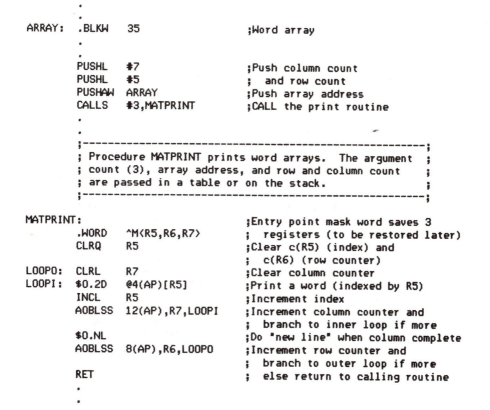

```
        .
        .
        .
ARRAY:  .BLKW    35                      ;Word array


        .
        .
        PUSHL    #7                      ;Push column count
        PUSHL    #5                      ; and row count
        PUSHAW   ARRAY                   ;Push array address
        CALLS    #3,MATPRINT             ;CALL the print routine
        .
        .
        .
;-----------------------------------------------------------;
; Procedure MATPRINT prints word arrays.  The argument      ;
; count (3), array address, and row and column count        ;
; are passed in a table or on the stack.                    ;
;-----------------------------------------------------------;

MATPRINT:                               ;Entry point mask word saves 3
        .WORD    ^M<R5,R6,R7>           ;  registers (to be restored later)
        CLRQ     R5                     ;Clear c(R5) (index) and
                                        ;  c(R6) (row counter)
LOOPO:  CLRL     R7                     ;Clear column counter
LOOPI:  $0.2D    @4(AP)[R5]             ;Print a word (indexed by R5)
        INCL     R5                     ;Increment index
        AOBLSS   12(AP),R7,LOOPI        ;Increment column counter and
                                        ;  branch to inner loop if more
        $0.NL                           ;Do "new line" when column complete
        AOBLSS   8(AP),R6,LOOPO         ;Increment row counter and
                                        ;  branch to outer loop if more
        RET                             ;  else return to calling routine
        .
        .
```

Figure 10.1.1

use of the macroinstruction $0.2D.   We can even eliminate that requirement if we make a slight adjustment to the routine.   The procedure of Figure 10.1.3 can be used to print any byte, word, or longword array.   It is called in exactly the same way as in Figure 10.1.1 or 10.1.2, *except* that one additional argument is passed, and it must be the first argument in the argument table (after the argument count, which must now be 4), or it must be the last argument stacked.   That additional argument is a longword containing 1, 2, or 4, according as the array consists of bytes, words, or longwords.   We leave it to the reader to examine the few changes that are made in the procedure and to devise appropriate calls to the procedure using CALLS and CALLG.   (Notice, incidentally, that any of these versions will also print *one-dimensional* arrays of length n, simply by interpreting them as 1 by n arrays.)

This little routine, which was introduced in Section 7.4, has evolved from a few lines of instruction which would print only a specific 6 by 6 word array, to a highly useful procedure which will print any matrix, regardless of its shape or the structure of its entries.   Thus rather than being applicable in a single program, our latest effort would seem to be useful in any program whatever that deals with matrices of any kind.   Adding further to its utility is the fact that since any needed

```
              .
              .
              .
ARRAY:  .BLKW    35                    ;Word array


              .
              .
TABLE:  .LONG    3                     ;Argument count
        .ADDRESS ARRAY                 ;Array address
        .LONG    5                     ;Number of rows
        .LONG    7                     ;Number of columns
              .
              .
        CALLG    TABLE,MATPRINT        ;CALL the print routine
              .
              .
        ;----------------------------------------------------------;
        ; Procedure MATPRINT prints word arrays.  The argument     ;
        ; count (3), array address, and row and column count       ;
        ; are passed in a table or on the stack.                   ;
        ;----------------------------------------------------------;

MATPRINT:                              ;Entry point mask word saves 3
        .WORD    ^M<R5,R6,R7>          ;  registers (to be restored later)
        CLRQ     R5                    ;Clear c(R5) (index) and
                                       ;  c(R6) (row counter)
LOOPO:  CLRL     R7                    ;Clear column counter
LOOPI:  $0.2D    @4(AP)[R5]            ;Print a word (indexed by R5)
        INCL     R5                    ;Increment index
        AOBLSS   12(AP),R7,LOOPI       ;Increment column counter and
                                       ;  branch to inner loop if more
        $0.NL                          ;Do "new line" when column complete
        AOBLSS   8(AP),R6,LOOPO        ;Increment row counter and
                                       ;  branch to outer loop if more
        RET                            ;  else return to calling routine
              .
              .
```

Figure 10.1.2

registers have been saved and restored, the user of this procedure need never be concerned with register use, only with properly transmitting the arguments to the procedure, either on the stack (CALLS) or in a table (CALLG). But now how can a user program take advantage of this procedure? It would appear that any time a program needed it, the source code for MATPRINT would have to be copied into that program. Such copying is tedious at best, and it is an area of potential error. It would seem more sensible to write MATPRINT's source code just once, and then somehow append it to the source code of any program that required it. This can be done, since the operating system provides utilities that give the user the capability of appending files of ASCII text. But what we are seeking is a more ambitious scheme which is far more efficient and user convenient.

Consider the following device. We write the source code for MATPRINT (such as shown in Figure 10.1.3) *and assemble it* into an *object file*. We now write a main source program, say MAIN, which calls MATPRINT, but we do *not* include in it the source code for MATPRINT. Instead, we assemble the code for MAIN

```
;----------------------------------------------------------------;
; Procedure MATPRINT prints byte, word or longword               ;
; arrays. The argument count (4), structure code,                ;
; array address, and row and column count are passed             ;
; in a table or on the stack. The structure code is              ;
; 1 (byte), 2 (word) or 4 (longword).                            ;
;----------------------------------------------------------------;

MATPRINT:
        .WORD    ^M<R5,R6,R7>          ;Entry point mask word saves 3
                                       ;  registers (restored later)
        CLRQ     R5                    ;Clear c(R5) (array index) and
                                       ;  c(R6) (row counter)
LOOP0:  CLRL     R7                    ;Clear column counter
LOOP1:  CMPL     #2,4(AP)              ;Is array "word-structured"?
        BLSS     LONG                  ;No -- "longword-structured"
        BGTR     BYTE                  ;No -- "byte-structured"
        $0.2D    @8(AP)[R5]            ;Print a word (indexed by R5)
INCEX:  INCL     R5                    ;Increment index
        AOBLSS   16(AP),R7,LOOP1       ;Increment column counter and
                                       ;  branch to inner loop if more
        $0.NL                          ;"New line" when column complete
        AOBLSS   12(AP),R6,LOOP0       ;Increment row counter and
                                       ;  branch to outer loop if more
        RET                            ;  else return to calling routine
        ;
LONG:   $0.4D    @8(AP)[R5]            ;Print a longword (indexed by R5)
        BRB      INCEX                 ;  and return to main procedure
        ;
BYTE:   $0.1D    @8(AP)[R5]            ;Print a byte (indexed by R5)
        BRB      INCEX                 ;  and return to main procedure
```

Figure 10.1.3

and then, somehow, "tack onto" MAIN's object file the object code for MAT-
PRINT. Our motives here are that not only does this not require the copying of
MATPRINT's source instructions into the source program MAIN, it does not even
require an assembly of MATPRINT, that having been done once and for all. Some
informal terminology will be useful for this discussion. We shall say that a **module**
is a segment of assembly language source code which undergoes an assembly, or
is the object file that results from such an assembly. (This term is used in a variety
of ways, and in fact we shall shortly use it in another way ourselves. For the time
being the description given above will serve our purposes.) Our objective can
now be phrased as follows. We create a "main module" (the program referred
to as MAIN above) and a "procedure module" containing the procedure MAT-
PRINT. Each of these undergoes a separate assembly, resulting in *two* object
files, as shown in Figure 10.1.4. These two object modules are now joined to
form a single module. This much is fairly straightforward and easily accomplished.
But the critical step, and one that at first glance seems to be beyond our ability to
accomplish, is the establishment of a **linkage** between the *main* module's reference
to MATPRINT and the entry point MATPRINT in the *procedure* module, as
indicated by the arrow in the figure.

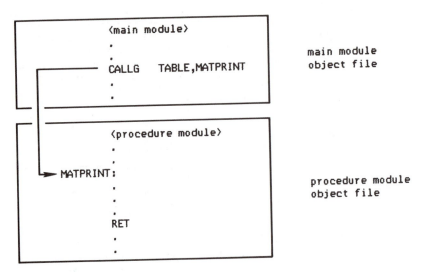

Figure 10.1.4

10.2 EXTERNALLY DEFINED SYMBOLS AND THE .*EXTERNAL* DIRECTIVE

To see what problems we face in attempting to bring about the appending of object modules, consider first what will happen when there is a reference in MAIN to MATPRINT. The assembler will generate the error shown in Figure 10.2.1, and the source of the problem is clear: We have made a reference to a symbol, MAT-PRINT, which is not defined within this module. Somehow we are going to have to notify the assembler *in advance* that it will encounter this undefined symbol and, so to say, to "ignore" the problems that it poses. That is, we wish to inform the assembler that MATPRINT is an **externally defined symbol** or, more simply, an **external symbol**, a symbol whose definition is *external* to the present source module. This is accomplished by including the name of the external symbol in a .EXTERNAL directive; Figure 10.2.2 shows that by declaring MATPRINT to be external, we have suppressed the error message that was generated previously. But has anything been accomplished here other than the suppression of an unwanted message? The answer is "yes," but to see what that is we need a deeper understanding of what the "procedure or subroutine linkage" problem is, and what must be done to solve it.

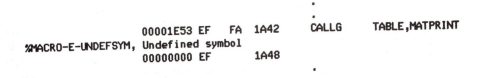

```
                        00001E53 EF   FA  1A42    CALLG      TABLE,MATPRINT
%MACRO-E-UNDEFSYM, Undefined symbol
                        00000000 EF       1A48
```

Figure 10.2.1

```
00000000 EF    00001E53 EF    FA  1A42    CALLG      TABLE,MATPRINT
                                            .
                                            .
```

Figure 10.2.2

10.3 OBJECT MODULE LOADING AND RELOCATION

Figure 10.3.1 is an expanded version of Figure 10.1.4, showing the addresses and machine codes, generated by the assembler, which are found in the main and procedure module object files, and there are a number of important observations that we shall make about it. First, notice that the procedure module contains a .END statement, but we have included *no* transfer or start address in that directive. The reason for this construction is twofold. The .END is required, for without it the assembler will not know when it has come to the end of the source file. Now

```
             0000                    .EXTERNAL MATPRINT
             0000                    ;
00000004     0000     TABLE:  .LONG     4
00000002     0004             .LONG     2
00000014'    0008             .ADDRESS  ARRAY
00000005     000C             .LONG     5
00000007     0010             .LONG     7
             0014                    ;
0000005A     0014     ARRAY:  .BLKW     35
             005A                    ;
             005A     START:                              main module
                              .                           object file
                              .
        FA   0070             CALLG     TABLE,MATPRINT
        AF   0071
        8D   0072
        EF   0073
00000000'    0074             <displacement to MATPRINT>
                              .
                              .
             0084             .END      START
```

```
   00E0  0000   MATPRINT: .WORD    ^M<R5,R6,R7>
                          .
   04    003A            RET                          procedure module
                          .                           object file
         0067            .END
```

Figure 10.3.1

recall that the transfer address is the address to be put in the program counter when execution of the object code is to begin. No transfer address for the procedure module is specified, because MATPRINT does not "begin" at all; rather, it owes its execution to the main module, which *passes control* to it via the CALLG instruction, once the main module has been "started." (We shall shortly have more to say about this transfer address, or more properly the absence of it.) Second, the longword at 00000074 in the main module requires some repair. This is the reference to MATPRINT, the displacement to which the assembler was unable to generate, since it did not know the *value* of MATPRINT. Notice, however, that the assembler did leave a longword in the main module object file, so there is some hope ultimately of putting the correct PC displacement here. Finally, we see that there is something quite wrong with the addressing scheme, for as shown, both the main module and the procedure module source code *occupy the same physical memory*, which of course is not possible. In this section we focus our attention on this and one additional problem.

We know that when the assembler translates a source file, many of its constructions are dependent on the addresses at which various source program elements are located—moving the address of a location to a register, and branching to some location, are two examples of instructions in which knowledge of an address is essential to the assembler. As we have already noted, the assembler maintains a *location counter* to keep track of these addresses, and the *initial value* given to this counter is called the **Assembly Load Address** (or **ALA**, for short), since it is the address at which the assembler *assumes* that the object module will ultimately be loaded into main memory. Unless it is informed otherwise, the assembler uses the address 00000000 as a *default* ALA. It is for this reason that both modules in Figure 10.3.1 *show* a beginning address of 00000000 and thus *appear* to overlap in memory.

But what happens when these modules are actually loaded into memory? The responsibility for the task of loading object modules into main memory falls to an operating system utility which we shall call the **object module loader**. The loader must locate the object file (on a disk, perhaps) and bring it into memory, byte by byte, *beginning at some address*. The address at which an object module is loaded in memory is called the module's **Physical Load Address**, or **PLA**, and it may not coincide with its ALA (the assembler's assumed load address). Indeed, in Figure 10.3.2 we show the first of the modules of Figure 10.3.1 as having been brought into physical memory by the loader at physical load address 0000080B. Now the loader must also bring into main memory a second module, the procedure module, and it cannot load it also at 0000080B, since that area of memory is currently occupied by the main module. But the last byte occupied by the main module has address 0000088E, and thus the procedure module *can* be loaded beginning at 0000088F. (The .END directive of the main module appears to "occupy" address 0000088F, but of course that directive does not occupy memory at all; the address shown, 0000088F, is simply the address of the *next available* byte of memory.) If a third module were to be appended to these two, it could be loaded beginning at 000008F6.

```
              080B                    .EXTERNAL MATPRINT
              080B                    ;
00000004      080B      TABLE:        .LONG    4
00000002      080F                    .LONG    2
0000081F      0813                    .ADDRESS ARRAY
00000005      0817                    .LONG    5
00000007      081B                    .LONG    7
              081F                    ;
0000005A      081F      ARRAY:        .BLKW    35
              0865                    ;
              0865      START:
                                        .
                                        .
FA            087B                    CALLG    TABLE,MATPRINT
AF            087C
8D            087D
EF            087E
--------      087F                    <displacement to MATPRINT>
                                        .
                                        .
              088F                    .END     START
```

main module
object file

```
00E0          088F      MATPRINT:  .WORD    ^M<R5,R6,R7>
                                     .
04            08C9                 RET
                                     .
              08F6                 .END
```

procedure module
object file

Figure 10.3.2

Our showing a physical load address of 0000080B is somewhat arbitrary, but in general the loader will *not* place a module at 00000000, since an area in low memory is needed by the operating system to hold certain information required for program *execution*. Just exactly how many bytes are required may depend on the particular operating system, but our point is that object modules, when loaded into memory for ultimate execution, are *relocated* away from their assembly load addresses. That subsequent modules are "packed up against" the preceding module is simply the loader's way of using memory in as efficient a way as possible.

In addition to making some choices regarding physical load addresses for modules to be loaded into memory, the loader has a further task. Some of the references in the modules being loaded may be to symbols that are *sensitive to relocation*, and if a module is loaded at some address which differs from its assumed assembly load address, these relocation sensitive references will no longer be correct, and thus some repairs will have to be made. As a case in point, refer again to Figure 10.3.1 and note the longword at location 00000008 of the main module. This is the *address* ARRAY, and it appears on that listing as 00000014. This is correct, of course, for ARRAY does have the value 00000014, *provided* that the load address of the module is 00000000, as assumed by the assembler. But now the loader has chosen to move this module to a new physical load address, 0000080B. The reference at 00000008 (which will now be 00000813) is no longer correct and will have to be modified. As we see from Figure 10.3.2, the loader has made the necessary repair, and the contents of 00000813 is indeed 0000081F, the relocated value of ARRAY. This happens to be the only relocation-sensitive reference that appears in Figure 10.3.1, but any others would have to be handled in a similar fashion.

How can the loader make these repairs? The task is quite simple, *provided* that the loader has certain information. First, it must know *where* the relocation sensitive references are. And it must also know the assembly load address, ALA. Once it has these two pieces of information, and it has made a decision regarding the module's PLA, a longword A whose contents is relocation sensitive is adjusted as follows:

$$\text{Relocated-A is given the value } c(A) + PLA - ALA$$

In the specific example at hand, $A = 00000008$, Relocated-A $= 00000813$, $c(A) = 00000014$, ALA $= 00000000$, and PLA $= 0000080B$. Thus

$$\text{Relocated-A is given the value } c(A) + PLA - ALA, \text{ or}$$
$$00000813 \text{ is given the value}$$
$$00000014 + 0000080B - 00000000 = 0000081F$$

We shall look at one more example of this "relocation" task, in which we have intentionally complicated matters a bit by arbitrarily making the assembler's load address 00000F2C and the loader's physical load address 0000054A. As we see from Figure 10.3.3, there are three relocation-sensitive references that need to be repaired upon loading, at 0000104C, 00001054, and 000010A2. When the module is loaded into memory (Figure 10.3.4), these references are each adjusted by *adding* the factor

$$PLA - ALA = 0000054A - 00000F2C = FFFFF61E$$

For example, the reference in Figure 10.3.3 to DATA at 0000104C is adjusted to

$$00000F2C + FFFFF61E = 0000054A$$

at (the relocated address) 0000066A in Figure 10.3.4, and as we see, this is the correct value of the (relocated) symbol DATA. The other two relocations proceed in an identical fashion, using the number FFFFF61E as the relocation factor. Finally, note that the reference to DATA at 0000109C need *not* be repaired, since it is given there as a program counter displacement, not as an absolute address— as a PC displacement, it is *insensitive* to relocation.

```
00000FD4  0F2C          DATA:      .BLKL 42
00000200  0FD4          VECTOR:    .LONG 512
                                   .
                                   .
       D0  104A                    MOVL  #DATA,R4
       8F  104B
00000F2C' 104C
       54  1050
       D1  1051                    CMPL  (R4)+,@#VECTOR
       84  1052
       9F  1053
00000FD4' 1054
       13  1058                    BEQL  CONTINUE
       42  1059
                                   .
                                   .
       D4  109C          CONTINUE: CLRL  DATA
       CF  109D
     FE8C  109E
       D6  10A0                    INCL  @#DATA
       9F  10A1
00000F2C' 10A2
                                   .
```

Figure 10.3.3

```
000005F2  054A          DATA:      .BLKL 42
00000200  05F2          VECTOR:    .LONG 512
                                   .
                                   .
       D0  0668                    MOVL  #DATA,R4
       8F  0669
0000054A  066A
       54  066E
       D1  066F                    CMPL  (R4)+,@#VECTOR
       84  0670
       9F  0671
000005F2  0672
       13  0676                    BEQL  CONTINUE
       42  0677
                                   .
                                   .
       D4  06BA          CONTINUE: CLRL  DATA
       CF  06BB
     FE8C  06BC
       D6  06BE                    INCL  @#DATA
       9F  06BF
0000054A  06C0
                                   .
                                   .
```

Figure 10.3.4

We see from these examples that relocation is really a fairly trivial affair, and that the loader need only know where the relocation-sensitive longwords are and what the assembler's presumed load address was. It can then modify these by adding the relocation factor PLA − ALA, an activity that is called **object module editing**. Thus the utility we have been referring to as a loader might more appropriately be called a **loader-editor**.

It is clearly the responsibility of the assembler to notify the loader-editor of just where the relocation-sensitive instruction components are, and there is a wide variety of ways in which it might do this. What we shall describe is a technique in use by some assemblers and operating system loader-editors, and although it differs from actual practice for the VAX operating system, it has conceptual simplicity on its side. It is quite easy for the assembler to determine that one of its constructions is sensitive to relocation, and as we noted in Section 6.6, it even "flags" these constructions with an apostrophe on the program listing. Whenever it encounters such a longword, it enters its *address*, relative to the assembly load address, in a **relocation table**. This table is included as a "supplement" to the file of actual machine code, as shown in Figure 10.3.5. Notice that the assembler must also include in this file its assumed load address, so that the loader-editor can properly adjust the instruction components which are sensitive to relocation, once the physical load address has been determined. Finally, observe that we also show a "transfer address," the address at which the program counter is to be set once the module has been loaded for execution. This address, which is also *relocation sensitive*, is known to the assembler, since it is found in the .END directive.

Given what has just been said about the noting in the object file of the module's transfer address, the reader may feel that the assembler would not know how to deal with a module such as the "procedure module" of Figure 10.3.1, which for the reasons we have already stated, has *no* transfer address. In fact, for the sake of *uniformity*, so that all object files will have identical components, the assembler will include a transfer address entry for such a module as well. To signal that the module does *not* actually have a transfer address, the assembler need only use an address which must be *invalid*, such as FFFFFFFF. In this way both the "main module" and the "procedure module" of Figure 10.3.1 will have structurally identical object files, each of which will look like that of Figure 10.3.5.

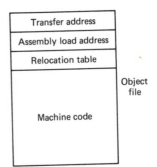

Figure 10.3.5

10.4. THE RESOLUTION OF EXTERNAL REFERENCES

We are now in a position to treat the problem that prompted this lengthy investigation: How can the main module invoke the procedure MATPRINT, which resides in another object module? By now we have managed to load both the main and procedure modules into main memory at some physical addresses, and any instruction components that were affected by the relocation have been repaired. In fact, the layout of memory as shown in Figure 10.3.2 shows a module which is *executable* except for the missing displacement to MATPRINT at 0000087F. But this is easily inserted, for we know that upon execution, by the time the processor has fetched this displacement, c(PC) will be 00000883, and since the value of MATPRINT is 0000088F, the displacement should evidently by 0000088F − 00000883 = 0000000C. We can thus substitute this displacement for the "————————" shown in the figure at 0000087F and execute the resulting machine code.

The operating system utility program responsible for this substitution is called a **linker**, since it establishes the *linkages* between modules, necessitated by one module making a reference to a symbol defined in another module. As simple as this displacement calculation has been for *us*, we must view the task of resolving this **external reference** as it appears to the linker. In particular, the linker must know just *where* in the object module such references occur, and to *what* they refer—that is, to what external symbols they are references. One of the consequences of the .EXTERNAL directive discussed in Section 10.2 is the construction by the assembler of an **external reference table**, to be included with the object file. This table includes the names of all symbols declared as external, and the (relative) locations within the object module where references to these symbols occur. For example, this table for the main module of Figure 10.3.1 might contain the entry

MATPRINT   00000074

A little reflection will reveal that this is *not* adequate information for the linker to resolve the reference. To see why, consider what will happen if, instead of as shown in Figure 10.3.1, MATPRINT had been called with the instruction

CALLG   TABLE,@#MATPRINT

so that after loading and relocation, main memory would contain

FA	087B	CALLG TABLE,@#MATPRINT
AF	087C	
D3	087D	
9F	087E	
————————	087F	⟨value of MATPRINT⟩

a variation of what is shown in Figure 10.3.2. What should be placed at 0000087F is now the actual *value* of MATPRINT (0000088F) rather than the *displacement to* MATPRINT. Thus the external reference table is going to have to carry information as to the type of construction to be found at the specified location. Therefore, this entry should read

MATPRINT 00000074 displacement

or perhaps

MATPRINT 00000074 value

But even this is insufficient information. Suppose, for example, that since we know that the procedure module will be loaded immediately following the main module, and thus that MATPRINT will be relatively close to the CALLG instruction that invokes it, we write the instruction as

```
FA   087B      CALLG   TABLE,W^MATPRINT
AF   087C
D3   087D
CF   087E
----  087F      ⟨displacement to MATPRINT⟩
```

Evidently the "displacement to MATPRINT" should be a *word* displacement (notice the PC addressing mode, CF), and the object module will surely be corrupted if the linker simply assumes a *longword* displacement. Thus this information will also need to be passed in the external reference table:

MATPRINT   0000007E   displacement   word

The object file for the main module will now appear as in Figure 10.4.1, which shows the inclusion of the external reference table. If a module makes no external references, the assembler, for the sake of uniformity of object file structure, should build this table anyway, although in this case the table would be empty.

Now in addition to knowing *where* external references are made, and to *what* they are references, the linker must also know the *value* of the reference, so that the value, or possibly the displacement to the symbol, can resolve the reference. In Figure 10.3.1, the reference is to MATPRINT, and MATPRINT's value, relative to the assembly load address of *its* module, is 00000000. (This value is sensitive to relocation, and as we see from Figure 10.3.2, MATPRINT's final value is 0000088F.) But here we encounter a problem, for although MATPRINT appears on the listings of Figures 10.3.1 and 10.3.2, its value is nowhere contained in its object file. To see why, let us review the assembly process. The assembler creates a symbol table, which it needs on its second pass through the source program, and each entry in the table consists of the *name* of a symbol, together with its *value* relative to the assembly load address. It is this value (of MATPRINT, for example) that is needed to resolve the main module's reference to the procedure module's address, but unfortunately, the assembler does not keep the symbol table when assembly is complete, for under ordinary circumstances the symbol table would

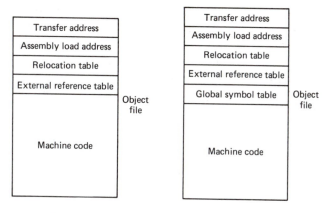

| Transfer address |
| Assembly load address |
| Relocation table |
| External reference table |
| Machine code |

Figure 10.4.1

| Transfer address |
| Assembly load address |
| Relocation table |
| External reference table |
| Global symbol table |
| Machine code |

Figure 10.4.2

serve no further purpose. But here we see that at least part of the table is critical to external reference resolution, and thus we must have some means of notifying the assembler that certain table entires should be maintained after assembly, as a part of the object file. Such a symbol is called a **global symbol**, since its intended use in other modules makes it *global*, rather than being purely *local* to the module in which it is defined. That part of the symbol table which consists of the globally declared symbols is carried along with the module's object file, in a **global symbol table**. Figure 10.4.2 shows this latest (and final) extension to the object file.

A symbol is declared to be **global** in one of the following three ways. First, and the way we much prefer, it may be so declared by following its definition, as a label, with *two* colons rather than one; for example,

MATPRINT::

or if the symbol is defined by direct assignment, it may be declared as global by using the double-equal-sign construction:

FLAG = = 7

The second technique for global declaration is to use the name of the symbol in a .GLOBAL directive, thus:

.GLOBAL   MATPRINT

We decline to use this construction, however, for .GLOBAL does more than we have indicated here. In fact, if a symbol in a .GLOBAL directive *is* defined within a module, it is made global as above; however, if it is *not* defined there, .GLOBAL is treated as if it were .EXTERNAL—the symbol is declared "global" in the sense that it is not "local" to the present module. We consider .EXTERNAL to be far more explicit (and thus more clear).

Finally, any symbol appearing in a .ENTRY directive is made global. We have already indicated that we shall not use .ENTRY because of its tendency to "hide" the symbol name. But now we see that .ENTRY also declares the symbol to be global, *whether we want it global or not*. The declaration of a symbol as global when it is not intended for such use can cause problems when the program's executable module is constructed.

Figure 10.4.3 shows the final version of Figure 10.3.2, in which MATPRINT has been declared as global, and the displacement to it (at 0000087F) has been filled in. (We have also removed the .END statements, since they contribute no machine code to the executable module.)

There are still a couple of matters that need to be disposed of. In the main module program listing of Figure 10.3.1 we find the following construction:

FA	0070	CALLG TABLE,MATPRINT
AF	0071	
D3	0072	
EF	0073	
00000000′	0074	⟨displacement to MATPRINT⟩

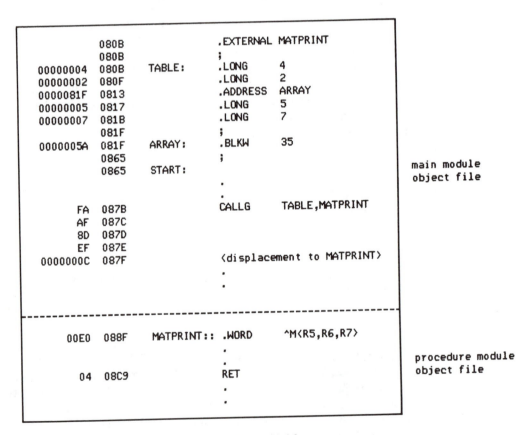

Figure 10.4.3

Note first that the contents of 00000074 is flagged with an apostrophe as being sensitive to relocation. But as a *displacement*, it should be *insensitive* to relocation. All of this is true, and the fault lies in our interpretation of the apostrophe. We need to take it as an indication that the symbol (MATPRINT) whose value will ultimately determine the displacement *is* sensitive to relocation.

We commented earlier that the assembler has left a longword at 00000074 for the unknown displacement. In fact, the longword it left there has value 00000000. Is this simply a convenient way for the assembler to leave 4 "open" bytes in the object module? The answer is "no"; if the assembler had intended to do this, it could merely have advanced its location counter by 4 at this point and not bothered inserting any particular value at all. Rather, the *value* 00000000 has some significance. To see what it is, consider the following modification of the CALLG instruction shown above.

FA	0070	CALLG TABLE,MATPRINT + 4
AF	0071	
D3	0072	
EF	0073	
00000004'	0074	⟨displacement to MATPRINT + 4⟩

Here we assume that the procedure MATPRINT has two entry points, perhaps with different entry point mask words used for different purposes, and that those mask words are at MATPRINT and MATPRINT + 4. In this example we wish to enter the procedure at MATPRINT + 4, as indicated in the CALLG instruction. Observe how the assembler has treated the unknown displacement. Instead of simply leaving a longword, with a value 00000000 for lack of any better value, the assembler has constructed the longword 00000004. It should be clear why this has been done. For although the linker is able to find the value of MATPRINT from the procedure module's object file global symbol table, it would not know to offset that value by 4 without the information given above. We can now give a detailed description of what is required to resolve an external reference. We assume that the object files in question have already been loaded and relocated, and in addition that their external reference table and global entry table entries have also been relocated.

1. Locate the (relocated) value of the external symbol in some module's global symbol table.

2. *Add to* this symbol value the contents of the longword that represents the unresolved reference. (If the reference is given as a byte or a word instead, sign extend its value to a longword.)

3. If the reference is given by the *value* of the symbol, use the value calculated in step 2 as the reference. If the reference is given as a *displacement* to the symbol, subtract from the value calculated above the address of the byte immediately following the current (byte, word, or longword) reference and use the result (possibly truncated to a byte or word) to replace the unknown displacement.

We close this section by dealing with an anomaly that we observed in Chapter 7. In discussing *program counter displacement mode* addressing, we noted that when the assembler encountered a *forward* reference in an instruction using this mode, it took that reference as *unknown*, even though by the time it had completed its first pass, it did in fact have a value for the symbol in question. In particular, the symbol DATA2 in Figure 7.6.9, whose value was ultimately known to be 00000542, nonetheless yielded the following construction:

$$
\begin{array}{lll}
\text{D4} & \text{043C} & \text{CLRL} \quad \text{DATA2} \\
\text{EF} & \text{043D} & \\
00000542' & \text{043E} &
\end{array}
$$

We commented that 00000542 was *not* the correct displacement, and in fact it is the *value* of DATA2. However, suppose that we interpret the 00000542 exactly as we treated the number 00000004 above, in reference to the construction MATPRINT + 4. In that case the 00000004—the offset from the global symbol MATPRINT—was replaced by the displacement to MATPRINT + 4, once the value of MATPRINT was known. In an analogous fashion, we can consider the number 00000542 to be an offset from ????????, and thus ultimately is to be replaced, *by the linker*, with the displacement to ???????? + 542 = ???????? + DATA2. What unknown address does ???????? represent? The answer is, the module's *physical load address*! We leave it to the reader to verify that with these interpretations, the linker will replace the *value* of DATA2 that appears in this longword with the *displacement* to DATA2, as we expected to find here in the first place.

10.5 THE *VAX* LINKER AND OBJECT MODULE LINKING

In the VAX operating system, as is the case in many others, a single utility program takes on the tasks of object module loading and relocating, and of establishing intermodule linkages. The program is typically called a **linker**, although **loader-editor-linker** might be more suggestive of its total task. If the reader reviews each aspect of this task, it will be apparent that with sufficient information (provided by the numerous tables which we have assumed have been appended by the assembler to the object file), there is nothing particularly difficult about the preparation of a collection of object modules for execution. On the other hand, we do not want to leave the impression that the linker's performance is trivial; the VAX linker, as with many others, is a highly complex piece of software, whose capabilities extend far beyond what we have described here.

In this chapter we have approached the linking problem from the viewpoint of a central mainline programming module, to which is "tacked on" some procedure module. In practice, however, the linker does not view the process as being "mainline module" oriented at all. Rather than viewing its task as linking modules *to* some main module, it sees a collection of modules that are linked *together*. That some of them may contain external procedures is of no consequence to the linker, since in fact it has no way of knowing this. (Recall that the assembler has constructed object files which are structurally *identical*, as shown in Figure 10.4.2.) The linker will simply load each file, in the order in which they are presented to it; then each module will be edited for relocation-sensitive components; and finally, intermodule linkages will be established where necessary.

If the linker loads, relocates, and links a collection of object files without viewing any of those files as "*the* mainline" program, what does it use as the resulting executable module's "start address?" We have already noted that each module has a start address, even if some of these may be "invalid"—a device used by the assembler to indicate *no* start address. Having loaded and linked the modules, the linker looks for a *valid* start address among the modules. If it finds *one and only one* valid transfer address, it uses it (relocated) as the executable module's start address. If it finds more than one valid transfer address, or if it finds none, it will report an appropriate "transfer address error."

The user may have the impression that modules containing external subroutines or procedures are linked to modules that invoke them, and thus modules which enter into a linking are collections of *executable* machine code. This is, in fact, most frequently the case, but a review of the total load-edit-link procedure will reveal that there are no such requirements. Modules to be linked need only to have been produced by the assembler, and they might not contain any executable code at all. As a simple example, consider the program segment of Figure 7.4.7. Recall that we had a collection of strings (each of which consisted of a collection of ASCII codes, terminated by a NUL character), and a vector or array of the *addresses* of those strings. If those strings were to be used in a number of programs,

```
              (File of string addresses)

              .EXTERNAL STRING1,STRING2,STRING3,STRING4,STRING5
              ;
ADDR::        .ADDRESS STRING1
              .ADDRESS STRING2
              .ADDRESS STRING3
              .ADDRESS STRING4
              .ADDRESS STRING5
              ;
ENDADDR::
              .END


              (File of strings)

STRING1:: .ASCIZ    /first string/
STRING2:: .ASCIZ    /second string/
STRING3:: .ASCIZ    /third string/
STRING4:: .ASCIZ    /fourth string/
STRING5:: .ASCIZ    /fifth string/
          ;
          .END
```

Figure 10.5.1

```
;-----------------------------------------------------;
; Print a collection of strings, the array of addresses ;
; of which is external to the present module.          ;
;-----------------------------------------------------;

        .EXTERNAL ADDR,ENDADDR    ;Beginning and ending addresses
                                  ;  of string addresses

START:  .WORD    ^M<>             ;(Entry mask word)

        MOVAB    ADDR,R4          ;Put address of address of
                                  ;  first string in R4
LOOP:   $0.STR   @(R4)+           ;Print a string
        $0.NL                     ;  and a "new line"
        CMPL     R4,#ENDADDR      ;Last string printed?
        BLSSU    LOOP             ;No -- print next string
        $EXIT                     ;  else exit to operating system

        .END     START
```

Figure 10.5.2

we might consider creating a source file consisting just of the strings themselves, and another source file consisting of their addresses. After assembly, these two files could then be linked to any other object module that needed them. Examples of two files of this type are shown in Figure 10.5.1, and the reader should note which symbols are declared as global or external in each module. A main program could now reference either STRING1, ..., STRING5, or ADDR and ENDADDR, or both. Figure 10.5.2 shows a main program which simply prints the strings, in a fashion similar to that of the segment of Figure 7.4.7, when these three modules are linked and executed.

10.6 THE STRUCTURE OF *VAX* OBJECT FILES

In discussing external and global symbols, relocation, and linking, we stated that it is conceptually convenient to think of the assembler as creating *tables* of information—notes, so to say, which are sort of "paper clipped" to the file of object code when it is passed along to the linker for modification to an executable module. Some assemblers produce object files which are very close to what we have described, but this is not true of the VAX. In fact, the VAX assembler produces object modules which are quite complex from the programmer's point of view. Embedded *within* the machine codes for the user's instructions are "code bytes" which give various kinds of information to the linker concerning relocation and the resolution of external references. The linker must scan this file, decoding these various code bytes, and make appropriate adjustments in the object code built by the assembler. Thus although we might think of the linker's task as that of referencing the various tables and then *patching* the object module to make it executable, in fact the VAX linker must create a *new* executable module *from* the information contained in the object modules. Thus what we see on program listings as "the object code" is quite a bit different from the actual object file, which contains in addition to this object code, the various code bytes which the linker must then interpret. Thus VAX object files are really "recipes" for the linker, from which it builds executable files. We decline to give further details of VAX object files, since this would lead us beyond the intended scope of the book, and the details would not materially enhance what has already been accomplished—an understanding of the *problems* and *processes* involved, however they might be dealt with in practice on a particular machine.

10.7 POSITION-INDEPENDENT CODE AND PROGRAM RELOCATION

We noted in Section 6.5, and again in Section 7.6, that certain constructions are *insensitive to relocation*, that is, that they consist exclusively of **position-independent code**. For example, program counter displacement mode instructions are position independent, whereas absolute mode instructions are not. We did not make a great fuss about position-independent code earlier, nor do we intend to here. But we shall give an example that will indicate that object files which are insensitive to relocation can result in substantial savings in time in some environments.

A user program, which may reference several external modules, is typically loaded, relocated, and linked once and for all. The resulting executable module, with a *fixed* physical load address, is then stored (on disk, say), and whenever it needs to be executed, it is brought into main memory *at that load address*, the program counter is set to the transfer address, and control is given to the program. But consider now an operating system utility program, which may consist of thousands of lines of instructions, which is stored on disk. A serious problem that may be encountered here is that each time the program needs to be brought into memory for execution, that segment of main memory that was used to link the program may not be available. That is, due to the dynamic nature of the memory used by the operating system, available memory is constantly growing and shrinking, and thus we cannot be certain that a particular segment of memory will always be available for loading this utility. The linker can cope with this problem in the following way. The utility program is, in fact, *not* relocated; instead, the relocation tables for all the modules that make up this program *are saved* with the program. Then when the module is brought into memory for execution, at some available location in memory (which will vary from execution to execution), a relocator can "patch" the relocation-sensitive components. For a large program, with much position-dependent code, this can involve a fair amount of effort, at a time in the operating system's overall task at which processor time is at a premium. But if the program consists exclusively of position-independent code, it can be "dropped into main memory" *anywhere* and execution begun immediately.

We do not claim that the writing of position-independent code is a trivial matter. In general, it is fairly difficult and requires constructions that the average programmer would view as awkward. As an interesting exercise, the reader is encouraged to rewrite a working program in position-independent code, insofar as possible.

10.8 EXERCISES

10.1.1. Suppose that a procedure, in its source code form, requires 2000 bytes of text, and that its assembled object module makes up 420 bytes. Show that the appending of the object module of the procedure to the object module of any mainline program that invokes it is far more efficient than the *copying* of the procedure's source code into the source code of the mainline program, by calculating the total storage required by the procedure (in both its source and object forms), using each technique, if the procedure is needed by 12 main programs.

10.1.2. Explain why CALLG to MATPRINT (or to any other procedure) is usually more convenient than CALLS when the procedure must be called several times in a main program.

10.3.1. It was stated that the assembler might use the transfer address FFFFFFFF to indicate that the module has *no* transfer address. Why is FFFFFFFF not a valid transfer address?

10.3.2. Explain how the assembler can determine that an instruction component is sensitive to relocation.

10.3.3. What would be the consequences to Figure 10.3.2 if the loader has loaded the procedure module *first*, at 0000080B, followed by the main module? In particular, at what address would the main module be loaded?

10.4.1. Suppose that each of the following constructions is loaded in physical memory at 00000264, and that EXSUB = 000002A7. Show what code will be generated by the assembler in each case, and what modifications to it will be made by the linker.

   (a) JSB EXSUB   **(b)** JSB EXSUB + 14
   (c) JSB EXSUB − 4   **(d)** JSB @#EXSUB
   (e) JSB @#EXSUB + 7   **(f)** MOVAB EXSUB,R4
                                     JSB (R4)
   (g) JSB W'EXSUB   **(h)** JSR B'EXSUB + 2
   (i) JSB B'EXSUB + 104

10.4.2. Construct the transfer address, relocation table, external reference table, and global symbol table for the module shown in Figure 10.8.1.

10.4.3. Figure 10.8.2 is a variation of the program listing of Figure 10.8.1, in which the entry point EXSUB + 2 has been invoked with BSBW instead of JSB. Why has the assembler generated the word FFF5 at 0000000B, what is its significance, and how is it treated by the linker?

10.4.4. Consider the two modules MOD1 and MOD2 as shown in Figure 10.8.3. Suppose that MOD1 is loaded at 00000200, and MOD2 is loaded immediately behind it.
   (a) What will be the PLA for MOD1 and MOD2?
   (b) What is the executable module's transfer address?
   (c) State explicitly what the machine code for the executable module will be.
   (d) Answer parts (a) through (c) if MOD2 is loaded at 00000200, and MOD1 is loaded immediately behind it.
   (e) If the executable module is executed, what longword will be moved into R4?

```
            0000       1                    .EXTERNAL EXSUB, CONST
00000008    0000       2      ARRAY:: .BLKB    8
    0000    0008       3      BEGIN:  .WORD    ^M<>
      16    000A       4              JSB      EXSUB+2
      EF    000B
00000002'   000C
      D4    0010       5              CLRL     R2
      52    0011
      90    0012       6      LOOP:   MOVB     CONST,ARRAY[R2]
      EF    0013
00000000'   0014
    AF42    0018
      E5    001A
      D6    001B       7              INCL     R2
      52    001C
      D1    001D       8              CMPL     R2,#8
      52    001E
      08    001F
      19    0020       9              BLSS     LOOP
      F0    0021
            0022      10              $EXIT
            002E      11              .END     BEGIN
```

Figure 10.8.1

10.4.5. Verify the statement at the end of Section 10.4, that the reference to DATA2 in Figure 7.6.9 can be interpreted as the displacement to PLA+DATA2.

10.5.1. Referring to the source files of Figure 10.5.1, write a program to print the characters in STRING4, in one case by referencing STRING4 directly, and in another by referencing ADDR+12.

```
            0000       1                    .EXTERNAL EXSUB, CONST
00000008    0000       2      ARRAY:: .BLKB    8
    0000    0008       3      BEGIN:  .WORD    ^M<>
      30    000A       4              BSBW     EXSUB+2
   FFF5'    000B
      D4    000D       5              CLRL     R2
      52    000E
      90    000F       6      LOOP:   MOVB     CONST,ARRAY[R2]
      EF    0010
00000000'   0011
    AF42    0015
      E8    0017
      D6    0018       7              INCL     R2
      52    0019
      D1    001A       8              CMPL     R2,#8
      52    001B
      08    001C
      19    001D       9              BLSS     LOOP
      F0    001E
            001F      10              $EXIT
            002B      11              .END     BEGIN
```

Figure 10.8.2

```
        <Module MOD1>                              <Module MOD2>

            .EXTERNAL DATA1                             .EXTERNAL DATA2
DATA2:: .LONG      ^X708F27          DATA1:: .LONG      DATA2
START:  .WORD      ^M<>                       .END
        MOVL       @DATA1,R4
        HALT
        .END       START
```

Figure 10.8.3

10.5.2. Consider the "program" of Figure 10.8.4. (The bytes consist of the numbers of days in the months of a non-leap year.) Write a program to print the number of days in a given month, where the month is input (via $I.1D) as a number between 1 and 12.

```
DAYS::  .BYTE    31,28,31,30,31,30,31,31,30,31,30,31
        .END
```

Figure 10.8.4

10.5.3. (*Continuation of Exercise 10.5.2.*)   Create an object file whose only "instruction" is

MONTH:: .ASCII /JANFEBMARAPRMAYJUNJULAUGSEPOCTNOVDEC/

Then write a program, as in Exercise 10.5.2, except that the input is a string of three uppercase characters that specify the month. (*Suggestion:* Since three-character compares will be required, consider comparing the two low-order characters first, using CMPW, and if a match occurs, then use CMPB to see if the third characters match. If not, go on to the next triple of characters.)

10.5.4. (*Continuation of Exercise 10.5.3*) Rewrite Exercise 10.5.3 so that both a month *and* year, separated by a comma, are entered; for example,

JUL,1917

The program should print the number of days in the month, and it should now account for leap years. (But do not bother to adjust for years that are a multiple of 400.)

10.5.5. Suppose that a symbol is declared within a module to be *global*, but that it is not intended to be used in that way. (The .ENTRY directive declares symbols to be global, whether we want them to be or not.) What possible unpleasant consequences could this have at *link time* if a number of modules with numerous external references are linked together?

11 CHAPTER

EXCEPTIONS AND CONDITION HANDLING

11.1 ERRORS

In Chapter 2 we first introduced the concept of **integer overflow**, a kind of "error" with which we have been coping on and off ever since. The context in which this phenomenon first arose was 4-bit-"word" signed addition, and we saw that in some cases, the addition of 4-bit words resulted in numbers which were too large to be represented in the 3 bits available for holding the "size" of a twos-complement number. We found that although there was no hope of *repairing* these results, we were at least *notified* of the error, since the PSW V-bit was set when such an overflow occurred. Thus typically we treated integer overflow as an error when the numbers in question were interpreted as *signed*, but such an overflow played no role in the correctness of results when the numbers were treated as *unsigned*— in the latter case, *carries* out of the high-order bit were the events of significance.

The reader may have encountered one or two other errors in the course of executing programs. One of these is **integer divide by 0**, and although we have not discussed it explicitly, it is evident what causes it. Two others—**reserved operand** and **reserved instruction**—may also have been seen, but in the environments in which we have been executing so far, these would probably result from severe errors in program logic—errors which are typically caused by our losing control of the program counter, branching off into some "unknown" area of memory, and thus attempting to execute random bytes of memory. Indeed, loss of control can be so severe that the executing "program" may attempt to make references to memory locations that have not even been allocated as valid memory for the particular user. In these cases, an **access violation** error will normally occur.

11.2 TRAPS AND FAULTS

An event such as an integer overflow or an attempt to execute a reserved instruction is detected by the hardware, and the action taken by the hardware depends on the event itself. In some cases the problem is detected at the end of execution of the instruction, and the status of the processor is sufficiently altered that there is no hope of making any repairs and then reexecuting the instruction. Such an event is called a **trap**. In other cases, however, whatever problem is encountered by the processor may be detected early enough in its execution cycle that no nonrecallable effects have taken place. Such an event is called a **fault**. We use the term **exception** to denote *either* a trap *or* a fault. For our purposes, the most significant difference between these two has to do with how the processor handles the program counter upon completion of its dealing with the exception. Specifically:

> **TRAP.** When an event occurs which is treated by the processor as a *trap*, the processor leaves the program counter pointing at the next instruction.
> **FAULT.** When an event occurs which is treated by the processor as a *fault*, the processor backs up the program counter so that it is once again pointing at the first byte of the instruction that caused the fault.

It is clear that in the event of an exception, processing cannot simply be allowed to continue. For if the exception was a trap, then in effect any problems that may be inherent in the instruction would simply be ignored, since the PC is pointing at the *next* instruction. If the exception was a fault, then since the PC is again pointing at that same instruction, without some intervention on the part of the processor we would be doomed to execute that instruction forever. In fact, when an exception is detected by the processor, it *saves* the current processor status (PSL) and program counter on the stack, as shown in Figure 11.2.1. A *new* PC is then obtained (from somewhere), so that not only is processing of the current taks *interrupted*—processing has resumed *elsewhere*—but since the PC and PSL

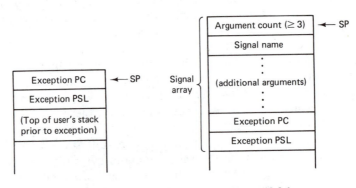

Figure 11.2.1   Figure 11.3.1

at the time of the exception have been saved, there is hope ultimately of returning to the execution of the program that caused the exception.

11.3 EXCEPTION HANDLING

Section 11.2 raises a number of questions with which we shall deal in this section, and in fact we need to be a little more truthful about the action taken by the processor in the event of an exception. First, the processor pushes the PSL and PC onto the stack, but in almost all cases this stack is *not* the user's stack, as declared in Figure 11.2.1. In fact, it is a stack used by the *operating system*. We shall shortly justify this small dishonesty when we show that the exception PSL and PC *do* appear almost immediately on the *user's* stack. In addition to pushing the PSL and PC, the processor may also push some arguments that specify the type of exception that occurred. Having saved this critical information about the exception, the processor now loads the program counter with a new value, obtained from a *fixed* location in a portion of main memory reserved for the operating system. (The fixed location in question is taken from a block of storage called the **System Control Block**.) This activity—the stacking of the current PSL and PC, together possibly with other information, and the obtaining of a new PC from some fixed location in main memory—is referred to as a **trap sequence** (not to be confused with the use of the word *trap* in Section 11.2 as an exception of a particular type, although the two are clearly closely related; exceptions—traps and faults—cause the processor to execute trap sequences.)

Since during the course of the trap sequence a new value for the PC has been loaded, execution picks up at some new location. The routine that is now executing, which is part of the operating system, is called an **exception service routine**, and its action is to build on the *user* stack a collection of longwords called a **signal array**. Figure 11.3.1 shows the form of the signal array, and we note that at the bottom of it reside the PSL and PC of Figure 11.2.1. Included in this array is the **signal name**, a unique bit configuration by means of which we can identify the exception. (Depending on the type of exception, some additional arguments may also be placed in this array by the hardware or by the service routine.) Notice that the signal array also contains, at its top, the argument count—the number of entries in the array exclusive of the argument count itself. This argument count must be at least 3, since the signal name, exception PC, and exception PSL will always be in the array.

Now that the signal array has been constructed, control is passed to another operating system routine, called an **exception dispatcher**, whose task it is to locate the routine that will actually *handle* the exception—deal with it in some reasonable way. The routine that ultimately deals with the exception is called an **exception handler** or **condition handler**, and we shall see that an executing process can have a number of exception handlers *present* simultaneously (although only one of them can be *active* at any given time). Since the exception dispatcher must be able to keep track of the active handler, it begins by building on the stack another array,

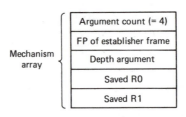

Figure 11.3.2

called a **mechanism array**. This array is shown in Figure 11.3.2, and the keys to exception handling are this array (which is used by the exception dispatcher) and the signal array (which is used by the handler itself, to determine the exception type and possibly to return to program execution, using the saved PC and PSL). The mechanism array always contains four arguments, in addition to the argument count itself, as follows.

(a) Frame Pointer of Establisher Frame

We shall see when we come to examine just how exceptions are handled that the critical pieces of information required for handling exceptions will reside on the stack, and in fact that an exception handler is invoked by the dispatcher with a CALL-type instruction. Thus it is essential that the dispatcher know where to locate the stack frame of the routine that has established the exception handler. This first longword contains that frame pointer.

(b) Depth Argument

We shall note later that it is possible for an exception handler to invoke another exception handler, in the event the first handler chooses not to manage the exception. Indeed, this passing along of the exception (called resignaling) might take place a number of times. The depth argument keeps track of how many times handlers have resignaled the exception.

(c) Saved R0 and R1

Recall from Chapter 9 that one of the conventions established by Digital Equipment Corporation concerning *procedures* is that c(R0) and c(R1) are *not* saved upon entering a procedure, but rather that these two registers are used for the transmission of information back to the calling routine. (We have adhered to that convention in some of our examples, and have not in others.) However, upon the occurrence of an exception, these register contents *must* be saved, since although they may not be in use by the routine that called a procedure, they are possibly in use by the procedure itself—the procedure whose execution resulted in the exception. The exception dispatcher places the current contents of these registers in the mechanism array for later restoration.

11.4 USER-WRITTEN EXCEPTION HANDLERS

We noted in Chapter 9 (in particular, Section 9.11) that one of the components of a CALL frame was the longword that was the last longword built by CALLx—it was at this longword that FP was pointing, and its contents was 0 (see, for example, Figure 9.11.1). We commented there that we would discuss the topic later. Now is the time.

To begin with, what should an exception (condition) handler do? That is, if a user-written exception handler executes as the result of some exception, what action should it take to respond to the condition? We cannot reasonably answer this question, for it depends on the current circumstances as well as on the type of exception. However, later in this section and in the next we shall see examples of handlers that make reasonable responses relative to their particular environments.

If the decision is made that during the course of execution of a procedure, a user-written exception handler should be active, the *address* of that handler must be put in the top longword of the CALL frame. This can be done, and frequently is done, immediately upon entering the procedure: for example,

```
PROC: .WORD   ^M⟨entry mask⟩      ;Save registers, etc.
      MOVAB   HANDLER,(FP)        ;Establish exception handler
```

MOVAB, of course, could as well be MOVAW or MOVAL, or even

```
MOVL   #HANDLER,(FP)
```

Since the address of the exception handler (HANDLER) in the longword at the top of the CALL frame will *not* be 0, the exception dispatcher will now be able to determine, should an exception occur in the course of execution of the procedure, that there is a user-written routine that is to be executed. The dispatcher will pass control to it in a familiar way which we shall examine shortly.

We should mention that even if an exception handler is to be active during the execution of a procedure, it need not be so during the *entire* execution; user-written handlers can be activated and deactivated selectively during execution, as illustrated in Figure 11.4.1.

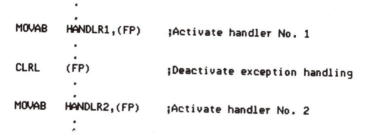

```
      .
      .
MOVAB   HANDLR1,(FP)      ;Activate handler No. 1
      .
      .
CLRL    (FP)             ;Deactivate exception handling
      .
      .
MOVAB   HANDLR2,(FP)      ;Activate handler No. 2
      .
      .
```

Figure 11.4.1

Suppose now that an exception occurs during execution of some procedure, so that the operating system routines build the signal array and mechanism array on top of the user stack. Suppose further that some user-written exception handler is active—that its address is in the top longword of the CALL frame created by invoking the procedure and thus is being pointed at by the procedure's frame pointer. The exception dispatcher passes control to this handler by means of a standard procedure CALL. Thus the writing of exception handlers is nothing really new, since they are written just as any other procedure is, with an entry point mask word and a concluding RET instruction, although we need to make

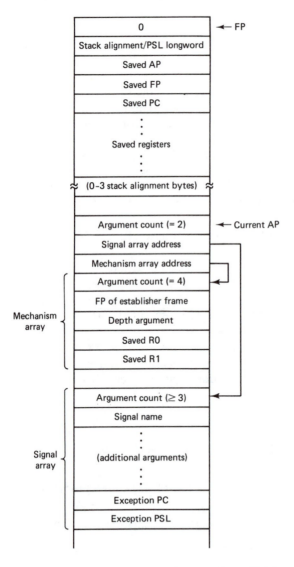

Figure 11.4.2

some comments about the effects of RET in this special case. Figure 11.4.2 shows a typical stack frame as it exists upon completion of the dispatcher's CALL to the user-written exception handler. Observe that the signal array and mechanism arrays are at the bottom of the stack frame, immediately above the user's stack as it existed prior to the occurrence of the exception; that the top of the stack frame is nothing but a standard CALL frame; and that the argument pointer is pointing at an argument count (2), followed by an argument list. All of this is precisely what we expect to occur when CALLx is invoked. There are, however, two small details which we need to mention. First, two longwords in the stack frame have been left intentionally unlabeled, since they are of no concern to us in the present discussion. Second, since the argument list is on the stack, immediately below the CALL frame, it would *appear* that the exception dispatcher has issued a CALLS instruction. But, in fact, it has not, for a glance at the CALL frame in an actual example (see Figure 11.4.6, for example) discloses that the "stack alignment/PSL" longword, immediately below the top of the stack, has its "CALLS" bit (bit 29) set to 0. We shall see below how that argument list is ultimately dealt with—it is removed from the stack.

Once control has been passed to the exception-handling procedure, it can use the argument pointer, AP, to locate the addresses of the mechanism array (which is frequently not of interest to it) and of the signal array. The latter array contains the desired information concerning the type of trap or fault, together with the offending PC and PSL, and the handler can now take some appropriate action.

As an example of a simple exception handler we offer the procedure of Figure 11.4.3. Actually, the only "handling" the routine does is to print a message as to

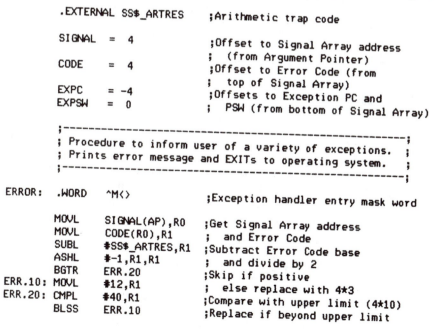

```
        .EXTERNAL SS$_ARTRES        ;Arithmetic trap code

        SIGNAL   = 4                ;Offset to Signal Array address
                                    ;  (from Argument Pointer)
        CODE     = 4                ;Offset to Error Code (from
                                    ;  top of Signal Array)
        EXPC     = -4               ;Offsets to Exception PC and
        EXPSW    = 0                ;  PSW (from bottom of Signal Array)

        ;----------------------------------------------------------------;
        ; Procedure to inform user of a variety of exceptions.  ;
        ; Prints error message and EXITs to operating system.   ;
        ;----------------------------------------------------------------;

ERROR:  .WORD    ^M<>               ;Exception handler entry mask word

        MOVL     SIGNAL(AP),R0      ;Get Signal Array address
        MOVL     CODE(R0),R1        ;  and Error Code
        SUBL     #SS$_ARTRES,R1     ;Subtract Error Code base
        ASHL     #-1,R1,R1          ;  and divide by 2
        BGTR     ERR.20             ;Skip if positive
ERR.10: MOVL     #12,R1             ;  else replace with 4*3
ERR.20: CMPL     #40,R1             ;Compare with upper limit (4*10)
        BLSS     ERR.10             ;Replace if beyond upper limit
```

Figure 11.4.3

```
        BITL    #3,R1               ;Make sure multiple of 4
        BNEQ    ERR.10              ;  and replace if not

        $0.NL                       ;Clear current print line,
        $0.STR  EXCTYP              ;  generate header and the message
        $0.STR  @MESVEC-4(R1)       ;  appropriate to the error
        $0.NL                       ;(new line)

        MOVZBL  (R0),R1             ;Get number of arguments in
                                    ;  Signal Array
        $0.STR  EXCPC               ;Generate header and
        $0.4H   EXPC(R0)[R1]        ;  exception PC
        $0.NL                       ;(new line)
        $0.STR  EXCPSW              ;Generate header and
        $0.4H   EXPSW(R0)[R1]       ;  exception PSW
        $0.NL                       ;(new line)

        $EXIT                       ;Exit to operating system
                ;Message addresses and message texts

MESVEC: .ADDRESS INT_OV,INT_DV,UNCLAS,DEC_DV,UNCLAS
        .ADDRESS DEC_OV,SUB_OR,FPT_OV,FPT_DV,FPT_UV


INT_OV: .ASCIZ  /Integer overflow (T)/
INT_DV: .ASCIZ  /Integer divide-by-zero (T)/
UNCLAS: .ASCIZ  /(unclassified exception)/
DEC_DV: .ASCIZ  /Decimal divide-by-zero (T)/
DEC_OV: .ASCIZ  /Decimal overflow (T)/
SUB_OR: .ASCIZ  /Subscript out-of-range (T)/
FPT_OV: .ASCIZ  /Floating point overflow (F)/
FPT_DV: .ASCIZ  /Floating point divide-by-zero (F)/
FPT_UV: .ASCIZ  /Floating point underflow (F)/

EXCTYP: .ASCIZ  /Exception type: /
EXCPC:  .ASCIZ  /PC =/
EXCPSW: .ASCIZ  /PSW =/
```

Figure 11.4.3 (continued)

the cause of the exception, and the contents of the PC and PSL at the time of the
exception. The procedure then $EXITs to the operating system. The program-
ming is quite straightforward, with the exception of the reference to the external
symbol SS$_ARTRES, which requires some explanation. SS$_ARTRES is a symbol whose value is established by the operating system, and it is used to determine
the values of the signal names for *arithmetic exceptions*, in the following way.
Associated with each such exception is a code, and these are shown in Figure
11.4.4. The signal name for each trap or fault is obtained by multiplying the code
shown in Figure 11.4.4 by 8 and adding the result to the value of SS$_ARTRES:

$$\text{signal name} = \text{SS\$\_ARTRES} + 8 \cdot \text{code}$$

The exception handler of Figure 11.4.3 generates a specific message for each
of the codes 1, 2, 4, 6, 7, 8, 9, and 10. Other arithmetic traps and faults (which,

FIGURE 11.4.4

Code	Exception	Type
1	Integer overflow	Trap
2	Integer divide-by-zero	Trap
3	Floating overflow[a]	Trap
4	Decimal or floating[a] divide-by-zero	Trap
5	Floating underflow[a]	Trap
6	Decimal overflow	Trap
7	Subscript out of range	Trap
8	Floating overflow	Fault
9	Floating divide-by-zero	Fault
10	Floating underflow	Fault

[a]On all VAX models except some early 11/780 models, these floating-point errors are *faults* 8, 9, and 10.

in fact, should not occur), and other exceptions which are not arithmetic in nature (for example, *access violation* or *reserved instruction* errors) are put into a catch-all category of "unclassified exception." For example, if an "integer divide-by-zero" trap occurs, the signal name will be SS$_ARTRERS + 8·2; subtracting the value of SS$_ARTRES from the signal name and dividing by 8 will isolate the arithmetic code. (In the procedure, we divide only by 2, since we ultimately need four times the code, to be used as a longword offset from the beginning of an address table.) With this information the reader should have little difficulty following the execution of this exception handler.

It will be instructive to see exactly what happens in practice if a mainline routine invokes a procedure, which in turn establishes this exception handler, and

```
0000080B      START:  .WORD  ^M<>                ;Entry mask word
                       .
                       .
0000083B              PUSHL  #^X12345678         ;Push two arguments
00000841              PUSHL  #^X0020426A         ;  on the stack
00000847              CALLS  #2,EVAL             ;  and call the procedure
0000084E              <next instruction>         ;(RET returns here)
                       .
                       .
0000095A      EVAL:   .WORD  ^M<IV,R5,R6>        ;Entry mask word
0000095C              MOVAB  ERROR,(FP)          ;Establish error handler
                       .
                       .
00000B89              INCB   X                   ;(Causes "integer overflow")
00000B8F              <next instruction>
                       .
                       .
00000CB1      ERROR:  .WORD  ^M<>                ;Exception handler entry
                       .
                       .
```

Figure 11.4.5

then an error occurs in the course of the procedure's execution. Figure 11.4.5 shows a mainline which, having pushed two arguments on the stack, invokes a procedure named EVAL with a CALLS instruction. (Note that EVAL enables "integer overflow" trapping, as well as saving two registers.) EVAL then establishes the procedure ERROR of Figure 11.4.3 as an exception handler, by placing the address of that routine in the longword being pointed at by the Frame Pointer of its (EVAL's) CALL frame. The addresses shown in the figure are the actual

Stack frame address	contents		meaning	
7FFAD710	00000000	← FP	Error handler address	CALL frame
7FFAD714	00000020		SPA/PSW longword	built
7FFAD718	7FFAD778		Saved AP	by dispatcher's
7FFAD71C	7FFAD75C		Saved FP	call to ERROR
7FFAD720	80000014		Saved PC	
7FFAD724	————			
7FFAD728	00000002	← AP	Argument count	Argument list for
7FFAD72C	7FFAD74C		Signal array address	exception handler
7FFAD730	7FFAD734		Mechanism array address	ERROR
7FFAD734	00000004		Argument count	
7FFAD738	7FFAD75C		FP of establisher	
7FFAD73C	00000000		Depth argument	Mechanism array
7FFAD740	Saved R0		Saved registers	
7FFAD744	Saved R1		0 and 1	
7FFAD748	————			
7FFAD74C	00000003		Argument count	
7FFAD750	0000047C		"Int overflow" signal	Signal
7FFAD754	00000B8F		Exception PC	array
7FFAD758	03C0002A		Exception PSL	
7FFAD75C	00000CB1		Exception handler address	CALL frame
7FFAD760	20600000		SPA/PSW longword	built
7FFAD764	7FFAD7CC		Saved AP	by mainline's
7FFAD768	7FFAD784		Saved FP	call to EVAL
7FFAD76C	0000084E		Saved PC	
7FFAD770	Saved R5		Saved registers	
7FFAD774	Saved R6		5 and 6	
7FFAD778	00000002	(← AP)	Argument count	Argument list
7FFAD77C	0020426A		Argument 1	for procedure
7FFAD780	12345678		Argument 2	EVAL
7FFAD784	————		Top of user's stack prior	
7FFAD788	————		to CALLS #2,EVAL	

Figure 11.4.6

Exceptions and Condition Handling   Chap. 11

memory addresses occupied by these instructions *during execution*, rather than the assembler's default addresses as we have ordinarily shown. Once EVAL is executing, we assume that the INCB instruction at 00000B89 causes an "integer overflow" trap. As we know, the processor will execute a trap sequence into the operating system, which builds, on the user's stack, the signal and mechanism arrays. Control is then passed to ERROR, the procedure whose address is in the longword pointed at by EVAL's frame pointer. The stack frame at this point is shown in Figure 11.4.6. This stack frame corresponds to that of Figure 11.4.2, and the reader should go through the frame verifying that each longword is as expected. Of particular note, however, are the following. The "SPA/PSW longword" at 7FFAD714 reflects in part the PSW from EVAL, and we observe that the "integer overflow trap" bit (bit 5) is on. The "Saved FP" at 7FFAD71C is EVAL's FP, of course, and notice that its value, 7FFAD75C, is the same as the "Establisher FP" at 7FFAD738 since in fact it was EVAL that established the exception handling. The signal name at 7FFAD750 is 0000047C. In the particular version of the operating system under which this program was executed, SS$_ARTRES had the value 00000474, and if this number is subtracted from 0000047C, we obtain $8 = 8 \cdot 1$. Thus the arithmetic exception code is 1—integer overflow, as seen from Figure 11.4.4. Finally, we note that the longword at EVAL's FP (7FFAD75C) contains 00000CB1, which is the address of the entry point to ERROR, EVAL's exception handler.

11.5. EXCEPTION HANDLERS FOR MAINLINE PROGRAMS

So far we have discussed the establishing of exception handlers only for a *procedure* that is invoked by some mainline program, for it is only in the context of procedures that we have discussed the concept of stack frames and frame pointers. But it is possible for a mainline program to establish its own exception handling, in a fashion identical to that used by an invoked procedure. For a mainline program *has* an associated frame pointer, and in fact it has a stack frame with much the same appearance as a procedure's CALL frame.

We know that when a program is executed, some few actions need to be taken by the operating system. In particular, the executable module must be loaded into main memory. Then the user's stack pointer must be set to some value. Information about the execution environment is obtained from the program entry mask word. Finally execution is begun by putting the program's transfer address in the program counter. But, in fact, the operating system treats the user's program very much as if it were a *procedure*. It establishes a frame pointer (pointing at a longword initially containing a 0), a "SPA/PSW longword" whose bits are set according to the program's entry mask word, and a *return address* (saved PC), which is an address in the operating system itself. Thus it is even possible for a mainline program to execute RET, and control will be "returned" to the operating system routine that "invoked" the mainline. (The effect of this RET will not be appreciably different from that of $EXIT.) All of this accounts for the fact that a mainline program's entry point has the same appearance as that of a procedure—from the operating system's standpoint they are the same kinds of structures.

11.6 MULTIPLE EXCEPTION HANDLERS

Although not more than one exception handler can be *active* at any given time, multiple handlers can be *present*, in the sense that procedure A can establish a handler, and then A calls procedure B, which in turn establishes its own handler. Thus the handlers for both A and B are present, with the active handler being that established by the currently executing procedure. As an example of this situation, consider the mainline program of Figure 11.6.1, which establishes the procedure ERROR of Figure 11.4.3 as its exception handler. This mainline then invokes the procedure EVAL, which establishes a small exception handler, ERR, the purpose of which is to deal only with "integer divide by zero" exceptions. It does so simply by printing a message to notify the user that a division by zero has taken place, where it took place, and it then simply *resumes* execution of EVAL. (Depending on the circumstances, this may be a reasonable response to this kind of error, since neither operand is changed upon division by zero.) Notice that execution can be resumed, since division by zero is a *trap* exception, and thus the PC is pointing at the next instruction when the trap occurs. On the other hand, if some other type of error occurs within the processing of EVAL, the handler ERR does *not* deal with it. Rather, it invokes the handler ERROR to manage it—to print an appropriate message and then to $EXIT.

Suppose that the mainline routine has invoked EVAL, and that in the course of EVAL's execution, an "integer divide by zero" error occurs. Then the operating system will build, on the user's stack, the signal array and the mechanism array. The exception dispatcher, seeing that EVAL has established an exception handler, will create a CALL frame on the stack and invoke ERR. Since ERR detects that the exception is in fact a result of a division by zero, it prints a message and the offending PC, and it now wishes to *resume* execution at the next EVAL instruction. It does so by putting the value SS$_CONTINUE in R0 and executing RET, and we must examine the operating system's response to this RET. We have already noted (see Figures 11.4.2 and 11.4.6) that the "saved PC" in the CALL frame built upon invoking the exception handler is *not* a PC value in the user's program, but rather is an address in the operating system routines. RET clears the CALL frame and restores various pointers, and then control is passed to this operating system routine. This routine examines the contents of R0, and in this case finds it to be the value SS$_CONTINUE (a symbol whose value is defined and declared as global by the operating system, just as SS$_ARTRES is). The operating system's response is to clear the argument list pointed at by AP from the stack, restore the contents of R0 and R1 from the mechanism array, and set the stack pointer SP to the exception PC longword in the signal array. This routine then executes REI (*Return from Exception or Interrupt*), which has the effect of popping the top two longwords from the stack into the program counter and the processor status longword. (See Appendix A for further details of REI, although some of these are meaningful only in an *interrupt* context.) Since by now the stack pointer is pointing at the exception PC, that PC value is restored, and thus execution resumes at the location immediately following the instruction that caused the division by zero.

Suppose now that in the course of execution of EVAL, an error *other than* a division by zero occurs. Then as we see from Figure 11.6.1, the exception handler ERR places the value SS$_RESIGNAL in R0 and executes RET. (SS$_RESIGNAL is another operating system globally declared symbol.) The operating system

```
START:  .WORD    ^M<>                    ;Mainline entry point
        MOVAB    ERROR,(FP)              ;Establish mainline exception
                                         ;  handler
          .
          .
          .
        PUSHL    X                       ;Push two arguments
        PUSHL    Y                       ;  on the stack
        CALLS    #2,EVAL                 ;  and invoke procedure EVAL
          .
          .
          .
EVAL:   .WORD    ^M<IV,R5,R6>            ;Procedure entry point
        MOVAB    ERR,(FP)                ;Establish procedure exception
                                         ;  handler
          .
          .
          .
        .EXTERNAL       SS$_ARTRES,SS$_RESIGNAL,SS$_CONTINUE

        SIGNAL  =  4                     ;Offset to Signal Array address
                                         ;  (from Argument Pointer)
        CODE    =  4                     ;Offset to Error Code (from
                                         ;  top of Signal Array)
        EXPC    =  -4                    ;Offset to exception PC
                                         ;  (from bottom of Signal Array)

ERR:    .WORD    ^M<>                    ;Exception handler entry point
        MOVL     SIGNAL(AP),R0           ;Get Signal Array address

        CMPL     CODE(R0),-             ;Compare Signal Name against
                 #SS$_ARTRES+<8*2>      ;  "divide-by-zero" signal name
        BEQL     CONT                    ;Skip if "divide-by-zero"
        MOVL     #SS$_RESIGNAL,R0        ;  else set R0 to "resignal the
                                         ;  exception"
        RET                              ;  and return to operating system

CONT:   $0.NL                            ;Clear current print line
        $0.STR   DIVBY0                  ;  and print message
        MOVZBL   (R0),R1                 ;Get number of arguments in
                                         ;  Signal Array
        $0.4H    EXPC(R0)[R1]            ;  and print exception PC
        $0.NL                            ;(new line)

        MOVL     #SS$_CONTINUE,R0        ;Set R0 to "continue"
        RET                              ;  and return to operating system

DIVBY0: .ASCIZ  /Divide-by-zero at PC =/
```

Figure 11.6.1

routine that begins execution as a result of this RET clears the argument list (pointed at by AP) from the stack and then passes control back to the *exception dispatcher*, with the information that the exception has been **resignaled**—that is, that the dispatcher is to search for another exception handler to manage the error. The dispatcher treats this task as follows. Since the mechanism array (which is still on the stack) contains the FP of the procedure that established the current exception handler (in this case, EVAL), the dispatcher can locate the CALL frame associated with the call to EVAL and thus can determine the "saved FP" in that frame. But that saved FP is the FP of the *mainline* routine. And the longword pointed at by that frame pointer contains the address ERROR. In this way the dispatcher can rebuild the stack frame, this time invoking the handler ERROR. In the course of doing so, it replaced the "establisher FP" longword in the mechanism array with the frame pointer of the mainline program (which established ERROR as an exception handler) and increments the *depth pointer* to indicate that exception handling is one level "deeper" than the level of the procedure that caused the error.

11.7 DEFAULT EXCEPTION HANDLERS

Suppose now that in Figure 11.6.1 the mainline routine had established ERROR as an exception handler (as shown), but that EVAL had established *no* exception handler. What will take place if an error (division by zero, or any other type of error, for that matter) occurs during execution of EVAL? The exception dispatcher will note that the currently executing procedure (EVAL) has *not* established a handler, and thus it will automatically resignal to locate a handler at a lower level in the chain of procedure calls. Since the mainline routine has established a handler (ERROR), it is to this procedure that control will be passed (and, as above, the depth argument in the mechanism array will be incremented by 1).

If no routine (including the mainline) in the chain of CALLs to procedures has established an exception handler, the dispatcher will ultimately work its way down to the mainline. Failing to find a nonzero entry at the top of any CALL frame, the dispatcher will hand control over to an operating system established exception handler, called the **catch-all exception handler**. It is messages from this handler that the reader has seen so far as a result of execution errors.

11.8 FURTHER COMMENTS ON EXCEPTION HANDLING

We have examined some of the details of exception handling, but the process is quite complex and contains other details which have not been touched on here. Similarly, although we have given examples of handlers that respond to errors in various ways—by exiting, continuing or resignaling, for example—there are several other actions an exception handler might take, including aborting execution of the procedure that generated the exception and resuming execution back at that procedure's caller. Of course, in dealing with specific errors we have focused our attention on the arithmetic traps and faults, whereas in practice we might also need to concern ourselves with, for instance, reserved operand or memory access exceptions. Further details can be found in the Digital Equipment Corporation *VAX/VMS System Services Reference Manual.*

The reader will have noted that in this chapter we have for the first time taken extensive advantage of routines that are supplied *by the operating system*, rather than writing any of the needed programming ourselves. This stems from necessity rather than indolence, for when the processor executes a *trap sequence* in response to some kind of event, the new PC that is obtained is in an area of memory which is *protected*—is *not valid* for access by the ordinary user. Thus we *must* let the operating system routines establish the various arrays and frames that we have seen in this chapter.

11.9 EXERCISES

11.3.1. (a) How do the results of the processor's execution of a *trap sequence* differ in concept from the results of execution of the JSB instructions? (Both sequences stack the current program counter contents and obtain a new PC from somewhere.)

(b) What is the significance of the processor's saving of the PSL contents on the stack when a trap or fault occurs?

(c) When the time comes to return from a subroutine, RSB simply pops the top of the stack into the program counter. It has the effect of

$$\text{JMP} \quad @(SP)+$$

Why will this instruction *not* do for returning from a trap sequence?

(d) How can the PC *and* PSL be restored from the stack at the conclusion of processing of a trap sequence? In particular, show that neither of the two sequences

```
JMP     @(SP)+          BICPSW   #^XFFFF
BICPSW  #^XFFFF         BISPSW   4(SP)
BISPSW  (SP)+           MOVL     (SP)+,(SP)
                        JMP      @(SP)+
```

will quite do. Show, however, that the operation REI (Appendix A) does exactly what is required here in restoring both PC and PSL from the stack.

11.4.1. Why will the address of a user-written exception handler never be zero? (This fact is critical to the exception dispatcher's treatment of the top longword of a procedure's CALL frame.)

11.4.2. Why does the instruction

$$\text{CLRL} \quad (FP)$$

deactivate exception handling? (See Figure 11.4.1.)

11.4.3. In the exception-handling procedure ERROR of Figure 11.4.3:

    (a) What will be the signal longword at the top of the signal array if the exception is *not* arithmetic in nature? In particular, how does ERROR treat such a nonarithmetic exception?

    (b) Why is it not necessary to save R0 and R1 (by specifying them, for example, in ERROR's entry mask word), since they are used in this procedure?

    (c) Verify that if c(R0) = signal array address and c(R1) = number of arguments in signal array, a longword reference to $-4(R0)[R1]$ will access the exception PC. Why will not 8(R0) do just as well to reference this stacked PC?

11.4.4. Referring to Figure 11.4.6, explain the contents of each of the longwords in the stack frame whose address is given below.

    (a) 7FFAD710   **(b)** 7FFAD718   **(c)** 7FFAD71C

    (d) 7FFAD72C   **(e)** 7FFAD730   **(f)** 7FFAD738

    (g) 7FFAD754   **(h)** 7FFAD758   **(i)** 7FFAD768

    (j) 7FFAD76C   **(k)** 7FFAD778 to 7FFAD780

11.4.5. Since an exception handler is a procedure, it can itself establish an exception handler. What could be the consequences of an exception handler that establishes itself as its own exception handler?

11.6.1. Suppose that a mainline program establishes a procedure ERROR as its exception handler, but that ERROR establishes *no* exception-handling procedures. Suppose that an error occurs in the mainline which causes ERROR to execute, and in the course of ERROR's execution an exception occurs. Since ERROR has established no exception handler, the exception should be resignalled to the mainline, and it appears that the possibility exists for an infinite recursion of calls to ERROR. But, in fact, ERROR is not reinvoked. Why not?

11.6.2. In the routine of Figure 11.6.1, suppose that we replace the instructions

```
                MOVL    #SS$_CONTINUE,R0
                RET
```

by the instructions

```
                MOVAL   EXPC(R0)[R1],SP
                REI
```

Explain why either sequence will have the effect of continuing execution at the exception PC, with the PSL restored to its condition immediately after execution of the offending instruction. In what ways do these sequences of instructions differ? Could the MOVAL operation be replaced by MOVAB? Explain.

11.6.3. As in Exercise 11.6.2, suppose that we execute the sequence of instructions

```
                MOVAL   EXPC(R0)[R1],SP
                MOVAB   ADDR,(SP)
                REI
```

Show that execution resumes at ADDR rather than at the exception PC, and thus that "continuing" can be done selectively—that execution need not always resume at the place at which the exception occurred.

12 FLOATING-POINT DATATYPES

12.1 INTRODUCTION

The first few sections of this chapter deal with the differences between fixed-point (integer) and floating-point (fractional) data, how each type is interpreted, and the considerations that play a role in the development of a representation scheme for floating-point data—numbers that contain both an integer and a fraction part. The reader whose only interest is in the representations of the various floating-point formats as implemented on the VAX, and the operations that affect these datatypes, may omit these early sections and resume the development at Section 12.9.

12.2 FIXED-POINT DATA

Although we have spent quite a bit of time manipulating numerical data, to date the only such data have consisted of *integers*—whole numbers. But the reader is doubtless aware that there are circumstances in which whole numbers are simply inadequate or at least inappropriate. As an example, consider the (conceptually) simple task of balancing one's checkbook. This requires that we be able to add deposits, subtract withdrawals, and maintain a current balance. But by the very nature of our monetary system, based as it is on dollars and fractional dollars, the most natural numerical scheme for this task is one in which we can maintain two *decimal places*; we must be able to work in hundredths of dollars, with numbers such as 12.47, 748.92, −56.65, and so on. It would appear that the whole-number system in which we have operated so far would be inappropriate for these purposes.

If we revise our approach to, or at least interpretation of, this task, we find that the currently available system is quite adequate. We simply agree to view our bank balance and the various transactions that affect it in *whole pennies* rather than in *fractional dollars*. Thus the three dollar amounts mentioned above become penny amounts 1247, 74892, and −5665, and we already have a completely satisfactory set of machine operations that will manipulate these data. And if we make use of longword data throughout, we can manage amounts up to 2 billion pennies or so, or equivalently about 20 million dollars. There are certainly no dangers of any integer overflows, and in fact this range would probably be adequate to manage most of the accounting for even a modest-sized corporation. (Longwords would not suffice for the larger corporations, but even the federal government could work in pennies and not exhaust the capacities of quadwords.)

Now although we may be *performing* operations with integer data (pennies), we are still *thinking* of the data in terms of whole and fractional dollars. That is, although the actual contents of a register or memory location might be 1247, we interpret that value as 12.47 instead, there being an *implied decimal point* two digits from the right end of the number representation. Thus in this particular environment, any collection *dddddddddd* of digits is interpreted *by us* as representing the whole and fractional number *ddddddd.dd*, where we have used the symbol '.' to indicate the position of the implied decimal point. Since the position of the implied decimal point is *fixed* (in this case, two digits from the right end) for *all* the numbers we will be dealing with during this task, these numbers are referred to as **fixed-point numbers.**

It is important to understand that we have not suddenly endowed the integer operations (such as ADDL, INCL, and so on) with the ability to manipulate data that consist in part of an integer and in part of a fraction. It is only our interpretation that gives this appearance. Thus although we might impose an implied decimal point on the data, and in fact we might even output the integer 1247 on the terminal screen as $12.47, we are still manipulating the familiar integer datatypes. Indeed, we could as well say that the integer data we have used throughout the text are fixed-point data, with the implied decimal point at the extreme right end of the number: *dddddddddd.*.

Next consider the following problem. We invest $512,872.37 at 10.8%, compounded daily, and we wish to calculate the first day's interest. As 10.8% yearly interest amounts to approximately 0.03% daily interest, we are going to be multiplying the principal by the number 0.0003, and to manage both the principal and the interest rate as fixed-point numbers will require 10 decimal digits, with the implied decimal point four digits from the right end of the number: The principal is 5128723700 (512872.3700) and the interest rate is 3 (.0003). Observe that the principal must be represented by a decimal number so large that it will not fit in a longword, even though the number of pennies (51287237) in the principal is comfortably accommodated in 32 bits. The source of the difficulty is clear: We are dealing with two numbers which are vastly different in orders of magnitude.

Floating-Point Datatypes   Chap. 12

But even if we ignore this difficulty, there is a further problem. When the principal is multiplied by the daily interest rate, the result is 15386171100. But how are we to interpret this number? We cannot claim that it is also a fixed-point number of the same type as the principal and interest, for this would lead to a daily interest of 1538617.1100 = $1,538,517.11, which is clearly absurd; the correct result is 153.85171100, or approximately $153.85. The problem stems from the fact that fixed-point additions and subtractions yield results which have the same fixed-point representations, whereas fixed-point multiplications and divisions do not; the results must be appropriately *scaled*, either right or left. We could, of course, write some programming that would deal with this, and there is no reason why hardware could not be devised to do the scaling for us, although note that in either case some truncation would have to take place. The most accurate representation of the result after scaling would be 1538517 (with the assumed decimal point four digits from the right end of the number as before, that is, 153.8517).

12.3 FLOATING-POINT DATA

What is needed to manage the problem that arose in the preceding example is some representation of a fractional number in which the assumed decimal point, rather than being in a *fixed* location relative to some reference point in the number, is allowed to *float* across the number, into whatever position is most natural or useful relative to the magnitude of the number. Thus the principal is perhaps most easily treated as the integer 51287237 (with the decimal point two places from the right end of the number) and the interest could simply be represented by the number 3 (the decimal point being four places from the right end). Another possible choice would be to represent the principal as the number .51287237 (with the decimal point six places to the *right* of the *left* end of the number), and the interest as .3 (with the decimal point three places to the *left* of the *left* end of the number).

No matter how we choose to represent a number in this **floating-point representation,** it is clear that three pieces of information are required to be able to determine the actual value of the number whose representation is given, two of which will need to be explicit. First, of course, we need to know the magnitude of the number (51287237, or 3, or whatever). Next, we need to know where the decimal point is *assumed* to be in that representation. (The decimal point, after all, is not a part of the number's internal representation in main memory. However, we might agree, for example, that the decimal point is always assumed to be immediately preceding the most significant digit, or perhaps immediately succeeding the least significant digit.) If we agree in advance on some convention regarding the placement of the decimal point, there is no need explicitly to convey this information in the data that represent the floating-point data. Finally, we shall have to know how many places, left or right, the assumed decimal point must be shifted to yield the actual value of the number in question. As an example, if we agree that the assumed decimal point of a number always immediately follows its least significant digit, then the number .0003 can be represented as 3 [−4], and 1200 can be represented as 12 [+2], where the numbers in brackets represent the required scalings, positive numbers indicating a decimal point shift to the right, negative numbers indicating a decimal point shift to the left. On the other hand, if we assume a decimal point immediately preceding the most significant digit, these representations would be .0003 = 3 [−3] and 1200 = 12 [+4]. Notice that in doing the shifting it may be necessary to supply missing 0s, as has been done above.

The reader will recognize that what has been done in these last few examples is simply to write each of these numbers in **scientific notation,** in which the number is scaled down to a number of modest size, and then scaled back up to its equivalent value by multiplying by an appropriate power of 10:

$$.0003 = 3 [-3] = 0.3 \cdot 10^{-3}$$

$$1200 = 12 [+4] = 0.12 \cdot 10^{+4}$$

No matter what convention we adopt concerning the placement of the assumed decimal point in a floating-point number, it is clear that two pieces of information are still required uniquely to determine its value: the *magnitude* of the number, and the *scaling factor*. Thus we shall concentrate our efforts on efficient and reasonable ways of representing this needed information.

Now it has been all very well in our previous discussions to deal in the familiar decimal number system, but when it comes to the actual implementation of floating-point numbers on a computer, we must revert to a binary system, since it is in this system that numbers are held internally. But except for the number base, all the observations and conclusions we have already made are still valid. In particular, the concepts of assumed decimal point—which in this setting we refer to as **binary point**—scaling factor, and magnitude carry over with only the obvious changes required by the base 2 representation. In the following examples, we give a number in (a) its decimal representation, (b) its binary representation as a whole number and (base-2) fraction, (c) its binary representation scaled so that the binary point immediately precedes its most significant digit, and (d) its "magnitude/assumed decimal point/scaling factor" form, where as before we *assume* the binary point immediately preceding the most significant binary digit.

$$12_{10} \quad = 1 \cdot 10^1 + 2 \cdot 10^0 \tag{a}$$

$$= 1 \cdot 2^3 + 1 \cdot 2^2 + 0 \cdot 2^1 + 0 \cdot 2^0$$

$$= 1100._2 \tag{b}$$

$$= (1 \cdot 2^{-1} + 1 \cdot 2^{-2}) \cdot 2^4$$

$$= .11 \cdot 2^4 \tag{c}$$

$$= 11 [4] \tag{d}$$

$$5.75_{10} \quad = 5 \cdot 10^0 + 7 \cdot 10^{-1} + 5 \cdot 10^{-2} \tag{a}$$

$$= 1 \cdot 2^2 + 0 \cdot 2^1 + 1 \cdot 2^0 + 1 \cdot 2^{-1} + 1 \cdot 2^{-2}$$

$$= 101.11_2 \tag{b}$$

$$= (1 \cdot 2^{-1} + 0 \cdot 2^{-2} + 1 \cdot 2^{-3} + 1 \cdot 2^{-4} + 1 \cdot 2^{-5}) \cdot 2^3$$

$$= .10111 \cdot 2^3 \tag{c}$$

$$= 10111 \ [3] \tag{d}$$

$$.09375_{10} = 9 \cdot 10^{-2} + 3 \cdot 10^{-3} + 7 \cdot 10^{-4} + 5 \cdot 10^{-5} \tag{a}$$

$$= 0 \cdot 2^{-1} + 0 \cdot 2^{-2} + 0 \cdot 2^{-3} + 1 \cdot 2^{-4} + 1 \cdot 2^{-5}$$

$$= .00011_2 \tag{b}$$

$$= (1 \cdot 2^{-1} + 1 \cdot 2^{-2}) \cdot 2^{-3}$$

$$= .11 \cdot 2^{-3} \tag{c}$$

$$= 11 \ [-3] \tag{d}$$

The reader may infer from these three examples that *any* decimal number, with integer and fractional parts, will have a base-2 representation. To show that this is not the case, consider the especially simple example of the decimal fraction $1/10 = 0.1$, and suppose it *could* be written in binary. Then for some appropriate positive integer n, we would have

$$.1_{10} = a_1 \cdot 2^{-1} + a_2 \cdot 3^{-2} + \cdots + a_n \cdot 2^{-n}$$

$$= (a_1 \cdot 2^{-1} + a_2 \cdot 2^{-2} + \cdots + a_n \cdot 2^{-n}) \cdot 2^n \cdot 2^{-n}$$

$$= (a_1 \cdot 2^{n-1} + a_2 \cdot 2^{n-2} + \cdots + a_{n-1} \cdot 2^1 + a_n \cdot 2^0) \cdot 2^{-n}$$

where each $a_i = 0$ or 1. Since the quantity in parentheses in the last expression is a positive integer, if we denote it by k the equation becomes

$$.1_{10} = k \cdot 2^{-n}$$

or equivalently,

$$2^n = 10 \cdot k$$

But this is impossible, since no power of 2 is an integer multiple of 10. This contradiction leads us to the conclusion that no such sum of powers of 2 as shown above can equal 1/10, and thus the best we can do is to *approximate* 1/10 as a number written in base 2. (None of this should come as a surprise; after all, in *decimal* there is no finite representation of the number 1/3.)

12.4 A REPRESENTATION SCHEME FOR FLOATING-POINT NUMBERS

In developing a system for representing floating-point numbers internally in main memory, we shall be working with the 8-bit byte structure. Just as the 4-bit "word" of Chapter 2 was unrealistically small, we shall see that a byte is simply not large enough to hold the information required for specifying a useful range of floating-point numbers. But the 4-bit "word" was valuable in discovering and developing concepts and techniques, which were then easily transferred to larger structures, and this same idea will prove to hold here—8-bit structures are indeed too small for any but the most trivial processing, yet they are small enough to be manageable, while being just large enough to lead us to some important insights into the structure of floating-point representations.

Since we need to hold both the size and the scaling factor—which we shall refer to as the **magnitude** and **exponent,** respectively—of a floating-point number in 8 bits, we shall divide these bits somewhat arbitrarily as follows:

bits 7:5 = signed exponent, with bit 7 acting as the exponent's sign bit; thus the range of exponents is 100 to 011 or, in decimal, -4 to $+3$

bits 4:0 = magnitude of the number, with the binary point assumed to be immediately to the left of bit 4

With this scheme the internal representation of a floating-point number will be

$$e\ e\ e\ _\wedge m\ m\ m\ m\ m$$

where the e's and m's represent exponent bits and magnitude bits, respectively, and as usual the symbol '$_\wedge$' represents the position of the assumed binary point. For example, the byte whose contents is 01011010, when interpreted as a floating-point number representation, means

$$\text{exponent} \ = 010 = 2$$
$$\text{magnitude} = 11010 = {}_\wedge 11010 = .11010$$

Thus the number represented is $.11010 \cdot 2^2 = 11.010$, which in decimal is 3.25. In a similar fashion, 11110100 would be interpreted as

$$\text{exponent} \ = 111 = -1$$
$$\text{magnitude} = 10100 = {}_\wedge 10100 = .10100$$

which is the number $.10100 \cdot 2^{-1} = .0101$ or, in decimal .3125.

Notice that in this binary representation, the position of the assumed binary point is somewhat more explicit than it was in our earlier, less formal discussion, in which we assumed that the decimal point was immediately to the left of the most significant digit. Here the binary point is positioned relative to the *bit positions in the byte* (specifically, to the left of bit 4), *not* relative to the most significant digit (bit) of the number's magnitude. To see this, we need only observe that

$00110100 = 001{.}10100 = .10100 \cdot 2^1$ and $01001010 = 010{.}01010 = .01010 \cdot 2^2$ are both representations of the decimal number 1.25. In the first case the assumed binary point is immediately to the left of the most significant digit of the magnitude; in the second case it is not. Since the multiple representations of one and the same floating-point number, as illustrated above, are undesirable from the standpoint of some of our future considerations, we adopt the following convention, which will guarantee the uniqueness of the representation: A floating-point number is always represented in such a way that the most significant bit of its magnitude is in bit position 4. (There are also a few undesirable consequences of this convention; some of these are discussed below, and others are explored in the exercises.)

The reader may have noted that to date no mention has been made of *negative* floating-point numbers. They have been postponed because their introduction will force us to rethink the structure we have devised so far and which seems to hold some promise. To see what the difficulties are, consider the floating-point number 4. This would be written as $011{.}10000 = .10000 \cdot 2^3 = 100.00_2$ according to our conventions. But then how is -4 to be represented? With our extensive background with twos-complement numbers, we might naturally take the following approach. Since 5 binary bits are available to us for the magnitude portion of the number, consider those bits as representing *signed* numbers, with the high-order bit (bit 4) serving as the sign bit. Then -4 would be written as 11100 (the two's complement in 5 bits of 00100), and since again a scaling factor of 3 is required, the floating-point number -4 should be represented as $011{.}11100$. Unfortunately, the interpretation of this number, by our earlier conventions, is $.11100 \cdot 2^3 = 111.00_2 = 7_{10}$. The source of the problem is clear: We have no way of telling whether the leading 1 in a magnitude representation is to be interpreted as the sign bit of a negative number or as the most significant bit of a positive number. The problem can be traced directly to our convention that the most significant bit of the magnitude is to occupy bit 4.

Evidently if we plan to adhere to this convention and still introduce negative magnitudes, we are going to have to devise some scheme in which the sign is *not* bit 4—that is, the sign bit must somehow be kept separate from the magnitude itself, and hence some scheme other than our traditional two's-complement representation is required. In fact, we have already investigated a representation which precisely serves these purposes, the **sign-magnitude** number representation system of Chapter 2. Recall that in that earlier investigation we abandoned the sign-magnitude system for two principal reasons. First, it did not well accommodate the *unsigned* number system which we had already developed. That objection is no longer valid here, for we shall not be dealing with unsigned floating-point numbers. Second, the algorithms for doing arithmetic in the sign-magnitude system were rather more complicated than what we were seeking, since, for example, in order to add two sign-magnitude numbers, decisions had to be made about their signs. Those complications are something with which we shall now simply have to deal.

The **sign-magnitude floating-point representation** of a number now takes the following form.

(2) Floating-Point Format-1 (FPF-1)

The FPF-1 representation of a floating-point number is

$$s \quad e \, e \, e \,{}_{\wedge} m \, m \, m \, m$$

where s is the sign bit for the magnitude (with 0 meaning positive and 1 meaning negative, as usual), the e's are the exponent bits, interpreted as a *signed* 3-bit integer, and the m's are the magnitude bits, with the most significant bit of the magnitude occupying the high-order bit of the magnitude field. The value of the number so represented is

$$\pm 0.mmmm \cdot 2^{eee} \quad (+ \text{ if } s = 0, - \text{ if } s = 1)$$

There are a number of observations to be made about this structure. First, note that the sign bit s has been split off from the magnitude bits m. The reason for this is *not* so much that we want to isolate the sign bit, but rather that we wish to keep the exponent and magnitude bits *adjacent*, for reasons that will shortly be clear. Second, observe that while the magnitude of the number is now written in the sign-magnitude format, the exponent is still represented as a twos-complement number. Finally, note that we have had to sacrifice one bit in order to hold the sign, the consequence being a reduction in the number of magnitude bits from 5 down to 4, a reduction that implies a loss in the range of the floating-point numbers which can be represented in 8 bits.

We can now easily deal with the example that led to this modification of our structure, the numbers $+4$ and -4. Specifically,

$$+4 = +100.0_2 = +.1000 \cdot 2^3 = 0 \; 011_{\wedge}1000 = 00111000$$

$$-4 = -100.0_2 = -.1000 \cdot 2^3 = 1 \; 011_{\wedge}1000 = 10111000$$

One of the activities with which we shall have to become involved when doing arithmetic computations with floating-point numbers is the *shifting*, right or left, of the magnitude bits, together with corresponding adjustments to the exponent bits in order to preserve the number's value. As an example, consider the operation of addition. Note that to add two numbers of the form $a \cdot 2^x$ and $b \cdot 2^y$, they must be adjusted so that their powers of 2 are identical, since then we have

$$a' \cdot 2^z + b' \cdot 2^z = (a' + b') \cdot 2^z$$

As a simple example, consider the sum $1.5 + 0.25$. In the floating-point format the problem becomes

$$1.5 + 0.25 = (0 \; 001 \; 1100) + (0 \; 111 \; 1000)$$

Now we can make the exponent portions of these representations agree if we adjust the representation of 0.25 as follows:

$$0.25 = 0 \; 111 \; 1000 = 0 \; 001 \; 0010$$

That is,

$$.1 \cdot 2^{-1} = .001 \cdot 2^{+1}$$

The addition can now be performed, and we obtain

$$1.5 + 0.25 = (0\ 001\ 1100) + (0\ 001\ 0010) = 0\ 001\ 1110$$

which is the desired result, 1.75.

The process of shifting the magnitude and making corresponding adjustments in the exponent (or, conversely, changing the exponent and making corresponding adjustments in the magnitude by shifting) is called **scaling**, and a further example will show that it can lead to some problems. Consider the sum 2.5 plus 5.5:

$$2.5 + 5.5 = (0\ 010\ 1010) + (0\ 011\ 1011)$$

The 2.5 can be scaled so that its exponent portion agrees with that of 5.5:

$$2.5 = 0\ 010\ 1010 = 0\ 011\ 0101$$

and the addition can now take place:

$$2.5 + 5.5 = (0\ 011\ 0101) + (0\ 011\ 1011) = 0\ 011\ 1.0000$$

We have a slight problem here, for the addition of the magnitudes has resulted in an "overflow" beyond the assumed binary point, a situation that did not arise in the preceding example. However, we can easily repair this situation simply by scaling the result back so that it agrees with our convention: We shift the magnitude one bit position to the right, and at the same time we increase the exponent by 1. This yields

$$2.5 + 5.5 = 0\ 011\ 1.0000 = 0\ 100\ 1000$$

The scheme *appears* to work, since in binary,

$$0\ 100\ 1000 = .1 \cdot 2^4 = 1000. = 8.0_{10}$$

until we recall that the exponents are *signed* numbers, with the highest order of the 3 bits acting as the *sign* bit. Thus, in fact, the exponent bits 100 represent -4, not $+4$. The actual value of the result then is not 8.0_{10} but

$$0\ 100\ 1000 = .1 \cdot 2^{-4} = 1. \cdot 2^{-5} = 0.03125_{10}$$

The source of the incorrectness of the result is now clear—there has been an overflow into the exponent's sign bit—and it was only our inattention to detail that caused us to fail to recognize it immediately.

Although this overflow into the exponent's high-order bit is easy enough for *us* to detect, it turns out to be far more troublesome when the addition process, as illustrated above, is implemented on a computer, either by software (a subroutine or function, perhaps) or in the processor's circuitry. To see why, we note first that just because an addition results in a negative exponent does not mean necessarily that the result of the addition is incorrect. For example,

$$0.125 + 0.1875 = (0\ 110\ 1000) + (1\ 110\ 1100)$$
$$= 0\ 110\ 1.0100 = 0\ 111\ 1010 = 0.3125$$

which is quite correct. It seems evident that the correctness or incorrectness of the result depends not simply on the state of the sign bit *after* the addition (and any subsequent required scaling), but rather on whether that bit *changed* its state in the course of the addition. It is this phenomenon that is somewhat difficult to detect. This will be more obvious if we try to implement the addition with the instructions that we currently have on hand. For example, in adding 2.5 and 5.5, we might begin by decomposing each floating-point representation into its individual components. Suppose, for example, that we place the magnitudes in 8-bit bytes in such a way that the implied binary point is between bits 4 and 3. (This requires some bit manipulation, but with the arithmetic shift and bit-clear instructions, it is not difficult.) Suppose further that the exponent portion of the representation is placed in the low-order bits of some byte. This decomposition technique when applied to 2.5 and 5.5 yields

$$2.5 = 0\ 010\ 1010:\quad \text{exponent byte} = 00000\ 010$$
$$\text{magnitude byte} = 0000\ 1010$$
$$5.5 = 0\ 011\ 1011:\quad \text{exponent byte} = 00000\ 011$$
$$\text{magnitude byte} = 0000\ 1011$$

By comparing the exponent bytes, we can easily determine that the number with the smaller exponent—2.5—must be adjusted by shifting its magnitude byte to the right by 1, and then adding 1 to its exponent byte. Now that the exponents agree, we can add the magnitude bytes:

$$0000\ 0101 + 0000\ 1011 = 0001\ 0000$$

Since bit 4 of the resulting byte is 1, evidently an "overflow" beyond the assumed binary point has occurred. We compensate by shifting the sum one bit to the right and adding 1 to the (common) exponent. The resulting exponent and magnitude bytes are

$$\text{exponent} = 00000100,\quad \text{magnitude} = 0000\ 1000$$

and it would not be difficult to reassemble these structures back into the 8-bit floating-point format. Once more we may observe that the value in the exponent byte is negative (-4), since bit 2 of that byte is 1, but without looking back at the exponent bytes of the addends, we have no way of determining whether there has been an "exponent overflow." The negative exponent may very well be correct, as we saw in an earlier example.

The procedure of Figure 12.4.1 implements the technique just described, with the sole exception that the exponents are held in 32 bits, as *signed* longwords, a device that facilitates the comparing of the exponents. The function FADD_1

```
;-------------------------------------------------------;
; Function FADD_1 -- adds two FPF-1 floating point      ;
; numbers of like sign with the result returned in the  ;
; low-order byte of R0.  FADD_1 is invoked with CALLG   ;
; or CALLS, the numbers to be added in a table or on    ;
; the stack,  in the low-order bytes of longword        ;
; arguments.  No provision is made for detection of     ;
; exponent overflow.                                    ;
;-------------------------------------------------------;

FADD_1: .WORD    ^M<R1,R2,R3,R4> ;Entry point -- save registers
        MOVZBL   4(AP),R2         ;Get 1st floating point number
        BSBB     FA0800           ;  and decompose it
        MOVQ     R2,R0            ;Put decomposition in R0 and R1
        MOVZBL   8(AP),R2         ;Get 2nd floating point number
        BSBB     FA0800           ;  and decompose it
        SUBL3    R1,R3,R4         ;Subtract exponents
        BLSS     FA0100           ;c(R1) is larger exponent
        MOVL     R3,R1            ;  else put larger exponent in R1
        MNEGL    R4,R4            ;Change sign of exponent difference
        ASHL     R4,R0,R0         ;  and shift smaller magnitude
        BRB      FA0200           ;(Skip around)
FA0100: ASHL     R4,R2,R2         ;Shift smaller magnitude
FA0200: ADDL     R2,R0            ;Add magnitudes
        BITW     #^X0100,R0       ;"Overflow" past binary point?
        BEQL     FA0300           ;No -- skip around
        ASHL     #-1,R0,R0        ;  else shift magnitude of sum
        INCL     R1               ;  and adjust exponent
FA0300: ASHL     #-4,R0,R0        ;Shift magnitude to bits 3:0
        ASHL     #4,R1,R1         ;Move exponent up in R1
        BICB     #^X80,R1         ;  and clear bit 7 (sign bit)
        TSTB     4(AP)            ;Check the sign of the numbers
        BGEQ     FA0400           ;  and skip around if "+"
        BISB     #^X80,R1         ;  else turn on sign bit
FA0400: BISB     R1,R0            ;Put sign and exponent bits in sum
        RET                       ;  and return from function FADD_1

;-------------------------------------------------------;
; Subroutine FA0800 -- decomposes an 8-bit floating     ;
; point number into its magnitude (R2<7:4>) and signed  ;
; exponent (R3<31:0>).  The sign bit is discarded.      ;
;-------------------------------------------------------;

FA0800: MOVL     R2,R3            ;Duplicate floating point number
        BICB     #^X8F,R3         ;Isolate exponent bits
        ROTL     #-7,R3,R3        ;Move exponent to bits 31:29
        ASHL     #-29,R3,R3       ;Shift to bits 2:0, preserving sign
        BICB     #^XF0,R2         ;Isolate floating point magnitude
        ASHL     #4,R2,R2         ;  and shift up to bits 7:4
        RSB                       ;Return to main procedure
```

Figure 12.4.1

will add only floating-point numbers of *like* sign, and the sum is returned in the floating-point format in the low-order byte of R0. The programming is quite straightforward (although it could have been simplified by employing some of the concepts of Chapter 15). The instructions between FA0200: and FA0300: determine whether the sum of the magnitudes has "overflowed" past the assumed binary point and, if it has, provide for shifting the magnitude one bit position to the right and adding one to the common exponent. It is in this last step that a carry into the high-order bit of the exponent may occur, and we observe that the programming makes no provision for detecting this. To do so is more awkward than difficult, but it does require a few lines of instruction to determine whether a resulting negative exponent was caused by overflow or not. (The reader is asked in the exercises what instructions these might be, and suggestions for modification of the scheme to make this determination easier are also given there.)

Since it is the sign bit in the exponent portion of the floating-point representation that seems to be giving so much trouble, we shall revert to a modified unsigned interpretation, but in such a way that we do not simultaneously lose the signed exponent concept. The technique we use involves a *reinterpretation* of the 3 exponent bits—the **excess-4** interpretation—which is described in Figure 12.4.2. The reason for the term "excess-4" should be clear—the *interpretation* of the actual value of the exponent is the *excess beyond 4* of the unsigned binary value of the exponent. Specifically, if we let u be the unsigned value of the exponent, the actual (interpreted) value of the exponent is

$$e = u - 4$$

Such an exponent is referred to as a **biased exponent**. The immediate desired effects of this reinterpretation are: (1) the arithmetic we have already developed (Figure 12.4.1) applies with only trivial changes; and (2) the "exponent overflow" occurs now *not* from 011 to 100, but rather from 111 to (1)000, a phenomenon that is much more easily detected. As is almost always the case in such improvements, we pay a price somewhere else, but in this case the costs are minor. Specifically, the value of the number is slightly more difficult *for us* to construct, since we must now adjust the exponent portion of the representation prior to the evaluation. Some arithmetic—multiplication, for example—is made trivially more complex.

FIGURE 12.4.2

3-bit configuration	Signed binary interpretation	Unsigned binary interpretation	Excess-4 interpretation
111	-1	7	$+3$
110	-2	6	$+2$
101	-3	5	$+1$
100	-4	4	0
011	$+3$	3	-1
010	$+2$	2	-2
001	$+1$	1	-3

Floating-Point Datatypes   Chap. 12

But we shall see (Figure 12.4.3) that it is now very easy to detect exponent overflows and to warn the user that the resulting sum is incorrect.

A further consequence of this change in exponent interpretation is perhaps not so obvious: The low-order 7 bits of two floating-point numbers may now be *compared* arithmetically by means of a CMPB operation, to determine which has the larger absolute value. This could not have been done in the earlier notation, as the reader should verify; of course, even in that less convenient form, the comparison could still have been made, although much less easily.

Before implementing addition for this latest floating-point format, we add one more feature to it. We have established the convention that, to ensure the uniqueness of representations of floating-point numbers, the most significant bit of the magnitude shall occupy bit 3—the highest order of the magnitude bits— and that all numbers will be scaled where necessary to adhere to this convention. But if this is the case, then the actual appearance of that bit is redundant—we may as well *assume* that the high-order bit of the magnitude is 1, without specifically writing it, and this leaves us 4 additional bits for the representation of the magnitude. This assumed 1, in the most significant position of the magnitude bits, is called a **hidden bit**, it never actually appears in the representation, and its use has a number of consequences. First, it contributes further to the difficulty *we* have in interpreting a floating-point representation, since we must now insert the "hidden" bit upon evaluation of the number, and we must remove it when writing values in this format. In addition, it forces us into a special case which is discussed in the next section (although, in fact, that special case has been with us all along). On the positive side, it expands the range and accuracy of numbers that can be represented.

(b) Floating-Point Format-2 (FPF-2)

The FPF-2 representation of a floating point number is

$$s \quad b \; b \; b \quad {}_{\wedge} \quad (1) \; m \; m \; m \; m$$

where s is the sign bit for the magnitude, the b's are the biased exponent bits, interpreted as an *excess-4* 3-bit integer, and the m's are the magnitude bits, the magnitude of the number being represented by these bits preceded by an implied 1.

Floating-point representations in which the most significant bit of the magnitude is the highest-order position of the magnitude bits (in this case, the "hidden" bit), are called **normalized** floating-point representations. The process of scaling the representations where necessary to achieve this configuration is called floating-point-representation **normalization**.

For the record, we give a few examples of floating-point numbers written in this format. The "hidden" bit is shown in parentheses.

```
;-------------------------------------------------------------;
; Function FADD_2 -- adds two FPF-2 floating point            ;
; numbers of like sign with the result returned in the        ;
; low-order byte of R0.  FADD_2 is invoked with CALLG         ;
; or CALLS, the numbers to be added in a table or on          ;
; the stack, in the low-order bytes of longword               ;
; arguments.  FADD_2 returns with the Carry bit set in        ;
; the event of an exponent overflow (in which case            ;
; C(R0) is unpredictable).                                    ;
;-------------------------------------------------------------;

FADD_2: .WORD   ^M<R1,R2,R3,R4> ;Entry point -- save registers
        MOVZBL  4(AP),R2        ;Get 1st floating point number
        BSBB    FA0800          ;   and decompose it
        MOVQ    R2,R0           ;Put decomposition in R0 and R1
        MOVZBL  8(AP),R2        ;Get 2nd floating point number
        BSBB    FA0800          ;   and decompose it
        SUBL3   R1,R3,R4        ;Subtract exponents
        BLSS    FA0100          ;c(R1) is larger exponent
        MOVB    R3,R1           ;   else put larger exponent in R1
        MNEGL   R4,R4           ;Change sign of exponent difference
        ASHL    R4,R0,R0        ;   and shift smaller magnitude
        BRB     FA0200          ;(Skip around)
FA0100: ASHL    R4,R2,R2        ;Shift smaller magnitude
FA0200: ADDB    R2,R0           ;Add magnitudes
        BITB    #^X20,R0        ;"Overflow" past binary point?
        BEQL    FA0300          ;No -- skip around
        ASHL    #-1,R0,R0       ;   else shift magnitude of sum
        INCB    R1              ;   and adjust exponent
FA0300: BICB    #^X10,R0        ;Clear "hidden" bit and
        ASHL    #4,R1,R1        ;   move exponent up in R1
        TSTB    R1              ;Was there exponent overflow?
        BGEQ    FA0400          ;No -- skip around
        BISB    #1,4(FP)        ;   else set caller's C-bit
        RET                     ;   and return
FA0400: TSTL    R3              ;Check the sign of the numbers
        BGEQ    FA0500          ;   and skip around if "+"
        BISB    #^X80,R1        ;   else turn on sign bit
FA0500: BISB    R1,R0           ;Put sign and exponent bits in sum
        RET                     ;   and return from function FADD_2


;-------------------------------------------------------------;
; Subroutine FA0800 -- decomposes an 8-bit floating           ;
; point number into its magnitude (R2<4:0>, with R2<4>        ;
; being the "hidden" high-order bit) and unsigned             ;
; exponent (R3<2:0>).  The sign bit is discarded.             ;
;-------------------------------------------------------------;

FA0800: MOVL    R2,R3           ;Duplicate floating point number
        BICB    #^X8F,R3        ;Isolate exponent bits
        ASHL    #-4,R3,R3       ;   and shift to bits 2:0
        TSTB    R2              ;Sign bit on?
        BGEQ    FA0850          ;No -- skip around
        BISL    #^X80000000,R3  ;   else set bit 31 of exponent reg.
FA0850: BICB    #^XF0,R2        ;Isolate floating point magnitude
        BISB    #^X10,R2        ;Turn on "hidden" bit
        RSB                     ;Return to main procedure
```

Figure 12.4.3

$$0\ 101\ 1000 = +.(1)1000 \cdot 2^{5-4} = +.11000 \cdot 2^1$$
$$= +1.1000_2 = +1.5_{10}$$
$$1\ 011\ 0100 = -.(1)0100 \cdot 2^{3-4} = -.10100 \cdot 2^{-1}$$
$$= -.01010_2 = -0.3125_{10}$$
$$0\ 111\ 1110 = +.(1)1110 \cdot 2^{7-4} = +.11110 \cdot 2^3$$
$$= +111.10_2 = +7.5_{10}$$

Figure 12.4.3 shows the function FADD_2, which adds floating-point numbers (with like sign) which are written in this latest representation. The principal difference between FADD_1 and FADD_2, in addition to managing the "hidden" bit, is that the latter also deals with exponent overflows, by setting or clearing the PSW C-bit, according as the overflow did or did not occur. The calling routine can thus determine when the addition did not proceed properly due to this overflow.

12.5 THE FLOATING-POINT NUMBER ZERO

The reader may have observed that we have assiduously avoided any mention of the floating-point number zero. This was not an oversight, nor was it omitted from our discussions on the grounds that its representation is so trivial as not to deserve mention. Quite the contrary is true, since in fact we have *no* way of representing this number. In our very first attempt at floating-point representations, zero could have been written as *any* representation having 0s in the magnitude bits. But the moment we decided, for reasons of uniqueness of the representation, that the most significant bit of the magnitude should occupy the highest-order position of the magnitude bits, we eliminated the representation of 0, since that number has no most significant bit. Thus 0 has no representation in the format FPF-1, and it certainly has none in the format FPF-2, which actually forces a 1 (the hidden bit) into the number's magnitude.

The reader may also have noted that in describing the excess-4 exponents in the table of Figure 12.4.2, we did *not* include the representation 000, whose value would be interpreted as -4. The reason for this is that this exponent is reserved for a special case, the representation of the floating-point number 0.

Floating-Point Zero. A floating-point number 0 representation is any representation in which the sign and exponent bits are all 0. The magnitude bits play no role in the representation.

It is clear that by adopting this convention, we have made the representation of 0 a special case, and that it *cannot* be manipulated as the other floating-point representations are. That is, routines which deal, say arithmetically, with floating-point numbers must test for and treat zero as a separate case.

12.6 FLOATING-POINT RANGES AND PRECISION

We have already commented that not every number has a representation in floating-point format, and in fact in devoting just 8 bits to the representation, only a handful of numbers do. But even in this limited case it will be worth looking at just which numbers do have such a representation, and which numbers can be approximated in this format.

Evidently the numbers that can be represented are in the range

$$x\ 001\ 0000 \quad \text{to} \quad x\ 111\ 1111 \quad (x = 0,1)$$

That is,

$$1\ 001\ 0000 = -0.0625_{10} \quad \text{to} \quad 1\ 111\ 1111 = -7.75_{10}$$

$$0\ 001\ 0000 = +0.0625_{10} \quad \text{to} \quad 0\ 111\ 1111 = +7.75_{10}$$

together with the special case, $0\ 000\ xxxx = 0.0$. But it is equally evident that not *every* decimal within these ranges can be represented *exactly*, and thus we ask: If a decimal number cannot be represented in the floating-point format, to what degree of accuracy can it be approximated? The question is not easily dealt with, but some experimentation reveals that in general at best only one decimal digit of accuracy can be oriented. For example, it is clear that any integer from 1 to 7 can be represented exactly. In fact, any decimal number between 1.0 and 2.0 can be represented with accuracy to two digits. For example, 1.34 can be represented as $0\ 101\ 0110$, whose actual value is 1.375 but which is still correct to two digits. However, the closest we can come to a representation of 4.6 is

$$0\ 111\ 0010 = 4.5_{10} \quad \text{or} \quad 0\ 111\ 0011 = 4.75_{10}$$

Thus the best precision we can claim for any decimal number within the range of numbers that can be represented in this 8-bit format is single-digit precision.

It should be clear that improved precision could be obtained if more bits were devoted to the number's magnitude. (For example, in *five* bits, with one additional hidden bit, 4.6 can be approximated by $0\ 111\ 00101 = 4.625$.) Thus in general the degree of *precision* of the representation is related to the number of magnitude bits, while the *range* of the numbers that can be represented depends on the number of bits that are allocated to the exponent.

12.7 TRUNCATION VERSUS ROUNDING

Consider the addition problem

$$3.125_{10} + 0.59375_{10}$$

Each of these numbers has a FPF-2 representation, yet their sum—3.71875—does not. To see where the problem lies, consider the details of the addition shown in Figure 12.7.1. The expression at line (c) shows the representation of line (b), including the implied binary-point position and the hidden bit. At line (d) the

Floating-Point Datatypes   Chap. 12

FIGURE 12.7.1

$$\begin{array}{ll}
\text{(a)} & 3.125_{10} + 0.59375_{10} \\
\text{(b)} & = 0\ 110\ 1001 + 0\ 100\ 0011 \\
\text{(c)} & = {}_{\wedge}(1)1001 \cdot 2^2 + {}_{\wedge}(1)0011 \cdot 2^0 \\
\text{(d)} & = {}_{\wedge}11001 \cdot 2^2 + {}_{\wedge}00100[11] \cdot 2^2 \\
\text{(e)} & = {}_{\wedge}11101[11] \cdot 2^2 \\
\text{(f)} & = {}_{\wedge}(1)1101[11] \cdot 2^2 \\
\text{(g)} & = 0\ 110\ 1101 \\
\text{(h)} & = 3.625_{10}
\end{array}$$

second number is scaled down so that its exponent aligns with that of the first number. But notice that 2 bits have been shifted out of the 5 bits allocated for the magnitude. These are shown in brackets. The addition of the magnitudes is now possible, and this is done at line (e). In converting back to FPF-2 representation in line (f), we once again "hide" the most significant bit and take the next highest 4 bits as the magnitude bits. But observe that this requires dropping the 2 bits that had been shifted down in the course of exponent alignment. Lines (g) and (h) complete the process.

The inaccuracy of the representation of the sum is evidently tied directly to this **truncation** or **chopping** of the two shifted bits, and it is equally clear that there is no way to avoid this truncation, since we are restricted to 4 actual magnitude bits. However, it seems that a more accurate (but still not precise) representation could be achieved if the two shifted bits [11] had been allowed to "overflow" into the next-higher bit position—that is, if the result had been "rounded up." Thus if we allow these shifted bits to influence their immediate predecessor, the last three steps of Figure 12.7.1 would be

$$\text{(f)} = {}_{\wedge}(1)1101[11] \cdot 2^2$$

$$\text{(f}') = ({}_{\wedge}(1)1101 + {}_{\wedge}(0)0001) \cdot 2^2$$

$$\text{(g)} = 0\ 110\ 1110$$

$$\text{(h)} = 3.75_{10}$$

which is a better approximation to the actual result, 3.71875. The approach we have taken here is the following: If the highest order of the bits to be truncated is a 1, we allow it to "overflow" into the next-higher bit position, which is accomplished by adding 1 to that next bit. If it is 0, we make no such adjustment. We can remove the decision making here simply by adding 1 to the highest order of the bits to be truncated. Thus line (f') above could be replaced by

$$\text{(f}'') = ({}_{\wedge}(1)1101[11] + {}_{\wedge}(0)0000[10] \cdot 2^2$$

The **rounding** of arithmetic results is thus accomplished as follows. The floating-point representations of the numbers that enter into the arithmetic are expanded out to two additional bits, which are taken as additional low-order bits of the magnitude, and which are given the initial value 00. These bits are called **guard bits,** and upon completion of the arithmetic operation, rounding is achieved by adding the bit configuration 10 to the guard bits, prior to the truncation back to 4 magnitude bits (or 5, including the hidden bit). Using guard bits, the computations of Figure 12.7.1 are given in Figure 12.7.2, where the guard bits are shown in *italics*. Notice that the guard bits have been inserted at line (c), and that the shifting in line (d), required to align the exponents, has shifted the guard bits of the second addend out of the 7 bits allocated for the magnitude, and they are replaced by the two low-order bits of the original magnitude. The rounding takes place in line (e), where 0000010 is added to the magnitude of the result (equivalent to adding *10* to the guard bits), and the guard bits are then discarded in line (f), where the truncated bits are shown in square brackets. The listing of Figure 12.7.3 shows the modification of the function FADD_2 of Figure 12.4.3 to achieve rounding. The differences involve the saving of the guard bits when the floating-point representation is decomposed by the subroutine at FA0800; the addition of the bit configuration *10* at FA0300, and the subsequent further testing for possible overflows beyond the assumed binary point.

The reader may be puzzled that we have allowed for *two* guard bits, for it would appear that only the higher order of these could affect the end result. Indeed, this is the case *for addition*, where shifting always takes place only to the right, into lower-order bits. But in the case of subtraction—equivalently, an addition in which the addends have opposite signs—there can be a subsequent shifting *to the left*, into *higher*-order bits. Consider, for example, the addition problem

$$1.0 + (-0.421875)$$

We present the result in Figure 12.7.4, and then explain several of the critical steps.

FIGURE 12.7.2

(a) $3.125_{10} + 0.59375_{10}$

(b)   = 0 110 1001 + 0 100 0011

(c)   = $_\wedge(1)100100 \cdot 2^2 + _\wedge(1)001100 \cdot 2^0$

(d)   = $_\wedge1100100 \cdot 2^2 + _\wedge0010011 \cdot 2^2$

(e)   = $(_\wedge1110111 + _\wedge0000010) \cdot 2^2$

(f)   = $_\wedge(1)1110[01] \cdot 2^2$

(g)   = 0 110 1110

(h)   = 3.75_{10}

The development proceeds as usual through step (d), the numbers being decomposed into their magnitudes and powers of 2, with 2 guard bits being appended (shown again in italics). Since the signs are *not* the same, a *subtraction* is involved, and in a sign-magnitude system, this is achieved by *negating* the number with smaller absolute value and then adding. Since the second number (0.42185) has smaller absolute value, we negate it in line (e) by taking its *7-bit twos-com-*

```
;-----------------------------------------------------------;
; Function FADD_2R -- adds two FPF-2 floating point         ;
; numbers of like sign with the rounded result returned     ;
; in the low-order byte of R0.  FADD_2R is invoked with     ;
; CALLG or CALLS, the numbers to be added in a table or     ;
; on the stack, in the low-order bytes of longword          ;
; arguments.  FADD_2R returns with the Carry bit set in     ;
; the event of an exponent overflow (in which case          ;
; C(R0) is unpredictable).                                  ;
;-----------------------------------------------------------;

FADD_2R:.WORD    ^M<R1,R2,R3,R4> ;Entry point -- save registers
        MOVZBL   4(AP),R2        ;Get 1st floating point number
        BSBB     FA0800          ;   and decompose it
        MOVQ     R2,R0           ;Put decomposition in R0 and R1
        MOVZBL   8(AP),R2        ;Get 2nd floating point number
        BSBB     FA0800          ;   and decompose it
        SUBL3    R1,R3,R4        ;Subtract exponents
        BLSS     FA0100          ;c(R1) is larger exponent
        MOVB     R3,R1           ;   else put larger exponent in R1
        MNEGL    R4,R4           ;Change sign of exponent difference
        ASHL     R4,R0,R0        ;   and shift smaller magnitude
        BRB      FA0200          ;(Skip around)
FA0100: ASHL     R4,R2,R2        ;Shift smaller magnitude
FA0200: ADDB     R2,R0           ;Add magnitudes
        BITB     #^X80,R0        ;"Overflow" past binary point?
        BEQL     FA0300          ;No -- skip around
        ASHL     #-1,R0,R0       ;   else shift magnitude of sum
        INCB     R1              ;   and adjust exponent
FA0300: ADDB     #2,R0           ;Add 1 to first "guard" bit
        BITB     #^X80,R0        ;"Overflow" past binary point?
        BEQL     FA0350          ;No -- skip around
        ASHL     #-1,R0,R0       ;   else shift magnitude of sum
        INCB     R1              ;   and adjust exponent
FA0350: BICB     #^X40,R0        ;Clear "hidden" bit and
        ASHL     #-2,R0,R0       ;   shift magnitude to bits 3:0
        ASHL     #4,R1,R1        ;Move exponent up in R1
        TSTB     R1              ;Was there exponent overflow?
        BGEQ     FA0400          ;No -- skip around
        BISB     #1,4(FP)        ;   else set caller's C-bit
        RET                      ;   and return
FA0400: TSTL     R3              ;Check the sign of the numbers
        BGEQ     FA0500          ;   and skip around if "+"
        BISB     #^X80,R1        ;   else turn on sign bit
FA0500: BISB     R1,R0           ;Put sign and exponent bits in sum
        RET                      ;   and return from function FADD_2R
```

Figure 12.7.3

```
;-------------------------------------------------------;
; Subroutine FA0800 -- decomposes an 8-bit floating     ;
; point number into its magnitude (R2<6:2>, with R2<6>  ;
; being the "hidden" high-order bit) and unsigned       ;
; exponent (R3<2:0>).  The sign bit is placed in R3<31> ;
;-------------------------------------------------------;

FA0800: MOVL    R2,R3           ;Duplicate floating point number
        BICB    #^X8F,R3        ;Isolate exponent bits
        ASHL    #-4,R3,R3       ; and shift to bits 2:0
        TSTB    R2              ;Sign bit on?
        BGEQ    FA0850          ;No -- skip around
        BISL    #^X80000000,R3  ; else set bit 31 of exponent reg.
FA0850: BICB    #^XF0,R2        ;Isolate floating point magnitude
        ASHL    #2,R2,R2        ; and shift up to bits 5:2
        BISB    #^X40,R2        ;Turn on "hidden" bit
        RSB                     ;Return to main procedure
```

Figure 12.7.3 (continued)

plement. Now this second number, in its negated form, still requires a shift right by 2 to align the exponents, and this is done in line (f). But notice that the vacated high-order bits are filled with 1s, not 0s, since this number had been negated. The addition can now take place, and the result at line (g) shows that a 1 has overflowed past the assumed binary point. But this must *always* take place, when a smaller

FIGURE 12.7.4

$$
\begin{array}{lll}
\text{(a)} & & 1.0_{10} + (-0.421875_{10}) \\
\text{(b)} & = & 0\ 101\ 0000 + 1\ 011\ 1011 \\
\text{(c)} & = & _{\wedge}(1)000000{\cdot}2^1 - _{\wedge}(1)101100{\cdot}2^{-1} \\
\text{(d)} & = & _{\wedge}1000000{\cdot}2^1 - _{\wedge}1101100{\cdot}2^{-1} \\
\text{(e)} & = & _{\wedge}1000000{\cdot}2^1 + _{\wedge}0010100{\cdot}2^{-1} \\
\text{(f)} & = & _{\wedge}1000000{\cdot}2^1 + _{\wedge}1100101{\cdot}2^1 \\
\text{(g)} & = & 1_{\wedge}0100101{\cdot}2^1 \\
\text{(h)} & = & _{\wedge}0100101{\cdot}2^1 \\
\text{(i)} & = & _{\wedge}1001010{\cdot}2^0 \\
\text{(j)} & = & (_{\wedge}1001010 + _{\wedge}0000010){\cdot}2^0 \\
\text{(k)} & = & _{\wedge}1001100{\cdot}2^0 \\
\text{(l)} & = & _{\wedge}(1)0011[00]{\cdot}2^0 \\
\text{(m)} & = & 0\ 100\ 0011 \\
\text{(n)} & = & 0.59375_{10}
\end{array}
$$

Floating-Point Datatypes   Chap. 12

number is subtracted from a larger, and in fact this 1 is *not* a part of the result. Thus, as shown in line (h), this leading 1 is *discarded*. But notice that the resulting magnitude is not *normalized*—that is, the most significant bit is not the hidden 1. Thus in line (i) we shift the magnitude *to the left* and adjust the exponent down to 0. At line (j) the rounding factor *10* is added into the guard bits, which are then truncated at line (1). Finally, in line (m) we rebuild the FPF-2 representation of the result, using the positive sign (leading bit = 0), since it was the positive addend which had the larger magnitude.

The reader is asked to show that if only *one* guard bit had been maintained in this process, the critical guard bits *10* of line (j), to which the rounding bits *10* were added, would be the bit combination *00* instead, and no rounding up would have taken place.

With the introduction of mixed-sign addition, there is a further type of error that may occur and of which we have not yet made mention—exponent *underflow*. **Floating-point underflow** occurs when the nonzero result of an operation is too small, in absolute value, to be represented in the floating-point format. As an example, consider the addition $+0.125 + (-0.12109375)$. In the FPF-2 representation, this addition is

$$0\ 010\ 0000 + 1\ 001\ 1111$$

Without going through all the details, we find that after complementing and scaling the second of these numbers, the addition reduces to

$$_\wedge 1000000 \cdot 2^{-2} + _\wedge 10000010 \cdot 2^{-2}$$

$$= 1_\wedge 0000010 \cdot 2^{-2}$$

As before, the "overflow" 1 is discarded, and now in order to normalize the resulting representation, a shift left of five places would be required. But this would necessitate adjusting the exponent to -7, which exponent simply does not exist in our excess-4 system. Since there is no way to salvage the situation, we can only indicate that the operation has resulted in a nonrepresentable number. (This is the low-order counterpart of exponent overflow, which occurs when the absolute value of a result requires too *large* an exponent to be represented in the floating-point format).

We offer in Figure 12.7.5 a function FADD that returns the sum of two FPF-2 floating-point numbers whether of the same or opposite sign. It deals with exponent overflow, as before, and also exponent *underflow*. The programming is a vast diversion from that of FADD_2 or FADD_2R, for most of the work is done in memory (on the stack) rather than in registers, since registers cannot be indexed, nor can their individual bytes (other than the low-order one) be referenced. The differences result from the necessity for keeping track of the ultimate sign of the result and for the complementing of one of the numbers. It is by no means as straightforward as the previous functions, but by traversing the algorithm with a specific example, the reader will encounter each of the steps shown in Figure 12.7.4.

```
;----------------------------------------------------------------;
; Function FADD -- adds two FPF-2 floating point numbers of      ;
; like or opposite signs, with the rounded result returned       ;
; in the low-order byte of R0.  FADD is invoked with CALLG        ;
; or CALLS, the numbers to be added in a table or on the         ;
; stack, in the low-order bytes of longword arguments.  In       ;
; the event of exponent overflow or underflow, FADD returns      ;
; with the C-bit or V-bit set, respectively, and c(R0) is        ;
; unpredictable.                                                  ;
;----------------------------------------------------------------;

FADD:    .WORD    ^M<R1>                     ;Save one scratch register
         MOVZBL   4(AP),-(SP)                ;Stack first
         MOVZBL   8(AP),-(SP)                ;  and second numbers
         MOVL     4(SP),-(SP)                ;Make a copy of first number
         MOVB     (SP),-(SP)                 ;Then duplicate numbers on
         MOVB     5(SP),-(SP)                ;  stack, as bytes
         BICW     #^X8F8F,(SP)               ;Clear off sign and magnitude bits
         CLRL     R0                         ;Get a zero index
FA0020:  BITL     #^XF0,2(SP)[R0]            ;Is addend = 0?
         BNEQ     FA0040                     ;No -- skip around
         MOVL     6(SP)[R0],R0               ;Yes -- put other number in R0
         RET                                 ;  and return
FA0040:  ASHL     #1,2(SP)[R0],2(SP)[R0]     ;Shift sign bit to next byte
         AOBLEQ   #2,R0,FA0020               ;(Do for all 3 longwords)
         MOVL     #-1,R1                     ;Set indicator
         CLRL     R0                         ;Get a zero
         CMPB     3(SP),7(SP)                ;Same signs?
         BEQL     FA0100                     ;Yes -- continue processing
         MOVL     #2,R1                      ;  else reset position indicator
         CMPB     2(SP),6(SP)                ;Compare the two numbers
         BLSSU    FA0060                     ;Skip if first less than second
         BGTRU    FA0080                     ;  or second less than first
         RET                                 ;  else return with c(R0) = 0
FA0060:  XORB     #1,11(SP)                  ;Toggle the sign of result
         DECL     R1                         ;Decrement position indicator
FA0080:  DECL     R1                         ;Decrement position indicator
         BISB     #2,11(SP)                  ;Set "opposite signs" flag

FA0100:  ASHL     #1,2(SP)[R0],2(SP)[R0]     ;Shift magnitude up one more,
         BISL     #^X40,2(SP)[R0]            ;  and set "hidden" bit
         BICL     #^XFF80,2(SP)[R0]          ;Clear off sign/exponent bits
         CMPL     R0,R1                      ;At "sign change" position?
         BNEQ     FA0120                     ;No -- skip
         MNEGL    2(SP)[R0],2(SP)[R0]        ;  else negate smaller magnitude

FA0120:  AOBLEQ   #1,R0,FA0100               ;Do next number
         CLRL     R0                         ;Get zero index
         SUBB3    (SP),1(SP),R1              ;Subtract exponents,
         CVTBL    R1,R1                      ;  convert to signed longword
         ASHL     #-4,R1,R1                  ;  and shift difference down
         BEQL     FA0200                     ;They agree -- no scaling required
         BLSS     FA0140                     ;Second exponent greater than first
         INCL     R0                         ;  else reset index
         MNEGL    R1,R1                      ;  and change sign of difference
```

Figure 12.7.5

```
FA0140:  ASHL    R1,2(SP)[R0],2(SP)[R0]  ;Shift magnitude down to right
         BICL    #^X80,2(SP)[R0]         ;  and turn off sign bit

FA0200:  MOVB    (SP)[R0],10(SP)         ;Save exponent of result
         ADDB3   2(SP),6(SP),R0          ;Add magnitudes
         BITB    #2,11(SP)               ;Opposite signs?
         BNEQ    FA0300                  ;Yes -- rescale
         TSTB    R0                      ;Overflow past assumed binary point?
         BGEQ    FA0400                  ;No -- skip around
         ASHL    #-1,R0,R0               ;  else scale magnitude down
         ADDB    #^X10,10(SP)            ;  and adjust exponent
         BGEQ    FA0400                  ;Continue if no exponent overflow
FA0220:  BISB    #1,4(FP)                ;  else set caller's C-bit
         RET                             ;  and return

FA0300:  BICB    #^X80,R0               ;Turn off "subtraction carry"
FA0320:  BITB    #^X40,R0               ;"Hidden" bit here?
         BNEQ    FA0400                  ;Yes -- properly scaled
         ASHL    #1,R0,R0                ;  else shift left
         SUBB    #^X10,10(SP)            ;  and adjust exponent
         BGTR    FA0320                  ;Check next bit if no "underflow"
         BISB    #2,4(FP)                ;  else set caller's V-bit
         RET                             ;  and return

FA0400:  ADDB    #2,R0                   ;Add 1 to high-order guard bit
         BGEQ    FA0420                  ;Skip if no overflow
         ASHL    #-1,R0,R0               ;  else shift down
         ADDB    #^X10,10(SP)            ;  and adjust exponent
         BLSS    FA0220                  ;Exponent overflow!
FA0420:  ASHL    #-2,R0,R0               ;Shift down
         BICB    #^X10,R0               ;Remove "hidden" bit
         BISB    10(SP),R0               ;  and insert exponent
         BITB    #1,11(SP)               ;Sign bit "negative"?
         BEQL    FA0440                  ;No -- done
         BISB    #^X80,R0               ;  else set sign bit
FA0440:  RET                             ;Return from procedure
```

Figure 12.7.5 (Continued)

12.8 CLOSING COMMENTS

The 8-bit floating-point representations developed in the preceding sections are clearly too small to be of real use. But we have discovered many important aspects of such representations, and the transitions to more practical formats should now cause us no problems. It is important to note that the final representation that we devised—FPF-2—is not *the* floating-point representation, since in fact there are several such formats currently in use by various computer systems. To see why the representation is not unique, we need only review the processes we went through to arrive at FPF-2. There were numerous decisions that we made—how many bits to allocate to the exponent and to the magnitude, which bit to use as a sign bit, the biasing of the exponent, how many guard bits to use, and so on—and in each case there was little if anything to dictate that one of several choices *had to* be made. The particular scheme that we developed is compatible with the floating-point representations used on the VAX, as will be seen in the next section. Other systems may make other choices, thus arriving at different (but no less useful) formats.

12.9 *VAX FLOATING-POINT REPRESENTATIONS*

The VAX hardware supports four types of floating-point data, referred to as **F_floating, D_floating, G_floating,** and **H_floating,** although some VAX models, depending on their configurations, implement only the first two of these.* Each occupies 4, 8, or 16 bytes (one, two, or four longwords), and each allocates a single bit for the **sign,** some contiguous bits for the **exponent,** and the remaining bits for the **magnitude** or **fraction.** The exponent bits are in excess-*n* form, and the magnitude bits assume a hidden high-order bit, which is taken to be immediately to the right of the implied binary point. We shall go into some detail in the discussion of F_floating format numbers, the remaining representations being analogous.

An F_floating representation occupies a 32-bit longword. Bit 15 is the sign bit, bits 14:7 are the biased excess-128 exponent, bits 6:0 are the more significant bits of the magnitude (after the hidden bit, which is the most significant magnitude bit), and bits 31:16 form the less significant magnitude bits, with bit 16 the least significant of these (see Figure 12.9.1). Thus there are 24 magnitude bits, including the hidden bit, and these we number from 23 down to 0, 0 being the least significant. Figure 12.9.2 gives another view of the two words that make up this representation, which makes more evident the ordering of magnitude bits, from high order to low order.

The range of values that can be taken on by F_floating format numbers is approximately $\pm 2.9 \cdot 10^{-39}$ to $\pm 1.7 \cdot 10^{+38}$. The 24 magnitude bits yield a precision that is approximately equal to seven decimal digits. These concepts are summarized below, followed without further comment by the descriptions of the other floating-point representations. The reader should note, however, that while both D_floating and G_floating numbers occupy 8 bytes, they differ in their allocations of exponent and magnitude bits, and thus they yield different ranges and levels of precision. In each format the (binary) value of the floating-point number is

$$\pm 0.1mm \ldots mm \cdot 2^{(\text{exponent} - 2^{n-1})}$$

where *mm...mm* are the magnitude bits, *n* is the *number* of exponent bits, and the sign is positive if $s = 0$, negative if $s = 1$. The number whose sign and exponent bits are all 0 is taken to be the floating-point number 0, regardless of the value of the magnitude bits. Any number whose sign is 1 and whose exponent

---

*The single-chip version of the VAX processor, the MicroVAX, does not directly implement floating-point numbers. Those models that include the optional Floating Point Unit (FPU) chip implement operations in the F_floating, G_floating, and D_floating instruction groups—those and other floating-point data types and instructions can be emulated via software on models without the FPU chip. In a similar fashion, larger VAX models whose processors support only F_ and D_floating numbers can also emulate G_ and H_floating numbers in software.

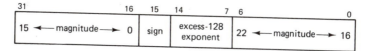

Figure 12.9.1

bits are all 0 is invalid, and reference to such a number will result in a *reserved operand exception*.

(a) F_Floating Representation

Numbers written in F_floating format occupy 32 bits (4 bytes), numbered from 31 down to 0. Bit 15 is the sign bit. Bits 14:7 form the biased excess-128 exponent. A single hidden magnitude bit, with value 1, is assumed immediately to the right of the implied binary point. The remaining magnitude bits, in order of decreasing significance, are 6:0 and 31:16. F_floating numbers take on a range of values approximately $\pm 2.9 \cdot 10^{-39}$ to $\pm 1.7 \cdot 10^{+38}$, to a precision of approximately seven decimal digits.

(b) D_Floating Representation

Numbers written in D_floating format occupy 64 bits (8 bytes), numbered from 63 to 0. Bit 15 is the sign bit. Bits 14:7 form the biased excess-128 exponent. A single hidden magnitude bit, with value 1, is assumed immediately to the right of the implied binary point. The remaining magnitude bits, in order of decreasing significance, are 6:0, 31:16, 47:32, and 63:48. D_floating numbers take on a range of values approximately $\pm 2.9 \cdot 10^{-39}$ to $\pm 1.7 \cdot 10^{+38}$, to a precision of approximately 16 decimal digits [see Figure 12.9.3(a)].

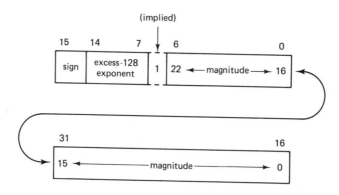

Figure 12.9.2

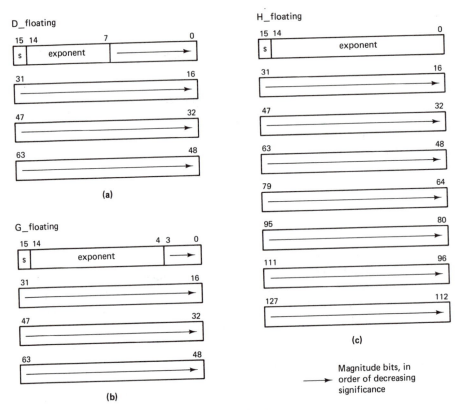

Figure 12.9.3

(c) G_Floating Representation

Numbers written in G_floating format occupy 64 bits (8 bytes), numbered from 63 down to 0. Bit 15 is the sign bit. Bits 14:4 form the biased excess-1024 exponent. A single hidden magnitude bit, with value 1, is assumed immediately to the right of the implied binary point. The remaining magnitude bits, in order of decreasing significance, are 3:0, 31:16, 47:32, and 63:48. G_floating numbers take on a range of values approximately $\pm 5.6 \cdot 10^{-309}$ to $\pm 0.9 \cdot 10^{+308}$, to a precision of approximately 15 decimal digits [see Figure 12.9.3(b)].

(d) H_Floating Representation

Numbers written in H_floating format occupy 128 bits (16 bytes), numbered from 127 down to 0. Bit 15 is the sign bit. Bits 14:0 form the biased excess-16384 exponent. A single hidden magnitude bit, with value 1, is assumed immediately to the right of the implied binary point. The remaining magnitude bits, in order of decreasing significance, are 31:16, 47:32, 63:48, 79:64, 95:80, 111:96, and 127:112. H_floating numbers take on a range of values approximately $\pm 8.4 \cdot 10^{-4933}$ to $\pm 5.9 \cdot 10^{+4931}$, to a precision of approximately 33 decimal digits [see Figure 12.9.3(c)].

12.10 FLOATING-POINT DIRECTIVES

The assembler directives that deal with floating-point data either allocate storage for floating-point numbers (analogous to .BLKW) or generate floating-point values (analogous to .WORD). They are as follows:

.BLKD, .BLKF, .BLKG, .BLKH The single argument for each of these directives is a numerical-valued expression. The effect is the generation by the assembler of a block of storage consisting of $n \cdot v$ bytes, where $n = 4$ (for .BLKF) 8 (for .BLKD and .BLKG), or 16 (for .BLKH), and v is the value of the expression. For example,

$$.BLKG \quad 2*\langle\langle 1+7\rangle/3\rangle$$

will allocate 32 bytes at the current position of the assembler's location counter, since for .BLKG, $n = 8$, and the value of the expression is 4.

.D_FLOATING, .F_FLOATING, .G_FLOATING, .H_FLOATING Each of the directive takes one or more floating-point literal arguments, and for each the assembler generates 8, 4, 8, or 16 bytes, respectively, containing the floating-point literal(s) in the specified format. Literals may be entered in their integer/fraction form (for example, 127.92884) or in an integer/fraction/exponent form (the **scientific notation**), in which the exponent is specified by the character "E" followed by a signed integer, interpreted as that integer power of 10. For example, 1.2792884E2 is interpreted as $1.2792884 \cdot 10^2 = 127.92884$, which could also be represented by $12792.884E-2 = 12792.884 \cdot 10^{-2}$.

.DOUBLE, .FLOAT These directives are equivalent to .D_FLOATING and .F_FLOATING, respectively.

12.11 FLOATING-POINT OPERATIONS

The VAX implements numerous operations on floating-point datatypes, including logical, arithmetic, and data transfer and conversion operations. Since these have already been discussed for the integer datatypes, and since their effects do not differ substantially for floating-point operands, we simply list these operations below; the reader will find the details in Appendix A. These operations all have variations that act on the four datatypes—F, D, G, and H—although once again we advise that not all VAX systems implement G_floating and H_floating datatypes and their operations.

Data transfer operations

CVT   MNEG   MOV   MOVA   PUSHA

Arithmetic operations

ADD   CLR   DIV   MUL   SUB

Miscellaneous operations

ACB   CMP   TST

In addition to the reserved operand exception already mentioned, some of these operations may result in *floating-point overflow* (in which the result has too large an exponent to be held in the allocated exponent bits) or *floating-point underflow* (in which the nonzero result is too small to be represented with the given exponent bits). The processor will always treat floating-point overflow as an exception; whether or not the processor treats underflow as an exception depends on the state of the FU bit (bit 6) in the PSW. If this bit is set at the time a floating-point underflow occurs, the processor will treat that event as an exception (and in particular, as a *fault*; see Chapter 11). This bit may be set or cleared by using the BISPSW and BICPSW operations.

There are two further operations that apply to floating-point operands which do not have integer datatype counterparts, and which perform rather complex operations for the evaluation of mathematical functions. These are EMOD (an extended multiply operation which splits the resulting product into its integer and fractional parts) and POLY (which evaluates polynomial functions, given the function's argument and coefficients). These are not discussed here; the interested reader is directed to the Digital Equipment Corporation *VAX Architecture Handbook*.

12.12 ADDRESSING MODE CONSIDERATIONS

All addressing modes are valid for the floating-point operations. For modes 8 (autoincrement), 7 (autodecrement) and 4 (index) we need to know the *context* of the operation, and for the floating-point operations, the context depends on the operation type. As is expected, the contexts of F_, D_, G_, and H_floating operations are 4, 8, 8, and 16 bytes, respectively. For example,

MOVD   X,(R3)+

will move the D_floating number at X into the 8-byte structure whose address is in R3, and c(R3) will have been incremented by 8.

The short literal "modes" (modes 0, 1, 2, and 3) are also valid for floating-point operations, but the range of floating-point numbers that can be generated by a short literal is extremely limited. To see why, we need to know how the processor interprets a short literal floating-point number of type F_, D_, G_, or H_floating. Recall that in short literal mode, the "mode" byte must have its two high-order bits, 7:6, equal to 0, the operand itself then consisting of bits 5:0. In floating-point operations, these bits are divided between exponent bits and mag-

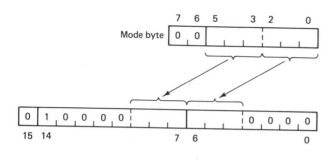

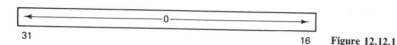

Figure 12.12.1

nitude bits as follows: Bits 5:3 are used as the low-order (least-significant) exponent bits, and bits 2:0 are used as the high-order (most-significant) magnitude bits. Furthermore, both the number itself and the exponent are assumed to be non-negative, the latter implying that the high-order exponent bit is 1. Thus the resulting floating-point operand can be thought of as a normally formed floating-point number in which the sign bit is 0; the high-order exponent bit is 1, the three low-order exponent bits are bits 5:3 of the short literal mode byte, the remaining exponent bits being 0; and the three high-order bits of the magnitude are bits 2:0 of the short literal mode byte, all other magnitude bits being 0. Figure 12.12.1 illustrates this scheme for F_floating operands, the situation being analogous for D_, G_, and H_floating operands.

As an example of this construction, consider the mode byte 00010110. This decomposes into bits 7:6, 5:3, and 2:0 as

$$00 \ 010 \ 110$$

so that we have 010 as the low-order exponent bits and 110 as the high-order magnitude bits. Thus the floating-point number generated (shown here in its F_floating form) is

$$\underbrace{0000000000000000}_{\text{magnitude (low order)}} \ \underbrace{0}_{\text{sign}} \ \underbrace{10000 \ 010}_{\text{exponent}} \ \underbrace{110 \ 0000}_{\text{magnitude (high order)}}$$

= ^X00004160, whose value in decimal is 3.5. We leave it to the reader to verify that the smallest floating-point number that can be generated by a short literal construction is the number 0.5, which is generated by the mode byte 00000000, and the largest such is 120.0, generated by the mode byte 00111111.

Care must be taken when *forcing* a short literal construction by using the symbol S^. For even if the number in question is in the range 0.5 to 120.0, it may not be one of the few numbers in that range which can be generated as a floating-point short literal. Numbers outside that range will generate short literals that are quite incorrect. This results from the method used by the *assembler* to construct the short literal—the "mode" byte—which is as follows. When the assembler is asked to construct a short literal to be used as a floating-point number, it constructs it as a floating-point number which is *consistent with the context of the operation*. That is, if the context of the operation is, say, D_floating, the assembler constructs the specified number as a D_floating number. It then takes the three low-order exponent bits and uses them as bits 5:3 of the short literal mode byte, and it takes the three high-order magnitude bits and uses them as bits 2:0 of that byte. It does so without regard to the correctness or incorrectness of the representation. For example, the number 341 in the instruction

$$\text{MOVF } S\hat{}\#341.,R4$$

will be treated as follows. 341., in F_floating format is

$$1000000000000000 \quad 0 \quad 10001001 \quad 0101010$$

The "mode" byte that is constructed will have 00 as bits 7:6, the three low-order exponent bits 001 as bits 5:3, and the three high-order magnitude bits 010 as bits 2:0; thus the constructed byte will be 00001010 = 0A. But as a floating-point short literal, the value of this byte is (decimal) 1.25. The source of the inaccuracy is not only the truncation of significant magnitude bits, but also the far more serious loss of an exponent bit.

12.13 EXERCISES

12.3.1. It was stated in Section 12.3 that no power of 2 is a multiple of 10. Justify this statement.

12.3.2. Some fractional numbers (1/10, for example) can be written as the finite sum of powers of 10, whereas others cannot (for instance, 1/3). Show that any number which can be written as a finite sum of powers of 2 also has a finite decimal representation.

12.4.1. One of the consequences of adopting the convention that the most significant bit of the magnitude of a floating-point number (having 3 exponent bits and 5 magnitude bits) is in bit position 4 is that it reduces the *range* of the numbers that can be represented. Show that the smallest nonzero number that can be represented in this format is

$$10010000 = .1 \cdot 2^{-4} = .00001 = 0.03125_{10}$$

if we adhere to this convention, while the smallest such is 0.001953125 if we do not.

12.4.2. State the smallest and largest (in absolute value) numbers that can be written using the FPF-1 representation.

12.4.3. What is the representation of the number 0 in the FPF-1 format?

12.4.4. Show that in adding two FPF-1 numbers, overflows of the sum beyond the assumed binary point can never exceed a single binary digit.

12.4.5. Add appropriate instructions to the procedure of Figure 12.4.1 to determine if a 1 in the exponent's sign bit resulted from exponent overflow. (*Suggestion:* If the exponent was *originally* 1, bits 31:3 of the exponent's longword will also be 1s.)

12.4.6. Show that the detection of exponent overflow during the addition of FPF-1 numbers is simplified if the exponents reside in bits 7:5 of a byte, rather than in bits 2:0, as in the function FADD_1 of Figure 12.4.1. What changes in the programming of FADD_1 would be required to implement this change?

12.4.7. In the FPF-1 representation, why cannot the 7-bit combination of exponent and magnitude be used to compare the relative sizes of the two numbers? Specifically, assuming that two such representations reside in bytes labeled X and Y, show that the instruction

CMPB X,Y

will give *no* information about the relative sizes of the two numbers. How *can* these numbers be compared as to relative size? Show, however, that

CMPB X,Y

will give information about their relative sizes for numbers written in FPF-2 format.

12.5.1. Show that neither of the functions FADD_1 or FADD_2 will properly deal with additions in which one of the addends is the floating point 0.

12.7.1. Write the following numbers in FPF-2 format, and calculate the sums, assuming *no* rounding of the result (that is, assuming no use of guard bits).
   (a) 3.125 + 1.0625   **(b)** 3.125 + (−1.0625)
   (c) 1.5 + 0.9375   **(d)** 1.5 + (−0.9375)

12.7.2. Calculate the sums shown in Exercise 12.7.1, assuming the use of two guard bits for rounding purposes.

12.7.3. When the twos-complement of 0.421875 was shifted right at line (f) of Figure 12.7.2, why were 1s used to fill the vacated bits?

12.7.4. It was shown at line (g) of Figure 12.7.2 that a 1 overflowed beyond the binary point, but it was stated that this was to be *expected* and that the 1 was to be *discarded*. Justify the statement and the procedure.

12.7.5. Show that if only one guard bit had been used in the floating-point representations of Figure 12.7.2, *no* rounding would have taken place.

12.7.6. The function FADD of Figure 12.7.5 is complicated somewhat by the fact that if, after twos-complementing, the negated number still needs to be shifted to accommodate exponent alignment, 1s must be used to fill the vacated bits. Could this problem have been eliminated if the shifting for exponent alignment had taken place *prior to* twos-complementing? Explain, and take into account any further consequences of making such a change.

12.9.1. Write the hexadecimal form of the F_, D_, G_, and H_floating representations of each of the following decimal numbers.
   (a) 3.125   **(b)** −134.8203125   **(c)** 1024.525
   (d) 1/8192   **(e)** 0.76953025   **(f)** −3.078121

12.9.2. Show what decimal number is represented by each of the following hexadecimal numbers, interpreted as representing an F_floating number.
   (a) 0000C0A0   **(b)** 8000C0A0   **(c)** C000510F

12.12.1. Write a table of all numbers that can be represented as a short literal.

12.12.2. Tell what numbers each of the following short literals represents.

    (a) 39   **(b)** 0F   **(c)** 1A   **(d)** 2D   **(e)** 38

12.12.3. Tell what short literal the assembler will generate for each of the decimal numbers shown below, and state the actual value of the short literal that is generated.

    (a) 3.75   **(b)** 0.0625   **(c)** 15.0   **(d)** 121.0   **(e)** 0.0

13 NUMERICAL STRING DATATYPES*

13.1 STRINGS OF DIGITS

Since our earliest considerations of numbers and computer number systems we have had to contend with the complications caused by the need for (or, minimally, the desirability of) a dual representation for integers. Because of physical characteristics of main memory units and registers, the base-2 representation system is the most natural for the hardware, and most general-purpose computers perform twos-complement arithmetic on such binary number representations. Of course, *we* are most comfortable with decimal (base-10) representations. Conflicts arise when *both* representations are required in a particular application, and in fact this is normally the case. The user may input to a program some datum, say 17294, which appears to the *user* to be a number, but which appears to the *computer system* to be simply a string of 5 ASCII-coded decimal digits. If arithmetic needs to be done on this "number" 17294, it must be in its *binary* representation, not its representation as a string of decimal characters. And if some result is to be reported to the user, perhaps by printing on the user's terminal, then it should be in the form of an appropriate string of numerical characters; the binary representation of the result will not be useful here. Thus to make the computing system useful, we must accept this dual representation and the fact that numbers will have

---

*The single-chip version of the VAX processor, the MicroVAX, does not implement these data types *directly* in the CPU. However, the processor hardware does indicate to the operating system that an instruction in this group has been attempted, and the operating system then invokes system software to emulate that operation. Thus to the user, the appearance is that the instruction has been executed directly by the CPU.

to be converted between these representations, for their internal and external uses. Fortunately, such conversions are not particularly difficult, and we shall see an example of one such below.

Almost from the beginning of electronic computing, efforts have been put forth to maintain the "decimal" nature of integer data stored internally, even at the expense of complicating some of the operations that must go on in the central processing unit. In this chapter we introduce three new datatypes which are variations on the integer datatype in that they allow for the storage of integer data, but in a form which is more "human-oriented" than the twos-complement binary representation that we have used to date.

13.2 LEADING SEPARATE NUMERIC STRINGS

When a number such as −72691 is presented to a computing system via the keyboard of an ASCII-coded terminal, the keyboard in fact generates an array of six numbers:

$$31 \quad 39 \quad 36 \quad 32 \quad 37 \quad 2D$$

Each of these bytes represents the ASCII code for a *character* in the string of characters −, 7, 2, 6, 9, 1. These 6 bytes are given in their hexadecimal representation, and they are shown in the order in which they would normally appear in main memory, with addresses increasing from right to left. There are three comments that we wish to make about this "representation" of −72691. First, as an internal representation of a number, it is quite "human-readable"—far more so than, say, the *binary* representation FFFEE40D. Second, if this number is to be *printed* (on a terminal screen, say), and if the device on which the printing is to take place is ASCII coded, we find that there is nothing to do other than to transmit these 6 bytes *as they are*. Third, if any arithmetic or logical manipulations are to be performed on this number, the representation in which we find it here is totally inappropriate.

This representation of an integer, in which the data stored are the ASCII codes for the numerical characters that make up the decimal representation of the integer (together with the sign character), is precisely what is needed for communication with the outside world. We shall declare it to be a formal datatype, and in so doing we need only establish a couple of conventions. Evidently the two critical pieces of information about such a string of numerical characters are: (1) where in main memory they begin, and (2) how many such characters there are. Thus any such numeric string can be uniquely defined by specifying (1) an *address* (of the first byte), and (2) a *length* (the number of bytes), and it is here that we must establish some standards.

Leading Separate Numeric String. A leading separate numeric string is a collection of contiguous bytes with the following properties.

1. The first (lowest addressed) byte contains the ASCII code for a plus sign (2B), minus sign (2D), or space character (20).

Contents	Address	Character
2 D	ADDR	–
3 7	ADDR+1	7
3 2	ADDR+2	2
3 6	ADDR+3	6
3 9	ADDR+4	9
3 1	ADDR+5	1

Figure 13.2.1

2. Each byte beyond the lowest-addressed byte contains the ASCII codes for one of the decimal characters 0 to 9 (30 to 39 in hexadecimal), with the more significant decimal digits of the numeric string occupying the lower-addressed locations.

The address of the lowest-order byte (the "sign" byte) is the **address** of the leading separate numeric string. The number of decimal characters in the string (and thus not counting the sign character) is the **length** of the leading separate numeric string. By convention, the length may not exceed 31. A string of length 0 (consisting only of a sign byte) has by definition the value 0. A string whose length is longer than what is required to hold the specified decimal number is padded with leading (ASCII) 0s, each of which contributes one to the length argument.

Figure 13.2.1 shows the leading separate representation of the number -72691. Its address is ADDR, and its length is 5 (*not* 6, since the sign byte is not counted in the length arugment). Notice that if we want a representation of the number 72691, considered either as positive or perhaps unsigned, we could change c(ADDR) to 2B (plus sign) or 20 (space character). But in any event we must be aware that some leading sign byte is always assumed in this format.

We commented earlier that whereas a format such as leading separate numeric might be convenient for input and output, it will not do for arithmetic or logical

```
;-----------------------------------------------------------;
; Function CVTSL -- converts a leading separate numeric      ;
; string to a signed binary longword.                        ;
;                                                            ;
; CVTSL is invoked by creating a general or stacked          ;
; argument list, with the address of the first byte (the     ;
; sign byte) at the bottom of the argument list, and the     ;
; length of the string (not including the sign byte) at      ;
; the top of the argument list. If the value of the          ;
; string is too large to be held in a longword, the pro-     ;
; cedure returns with the PSW V-bit set. Otherwise the       ;
; longword value of the numeric string is returned in R0.    ;
;-----------------------------------------------------------;

CVTSL:  .WORD   ^M<R2,R3>       ;Save two registers
        CLRQ    R0              ; and clear R0 and R1
        ADDL3   4(AP),8(AP),R3  ;Get addresses of last numeric byte
        MOVAB   @8(AP),R2       ; and sign byte
```

Figure 13.2.2

```
CVT100:  CMPL   R2,R3              ;Done all bytes?
         BGEQU  CVT300             ;Yes -- set sign and return
         INCL   R2                 ;Move up pointer and
         MULL   #10,R0             ;  multiply current number by 10
         BLSS   CVT200             ;(Error if overflow)
         BICB3  #^XF0,(R2),R1      ;Get numerical value of byte
         ADDL   R1,R0              ;  and accumulate this digit
         BGEQ   CVT100             ;Do next byte (if no overflow)

CVT200:  BISB   #2,4(FP)           ;Set V-bit in caller's PSW to
         RET                       ;  indicate overflow

CVT300:  CMPB   @8(AP),#^A/-/      ;Minus sign?
         BNEQ   CVT400             ;No -- skip around
         MNEGL  R0,R0              ;  otherwise change sign
CVT400:  RET                       ;Return to caller
```

Figure 13.2.2 (Continued)

processing. But conversion to integer datatype is quite easy, and we offer in Figure 13.2.2 a sample procedure that converts such strings to longword integer format. Although the function CVTSL does test for "integer overflow," note that it does *not* check to ensure that the sign byte or decimal have valid ASCII codes, nor does it test for the validity of the length argument. None of these tests would be difficult to incorporate into the programming. We leave it to the reader to develop a procedure CVTLS to convert from longword format to the leading separate numeric string datatype, a task which is only minimally more difficult than that shown here.

13.3 TRAILING NUMERIC STRINGS

The term *leading separate numeric string* introduced in the preceding section is motivated by the fact that the *string* (of characters) represents a *numeric* quantity, and the sign of the quantity is maintained as a *separate* byte, which in fact is the *leading* (lowest-addressed) byte of the string, immediately preceding the most significant digit of the string. In contradistinction to these strings are those in which the sign *trails*—follows—the digits that make up the numeric string. Such strings have been in use since the early days of computing and were especially useful in a *punch card* environment. However, in this format the sign of the numeric string, although it follows the digits of the number, is typically not a *separate* byte (and for this reason we do *not* apply the descriptive phrase "trailing separate"). Rather, the last (least significant) digit is *modified* in such a way that this byte carries information not only about the last digit but also about the sign as well. As a simple scheme in which both sign and numeric information can be transmitted in a single byte, consider the following. Each byte of the string, except for the last byte, contains the ASCII code for one of the digits 0 to 9. The last, highest-addressed byte contains (1) the ASCII code for the least significant digit if the numeric string represents a *nonnegative* or *unsigned* number; or (2) the ASCII code for the least significant digit, modified by having bit 6 *set*, if the number string represents a *negative* number. In this format, then, the number 475 (positive or unsigned) would be stored as

$$35 \quad 37 \quad 34$$

with the ASCII codes for the numeric characters shown in hexadecimal, and written in the usual right-to-left order of increasing addresses. The number -475 would be represented as

$$75 \quad 37 \quad 34$$

where we note that 75 is simply 35—the ASCII code for the least significant digit, 5—with bit 6 turned on. Our interpretation of the 75 is that it represents an ASCII 5 and *also* represents a negative sign for the numeric string. This type of string is one example of a **trailing numeric string,** and we shall examine another shortly. In the meantime note that the second and third columns of Figure 13.3.1 show the possible values of the last digit of a nonnegative and negative, respectively, trailing numeric string in the format introduced above—the so-called **zoned numeric format.**

A second standard type of trailing numeric string is called the **overpunch numeric format,** a term which comes historically from the fact that when a number was punched into a card, the last digit was overpunched—the last digit was punched, and the card was then backed up to that last card column and a second code was punched in the card, thus *overpunching* the last digit. The least-significant digits, together with sign information, for trailing numeric strings in this overpunch format are shown in the last two columns of the table for Figure 13.3.1.

Now that we have seen two examples, we give a general description of a trailing numeric string.

Trailing Numeric String. A trailing numeric string is a collection of contiguous bytes with the following properties.

1. With the exception of the last (highest-addressed) byte, each byte contains the ASCII code for one of the decimal characters 0 to 9 (30 to 39 in hex-

FIGURE 13.3.1 TRAILING NUMERIC STRING DATA: REPRESENTATION OF LEAST-SIGNIFICANT DIGIT AND SIGN

Digit	Zoned +	Zoned −	Overpunch +	Overpunch −
0	30	70	7B	7D
1	31	71	41	4A
2	32	72	42	4B
3	33	73	43	4C
4	34	74	44	4D
5	35	75	45	4E
6	36	76	46	4F
7	37	77	47	50
8	38	78	48	51
9	39	79	49	52

adecimal), with the more-significant decimal digits of the numeric string occupying the lower-addressed locations.
2. The last (highest-addressed) byte contains information which specifies both
the value of the least-significant digit of the numeric string and the sign of
the numeric string.

The address of the lowest-addressed byte (most-significant digit) is the **address** of
the trailing numeric string. The number of bytes in the string is the **length** of the
trailing numeric string. By convention, the length may not exceed 31. A string
of length 0 contains no bytes and by definition has the value 0. Such a string may
have an address which is invalid, since the address is not used in the evaluation of
the numeric string.

Observe that in the description of a trailing numeric string, we have specified
that the last byte contains both digit and sign information, but we have not specified
just *how* that information is to be encoded. In fact, the particular form of this
last byte is left unspecified, and thus we evidently have a variety of possible trailing
numeric formats, two of which have already been discussed—zoned numeric and
overpunch numeric. As the reader may well expect, this lack of definiteness,
which is prompted by the fact that several different encodings are of practical and
historical importance, will return to haunt us when we attempt actually to manipulate these strings in some specific fashion.

13.4 PACKED DECIMAL STRINGS

The reader has undoubtedly observed that leading separate and trailing numeric
strings, although convenient in that they contain the actual ASCII code for the
decimal numbers they represent, are also quite expensive of memory. Each digit—
"tens" place—requires a byte of storage, so that even relatively small decimal
numbers may take up inordinate amounts of memory. As a compromise, in which
we can halve the amount of storage required while maintaining the essential decimal
quality of the representation, consider the **binary-coded-decimal (BCD)** representation, which results from the following observation. A decimal digit, when written
in its ASCII form, is a (hexadecimal) number between 30 and 39, inclusive. That
is, such a representation has the form 00110000 to 00111001, in binary. If we
simply drop the high-order nibble (0011) in each such representation, the remaining
nibble transmits as much information as before, but with only half the bits required.
For example, the number 1938, which requires 4 bytes when written as, say, a
trailing numeric string in zoned format [Figure 13.4.1(a)], requires only 2 bytes in
its BCD encoding [Figure 13.4.1(b)].

In going from a pure ASCII encoding to BCD code, we gain storage but, as
usual, we pay a price. For if a string of decimal characters is input in its ASCII
format, we must expend some effort in compressing it to its BCD form. Similarly,
if it is desired, say, to print a BCD string on an ASCII-coded device, the string
must be expanded into its ASCII code. These are tasks which were unnecessary

0011 , 0001	31 = '1'	
0011 , 1001	39 = '9'	
0011 , 0011	33 = '3'	
0011 , 1000	38 = '8'	

(a)

0001 , 1001	19
0011 , 1000	38

(b)   Figure 13.4.1

in the leading separate and trailing numeric formats, since in those cases the ASCII codes for the digits were left intact.

The example of Figure 13.4.1 suggests that in declaring binary-coded-decimal strings as a formal datatype, some conventions are going to have to be established. In particular, we need to have some way of expressing the sign of the number. What are we to do with the BCD representation of a decimal number with an *odd* number of digits? In this case there will be a nibble that is unused, and some agreements will have to be made concerning its interpretation. We deal with both of these potential problems in the following definition.

Packed Decimal String. A packed decimal string is a collection of contiguous bytes with the following properties.

1. Each byte consists of two nibbles, and each nibble (except the low-order nibble of the highest-addressed byte) contains the binary-coded-decimal representation of a decimal digit; that is, each nibble contains one of the numbers 0000 to 1001. The more significant digits in the packed decimal string correspond to the lower-addressed bytes in the string, and within each byte, the high-order nibble represents the more significant decimal digit.

2. The highest-addressed byte in the string contains, in its high-order nibble, the least significant digit in the packed decimal string. The low-order nibble of the highest-addressed byte contains the sign of the decimal string, as follows:

$$10, 12, 14, \text{ or } 15 \ (A, C, E, \text{ or } F) \text{ represents } '+'$$

$$11 \text{ or } 13 \ (B \text{ or } D) \text{ represents } '-'$$

(Of these, C and D are the preferred sign encodings.)

The address of the lowest-addressed byte (which contains the most significant digit) is the **address** of the packed decimal string. The number of digits in the string is the **length** of the packed decimal string. If the length of the string is *even*, the string is assumed to contain a zero (0000) in its most significant nibble, although that zero does not contribute to the length of the string. By convention, the length may not exceed 31. A string of length 0 consists of a single byte, with a zero in the high-order nibble and a sign in the low-order nibble. Figure 13.4.2 shows the contents of the consecutive bytes that represent a packed decimal string of length n.

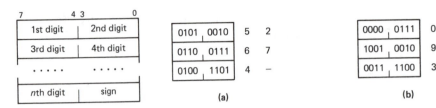

Figure 13.4.2

Figure 13.4.3

As examples of packed decimal strings, consider those of Figure 13.4.3. The number -52674 of Figure 13.4.3(a) has length 5. Note the sign code (1101 = D) in the low-order nibble of the highest-addressed byte. The number $+7923$ of Figure 13.4.3(b) has length 4, but observe that a zero nibble has been prefixed to it so that its four digits, together with the sign nibble and this extra zero, will take up an even number of nibbles. In general, if L is the length of a packed decimal string, the number of bytes occupied by the string will be $[L/2] + 1$, where $[x]$ represents "the greatest integer not exceeding x.

The conversion of a packed decimal string to a corresponding binary number is just slightly more difficult than the conversion of, say, a leading separate string (Figure 13.2.2), since the bytes of a packed string must be separated into their individual nibbles. However, as Figure 13.4.4 shows, with the use of the shift (ASHL) and mask (BICB) instructions, the conversion is quite straightforward (and would even be more so with the use of some of the concepts of Chapter 15). We shall see in the next section that the conversion is also quite unnecessary, since the VAX provides a hardware operation that performs the function of the procedure CVTPL.

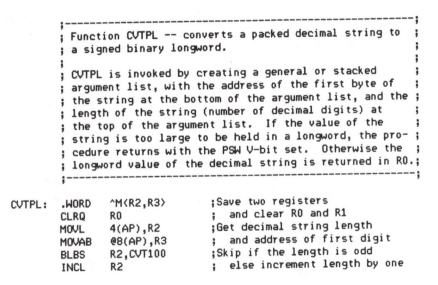

```
;------------------------------------------------------------;
; Function CVTPL -- converts a packed decimal string to      ;
; a signed binary longword.                                  ;
;                                                            ;
; CVTPL is invoked by creating a general or stacked          ;
; argument list, with the address of the first byte of       ;
; the string at the bottom of the argument list, and the     ;
; length of the string (number of decimal digits) at         ;
; the top of the argument list. If the value of the          ;
; string is too large to be held in a longword, the pro-     ;
; cedure returns with the PSW V-bit set. Otherwise the       ;
; longword value of the decimal string is returned in R0.    ;
;------------------------------------------------------------;

CVTPL:  .WORD   ^M<R2,R3>        ;Save two registers
        CLRQ    R0               ;  and clear R0 and R1
        MOVL    4(AP),R2         ;Get decimal string length
        MOVAB   @8(AP),R3        ;  and address of first digit
        BLBS    R2,CVT100        ;Skip if the length is odd
        INCL    R2               ;  else increment length by one
```

Figure 13.4.4

```
CVT100: MOVB    (R3),R1         ;Get 2 nibbles
        ASHL    #-4,R1,R1       ;  and isolate high-order nibble
        BSBB    CVT500          ;Convert to binary
        MOVB    (R3)+,R1        ;Get same 2 nibbles back
        BICB    #^XF0,R1        ;  and isolate low-order nibble
        DECL    R2              ;Decrement digit counter
        BEQL    CVT200          ;  and skip if done
        BSBB    CVT500          ;  else convert to binary
        SOBGTR  R2,CVT100       ;Do next pair of nibbles

CVT200: CMPB    R1,#11          ;Is sign 'negative'?
        BEQL    CVT250          ;Yes -- skip
        CMPB    R1,#13          ;Other form of 'negative'?
        BNEQ    CVT300          ;No -- skip out to return
CVT250: MNEGL   R0,R0           ;Change sign to negative
CVT300: RET                     ;Return to caller

        ;Subroutine to convert nibble to binary and accumulate
        ;  packed decimal result in longword

CVT500: MULL    #10,R0          ;Multiply accumulator by 10
        BLSS    CVT600          ;(error if overflow to sign bit)
        ADDL    R1,R0           ;Add in nibble
        BLSS    CVT600          ;(error if overflow to sign bit)
        RSB                     ;Return to CVTPL

CVT600: BISB    #2,4(FP)        ;Set V-bit in caller's PSW
        TSTL    (SP)+           ;Clear return PC from stack
        RET                     ;  and return to caller with
                                ;  error indicator (V-bit) set
```

Figure 13.4.4 (Continued)

13.5 CONVERSIONS BETWEEN DATATYPES

The various datatypes discussed in the preceding sections may be converted to one another by means of operations provided by the VAX hardware. Since a number of new concepts are introduced here, we shall take some pains in describing a few of these operations.

We noted in Section 13.4 that it is possible to convert a packed decimal string to its corresponding twos-complement binary representation as a longword, and the function of Figure 13.4.4 does just that. Observe that the function checks for integer overflow, but despite that feature, it still has some deficiencies, which are discussed in the exercises of Section 13.4. One of those deficiencies is that it does *not* check to see that the string being converted is even in valid BCD form. With these thoughts in mind, we shall examine the *hardware operation* CVTPL, which converts a packed decimal string to its corresponding twos-complement binary longword form, just as our *function* CVTPL did. The details of CVTPL are given in Appendix A.

The format of the operation CVTPL is

$$CVTPL \quad srclen.rw, srcaddr.ab, dest.wl$$

where the arguments *srclen* and *srcaddr* are the length and address that define the packed decimal string; *dest* is, of course, the longword destination of the conversion. The effect of the operation is what we expect—the generation of a longword whose value is equivalent to that of the decimal string. We shall focus our attention on two aspects of the operation's execution: things that can go wrong, and some interesting side effects.

There are two ways in which hardware errors can be generated when attempting to convert from packed decimal to binary format. As noted above, the packed decimal string may simply represent a number which exceeds the largest (signed) integer that can be held in a 32-bit longword. If this is the case, the processor will generate an *integer overflow trap* (provided of course, that integer overflow trapping is enabled; see Section 6.7 and Chapter 11). And if the length of the string (*srclen*) is not in the range 0 to 31, then a *reserved operand fault* will be generated by the processor. In addition to these errors, which *are* detected by the hardware, there is one other event that may produce incorrect results: namely, that the string contains an invalid nibble, a 4-bit code that does not represent a decimal digit or a valid sign code. This type of error is *not* detected by the hardware.

In addition to effecting the desired conversion, CVTPL also provides some potentially useful information, and it does so by returning this information in some of the *general-purpose registers*! In particular, the instruction alters the contents of R0, R1, R2, and R3, an obvious source of severe errors if these side effects are not anticipated by the programmer. In the specific case of CVTPL, the contents of R0, R2, and R3 are cleared (to zero), and upon execution, R1 is given as a value the *address* of the byte containing the most-significant digit of the packed decimal string, thus the byte whose high-order nibble is the most-significant digit, or whose high-order nibble is 0000 and whose low-order nibble is the most-significant digit in the string.

All the numeric string conversion and arithmetic operations (Section 13.6) have side effects similar to those described above. For the sake of uniformity, the conversion operations have been designed to return information in registers R0 to R3. The arithmetic operations return information in R0 to R3, or R0 to R5. In either event, the even-numbered registers always return with the value zero.

The companion operation to CVTPL is

$$CVTLP \quad src.rl,destlen.rw,destaddr.ab$$

which converts longwords to packed decimal strings, that is, generates the packed decimal string with length and address *destlen* and *destaddr*, respectively, and having the value of the longword *src*. As with CVTPL, a *reserved operand fault* will occur if the *destlen* operand is not in the range 0 to 31. There is another type of error which can occur in this case, and it is one that *may* be trapped by the hardware. It is a **decimal overflow trap,** and it occurs if the receiving packed decimal string is too small (specifically, does not contain sufficiently many decimal digits positions) to hold the decimal value of the longword, together with a sign nibble. For example, if a longword contains the (decimal) number -12832, and if the length operand in CVTLP is specified as 5 or greater, the conversion can take place. But if the length operand is less than 5, a decimal overflow occurs.

We stated above that in the event of a decimal overflow, the hardware *may* generate a trap—either abort execution or begin execution of a user-written condition handler (as described in Chapter 11). What determines this action is the state of bit 7 of the processor status word (PSW). If this bit—denoted DV, for *Decimal oVerflow*—is *set* when the overflow occurs, execution will be terminated and control passed to an error-handling routine. If this bit is *clear* when the overflow takes place, no such trap will occur; rather, the conversion will be incorrect, but execution will simply continue with the next instruction. The setting and clearing of bit 7 of the PSW may, of course, be accomplished with the BISPSW and BICPSW operations. But this bit is more easily manipulated in the entry mask word for a program or procedure, for by default it is cleared, and it may be set by declaring its mnemonic DV in the mask word, thus:

.WORD   ^M⟨DV, ...⟩

just as integer overflow trapping can be enabled by specifying IV in the mask word (see Section 6.7).

CVTLP also generates values which are returned in R0 to R3: namely, R0, R1, and R2 are cleared, and R3 contains the address of the byte containing the most-significant digit of the packed decimal string.

In addition to the conversions between longwords and packed decimal strings (CVTPL and CVTLP), the VAX provides operations to convert between packed decimal and leading separate numeric strings (CVTPS and CVTSP), and between packed decimal and trailing numeric strings (CVTPT and CVTTP). For the most part these conversions are quite straightforward, and their details, together with their side effects on the general registers and the possible errors that they can generate, are given in Appendix A. However, the trailing numeric strings have a feature which requires that we devote some discussion to them. The reader will recall that when the trailing numeric strings were described in Section 13.3, we gave some *examples* of how the sign byte (which also contains the least-significant decimal digit) might be constructed, but we did not *dictate* a particular scheme, for the simple reason that a number of techniques have been developed and are in use. That is, there is no standard here to which we can point as *the* definition of a trailing numeric string. But if this is the case, how can we ever achieve any conversions in which this sign byte plays a role? The answer is that we cannot unless we allow the *user* to determine the coding of the byte containing the sign and least-significant digit. This is precisely what the VAX conversion operations do, and they do so in a completely flexible way, one that imposes absolutely no constraints or preconditions on the conversion. To see how the scheme works, we shall examine in some detail the operation CVTTP, which converts trailing numeric strings to packed decimal strings.

The format of the CVTTP operation is

$$\text{CVTTP} \quad scrlen.rw, srcaddr.ab, tableaddr.ab,$$
$$destlen.rw, destaddr.ab$$

The operands *srclen, srcaddr, destlen*, and *destaddr* require no explanation; they are the parameters used to define the source and destination strings. And it should be quite clear how the conversion takes place. Each byte of the trailing numeric string (the source operand) has its high-order nibble stripped off, to form one of the nibbles used to represent a digit in the packed decimal format. The only remaining question is: How is the last—highest-addressed—byte of the trailing numeric string converted to the highest-addressed byte of the packed decimal string, since there is no standard way in which that byte of the trailing numeric string is encoded? The answer is that the *unsigned value*—0 to 255—of the highest addressed byte is used as an *index* into a 256-byte *table*; the table entry at that index is used as the highest-addressed byte (and thus the highest-addressed two nibbles) in the packed decimal string. The address of the 0th entry of the table is the operand *tableaddr*.

As an example, consider the trailing numeric string

$$\text{4F} \quad 39 \quad 34 \quad 37 \quad 32$$

shown written right to left in order of increasing addresses. Assuming that the highest-addressed byte (4F) contains the last digit *and* the sign code, as represented in overpunch format (see Figure 13.3.1), this last byte is the encoding of the digit 6 and the minus sign. Thus this trailing numeric string represents the decimal number -27496. The conversion to packed decimal is straightforward for the low-order 4 bytes; they become the nibbles

$$49 \quad 27 = 01001001 \quad 00100111$$

The last trailing numeric byte—4F—is encoded into the byte which is the seventy-ninth ($= $ 4F) entry in the translation table. Presumably the byte at that entry contains 6D, the byte representing the least-significant digit 6, together with the 4-bit code for a minus sign (D), for packed decimal strings.

It would appear from this description that any conversion involving trailing numeric strings will require the construction of a 256-byte translation table. This is usually not the case, for we ordinarily know enough about the types of trailing numeric strings we are dealing with that only relatively small partial tables are required. Some suggestions in this direction are given in the exercises.

13.6 ARITHMETIC OPERATIONS ON PACKED DECIMAL STRINGS

That the VAX supports arithmetic operations on packed decimal strings is not unusual, for even some of the small and inexpensive microcomputers have for many years incorporated hardware in their processors to do some simple arithmetic on

BCD-encoded numbers. Some examples and further development of these ideas will be found in the exercises.

The operations supported by the VAX are the following.

ADDP4	ADDP6	ASHP	CMPP3	CMPP4
DIVP	MOVP	MULP	SUBP4	SUBP6

They are implemented *only* for packed decimal strings, as suggested by the letter 'P' in the operation mnemonics. If it is required that corresponding operations be performed on, say, trailing numeric strings, then of course these can be converted to packed decimal, operated on, and finally converted back to trailing numeric.

The operations listed above perform the functions which are suggested by their mnemonics and which correspond more or less to the familiar integer operations; the full details of each of these are given in Appendix A. We do make a few comments, however, about some aspects of these operations. Note that ADDP and SUBP come in two forms, a four-operand and a six-operand format. These correspond to the two- and three-operand forms of ADD and SUB, the additional operands being accounted for by the fact that each packed decimal string requires *two* arguments—its length and address—for its definition. The differences between CMPP3 and CMPP4 lie in the length operands—CMPP3 compares two decimal strings having a *common* length, whereas CMPP4 compares decimal strings each of which has its *own* length argument. Each of the operations uses R0 to R3, or R0 to R5, to return information about the packed decimal string operands. All of these operations are subject to a *reserved operand* error, which will occur if the length argument for a packed decimal string is outside the range 0 to 31. Most are also candidates for a *decimal overflow* error, which signifies that a receiving field is not sufficiently large to hold a packed decimal result. (Again we remind the reader that this error will generate a processor trap only if the DV bit—bit 7—of the PSW is set.) And DIVP can generate a *decimal divide-by-zero* error.

ASHP is, as its mnemonic suggests, a shift operation. However, it is sufficiently different from those we have already studied that a few comments about it are in order. In the case of ASHP, "shifting" means multiplication by a power of *10*, not a power of 2, since the string is naturally decimal instead of binary. But in addition, on *right* shifts, in which digits are *dropped* at the least significant end, provision is made for *rounding* the result so that, for example, the string 1287, shifted one place to the right (which we can interpret as a divide by 10), will result in 129, while the string 1284, shifted one place to the right, will result in 128.

Finally, we note that there is an assembler directive, .PACKED, which is relevant here. Analogous to .BYTE, .WORD, and so on, .PACKED is a data allocation directive. Specifically:

.PACKED   The .PACKED directive has as its argument a *string* of decimal characters, optionally preceded by a plus or minus sign. The effect of the directive is to instruct the assembler to construct the packed decimal string having the specified value. If the number of characters in the string (exclusive of the sign) is even, the assembler will append a leading-zero nibble to the packed decimal string. The assembler always generates a packed string of minimal length; however, longer packed decimal strings can be generated by inserting leading zeros into the specified string: for example,

```
      3C 12   .PACKED   123
   4C 23 01   .PACKED   1234
3D 12 00 00   .PACKED   -0000123
```

13.7 A PROGRAMMING EXAMPLE

As an example of the use of some of these packed decimal operations, we offer the program of Figure 13.7.1. Aside from being an illustrative example, there is little to distinguish it, except that it can deal with very large numbers—far larger than what can be held in a longword, for example. The purpose of the program is to accept decimal numbers input from the keyboard *without* a leading sign (and thus assumed to be positive), add them up, and then find the average of the numbers, correct to one decimal place. Numbers are input one after another until an equal sign (=) is entered as the first input character, used to signal termination of the numerical input.

At the top of the program are some work areas and a keyboard buffer; the program begins by clearing the 8-byte area named SUM and ensuring that it will be interpreted as a +0. Strings are then input from the keyboard (at GETNUM), checked for the equal sign, and then the length of the string is determined. (Recall that the input macroinstruction **$I.STR** does not count input characters; rather, it appends a NUL byte to the input string.) The input string is now in the form of a leading separate numeric string (note that it is preceded by an ASCII plus sign), which is then converted to packed decimal, of length 15. (This length, which is common to all the packed strings, ensures that all 16 nibbles of their quadword storage will be used.) This is then multiplied by 10 by means of the ASHP operation to yield the one decimal place of precision, and accumulated at SUM. When all the numbers have been entered, their sum is divided by the contents of the counter R9 (which is converted from binary to packed decimal), and the result is printed.

13.8 CLOSING COMMENTS

In dealing with numerical data, the user has a choice of many different data types. When the data are most naturally in whole-number (integer) form, then byte, word, and longword types are available, as are quadword and octaword as well, although *processing* on the latter two is in general not well implemented. If the data are fractional, the floating-point types of Chapter 12 are appropriate. For these reasons the reader may be surprised not only that we describe the decimal string types of this chapter, even for reasons of history, but the more so that a modern computer would actually provide hardware to *effect* these operations. But

```
;-----------------------------------------------------------;
; Read an arbitrary number of packed decimal strings        ;
; and calculate and print their average.                    ;
;-----------------------------------------------------------;

SUM:    .BLKQ   1                   ;Sum accumulated here
WORK1:  .BLKQ   1                   ;Packed decimal string
WORK2:  .BLKQ   1                   ;  work areas
INPUT:  .BYTE   ^A/+/               ;Assumed ASCII plus-sign
        .BLKB   16                  ;Input buffer

START:  .WORD   ^M<DV>              ;Entry point (enable decimal
                                    ;  overflow trapping)
        CLRQ    SUM                 ;Make SUM a packed
        MOVB    #12,SUM+7           ;  decimal (+) zero
        CLRL    R9                  ;R9 used as number counter

GETNUM: $I.STR  INPUT+1             ;Get a leading separate number
        CMPB    INPUT+1,#^A/=/      ;Check 1st byte for "="
        BEQL    FINISH              ;Is "=" -- finish up
        INCL    R9                  ;  else increment counter
        MOVAB   INPUT+1,R0          ;Set pointer to 1st number

TEST:   TSTB    (R0)+               ;Test for terminating <NUL>
        BNEQ    TEST                ;Isn't <NUL> -- test next byte
        SUBL    #INPUT+2,R0         ;Subtract to get string length
        CVTSP   R0,INPUT,-          ;Convert to
                #15,WORK1           ;  packed decimal,
        ASHP    #1,#15,WORK1,-      ;  shift left
                #0,#15,WORK2        ;  (multiply by 10)
        ADDP4   #15,WORK2,-         ;  and add to SUM
                #15,SUM
        BRB     GETNUM              ;Get next number

FINISH: CVTLP   R9,#15,WORK1        ;Change counter to packed decimal
        DIVP    #15,WORK1,-         ;  and divide into accumulated sum
                #15,SUM,-
                #15,WORK2
        CVTPS   #15,WORK2,-         ;Convert result backed to leading
                #16,INPUT           ;  separate string for printing
        MOVAB   INPUT+1,R0          ;Set pointer
SKIP:   CMPB    (R0)+,#^A/0/        ;Skip if
        BEQL    SKIP                ;  leading ASCII zero
        DECL    R0                  ;Adjust buffer pointer
PRINT:  CMPL    R0,#INPUT+16        ;At last ASCII decimal digit?
        BEQL    DONE                ;Yes -- handle as special case
        $O.CHR  (R0)+               ;  else print digit
        BRB     PRINT               ;  and deal with next digit

DONE:   $O.CHR  #^A/./              ;Print decimal point
        $O.CHR  (R0)                ;  and last character
        $O.NL                       ;Clear line
        $EXIT                       ;  and exit

        .END    START
```

Figure 13.7.1

consider for the moment the plight of the accounting department of a large corporation. If that business's accounts—gross sales, for example—involve numbers in perhaps the 100 million dollar range, how can accounting programs deal with these amounts? As integers, they would have to be dealt with in penny amounts, and these numbers (10,000,000,000) are too large for longwords. They could be handled as floating-point numbers, but the reader familiar with the material of Chapter 12 is aware that certain inaccuracies creep into these representations, inaccuracies that may be of no significance in, say, scientific programs, but which are intolerable when dealing with corporate stockholders. But decimal strings, limited only by the 31-character constraint, can hold numbers in the range

$$\pm 9,999,999,999,999,999,999,999,999,999,999$$

and can do so with complete accuracy.

This gives perhaps one justification for the use of numbers which maintain their decimal character even when machine resident, and there are others. Suffice it to say that except in special environments, decimal strings are not frequently used in day-to-day programming. But when they are desired or required, we see that the VAX implements them quite fully and in ways that are most convenient to the user.

13.9 EXERCISES

13.2.1. Write the bytes that make up the leading separate numeric strings for each of the following decimal numbers and specify the length of each string. (Write the bytes so that higher addresses are at the left.)
   (a) 1274   **(b)** −1274   **(c)** +80299340521

13.2.2. State the decimal number whose leading separate numeric string representations are given below. (Assume that byte addresses increase right to left.)
   (a) 39 34 32 30 30 31 20   **(b)** 30 30 30 37 2D
   (c) 30 30 30 2B   **(d)** 2d

13.2.3. Determine what the function CVTSL of Figure 13.2.2 will do if the string length argument passed to it is 0.

13.2.4. Show that the function CVTSL of Figure 13.2.2 will set the PSW V-bit if an attempt is made to convert any positive number that exceeds the largest positive number which can be held in a longword. However, show also that CVTSL does *not* successfully convert the largest *negative* number. Explain how this deficiency might be repaired.

13.2.5. Modify the function CVTSL of Figure 13.2.2 so that it detects "numbers" that do not begin with a valid sign or blank character, or which contain bytes whose contents are not the ASCII codes for decimal digits, or which have invalid lengths (outside the range 0 to 31).

13.2.6. Write a procedure CVTLS that converts a longword signed integer to its leading separate numeric string format. What arguments need to be transmitted to the procedure? What possible errors may occur?

13.3.1. Write the bytes that make up the trailing numeric strings, assuming the *zoned format* of Figure 13.3.1, for each of the following decimal numbers, and specify the length of each string. (Write the bytes so that higher addresses are at the left.)

(a) 1274   (b) −1274   (c) +80299340521

13.3.2. State the decimal number whose trailing numeric string representations are given below. (Assume the *zoned format* of Figure 13.3.1, and that byte addresses increase right to left.)

(a) 39 34 32 30 30 31   (b) 74 30 30 37

(c) 30 30 30   (d) 70

13.3.3. Write the bytes that make up the trailing numeric strings, assuming the *overpunch format* of Figure 13.3.1, for each of the following decimal numbers and specify the length of each string. (Write the bytes so that higher addresses are at the left.)

(a) 1274   (b) −1274   (c) +80299340521

13.3.4. State the decimal number whose trailing numeric string representations are given below. (Assume the *overpunch format* of Figure 13.3.1, and that byte addresses increase right to left.)

(a) 49 34 32 30 30 31   (b) 51 30 30 37

(c) 7D 30 30   (d) 7B

13.3.5. Write a function CVTTZL to convert trailing numeric strings to longword binary format, where the zoned format of Figure 13.3.1 is used to encode the least-significant digit and sign. What arguments need to be transmitted to the procedure? What possible error may occur?

13.3.6. Write a function CVTTOL to convert trailing numeric strings to longword binary format, where the overpunch format of Figure 13.3.1 is used to encode the least-significant digit and sign. What arguments need to be transmitted to the procedure? What possible errors may occur?

13.3.7. Write a procedure CVTLTZ to convert a longword to trailing numeric string format, where the zoned format of Figure 13.3.1 is used to encode the least-significant digit and sign. What arguments need to be transmitted to the procedure? What possible errors may occur?

13.3.8. Write a procedure CVTLTO to convert a longword to trailing numeric string format, where the overpunch format of Figure 13.3.1 is used to encode the least-significant digit and sign. What arguments need to be transmitted to the procedure? What possible errors may occur?

13.4.1. Write the bytes that make up the packed decimal strings for each of the following decimal numbers and specify the length of each string. (Write the bytes so that higher addresses are at the left.)

(a) 1274   (b) −1274   (c) +80299340521

13.4.2. State the decimal number whose packed decimal string representations are given below. (Assume that byte addresses increase right to left.)

(a) 4C 27 30 00   (b) 4D 27

(c) 0D   (d) 2D

13.4.3. Show that if L = length of a packed decimal string, the string occupies [L/2] + 1 bytes, where [x] represents "the greatest integer not exceeding x."

13.4.4. Show that the function CVTPL of Figure 13.4.4 will *not* convert the largest negative integer to a longword. Show also that it does not detect an invalid BCD code (outside the range 0000 to 1001) or an invalid sign nibble. Suggest how these deficiencies can be corrected.

13.4.5. Write a procedure CVTLP that converts a longword signed integer to its packed decimal string format. What arguments need to be transmitted to the procedure? What possible errors may occur?

13.5.1. Determine the contents of the consecutive bytes, the first of which has address BASE, which are generated by each of the following CVTLP instructions, assuming that R6 contains the (decimal) number 742381.

(a) CVTLP R6,#6,BASE   (b) CVTLP R6,#9,BASE
(c) CVTLP R6,#5,BASE   (d) CVTLP R6,#34,BASE
(e) CVTLP R6,#0,BASE   (f) CVTLP R6,#7,BASE

13.5.2. By experimentation, determine the values of the longwords generated by the operation CVTPL when applied to each of the following *invalid* packed decimal strings (shown right to left in order of increasing addresses).

(a) 32   41   26; length = 5
(b) 3C   41   2A; length = 5
(c) 3D   4B   15; length = 4

From these examples deduce, as far as possible, what basic processor operations are being performed by the machine instruction CVTPL.

13.5.3. Show that the scheme of Figure 13.9.1 below will deal with conversion from trailing numeric to packed decimal, where we assume that the zoned format of Figure 13.3.1 is used to encode the least-significant digit and sign of the trailing numeric string.

```
POSNOS: .BYTE    ^X0C          ;These bytes represent
        .BYTE    ^X1C          ;  the packed decimal
        .BYTE    ^X2C          ;  numbers +0 to +9,
        .BYTE    ^X3C          ;  and thus correspond
        .BYTE    ^X4C          ;  to the zoned format values
        .BYTE    ^X5C          ;  ^X30 - ^X39
        .BYTE    ^X6C          ;Thus POSNOS must
        .BYTE    ^X7C          ;  be entry no. ^X30
        .BYTE    ^X8C          ;  (= decimal 48) in
        .BYTE    ^X9C          ;  the translation table

FILLER: .BLKB    ^X70 - ^X3A   ;The contents of the bytes in
                               ;  this "filler" block are
                               ;  immaterial to the translation
                               ;  of zoned trailing numeric to
                               ;  packed decimal, and thus any data
                               ;  may be placed here.  However,
                               ;  this block must contain precisely
                               ;  54 bytes

NEGNOS: .BYTE    ^X0D          ;These bytes
        .BYTE    ^X1D          ;  represent the
        .BYTE    ^X2D          ;  packed decimal
        .BYTE    ^X3D          ;  numbers -0 to -9,
        .BYTE    ^X4D          ;  and thus
        .BYTE    ^X5D          ;  correspond
        .BYTE    ^X6D          ;  to the
        .BYTE    ^X7D          ;  zoned format
        .BYTE    ^X8D          ;  values
        .BYTE    ^X9D          ;  ^X70 - ^X79

TBLADDR = POSNOS - ^X30        ;Address of beginning of
                               ;  translation table
```

Figure 13.9.1

13.5.4. Use a scheme analogous to that of Exercise 13.5.3 to construct a table for the translation to packed decimal from trailing numeric, where we assume the overpunch format of Figure 13.3.1.

13.5.5. Use a scheme analogous to that of Exercise 13.5.3 to construct a table for the translation from packed decimal to trailing numeric, where we assume the overpunch format of Figure 13.3.1.

13.6.1. A popular microcomputer implements some special hardware to assist in the management of BCD number representations. However, unlike the VAX, it does *not* have special instructions to ADD such representations, for example. Rather, the standard twos-complement binary ADD is used, and then the result is "adjusted" to make it correspond to what the result should have been if BCD representations had been added. The computer has the 8-bit byte as its principal integer datatype, and it has the usual condition codes N, Z, V, and C, which behave much as they do on the VAX. But in addition, there is a **half-byte carry indicator H,** which is set on carries *out of bit 3* of the byte being operated on. Finally, the processor implements an instruction, called **Decimal Adjust,** which functions as follows. Suppose that two bytes each contain two BCD codes; that is, the high- and low-order nibbles of each of the bytes is in the range 0000 to 1001. If these two bytes are added, for example, we cannot expect the 8-bit result to consist of two nibbles whose values are equivalent to the sum of the two 2-digit BCD representations. It is the purpose of Decimal Adjust to "fix" the result so that it *does* represent the sum of the BCD numbers. As an example, consider the bytes

$$0011\ 0100 \quad (= BCD\ 34)$$
$$0101\ 0110 \quad (= BCD\ 56)$$

The sum of these is 0111 1010, which is *not* a BCD representation. But if Decimal Adjust is applied to this result, it will convert it to 1001 0000, the BCD representation of 90, which is the sum of 34 and 56. Explain how, based on the condition codes, the H-indicator, and the states of the high- and low-order nibbles *after* the addition, Decimal Adjust can make this appropriate adjustment.

14 CHARACTER STRINGS

14.1 CHARACTER STRINGS

In Chapter 4, and again in Chapter 9, we defined a character string to be a collection of contiguous bytes that contained the ASCII codes for characters. We repeat that definition here; the description is just slightly relaxed, in that we do not insist that the bytes contain character codes.

Character String. A character string is a (perhaps empty) collection of contiguous bytes. The **address** of the string is the address of the first (lowest-addressed) byte of the string; the **length** of the string is the number of bytes in the collection. Evidently the length must be nonnegative.

Observe that in this definition we have not insisted that the bytes in a character string actually contain the ASCII codes for characters; as we know, those ASCII codes are all 7 bits long (more properly, bit 7 is always 0), whereas we allow a byte in a character string as defined here to be any collection of 8 bits. This relaxation in the definition adds some flexibility when it comes to interpreting some of the character string instructions examined later in the chapter.

The reader may also have encountered character strings in Appendix D, in which macroinstructions are defined for the input and output of strings. In those cases, a "string" means something slightly different from what we have defined here—as far as the macroinstructions are concerned, a string means a collection of bytes that ends in a NUL byte (a byte whose contents is 0). However, it is not difficult to reconcile these two definitions, and the procedures PRSTR1 and PRSTR2

```
;----------------------------------------------------------;
;  Procedures PTSTR1 and PTSTR2 -- print a character       ;
;  string whose address and length are specified.          ;
;                                                          ;
;  Calling sequence:      CALLx    arg,PTSTRn              ;
;                                                          ;
;  where either CALLG or CALLS is valid, provided AP       ;
;  points at a 3-longword array as follows:               ;
;                                                          ;
;                    .LONG   2              <-- AP         ;
;                    .LONG   <length>                      ;
;                    .LONG   <addr>                        ;
;                                                          ;
;  where <length> is the length of the string and <addr>  ;
;  is the address of the first (lowest addressed) byte     ;
;  of the string.                                          ;
;----------------------------------------------------------;

PRSTR1: .WORD   ^M<R2,R3>       ;Entry point mask word
        MOVL    4(AP),R2        ;Get string length
        MOVAB   @8(AP),R3       ;  and string address
        MOVB    (R3)[R2],-(SP)  ;Save <last character>+1 on stack
        CLRB    (R3)[R2]        ;  and replace it with NUL
        $0.STR  (R3)            ;Use standard routine to print
                                ;  string
        MOVB    (SP)+,(R3)[R2]  ;Replace character
        RET                     ;  and return to caller

PRSTR2: .WORD   ^M<R2,R3>       ;Entry point mask word
        MOVL    4(AP),R2        ;Get string length
        MOVAB   @8(AP),R3       ;  and string address
        BRB     PR.200          ;Skip down to start print loop
                                ;  (deals with empty string case)
PR.100: $0.CHR  (R3)+           ;Use standard routine to print
                                ;  character
PR.200: SOBGEQ  R2,PR.100       ;Print next character
        RET                     ;  or return to caller if done
```

Figure 14.1.1

of Figure 14.1.1 show two possible ways to output character strings as defined here, in terms of their addresses and lengths.

14.2 BASIC CHARACTER STRING OPERATIONS*

The most fundamental operation we can perform on a string is to copy it to some other location in main memory. The operation's mnemonic is MOVC (*MOVe Character string*), and as we shall see, it comes in two forms.

*The single-chip version of the VAX processor, the MicroVAX, implements *directly* in hardware *only* the two "move character string" operations MOVC3 and MOVC5. In the event that another operation in the group described here is encountered, the processor hardware informs the operating system of that event, and the operating system then invokes system software to emulate the operation. Thus to the user, the appearance is that the instruction has been executed directly by the CPU.

```
        .
        .
        .
BLOCK:  .LONG    12743221,904,-22488729,18,0,-1,442981
        .
        .
        MOVC3   #28,BLOCK,NEWBLK
        .
        .
```

Figure 14.2.1

What is required to copy a string from one place to another are clearly (1) the defining characteristics of the string to be copied (its beginning address and length), and (2) the address of the destination of the copy. Indeed, the more primitive version of MOVC performs precisely this function.

(a) MOVC3   *MOVe Character string, 3-operand*

MOVC3 has the format

$$\text{MOVC3} \quad len.rw, srcaddr.ab, destaddr.ab$$

Its effect is to copy the *len* bytes between *srcaddr* and *srcaddr* + *len* − 1 to the bytes with addresses from *destaddr* to *destaddr* + *len* − 1. In addition to the actual move, MOVC3 sets registers 0 to 5 to various values, and the user must be aware of these side effects to avoid unexpected programming errors. The details are explained in Appendix A.

Observe that although we may think of these collections of bytes as representing strings of characters, there is nothing in the definition of a character string or the description of MOVC3 which dictates that the bytes in question must contain the ASCII codes for characters. Thus, in fact, MOVC3 may be used to copy *any* block of bytes from one location to another. The program segment of Figure 14.2.1 shows how we can take advantage of this instruction to do multiple MOVs with a single instruction.

A five-operand version of MOVC copies the characters of one string to another string, even though the strings may be of *different* length. Put in less character-oriented terms, a block of *m* bytes may be copied from a source location to a destination block of length *n*, where *m* is not necessarily equal to *n*. If *m* > *n*, only *n* source bytes are transferred (so that bytes are not moved beyond the end of the destination block). But if *m* < *n* all *m* source bytes are copied to the destination block, but that block still contains bytes which have not been copied into. In this case, the remaining bytes of the destination block are filled with a "character" (byte) specified by the instruction.

(b) MOVC5   *MOVe Character string, 5-operand*

MOVC5 has the format

$$\text{MOVC5} \quad srclen.rw, srcaddr.ab, fill.rb,$$
$$destlen.rw, destaddr.ab$$

and executes as follows. If *srclen* ≥ *destlen*, the *destlen* bytes from *srcaddr* to *srcadd* + *destlin* − 1 are copied to the byte locations from *destaddr* to *destaddr* + *destlen* − 1. If *srclen* < *destlen*, the *srclen* bytes from *srcaddr* to *srcaddr* + *srclen* − 1 are copied to the byte locations from *destaddr* to *destaddr* + *srclen* − 1, and the bytes from *destaddr* + *srclen* to *destaddr* + *destlen* − 1 are filled with the byte value *fill*. As with MOVC3, registers 0 to 5 are given values by MOVC5, which side effects can be useful to the programmer (see Appendix A for the details).

MOVC5 has an interesting capability that the reader may already have noted. Suppose that it is necessary to fill a block of storage with zeros (perhaps to initialize some values). This can be done using MOVC5, if we simply let the fill character be 0, and then specify that *no* "characters" be moved to the destination:

$$\text{MOVC5} \quad \text{\#0,DUMMY,\#0,\#N,BLOCK}$$

In this case, 0 bytes are copied, and then the remaining N bytes of BLOCK (that is, all of them) are filled with the "fill character" 0. Note that in this case the address DUMMY can be any address at all, since no bytes are actually copied from that location. Thus MOVC5 can be used as a "byte fill" operation, much as MOVC3 can be used as a "byte copy" operation.

Another type of operation which is quite useful when dealing with character strings (or blocks of byte storage, for that matter) is *comparison*, in which we can determine if two strings are identical or, if they are different, which is the lexicographic predecessor. As with MOVC, the comparison operation comes in both a three- and a five-operand form, and the distinction is essentially the same.

(c) CMPC3   *CoMPare Character strings, 3-operand*

CMPC3 has the format

$$\text{CMPC3} \quad \textit{len.rw,src1addr.ab,src2addr.ab}$$

and compares the byte at *src1addr* with the byte at *src2addr*. If these bytes are equal, the next pair of bytes is compared (that is, the bytes at *src1addr* + 1 and *src2addr* + 2); if they are equal, the next pair is compared; and so on. The pairwise comparison continues until either (1) the bytes are unequal, or (2) *len* bytes have been compared. When the comparisons terminate (for either reason), the condition codes are set as follows:

N ← {byte of 1st string LSS corresponding byte of 2nd string};
Z ← {byte of 1st string EQU corresponding byte of 2nd string};
V ← 0;
C ← {byte of 1st string LSSU corresponding byte of 2nd string};

In addition to the setting of the condition codes, the contents of R0 to R3 are also set, as described in Appendix A.

The principal use of CMPC3 is the comparison of character strings, of the same length, to determine their lexicographic (dictionary) order. Suppose, for example, that located at STR1 and STR2 are the following strings of length 7 (shown here as generated by .ASCII directives):

$$\text{STR1:} \quad .\text{ASCII} \quad /\text{Kittens}/$$
$$\text{STR2:} \quad .\text{ASCII} \quad /\text{Kitchen}/$$

The effect of the instruction

$$\text{CMPC3} \quad \#7,\text{STR1},\text{STR2}$$

is to compare the bytes of the strings, character by character and beginning with the bytes at STR1 and STR2. The comparisons will reveal equality for the first three characters, but the comparison will terminate on the fourth character, since "c" < "t". At that point *all* condition codes will be 0, and this would be interpreted as meaning that the second string is "less than" the first string. In addition, c(R0) will be 4, c(R1) will be STR1 + 3, and c(R3) will be STR2 + 3. (See Appendix A for descriptions of the settings of these registers.)

If two character strings are not of equal length, CMPC3 may not yield a satisfactory method of comparison. Consider the words "cat" and "catenation," for example. If we use a length of 3, CMPC3 will tell us that the strings are identical, which is false. But if we use a length of 10 (the length of the second string), CMPC3 will be comparing characters that do not even belong to the first string. What is normally done in this case (and what the reader has doubtless done dozens of times) is to "pad out" the shorter string, say with spaces or blanks, so that its length is the same as that of the longer string, and then, in effect, use CMPC3 to do the compare. Thus we would be comparing "catƀƀƀƀƀƀƀ" with "catenation" and assuming that the blanks (shown here as ƀ) are taken to be *smaller* than any alphabetic character (a statement which is true of their ASCII codes), we would conclude that "cat" is smaller than "catenation," This "padding out" of the shorter string is precisely the function of the five-operand version of CMPC.

(d) CMPC5   *CoMPare Character strings, 5-operand*

CMPC5 has the format

$$\text{CMPC5} \quad \textit{src1len.rw,src1addr.ab,fill.rb,}$$
$$\textit{src2len.rw,src2addr.ab}$$

CMPC5 has the conceptual effect of extending the shorter of the two strings by padding it with trailing *fill* characters and then performing exactly the comparison of CMPC3 on the (now equal length) strings. Again, the details are given in Appendix A, as are the effects on the contents of R0 to R3.

```
;----------------------------------------------------------------;
; Procedure SEARCH -- search for a specified character           ;
; in a string whose address and length are given.               ;
;                                                                ;
; Calling sequence:      CALLx    arg,SEARCH                     ;
;                                                                ;
; where either CALLG or CALLS is valid, provided AP             ;
; points at a 4-longword array as follows:                      ;
;                                                                ;
;                    .LONG   3               <-- AP             ;
;                    .LONG   <char>                             ;
;                    .LONG   <length>                           ;
;                    .LONG   <addr>                             ;
;                                                                ;
; where <char> is the character to be searched for (in          ;
; longword form), <length> is the length of the string          ;
; and <addr> is the address of the first (lowest                ;
; addressed) byte of the string.                                ;
;----------------------------------------------------------------;

SEARCH: .WORD   ^M<>              ;Entry point mask word
        MOVAB   @12(AP),R1        ;Get string beginning address
LOOP:   CMPB    4(AP),(R1)+       ;Compare specified character
                                  ; with string character
        BEQL    FOUND             ;Matches -- skip out
        SOBGTR  8(AP),LOOP        ;Try for match on next character
        BISB    #4,4(FP)          ;If no match found, set user's
        RET                       ; Z-bit and return

FOUND:  DECL    R1                ;Adjust pointer back by 1
        RET                       ; and return
```

Figure 14.2.2

An activity that is frequently necessary when dealing with character strings is the *searching* of a string for a particular character. In fact, the function SEARCH of Figure 14.2.2, when passed a string address and length, and a character to search for, returns in R1 the address in the string of the first instance of the specified character. If the character is not found, R1 contains the address of the byte one byte beyond the end of the string, and the PSW Z-bit is set (to indicate failure). The reader should find the programming to be perfectly direct.

Since the searching for a specific character is done often in some environments (especially in some operating system routines, where strings of characters have to be "parsed"—decomposed into their various components), the VAX implements an operation which has almost exactly the same effect as the function SEARCH of Figure 14.2.2.

(e) LOCC   *LOCate Character*

LOCC has the format

$$LOCC \quad char.rb, len.rw, addr.ab$$

where *char* is the character to be located, and *len* and *addr* define the string to be searched. LOCC concludes execution with the character's address in R1 if the character was found, and if the character was not found, the PSW Z-bit is set and R1 contains the address of the byte following the string. The complete details, and in particular the setting of R0 and R1, are given in Appendix A.

LOCC has a companion instruction whose mnemonic is SKPC which scans a string for the first instance of a character *different from* a specified character.

(f) SKPC   SKiP Character

SKPC has the format

$$\text{SKPC} \quad char.rb,len.rw,addr.ab$$

and searches the string defined by *len* and *addr* for the first instance of a byte different from *char*. SKPC sets the condition codes and registers R0 and R1 in exactly the same fashion as LOCC.

Another activity that takes place frequently not only in an operating system environment but also in many user programs is the searching of a string for a particular substring. A program may ask a question, for example, and then might have to scan the user's response for an instance of the string "yes" or, failing that, the string "no." It is not difficult to write a procedure which determines if one string is found as a substring of a second string, and if so, where in the second string it is found. But, in fact, the VAX implements precisely this operation.

(g) MATCHC   MATCH Character string

MATCHC has the format

$$\text{MATCHC} \quad objlen.rw,objaddr.ab,srclen.rw, srcaddr.ab$$

The effect of MATCHC is to determine whether or not the string defined by *srclen* and *srcaddr* contains an instance of the string defined by *objlen* and *objaddr* as a substring. If it does, the PSW Z-bit is set and R3 is set to the address in the source string of the byte after the last byte matched. This information, together with the length of the object string, can be used to determine where in the source string the match begins. Registers 0 through 2 are also set in somewhat useful ways, and the reader may refer to Appendix A for complete details.

We close this section with a simple example which uses several of the basic string operations and which is similar to the programming segment of Figure 7.4.7. We wish to input some strings through the keyboard, using the macroinstruction **$I.STR.** Recall that that macroinstruction will create strings which end in a NUL character (ASCII code = 0). Having input the string, we wish to store it in a large block of bytes intended for string storage in such a way that the strings saved in the block are in lexicographic (dictionary) order. Now if a new string has to be added somewhere in the middle of the block of strings in order to maintain the order, an excessive amount of moving of bytes may be involved. Thus instead we agree always to add a new string to the end of the block of strings. However, to keep the dictionary ordering of the strings, we also maintain an array of *string addresses*; it is the string addresses that maintain the dictionary order, for the *linear* order of the string addresses in the array of addresses determines the proper order of the strings. A simple example will illustrate the process. Suppose that the block currently contains the following three strings at the addresses shown:

00000974	BLOCK:	"the quick brown fox⟨NUL⟩"
00000988		"the cat and the fiddle⟨NUL⟩"
0000099F		"the sky is falling⟨NUL⟩"
000009B2		⟨first free byte in BLOCK⟩

As we see, the strings are not in dictionary order. But an array of their addresses in essence puts them in order as follows:

VECTOR	00000988
	00000974
	0000099F

If a new string, say

"the cow jumped over the moon⟨NUL⟩"

were to be inserted, it would simply be added at the end of the block, namely at 000009B2, and its address (000009B2) would then be put in the array of addresses as the *second* entry, between 00000988 and 00000974. This would necessitate moving the last two addresses down one position to make room for the new address, but this is preferable to "unpacking" the relatively large block of bytes.

Figure 14.2.3 shows the block of bytes (sufficient to accommodate 2000 characters) and the array used to hold the string addresses (100 such), together with two procedures. One of these simply prints the strings currently stored (and is almost identical to the segment of Figure 7.4.7), and the other provides for the addition of a new string to the collection. R6 contains the number of strings that are currently saved (initialized to 0), and R7 contains the address of the first free byte in the block that holds the strings. Since the procedures are not passed any arguments, they should be invoked with

CALLS   #0,procedure_name

```
BLOCK:   .BLKB    2000            ;Storage for strings
VECTOR:  .BLKL    100             ;Storage for string addresses
KBBUFF:  .BLKB    81              ;81-byte keyboard buffer

START:   .WORD    ^M<>            ;Program entry point
         CLRL     R6              ;Set VECTOR addresses count to 0
         MOVAB    BLOCK,R7        ;Put address of 1st free byte in R7
           .
           .
;-------------------------------------------------------------;
; Procedure PRINT -- prints strings currently stored, in      ;
; lexicographic order (i.e., via their addresses in VECTOR)   ;
;-------------------------------------------------------------;

PRINT:   .WORD    ^M<R0,R1>       ;Save two registers
         MOVAL    VECTOR,R0       ;Set R0 to VECTOR address
         MOVL     R6,R1           ;   and R1 to address count
         BRB      PRT.40          ;Skip to do initial SOB
PRT.20:  $O.STR   @(R0)+          ;Print a string
         $O.NL                    ;   (and generate a "new line")
PRT.40:  SOBGEQ   R1,PRT.20       ;Decrement counter and print next
         RET                      ;Return when printed all strings
           .
           .
;-------------------------------------------------------------;
; Procedure ADDSTR -- adds a new string to those currently    ;
; stored in BLOCK, and inserts its address in VECTOR          ;
;-------------------------------------------------------------;

ADDSTR:  .WORD    ^M<R0,R1,R2,-   ;Save registers
                  R3,R4,R5>
         $I.NL                    ;Clear keyboard buffer
         $I.STR   KBBUFF          ;   and get a string
         LOCC     #0,#81,KBBUFF   ;Find the terminating NUL in KBBUFF
         SUBL3    #KBBUFF-1,R1,R4 ;C(R4) = length of new string
         MOVL     R6,R5           ;Copy address count
         ASHL     #2,R5,R5        ;   and calculate last address
         ADDL     #VECTOR,R5      ;   plus 4
         BRB      ADD.40          ;Skip to do initial R5 decrement
ADD.20:  LOCC     #0,#81,@(R5)    ;Find terminating NUL in string
         SUBL     R5,R1           ;Length, not including NUL
         CMPC5    R1,@(R5),#0,-   ;Compare stored string with
                  R4,KBBUFF       ;   new string (in KBBUFF)
         BLEQ     ADD.60          ;Found position if smaller
         MOVL     (R5),4(R5)      ;   else move address up in VECTOR
ADD.40:  ACBL     #VECTOR,#-4,-   ;Decrement c(R5) by 4 and compare
                  R5,ADD.20       ;   next string if more addresses
ADD.60:  MOVL     R7,4(R5)        ;Put address in VECTOR,
         MOVC3    R4,KBBUFF,(R7)  ;   put string in BLOCK,
         MOVL     R3,R7           ;   set "1st available byte" address
         INCL     R6              ;   and increment address counter
         RET                      ;Return
           .
           .
```

Figure 14.2.3

14.3 CHARACTER STRINGS AND TRANSLATION TABLES

We noted in Section 4.7 the desirability of the *standardization* of character encoding schemes—if two computer installations use the same character codes (ASCII, for example), these installations will have no difficulty in communicating with one another. Early in the history of character processing the situation was fairly chaotic, with many different coding schemes being used in a variety of environments. Nowadays there are only a few standard encodings (except for special-purpose codes, which we need not discuss), but inasmuch as there is more than *one* such, it is necessary to be able to *translate* one coding scheme to another, to provide communication between systems that use different codes.

As a concrete example of the communication problem, suppose that computer installation *A* wishes to send a magnetic tape, containing a text file, to computer installation *B*. However, *A*'s file is encoded in the EBCDIC scheme, while *B*'s system deals only with ASCII code. (EBCDIC stands for *Extended Binary-Coded Decimal Interchange Code*, an encoding in wide use, especially among IBM installations.) The task, of course, is to take each EBCDIC-encoded character and convert—translate—it to ASCII prior to writing it to the tape. Now an EBCDIC-encoded character requires 8 bits (recall that an ASCII-coded character requires only 7 bits), and thus there are 256 possible 8-bit codes which have to be dealt with. On the other hand, since there are only about 110 of these which we think of as representing "alphanumeric" characters, evidently many of the EBCDIC codes will *not* be able to be translated to ASCII. Although it is possible to devise a translating *function* that will implement the code conversion, the function is quite complex, a result of the fact that the EBCDIC coding scheme is not as "rational" as ASCII. (For example, whereas the EBCDIC codes for the characters A to I are consecutive integers, the code for the character J is *eight* more than the code for the character I. The conversion function must examine a wide collection of special cases such as this, and these contribute to its complexity.) As an alternative to a complex function to do the conversion, we adopt the following simple scheme. We construct a 256-byte table, each of whose entries is the ASCII code for the character whose EBCDIC code is the *position* in the table. For example, the EBCDIC code for the character *Q* is hexadecimal D8 = decimal 216. Thus the 216th entry in the table (starting with entry number 0) is the ASCII code for *Q*, namely hexadecimal 51 = decimal 81. Thus the translation table will appear as in Figure 14.3.1, where we have assumed for the sake of definiteness a beginning address of 00001000. To do the translation from EBCDIC to ASCII is now trivial, for if we assume that R4 points at the EBCDIC (source) characters and that R5 points at the corresponding ASCII (destination) characters, the instructions

```
MOVZBL   (R4)+,R0
MOVB     TABLE[R0],(R5)+
```

will do the conversion. By now it should be clear that the scheme has nothing to do with the particular encoding scheme—ASCII, EBCDIC, or whatever—any code may be converted to any other code as easily as shown here. All that is

```
00001000        TABLE:  .BYTE   ..      ;ASCII code corresponding
                                        ;  to EBCDIC ^X00
00001001                .BYTE   ..      ;ASCII code corresponding
                                        ;  to EBCDIC ^X01
   .
   .
000010D8                .BYTE   ^X51    ;ASCII code for 'Q' --
                                        ;  corresponds to EBCDIC ^XD8
   .
   .
000010FF                .BYTE   ..      ;ASCII code corresponding
                                        ;  to EBCDIC ^XFF
```

Figure 14.3.1

required is the appropriate table and the two lines of instructions shown above. Indeed, an installation might have several such conversion tables available as separate object modules with global table addresses, which can be linked into programs as needed.

In addition to the "move character string" (MOVC) operation introduced in the preceding section, the VAX also implements a "move translated character string" operation which has the effect of the translation process described above, but which translates and moves entire strings with a single instruction, rather than a single character at a time.

(a) **MOVTC**   *MOVe Translated Characters*

MOVTC has the format

$$MOVTC \quad srclen.rw, srcaddr.ab, fill.rb, tableaddr.ab,$$
$$destlen.rw, destaddr.ab$$

Each 8-bit source string byte is translated by using its value as an index into a 256-byte table, and the translated value is placed in the destination string. If the source string's length is greater than or equal to the destination string's length, only the first *destlen* bytes are translated and moved. If the destination string is longer, the entire source string is translated, and the remaining destination string bytes are filled with the *fill* byte. The operation has some useful side effects on registers R0 to R5, which are described in Appendix A.

An operation that is similar to MOVTC is one which translates one string to another, as MOVTC does, but with two differnces. First, there is no fill character, for character translation and transfer terminates if the source string "empties" or the destination string "fills." That is the maximum number of characters translated and moved is minimum{*srclen, destlen*}. Second, translation and transfer will also terminate prematurely if a *specified* byte is detected as a *translated* value.

(b) MOVTUC — *MOVe Translated string Until "escape" Character*

MOVTUC has the format

$$\text{MOVTUC} \quad srclen.rw, srcaddr.ab, escape.rb, tableaddr.ab, destlen.rw, destaddr.ab$$

Characters in the source string are translated as usual by means of the specified table and moved to the destination string until one of three things occurs: (1) the number of characters moved is *srclen*; (2) the number of characters moved is *destlen*; or (3) a character translates to the value *escape*. This value, which triggers termination of the translation and transfer, is called an *escape value*. Notice that *escape* is a *translated* value, not a source byte value. Observe also that the translation terminates *prior to* the "escape value" being moved to the destination string. Further details of MOVTUC, as well as its effects on the contents of R0 to R5, are given in Appendix A.

As a simple example of the use of MOVTUC, consider a collection of ASCII characters which are divided into "lines" as follows. A *line* of characters is just any collection that ends in a NUL character (ASCII code = 0). Thus a "line" is the collection we would obtain from a .ASCIZ directive, or from the input macroinstruction **$I.STR**. Assume now that it is desired to send each such line to a printer, but suppose the printer hardware requires that it be sent EBCDIC code, and that such a line of code must end in a carriage return/line feed combination, not a NUL. Finally, we suppose that no such line contains more than 80 characters (not including the NUL). Figure 14.3.2 is a sample of the type of block of characters we might have to deal with; the NULs are *shown* here as ⟨NUL⟩, although in fact they are simply 0 bytes embedded in the text. Figure 14.3.3 shows a segment of instructions which uses MOVTUC to translate ASCII characters in BLOCK to EBCDIC, to put the translated characters in PTRBUFF for printing, and to "escape" upon detection of the *zero* which is the translation of the NUL—the ASCII "line" terminating character. Notice that the translation table ASC2EBC need only be 128 bytes long. (Why?) As explained in Appendix A, upon termination of MOVTUC, R1 will contain the address in the source string of the character that

FIGURE 14.3.2

> When, in the course of human events, it⟨NUL⟩becomes necessary for one people to dissolve⟨NUL⟩the political bands which have connected⟨NUL⟩them with another, and to assume among the⟨NUL⟩powers of the earth, the separate and equal⟨NUL⟩station to which the laws of nature and of⟨NUL⟩nature's God entitle them, a decent respect⟨NUL⟩to the opinions of mankind requires that⟨NUL⟩they should declare the causes which impel⟨NUL⟩them to the separation.⟨NUL⟩

```
CRLF:     .BYTE    ^X0D,^X25          ;EBCDIC Carriage return/line feed codes

ASC2EBC:                              ;ASCII to EBCDIC translation table

          .BYTE    0                  ;Code corresponding to ASCII 0 = NUL
                                      ;  (This is the "escape" code)

          .BYTE    ..                 ;EBCDIC code dorresponding to ASCII 1
     .
     .
          .BYTE    ..                 ;EBCDIC code corresponding to ASCII 127

BLOCK:                                ;Block of ASCII characters to be translated

PTRBUFF:  .BLKB    82                 ;Printer buffer for no more than 80
                                      ;  translated EBCDIC characters)
     .

INIT:     MOVAB    BLOCK,R6           ;Put BLOCK address in R6
     .
          MOVTUC   #81,(R6),#0,-      ;Translate "line" of ASCII text to EBCDIC,
                   ASC2EBC,#80,-      ;  put resulting code in PTRBUFF, and
                   PTRBUFF            ;  "escape" when translated byte = 0
          MOVW     CRLF,(R5)          ;Put CR/LF into destination buffer
          MOVL     R1,R6              ;Reset c(R6) to address
          INCL     R6                 ;  of next "line" in BLOCK
     .
     .
```

Figure 14.3.3 (Continued)

caused the "escape," and R5 will contain the address in the destination string of the byte that *would* have received the "escape" character. It is clear how the present programming segment takes advantage of these values.

The last two character string operations we shall deal with also reference "tables" as do all the others in this section, but we hesitate to call these "translation tables," since they are not normally used to translate from one encoding to another. As before, when a byte in a string is referenced, that byte's 8-bit value is used as an index into a 256-byte table. However, in these cases, the table entry is used as a "code" to indicate something about the string character—that it is numeric, or alphabetic, that it is uppercase, and so on—rather than to generate a new encoding for that character. We shall describe the operations and then look at two simple examples, which illustrate how the operations might be used in practice.

(c) SCANC   *SCAN* Character string

SCANC has the format

$$\text{SCANC} \quad len.rw,addr.ab,tableaddr.ab,mask.rb$$

The effect of the operation is to scan the string specified by the *len* and *addr* operands and as each byte is encountered, to use its 8-bit value as an index into the 256-byte table whose beginning address is *tableaddr*. The table entry is then ANDed with the *mask* operand. This process continues until the result of the AND is nonzero or *len* consecutive bytes have yielded a zero result when their table values are ANDed with *mask*. R0 contains the number of bytes remaining in the string (including the byte that resulted in a nonzero AND with *mask*) and R1 contains the address of the byte in the string which resulted in the nonzero AND (or the address of the byte one byte beyond the end of the string, if no such byte ANDed to zero). R2 and R3 are also affected in less interesting ways, as described in Appendix A.

(d) SPANC   *SPAN Character string*

SPANC has the format

$$\text{SPANC}\quad len.rw,addr.ab,tableaddr.ab,mask.rb$$

The effect of the operation is to scan the string specified by the *len* and *addr* operands and, as each byte is encountered, to use its 8-bit value as an index into the 256-byte table whose beginning address is *tableaddr*. The table entry is then ANDed with the *mask* operand. This process continues until the result of the AND is zero or *len* consecutive bytes have yielded a nonzero result when their table values are ANDed with *mask*. R0 contains the number of bytes remaining in the string (including the byte that resulted in a zero AND with *mask*) and R1 contains the address of the byte in the string which resulted in the zero AND (or the address of the byte one byte beyond the end of the string if there was no such byte). R2 and R3 are also affected, as described in Appendix A.

We see that the effect of SCANC is to "scan" across a string until some event occurs (an AND has a nonzero result), and SPANC is its complementary operation—SPANC "scans" the string until some event *fails* to occur (an AND does *not* have a nonzero result). Evidently SPANC is unnecessary, since the effects of SPANC can be achieved by using SCANC and the *ones-complement* of the specified mask byte.

Although it is clear just what SCANC and SPANC do, it may not be clear *why* they do it or how the programmer might put these operations to use. Consider for the moment the task of locating, in a character string, the first instance of a plus-sign (+). We already have a construction for this, LOCC, where the character to be searched for could be written as #^A/+/. But now we modify the task a bit and request the first instance of *any* arithmetic operator: +, −, *, or /. Of course, we could use LOCC here as well, but the programming would be awkward at best. Suppose, instead, that we construct a table (similar to the translation tables we have already used) in which the entries at the positions of these arithmetic operators is, say, 1, and such that all the remaining (252) entries are *even*. Then the instruction

$$\text{SCANC}\quad length,address,table,\#1$$

will locate the first character whose table entry is *odd*, that is, the first instance of an operator.

In closing we offer two sample program segments, each of which uses SCANC to locate a character from a class of characters, and the second of which also uses SPANC to advantage. We have seen routines earlier which have approximately the same effects, but the methods are vastly different. The segment of Figure 14.3.4 converts each lowercase character in a character string to uppercase, as did the procedure LC2UC of Figure 9.13.7. Notice that the table has been constructed to group together all the "control" characters (not needed here, but rather for the segment of Figure 14.4.5), all the numeric characters, the uppercase characters, lowercase characters, and finally the "special" characters (mainly punctuation). NUL is a special case. For the purposes of Figure 14.3.4 it would have been sufficient simply to be able to distinguish between lowercase, non-lowercase, and NUL. (Notice the use of the "repeat" notation—[...]—in the .BYTE directives, to indicate repeated instances of the same byte value. See Appendix B, Section B.10).

The action of the instructions of Figure 14.3.4 is quite straightforward, but observe in particular the use of R1 as a buffer pointer. Beginning at the start of the string, the string is scanned for a lowercase alphabetic *or* a NUL, the string-terminating character. (This is done by means of the mask byte 00100001—the 1 in bit position 5 locates uppercase characters, while the 1 in position 0 detects the NUL.) When found, if it is a NUL, the scan is complete. If it is not a NUL, it must be a lower case character, which is then converted to uppercase.

```
TABLE:  .BYTE   ^B00000001              ;ASCII NUL
        .BYTE   ^B00000010[32]          ;"Control" characters and "space"
        .BYTE   ^B00000100[15]          ;Special characters (! - /)
        .BYTE   ^B00001000[10]          ;Numeric characters (0 - 9)
        .BYTE   ^B00000100[7]           ;Special characters (: - @)
        .BYTE   ^B00010000[26]          ;Upper-case alphabetic (A - Z)
        .BYTE   ^B00000100[6]           ;Special characters ([ - `)
        .BYTE   ^B00100000[26]          ;Lower-case alphabetic (a - z)
        .BYTE   ^B00000100[5]           ;Special characters ({ - DEL)

LINE:   .BLKB   81                      ;String to be converted
        .
        .
        .
        MOVAB   LINE,R1                 ;Set pointer to begining of string
FIND:   SCANC   #81,(R1),TABLE,-        ;Search string for a lower-case
                #^B00100001             ;  alphabetic or NUL
        TSTB    (R1)                    ;NUL?
        BEQL    DONE                    ;Yes -- done converting line
        BICB    #^X20,(R1)+             ;  else convert to upper-case
        BRB     FIND                    ;  and treat next character

DONE:   .
        .
```

Figure 14.3.4

Character Strings   Chap. 14

```
TABLE:  .BYTE   ^B00000001              ;ASCII NUL
        .BYTE   ^B00000010[32]          ;"Control" characters and "space"
        .BYTE   ^B00000100[15]          ;Special characters (! - /)
        .BYTE   ^B00001000[10]          ;Numeric characters (0 - 9)
        .BYTE   ^B00000100[7]           ;Special characters (: - @)
        .BYTE   ^B00010000[26]          ;Upper-case alphabetic (A - Z)
        .BYTE   ^B00000100[6]           ;Special characters ([ - `)
        .BYTE   ^B00100000[26]          ;Lower-case alphabetic (a - z)
        .BYTE   ^B00000100[5]           ;Special characters ({ - DEL)

LINE:   .BLKB   81                      ;String to be converted
        .
        .
        MOVAB   LINE,R1                 ;Set pointer to begining of string
FIND:   SCANC   #81,(R1),TABLE,-        ;Search string for a control
                #^B00000011            ;  character or NUL
        TSTB    (R1)                    ;NUL?
        BEQL    DONE                    ;Yes -- done packing line
        MOVL    R1,R6                   ;  else save string position
        SPANC   #81,(R1),TABLE,-        ;Skip over contiguous
                #^B00000010            ;  control characters
        MOVAB   LINE+80,R0              ;Get last character address and make
        SUBL    R1,R0                   ;  it maximum possible character count
        MOVC3   R0,(R1),(R6)            ;Move end of string down in LINE
        MOVL    R6,R1                   ;Copy string position and look for
        BRB     FIND                    ;  next control character

DONE:   .
        .
```

Figure 14.3.5

The program segment of Figure 14.3.5 removes blanks, tabs, and "control" characters (such as backspace, form feed, and so on) from a string. Its effect is the same as that of the procedure PACK of Figure 9.13.7, but its technique is completely different. Notice that it uses the same table of mask values that the preceding example did. The approach to removing control characters and thus packing them out of the string is the following. We search the string for a control character. Having found it, we note where it was and then *skip* (using SPANC) any contiguous control characters until we find a byte that is *not* a control character. At this point the rightmost portion of the string is moved in such a way that the contiguous control characters are *overlaid*.

14.4 EXERCISES

14.1.1. Write a procedure INSTR that will read from the terminal keyboard a string of specified length. INSTR is to be passed the string length and the address of the first byte of the receiving buffer.

14.2.1. Write a procedure that emulates the action of MOVC3, including the setting of registers and condition codes.

14.2.2. How does

$$\text{MOVC3} \quad \#4,X,Y$$

differ from

$$\text{MOVL} \quad X,Y$$

14.2.3. It was stated that the CMPC3 instruction which compared the strings "Kittens" and "Kitchen" (in that order) resulted in *all* the condition codes being cleared. Why? Why was this interpreted as meaning that "Kitchen" precedes "Kittens"?

14.2.4. What is the purpose of the particular way in which the carry bit C is set upon execution of CMPC3 or CMPC5?

14.2.5. Write a procedure that emulates the action of SKPC, including the setting of registers and condition codes.

14.2.6. Write a procedure that emulates the action of MATCHC, including the setting of registers and condition codes.

14.2.7. Write a procedure that uses successive applications of LOCC to emulate the operation MATCHC.

14.2.8. In the programming of Figure 14.2.3, explain why R0 and R1 could or could not be used to hold the string count and the address of the first free byte.

14.2.9. Show that the procedure ADDSTR of Figure 14.2.3 could be simplified if the input statement were changed to

$$\text{\$I.STR} \quad \text{(R7)}$$

Describe what other changes would then have to be made.

14.2.10. The principal motivation behind the design of the programming of Figure 14.2.3 was to avoid moving large blocks of bytes so as to maintain the strings in lexicographic order. But could not MOVC3 be used to move these blocks? In particular, suppose that it was necessary to open up the block of strings at BLOCK + 739 to accommodate a new string of length 32 characters, and that the block currently contained 1328 bytes. We could execute the instruction

$$\text{MOVC3} \quad \#1328-739,\text{BLOCK}+739,\text{BLOCK}+739+32$$

But is there a problem when the source string (beginning at BLOCK + 739) *overlaps* the destination string.

14.3.1. Punch cards, although no longer in widespread use, can still be useful machine-readable "documents" in some environments. The standard punch card consists of 80 columns of 12 rows each, and thus the number of *possible* different punch combinations in a column is 2^{12}, although the vast majority of these is not used; they are not punch combinations which represent a character. The device that reads the card will then present to the processor these 12 bits in the form of a 12-bit "word" in which a 1 means that a hole is punched in that row, and a 0 means the row is unpunched. (These 12 bits may for convenience be expanded out to a full 16-bit word by padding 0s as the low-order 4 bits.) Find a table of card codes (sometimes called *Hollerith codes*) and devise a scheme for converting these 12-

bit "punches" to ASCII code. Is it reasonable for this conversion to be "table driven?" Partially "table driven?"

14.3.2. Write a procedure that emulates the action of MOVTC, including the setting of registers and condition codes.

14.3.3. Write a procedure that emulates the action of MOVTUC, including the setting of registers and condition codes.

14.3.4. Why did the translation table ASC2EBC of Figure 14.3.3 need be only 128 bytes long?

14.3.5. Consider the line of assembly code

label: op opnd1,opnd2 ;comment

Explain how the VAX assembler can use SCANC and SPANC, possibly with the assistance of other operations, such as MATCHC and LOCC, to locate the various components of this source line. That is, to be able to translate the source code, the assembler must be able to determine which part of it is operation, which is operand, and so on. Show that the character string operations can be extremely useful in this endeavor.

14.3.6. Tell what will be printed when the program segment of Figure 14.4.1 is executed. This suggests the possibility of using computers to *decode* hidden messages, and of course it is also possible for them to *encode* English text into data such as shown here. (In fact, these longwords were generated by a corresponding encoding program.) An analysis of the scheme used here reveals that it is so simple that it would not offer even a novice cryptographer much of a challenge. Consider as an alternative the technique of using a *translation table*, such as those implemented in Section 14.3, to encode English text. With the character string operations we have available, it is clear that such encodings would be very easy to accomplish, yet the resulting encryption, called a **substitution cypher,** is the easiest of codes to "break." However, devise some schemes that do use translation tables and yet are far more secure than what was just proposed. (*Suggestion*: Consider what kind of code would be generated if a simple translation were considered to be *circular*, with its last entry immediately adjacent to its first; and while the same table is used without modification for the translation of each character, the "beginning" of the table is *changed* for each character, perhaps by letting the beginning of the table be defined somehow in terms of the value of the last character translated.)

```
CODE:      .LONG    ^X42BBA30B,^X4103A30B,^X03437A39
           .LONG    ^X032393B9,^XAB7B433B,^XFBA2E801
           .
           .
           MOVAL    CODE,R8
DECODE:    ROTL     #13,(R8),(R8)+
           LOCC     #0,#4,-4(R8)
           BEQL     DECODE

           $0.STR   CODE
```

Figure 14.4.1

```
ASC2INT:  .WORD    ^M<R1,R2,R3>
          MOVL     4(AP),R1
          MOVAB    @8(AP),R2
          CLRL     R0
          BRB      ASC.40
ASC.20:   MULL     #10,R0
          MOVZBL   (R2)+,R3
          BICB     #^A/0/,R3
          ADDL     R3,R0
ASC.40:   SOBGEQ   R1,ASC.20
          RET
```

Figure 14.4.2

14.3.7. Write a "calculator" program that accepts from the keyboard strings of numeric characters and operators and prints the numeric value of the string. An example of the sort of strings we have in mind is

$$12 + 96 - 4*17$$

We assume the use of decimal digits only; that the string contains no blanks or tabs; that only the operators $+$, $-$, $*$, and $/$ are used; that execution always takes place left-to-right (that is, that there is no operator priority); that there is no monadic (unary) use of $+$ and $-$; and that there can be no errors in the input string.

Since the decimal characters in the strings will have to be converted to binary integers, we offer in Figure 14.4.2 a procedure that is passed the arguments

```
.LONG   2
.LONG   ⟨length⟩
.LONG   ⟨address⟩
```

where ⟨address⟩ is the address of the first (highest power of 10) digit and ⟨length⟩ is the number of digits. The procedure returns in R0 the value of the string, but note that it makes no provision for overflows and it does not verify that all the characters it deals with are decimal digits.

There are a number of possible ways in which the basic program can be expanded. For example, error checking can be introduced; the monadic use of $+$ and $-$ can be permitted; operator hierarchy can be provided for, and with it the use of parenthesizing (although this last expansion is far more involved than the preceding ones).

CHAPTER

15

VARIABLE-LENGTH BIT FIELDS

15.1 A BINARY-TO-HEXADECIMAL CONVERSION ALGORITHM

Consider the following simple problem. We wish to display, in its hexadecimal representation, the contents of some register, say R2. Clearly, what we need to do is to divide the register into 4-bit groups, evaluate each group (as a number between 0 and 15), and then display the appropriate character 0...9 or A...F, depending on the 4-bit value. (We assume that some routine, $O.CHR, is available which will print a single character on the user's terminal.) The programming segment of Figure 15.1.1 accomplishes this in a straightforward fashion. The slight annoyance encountered here, where the resulting converted number must be tested to see if it exceeds an ASCII 9 and, if so, must be further adjusted into the A...F range, can be eliminated by building a table of the hexadecimal digits and using the value of the 4-bit group to index the table. This improvement is shown in the segment of Figure 15.1.2.

At the center of this little algorithm are the two instructions

```
LOOP:   ASHL   R9,R2,R3
        BICL   # - 16,R3
```

and it will be worth taking a moment to examine their effect. The shift instruction ASHL shifts the desired 4-bit group to the right in such a way that they end up in bits 3:0 of R3. But because of the way ASHL does a right shift, we have no assurance that the contents of R3 now represents the numerical value of the 4-bit

445

```
;----------------------------------------------------------;
; Segment to print on the user's terminal the contents     ;
; of R2 by generating the ASCII code for each nibble.       ;
;----------------------------------------------------------;
        .
        .
        MOVL    #-28,R9         ;Initialize shift-right count
LOOP:   ASHL    R9,R2,R3        ;Shift a 4-bit group to right
        BICL    #-16,R3         ;Zero out all but 4 low-order
                                ;  bits (mask = ^XFFFFFFF0)
        ADDB    #^A/0/,R3       ;Convert to ASCII
        CMPB    R3,#^A/9/       ;Does result exceed ASCII 9?
        BLEQ    PRINT           ;No -- go print ASCII character
        ADDB    #7,R3           ;  else adjust into 'A...F' range
PRINT:  $O.CHR  R3              ;Print the character
        ACBL    #0,#4,R9,LOOP   ;Add 4 to shift count and
                                ;  process next 4 bits
        .
        .
```

Figure 15.1.1

group in question—some of the higher-order bits of R3 (bits 31:4) may also be set. Of course, it is precisely the purpose of the BICL instruction to clear those higher-order bits and thus to ensure that c(R3) is now the actual numerical value of the 4-bit group in question. This is crucial, for in subsequent instructions c(R3) is used as a *number*—for example, as a table index in the program segment of Figure 15.1.2.

A little reflection will reveal that the manipulations performed on these bits were required because that group of bits cannot be directly *addressed* (as a byte or word can be), nor can arithmetic be performed on them *as they stand*, that is, without first isolating them in, say, a register. Yet the situation we have encoun-

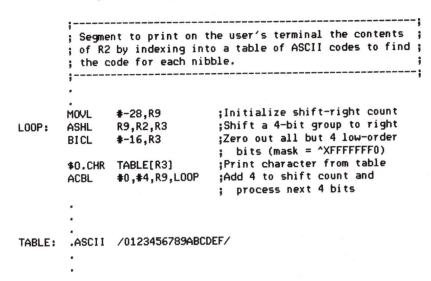

```
;----------------------------------------------------------;
; Segment to print on the user's terminal the contents     ;
; of R2 by indexing into a table of ASCII codes to find    ;
; the code for each nibble.                                 ;
;----------------------------------------------------------;
        .
        .
        MOVL    #-28,R9         ;Initialize shift-right count
LOOP:   ASHL    R9,R2,R3        ;Shift a 4-bit group to right
        BICL    #-16,R3         ;Zero out all but 4 low-order
                                ;  bits (mask = ^XFFFFFFF0)
        $O.CHR  TABLE[R3]       ;Print character from table
        ACBL    #0,#4,R9,LOOP   ;Add 4 to shift count and
                                ;  process next 4 bits
        .
        .
        .
TABLE:  .ASCII  /0123456789ABCDEF/
        .
        .
```

Figure 15.1.2

tered here—a collection of contiguous bits, buried somewhere in the middle of a larger structure, is to be considered as representing a numerical value—is by no means unusual, as other examples in the remainder of this chapter will demonstrate. As we shall see, the VAX can perform certain operations on these groups of contiguous bits, and thus we can consider them to be an additional datatype. Although the operations are fairly primitive in comparison with those which apply to some of the other datatypes with which we are already familiar, nonetheless they make manipulations such as were required in the program segments of this section significantly more convenient.

15.2 VARIABLE-LENGTH BIT FIELDS

If, as in Section 15.1, we are interested in groups of bits and we want the VAX to give us some assistance in managing these groups, the processor is going to need some information in order to identify just which bits are being referenced. In particular, the processor will evidently need to know (1) how many contiguous bits make up the group in question, and (2) just where those bits are. Part (1) is no problem, since this information can simply be passed to the processor as a numerical value. But (2)—where the bits are located—presents more of a difficulty, since in the VAX architecture the byte is the smallest data type that is directly (numerically) addressable. Nonetheless, the appropriate information can be passed to the processor by specifying some address (of a byte, word, and so on, or even a register designator), which we can think of as being the "address of bit 0" of that structure, and then specifying a **bit offset** from that "bit 0 address." For example, the 6-bit group shown in Figure 15.2.1, consisting of bits 10:5 of the word whose address is 0F2D, can be described by specifying the length of the group (6), the address 0F2D, and the bit offset 5, which indicates that the low-order bit of the 6-bit group is 5 bits *above* the address 0F2D. In a sense, the address and bit offset specify the "address" of the group of bits. In any event, this information uniquely defines these 6 bits, and we shall see in Section 15.3 that the hardware can perform some useful operations on these rather randomly placed, random-length substructures. In the meantime, we shall formalize some of the terminology.

A **variable-length bit field** consists of a (possibly empty) collection of contiguous bits defined by the following specifiers:

Its **size**, or **length**, which is a number between 0 and 32, inclusive.

Its **base address,** which is any address obtainable from an address access operand, or which is a register (in which case the bit field is a subfield of $R[n]$ or of $R[n+1]'R[n]$).

Its **position** relative to the base address, which represents the bit offset of the

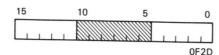

0F2D   **Figure 15.2.1**

Figure 15.2.2   Figure 15.2.3

low-order bit of the field from the low-order bit of the byte whose address is the base address. Unless the base address is a register, the position may be any signed number that can be held in a 32-bit longword. If the position is *positive*, the bit 0 offset is into higher-order bits; if *negative*, the offset is into lower-order bits. If the base address is a register R[n], the position must be in the range 0 to 31. If the base address is a register and the size and position are such that *position* + *size* > 32, then the bit field is taken as a subfield of the 64-bit concatenation of R[n + 1] with R[n] (R[n + 1]'R[n], with the high-order 32 bits in R[n + 1], the low-order 32 bits in R[n]).

Some examples will help to clarify these concepts. The bit field of Figure 15.2.1 is described by base address = 0F2D, position = 5, and size = 6. As a similar example, consider the field shown in Figure 15.2.2, in which base address = A (a symbolic address), position = 14, and size = 15. Note that in this case the field does not begin within the byte whose address is given as the base address. Observe also that we could as well have described this field by base address = A + 1, position = 6, and size = 15. As a more extreme example of this phenomenon, consider the field of Figure 15.2.3, where base address = A, position = 341, and size = 12.

To see what occurs when a register is used as the base address, consider the field of Figure 15.2.4, in which base address = R7, position = 26, and size = 9. Since *position* + *size* > 32, the low-order 6 bits of the field are bits 31:26 of R7, while the high-order 3 bits are bits 2:0 of R8. Thus in this case, the bit field is taken as a subfield of the 64-bit concatenation of R8 with R7.

We close this section with an example (Figure 15.2.5) of a bit field in which the position is given as a *negative* bit offset—base address = A, position = −10, and size = 21—although again we note that this field could also be defined by base address = A-2, position = 6, and size = 21.

It should be clear from these examples that with the exception of subfields of registers, the same bit field can be referenced in a variety of ways, the particular method in each case being dictated by programmer convenience and/or the surrounding programming environment.

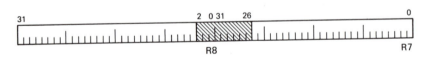

Figure 15.2.4

Variable-Length Bit Fields   Chap. 15

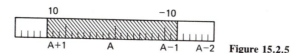

Figure 15.2.5

15.3 VARIABLE-LENGTH BIT FIELD OPERATIONS

Of the operations that the VAX is capable of performing on variable-length bit fields, two of the most useful are the "move" and "compare" operations. As the names suggest, they move a field (to somewhere) and compare a field with some number. In each case the destination of the operation is a *longword*, and this leads immediately to the following question. If a bit field, whose size S is not necessarily 32, is "moved" to a longword destination, then to which S bits in the destination is the field moved, and what becomes of the remaining 32-S bits in the destination? We can gain some insight into the answer to this question by reviewing the actions of the various familiar "move byte" operations.

Since our concern here is what happens when a similar structure (a bit field) is moved to a larger structure (a longword), we shall concentrate on the effects of moving a byte to a word or longword. For the sake of definiteness, let the destination be a longword, and in particular we may as well assume that it is one of the general-purpose registers, say R0. Let the byte in question have the symbolic address BYTE (although, of course, it could also be the low-order byte of some other register). As we know, the effect of the instruction

$$\text{MOVB} \quad \text{BYTE,R0}$$

is to replace the low-order 8 bits of R0 with the contents of BYTE, with bits 31:8 of R0 being unaffected. A second type of "move byte," used when we want to convert the numerical value of an 8-bit byte to a 32-bit longword, but without regard to sign is

$$\text{MOVZBL} \quad \text{BYTE,R0}$$

In this case, bits 31:8 of R0 are replaced with 0s. Finally,

$$\text{CVTBL} \quad \text{BYTE,R0}$$

puts c(BYTE) in bits 7:0 of R0 and then extends the sign bit, bit 7, into the remaining 24 bits of the register, thus giving a longword *signed* version of the numerical contents of BYTE.

We are now in a position to deal with just how the processor views a variable-length bit field. Suppose that a field has base address B, position P, and size S. Then, depending on our needs at the time, the S bits in positions $P+S-1:P$ of B may be interpreted as an *unsigned* S-bit number; or it may be considered as a *signed* S-bit number, with the high-order bit (in position $P+S-1$) acting as the sign bit. Although the VAX does not have a bit field "move" operation analogous to MOVB, it does have the equivalents of MOVZBL and CVTBL. The operations are referred to as **extraction** operations (mnemonic EXTV), since they "extract" some bits from a field and then "move" them in some fashion to a longword. These two operations are described here, with more formal descriptions and further details given below.

The operator EXTZV moves a bit field with base address B, position P, and size S to a longword destination. The bits of the field replace the low-order S bits of the destination; and the high-order 32-S bits of the destination are replaced with 0s. The source field is unaffected. If S = 0, the destination longword is cleared.

The operator EXTV moves a bit field with base address B, position P, and size S to a longword destination. The bits of the field replace the low-order S bits of the destination, and the high-order 32-S bits of the destination are replaced with the high-order bit of the source field (= bit S-1 of the destination, *after* the move). The source field is unaffected. If S = 0, the destination longword is cleared.

Thus EXTZV moves a bit field to a longword with zero-extend, while EXTV moves a bit field to a longword with sign-extend. These two operators are diagrammed in Figure 15.3.1 and are formally described as follows:

(a) **EXTZV** *EXT*ract with *Z*ero-extend *V*ariable-length bit field

  EXTV   *EXT*ract with sign-extend *V*ariable-length bit field

The formats of the "extract" operators are

$$\text{EXTZV} \quad pos.rl, size.rb, base.vb, dest.wl$$

and

$$\text{EXTV} \quad pos.rl, size.rb, base.vb, dest.wl$$

EXTZV

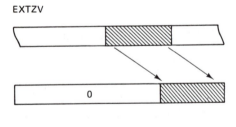

EXTV

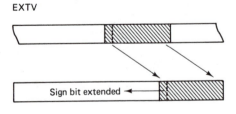

Figure 15.3.1

where *pos.rl* is the bit field's position (given as a longword), *size.rb* is the field size (given as a byte), *base.vb* is the base address, and *dest.wl* is the destination longword.

As a simple example, consider a 16-bit word with symbolic address WORD whose contents is ^XF27C (= 1111001001111100 in binary). The instruction

$$\text{EXTZV} \quad \#4,\#6,\text{WORD,R9}$$

will extract the field 100111 from WORD and move it, with zero-extend, to R9. Thus at the completion of the instruction, we will have c(R9) = ^X00000027. In a similar fashion,

$$\text{EXTV} \quad \#4,\#6,\text{WORD,R9}$$

will put the number ^XFFFFFFE7 in R9, the leading 1s resulting from the sign-extend property of EXTV and the fact that the high-order bit of the field being moved is a 1. Thus we see that if we choose to interpret this field 100111 as *unsigned*, representing the decimal number 39, EXTZV has moved the field to R9, giving R9 the value ^X27, thereby generating a 32-bit longword containing the number 39. On the other hand, if we choose to interpret 100111 as a *signed* number, with decimal value −25, then EXTV has produced in R9 the 32-bit equivalent of −25, namely ^XFFFFFFE7.

We can now use this operator further to simplify the programming segment of Section 15.1. Recall that in that algorithm we needed to isolate a group of 4 bits of R2 and then to use the value represented by those bits as an index (see Figure 15.1.2). But note that this 4-bit field was considered as *unsigned*—we want to treat, for instance, the bit configuration 1101 as a representation of the number

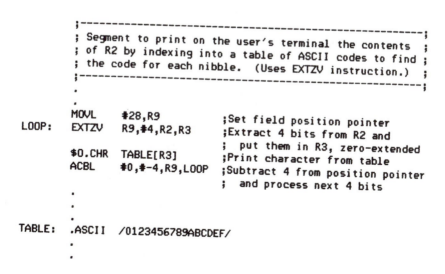

```
;-------------------------------------------------------------;
; Segment to print on the user's terminal the contents        ;
; of R2 by indexing into a table of ASCII codes to find       ;
; the code for each nibble.  (Uses EXTZV instruction.)         ;
;-------------------------------------------------------------;
        .
        .
        MOVL    #28,R9          ;Set field position pointer
LOOP:   EXTZV   R9,#4,R2,R3     ;Extract 4 bits from R2 and
                                ;  put them in R3, zero-extended
        $O.CHR  TABLE[R3]       ;Print character from table
        ACBL    #0,#-4,R9,LOOP  ;Subtract 4 from position pointer
                                ;  and process next 4 bits
        .
        .
        .
TABLE:  .ASCII  /0123456789ABCDEF/
        .
        .
        .
```

Figure 15.3.2

13, not −3—and thus EXTZV is precisely the operation we want. The final improved version of the algorithm is shown in Figure 15.3.2.

Now that we have some experience with the "extract" operators, we can deal with the variable-length-bit-field "compare" operations in a far more cursory fashion. The operators' mnemonics are CMPZV and CMPV, and they each compare a bit field with a longword integer, *in that order*. In effect, they simply use EXTZV and EXTV, respectively, to construct in a temporary register a longword from the bit field, and then compare this constructed longword with the specified longword (exactly as CMPL does).

(b) CMPZV   *CoMP*are with *Z*ero-extend *V*ariable-length bit field

CMPV   *CoMP*are with sign-extend *V*ariable-length bit field

The formats of the "compare" operators are

$$\text{CMPZV} \quad pos.rl, size.rb, base.vb, src.rl$$

and

$$\text{CMPV} \quad pos.rl, size.rb, base.vb, src.rl$$

where *pos.rl* is the bit field's position (given as a longword), *size.rb* is the field size (given as a byte), *base.vb* is the base address, and *src.rl* is the source longword to which the field is to be compared.

A temporary register *temp* is given the value

0 if *size* = 0
Zero-extended field for CMPZV
Sign-extended field for CMPV

temp is then compared with *src* as longwords; that is, *temp* − *src* is calculated and the condition codes are set according to the result:

N is set if *temp* < *src*, cleared otherwise.
Z is set if *temp* = *src*, cleared otherwise.
V is cleared.
C is set if the *unsigned* value of *temp* is less than the *unsigned* value of *src*; cleared otherwise.

Knowing the states of the condition codes is essential since, like CMPL, a CMPZV or CMPV is almost always followed by some conditional branch instruction, which, of course, depends on these condition codes.

         Variable-Length Bit Fields   Chap. 15

Since CMPZV (CMPV) is essentially EXTZV (EXTV) followed by CMPL, operations which are by now familiar to us, there is little more that needs to be said about these operators, but we offer one simple example before moving on to the next field operation. Let FIELD be the address of a word containing ˆXF0A7 and SRC be the address of a longword containing ˆX4072C5D2. Consider the instruction

$$\text{CMPZV} \quad \#1,\#13,\text{FIELD},\text{SRC}$$

Then *temp* gets the value ˆX00001853, and thus the condition codes are set as follows: N = 1; Z = 0; (V = 0); C = 1. For the instruction

$$\text{CMPV} \quad \#1,\#13,\text{FIELD},\text{SRC}$$

temp is given the value ˆXFFFFF853 and thus N = 1; Z = 0; (V = 0); C = 0.

Just as we can "move" a bit field to a longword, we can also transfer a longword to a field, but this type of move is somewhat simpler than what occurs with EXTZV or EXTV, since no zero-extend or sign-extend comes into play.

(c) **INSV**   *INS*ert into Variable-length bit field

The format of INSV is

$$\text{INSV} \quad src.rl,pos.rl,size.rb,base.vb$$

where *src.rl* is the source longword to be moved, *pos.rl* is the bit field's position (given as a longword); *size.rb* is the field size (given as a byte), and *base.vb* is the base address. The low-order *size* bits of *src* (that is, bits $size-1{:}0$) are moved into the bit field into positions $pos+size-1{:}pos$. The action of INSV is diagrammed in Figure 15.3.3.

As an example, consider again the symbolic addresses FIELD and SRC as given above, with c(FIELD) = ˆXF0A7 and c(SRC) = ˆX4072C5D2. The instruction

$$\text{INSV} \quad \text{SRC},\#4,\#7,\text{FIELD}$$

will move the low-order 7 bits of SRC, 1010010, into FIELD, beginning in position 4 and extending through position 10. Thus after execution of this instruction we will have c(FIELD) = ˆXF527.

INSV

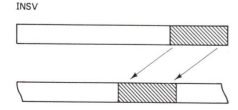

Figure 15.3.3

We close this section with two operations on bit fields which, although some-times useful in special programming environments, are used relatively infrequently compared with the other operators we have described above. The operators in question search a bit field for the *first* bit that is *set* (or *cleared*) and return infor-mation about that bit's position in a specified longword.

(d) **FFC**   *Find First Cleared* bit in variable-length bit field
   FFS   *Find First Set* bit in variable-length bit field

The formats of the "find first" operators are

$$\text{FFC} \quad pos.rl, size.rb, base.vb, bitpos.wl$$

and

$$\text{FFS} \quad pos.rl, size.rb, base.vb, bitpos.wl$$

where *pos.rl* is the bit field's position (given as a longword), *size.rb* is the field size (given as a byte), *base.vb* is the base address, and *bitpos.wl* is the (longword) position of the first bit in the field that was found to be cleared or set, respectively. *bitpos* is returned as a position relative to the *base, not* relative to the low-order bit of the variable-length bit field. If no (cleared or set) bit is found in the specified field, *bitpos* is given the value of the position of the bit one position to the left of the specified field. If *size* = 0, *bitpos* is set to *pos*. If the specified (cleared or set) bit is found in the field, the condition code Z-bit is cleared; if the specified bit is not found, or if *size* = 0, the Z-bit is set.

A couple of examples will suffice to clarify the actions of these operators. Suppose that c(FIELD) = ^XA0375 and we wish to find the first clear bit in the field whose base address is FIELD, position is 8, and size is 6. (This field consists of the bits 000011.) Then the instruction

$$\text{FFC} \quad \#8, \#6, \text{FIELD}, \text{R9}$$

will return in R9 the value 10, the position of the first clear bit in that field, and the Z-bit will be set to 0. (Note that it does *not* return the value 2, the bit position *within that field* of the first clear bit.) On the other hand, the instruction

$$\text{FFS} \quad \#10, \#6, \text{FIELD}, \text{R9}$$

will return the value 16 in R9 and the Z-bit will be set to 1, as the reader can easily verify.

15.4 A BIT FIELD PROGRAMMING EXAMPLE

The following programming segments use most of the variable-length bit field operators. Some simplifications have been made here so that we might concentrate on the bit field manipulations and not have them obscured by many details which, in practice, may well be desirable if not actually required. Thus arguments are passed back and forth to subroutines via registers, whereas good programming practice might dictate the use of the stack and procedure calls instead; registers used in subroutines are not saved and restored as they normally would be; and so on. The reader's indulgence is sought here; we focus our attention on the uses of FFC, INSV, etc., and ignore any structural deficiencies.

Consider a program in which it is required to create a large number of short character strings of varying lengths, but each of length not to exceed 32. We set aside a block of CHRNUM bytes to hold these strings (the block labeled STRING in the accompanying program listings). However, the situation is not static, for

```
STRING: .BLKB    CHRNUM        ;Block to hold strings
BITMAP: .BLKB    <CHRNUM-1>/8+1 ;'Bytes in use' bitmap

;-----------------------------------------------------------;
; Subroutine 'LOCATE' -- finds the first byte in STRING ;
; which begins a block of N contiguous bytes currently  ;
; not in use, by searching BITMAP for the first set of  ;
; N contiguous cleared bits.                            ;
;                                                       ;
; R0 contains the number N of bytes to locate.  Upon    ;
; return, R0 contains N and R1 contains the address in  ;
; the block STRING of the start of N contiguous free    ;
; bytes.                                                ;
;-----------------------------------------------------------;

LOCATE: MOVAB    BITMAP,R1     ;Set BITMAP pointer
        CLRQ     R2            ;R2 is variable field 'position'
                              ;(R3 is high-order 32 bits used
                              ; in EDIV instructions)

LOC.10: FFC      R2,#32,(R1),R2 ;Look for 1st clear bit in map
        BNEQ     LOC.30         ;Found it -- skip out
LOC.20: EDIV     #8,R2,R4,R2    ; else divide current 'position'
                              ; into 0-4 bytes, new 'position'
        ADDL     R4,R1         ;Adjust BITMAP pointer
        BRB      LOC.10        ; and look again for clear bit

LOC.30: EDIV     #8,R2,R4,R2   ;Divide current 'position'
                              ; into 0-4 bytes, new 'position'
        ADDL     R4,R1         ;Adjust BITMAP pointer
        CMPV     R2,R0,(R1),#0 ;Are N contiguous bits clear?
        BEQL     LOC.40        ;Yes -- found desired block
        FFS      R2,#32,(R1),R2 ; else find first set bit
        BRB      LOC.20        ; and start search over again

LOC.40: SUBL     #BITMAP,R1    ;Get number of BITMAP bytes,
        ASHL     #3,R1,R1      ; multiply by 8 and
        ADDL     R2,R1         ; add current 'position' to get
                              ; number of bytes in STRING
        ADDL     #STRING,R1    ;Generate byte address in STRING
        RSB                    ; and return to caller
```

Figure 15.4.1

once a string is placed in this block of memory, it need not remain there until the completion of program execution; it may well be deleted later, and the bytes it had occupied may then be used for another newly created string. It is clear that one of the major problems we have in this program is to manage this rather dynamic area STRING. For whenever a new string is to be added to the collection, we must be able to determine *where* it can be added—that is, just where in the block STRING there are sufficiently many currently unused contiguous bytes to hold this new string. When a string is removed from the block of storage, we must somehow mark the bytes it formerly occupied as "no longer in use."

To deal with this problem and manage this block of memory in a fairly efficient fashion, we create a **bitmap,** which reflects the current status of the block STRING, in the following way. To each byte in STRING there is assigned a *bit* in the map (which, in the following programming segments, is labeled BITMAP). If that bit is *set* (1), the corresponding byte in STRING is currently occupied; if that bit is *clear* (0), the corresponding byte is free. Note that although the bitmap itself takes up some storage (one-eighth of the storage required by STRING itself), the map can be scanned far more efficiently than the block STRING can, even assuming that we had some means of looking at the bytes of STRING and determining whether they were currently occupied.

There are clearly a number of tasks that need to be dealt with here: Strings must be inserted into STRING, their addresses and lengths must be kept track of, and so on. We concentrate on three of these. The first job, written as a subroutine, is to search the bitmap to find sufficiently many contiguous bytes (in

```
;------------------------------------------------------------;
; Subroutines 'FREE' and 'INUSE' -- clear or set bits        ;
; in BITMAP to correponding bytes in STRING                  ;
; are 'free' or 'in use'.                                     ;
;                                                            ;
; R0 contains the number N of bytes in STRING and R1         ;
; contains the address in STRING of the first of those       ;
; N bytes.                                                   ;
;                                                            ;
; R0 and R1 are returned unaffected.                         ;
;------------------------------------------------------------;

FREE:    CLRL    R5              ;Establish 32 0's
         BRB     IN.10           ;   and enter main routine

INUSE:   MOVL    #-1,R5          ;Establish 32 1's

IN.10:   CLRL    R3              ;(R3 is high-order 32 bits used
                                 ;   in EDIV instruction)
         SUBL3   #STRING,R1,R2   ;Get number of STRING bytes
         EDIV    #8,R2,R4,R2     ;Number of BITMAP bytes (R4)
                                 ;   and field 'position' (R2)
         ADDL    #BITMAP,R4      ;Generate BITMAP address
         INSV    R5,R2,R0,(R4)   ;   and put 0's or 1's in BITMAP
         RSB                     ;Return to caller
```

Figure 15.4.2

STRING) to hold a new string. It is clear that we must pass to this subroutine (shown in Figure 15.4.1) the number of bytes required by the new string, and we want the subroutine to return to us the address in STRING of the first byte of a sufficiently large contiguous block of storage for that string. The remaining two tasks we deal with involve the marking of bits in the bitmap as representing "free" or "in use" bytes in STRING, and this is done in the subroutines of Figure 15.4.2.

With this understanding of the environment, and assuming that all the bits in BITMAP are initially cleared, the reader should have little difficulty in following the logic of these subroutines. In particular, LOCATE finds the beginning address of a block of N currently free bytes in STRING. But note that the routine *assumes* that success is guaranteed—no provision is made for failing to find these free bytes. This is simply another problem that has been swept under the rug in the interest of simplicity.

15.5 EXERCISES

15.1.1. Modify the program segment of Figure 15.1.1 or 15.1.2 to display the contents of R2 in *binary*, as a sequence of 32 0s and 1s.

15.1.2. Modify the program segment of Figure 15.1.1 or 15.1.2 to display the contents of R2 in *octal* (base 8), as a sequence of 11 digits, each in the range 0 to 7. (There is a problem here, since 32 is not a multiple of 3. Thus the leftmost octal digit will represent only the *two* high-order bits, 31:30, of R2. Consequently, this leading digit will evidently have to be treated as a special case.)

15.2.1. Assume that the quadword whose symbolic address is QUAD contains the number ˆXF02C81AA27E446AE. State what bit configuration is determined by each of the following sets of variable-length bit field specifiers. (We use the following abbreviations: B = base address, P = position, S = size.)

(a) B = QUAD	**(b)** B = QUAD+1	**(c)** B = QUAD+3
P = 19	P = 11	P = −5
S = 7	S = 7	S = 7
(d) B = QUAD	**(e)** B = QUAD+4	**(f)** B = QUAD−2
P = 52	P = −3	P = 18
S = 5	S = 0	S = 21

15.2.2. Assuming the same value of c(QUAD) as in Exercise 15.2.1, find *two* representations, in terms of base address, position and size, for each of the bit fields given below. In one of the representations the position specifier is to be the smallest possible nonnegative number, whereas in the other, the position specifier is to be the smallest possible (in absolute value) negative number. (Note that there may be several fields in QUAD having these same bit configurations, and thus the representations need not be unique.)

(a) 111111	**(b)** 0000011	**(c)** 110101
(d) 1011	**(e)** 111000	**(f)** 00000

15.3.1. Modify the program segment of Figure 15.3.2 to display the contents of R2 in *binary*, as a sequence of 32 0s and 1s.

15.3.2. Modify the program segment of Figure 15.3.2 to display the contents of R2 in *octal* (base 8), as a sequence of 11 digits, each in the range 0 to 7. (Note that the same problem occurs here that was mentioned in Exercise 15.1.2: 3 does not divide 32, and thus the leftmost octal digit represents only the *two* bits 31:30 of R2. But show that this problem, and the necessity to treat these two bits as a special case, can be eliminated by clearing R3 prior to executing the algorithm. Could this or a similar technique have simplified Exercise 15.1.2?)

15.3.3. Assume that initially c(R7) = 13 and that LONG is the symbolic address of a longword containing the number ^X1043C2F. State what will be the contents (in hexadecimal) of R7 after execution of each of the following instructions.

(a) EXTV   #1,#6,LONG,R7   (b) EXTZV   #1,#6,LONG, R7

(c) EXTZV   R7,#5,LONG − 1,R7   (d) EXTV   # − 4,R7, LONG + 1,R7

(e) EXTV   R7,R7,LONG,R7   (f) EXTZV   #7,#0, LONG + 3,R7

15.3.4. We have observed that, unlike MOVB, for example, there is no VAX instruction to "move" a variable-length bit field or size S to a longword destination in such a way that only the low-order S bits of the destination are affected; as we know, the remaining bits in the destination are replaced with 0s or 1s by EXTV and EXTZV. However, write a few instructions that will have the effect of simply *replacing* the low-order S bits of the destination longword with the specified bit field, without affecting the remaining bits of the destination.

15.3.5. Let c(R6) = ^X2FC and let LONG be the symbolic address of a longword whose contents is ^X3A0E73C3. For each of the following constructions, determine whether the indicated branch (to TARGET) will be executed or ignored.

(a) CMPV   #3,#6,LONG,R6   (b) CMPV   #3,#6,R6,LONG
    BGTR   TARGET   BGTR   TARGET

(c) CMPZV   #3,#6,LONG,R6   (d) CMPZV   #3,#6,R6,LONG
    BGTR   TARGET   BGTR   TARGET

(e) CMPV   #3,#4,LONG + 1,R6   (f) CMPZV   #13,#14, LONG − 1,R6
    BLSSU   TARGET   BGEQ   TARGET

(g) CMPZV   #0,#32,LONG,R6   (h) CMPV   #29,#3,LONG,R6
    BLSS   TARGET   BLSS   TARGET

15.3.6. Assume that c(R10) = ^X4027A53 and that the (16-bit) word whose address is WORD contains ^XAB3F. State what will be the contents of WORD after execution of each of the following INSV instructions.

(a) INSV   R10,#5,#7,WORD   (b) INSV   R10,#0,#4, WORD

(c) INSV   R10,#15,#3,WORD − 1   (d) INSV   R10,#15, #3,WORD

15.3.7. Let c(R4) = ^X102A03F5. What will be the contents of R5 and the state of the Z-bit after execution of each of the following instructions?

(a) FFC   #0,#6,R4,R5   (b) FFC   #4,#4,R4,R5

(c) FFS   #7,#13,R4,R5   (d) FFS   #10,#13,R4,R5

(e) FFS   #10,#5,R4,R5   (f) FFC   #28,#0,R4,R5

15.4.1. Although some attention must be paid to the details of writing the subroutines of Section 15.4, it should be clear that with the aid of FFC, INSV, and so on, the managing of the bits in BITMAP is not a difficult task. The reader is asked to reflect on the following question: How could one implement the subroutines LOCATE, FREE, and INUSE in a *high-level* language—Pascal or FORTRAN, for example? The answer should imply that despite the ease of programming afforded by these languages, there are some tasks which are best implemented at a machine level. (This phenomenon will frequently occur in an environment in which the fundamental unit of information is the *bit*; most high-level languages do not handle bit structures in an efficient fashion.)

15.4.2. How could the subroutines of Section 15.4 be modified to manage strings of arbitrary length? (Assume some reasonable upper bound on the maximum number of characters in a string, say 1000. The important question is: What changes need to be made if the string length is not ≤ 32?)

15.4.3. Consider an operating system that must manage disk storage; that is, since files are constantly being created on and deleted from the disk, the system must know at all times which disk "units" (blocks or sectors) are free and which are in use. Show that if files are always stored in *contiguous* disk blocks (a scheme used by a currently popular Digital Equipment Corporation operating system), the BITMAP handling scheme of Section 15.4 is almost ready-made for a disk management utility. Specifically, rewrite the subroutines LOCATE, FREE, and INUSE on the assumption that the disk contains 65536 blocks, numbered 0 to 65535, all of which are initially free, and that no file will exceed 32767 blocks in length. The routines will then refer to "block addresses on the disk" rather than "byte addresses in the block STRING." The LOCATE routine should also deal with the case in which the desired number of contiguous blocks *cannot* be found, perhaps by returning in R1 the number -1 as a block address, to signify failure.

LINKED
LISTS AND
QUEUES

16.1 LINKED LISTS

Since the very earliest of our programming efforts we have taken advantage of the **linear list** structure, in which data entries occupy *consecutive* memory locations and are then thought of by the programmer as a **single-** or **multidimensional array.** This viewpoint is further enhanced, from a programming standpoint, by the autoincrement addressing mode, and in fact even our first "serious" program, determining the largest of a collection of numbers (see Figure 6.4.2, for example), employed this mode. Indeed, this mode, or an equivalent means of "stepping through memory," has prevailed in computers almost from their very beginnings, a fact that attests to the importance of the list structure. As we know, the VAX also implements *index* mode, a mode that allows even the assembly language programmer to view contiguous memory as an "array" or "subscripted variable" in much the same fashion as the high-level-language programmer.

As useful as the array *concept* may be, there are circumstances under which the *implementation* of an array as a collection of consecutive locations is inappropriate. As an example of one such set of circumstances, consider the task of maintaining a small inventory of, say, approximately 100 household appliance repair parts. Each inventory entry consists of a part's identifying number and its count (number on hand), and thus we may assume that a given part can be represented as a pair of longwords. We suppose that for the purpose of searching through this list of parts, we choose to maintain the inventory list in order of *increasing* part number. This will make it quite easy to locate a given part, and even though some problems of a maintenance nature arise, in this particular instance they are minor. To see what these are, suppose that one of our parts is dropped from the inventory, perhaps as a result of its use being discontinued. Then unless that part just happens to be at the *end* of the list (highest part number), we shall have to remove it from the list by moving all its successors up one entry (two longwords) in the list, thereby "covering up" the deleted part. If a new entry is added to the inventory, we must find out where in the list the new part number belongs (according to the prescribed increasing order) and then "unpack" the list by moving each subsequent entry down two longwords, to allow for the insertion of the new entry.

Neither of these maintenance tasks is especially difficult to implement, and in a list of just 100 or so entries, they are also not time consuming. But suppose, instead, that we are dealing with an inventory of, say, hundreds of thousands of parts. (Such examples are not farfetched; the Department of the Army or a major automobile manufacturer, for example, must have to deal with such inventory lists.) Now each transaction—searching the list for a given part, "packing the list" by moving entries up in the list, or "unpacking the list" by moving them down in the list—can involve the comparing and/or moving of perhaps hundreds of thousands of entries. This data movement can become quite expensive of processor time, and if a number of users are accessing the inventory list simultaneously (as is most often the case in a timesharing inventory system), the situation may ultimately reach the saturation point, at which requests for insertions and deletions are being received faster than they can be processed.

As a second example of a situation in which the implementation of an array structure is complicated by the circumstances of the array of entries or their intended use, consider again the simple inventory example above, in which we have a hundred or so parts stored in part number order in consecutive memory locations. Suppose this time, however, that an entry consists not simply of the part number and count of parts on hand, but rather also contains a *part description*—a string of ASCII-coded characters. Although there is no problem in including these characters together with the part information, there may be a difficulty in determining just how many bytes to allocate for the description. Some parts may need only a word or two ("water pump," for instance, may be adequate), whereas others may require rather extensive wording to be completely descriptive ("washing machine agitator, 2″ shaft, left-hand thread"). On the one hand, it would be quite wasteful of memory to *preallocate* for *each* part the maximum amount of bytes that *any* part would ever require for its description, since in most cases many of these bytes would simply not be used. But on the other hand, if a *variable* number of bytes is used by each entry, then how are we to tell precisely at which memory location each entry begins? In the scheme described initially, in which the entries each occupied two longwords and were contiguous, we knew that the beginning of the *next* inventory entry was always 8 bytes down from the current entry, or equivalently, that the nth entry occupies bytes

$$\text{INVENT} + 8 \cdot (n - 1) \quad \text{to} \quad \text{INVENT} + 8 \cdot n - 1$$

where INVENT is the address of the beginning of the list (see Figure 16.1.1). We

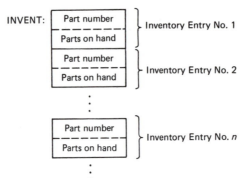

INVENT:

| Part number | } Inventory Entry No. 1 |
| Parts on hand | |

| Part number | } Inventory Entry No. 2 |
| Parts on hand | |

| Part number | } Inventory Entry No. *n* |
| Parts on hand | |

Figure 16.1.1

can resolve the present problem by including, with each entry, its length.   Figure 16.1.2 shows an example of this scheme, where the field labled *length* is the total length of the entry in bytes, or perhaps is simply the number of bytes in the description field.   But observe that if we do this (and some such scheme evidently is required), we cannot *directly* locate a given entry in the list as was done above; rather, we must find any entry by passing through its predecessors, since it is only in this way that we can determine where the *next* entry begins.   For example, to locate the third entry, we start at the first entry and *calculate*, using the *length* field, the beginning of the second entry.   Once at the second entry, we may use

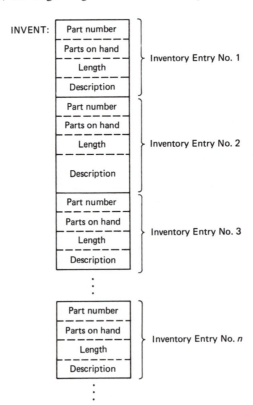

INVENT:

Inventory Entry No. 1
- Part number
- Parts on hand
- Length
- Description

Inventory Entry No. 2
- Part number
- Parts on hand
- Length
- Description

Inventory Entry No. 3
- Part number
- Parts on hand
- Length
- Description

Inventory Entry No. *n*
- Part number
- Parts on hand
- Length
- Description

Figure 16.1.2

its *length* field to locate the beginning of the third entry. That is, even knowing where the first entry is located, there is no way for us to determine where the third entry is without "passing through" the second entry.

It is clear that the storage technique of this last example has the advantage of being able to manage entries that require a variable amount of storage. It is equally clear what price we have paid for this capability—we have lost our "direct access" ability. But the scheme holds some promise, and in fact if we modify it just slightly we obtain a storage technique that also provides a partial solution to the first problem discussed above—the management of very large lists which must be maintained in a specified order. The *length* fields shown in Figure 16.1.2 are used, say, to indicate the number of characters in the description of the item, and this can be used to determine where the next entry begins. [In fact, the $(n + 1)$st entry begins at $N + 12 + 4*length$, where N is the address of the beginning of the nth entry, assuming that *length* itself is stored as a longword.] But suppose that instead of *suggesting* (by means of the *length* field) where the next entry is, we state its address *explicitly*, so that an entry would now appear as in Figure 16.1.3, where we have rather arbitrarily chosen the entry's first longword field to hold the address of the *next* entry. Two consequences emerge from this development. First, it is clear that just how much "data" the entry might contain is no longer of any consequence to the calculation of the address of the next entry, since in fact that address is now given explicitly. Second, evidently the $(n + 1)$st entry need no longer immediately follow the nth entry in *physical* memory—it can actually be located anywhere, since we are told exactly where it is without the necessity to do any calculations.

Before examining some of the details of the implementation and management of structures of the sort just discovered, we establish some terminology and notation. A linearly ordered collection of data, the entries of which are all of the same fixed length (number of bytes) and which occupy consecutive memory locations, is called a **dense list** or an **array**. This is the data structure with which we have been dealing since Chapter 6. Dense lists have the property that each entry has a **position, subscript,** or **index** in the list, and the location of each entry can easily be calculated once the address of the first byte of the list, the number of bytes in each entry, and the position in the list of the desired entry are known.

A linearly ordered collection of data, each entry of which contains the *address* of the *succeeding* entry, is called a **linked list.** The specified address is called a **pointer** or **link** to the next entry. If an entry A has the address of entry B as its link or pointer, we say that **A points at B, B is pointed at by A,** that **B is A's successor,** and that **A is B's predecessor.** Since a linked list may obviously contain

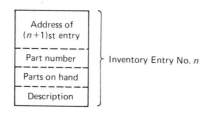

Figure 16.1.3

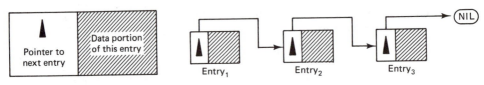

Figure 16.1.4

Figure 16.1.5

only finitely many entries, then unless some entry is one of its own "ancestors," so to say, some entry must have *no* successor. Such an entry is called the **terminal entry**, and for the sake of consistency, we give it a pointer as well, but one that we can recognize as *not* pointing at any subsequent entry. Such a pointer is named **NIL**, and in the sample programming we shall use the address 0 to indicate a NIL pointer, since we can ensure that no linked list entry will ever be located at physical memory location 00000000.

Observe that we have not specified what data are contained in a linked list entry or of how many bytes it consists, for although those details must be dealt with in practice, they have no bearing on the description given above. And nothing has been said about the address of the successor of an entry (that is, that entry's link or pointer), since in fact just where in memory the entries are located is of no consequence to the linked list concept. Compare this situation with that of the dense list. (In practice, of course, we will have to be assigning physical memory to new list elements, for instance, and then the actual locations will be of considerable practical importance.) Figure 16.1.4 shows a linked list entry in which the link, or pointer, appears as the first longword in the entry, again an arbitrary choice but one about which we shall be quite consistent. We have used the symbol ▲ to indicate the pointer field of the entry. In Figure 16.1.5 is shown a linked list

```
00000000   0000            NIL = 0                    ;Definition of NIL pointer
                             .
                             .
0000168A   0231   ENTRY1:  .ADDRESS  ENTRY2           ;Link to next entry
001077B8   0235            .LONG     1079224          ;Part number
000000AE   0239            .LONG     174              ;Parts on hand
           023D            .ASCIZ    #Water pump#
                             .
                             .
00000000   064A   ENTRY3:  .ADDRESS  NIL              ;Terminal entry -- NIL pointer
0028CEEA   064E            .LONG     2674410          ;Part number
00000011   0652            .LONG     17               ;Parts on hand
           0656            .ASCII    #Washing machine agitator -- #
                           .ASCIZ    #2" shaft -- LH thread#
                             .
                             .
0000064A   168A   ENTRY2:  .ADDRESS  ENTRY3           ;Link to next entry
001F61AF   168E            .LONG     2056623          ;Part number
00000403   1692            .LONG     1027             ;Parts on hand
           1696            .ASCIZ    #1/4" washers#
                             .
                             .
```

Figure 16.1.6

containing three entries, in which each link is diagrammed as an arrow from the link field of one entry to its successor entry. Finally, Figure 16.1.6 shows a portion of memory which contains three linked list entries similar to what would be required for the inventory example described earlier in this section. Note that the entries are not in contiguous memory locations, and in fact even though ENTRY2 precedes ENTRY3 *logically* (since it has a smaller part number and as we see it "points to" ENTRY3), ENTRY2 is actually located at a *higher* physical memory address.

16.2 BASIC OPERATIONS ON LINKED LISTS

The discussions of Section 16.1 indicate that there are three principal activities that play a role when dealing with and maintaining linked lists: *searching* for a given entry (or perhaps for a new entry's predecessor); *inserting* a new entry in the linked list; and *deleting* an existing entry from the list. We shall see that each of these is quite easily managed, although for the time being we shall *not* discuss the searching of a list for a given entry; there are some problems here with which we have yet to deal.

Recall that to insert an entry in an ordered dense list (array), it was necessary to unpack the list, since the new entry had to fit *physically* between its predecessor and successor. In the case of a linked list, however, although the new entry must reside *logically*—in the sense of the links—between its predecessor and successor, just where in *physical* memory it might be placed is of no consequence (except, of course, that those memory locations must be currently unoccupied). Thus all that is required is that the link from the new entry's predecessor to that predecessor's successor be *broken* and the new entry inserted between these two existing entries. The situation is diagrammed in Figure 16.2.1, where the new entry is labeled *entry* and its predecessor is labeled *pred*. The assembly language implementation of an insertion is actually trivial, as shown in the procedure INS_LIST of Figure 16.2.2. The procedure is passed the address of the predecessor and of the new entry, and the reader should have no difficulty verifying that the links are properly set and adjusted to insert the new entry in the list immediately following *pred*. There are, however, three comments that need to be made here. First, the procedure evidently assumes that the entries in the linked list have their pointers (to the next list entry) as the *first* longword in the entry. Second, no provision is made here to put anything in the new entry except the link to the next entry; any further information required in the data portion of the entry (part numbers, descriptions,

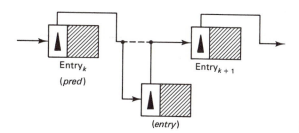

Entry$_k$
(*pred*)

Entry$_{k+1}$

(*entry*)

Figure 16.2.1

```
;--------------------------------------------------------;
; Procedure INS_LIST -- insert entry in a linked list    ;
;                                                        ;
; Argument list:      .LONG    2                         ;
;                     .ADDRESS <new entry's predecessor> ;
;                     .ADDRESS <new entry>               ;
;--------------------------------------------------------;
        ;
INS_LIST:
        .WORD   ^M<>            ;(Save no registers)
        MOVL    @4(AP),@8(AP)   ;Put <pred pointer> at 'entry',
        MOVL    8(AP),@4(AP)    ; put <entry address> at 'pred'
        RET                     ; and return
```

Figure 16.2.2

and so on) still needs to be inserted in memory following the link itself (that is, beginning at *entry* + 4). Finally, the space for this new entry must come from some pool of free memory, and that memory must be managed somehow. These details are not included in Figure 16.2.2, but at the end of this section we provide a complete program which calls this procedure (as well as others), and the reader will then see one way in which free memory can be managed.

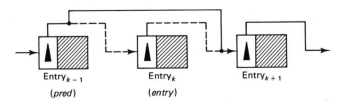

Entry$_{k-1}$ Entry$_k$ Entry$_{k+1}$

(*pred*)   (*entry*)

Figure 16.2.3

The deletion of a linked list entry is equally easy, both conceptually and in practice. All that needs to be done is to "short-circuit" the entry's predecessor's link, from the entry itself to the entry's successor, as indicated in Figure 16.2.3. The effect is to remove *entry* from the list, although of course that entry's data is still in main memory. Figure 16.2.4 shows a procedure DEL_LIST which, when

```
;--------------------------------------------------------;
; Procedure DEL_LIST -- delete entry from a linked list  ;
;                                                        ;
; Argument list:      .LONG    1                         ;
;                     .ADDRESS <entry's predecessor>     ;
;--------------------------------------------------------;
        ;
DEL_LIST:
        .WORD   ^M<>            ;(Save no registers)
        MOVL    @4(AP),-(SP)    ;Put <'pred' pointer> = <'entry'
                                ; address> on stack
        MOVL    @(SP),@4(AP)    ;Replace <'pred' pointer> by
                                ; <'entry' pointer>
        RET                     ; and return
```

Figure 16.2.4

passed the address of an entry's *predecessor*, will remove the entry itself from the list, by the "short-circuiting" of pointers described above. Once again notice that the procedure assumes that the link to the next entry is always the first longword of an entry.

16.3 LINKED LISTS WITH HEADER ENTRIES

The reader may have observed a serious deficiency with the linked list implementations we have devised so far. The insertion or deletion of an entry relies heavily on the entry's *predecessor*, and if the entry in question happens to be the *first* entry in the linked list, it has no predecessor. Thus with the techniques we have so far, and in particular using the procedures INS_LIST and DEL_LIST, it is not possible to remove the *first* entry from a list, nor is it possible to insert a new entry *ahead of* the (current) first entry in a linked list. But the situation is easily repaired, and the repair is such that we need make no changes in the procedures that have been devised so far.

Evidently what is needed to salvage this situation is to ensure that every linked list always have a "prefirst" entry, that is, an entry which *always* exists (even if the list is empty), and which points at the *first* entry of a nonempty list. Such an entry is called a list **header**; an example is shown in Figure 16.3.1, and we have indicated that the data portion of the header entry contains no data of significance. In fact, the header entry need contain nothing except the link to the first entry, although there are cases in which the header is made to match, in structure, at least, the data-bearing entries in the list for the sake of consistency. The reader should verify that the techniques diagrammed in Figures 16.2.1 and 16.2.3 are still valid and that INS_LIST and DEL_LIST will function properly without change, even if *pred* is the list header. Finally, note that when a linked list is created (and thus is initially empty), all that is required is establishing a header entry with a NIL link.

We now add a "search" routine to our small repertoire of linked list procedures. The procedure SRCH_LIST is shown in Figure 16.3.2, and as we see, it requires as arguments the address of the list header and the (longword) data for which the list is to be searched. The procedure assumes that the list is sorted in increasing order on this portion of the entry's data and that this longword is the first of the data portion of each entry, that is, that it immediately follows the link in each entry. The procedure returns information in R0 and the PSW C-bit as follows. If the specified data were found, the address of that entry's *predecessor* is placed in R0 and the C-bit is cleared. However, if the given entry is *not* found, the address of the list entry which *should* precede the entry is placed in R0, and

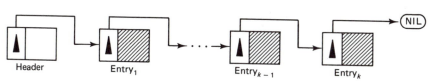

Header Entry₁ Entryₖ₋₁ Entryₖ

Figure 16.3.1

```
;----------------------------------------------------------;
; Procedure SRCH_LIST -- search for an entry in a linked   ;
; list.  The list is assumed sorted on the first long-     ;
; word data (beyond the link), in increasing order.        ;
; Returns with entry's predecessor's address in R0 and     ;
; C-bit clear if found, set if not found.                  ;
;                                                          ;
; Argument list:            .LONG      2                    ;
;                           .LONG      <entry to be         ;
;                                       searched for>       ;
;                           .ADDRESS   <header entry>       ;
;----------------------------------------------------------;
;
SRCH_LIST:
         .WORD    ^M<R6>          ;(Save one register)
         MOVAL    @8(AP),R6       ;Get <header address>
SRCH.1:  MOVL     R6,R0           ;Copy entry's address
         MOVL     (R6),R6         ; and get successor address
         BEQL     SRCH.2          ;Exit if NIL link
         CMPL     4(R6),4(AP)     ;Compare against passed argument
         BGTR     SRCH.2          ;Exit if gone too far or
         BLSS     SRCH.1          ; try next entry if not far enough
         RET                      ;Found desired entry -- return
SRCH.2:  BISB     #1,4(FP)        ;Set caller's C-bit
         RET                      ; and return
```

Figure 16.3.2

```
;----------------------------------------------------------;
; Procedure PRNT_LIST -- prints a linked list whose        ;
; entries are:             link to next entry  (longword)  ;
;                          part no.            (longword)  ;
;                          parts on hand       (longword)  ;
;                          description         (string)    ;
;                                                          ;
; Argument list:           .LONG       1                    ;
;                          .ADDRESS    <list header>        ;
;----------------------------------------------------------;
;
PRNT_LIST:
         .WORD    ^M<R6>          ;(Save one register)
         MOVAL    @4(AP),R6       ;Get <header address>
PRNT.1:  MOVL     (R6),R6         ;Get next entry address
         BNEQ     PRNT.2          ; and skip if non-NIL link
         RET                      ;Printing done -- return
PRNT.2:  $O.4D    4(R6)           ;Print part no.,
         $O.4D    8(R6)           ; parts on hand,
         $O.STR   SPACES          ; 5 spaces,
         $O.STR   12(R6)          ; description,
         $O.NL                    ; and generate a new line
         BRW      PRNT.1          ;Go do next entry

SPACES:  .ASCIZ   /     /
```

Figure 16.3.3

```
                    ;--------------------------------------------------------;
                    ; Program to manage (Insert, Delete and Print) entries   ;
                    ; in a linked list of Inventory Items.                   ;
                    ;--------------------------------------------------------;

                    .EXTERNAL INS_LIST,DEL_LIST,SRCH_LIST,PRNT_LIST

NIL     = 0                                 ;NIL "address"
BUFFER: .BLKB   4                           ;General use input buffer
HEADER: .ADDRESS   NIL                      ;List header (initialized with
                                            ;  NIL pointer)
LIST:   .BLKB   4000                        ;Area for inventory information

        ;Prompts, messages, dispatch vectors, etc.

SELECT: .ASCIZ  /IDPE/
VECTOR: .ADDRESS INSERT,DELETE,PRINT,EXIT

PRMT1:  .ASCIZ  /Select (I, D, P or E)/
PRMT2:  .ASCIZ  /Part No./
PRMT3:  .ASCIZ  /Parts on hand/
PRMT4:  .ASCIZ  /Description/

ERR1:   .ASCIZ  / already in list/
ERR2:   .ASCIZ  / not in list/

HEADNG: .ASCIZ  /      Part No.      On hand      Description/
ULINE:  .ASCIZ  /      --------      -------      -----------/

START:  .WORD   ^M<>               ;(No overflow trapping)

        MOVAB   LIST,R1            ;R1 always points to first free
                                   ;  byte in the block LIST

ASK:    $0.NL                      ;Clear print line
        $I.NL                      ;  and input buffer
        $0.STR  PRMT1              ;Ask for command
        $I.CHR  BUFFER             ;  and get it
        $I.NL                      ;(Clear input buffer)
        MOVAB   SELECT,R0          ;Set pointer
ASK.20: TSTB    (R0)               ;At end of selection codes?
        BEQL    ASK                ;Yes -- "ask" again
        CMPB    BUFFER,(R0)+       ;Found the "ask" code?
        BNEQ    ASK.20             ;No -- try the next one
        SUBL    #SELECT+1,R0       ;  else get code index,
        ASHL    #2,R0,R0           ;  multiply by 4
        JMP     @VECTOR(R0)        ;  and jump through dispatch vector

EXIT:   $EXIT                      ;Code was "E" (Exit)

INSERT: $0.STR  PRMT2             ;Code was "I" (Insert) --
                                  ;  ask for "part no."
        $I.4D   BUFFER            ;Get part no.
        $I.NL                     ;  (and clear input buffer)
```

Figure 16.3.4

```
        PUSHAL   HEADER          ;Set up for
        PUSHL    BUFFER          ; call to "search" procedure
        CALLS    #2,SRCH_LIST    ;Find where this part no. goes in list
        BCS      INS.20          ;Not found -- so it can be inserted
        $0.STR   PRMT2           ; otherwise notify
        $0.STR   ERR1            ; user that part already in list
        $0.NL                    ;(Generate "new line")
        BRW      ASK             ;Go get another selection
INS.20: PUSHAL   (R1)+           ;Push "first free byte" address
        PUSHAL   (R0)            ; and predecessor address
        CALLS    #2,INS_LIST     ;Put entry's link in list
        MOVL     BUFFER,(R1)+    ; and part no.
        $0.STR   PRMT3           ;Ask for "parts on hand"
        $I.4D    (R1)+           ;Get it, put in entry, and
        $I.NL                    ; clear input buffer
        $0.STR   PRMT4           ;Ask for "description"
        $I.STR   (R1)            ;Get it and put in entry
INS.40: TSTB     (R1)+           ;Look for string terminating NUL
        BNEQ     INS.40          ;Keep looking
        BRW      ASK             ; else go ask for next selection

DELETE: $0.STR   PRMT2           ;Code was "D" (Delete) --
                                 ; ask for "part no."
        $I.4D    BUFFER          ;Get part no.
        $I.NL                    ; and clear input buffer
        PUSHAL   HEADER          ;Set up for call to
        PUSHL    BUFFER          ; "search" procedure
        CALLS    #2,SRCH_LIST    ;Find where this part no. is in list
        BCC      DEL.20          ;Found it -- skip around
        $0.STR   PRMT2           ; else send
        $0.STR   ERR2            ; error message
        $0.NL                    ; and a "new line"
        BRW      ASK             ;Go get next selection
DEL.20: PUSHAL   (R0)            ;Stack predecessor's address
        CALLS    #1,DEL_LIST     ; and go delete entry
        BRW      ASK             ;Get next selection

PRINT:  $0.NL                    ;Code was "P" (Print) -- send "new line"
        $0.STR   HEADNG          ;Print heading,
        $0.NL                    ; "new line"
        $0.STR   ULINE           ; underlining
        $0.NL                    ; and another "new line"
        PUSHAL   HEADER          ;Push list header address
        CALLS    #1,PRNT_LIST    ; and invoke print procedure
        BRW      ASK             ;Get next selection

        .END     START
```

Figure 16.3.4 (continued)

the C-bit is set. As a concrete example, consider the searching of the inventory list of Figure 16.1.6 for a specified part number.

We are now in a position to write a complete linked list management program, and we shall do so using the small-scale inventory example as the illustrative list. Since we shall want to see that list from time to time, we provide in Figure 16.3.3 a list printing procedure for that particular linked list. Notice that it needs as an argument only the address of the list header. (See Figure 16.1.3 for the layout of the data portion of the list entries and Figure 16.1.6 for a sample list.)

Figure 16.3.4 shows an example of a complete inventory system of the sort we have been discussing, which allows for the insertion, deletion, and printing of items (linked list entries) consisting of a link (longword), part number (longword), parts-on-hand count (longword), and description (one or more ASCII bytes). The programming itself is quite simple, since it takes advantage of the procedures INS_LIST, DEL_LIST, SRCH_LIST, and PRNT_LIST. The heart of the mainline program is the few lines at ASK, which determines what function the user wishes to perform and then dispatches to small routines that invoke these procedures. As simple as it is, the reader should take particular note of the fashion in which free (available) storage is allocated each time a new entry is inserted.

16.4 THE MANAGEMENT OF AVAILABLE STORAGE IN LINKED LISTS

The inventory example of Section 16.3 discloses one of the deficiencies of the linked list concept as we have described it so far. When an item is inserted into the list, it requires 12 bytes for its link, part number, and parts-on-hand, together with some number of bytes for the part description. If the description requires on the average, say, 20 bytes, the 4000 bytes of storage that was preallocated will suffice for 125 parts, which is adequate for the kinds of inventories we have in mind, *provided* that the collection of parts is relatively static. But suppose now that the inventory list is quite dynamic—that even though the list never contains more than 100 or so parts at any one time, new parts are constantly being added to the inventory and older, obsolete parts are withdrawn from it. The problem with the program of Figure 16.3.4 is that whenever a part is removed from the inventory list (via DEL_LIST), no provision is made to *recover* the bytes which were occupied by that entry. Since the storage that is allocated to an entry can thus never be used by another entry, even if the original entry is deleted, we may soon run out of storage, despite the fact that only a modest number of parts are in the list. It is this problem that we intend to address in this section, and to do so for the specific inventory example, we must make a slight concession for the sake of uniformity of the entries in the list.

In the case of a dense list in which the active part of the list expands and contracts as entries are inserted and deleted, the only "available storage" management that is required is to keep track of the index of the first entry not in use, a number that increases by 1 when an entry is added and which decreases by 1 when an entry is removed. In the case of a linked list, however, the situation is complicated by two facts. First, the *amount* of storage occupied by a deleted entry may vary, and in fact we will *not* deal with this problem here, leaving an investigation of it to the exercises; that is, we assume for the present that *all* list entries have *identical* storage requirements. Second, the *location* of the storage that is returned to available memory upon a deletion is not necessarily related to other available storage in any reasonable way. When entries are added to the list, they may reside anywhere in physical memory, and thus when they are deleted a similar phenomenon occurs. In short, after several insertions of entries and subsequent deletions, the area occupied by the list entries, and consequently the area *unoccupied* as well, can become quite fragmented, even if that area was initially contiguous (as is the case in the example of Figure 16.3.4). But there is a simple and elegant solution to the problem of how to keep track of and, in particular, to "recover" the storage belonging to deleted entries in such a way that this memory can be used again. We simply *link available storage*, much as we do with occupied storage, in the following way. When the list is initially created (and is empty) and some storage is allocated for its entries, we break that storage down into groups of contiguous bytes, each group being large enough to hold the data for a single entry. (Recall that we are assuming that all the entries have *identical* storage requirements.) Links are then established from each of these blocks to the next, so that each block acts as an entry in a linked list. We then keep track of the address of the first such available block. Now when a new entry is inserted in the linked list, it takes as its storage the first available block, and the free storage successor of that first block now becomes the new "first available block." When an entry is deleted from the linked list, the memory occupied by that entry becomes the "first available block" of free storage, and a link is established from it to what *was* the first available block. In this way the same storage keeps getting used over and over, being occupied when an entry is created, but being recovered when that particular entry is deleted. Thus we never lose storage—every block is either occupied or available.

The program listing of Figure 16.4.1 is a modification of that of Figure 16.3.4, in which available storage is managed as described above. The changes are made

```
;------------------------------------------------------------;
; Program to manage (Insert, Delete and Print) entries  ;
; in a linked list of Inventory Items.  (Manages avail-  ;
; able storage as a linked list.)                        ;
;------------------------------------------------------------;

        .EXTERNAL INS_LIST,DEL_LIST,SRCH_LIST,PRNT_LIST

NIL     = 0                     ;NIL "address"
BUFFER: .BLKB   80              ;General use input buffer
HEADER: .ADDRESS NIL            ;List header (initialized with
                                ;  NIL pointer)
LIST:   .BLKB   4000            ;Area for inventory information
LISTEND:

        ;Prompts, messages, dispatch vectors, etc.

SELECT: .ASCIZ  /IDPE/
VECTOR: .ADDRESS INSERT,DELETE,PRINT,EXIT

PRMT1:  .ASCIZ  /Select (I, D, P or E)/
PRMT2:  .ASCIZ  /Part No./
PRMT3:  .ASCIZ  /Parts on hand/
PRMT4:  .ASCIZ  /Description (19 characters, maximum)/
```

Figure 16.4.1

```
ERR1:   .ASCIZ  / already in list/
ERR2:   .ASCIZ  / not in list/

HEADNG: .ASCIZ  /      Part No.      On hand    Description/
ULINE:  .ASCIZ  /      --------      -------    -----------/

START:  .WORD   ^M<>                ;(No overflow trapping)

        MOVAB   LIST+4000-32,R1 ;Set pointer
        CLRL    (R1)            ;  and put NIL at end of LIST
SETLNK: CMPL    R1,#LIST        ;At beginning of LIST area?
        BLEQU   ASK             ;Yes -- go ask user for option
        MOVL    R1,-32(R1)      ;Otherwise set link,
        SUBL    #32,R1          ;  adjust pointer
        BRB     SETLNK          ;  and do next 32-byte block

ASK:    $O.NL                   ;Clear print line
        $I.NL                   ;  and input buffer
        $O.STR  PRMT1           ;Ask for command
        $I.CHR  BUFFER          ;  and get it
        $I.NL                   ;(Clear input buffer)
        MOVAB   SELECT,R0       ;Set pointer

ASK.20: TSTB    (R0)            ;At end of selection codes?
        BEQL    ASK             ;Yes -- "ask" again
        CMPB    BUFFER,(R0)+    ;Found the "ask" code?
        BNEQ    ASK.20          ;No -- try the next one
        SUBL    #SELECT+1,R0    ;  else get code index,
        ASHL    #2,R0,R0        ;  multiply by 4
        JMP     @VECTOR(R0)     ;  and jump through dispatch vector

EXIT:   $EXIT                   ;Code was "E" (Exit)

INSERT: $O.STR  PRMT2           ;Code was "I" (Insert) --
                                ;  ask for "part no."
        $I.4D   BUFFER          ;Get part no.
        $I.NL                   ;  (and clear input buffer)
        PUSHAL  HEADER          ;Set up for
        PUSHL   BUFFER          ;  call to "search" procedure
        CALLS   #2,SRCH_LIST    ;Find where this part no. goes in list
        BCS     INS.20          ;Not found -- so it can be inserted
        $O.STR  PRMT2           ;  otherwise notify
        $O.STR  ERR1            ;  user that part already in list
        $O.NL                   ;(Generate "new line")
        BRW     ASK             ;Go get another selection

INS.20: MOVL    R1,R2           ;Copy "free storage" pointer
        MOVL    (R1),R1         ;  and set it to next 32-byte block
        PUSHAL  (R2)+           ;Push "first free byte" address
        PUSHAL  (R0)            ;  and predecessor address
        CALLS   #2,INS_LIST     ;Put entry's link in list
        MOVL    BUFFER,(R2)+    ;  and part no.
        $O.STR  PRMT3           ;Ask for "parts on hand"
        $I.4D   (R2)+           ;Get it, put in entry, and
        $I.NL                   ;  clear input buffer
        $O.STR  PRMT4           ;Ask for "description"
```

Figure 16.4.1   (continued)

```
              $I.STR   BUFFER            ;Get it and put in buffer
              MOVL     #19,R3            ;Set "maximum character" counter
              MOVAB    BUFFER,R4         ;  and buffer pointer
INS.40:       MOVB     (R4)+,(R2)+       ;Put "description" in
              SOBGTR   R3,INS.40         ;  32-byte block
              CLRB     (R2)              ;Put in trailing NUL and
              BRW      ASK               ;  go ask for next selection

DELETE:       $O.STR   PRMT2             ;Code was "D" (Delete) --
                                         ;  ask for "part no."
              $I.4D    BUFFER            ;Get part no.
              $I.NL                      ;  and clear input buffer
              PUSHAL   HEADER            ;Set up for call to
              PUSHL    BUFFER            ;  "search" procedure
              CALLS    #2,SRCH_LIST      ;Find where this part no. is in list
              BCC      DEL.20            ;Found it -- skip around
              $O.STR   PRMT2             ;  else send
              $O.STR   ERR2              ;  error message
              $O.NL                      ;  and a "new line"
              BRW      ASK               ;Go get next selection

DEL.20:       MOVAL    @(R0),R2          ;Copy deleted entry's address
              PUSHAL   (R0)              ;Stack predecessor's address
              CALLS    #1,DEL_LIST       ;  and go delete entry
              MOVAL    (R1),(R2)         ;Set deleted entry's pointer to
                                         ;  current "first available" block
              MOVAL    (R2),R1           ;  and make deleted entry new
                                         ;  "first available"
              BRW      ASK               ;Get next selection

PRINT:        $O.NL                      ;Code was "P" (Print) -- send "new line"
              $O.STR   HEADNG            ;Print heading,
              $O.NL                      ;  "new line"
              $O.STR   ULINE             ;  underlining
              $O.NL                      ;  and another "new line"
              PUSHAL   HEADER            ;Push list header address
              CALLS    #1,PRNT_LIST      ;  and invoke print procedure
              BRW      ASK               ;Get next selection

              .END     START
```

Figure 16.4.1 (continued)

at the expense of only a few lines of assembly code, but they are highly significant. In particular, the reader should note the following: At SETLNK the initial available storage (that is, all of the block LIST) is *linked* in blocks of 32 bytes; when a new entry is inserted, the "description" of the part is now limited to 19 characters, which with a trailing NUL and the 12 bytes comprising the link, part number, and parts-on-hand count make up 32 bytes; a new entry takes its storage from the pool of free storage as before, but now this free storage is linked in 32-byte blocks with R1 always pointing at the first of these; and when an entry is deleted, its storage is returned to this pool by making it the *first* of these linked "available blocks."

16.5 BIDIRECTIONAL LINKED LISTS

A review of the activities of the preceding sections reveals that much of what needs to be done in the management of a linked list involves *searching*—we must *find* an entry to be deleted, and we must *find* a new entry's predecessor, and of course we may simply wish to search the list to see if a given entry is present. There is something of a nuisance associated with the searching process as we have devised it and, in fact, more than a simple annoyance, it can also be fairly expensive of searching time, the most costly activity associated with linked list management. First, we note that when we are looking for an entry to insert or delete, we must find that entry's *predecessor*, and thus the searching algorithm itself must always keep track of the *last* entry examined. Second, searching always begins at the *beginning* of the list—at the header entry. (This is not, strictly speaking, always *required*, but it will be about half the time.) To see that both of these annoyances can be eliminated at small cost, consider the following example. Suppose that we have a linked list which is in increasing order according to one of its data fields (as is the inventory example) and we need to search the list for some entry, say X. We begin at the header and move through the list searching for a match of the specified field with the value X. If we find it, or if we find an entry greater than X before finding X, then in either case we are done—we can terminate the search and announce some result. Suppose next that we are to locate an entry whose field value is Y. If Y > X, we need only begin the search at our present point, X. But if Y < X, then since we have no means of *searching backward* through the list, we must again begin the search at the header entry. Suppose, however, that we add another link to each entry, a pointer to that entry's *predecessor*. Then movement through the list could take place in *either* direction, and the two aforementioned objections disappear.

A linearly ordered collection of data, each entry of which contains the *addresses* of the *preceding* and the *succeeding* entry, is called a **bidirectional linked list**. The specified addresses are called the **backward link (backward pointer)** and **forward link (forward pointer)**, respectively. If an entry A has the address of entry B as its forward link, we say that **A points at B, B is pointed at by A**, that **B is A's successor**, and that **A is B's predecessor**. Figure 16.5.1 shows a typical entry in a bidirectional linked list, where we have used the symbols ▲ and ▼ to represent the forward and backward links, respectively. Figure 16.5.2 shows some of the entries of such a list, where the forward links have been represented as heavy arrows, and the backward links are shown as lightly drawn arrows. Notice that the terminal entry has a NIL forward link, and that the header entry has a NIL backward link.

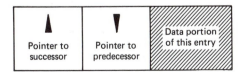

Figure 16.5.1

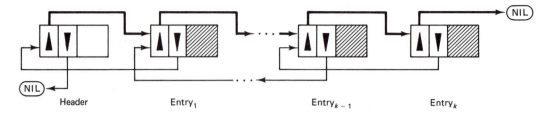

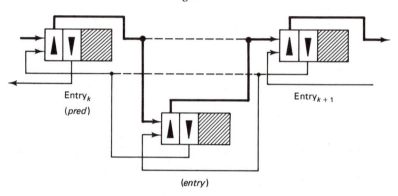

Header   Entry$_1$ Entry$_{k-1}$ Entry$_k$

Figure 16.5.2

Entry$_k$ Entry$_{k+1}$

(*pred*)

(*entry*)

Figure 16.5.3

The insertion and deletion of entries in the case of a bidirectional linked list is only slightly more involved than what has already been developed. In particular, Figure 16.5.3 diagrams what must be done for an insertion, and Figure 16.5.4 shows a procedure for the implementation of such an insertion. Notice that the arguments and the programming structure are almost identical to that of Figure 16.2.2, the

```
;-------------------------------------------------------------;
; Procedure INS_BLIST -- insert entry in a bidirectional      ;
; linked list                                                 ;
;                                                             ;
; Argument list:      .LONG     2                             ;
;                     .ADDRESS  <new entry's predecessor>     ;
;                     .ADDRESS  <new entry>                   ;
;-------------------------------------------------------------;
;
INS_BLIST:
        .WORD   ^M<R6,R7,R8>    ;(Save three registers)
        MOVAL   @4(AP),R6       ;Put 'pred' address in R6
        MOVAL   @8(AP),R7       ; and 'new entry' address in R7
        MOVAL   @(R6),R8        ;Get 'successor' address
        MOVAL   (R8),(R7)       ;Make <pred ptr> 'new entry' pointer
        MOVAL   (R6),4(R7)      ;Set 'new entry' backward pointer
        MOVAL   (R7),4(R8)      ;Reset 'successor' backward pointer
        MOVAL   (R7),@4(AP)     ;Set 'predecessor' pointer
        RET                     ; and return
```

Figure 16.5.4

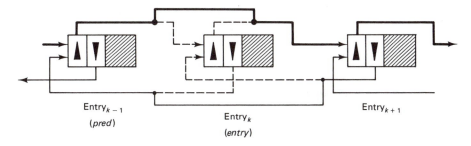

Entry$_{k-1}$
(pred)

Entry$_k$
(entry)

Entry$_{k+1}$

Figure 16.5.5

difference coming in the management of the backward link. In a similar fashion, Figure 16.5.5 shows what is required for the removal of an entry, and Figure 16.5.6 shows a procedure that achieves it. Notice in this case, however, that whereas the procedure of Figure 16.2.4 required the deleted entry's *predecessor*, here we may pass to the procedure the entry itself, since the backward link will yield the predecessor. We leave it to the reader to develop search routines, which will be slightly more complicated but far more efficient than what is presented in Figure 16.3.2. Some suggestions are offered in the exercises.

```
;----------------------------------------------------------;
; Procedure DEL_BLIST -- delete entry from a bidirec-      ;
; tional linked list                                       ;
;                                                          ;
; Argument list:        .LONG    1                         ;
;                       .ADDRESS <entry>                   ;
;----------------------------------------------------------;
;
DEL_BLIST:
        .WORD   ^M<R6,R7>       ;(Save two registers)
        MOVAL   @4(AP),R6       ;Get 'entry' address
        MOVAL   @(R6),R7        ;Get 'successor' address
        MOVAL   (R7),@4(R6)     ;Change predecessor's 'successor'
        MOVAL   @4(R6),4(R7)    ; and successor's 'predecessor'
        RET                     ;Return
```

Figure 16.5.6

16.6 THE *VAX* OPERATIONS *INSQUE* AND *REMQUE*

We devised the linked list concept as an improvement, from the standpoint of efficiency of some activities, of dense lists. Indeed, the concept is of such importance not only to user applications such as our inventory example, but also to operating systems applications, that the VAX implements the insertion and deletion procedures of Figures 16.5.4 and 16.5.6 as *hardware operations*! The two operations are called INSQUE and REMQUE (INSert into QUEue and REMove from QUEue, names that are explained in the next section), and their effects are almost precisely those of the procedures INS_BLIST and DEL_BLIST. The details of the operations, in particular their settings of the condition codes, are given in Appendix A.

(a) **INSQUE**   *INS*ert into *QUE*ue

INSQUE has the format

$$\text{INSQUE} \quad entry.ab, pred.ab$$

entry is the address of the entry to be inserted, and *pred* is the address of the predecessor of this new entry.   The effects of INSQUE are:

c($entry$)	$\leftarrow$ c($pred$)	Set forward link of new entry;
c($entry + 4$)	$\leftarrow$ $pred$	Set backward link of new entry;
c(c($pred$) + 4)	$\leftarrow$ $entry$	Reset new entry's successor's backward link;
c($pred$)	$\leftarrow$ $entry$	Reset new entry's predecessor's forward link.

(b) **REMQUE**   *REM*ove from *QUE*ue

REMQUE has the format

$$\text{REMQUE} \quad entry.ab, addr.ab$$

entry is the address of the entry to be removed (deleted), and *addr* simply maintains a copy of this address after execution of the operation, a feature that may be of importance if, for instance, the storage occupied by the deleted entry is to be recovered.   Specifically, the effects of REMQUE are:

c(c($entry + 4$))	$\leftarrow$ c($entry$)	Reset forward link of entry's predecessor;
c(c($entry$) + 4)	$\leftarrow$ c($entry + 4$)	Reset backward link of entry's successor;
$addr$	$\leftarrow$ $entry$	Copy address of deleted entry.

These two operations have an interesting and useful memory access checking feature which will ensure that the linked list cannot be left in an uncertain state as a result of some kind of access violation.   When an instruction is executed which involves the accessing of a memory location (as opposed to accessing a register), the processor determines whether the current user has valid access to that location. If not, the processor generates a fault, which is announced by the operating system as a memory access violation.   In the case of INSQUE and REMQUE, however, the references to *pred* and *entry*, given explicitly in the instruction itself, are not the only memory locations involved.   For the entry's predecessor and successor are also affected by deletions and insertions, and it is possible that although the entry itself is validly accessible, the entry's links are such that the predecessor or successor of the entry are *not* legitimately accessible to the current user. If INSQUE or REMQUE were allowed to proceed until such a violation revealed itself, it is possible that the linked list would have been partially modified when the access fault was detected. To avoid this possibility, the processor verifies *all* addresses before it modifies *any* addresses. That is, the processor verifies that it will be able to execute the instruction to completion before it begins that execution. In this way the user is always guaranteed that the list has the expected configuration as far as forward and backward pointers is concerned.

We leave it to the reader to modify the inventory management program of Figure 16.4.1 to take advantage of INSQUE and REMQUE and the bidirectionality of the list.

16.7 CIRCULAR LISTS AND QUEUES

One of the features of all our linked lists to date is that they have a *last* entry, that is, an entry with a NIL forward pointer. For bidirectional linked lists with header entries, the header entry itself always has a NIL backward pointer. These two NIL pointers, which are something of a special case, can be eliminated if we simply let the last entry point forward to the header, and let the header point backward to the last entry, as shown in Figure 16.7.1. Such a list is called a **circular bidirectional linked list**. It should be noted that in removing the NIL pointers by letting the list "wrap around on itself," we have also introduced some potential problem areas, such as the possibility of infinite list traversal. A few of these problems are investigated in the exercises. The reader should also verify that none of the procedures of Section 16.6, or the operations INSQUE and REMQUE, is affected by making the list circular.

We introduce some terminology that actually can be made to apply to any linked list but is normally used in the case of circular lists. The entry pointed at by the header entry (that is, the header's successor) is called the **head** of the list; the predecessor of the header (pointed at by the header's backward link) is called the **tail** of the list. A **queue** is a circular bidirectional linked list in which entries are always added at the tail and removed at the head. Notice that this definition

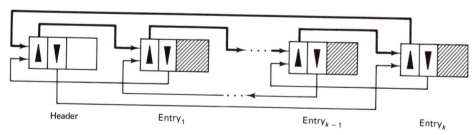

Header   Entry₁   Entry_{k-1}   Entry_k

Figure 16.7.1

does not make a queue a *structurally* new entity; in fact, it is nothing but a circular list. What distinguishes it is the fact that we have placed a constraint on the *activity* that can take place on the list—insertions and deletions take place only at the predecessor and successor of the header, respectively. (Compare this with the definition of a stack in Chapter 9, where the principal defining criterion was again a "constraint of activity"—insertions and deletions may take place only at the *top* of the structure.) Note also that the lists we have examined so far, and the examples which motivated the linked list concept, have the property that they are linked in some specific order according to some portion of the data field of each entry—the part number, for instance. In the case of a queue, however, no such ordering is involved, for there is never a question as to where a new entry is to be inserted; it is *always* inserted at the tail. In an analogous fashion, we need never "search for" an entry to delete; it is pointed at by the header's forward link.

Because of the fact that insertions and deletions always take place at the header entry, queue management is especially easy. If HEADER is the address of the header entry, then to insert a new entry (at the tail) we need only execute

$$\text{INSQUE} \quad entry,@\text{HEADER}+4$$

and to remove an entry (at the head) we can use

$$\text{REMQUE} \quad @\text{HEADER},addr$$

Since we frequently use a queue structure as a place to store information that is *waiting* to be processed, when an entry is *removed* from a queue it does not mean that we are done with it (as was the case earlier with general linked lists), but rather that we are just beginning with it. Thus the feature of REMQUE, which *saves* the address of the deleted entry, is most useful in this regard.

One of the conditions for which we must be on the lookout when dealing with queues is an *empty* queue. We did not have to worry so much about this in the case of the more general linked list, since whenever an entry was to be deleted, we first had to *search* for it (and if the list was empty, then of course we would not find it). But in the case of a queue, we never delete an entry with specific *contents*; rather, we delete a specific *positional* entry—the head entry. But it is trivial to detect that the queue is empty, for it is the only circumstance in which c(header) = header—that the header link (either forward or backward) points to itself. In fact, as revealed in Appendix A, both INSQUE and REMQUE use the condition codes to signal this empty queue condition.

16.8 EXERCISES

16.1.1. Implement a simple inventory system as a dense list, as shown in Figure 16.1.1, using the following guidelines.
   (a) Allocate, say, 400 longwords of storage for 200 entries, each consisting of a part number (maintained in increasing order) and a parts-on-hand field.

(b) Write a procedure to insert a new entry at a particular position in the dense list, and a procedure to remove a specified entry. A search procedure will also be required for the purposes of locating an entry to be deleted, and to find the position in the list of an entry to be added.

(c) Write a mainline program that initializes a list pointer (that keeps track of the first available free list longword), inserts several entries in the list, prints the list, deletes a few entries, prints the list again, and so on. That is, write a mainline routine that thoroughly tests the search, insert, and delete procedures.

16.1.2. Write a procedure, named INDEX, which, when passed the address of the first entry of a linked list and a "list index" I (that is, a positive number), will return in R0 the address of the Ith entry in the list. Assume that the list is structured as shown in Figure 16.1.3 and that indexing (subscripting) of the list entries begins at 1. Devise some means for the procedure to notify the calling routine if no such list entry exists—that is, that I is nonpositive, or that I exceeds the number of entries in the list. (*Suggestion:* A convenient and conventional method for the transmission of this information is through one of the PSW condition codes, say the C-bit.)

16.1.3. We stated that a terminal entry will have a NIL pointer, and that for the purposes of programming, we would use the address 0 as a NIL pointer, since we could ensure that no list entry would ever have 00000000 as its address.

(a) How can we be assured that no list entry will have a 0 address?

(b) In the segment of Figure 16.1.6 we made the direct assignment

$$NIL = 0$$

to establish a NIL pointer with the value 0. Could we just as well have made the *first* line of the program

$$NIL:$$

since it would assemble at location 00000000 and thus give NIL the value 0 also?

16.1.4. Mention was made of a linked list entry being one of its own "ancestors." What might be meant by that expression, and what would be the consequences of an entry that eventually pointed back to itself?

16.1.5. We defined what was meant by an entry being *the* terminal entry. Explain the use of the definite article *the*. Specifically, can a linked list have more than one terminal entry? If not, why not?

16.2.1. Write a procedure that will locate a given entry in a linked list. Evidently the procedure will need to know the address of the first list entry and the value of some entry field for which to search. How does the procedure manage requests for entries which are in fact not in the list? How is information returned by the procedure?

16.2.2. Why does the procedure DEL_LIST of Figure 16.2.4 require the use of the stack (which could as well have been a register) to hold the entry address? That is, why cannot the entry's pointer be put directly into the predecessor pointer? Should not the procedure "clean the stack" prior to its return?

16.3.1. The procedure SRCH_LIST can be improved somewhat as follows. Let some longword, say LAST_ACC, be used to keep track of the last list entry accessed, regardless of the purpose of that access. (LAST_ACC would be initialized to the header address.) When a "search" request is issued, SRCH_LIST looks at the entry whose address is in LAST_ACC. If that entry is the one requested, the search is over. If the data to be searched for are farther along the list than the data at the address in LAST_ACC, the search can begin at the entry whose address is in LAST_ACC. Otherwise, the search begins at the header entry, as in the version of SRCH_LIST as written. Write this improved version of SRCH_LIST.

16.3.2. The examples of linked lists that we have written, and the illustrative examples that motivated the definitions in the first place, have all centered around maintaining a list in some *logical* order based on some ordering of the list entries. In the inventory example the list is maintained in increasing part number order, and in other examples, lists might be maintained in, say, dictionary order of some key word in the entry. But observe that the definition of a linked list requires no such key field ordering. Consider, then, a linked list in which each new entry is simply linked from the *last* entry that was placed in the list. That is, logically each new entry goes at the end of the list, so that no particular logical order is maintained in the list. How would such a structure affect the search, insert, and delete routines that we have already written? What would such a list be good for? That is, what advantages would it have over a dense list?

16.3.3. One of the problems with which we are faced in practice when dealing with a linked list whose entries are ordered by some key field is that although the insertion and deletion of entries is extremely efficient, each of those activities requires the *locating* of a given entry, and the searching of a linked list is quite *in*efficient—if the list is several hundred thousand entries long, hundreds of thousands of compares will be required to find a given entry.

(a) Show that in general the number of compares will be on the average half the number of entries in the list. What will this number be if the improved searching of Exercise 16.3.1 is used?

(b) The searching of an ordered linked list (or even a dense list, for that matter) can be dramatically improved in the following way. Suppose that the key field on which the list is ordered can take on values from, say, 1 to 999. We construct an array (dense list) of 10 longwords the first of which contains the *address* of the first linked list entry whose key has a value between 0 and 99, the second of which contains the *address* of the first entry whose key value is between 100 and 199, and so on, the last entry containing the *address* of the first entry whose key value lies between 900 and 999. Now to locate a given entry by its key value, we go to the appropriate entry in the 10-entry array and find an address at which to begin the search. The effect is to require, on the average, a search of only one-twentieth of the list, rather than one-half of it. Such an array is called a list **index**, and a linked list with such an index array is called an **indexed list**. Revise the inventory program of Figure 16.3.4 to implement this scheme, on the assumption that part numbers are three digits long. (*Note:* This is by no means trivial, for the following reasons. If the list contains no part number in a certain range, the index array will have to reflect that fact, perhaps by containing a 0 address in that array entry. If the *first* list entry within a particular part number range is deleted from the list, the index array will have to be modified to reflect that change. Similarly, if an entry is added which comes at the *beginning* of a part number range, the index array entry will also have to be updated.)

(c) As an alternative to the index array of part (b) above, indicate how the list could be managed, and what changes would have to be made in the procedures that have already been written, if we maintained *ten* separate lists, one each to handle entries with part numbers between 0 and 99, between 100 and 199, and so on. How would the printing routine PRINT_LIST have to be modified in this case?

16.3.4. Add to the program of Figure 16.3.4 a "lookup" option, in which the user can specify a part number, and the program will announce the number of parts on hand and the description, provided that the part exists.

16.3.5. Add to the program of Figure 16.3.4 a "modify" option, in which the user can specify a part number and a new inventory, and the program will update that part's number on hand. (This would presumably be one of the most useful and used procedures in the program package.) Be certain to deal with errors such as occur when a specified part is not in the list and when the new "parts on hand" is not a valid integer.

16.4.1. The program of Figure 16.4.1 is designed to recover the storage released by deleted entries, and in providing for that feature, we made the concession of putting a 19-byte limit on the part description, so that every inventory item would require precisely 32 bytes. This was critical not to the *release* of storage upon a deletion, but rather to the *assignment* upon an insertion, so that free storage could be linked. The principal difficulty involved with an attempt to circumvent this fixed-length block is the following. Suppose that at the time a new entry needs to be inserted, the pointer to free storage points at a block of N bytes, and yet the new entry requires M bytes, where $M \neq N$. Discuss what would be involved in managing the free storage if the requirement of fixed-length entries is relaxed.

16.5.1. A problem may occur in a bidirectional linked list with a header entry which did not appear in the case of a simple forward linked list, namely, that it is now possible to "back into" the header entry by following the backward links, and it could be disastrous if we simply took the header as a *data* entry. Discuss several techniques by which we might recognize the header entry for what it is. (Some of these schemes may depend on knowing something about the valid data that the other entries can contain. But consider also the header entry's backward pointer.)

16.5.2. Rewrite the procedure SRCH_LIST of Figure 16.3.2 to take advantage of the fact that searching can take place in either direction in a bidirectional linked list. To be efficient, the "last entry accessed" will have to be noted, as in Exercise 16.3.1.

16.5.3. Rewrite the procedure INDEX described in Exercise 16.1.2 in the case of a bidirectional linked list.

16.5.4. Rewrite the program of Figure 16.4.1 so that the linked list is bidirectional, and thus the more efficient SRCH_LIST procedure of Exercise 16.5.2 can be used. Is it necessary bidirectionally to link the 36-byte blocks of free storage?

16.5.5. The links that determine the logical order of the entries in the linked lists we have discussed so far have been based on some field in the data portion of the entry (the part number, in the inventory example), and our latest effort employs both forward and backward links. But there is no reason why an entry cannot have other links in its records, links that perhaps order it is some other way and pertain to some other field in the entry. A list with these additional links is called a **multilinked list.** Add to the program of Exercise 16.5.4 a set of backward and forward links that order the list by "parts on hand" so that, for example, the list could be displayed in increasing order of size of inventory.

16.6.1. Rewrite the program of Exercise 16.5.4 using INSQUE and REMQUE instead of the procedures INS_BLIST and DEL_BLIST of Figures 16.5.4 and 16.5.6.

16.7.1. A queue, as defined in Section 16.7, is a structure which is very easily managed, the more so because of the INSQUE and REMQUE operations. But that definition is a bit more stringent than it needs to be, and in fact a queue can as well be constructed as a dense list. Suppose that we set aside an array of, say, 50 longwords for a queue. The first queue entry will go at the beginning of this array, the next immediately after it, and so on. The first entry to be removed will be at the beginning of the array, then the next array entry, and so on. Thus evidently what is needed to manage the queue is a **head pointer** and **tail pointer** so that we can keep track of what entry is "first" (at the head) and which is "last" (at the tail). But after 50 entries have been put on the queue, there is no more room in the array for additional entries, even if many entries have also been removed from the queue. Explain how the head and tail pointers, as well as the original array, must be managed so that the queue can always hold 50 entries at one time, regardless of how many entries may already have been added to and later removed from the queue.

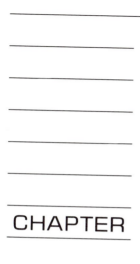

CHAPTER

17 PROGRAM SECTIONS

17.1 PROGRAM MODULARIZATION

Even our early programming efforts have been *modularized* to some extent. That is, we have made a conscious effort to divide programs into separate "pieces" or **modules** consisting of data to be read, data to be written, and pieces of related assembly code. In the beginning this was done primarily by dividing the program *instructions* up in such a way that the listing took on a modular appearance. (Refer, for instance, to Figure 6.6.1, in which the data are grouped at the end of the program listing, initialization instructions at the top, and two related groups of code at TEST and NEXT.) The subroutines and procedures of Chapter 9 greatly enhanced this modularity concept, and the concept of external routines as introduced in Chapter 10 extended the ease with which programs could be written by taking advantage of user-written "standard" external procedures and functions. Indeed, with a well-designed collection of procedures appropriate to a particular programming environment, mainline routines might consist of little more than a sequence of calls to various of these procedures. The macroinstruction constructions of Chapter 18 add further to this modularity.

We already know that none of this modular programming is *necessary*, in the sense that failure to write in this fashion will result in programs that do not execute properly. On the other hand, programs that are written rather randomly, with data and code interspersed, with many unnecessary jumps and branches, are programs that are very difficult to read and to maintain. As a short and simple example of this *genre*, consider the code of Figure 17.1.1, a complete program which actually does something useful. Its lack of modularity is the primary cause of the difficulty

```
X:      .WORD   0
        $I.1D   A
        BRB     B
A:      .BLKB   1
        .BYTE   0
C:      .WORD   0
B:      MOVW    A,C
        MULW    Z,A
        ADDW    Z+2,A
        MULW    C,A
        ADDW    Z+4,A
        JMP     DONE
Z:      .WORD   1,-2,4,0,6
P:      $0.2D   A
        BRW     Y
DONE:   MULW    C,A
        ADDW    W,A
        MULW    C,A
        ADDW    W+2,A
        BRW     P
W:      .WORD   0,6
Y:      $EXIT
        .END    X               Figure 17.1.1
```

in determining what it does, although the total absence of documentation and suggestive symbolic names are also contributing factors. Imagine what would be involved in reading, let alone maintaining, a program of several thousand lines of such code.

In this chapter we investigate another way in which a program can be modularized, by creating it in separate *sections*, each of which has its own *attributes*.

17.2 PROGRAM SECTIONS

Formally, a **program section** is any collection of assembler mnemonics or directives between two occurrences of the directive .PSECT (*Program SECT*ion), or between a .PSECT directive and the .END directive. The .PSECT directive may take any of a number of arguments, some of which are discussed in the remainder of this chapter. If a .PSECT directive has any arguments, the first such is always the **program section name**. If two program sections have the *same name*, the second section is taken to be a *continuation* of the first even if they are not contiguous in the source program, and the two program sections are treated as if the second were simply concatenated onto the first and contiguous with it in main memory.

Rather than attempt any further formalism here, we shall give a simple example. Figure 17.2.1 shows a program which has no real purpose other than as an illustrative example. (In particular, there are a number of bytes, words, and longwords which are declared and then never referenced. Actually, the programming does fill an array with consecutive integers, and it then prints the array.) The program contains five .PSECT directives. The first program section is named DATA1, and note that it contains some data—words and bytes which might be

```
        .PSECT  DATA1

ROW:    .BLKW   1
COL:    .BLKW   1
ARRAY:  .BLKW   36

FLAG1:  .BLKB   1
FLAG2:  .BLKB   1

TRUE:   .BYTE   -1

        .PSECT  CODE

START:  .WORD   ^M<>
        CLRL    R0
        MOVAW   ARRAY,R5
LOOP:   INCL    R0
        MOVW    R0,(R5)+
        CMPL    R5,#ARRAY+<2*36>
        BLSSU   LOOP

        .PSECT  DATA2

POWERS: .LONG   1,10,100,1000,10000,100000

X:      .WORD   2
Y:      .WORD   4
Z:      .WORD   8

        .PSECT  DATA1

A:      .WORD   1,2,3,4,5,6,7,8,9,10

        .PSECT  CODE

        CLRL    R0
PRINT:  $O.2D   ARRAY[R0]
        $O.NL
        INCL    R0
        CMPL    R0,#36
        BLSS    PRINT
        $EXIT

        .END    START
```

Figure 17.2.1

operated on by the program instructions. The second section is named CODE, and it contains the program entry point and some instructions. The third program section is named DATA2, and again it contains some data. The fourth section is *again* named DATA1, and as we shall see, it is treated as a continuation of the first instance of the DATA1 section. In a similar fashion, the last section is named CODE and is taken as a continuation of the earlier program section CODE. Before moving on to see how the assembler treats these constructions, we should note that despite the fact that DATA1 and DATA2 contain data, and that CODE contains assembler code, the *names* of the program sections are immaterial—they have no bearing on their contents. Our choice of names has simply been consistent with good documentation practices.

Figure 17.2.2 shows an assembly listing of the source program of Figure 17.2.1, and we see that some rather unusual and perhaps unexpected things have taken place. The first line is

.PSECT   DATA1

```
              00000000  1              .PSECT  DATA1
                0000    2
              00000002  0000  3 ROW:    .BLKW   1
              00000004  0002  4 COL:    .BLKW   1
              0000004C  0004  5 ARRAY:  .BLKW   36
                004C    6
              0000004D  004C  7 FLAG1:  .BLKB   1
              0000004E  004D  8 FLAG2:  .BLKB   1
                004E    9
           FF   004E   10 TRUE:   .BYTE   -1
                004F   11
              00000000 12              .PSECT  CODE
                0000   13
        0000  0000   14 START:  .WORD   ^M<>
     50   D4  0002   15              CLRL    R0
55 00000004'EF 3E  0004   16              MOVAW   ARRAY,R5
     50   D6  000B   17 LOOP:   INCL    R0
     85  50  B0  000D   18              MOVW    R0,(R5)+
0000004C'8F 55  D1  0010   19              CMPL    R5,#ARRAY+<2*36>
     F2   1F  0017   20              BLSSU   LOOP
                0019   21
              00000000 22              .PSECT  DATA2
                0000   23
                0000   24 POWERS: .LONG   1,10,100,1000,10000,100000
                0018   25
        0002  0018   26 X:      .WORD   2
        0004  001A   27 Y:      .WORD   4
        0008  001C   28 Z:      .WORD   8
                001E   29
              0000004F 30              .PSECT  DATA1
                004F   31
                004F   32 A:      .WORD   1,2,3,4,5,6,7,8,9,10
                0063   33
              00000019 34              .PSECT  CODE
                0019   35
     50   D4  0019   36              CLRL    R0
                001B   37 PRINT:  $O.2D   ARRAY[R0]
                0032   38              $O.NL
     50   D6  003E   39              INCL    R0
  24  50  D1  0040   40              CMPL    R0,#36
     D6  19  0043   41              BLSS    PRINT
                0045   42              $EXIT
                0051   43
                0051   44              .END    START
```

Figure 17.2.2

and, as we expect, the assembler has set its location counter to 00000000. The assembly continues, with data and storage being assigned to various locations, until the byte labeled TRUE is assigned a value at line 10. As we see, that byte occupies (relative) memory location 0000004E. The next line is another .PSECT directive:

.PSECT   CODE

But observe that the assembler has *reset* its location counter *back to zero* at the beginning of this program section. On the face of it we now have two collections of bytes occupying the same locations—the *data* from the program section DATA1 and the *instructions* from the section CODE. This is clearly not possible, but it will not be until Section 17.3 that we resolve this anomaly.

The program section CODE continues to location 00000019 (line 21), at which point in the program a new section, DATA2, is defined. Once again observe that the assembler's location counter is reset to zero. We encounter another .PSECT directive at line 30, but notice that this is a program section name which is already in use. Note also that this time the location counter is *not* reset to zero; rather, it is reset to the value it had the last time the program section DATA1 was *left*, namely 0000004F. This phenomenon occurs again at line 34, where the program section CODE is resumed.

Evidently the assembler maintains a location counter for *each* program section and, as suggested above, subsequent occurrences of an existing program section are then treated simply as continuations of the preceding ones. The assembler also assigns a two-digit number to each program section as it encounters it, and this number is used by both the assembler and the linker to identify, for example, the program section to which symbols belong.

Before examining how the code generated by the assembler is actually loaded into memory so that it avoids the apparent multiple occupancy we have observed, it will be illuminating to look at the symbol table generated by the assembler for this source program. We see from Figure 17.2.3 that POWERS, ROW, and START all have the value 00000000, but by now we suspect that this is not a conflict, since these symbols are in different program sections. Indeed, the symbol table itself indicates that POWERS is in section 04, ROW is in section 02, and

A	0000004F R	02
ARRAY	00000004 R	02
COL	00000002 R	02
FLAG1	0000004C R	02
FLAG2	0000004D R	02
LOOP	0000000B R	03
POWERS	00000000 R	04
PRINT	0000001B R	03
ROW	00000000 R	02
START	00000000 R	03
TRUE	0000004E R	02
X	00000018 R	04
Y	0000001A R	04
Z	0000001C R	04

Figure 17.2.3

START is in section 03. (There *is* a program section number 01, but it is not evident from the listing of Figure 17.2.2. This is discussed in Section 17.3.)

Finally, the fact that ARRAY and the instruction

$$MOVAW \quad ARRAY,R5$$

at line 16 are in *different* program sections accounts for the machine code that was generated, namely

$$55 \quad 00000004'EF \quad 3E \quad 0004 \quad 16 \quad MOVAW \quad ARRAY,R5$$

Note that the assembler has used displacement mode as expected, but it has generated a longword displacement and has *not* calculated that displacement, but rather, inserting the *value* ARRAY = 00000004, just as it would do if ARRAY were a forward reference, despite the fact that ARRAY *appears* to be a backward reference. But since ARRAY is not defined within this program section, the assembler has treated it as if it is currently undefined (which, in fact, it is, relative to this program section). Notice also that the assembler has used the value 00000004 for ARRAY, which is *correct* within ARRAY's program section (program section 02), but which is *incorrect* within the *current* program section, 03. Evidently there is more information in the code the assembler has generated at line 16 and will later pass to the linker than we can see; program section information about the address 00000004 must also be included here.

In summary, our investigations so far reveal that the assembler is treating these program sections almost as if it is dealing with three *separate* assemblies, and this is not a completely erroneous way to view the process. On the other hand, evidently the assembler does know the values of symbols in other sections. (For example, it knew that ARRAY in section DATA1 has the value 00000004 in that section, even when there was a reference to it during the assembly of program section CODE.) It seems evident that the resolving of references to symbols in different sections and the apparent conflict between sections occupying the same memory is going to require close cooperation between the assembler and the linker.

17.3 THE MANAGEMENT OF PROGRAM SECTIONS BY THE LINKER

We have seen that the assembler has generated the code for program sections as if all sections were to occupy the same physical memory, and of course that cannot actually occur. In fact, the program sections are assigned different memory blocks by the linker, and Figure 17.3.1 shows how these pieces of program sections are put together and loaded into main memory. We have shown the sections loaded with CODE in low memory addresses, then DATA1 and finally DATA2, in the higher addresses. The linker has loaded these sections in this order not because

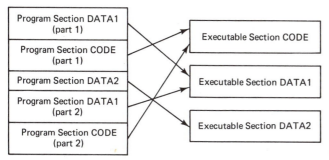

Figure 17.3.1

CODE contains the executable portion of the program (which fact neither the assembler nor the linker can really ascertain), but because, in general, sections are loaded in *alphabetic order*. (If we had named the CODE section INSTR instead, it would have been loaded last.)

Now that program sections are loaded into physical memory, the linker can proceed with the resolution of references that the assembler had not fully completed, such as the reference to ARRAY in line 16 of Figure 17.2.2.

What we have described here is *conceptually* quite simple, and in fact the task of the linker, as we have detailed it so far, is not especially difficult. However, as we mentioned in Chapter 10, the VAX linker is a complex program with many capabilities, and the object files produced by the assembler on which the linker operates are by no means as straightforward as we tend to view them—as simple sequences of executable machine code. But as in Chapter 10, the simplistic view is the most profitable one from our standpoint, and we shall continue to take it in our future dealings with the linker.

We can now deal with "program section 01," the "missing" section we noted when examining the symbol table of Figure 17.2.3. In fact, *every* source file always contains a program section, even if one is not explicitly created with a .PSECT directive. (This is just one more example of the system's devotion to consistency; since the linker wants always to deal with program sections, the assembler will force one if necessary, so that all object files will have the same basic structure.) The program section created by the assembler by default is named

. BLANK .

Notice the leading "period-space" and trailing "space-period." These characters are part of the program section name, and since the space character is *not* a valid character in the name of a *user-defined* program section, one of the effects of this naming is that the section . BLANK . will be loaded first in memory, since its name always precedes a user-defined name in lexicographic order. On the other hand, the user can create, or add to, the section . BLANK . by specifying the .PSECT directive *without* a name. Figure 17.3.2 shows a program segment that has this feature, together with a part of its symbol table, and Figure 17.3.3 shows how the linker would load these program sections in memory for execution.

```
          0000       1              ;Beginning of assembler's
          0000       2              ;  default  . BLANK .  program section
          0000       3
00000048  0000       4 ARRAY:       .BLKW        36
                                       .
                                       .
          016C      17              ;Beginning of user-defined program section
          016C      18
      00000000      19              .PSECT       DATA
          0000      20
00000001  0000      21 X:           .LONG        1
00000002  0004      22 Y:           .LONG        2
00000003  0008      23 Z:           .LONG        3
          000C      24
          000C      25              ;Continuation of  . BLANK .  program section
          000C      26
      0000016C      27              .PSECT
          016C      28
0000  016C          29 START:       .WORD        ^M<>
                                       .
                                       .
          0212      62              ;Continuation of user-defined program section
          0212      63
      0000000C      64              .PSECT       DATA
          000C      65
0000006C  000C      66 A:           .BLKL        24
000000FC  006C      67 VECTOR:      .BLKW        72
          00FC      68
          00FC      69              ;Continuation of  . BLANK .  program section
          00FC      70
      00000212      71              .PSECT
          0212      72
                                       .
                                       .
          025A      94              .END         START
```

Symbol table:

A	0000000C R	02
ARRAY	00000000 R	01
START	0000016C R	01
VECTOR	0000006C R	02
X	00000000 R	02
Y	00000004 R	02
Z	00000008 R	02

Figure 17.3.2

17.4 PROGRAM SECTION ATTRIBUTES

By now even the most patient reader must be asking: Why are we doing this? That is, although the use of program sections does seem to be a way to modularize programs (one of the goals stated at the outset of this chapter), the manner in which they do so seems unnecessarily complicated, and equivalent modularization

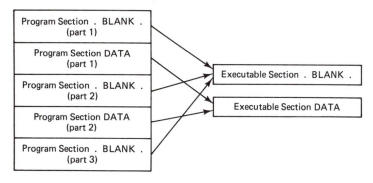

Program Section . BLANK .
(part 1)

Program Section DATA
(part 1)

Program Section . BLANK .
(part 2)

Program Section DATA
(part 2)

Program Section . BLANK .
(part 3)

Executable Section . BLANK .

Executable Section DATA

Figure 17.3.3

could be achieved more directly with familiar techniques. These valid objections are answered by stating a fact which we have not yet disclosed: The user not only has control over what code goes into a program section, but also those sections have *attributes* which can be dictated by the user and which control to some extent the treatment that will be given the code in these program sections upon linking and execution.

The format of the .PSECT directive is

.PSECT   *program-section-name,attribute-list*

where the program section name may be up to 31 characters in length and may include alphabetic and numerical characters, together with the special characters period (.), dollar sign ($), and underscore (_); however, a program section name may not begin with a numerical character. The attribute list is optional, and if it is not present, default attributes are used. (Our examples to date have specified no attributes.) There are numerous program section attributes that may be specified, but some of these apply primarily to a privileged or operating system environment and thus will not be discussed here. The interested reader is directed to the *VAX-11 MACRO Language Reference Manual* for details.

There are only three pairs of attributes which will be of concern to us, the first of which is **WRT** and its complement, **NOWRT**. We have observed on numerous occasions that physical memory which is not assigned by the operating system to a particular user is protected against access by that user. That is, various segments of memory are noted as being accessible by certain users but not others, and a violation of these established privileges will result in a *memory access violation* fault. This is, of course, a most desirable feature, for no user wants other users writing into his or her assigned memory, and even though reading another user's memory may not do any physical harm, it is still a violation of some sort. Now there are times when a user might want to protect some code not only from other users, but even from the *owner* of that code. By using the NOWRT (*NO WRiTe* access) attribute, a programmer can protect the code in a program section from being written into by instructions in the same or some other section of the program. Any attempt to write into a program section with the NOWRT attribute results in the same operating system generated memory access violation fault that occurs when a user attempts an access outside that user's assigned memory. NOWRT can be a most useful attribute to establish, especially when a program is in the developmental stage and the dangers of accidentally writing into some undesirable location are fairly great. The complementary attribute WRT (*WRiTe* access) is the default.

A second attribute associated with a program section has to do with *alignment*. We noted in Chapter 5 that certain structures have "natural" memory alignments—for example, although a longword *may* occupy any memory bytes, its natural alignment is that in which its low-order byte has an address that is a multiple of 4. We stated at that time that considerable processing time might be saved in some circumstances if memory structures were naturally aligned in order to eliminate multiple memory accesses. However, we did not give even a hint as to how this desirable alignment might be achieved, and in fact alignment of words, longwords, quadwords, and so on, depends on the *alignment attribute* of the program section in which the structure resides.

Each program section has an **alignment attribute** which determines two things: the alignment of the beginning of that program section, and the forced alignments which are permitted within that section. Alignment is given by an integer in the range 0 to 9, inclusive, which has the following properties. First, if the alignment attribute is the integer n, then when that program section is assigned actual memory by the linker, the address of the *first* byte of the section will be the smallest available byte whose address is a multiple of 2^n. Thus if, for example, $n = 4$, the program section will be loaded in memory beginning at the first available location whose address is a multiple of $2^4 = 16$.

The second property of the alignment attribute has to do with the forcing of alignments. We noted the desirability of aligning certain structures on particular memory boundaries, and this may be done with the **.ALIGN** directive. Specifically, the directive has the format

$$.ALIGN \quad n,expression \quad (0 \le n \le 9)$$

and it has the effect of moving the assembler's location counter up to the first value that is a multiple of 2^n. Any bytes that are skipped over in the process are filled with the value of the *expression*, and if this (optional) *expression* is not explicitly stated, the assembler will use the default value 0. However, no alignment may be specified which exceeds the alignment of the program section containing the .ALIGN directive. For example, longword alignment ($n = 2$) would *not* be permitted in a program section whose alignment was word ($n = 1$). Now the default alignment of a program section, and thus in particular, the alignment of the . BLANK . section, is $n = 0$—byte alignment. Thus it would not be possible, as suggested in Chapter 5, to specify

$$.ALIGN \quad 2$$

in an unnamed program section, in order to align longwords. We would first have to create a program section such as

.PSECT   NAME,2

and then, within that section, the .ALIGN directive above would be valid. (Notice that any program section alignment greater than 2 would also do here.)

As a convenience for the programmer, the assembler recognizes five keywords which may be used in place of the alignment specifier (integer n) in both the .PSECT and .ALIGN directives. These are

Keyword	n	2^n
BYTE	0	1
WORD	1	2
LONG	2	4
QUAD	3	8
PAGE	9	512

Thus the directives above could be replaced by

.PSECT   NAME,LONG
.ALIGN   LONG

17.5 THE GLOBAL NATURE OF PROGRAM SECTION NAMES

There is one further attribute of program sections which we need to discuss in some detail. Consider the two nonsense "programs" of Figure 17.5.1. Module-1 seems to be some sort of attempt at a mainline program, inasmuch as the .END directive references a legitimate program entry point. But from there the "program" does nothing other than load a number into R0. Module-2 is not even an executable affair, since it contains no transfer address. But if these two modules are *linked*, in the order "first Module-1, then Module-2," we find that the result is an executable module which is the same one we would have obtained from the source program

```
        ;Module-1                       ;Module-2

        .PSECT  SAMPLE                  .PSECT  SAMPLE

START:  .WORD   ^M<>                    $0.4H   R0
        MOVL    #^X12345678,R0          $EXIT
        .END    START                   .END

              (a)                             (b)
```

Figure 17.5.1

```
        .PSECT  SAMPLE

START:  .WORD   ^M<>
        MOVL    #^X12345678,R0
        $0.4H   R0
        $EXIT
        .END    START           Figure 17.5.2
```

shown in Figure 17.5.2. Evidently, Module-2 has simply been concatenated onto Module-1 by the linker, and we shall briefly investigate what has taken place here.

We already know that when the linker deals with a module containing several program sections, it loads them into different blocks of memory, but the code belonging to the various "pieces" of the *same* program section is simply concatenated in memory, so that it becomes contiguous, with the earlier declared pieces occupying lower memory addresses in the block of storage assigned to that section. Now when the linker sees two *different* modules, each containing a program section with the *same* name, it simply treats those sections uniformly as it does with section "pieces" belonging to a single module; it concatenates them into a common memory block. It is for this reason that the two lines of executable instruction

$$\text{\$0.4H} \quad \text{R0}$$
$$\text{\$EXIT}$$

of the module of Figure 17.5.1(b) were simply concatenated onto the end of the module of Figure 17.5.1(a), the result being, in effect, the program of Figure 17.5.2.

There are a couple of conclusions that we may draw from this little example. First, since the *order* in which the linker "sees" the program section is of considerable importance to the executable module it builds, it would not have done to link the modules of Figure 17.5.1 in the order "first Module-2, then Module-1." Second, the program sections need not even be named for this phenomenon to occur—even if the modules of Figure 17.5.3, were linked (in the correct order), the result would be the same as above, and if the resulting executable module were executed, the hexadecimal number 12345678 would be printed. What has happened here, of course, is that the default program section . BLANK . has served the function of the section named SAMPLE.

The examples of Figures 17.5.1 and 17.5.3 are certainly unusual if not bizarre, and it is clear that we would never consciously program in this way, linking together such *structurally incomplete* modules. Modules that are linked together typically contain or reference external subroutines or procedures, and the linkages take

```
        ;Module-1                        ;Module-2

START:  .WORD   ^M<>                     $0.4H   R0
        MOVL    #^X12345678,R0           $EXIT
        .END    START                    .END

           (a)                                (b)
```

Figure 17.5.3

place through global symbols and external references, not as a result of the identification of program section names. There is one case, however, in which the use of identical program section names *can* be used to advantage, but which does not lead to the strange piecemeal concatenated executable module, for the simple reason that the pieces of program sections with the same name are *not concatenated*—rather, they are *overlaid*.

One of the attributes that may be assigned to a program section is **CON** (*CON*catenate), and it directs the linker to concatenate program sections in different modules which have identical names and attributes. This is the action taken by the linker in the case of the modules of Figure 17.5.1, and the reason it did so is that CON is the default attribute. The complementary attribute (although perhaps *alternative attribute* would be a better term here) is **OVR**, which stands for *OVe*Rlay. The effect of specifying this attribute for program sections with identical names in *different* modules is that when these modules are linked, the linker assigns *the same memory* to all such program sections. That is, the physical memory ultimately occupied by the program section in one module is identical to that occupied by the program section of a second module. As an extremely simple example, consider the two modules of Figure 17.5.4. We recognize Module-1 as a complete, executable source program, albeit of little intrinsic interest. Module-2 consists only of a single piece of longword data. What is interesting here, of course, is the fact that the two modules declare identically named and attributed program sections, SHARED_VAR, consisting of a single longword, and having the OVR attribute. If these two modules are linked in the order "first Module-1, then Module-2," the effect is as shown in Figure 17.5.5(a): The program sections SHARED_VAR and XEQ from Module-1 are loaded into main memory, and *then* the program section SHARED_VAR of Module-2 is loaded into main memory, in exactly the same locations as those used by the SHARED_VAR program section of Module-1. As a consequence, the value ˆX87654321 of the longword VARBLE in Module-1 is *overlaid* by the value ˆX23242526 of the longword SHARE from Module-2. Thus when the executable module is executed, we will see the value 23242526 printed on

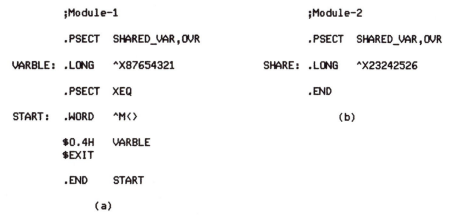

Figure 17.5.4

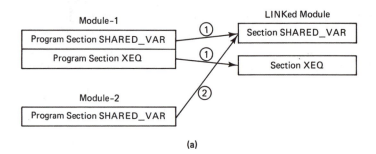

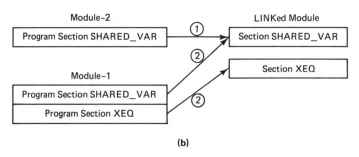

Figure 17.5.5

the terminal screen. The reader should verify that if the two modules are linked in the order "first Module-2, then Module-1," the resulting memory allocations will be as shown in Figure 17.5.5(b), and upon execution, the (hexadecimal) number 87654321 will be printed.

The phenomenon illustrated in the preceding paragraph is more than a curiosity, although the example given there is too simple to reveal any practical uses that this "overlay mode" might have. But consider now the following situation. We have a mainline program, perhaps with many "variables" (labeled bytes, words, longwords, and so on), and the mainline module also contains a procedure that must operate on a dozen or so of those data. There is no difficulty here, for since the procedure is a part of the main module, the module's "variables" are known also to the procedure. That is, there need be little or no argument passing in this case. But now suppose that we wish to excise the procedure from the main module and make it an *external* procedure, which again operates on these dozen or so pieces of data. How is the procedure to obtain its arguments from the calling routine? There are essentially three ways in which this can be done. First, the arguments can be transmitted as they usually are for a CALLx operation, but observe that in the present case this will require either building a large argument table (CALLG) or pushing many arguments on the stack (CALLS). Second, the arguments could be made *global* in the calling module and *external* in the module containing the procedure, in which case no arguments would have to be passed directly at all. But observe that the procedure then refers to the arguments *by name*—by the names they have in the procedure's .EXTERNAL directive—and this implies that these are the names that the *calling* routine *must* use for these "variables." This may severely limit the programmer's choice of structures and names in any program that invokes this procedure (and presumably the decision was made to write the procedure as a separate module exactly because it would be called by numerous routines in various environments).

The third way in which arguments can be passed to an external procedure is by means of a overlaid program section which is shared by the procedure's module and the module containing the procedure call. In this case, although the programmer must see to it that the OVR program section (or sections) in the calling routine has a specific name matching that in the module which contains the procedure, the names of the "variables" which reside in that program section are not material as they would be in the second option mentioned above. As an illustrative example, consider the program segment of Figure 17.5.6. The program deals with an array named ARRAY, which contains 24 words and which may be configured by the programmer in any suitable way: 3 by 8, 4 by 6, 12 by 2, 1 by 24, or whatever. That configuration is maintained in the bytes labeled ROWS and COLMNS. An array entry is determined by specifying a row and column number in ROW and

```
        .TITLE  MAINLINE_MODULE

        .PSECT  SHARED_ARRAY,OVR,WORD

ARRAY:  .BLKW   24

        .PSECT  CONFIGURATION,OVR

ROWS:   .BLKB   1
COLMNS: .BLKB   1

        .PSECT  PARAMETERS,OVR,BYTE

ROW:    .BLKB   1
COLUMN: .BLKB   1

        .PSECT

        .EXTERNAL PRNTRC

START:  .WORD   ^M<>

        MOVB    #3,ROWS         ;Establish array as being
        MOVB    #8,COLMNS       ; 3 rows by 8 columns
        .
        .
        MOVB    #3,ROW          ;Set row and column numbers
        MOVB    #6,COLUMN       ; to 3 and 6, respectively
        CALLS   #0,PRNTRC       ; and request printing of
                                ; that entry
        .
        .
        .END    START
```

Figure 17.5.6

COLUMN, respectively, presumably within the bounds specified in ROWS and COLMNS (although this is not checked within the program). As we see from the figure, the only thing the module shows as being done is the configuring of the array to be three rows of eight entries each, and then later the setting of ROW and COLUMN to 3 and 6, respectively, and the invoking of the procedure PRNTRC, where the third row, sixth column entry in the array is printed.

The procedure PRNTRC is shown in Figure 17.5.7 and does the straightforward computations required to locate a specific row and column entry in an array. Now in order that PRNTRC be able to print an array entry, it must know three things: the array address, the array configuration (number of rows and columns in the array), and the entry's row and column "subscripts." These five arguments could, of course, be passed to PRNTRC by means of an argument table or on the stack, but instead we have constructed, in the mainline module and in the procedure module, overlaid program sections through which these values will be transmitted. Thus the array itself, called ARRAY in the mainline module and MATRIX in the procedure module, is in a program section named SHARED_ARRAY. The configuration values ROWS and COLMNS are in a second program section with OVR attribute and named CONFIGURATION, and the desired row and column to be

```
        .TITLE  PROCEDURE_MODULE

        .PSECT  PARAMETERS,OVR

R:      .BLKB   1
C:      .BLKB   1

        .PSECT  SHARED_ARRAY,OVR,WORD

MATRIX: .BLKW   200

        .PSECT  CONFIGURATION,OVR

ROWS:   .BLKB   1
COLMNS: .BLKB   1

        .PSECT  PROCEDURE_PRNTRC,NOWRT

PRNTRC::.WORD   ^M<R6,R7>       ;Save two registers

        MOVZBL  R,R6            ;Get row number and
        DECL    R6              ;  subtract one
        MOVZBL  COLMNS,R7       ;Multiply (<row number> - 1)
        MULL    R7,R6           ;  by <number of columns>
        MOVZBL  C,R7            ;Now add
        DECL    R7              ;  (<column number> - 1)
        ADDL    R7,R6           ;  to get array index
        $0.2D   MATRIX[R6]      ;Print array entry
        RET                     ;  and return

        .END
```

Figure 17.5.7

printed are in PARAMETERS and named ROW and COLUMN in the mainline, R and C in the procedure module. The use of three program sections here is less necessary than illustrative, but if a single program section is used to transmit all five arguments to PRNTRC, there is a potential problem which is touched on in the exercises.

Let us examine what happens when the mainline module executes the instruction

MOVB   #6,COLUMN

The number 6 is moved into the byte labeled COLUMN, that is, the second byte of the two-byte program section named PARAMETERS. But since the linker has assigned the *same* memory to the program section*s* named PARAMETERS in both the mainline and the procedure modules, the effect of this instruction in the mainline module is the same as that of the instruction

MOVB   #6,C

in the procedure module. Thus the setting of one of these "shared variables" in one of the modules also sets it in the other, for the simple reason that the "variable" is occupying common space, referred to in one module by one name and in the other by another name. It is the shared nature of these data which precludes the necessity of the explicit transmission of argument values or addresses when the procedure is called.

Observe that in the procedure module of Figure 17.5.7, the array (named MATRIX in that module) has been allocated 200 words, whereas in the mainline module, the array (named ARRAY there) occupies only 24 words. This has been done to make PRNTRC more flexible, since as written it can deal with *any* array that does not require more than 200 words. But now the program sections SHARED_ARRAY do not have the same size in the two modules and thus, despite the best efforts of the linker, cannot be truly "overlaid" exactly. As an aid in seeing how the linker does react to this situation, we have obtained a **linker map** (or **load map** or **allocation map**) and reproduced a portion of it in Figure 17.5.8. It shows what memory has

Psect Name	Module Name	Base	End	Length
CONFIGURATION		00000B70	00000B71	00000002
	MAINLINE_MODULE	00000B70	00000B71	00000002
	PROCEDURE_MODULE	00000B70	00000B71	00000002
PARAMETERS		00000C08	00000C09	00000002
	MAINLINE_MODULE	00000C08	00000C09	00000002
	PROCEDURE_MODULE	00000C08	00000C09	00000002
SHARED_ARRAY		00000C0A	00000D99	00000190
	MAINLINE_MODULE	00000C0A	00000C39	00000030
	PROCEDURE_MODULE	00000C0A	00000D99	00000190

Figure 17.5.8

been allocated to each of the three program sections of concern to us here, and as we see, CONFIGURATION occupies the two bytes at 00000B70 and 00000B71, in *both* of the modules MAINLINE_MODULE and PROCEDURE_MODULE. In a similar fashion, the program section PARAMETERS occupies the two bytes at 00000C08 and 00000C09 in both modules. But observe that the program section SHARED_ARRAY occupies 400 bytes, those between 00000C0A and 00000D99. The *first* 48 of these, from 00000C0A to 00000C39, are the bytes occupied by ARRAY in the mainline module, while the *first* 400 of them (that is, all of them) correspond to the bytes assigned to MATRIX in the procedure module. Thus the "overlap" is in the first 48 bytes = 24 words, exactly as we would desire for the procedure PRNTRC to function properly.

(The reader who worries about such things will notice a "gap" in the addressing between the program sections CONFIGURATION and PARAMETERS in Figure 17.5.8. This was originally occupied by a program section which was removed from the load map listing as shown in the figure so as not to distract from those program sections of immediate interest. The program section in question is named IOBLOCKS, which the reader will find on the last page of the listing of Figure D.6.2 in Appendix D and which can be shown to consist of 148 bytes. The linker has placed it here to maintain the lexicographic ordering of program sections. IOBLOCKS is a part of the module which does the actual output to the terminal, and since that module is clearly required in this example, it was linked in with the mainline and procedure modules. The reason a .PSECT is needed here at all is that the construction "$FAB"—an operating system input/output macroinstruction—must be longword aligned.)

17.6 THE *FORTRAN "COMMON"* STATEMENT

To the reader familiar with the FORTRAN programming language, the "sharing" of "variables" introduced in the preceding section is doubtless reminiscent of variables that share COMMON areas in linked FORTRAN modules. The reason for this similarity is that a FORTRAN COMMON area is nothing more than a named program section of an appropriate size with OVR attribute. To illustrate this idea, we show in Figure 17.6.1 the variable declaration portion of a FORTRAN program containing four COMMON areas, three of them *named* (SHARED, PAR-

```
INTEGER*2 ARRAY(24)

BYTE      ROW,COLUMN,ROWS,COLMNS

BYTE      X1,X2,X3

INTEGER*4 Y1,Y2,Y3

COMMON    /SHARED/ARRAY/PARAMS/ROW,COLUMN/CONFIG/ROWS,COLMNS
COMMON    X1,X2,X3,Y1,Y2,Y3
```

Figure 17.6.1

Psect Name	Module Name	Base	End	Length
$BLANK		00000200	0000020E	0000000F
	SAMPLE$MAIN	00000200	0000020E	0000000F
CONFIG		00000210	00000211	00000002
	SAMPLE$MAIN	00000210	00000211	00000002
PARAMS		00000214	00000215	00000002
	SAMPLE$MAIN	00000214	00000215	00000002
SHARED		00000218	00000247	00000030
	SAMPLE$MAIN	00000218	00000247	00000030

Figure 17.6.2

AMS, and CONFIG), and one unnamed, or "blank COMMON" as is sometimes said. The four program sections generated by these COMMON areas, together with the space allocated to them by the linker, are shown in the partial linker load map of Figure 17.6.2, where we note that the unnamed COMMON area has been named $BLANK by the FORTRAN compiler. (Notice that the compiler has also TITLEd the object module SAMPLE$MAIN—a name derived from the *source* module's filename, SAMPLE.FOR.)

17.7 EXERCISES

17.1.1. What does the program of Figure 17.1.1 do?

17.5.1. What effect would there be on our discussion of Figure 17.5.4 if the longword ˆX23242526 of Module-2 had *not* been labeled?

17.5.2. Suppose that in Figure 17.5.4 we had *not* created the program section XEQ, but simply let the instructions of Module-1 belong to the program section SHARED_VAR. What effect would this have on the executable module, and upon execution, given the two possible orders in which the modules can be linked?

17.5.3. The procedure PRNTRC of Figure 17.5.7 would be even more useful if it were passed as an argument the *address* of the array in question, for then PRNTRC would not itself have to allocate any space for the array (such as the 200 words shown in the figure). Adjust the modules of Figures 17.5.6 and 17.5.7 to accommodate this modification.

17.5.4. Suppose that in the modules of Figures 17.5.6 and 17.5.7, we had simply declared *one* program section, say SHARED_STUFF, which contains ARRAY, ROWS, COLMNS, ROW, and COLUMN (which, equivalently, in the PROCEDURE_MODULE are named MATRIX, ROWS, COLMNS, R, and C, respectively). Show that in that case ARRAY (and in the PROCEDURE_MODULE, MATRIX) *must* appear at the very *end* of that program section, explain why, and discuss the consequences of failing to do so.

17.5.5. In the load map of Figure 17.5.8, evidently there is no code *between* the program sections PARAMETERS and SHARED_ARRAY, yet the program section PROCEDURE_PRNTRC fits *lexicographically* between these two. Explain why that program section has been loaded elsewhere. (This will require a little experimentation, but the reason has to do with the fact that the linker loads together program sections with the *same* attributes.)

17.5.6. It was stated that the "hidden" program section IOBLOCKS is (decimal) 148 bytes long, yet the load map of Figure 17.5.8 indicates that 151 bytes have been allocated to it. ($00000C08 - 00000B71 = 97_{16} = 151_{10}$.) Account for the additional 3 bytes.

17.5.7. Will the linker find any difficulty with the fact that the program section named PARAMETERS of Figure 17.5.6 has attribute BYTE, whereas the program section of the same name in Figure 17.5.7 does not?

17.6.1. Explain how two COMMON areas with the same name in different FORTRAN modules may have different sizes, how the variables in those areas are identified with one another, how such areas are loaded by the linker, and what care the FORTRAN programmer must take when dealing with this situation. Answer in terms of program sections. (Indeed, in terms of program sections, the questions have already been answered.)

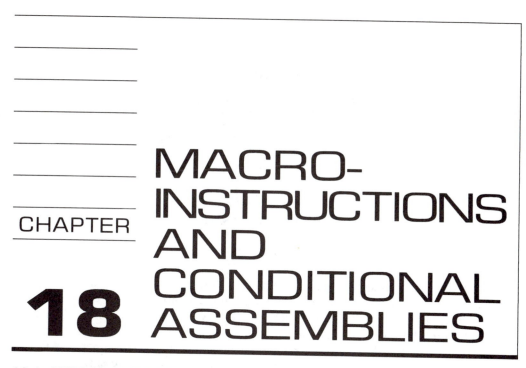

18 CHAPTER

MACRO-INSTRUCTIONS AND CONDITIONAL ASSEMBLIES

18.1 SUBROUTINES REVISITED

Consider a program in which at some point it is required that the contents of R1 be no larger than the contents of R2. That is, c(R1) and c(R2) must be in *increasing order*, and if they are not, then c(R1) and c(R2) are to be exchanged. This is certainly an easy task, and the few lines shown in Figure 18.1.1 will ensure that the register contents satisfy the requirement. Now if this condition is required a number of times in the program, we would probably write a small subroutine, such as the routine R1LEQR2 of Figure 18.1.2, to which we may JSB whenever necessary. (Notice that there is no need to bring in the more powerful *procedure* machinery here, since no arguments or results need to be passed to and from the routine.)

Consider next a program that contains a number of longword arguments labeled, say, ARG1, ARG2, ..., ARG12, and suppose that the first three of these need to be pushed onto the stack, perhaps to be used as arguments to a procedure invoked with a CALLS operation. All that is required, of course, is the three

```
        CMPL    R1,R2       ;In correct order: c(R1) <= c(R2)?
        BLEQ    DONE        ;Yes -- we're done
        PUSHR   #^M<R1>     ;  else save c(R1),
        MOVL    R2,R1       ;  replace R1 with c(R2)
        POPR    #^M<R2>     ;  and restore c(R2) from stack
DONE:   <next instruction>
```

Figure 18.1.1

```
;-------------------------------------------------;
; Subroutine to ensure that c(R1) <= c(R2)        ;
;-------------------------------------------------;

R1LEQR2: CMPL   R1,R2       ;In correct order: c(R1) <= c(R2)?
         BLEQ   DONE        ;Yes -- we're done
         PUSHR  #^M<R1>     ; else save c(R1),
         MOVL   R2,R1       ; replace R1 with c(R2)
         POPR   #^M<R2>     ; and restore c(R2) from stack
DONE:    RSB                ;Return to calling routine
```

Figure 18.1.2

instructions

$$
\begin{array}{ll}
\text{PUSHL} & \text{ARG1} \\
\text{PUSHL} & \text{ARG2} \\
\text{PUSHL} & \text{ARG3}
\end{array}
$$

If these same pushes are required numerous times within the program, then just as above we might be tempted to write a little subroutine to deal with this task, to which we jump when needed, such as that shown in Figure 18.1.3. A moment's reflection, however, reveals that this will not do at all, for the RSB instruction, which *should* pop the return address into the program counter, in fact pops c(ARG3) into the PC instead—the actual return address is buried in the stack. Thus it appears that each time the three arguments need to be stacked, we shall simply have to write these three PUSHL instructions. (The instructions *can* be written as a subroutine, although the return must be handled in a somewhat unorthodox fashion. A suggested construction is given in the exercises.)

```
SAV3ARGS: PUSHL   ARG1      ;Push three
          PUSHL   ARG2      ; longword arguments
          PUSHL   ARG3      ; onto the stack
          RSB               ;Return to calling routine
```

Figure 18.1.3

18.2 MACROINSTRUCTIONS

Despite the fact that the three PUSHL instructions of Section 18.1 are certainly easy enough to include in a program whenever needed, we would probably soon tire of doing so if the need arose very often. We might even consider the insertion of these instructions a likely mundane task for our *assembling clerk*, that assistant who was briefly brought on the scene in Chapter 6 to do assemblies for us, before being replaced by the VAX assembler, and who has been pretty much neglected ever since; it will be useful to reinstate him momentarily at this time. Suppose that we notify the clerk, in advance of his assembling our source program, that the three PUSHL instructions in question are going to have to be inserted in the program at a number of points, that those three instructions are "packaged" under the name SAV3ARGS, and that whenever he sees the term SAV3ARGS he is to replace it in the source program with

```
PUSHL   ARG1
PUSHL   ARG2
PUSHL   ARG3
```

These three lines of assembly language mnemonics then become part of the program, just as if the programmer had written them into the program. Notice that the clerk will not confuse this term with an operation mnemonic (since it is not in the list of mnemonics) or with an assembler directive (since it does not begin with a "dot"). There is no reason why the clerk cannot accommodate this request, although he—and we—will need to be careful to avoid a few problems that we shall discuss shortly.

What we have created here—the three PUSHL instructions, the term SAV3ARGS, and the instructions to the assembling clerk—is a kind of "super-instruction," a package of VAX instructions that has been *named*. Such a super-instruction is called a **macroinstruction**. The set of instructions that makes up the macroinstruction is called the **macroinstruction definition** (or **macrodefinition**). Thus in the present case the name of the macroinstruction is SAV3ARGS and its definition is given by the three PUSHL instructions shown above. When the clerk replaces the macroinstruction by its definition, he is said to **expand the macroinstruction** and the resulting instructions are referred to as the **macroinstruction expansion** (or **macroexpansion**). Finally, when the programmer makes reference to the macroinstruction in the source program, he or she is said to **invoke** or **call the macroinstruction**. (Throughout the remainder of this chapter we shall use the abbreviation *macro* for the word *macroinstruction* whenever it is convenient to do so.)

The process that the clerk must go through in expanding an instance of the macroinstruction SAV3ARGS is quite simple, but it is nonetheless worth examining in some detail. Recall that in assembling a program, the clerk will go through two passes. On the first pass, upon encountering the "pseudomnemonic" SAV3ARGS, the clerk sees that this symbol is the name of a macroinstruction, and he responds as follows. He inserts *into the source code* the macrodefinition—the three PUSHL instructions—but without any regard *at this time* to the *meaning* of these three lines of text. He next continues first pass processing with these three lines, but *now* he examines them, assigns addresses, gives values to symbols, and so on. These three instructions are encountered again on the second pass, when the assembly is completed.

18.3 THE *VAX* MACROINSTRUCTION ASSEMBLER

It will come as no surprise to the reader to find that the VAX assembler supports macroinstructions. That is, the programmer can *define* a macroinstruction—a named package of instructions—and then later invoke that package by name, and

```
                    0000    1        .MACRO   SAV3ARGS
                    0000    2        PUSHL    ARG1
                    0000    3        PUSHL    ARG2
                    0000    4        PUSHL    ARG3
                    0000    5        .ENDM
                                       .
                                       .
                    0BBD    84       SAV3ARGS
F53F CF   DD        0BBD             PUSHL    ARG1
FC7D CF   DD        0BC1             PUSHL    ARG2
FD7D CF   DD        0BC5             PUSHL    ARG3
                    0BC9    85       <next instruction>
                                       .
                                       .
```

Figure 18.3.1

the VAX assembler will react just as our clerk has—it will insert into the source
code the text that makes up the macro definition and then continue its first (and
later, second) pass assembly of that text. As an example, we show in the program
segment of Figure 18.3.1 the result of defining and then invoking the macroinstruction SAV3ARGS of Section 18.2. Observe first that we must signal to the
assembler that we are beginning the definition of a macroinstruction, and this is
done at line 1 by means of the assembler directive **.MACRO**—begin *MACRO*instruction definition. The .MACRO directive not only begins the macro definition,
it also *names* the macroinstruction, in this case SAV3ARGS. The three lines that
follow are, of course, the body of the definition. Finally, we must notify the
assembler of the end of the macrodefinition with the directive **.ENDM**—*END* of
*M*acroinstruction definition. Notice that the *definition* of the macroinstruction has
resulted in the generation of no machine code, a fact which is evident from the
listing of Figure 18.3.1 and which is also to be expected. The macrodefinition is
just that, a *definition* or *reference*, and in particular it is *not* a request to insert the
code for machine instructions into memory.

At line 84 the macro SAV3ARGS is *invoked* and now, as we expect, machine
code *is* generated. The three PUSHL instructions are inserted into the source

```
                    0000    1  .MACRO   SAV3ARGS   ;Macroinstruction definition
                    0000    2  PUSHL    ARG1       ;Push three
                    0000    3  PUSHL    ARG2       ;  longword arguments
                    0000    4  PUSHL    ARG3       ;  onto the stack
                    0000    5  .ENDM               ;(End of macro definition)
                                  .
                                  .
                    0BBD    84  SAV3ARGS           ;Invoke the macroinstruction
F53F CF   DD        0BBD        PUSHL    ARG1      ;Push three
FC7D CF   DD        0BC1        PUSHL    ARG2      ;  longword arguments
FD7D CF   DD        0BC5        PUSHL    ARG3      ;  onto the stack
                    0BC9    85  <next instruction>
                                  .
                                  .
```

Figure 18.3.2

program and assembled (the byte DD representing PUSHL, the mode byte CF indicating a word displacement of the program counter, and the *negative* word displacements Fxxx implying that the arguments themselves are in lower-addressed memory).

Contrary to our custom, we have not placed comments on the lines of instruction in the segment of Figure 18.3.1, either in the macrodefinition itself or at line 84 where the macroinstruction is invoked. There is no reason why lines of a macrodefinition cannot be commented, and in fact such documentation is to be encouraged. In Figure 18.3.2 we show the same program segment as that in Figure 18.3.1, in which we have placed comments on the lines that make up the definition of SAV3ARGS (as well as on line 84). The results are pretty much what are to be expected, but the feature of interest here is the macroexpansion itself, for it affords further insight into how the assembler treats the expansion of a macroinstruction. Notice that the comments, which we have placed on the three lines making up the definition of the macroinstruction (at lines 2 to 4) have been reproduced by the assembler when the macro is expanded (at line 84). This behavior results from a fact to which we alluded earlier, namely, that when the assembler expands a macroinstruction, it simply copies—character by character—*all* the *text* that makes up the macroinstruction's definition, into the source program at the point of the macro call, and *then* it begins its first pass assembly of the text it copied. Thus at the time this macrodefinition was copied, the assembler had no regard for *what* it was copying, and thus it copied comments and all. This totally slavish approach to macroexpansions, or at least the copying phase of them, can be the source of much error and confusion, and the programmer will need to exercise some care in certain cases which we shall see later in this chapter.

In Figures 18.3.1 and 18.3.2 we have shown a *listing* of the instructions and code generated when the macroinstruction is expanded. In fact, the VAX assembler will not normally list these since, by default, the assembler will generate the appropriate machine code and place it in the object file as desired, but it will *not* show on a listing the instructions and code that they generated. Thus the program segment listing of Figure 18.3.3 is what we would normally see. The three PUSHL instructions have been inserted at line 84, and the generated code has been placed in the object file at locations 00000BBD through 00000BC8; we simply are not shown this expansion. In the program listings of Figures 18.3.1 and 18.3.2 we have *forced* the listing of the macroexpansions by means of the assembler directive

```
0000    1   .MACRO  SAV3ARGS    ;Macroinstruction definition
0000    2   PUSHL   ARG1        ;Push three
0000    3   PUSHL   ARG2        ;  longword arguments
0000    4   PUSHL   ARG3        ;  onto the stack
0000    5   .ENDM               ;(End of macro definition)
            .
            .
0BBD   84   SAV3ARGS            ;Invoke the macroinstruction
0BC9   85   <next instruction>
            .
            .
```

Figure 18.3.3

```
                                    12A3     42        SAV3ARGS
       %MACRO-E-UNRECSTMT, Unrecognized statement       !
                                    .

                                    1407     84        .MACRO    SAV3ARGS
                                    1407     85        PUSHL     ARG1
                                    1407     86        PUSHL     ARG2
                                    1407     87        PUSHL     ARG3
                                    1407     88        .ENDM
                                    .
                                    .
```

Figure 18.3.4

.SHOW ME—*SHOW MacroExpansion*—which was included in the source program (but not shown in the figures) somewhere prior to line 84, where the macroinstruction was invoked. This directive's opposite number, **.NOSHOW ME,** is the default, as mentioned above. The programmer, by including these directives at appropriate points in the source program, can thus selectively turn on and off the listing of the macroexpansions. Finally, observe from Figure 18.3.3 that even though the macroinstruction's *expansion* was not listed, its *definition* was, at lines 1 through 5.

Figure 18.3.4 illustrates the consequences of attempting to invoke a macroinstruction prior to its definition; the assembler has declared the macro call to be an *unrecognized statement*. An easy method to avoid this problem is one which is followed by many programmers: Place *all* of a program's macrodefinitions at the

```
                              0224      7        .MACRO   SAV3ARGS
                              0224      8        PUSHL    ARG1
                              0224      9        PUSHL    ARG2
                              0224     10        PUSHL    ARG3
                              0224     11        .ENDM
                                       .

                              142B     43        SAV3ARGS
       EBD1 CF   DD  142B                        PUSHL    ARG1
       EDCD CF   DD  142F                        PUSHL    ARG2
       EDED CF   DD  1433                        PUSHL    ARG3
                                       .

                              15BB     65        .MACRO   SAV3ARGS
                              15BB     66        CLRL     R4
                              15BB     67        .ENDM
                                       .

                              1635     89        SAV3ARGS
       54       D4  1635                         CLRL     R4
                                       .
                                       .
```

Figure 18.3.5

physical beginning of the program, before any executable instructions. This will ensure that any macroinstruction is defined prior to its being called. However, it is not *necessary* to do this; macroinstruction definitions may appear *anywhere* in the source program, since these definitions do not result in the generation of any machine code and thus occupy no physical memory. (In this regard they behave like FORTRAN *FORMAT* and BASIC *DATA* statements, for like them, macro-definitions are purely *reference* statements.)

Can a macroinstruction be defined more than once? More properly, can two different macrodefinitions have the same name? Curiously enough, the answer is "yes," and to see the consequences of such a potentially dangerous (but possibly useful) practice, we shall examine the program segment of Figure 18.3.5. At lines 7 through 11, the macroinstruction SAV3ARGS is defined as before, and its expansion at line 43 is precisely what we expect and have seen a number of times already. But now at lines 65 through 67, SAV3ARGS is *redefined* as a CLRL instruction (which, of course, has nothing to do what *SAV*ing *3 ARG*ument*S*, all of which is immaterial anyway). At line 89 the macroinstruction is reinvoked, and as we see, it is now expanded as the CLRL instruction. The reader might infer from this, and quite correctly, that when a macroinstruction is defined, any previous

```
                             .
                             .
                    0224   7      .MACRO   SAV3ARGS
                    0224   8      PUSHL    ARG1
                    0224   9      PUSHL    ARG2
                    0224   10     PUSHL    ARG3
                    0224   11     .ENDM
                    0224   12
                    0224   13     .MACRO   SAV5ARGS
                    0224   14     SAV3ARGS
                    0224   15     PUSHL    ARG4
                    0224   16     PUSHL    ARG7
                    0224   17     .ENDM
                             .
                             .
                    142B   43     SAV3ARGS
    EBD1 CF   DD    142B          PUSHL    ARG1
    EDCD CF   DD    142F          PUSHL    ARG2
    EDED CF   DD    1433          PUSHL    ARG3
                             .

                    1635   89     SAV5ARGS
                    1635          SAV3ARGS
    E9C7 CF   DD    1635          PUSHL    ARG1
    EBC3 CF   DD    1639          PUSHL    ARG2
    EBE3 CF   DD    163D          PUSHL    ARG3
                    1641
    FDE6 CF       DD  1641        PUSHL    ARG4
0000176D'EF       DD  1645        PUSHL    ARG7
                             .
                             .
```

Figure 18.3.6

definition is lost, and consequently that when a macroinstruction is invoked (on pass one), what is expanded is the *current* definition of the macroinstruction.

Recall that in our illustrative sample problem we have assumed longword arguments ARG1, ARG2, ..., ARG12, and SAV3ARGS is a macroinstruction which pushes the first three of these onto the stack. Suppose now that in addition to needing to push ARG1, ARG2, and ARG3 onto the stack, we also require on occasion that ARG1, ARG2, ARG3, ARG4, and ARG7 be pushed onto the stack (in the stated order). We could write another macroinstruction, say SAV5ARGS, which consisted of the five appropriate PUSHL instructions, but we may as well take advantage of the fact that SAV3ARGS already takes care of part of the task, the pushing of the first three arguments. Figure 18.3.6 shows such a macro-instruction SAV5ARGS, which within its definition invokes the macroinstruction SAV3ARGS. When SAV5ARGS is invoked at line 89, we see that upon its expansion, first SAV3ARGS is expanded, and then the two additional PUSHL instructions are inserted, precisely the action we desire. (Notice that in this case, ARG1 through ARG4 are apparently backward references into lower memory, while ARG7 is evidently a *forward* reference.)

Finally, we resubmit the program segment of Figure 18.3.6, in which

			.		
			.		
		0224	7	.MACRO	SAV5ARGS
		0224	8	SAV3ARGS	
		0224	9	PUSHL	ARG4
		0224	10	PUSHL	ARG7
		0224	11	.ENDM	
		0224	12		
		0224	13	.MACRO	SAV3ARGS
		0224	14	PUSHL	ARG1
		0224	15	PUSHL	ARG2
		0224	16	PUSHL	ARG3
		0224	17	.ENDM	
			.		
			.		
		142B	43	SAV3ARGS	
EBD1 CF	DD	142B		PUSHL	ARG1
EDCD CF	DD	142F		PUSHL	ARG2
EDED CF	DD	1433		PUSHL	ARG3
			.		
			.		
		1635	89	SAV5ARGS	
		1635		SAV3ARGS	
E9C7 CF	DD	1635		PUSHL	ARG1
EBC3 CF	DD	1639		PUSHL	ARG2
EBE3 CF	DD	163D		PUSHL	ARG3
		1641			
FDE6 CF	DD	1641		PUSHL	ARG4
0000176D'EF	DD	1645		PUSHL	ARG7
			.		
			.		

Figure 18.3.7

SAV5ARGS (which invokes SAV3ARGS) is defined *prior to* the definition of SAV3ARGS (see Figure 18.3.7). At first glance this appears to be contrary to our earlier caution about invoking macroinstructions before they have been defined, but as we see from line 89, all appears to have gone well. The reader is asked to examine this situation and explain why it is different from that of Figure 18.3.4.

18.4 PASSING ARGUMENTS TO A MACROINSTRUCTION

Continuing with our principal example, let us suppose that three arguments from the list ARG1, ..., ARG12 need frequently to be pushed onto the stack, but we suppose now that these are *other than* ARG1, ARG2, and ARG3. As a concrete example, suppose that ARG1, ARG9, and ARG3 are to be stacked. Then even though we are still dealing with three arguments, the macroinstruction SAV3ARGS of Figure 18.3.1 will not do since it pushes the *wrong* three arguments, and SAV3ARGS cannot even be used to contribute to the solution as was the case in Figure 18.3.6. Of course, we could define another macroinstruction to do this task, but it is clear that if many different sets of three longwords need to be stacked, we will have to write a corresponding number of macroinstructions. What is needed here is a kind of "variable" macroinstruction, one that allows us to decide which arguments are to be stacked, but to postpone this decision until the time the macroinstruction is *invoked*. That is, we would like to be able to write a package of instructions of the form

```
PUSHL   ARGX
PUSHL   ARGY
PUSHL   ARGZ
```

and then to inform our clerk (or the VAX macroassembler) that when the macroinstruction is invoked, X is to take on the value 1, Y the value 2, and Z the value 3; or when the macroinstruction is invoked elsewhere in the program, X, Y, and Z are to have the values 1, 9, and 3, respectively. This would give us the desired flexibility to save any three of these arguments, but require that we write the macrodefinition only once.

We shall examine this concept from the clerk's point of view, for an investigation of what he or the assembler must do to honor such a request will give us some understanding of what information must be transmitted when the macroinstruction is defined and when it is invoked; and seeing how the macroexpansion takes place will also provide us with some valuable insights which we can use to avoid errors in the future. It is clear that the basic process involved is one of *substitution*—the clerk or assembler is being asked to *substitute* the values 1, 2, and 3 for X, Y, and Z, for example. Specifically, we are asking the clerk to enhance the macroexpansion process as follows. When a macroinstruction is invoked, the clerk should:

1. Locate the definition of the macroinstruction and insert that definition, on a character-by-character basis, into the source program.

2. Make a pass through the text just inserted and *replace*, for example, every instance of "X" with the character "1", "Y" with "2", and "Z" with "3".

3. Return to the beginning of the inserted and substituted text and continue the pass one assembly on it.

What is new here, of course, is step 2, the *substitution* of the characters 1, 2, and 3 for the characters X, Y, and Z. This should certainly not be beyond the clerk's abilities, provided that he is given enough information to do the job. Clearly, the required information consists of (1) the *names* of the symbols to be substituted for when the macroinstruction is invoked, and (2) the values to be used as substitutes for each of those symbols. It should be evident that requirement 1 must be dealt with at the time the macroinstruction is defined, and requirement 2 must be specified each time the macroinstruction is invoked.

To specify the *names* of the symbols for which a substitution is later to be made, we expand somewhat the description of the .MACRO directive. Specifically, this directive has the form

.MACRO   *macro-name*   [*argument-list*]

where *argument-list* is optional (as implied by the enclosing brackets), but if it is present it consists of a list of symbols, separated by *commas, spaces*, or *tab characters*. These symbols are called **formal arguments** or **formal parameters**, and the .MACRO directive as shown is called the **macroinstruction prototype statement**, since it acts as a *prototype* or *model* for the macroinstruction call. When the macroinstruction is *invoked*, each of the formal arguments is replaced by an **actual argument** or **actual parameter.** The clerk (or assembler) will then expand the macrodefinition and do the substitutions described above.

Now that we have this new construction at our disposal, we rewrite the macroinstruction SAV3ARGS to include three arguments X, Y, and Z, and then request upon invoking the macroinstruction that these be replaced by 1, 2, and 3, respectively. As we see from the program segment of Figure 18.4.1, things have not gone well. It appears that the assembler has simply ignored the request to substitute, but this is not the case. In fact, the assembler expanded the macrodefinition and then scanned it for instances of X, Y, and Z, but *it found none*. It *did* find, for example, an instance of the symbol ARGX, but it did not take this to be an instance of the formal argument X.

As disappointed as we might be with the assembler's inability to deal with this situation, that should be tempered with some gratitude, for a moment's reflection will reveal that if the assembler *had* made the substitutions we had in mind here, the situation would soon deteriorate to a state of chaos. For consider the macroinstruction POPL (which acts as a companion to the VAX *operation* PUSHL)

```
.MACRO   POPL P
MOVL     (SP)+,P
.ENDM
```

```
                          0000        1              .MACRO   SAV3ARGS  X,Y,Z
                          0000        2              PUSHL    ARGX
                          0000        3              PUSHL    ARGY
                          0000        4              PUSHL    ARGZ
                          0000        5              .ENDM
                                                       .
                                                       .
                          0402       37              SAV3ARGS  1,2,3
                    DD    0402                        PUSHL    ARGX
    %MACRO-E-UNDEFSYM, Undefined symbol
        00000000'EF      0403
                    DD    0408                        PUSHL    ARGY
    %MACRO-E-UNDEFSYM, Undefined symbol
        00000000'EF      0409
                    DD    040E                        PUSHL    ARGZ
    %MACRO-E-UNDEFSYM, Undefined symbol
        00000000'EF      040F
                                                       .
                                                       .
```

Figure 18.4.1

If the assembler made *all* substitutions for the formal argument P, the macro call

$$POPL \quad R6$$

would result in the expansion

$$MOVL \quad (SR6)+,R6$$

which is obvious nonsense.

There are essentially two ways in which we can deal with this problem, the more sophisticated of which we investigate in Section 18.6. In the meantime we note that a straightforward way of coaxing the assembler into making the desired substitutions involves redefining the macroinstruction of Figure 18.4.1 as follows.

```
.MACRO   SAV3ARGS  X,Y,Z
PUSHL    X
PUSHL    Y
PUSHL    Z
.ENDM
```

We are evidently being somewhat less ambitious here, and in fact as we see from Figure 18.4.2, when the macroinstruction is invoked, the entire argument ARG1, ARG2, and so on, must be passed as an actual argument, which is perhaps a bit more of a nuisance than simply passing the argument numbers 1,2 and so on. On the other hand, we see from the figure that this new version of SAV3ARGS is precisely what we were seeking—a macroinstruction whose instructions could be tailored to the need each time the macroinstruction was invoked.

```
                            0000        1        .MACRO   SAV3ARGS  X,Y,Z
                            0000        2        PUSHL    X
                            0000        3        PUSHL    Y
                            0000        4        PUSHL    Z
                            0000        5        .ENDM
                                                    .
                                                    .
                            0402       76        SAV3ARGS  ARG1,ARG2,ARG3
        FBFA CF     DD      0402                 PUSHL    ARG1
        FC1D CF     DD      0406                 PUSHL    ARG2
   00000A10'EF      DD      040A                 PUSHL    ARG3
                                                    .
                                                    .
                            0585      161        SAV3ARGS  ARG1,ARG9,ARG3
        FA77 CF     DD      0585                 PUSHL    ARG1
        FCA2 CF     DD      0589                 PUSHL    ARG9
   00000A10'EF      DD      058D                 PUSHL    ARG3
                                                    .
                                                    .
```

Figure 18.4.2

The macroinstruction SAV3ARGS of Figure 18.4.2 actually does more than
we had originally intended. For as the program segments of Figure 18.4.3 illustrate,
this latest version of SAV3ARGS will stack not only three longword arguments,
but will stack three of *anything* as longwords. Indeed, the passing of arguments
to a macroinstruction is far more powerful a concept than perhaps the reader
realizes. Almost *anything* can be passed as an actual argument, to replace a formal
argument, because of the way in which the assembler deals with argument replacement—pure substitution of characters. To give some indication of the power of
this concept, we show in Figure 18.4.4 a macroinstruction that passes as an argument
an entire VAX instruction. In this way we can "customize" macroinstructions for

```
                            0000        1        .MACRO   SAV3ARGS  X,Y,Z
                            0000        2        PUSHL    X
                            0000        3        PUSHL    Y
                            0000        4        PUSHL    Z
                            0000        5        .ENDM
                                                    .
                                                    .
                            0402       35        SAV3ARGS  ARG1,R7,ARG2
        FC21 CF     DD      0402                 PUSHL    ARG1
          57        DD      0406                 PUSHL    R7
        F7 AF       DD      0408                 PUSHL    ARG2
                                                    .
                                                    .
                            0722       62        SAV3ARGS  #1,R7,@DATA
          01        DD      0722                 PUSHL    #1
          57        DD      0724                 PUSHL    R7
        F9 BF       DD      0726                 PUSHL    @DATA
                                                    .
                                                    .
```

Figure 18.4.3

```
                     0000      1        .MACRO   CUSTOM   REG,INSTR
                     0000      2        CLRL     REG
                     0000      3        INSTR
                     0000      4        .ENDM
                                          .
                                          .
                     0A82      96       CUSTOM   R10,RSB
        5A    D4     0A82               CLRL     R10
              05     0A84               RSB
                                          .
                                          .
```

Figure 18.4.4

a variety of purposes, although we hasten to add that the example given here is purely illustrative and we claim no other merit for it. Notice that the body of the macroinstruction consists of a CLRL instruction whose operand is the formal argument REG (probably intended to be a *REG*ister, but by now we know that almost anything could be substituted here) and the argument INSTR, which we intend to be an *INSTR*uction. We see from the figure that when the macroinstruction is invoked with the actual arguments R10 and RSB, the macroinstruction becomes a two-instruction package which might in some circumstances be quite useful. Figure 18.4.5 shows another call to CUSTOM, in which we *intend* that R10 be cleared and then an INCW instruction be inserted. Unfortunately—and if we had thought a moment we could have anticipated it—the assembler has taken the spaces between INCW and @#DATA in the list of actual arguments to be valid argument separators, and thus to the assembler there were *three* arguments: R10, INCW, and @#DATA. Since only two arguments are required for the expansion of this macroinstruction, the third argument was simply *ignored*. Evidently what is needed here is some way of *grouping* this collection of characters so that the assembler will treat them as a *single* argument, that is, some means of including any of the separators (comma, space, or tab) within an actual argument. This is done with the angle brackets ⟨...⟩, and we see from Figure 18.4.6 that now the assembler has taken INCW @#DATA as a single argument, as desired. For-

```
                          0000      1        .MACRO   CUSTOM   REG,INSTR
                          0000      2        CLRL     REG
                          0000      3        INSTR
                          0000      4        .ENDM
                                               .
                                               .
                          0A82      68       CUSTOM   R10,INCW    @#DATA
%MACRO-E-TOOMNYARGS, Too many arguments in MACRO call        !
                          0A82
            5A    D4      0A82               CLRL     R10
                  B6      0A84               INCW
%MACRO-E-NOTENUFOPR, Not enough operands supplied    !
                                               .
                                               .
```

Figure 18.4.5

```
                          0000    1    .MACRO   CUSTOM   REG,INSTR
                          0000    2    CLRL     REG
                          0000    3    INSTR
                          0000    4    .ENDM
                                       .
                                       .
                                       .
                          0A82    68   CUSTOM   R10,<INCW      @#DATA>
                5A    D4  0A82         CLRL     R10
        00000402'9F   B6  0A84         INCW     @#DATA
                                       .
                                       .
```

Figure 18.4.6

mally, when the assembler encounters a pair of angle brackets in an actual macroinstruction argument, it treats the enclosed characters as a *single* argument, and in making the replacement of the corresponding formal argument in the macroexpansion, it *removes* the set of paired angle brackets.

If the angle brackets are used as grouping symbols for actual arguments, could a closing angle bracket ever appear as a character in an actual argument that requires grouping? The answer is "yes," but some adjustments are required. To see what the problems are, and how they may be eliminated, consider the totally contrived macroinstruction STRING of Figure 18.4.7, which does nothing but invoke the .ASCII directive. (In practice, of course, we would never write such a macroinstruction, but the .ASCII directive might well appear as *one* of several lines of source code in a more realistic macrodefinition.) We see from the figure that the argument /ABC/ has correctly generated the ASCII code for the three characters A, B, and C, but that the argument at line 38 has caused some problems because of the embedded spaces—the space between "The" and "sky" is taken by the assembler to be an argument separator, which accounts for the "Too many arguments" message. However, now the argument that remains is "/The" which has a leading delimiter "/" (required by the .ASCII directive) but not a corresponding trailing delimiter, which accounts for the "Unterminated argument" message. As expected, the construction at line 89, in which the string is enclosed in angle brackets, takes care of the matter; the embedded spaces now taken as a part of the *single* argument. Observe that an identical symptom appears at line 125, but for a different reason. The text for which we require the ASCII code is supposed to be

$$x + 2 > 3*y - 7$$

where the ">" symbol is to mean "greater than." Unhappily, the assembler has taken it to be the closing grouping symbol of a $\langle . . \rangle$ pair. This leaves the remainder of the string as "unwanted" arguments, and it also leaves "/x + 2" as an "unterminated argument."

There is no way out of this dilemma *unless* the assembler will accept some other characters as grouping symbols. In fact, almost *any* printing character may

```
              0000    1           .MACRO  STRING  X
              0000    2           .ASCII  X
              0000    3           .ENDM
                                     .
                                     .
              028C    25          STRING  /ABC/
     43 42 41 028C                .ASCII  /ABC/
                                     .
                                     .
              02CF    38          STRING  /The sky is falling/
%MACRO-E-TOOMNYARGS, Too many arguments in MACRO call  !
     65 68 54 02CF                .ASCII  /The
%MACRO-E-UNTERMARG, Unterminated argument              !
                                     .
                                     .
              05A3    89          STRING  </The sky is falling/>
   .  .  . 65 68 54 05A3          .ASCII  /The sky is falling/
     67 6E 69 . . .  05AF
                                     .
                                     .
              0A8C    125         STRING  </x + 2 > 3*y - 7/>
%MACRO-E-TOOMNYARGS, Too many arguments in MACRO call     !
     20 32 20 2B 20 78 0A8C       .ASCII  /x + 2
%MACRO-E-UNTERMARG, Unterminated argument                 !
                                     .
                                     .
```

Figure 18.4.7

be used as a grouping symbol, provided that the first (leftmost) instance of it is preceded by a circumflex (^). The next occurrence of that same symbol (but *not* preceded by a circumflex) is then taken as the rightmost grouping symbol. Figure 18.4.8 shows that the preceding problem is eliminated by choosing "#" as the grouping symbol: "^#...#". (The reader may feel that this matter of "grouping symbols" has now been put to rest. But consider actual arguments such as "^X1A4" in which the "^X" symbols are used to denote a *hexadecimal* number. The assembler will take "^X" as a leftmost grouping symbol, which of course is not what is intended. A further investigation of some of these annoyances is taken up in the exercises.)

We close this section with a final look at the assembler's process of the replacement of formal arguments with actual arguments. Consider the simple

```
              0000    1     .MACRO  STRING  X
              0000    2     .ASCII  X
              0000    3     .ENDM
                              .
                              .
              02D2    38    STRING  ^#/x + 2 > 3*y - 7/#
      .  .  . 2B 20 78 02D2 .ASCII  /x + 2 > 3*y - 7/
     37 20 2D . . .   02DE
                              .
                              .
```

Figure 18.4.8

```
              0000   1    .MACRO   CLEARWDS  A,B
              0000   2    CLRW     A                    ;Clear a couple
              0000   3    CLRW     B                    ;  of 16-bit words
              0000   4    .ENDM
                                .
                                .
                                .
              029A  56    CLEARWDS R3,@DATA
        53 B4 029A         CLRW    R3                   ;Clear R3 couple
000003A6'FF B4 029C         CLRW    @DATA               ;  of 16-bit words
                                .
                                .
```

Figure 18.4.9

macroinstruction of Figure 18.4.9, which merely clears two specified 16-bit words. Notice that the formal arguments are named A and B, and that the two lines which make up the body of the macrodefinition are commented. When the macroinstruction is expanded, with A taking on the value R3, observe that the *comment*

> ;Clear a couple

has been changed to

> ;Clear R3 couple

The "a" in the comment has been replaced by "R3"! (Note that the formal argument replacement has been done without regard to case, "a" being lowercase, the argument "A" being uppercase.) What has happened here is predictable and is more amusing than harmful, for there has been no impact on the executable instructions. However, the example does indicate just how unbending the assembler is when it comes to argument substitution. An intelligent clerk would probably not even scan the comments for possible argument replacement. In any event, the reader will recognize a warning here—the assembler will do *exactly* as it is told, and some forethought may be required to avoid unanticipated problems.

18.5 ELIDED ARGUMENTS, DEFAULT VALUES, AND KEYWORD ARGUMENTS

Consider the simple macroinstruction defined in the segment of Figure 18.5.1. It clears four longwords, but note that when it is invoked at line 30, one of its arguments, X2, is an **elided argument**—it is *not* supplied with an actual argument. The result is predictable, in that *nothing* (quite literally) has been substituted for X2, and the second CLRL instruction has been expanded as "CLRL   " with the expected error message.

Whenever an actual argument is elided, the formal argument in that position is replaced with *nothing*—more properly, the **empty string** of characters—and in most cases this will result in an unacceptable line of assembly language source code. It is possible, however, to supply **default values** to the arguments, values

```
                            0000    1     .MACRO  CLEAR   X1,X2,X3,X4
                            0000    2     CLRL    X1
                            0000    3     CLRL    X2
                            0000    4     CLRL    X3
                            0000    5     CLRL    X4
                            0000    6     .ENDM
                                            .
                                            .
                            028C    30    CLEAR   R2,,R4,(R7)+
                    52  D4  028C          CLRL    R2
                        D4  028E          CLRL
%MACRO-E-NOTENUFOPR, Not enough operands supplied         !
                    54  D4  028F          CLRL    R4
                    87  D4  0291          CLRL    (R7)+
                                            .
                                            .
```

Figure 18.5.1

that are to be used *if* no value is supplied when the macroinstruction is invoked. The assignment of default argument values is specified at the time the macroinstruction is defined, by declaring in the macroinstruction prototype statement the default value, together with the argument for which it is the default, as follows:

formal-argument-name = default-value

Figure 18.5.2 shows the macroinstruction CLEAR in which the first and second arguments have been given the default values R9 and R0, respectively. At line 30, CLEAR is invoked with its second argument, X2, elided. Notice that the default, R0, has been used by the assembler. Observe also, however, that even though X1 had been assigned a default (R9) in the prototype statement, it was *not* used, since X1 was given an actual value, R2.

The macroinstruction ARGLIST of Figure 18.5.3 is another example of a macroinstruction in which some of the formal arguments have been assigned default values. Notice that of the seven arguments, all but A2 have been given defaults.

```
                            0000    1     .MACRO  CLEAR   X1=R9,X2=R0,X3,X4
                            0000    2     CLRL    X1
                            0000    3     CLRL    X2
                            0000    4     CLRL    X3
                            0000    5     CLRL    X4
                            0000    6     .ENDM
                                            .
                                            .
                            028C    30    CLEAR   R2,,@#ARG-^X74,(R7)+
                    52  D4  028C          CLRL    R2
                    50  D4  028E          CLRL    R0
        000001A0'9F D4  0290          CLRL    @#ARG-^X74
                    87  D4  0296          CLRL    (R7)+
                                            .
                                            .
```

Figure 18.5.2

```
        0000     1     .MACRO  ARGLIST  A1=ARG1,A2,A3=ARG3,A4=ARG4,-
        0000     2                      A5=ARG5,A6=ARG6,A7=ARG7
        0000     3     .LONG   A1
        0000     4     .LONG   A2
        0000     5     .LONG   A3
        0000     6     .LONG   A4
        0000     7     .LONG   A5
        0000     8     .LONG   A6
        0000     9     .LONG   A7
        0000    10     .ENDM
                        .
                        .
        0373    59     ARGLIST  ,2*<ARG3-1>,,,,3
00003039 0373          .LONG   ARG1
00000016 0377          .LONG   2*<ARG3-1>
0000000C 037B          .LONG   ARG3
00011A3D 037F          .LONG   ARG4
00000000 0383          .LONG   ARG5
00000003 0387          .LONG   3
00000306 038B          .LONG   ARG7
                        .
                        .
```

Figure 18.5.3

Thus whenever ARGLIST is invoked, A2 *must* be given a replacement argument, but any (or all) of the others may be elided. At line 59 of Figure 18.5.3 we see a macro call in which A2 is given the value 2*⟨ARG3-1⟩ and A6 is given the value 3. The reader is asked to verify, perhaps by trying it, that if *only* A2 had been assigned the value 2*⟨ARG3-1⟩, all other arguments taking on their default values, the assembler would have been satisfied with the argument list

$$,2*\langle ARG3-1\rangle$$

That is, not even the trailing commas would have been needed in this case.

The macroinstruction ARGLIST of Figure 18.5.3 might generate a table of arguments to be passed to a procedure in a CALLG construction. It has seven arguments, which is the largest number that we have dealt with so far in our examples, but this is not an unusually large number. Although macroinstructions with dozens of arguments may not be the norm, neither are they especially rare. One of the annoyances that is evident from the call to ARGLIST in Figure 18.5.3 is that since A6 was to be replaced by the value 3, it was necessary to include all the commas between A2 and A6 in order to indicate that A3, A4, and A5 were elided; one could imagine how vexing the situation would be if a macroinstruction with, say, 30 arguments were called frequently, with only one or two actual arguments needed to be passed in each case. The VAX assembler circumvents the necessity to supply all the arguments by allowing the user to *name* the supplied arguments in a macroinstruction call. Specifically, the actual argument list may consist simply of the names of the *formal* arguments, followed by an equal sign, and the value to be assigned to that formal argument, thus:

formal-argument-name = actual-value

```
              0000     1        .MACRO   ARGLIST  A1=ARG1,A2,A3=ARG3,A4=ARG4,-
              0000     2                                    A5=ARG5,A6=ARG6,A7=ARG7
              0000     3        .LONG    A1
              0000     4        .LONG    A2
              0000     5        .LONG    A3
              0000     6        .LONG    A4
              0000     7        .LONG    A5
              0000     8        .LONG    A6
              0000     9        .LONG    A7
              0000    10        .ENDM
                                  .
                                  .
              0373    59        ARGLIST  A6=3,A2=2*<ARG3-1>
   00003039   0373             .LONG    ARG1
   00000016   0377             .LONG    2*<ARG3-1>
   0000000C   037B             .LONG    ARG3
   00011A3D   037F             .LONG    ARG4
   00000000   0383             .LONG    ARG5
   00000003   0387             .LONG    3
   00000306   038B             .LONG    ARG7
                                  .
                                  .
```

Figure 18.5.4

Such an argument is called a **keyword argument**, and as many such keyword arguments as necessary may be transmitted, all other arguments taking on their default values. Since the arguments are transmitted *by keyword name*, it is not necessary to list them in the order in which they appear in the macro prototype. Figure 18.5.4 shows again the macroinstruction ARGLIST of Figure 18.5.3, but this time the call at line 59 is given by keyword. Note that the value of A6 is given first, then the value of A2, illustrating that when transmitted by keyword, the order in which the arguments appear is immaterial. The reader is cautioned against attempting to pass arguments *both* positionally *and* by keyword, for example,

$$ARG6 = 3,,2*\langle ARG3 - 1\rangle$$

because of the difficulty of keeping track of the positionally declared arguments. (Notice that an extra comma has been required above, the first ending the keyword argument, the second to indicate the elided first argument, A1.)

18.6 THE CONCATENATION OF ARGUMENTS

Let us return to one of our earlier failures, namely, the attempt in Figure 18.4.1 to pass arguments to a macroinstruction. The macroinstruction defined there contained the instruction

PUSHL   ARGX

and it was our anticipation that when the macroinstruction was passed the argument

```
                              0000    1     .MACRO  SAV3ARGS  X,Y,Z
                              0000    2     PUSHL   ARG'X
                              0000    3     PUSHL   ARG'Y
                              0000    4     PUSHL   ARG'Z
                              0000    5     .ENDM
                                            .
                                            .
                              0278   41     SAV3ARGS  1,2,3
        FD84 CF   DD          0278          PUSHL   ARG1
        FDF4 CF   DD          027C          PUSHL   ARG2
   000004AD'EF    DD          0280          PUSHL   ARG3
                                            .
                                            .
                              04AD   74     SAV3ARGS  1,11,4
        FB4F CF   DD          04AD          PUSHL   ARG1
   000005BF'EF    DD          04B1          PUSHL   ARG11
        FDBD CF   DD          04B7          PUSHL   ARG4
                                            .
                                            .
```

Figure 18.6.1

$X = 1$, it would be expanded as

PUSHL   ARG1

Of course the X was not replaced with 1, and by now we would probably view these initial attempts as somewhat simplistic. Nonetheless, something can be salvaged here.

When we examined what went wrong in this example, we decided that while the assembler "saw" the term ARGX, it did *not* take it to be an instance of the symbol X; rather, it took ARGX as a single, indivisible term. What is required is that we somehow split the X off from the other characters, ARG, but if we try constructions such as

ARG,X   and   ARG X

the assembler will simply generate the expansions

ARG,1   and   ARG 1

That is, the comma and space have served to separate X from the rest of the term, but the resulting replacements have been disappointing. Evidently what is needed here is some notation which will signal the assembler that the replacement is to be made (as the comma and space did above), but also that the symbol used as the separator *is to be removed* when the substitution is made. The VAX macroassembler uses the apostrophe (') for this purpose, and the replacement process in this case is referred to as **concatenation,** since the string of characters making up the actual argument is *concatenated—chained—*onto whatever else is in the source code. The macrodefinition and two macro calls of Figure 18.6.1 show that this construction is precisely what is needed here. In each case the assembler recognizes an instance of the argument (X, Y, ...), replaces it with the actual argument (1,2 or whatever), removes the apostrophe, and then concatenates the two strings of characters that result from the removal of the apostrophe, to form a single string.

Figure 18.6.2 shows a macroinstruction which is more illustrative than practical, but it does indicate just what sorts of arguments can be passed to a macroinstruction. Notice that we have had to pass the colon (:) along with the label— LOOP:—the reason being that if the macrodefinition had contained the construction

LABEL': ...

then although it would have sufficed simply to specify the actual argument in the form LOOP, it would *not* be possible to generate this special instruction *without* a label, as was done in the macro call at line 67.

We have already noted, and seen by example, that when the assembler encounters an apostrophe in the replacement of a formal argument with an actual value, it removes the apostrophe. To be more precise, when in the course of expanding a macroinstruction, the assembler encounters an apostrophe *immediately preceding* a formal argument, it removes that apostrophe and replaces the formal argument with the real argument. And if the assembler finds an apostrophe *immediately following* a formal argument, that apostrophe is removed as above, together with the same replacement. Finally, if a formal argument is both *preceded and succeeded by* an apostrophe, both of those apostrophes are removed when the actual value replacement is made.

Our final example illustrates the assembler's treatment of the apostrophe construction as discussed above, and it has a couple of other interesting features. The macroinstruction GEN_INPUT_MACROS of Figure 18.6.3 does not generate any machine code when it is invoked—instead, it defines another macroinstruction. In fact, this macroinstruction *GEN*erates the definition of one of the *INPUT MACROS* $I.1B, $I.4D, and so on, which are described in Appendix D. There is actually a minor difference between the macroinstructions generated here and

```
          0000    1              .MACRO   SPECIAL   LABEL,INSTR,LENGTH,OPERAND
          0000    2   LABEL      INSTR'LENGTH      OPERAND
          0000    3              .ENDM
                   .
                   .
          0392   55              SPECIAL   LOOP:,CLR,B,R3
   53  94 0392        LOOP:      CLRB      R3
                   .
                   .
          03B8   67              SPECIAL   ,INC,W,LOOP-4
D3 AF  B6 03B8                   INCW      LOOP-4
                   .
                   .
```

Figure 18.6.2

```
        0000    1           .MACRO  GEN_INPUT_MACROS  BYTES,FORMAT
        0000    2
        0000    3           .MACRO  $I.'BYTES''FORMAT           ARG
        0000    4           PUSHAB  ARG
        0000    5           MOVW    #'BYTES,-(SP)
        0000    6           MOVW    #^A/I'FORMAT'/,-(SP)
        0000    7           CALLS   #2,...$
        0000    8           .ENDM   $I.'BYTES''FORMAT
        0000    9
        0000   10           .ENDM   GEN_INPUT_MACROS
                        .
                        .
        03A8   70           GEN_INPUT_MACROS  2,H
        03A8
        03A8               .MACRO  $I.2H   ARG
        03A8               PUSHAB  ARG
        03A8               MOVW    #2,-(SP)
        03A8               MOVW    #^A/IH/,-(SP)
        03A8               CALLS   #2,...$
        03A8               .ENDM   $I.2H
        03A8
        03A8   71           GEN_INPUT_MACROS  4,D
        03A8
        03A8               .MACRO  $I.4D   ARG
        03A8               PUSHAB  ARG
        03A8               MOVW    #4,-(SP)
        03A8               MOVW    #^A/ID/,-(SP)
        03A8               CALLS   #2,...$
        03A8               .ENDM   $I.4D
                        .
                        .
                07DB  215     $I.2H   DATA
      FD2F CF   9F  07DB       PUSHAB  DATA
        7E   02   B0  07DF       MOVW    #2,-(SP)
    7E 4849 8F   B0  07E2       MOVW    #^A/IH/,-(SP)
00000000'EF   02   FB  07E7       CALLS   #2,...$
                        .
                        .
```

Figure 18.6.3

those given in Figure D.6.1, and those of Appendix D are generated in a slightly different fashion. But the "$I.xx" macroinstructions generated by invoking GEN_INPUT_MACROS are in essence the same input "commands" the reader has employed throughout the book. By the end of this chapter we will be in a position to understand and appreciate all the details of the definitions given in Figure D.6.1.

The macroinstruction GEN_INPUT_MACROS has two formal arguments, BYTES and FORMAT. The body of the definition of this macroinstruction is a ".MACRO … .ENDM" construction, that is, a macrodefinition itself. We shall investigate just what macroinstruction is defined when GEN_INPUT_MACROS is invoked, but before doing so, note the .ENDM directives at lines 8 and 10. At line 8 we have written

.ENDM $I.'BYTES''FORMAT

rather than simply .ENDM. In effect we are telling the assembler that we are *END*ing the definition of the *M*acroinstruction named $I.'BYTES''FORMAT, a statement with which both we and the assembler concur. This "named" form of .ENDM has no more force than the unnamed version; its only function is for the *programmer* to verify that indeed the macrodefinition which is being ended *by the assembler* is the one specified. This can be a useful device to catch potential errors when much *nesting* of macrodefinitions takes place, enough so that some confusion is possible in the programmer's mind as to just which macroinstruction in the nest is being ended. If the assembler agrees with the programmer (and the assembler is much more proficient at keeping track of such things), it will continue the assembly. If for some reason the programmer has lost track of which macroinstruction is currently being defined and thus specifies the wrong macro name here, the assembler will respond with an appropriate error message (although it will not do so until the inner macroinstruction is actually invoked). At line 10 the .ENDM directive specifies that we are ending the definition of the outer macroinstruction GEN_INPUT_MACROS.

At line 70 of Figure 18.6.3 the macroinstruction GEN_INPUT_MACROS is invoked with the two actual arguments 2 and H. That is, BYTES takes on the value 2 and FORMAT takes on the value H (both of these values being *characters*, as we know). These two values are substituted for BYTES and FORMAT in the macro prototype statement of the inner macro, and thus this .MACRO directive defines $I.2H, with argument ARG. There are several features to note here. First, the actual arguments were passed down from the outer to the inner macroinstruction definition. Second, the apostrophes preceding *and* following the formal argument BYTES were both removed, as was the (remaining) single apostrophe preceding FORMAT. Finally, the formal argument ARG for what is now the macroinstruction $I.2H was *not* passed into it from the outer macroinstruction; this argument is part of the definition of the inner macroinstruction. At the next line of the macroexpansion, that argument is pushed onto the stack as an *address*. (Recall that the "operands" for the input macroinstructions must always be address access-type operands.) Then the argument BYTES—2, in this case—is pushed onto the stack, as a *word*, used by the actual input routine to determine the size of the structure to receive the data input through the keyboard. Next, the two ASCII characters I and FORMAT—H, in this case—are pushed onto the stack as a 2-byte word, again indicators used by the input routine to specify that the operation is input (I) and that the characters being input will be in the hexadecimal (H) representation. Observe that in the corresponding line in the macrodefinition—line 6—the formal argument FORMAT has both a preceding and succeeding apostrophe, both of which have been removed when FORMAT was replaced with the character H. Finally, the procedure ... $ is called; ... $ is the routine which actually does the input from the keyboard to the user's buffer having address ARG.

GEN_INPUT_MACROS is invoked again at line 71, and this time we see that the macroinstruction $I.4D is defined. Finally, to verify that the macroinstruction is now actually defined, $I.2H is itself invoked at line 215. Notice that this time, machine code is actually generated.

18.7 LOCAL LABELS

In some of the programs we have written we have had occasion to create *global symbols*, those whose names and values are carried along with the object file for subsequent use by the linker. We commented in Chapter 10 that all other user-created symbols of the program are *local*, a word used in contradistinction to the word *global*. Yet even local symbols have a certain "globalness" about them, at least within the module in which they are declared; for once a symbol is defined, either as a label or by direct assignment, that symbol is declared throughout the entire module, even across program sections, for example. (See Chapter 17 for a description of program sections.)

The VAX assembler supports symbols which are *very* local, in the sense that they are not even defined throughout the module in which they are declared—they are defined only within a small block of code, and outside that block their names and values are unknown to the assembler. These symbols might most naturally be called *local symbols*, but since that term is already in informal use (as above) and since these newly introduced symbols may be declared only as *labels*, we shall refer to them as **local labels.**

A local label has a *name* in the form **n$,** where n is a decimal integer in the range 1 to 65535. Thus 1$, 1024$, 65223$, and so on, are all valid local label names. Observe that this "symbol" name is in violation of the general rule for forming symbol names, as given in Section B.5, since it begins with a numerical character. The actual integer employed is of no consequence, being used simply to distinguish one local label from another. In particular, no *ordering* of any sort is imposed as a result of the integer numbers that appear in these labels. Local labels are declared and used exactly as normally formed labels are:

2791$: INCW   DATA[R3]

.

.

SOBLEQ   R10,2791$

However, local "symbols" may *not* be given values through the direct assignment (= or ==) construction.

Unlike a normally formed symbol, a local label is defined only within a **local label block** (or **local block,** for short), which is a block of contiguous code within the source program which is delimited by (1) the beginning of the source program; (2) any normally formed label; (3) a .PSECT directive (Chapter 17); or (4) the end of the source program. (There is an exception to all of this, not frequently

FIGURE 18.7.1

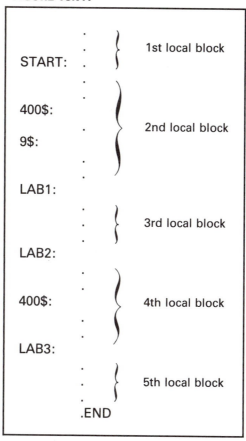

employed, which is noted at the end of this section.) Figure 18.7.1 is a diagram of a typical program, in which START, LAB1, LAB2, and LAB3 are normally formed labels, and we have noted the various local blocks. Observe that the use of 400$ as a label in both the second and fourth local blocks is *not* a conflict—multiple definition of label—since each use of this symbol 400$ is defined *only* within its own local block.

The module of Figure 18.7.2 is a complete program that does something useful (it is actually a solution to Exercise 8.10.2) and takes advantage of local labels. The local blocks lie between START and INIT, INIT and TEST, and TEST and the program end. Note the multiple use of the label 400$, each within its own local block. The machine code generated is straightforward, but the reader should examine the references to 400$ at lines 10, 19, and 23 to verify that those references are to addresses within the same block. Finally, notice that none of the local labels has been assigned an entry in the symbol table.

In Figure 18.7.3 we have changed the label TEST at line 20, and the reference to it, at line 11, to the local label 240$, and the result is an error that should have been anticipated. The label 240$ and the reference to it are in *different* local

```
                    000000A0    0000    1 NUM:      .BLKL     40
                    000000A4    00A0    2 COUNT:    .BLKL     1
                                00A4    3
                        0000    00A4    4 START:    .WORD     ^M<>
                                00A6    5           $I.4D     COUNT
                                00B8    6           $I.NL
                50      D4      00C4    7           CLRL      R0
                                00C6    8
                                00C6    9 400$:     $I.4D     NUM[R0]
        E7 50   C3 AF   F2      00DA   10           AOBLSS    COUNT,R0,400$
                        25      00DF   11           BRB       TEST
                                00E1   12
                        51      D4      00E1   13 INIT:     CLRL      R1
FF18 CF41   FF18 CF41   D1      00E3   14 400$:     CMPL      NUM[R1],NUM+4[R1]
                        14      00EC   15           BLEQ      235$
                FF0D CF41   DD  00EE   16           PUSHL     NUM[R1]
FF04 CF41   FF0C CF41   D0      00F3   17           MOVL      NUM+4[R1],NUM[R1]
    FF02 CF41   8E      D0      00FC   18           MOVL      (SP)+,NUM+4[R1]
            DD 51   50  F2      0102   19 235$:     AOBLSS    R0,R1,400$
                D8 50   F5      0106   20 TEST:     SOBGTR    R0,INIT
                                0109   21
                                0109   22 400$:     $0.4D     NUM[R0]
        E5 50   FF7E CF F2      011E   23           AOBLSS    COUNT,R0,400$
                                0124   24           $0.NL
                                0130   25           $EXIT
                                013C   26
                                013C   27           .END      START
```

Symbol table

```
NUM             00000000 R
COUNT           000000A0 R
INIT            000000E1 R
START           000000A4 R
TEST            00000106 R
```

Figure 18.7.2

blocks, and thus within the block between the normally formed labels START and INIT, 240$ is undefined. There are a number of ways to correct this error (including, of course, a return to the original version of Figure 18.7.2). One of these involves *overriding* the normal definitions of the initial and terminal points of a local label block with the **.ENABLE** and **.DISABLE** directives. Specifically, a local label block may be begun with the directive .ENABLE LOCAL_BLOCK. The local block is in effect until another .ENABLE LOCAL_BLOCK directive, or a .DISABLE LOCAL_BLOCK directive, is encountered. In the first case, the local block is terminated and a new local block is begun. In the second case, the local block is terminated. The difference between local blocks delimited by normally formed labels and .PSECT directives, and those delimited by .ENABLE/.DISABLE or .ENABLE/.ENABLE combinations is that in the latter case, the local block extends between the two directives, *irrespective* of any normally formed labels or .PSECT directives that might appear within that block. That is, .ENABLE LOCAL_BLOCK begins a block which effectively bridges the normally defined local blocks. Thus to eliminate the undefined symbol error of Figure 18.7.3, we need only start a local block, using a .ENABLE directive, somewhere prior to the reference at line 11 to 240$, and make sure that the block is not terminated (with a .DISABLE directive or another .ENABLE directive) until we get beyond the *definition* of 240$, at line 20. As we see from Figure 18.7.4 this error has been eliminated by inserting a .ENABLE directive at line 12 and a .DISABLE directive at line 25—the reference of 240$ at line 14 and its definition at line 23 are now both in the same local label block. However, we have (somewhat artificially) introduced another error—a multiple label definition error—by changing the label on the $O.4D command from 300$ (in Figure 18.7.3) back to 400$ (as in Figure 18.7.2), the thought being that inasmuch as that command lies *beyond* the .DISABLE LOCAL_BLOCK, there should be no symbol definition conflict. But there is a conflict, as we see, and the problem lies in the fact that although a local block is *begun* immediately by a .ENABLE directive, it is not *terminated* immediately by a .DISABLE directive. Rather, the current local block terminates with the first occurrence of a normally formed label or a .PSECT directive following the .DISABLE directive. Since neither of these occurred after the .DISABLE

```
             000000A0   0000    1 NUM:      .BLKL    40
             000000A4   00A0    2 COUNT:    .BLKL    1
                        00A4    3
                  0000  00A4    4 START:    .WORD    ^M<>
                        00A6    5           $I.4D    COUNT
                        00B8    6           $I.NL
              50    D4  00C4    7           CLRL     R0
                        00C6    8
                        00C6    9 400$:     $I.4D    NUM[R0]
   E7 50   C3 AF    F2  00DA   10           AOBLSS   COUNT,R0,400$
                    11  00DF   11           BRB      240$
   %MACRO-E-UNDEFSYM, Undefined symbol            !
                  0F'  00E0
                       00E1   12
                   51  D4  00E1  13 INIT:   CLRL     R1
FF18 CF41  FF18 CF41  D1  00E3  14 400$:    CMPL     NUM[R1],NUM+4[R1]
                14      15  00EC  15         BLEQ     235$
           FF0D CF41  DD  00EE  16          PUSHL    NUM[R1]
FF04 CF41  FF0C CF41  D0  00F3  17          MOVL     NUM+4[R1],NUM[R1]
      FF02 CF41    8E  D0  00FC  18          MOVL     (SP)+,NUM+4[R1]
         DD 51    50  F2  0102  19 235$:    AOBLSS   R0,R1,400$
            D8 50    F5  0106  20 240$:     SOBGTR   R0,INIT
                        0109   21
                        0109   22 300$:     $O.4D    NUM[R0]
   E5 50   FF7E CF    F2  011E  23          AOBLSS   COUNT,R0,300$
                        0124   24           $O.NL
                        0130   25           $EXIT
                        013C   26
                        013C   27           .END     START
```

Figure 18.7.3

```
000000A0    0000    1 NUM:      .BLKL     40
000000A4    00A0    2 COUNT:    .BLKL     1
            00A4    3
      0000  00A4    4 START:    .WORD     ^M<>
            00A6    5           $I.4D     COUNT
            00B8    6           $I.NL
       50 D4 00C4   7           CLRL      R0
            00C6    8
            00C6    9 400$:     $I.4D     NUM[R0]
E7 50  C3 AF  F2 00DA 10        AOBLSS    COUNT,R0,400$
            00DF   11
            00DF   12           .ENABLE   LOCAL_BLOCK
            00DF   13
       25 11 00DF  14           BRB       240$
            00E1   15
       51 D4 00E1  16 INIT:     CLRL      R1
            00E3   17 400$:     CMPL      NUM[R1],NUM+4[R1]
%MACRO-E-SYMOUTPHAS, Symbol out of phase
FF18 CF41    FF18 CF41  D1 00E3
            14 15 00EC 18       BLEQ      235$
       FF0D CF41    DD 00EE 19  PUSHL     NUM[R1]
FF04 CF41    FF0C CF41  D0 00F3 20        MOVL      NUM+4[R1],NUM[R1]
       FF02 CF41  8E  D0 00FC 21          MOVL      (SP)+,NUM+4[R1]
       DD 51  50  F2 0102 22 235$:        AOBLSS    R0,R1,400$
          D8 50   F5 0106 23 240$:        SOBGTR    R0,INIT
            0109   24
            0109   25           .DISABLE  LOCAL_BLOCK
            0109   26
            0109   27 400$:     $0.4D     NUM[R0]
%MACRO-E-MULDEFLBL, Multiple definition of label
            0109
E5 50  FF7E CF  F2 011E 28      AOBLSS    COUNT,R0,400$
            0124   29           $0.NL
            0130   30           $EXIT
            013C   31
            013C   32           .END      START
```

Figure 18.7.4

directive and prior to the redefinition of 400$ in Figure 18.7.4, the second definition of 400$ (line 27) and the first (line 17) are in the same local block. The matter is finally resolved in Figure 18.7.5 by placing a normally formed label on this $O.4D command, although there are numerous other solutions. Note that because of the label PRINT following the .DISABLE directive, the local block initiated at the .ENABLE directive finally ends at line 27.

18.8 AUTOMATICALLY GENERATED LOCAL LABELS

The typical user program frequently contains numerous branch instructions—conditional and otherwise—which are quite "local" in the sense that the destination of the branch is only a few bytes away from the branch instruction. A review of

```
000000A0        0000    1 NUM:      .BLKL    40
000000A4        00A0    2 COUNT:    .BLKL    1
                00A4    3
        0000    00A4    4 START:    .WORD    ^M<>
                00A6    5           $I.4D    COUNT
                00B8    6           $I.NL
        50  D4  00C4    7           CLRL     R0
                00C6    8
                00C6    9 400$:     $I.4D    NUM[R0]
    E7 50  C3 AF  F2    00DA   10           AOBLSS   COUNT,R0,400$
                00DF   11
                00DF   12           .ENABLE  LOCAL_BLOCK
                00DF   13
        25  11  00DF   14           BRB      240$
                00E1   15
        51  D4  00E1   16 INIT:     CLRL     R1
FF18 CF41  FF18 CF41  D1  00E3  17 400$:    CMPL     NUM[R1],NUM+4[R1]
        14  15  00EC   18           BLEQ     235$
        FF0D CF41  DD  00EE  19             PUSHL    NUM[R1]
FF04 CF41  FF0C CF41  D0  00F3  20          MOVL     NUM+4[R1],NUM[R1]
    FF02 CF41  8E  D0  00FC  21             MOVL     (SP)+,NUM+4[R1]
        DD 51  50  F2  0102  22 235$:       AOBLSS   R0,R1,400$
            D8 50  F5  0106  23 240$:       SOBGTR   R0,INIT
                0109   24
                0109   25           .DISABLE LOCAL_BLOCK
                0109   26
                0109   27 PRINT:    $O.4D    NUM[R0]
    E5 50   FF7E CF   F2  011E  28           AOBLSS   COUNT,R0,PRINT
                0124   29           $O.NL
                0130   30           $EXIT
                013C   31
                013C   32           .END     START
```

Figure 18.7.5

many of the sample programs in this book will reveal this phenomenon. Although the destination instruction of the branch must normally be labeled, that label usually serves no purpose of a more "global" nature. For such "target" locations the local labels not only will do but can also assist in program readability; when one sees a local label, one is led immediately to two conclusions: The references are quite nearby, and the label serves no globally significant function. But we have managed to survive without them for most of the book, and in fact most programmers use them only sparingly. The interested reader is directed to the program listing of the procedure ...$ in Figure D.6.2, where local labels are used in the fashion noted above.

It may be puzzling that we have included local labels here, because evidently, based on a description of them, local labels have nothing to do with the principal topic of this chapter, macroinstructions. In fact, there is a close connection between these two concepts, as the next example shows. Consider the task of replacing a number with its absolute value. This *might* be written as a subroutine or procedure, but only with difficulty, and instead we write it as a macroinstruction, as follows:

```
              .MACRO    ABS        ARG,SIZE=L
              TST'L     ARG
              BGEQ      DONE
              MNEG'SIZE ARG,ARG
    DONE:
              .ENDM
```

This little macroinstruction is perfectly straightforward, with ARG being the value to be replaced by its absolute value, and SIZE is the structure size of ARG—B, W, or L—with L (longword) being the default. Note that the label DONE seems not to label any instruction, and this is true. However, when the macroinstruction is *expanded*, DONE will have as its value the address of the *next* instruction, as desired. As Figure 18.8.1 reveals, DONE becomes a multiply defined label if the macroinstruction is invoked more than once in the same program. (Of course, if it were *not* to be invoked frequently, we would never have written it in the first place.) The problem is perfectly obvious, it should have been anticipated, and the solution is equally obvious—we simply pass the label name as one of the arguments, making certain that we never pass the same name twice. Figure 18.8.2 shows this repair, in which ABS is invoked with label arguments DONE1 and DONE2. The call at line 238 indicates that local labels can as well be used here, as we expect.

It is clear that if ABS is invoked many times in a program, the construction of a different label name each time is going to prove to be a nuisance, if not a problem, to the programmer. Because of the fact that the problem is of a book-

```
                        0000     1            .MACRO    ABS      ARG,SIZE=L
                        0000     2            TST'SIZE  ARG
                        0000     3            BGEQ      DONE
                        0000     4            MNEG'SIZE ARG,ARG
                        0000     5 DONE:
                        0000     6            .ENDM
                                 .
                                 .
                        048A     89           ABS       R8
              58   D5   048A                  TSTL      R8
              62   18   048C                  BGEQ      DONE
        58    58   CE   048E                  MNEGL     R8,R8
                        0491         DONE:
%MACRO-E-SYMOUTPHAS, Symbol out of phase
                                 .
                                 .
                        04E3     101          ABS       DATA,W
        FB19 CF    B5   04E3                  TSTW      DATA
              A8   18   04E7                  BGEQ      DONE
   FB10 CF    FB13 CF   AE   04E9             MNEGW     DATA,DATA
                        04F0         DONE:
%MACRO-E-MULDEFLBL, Multiple definition of label
                                 .
                                 .
```

Figure 18.8.1

```
                     0000    1           .MACRO  ABS  ARG,SIZE=L,LABEL
                     0000    2           TST'SIZE  ARG
                     0000    3           BGEQ       LABEL
                     0000    4           MNEG'SIZE  ARG,ARG
                     0000    5 LABEL':
                     0000    6           .ENDM
                                         .
                                         .
                     048A    89          ABS  R8,,DONE1
              58 D5  048A                 TSTL  R8
              03 18  048C                 BGEQ  DONE1
           58 58 CE  048E                 MNEGL R8,R8
                     0491      DONE1:
                                         .
                                         .
                     04E3    101          ABS  DATA,W,DONE2
        FB19 CF  B5  04E3                 TSTW  DATA
              07 18  04E7                 BGEQ  DONE2
FB10 CF FB13 CF  AE  04E9                 MNEGW DATA,DATA
                     04F0      DONE2:
                                         .
                                         .
                     0709    238          ABS  R0,B,12$
              50 95  0709                 TSTB  R0
              03 18  070B                 BGEQ  12$
           50 50 8E  070D                 MNEGB R0,R0
                     0710      12$:
                                         .
                                         .
```

Figure 18.8.2

keeping nature, a programmer might be inclined to argue thus: "I need to generate a number of labels, all distinct, which serve no purpose other than to act as the destination of the BGEQ operation in this macroinstruction. Thus I shall use local labels—1$, 2$, 3$, ...—since they will not use up the suggestive label names that could more profitably be used elsewhere, and also since it will be very easy to keep track of which labels are in use by one of these macroinstruction calls and which are not. I need only keep track of the last local label number used and then always use the next one." This scheme works so well for this task that it is even *implemented by the macroassembler*. That is, we can direct the assembler *automatically to generate* a new local label each time a macroinstruction is invoked. Such a label is called an **automatically generated local label**, and the assembler is directed to perform the generation as follows. The label to be generated must be one of the macroinstruction arguments; it is named and used as any formal argument is, but in the macroinstruction prototype statement the formal argument name is preceded by a question mark (?). If when the macroinstruction is invoked, that argument is elided, the assembler will substitute the *next* local label for it, where the assembler's automatically generated local label numbering begins at 30000$. If an actual argument is supplied for this formal argument, the substitution takes place as usual, with no automatic creation of a local label.

Figure 18.8.3 illustrates the automatic creation of labels—it is a more so-

```
                   0000    1          .MACRO ABS  ARG,SIZE=L,?LABEL
                   0000    2          TST'SIZE ARG
                   0000    3          BGEQ     LABEL
                   0000    4          MNEG'SIZE ARG,ARG
                   0000    5 LABEL':
                   0000    6          .ENDM
                                      .
                                      .
                                      .
                   048A   89          ABS   R8
            58  D5 048A               TSTL  R8
            03  18 048C               BGEQ  30000$
         58 58  CE 048E               MNEGL R8,R8
                   0491      30000$:
                                      .
                                      .
                                      .
                   04E3  101          ABS   DATA,W
       FB19 CF  B5 04E3               TSTW  DATA
            07  18 04E7               BGEQ  30001$
FB10 CF FB13 CF  AE 04E9              MNEGW DATA,DATA
                   04F0      30001$:
                                      .
                                      .
                                      .
                   071D  223          ABS   R5,B,GO
            55  95 071D               TSTB  R5
            03  18 071F               BGEQ  GO
         55 55  8E 0721               MNEGB R5,R5
                   0724      GO:
                                      .
                                      .
                                      .
```

Figure 18.8.3

phisticated and far more reasonable solution to the multiple label definition problem of Figure 18.8.1 than is the macroinstruction of Figure 18.8.2. Note that the calls at lines 89 and 101 leave the argument LABEL elided, and the assembler has created the labels 30000$ and 30001$. At line 223, the macroinstruction is called again, but this time a value—GO—has been substituted for the formal argument LABEL. On subsequent calls the automatic generation of labels would resume at 30002$, 30003$, ...

We close with a few comments about these automatically generated local labels. First, in the generation of local labels, the assembler does *not* start its local label numbering scheme over again at 30000$ if it enters a new local symbol block, *even though it could* without the danger of multiple label definitions. Thus assembler created local labels will range from 30000$ to 65535$, always increasing by 1 with each use, and thus the programmer is limited to 25,536 such label creations. (It is difficult to imagine that that will be a severe constraint in most cases.) Second, a number of different macroinstructions may use automatically generated local labels, and of course the assembler deals with that situation as expected, simply using the *next available* label number each time one is generated, regardless of which macroinstruction called for it. Next, a macroinstruction may require several created local labels; for example, the macroinstruction

.MACRO   CODE   ARG1,ARG2 = 7,ARG3,?LAB1,?LAB2,?DONE,?END

specifies four such labels, and if all four are elided, they will be given successive automatically generated local label values. Of course, some may be passed values and others elided, with the expected results. A formal argument preceded by a question mark may *not* be used as a keyword argument; any attempt to do so is simply ignored by the assembler. Thus if we attempt to call the macroinstruction ABS of Figure 18.8.3 with

ABS   ARG = R5,LABEL = DONE

the assembler will treat it exactly as if it had seen

ABS   ARG = R5

Finally, the reader will note that those arguments which are intended for automatic generation of local labels have consistently been placed *at the end* of the argument list. This is by no means necessary but has been done only because arguments at the end of an argument list may be elided without the necessity of including a number of successive commas—", , ,"—as would be the case if these were embedded in the argument list.

18.9 REPEAT BLOCKS

A **repeat block** is a kind of macroinstruction which differs in a number of significant ways from those we have already investigated. To begin with, while a repeat block specifies a "package" of VAX instructions that are to be inserted into the source program, it is not *named* as is an ordinary macroinstruction. Thus it cannot be invoked *by name*, nor is its name, together with its definition, set aside in a table of macroinstruction definitions. Instead, each time a repeat block is required in a program, it is defined at the point at which it is needed, and the assembler expands it when and where it encounters its definition. Second, a repeat block *always* contains *one and only one* formal argument, and the actual values that are to replace the formal argument are listed together with the definition of the repeat block. Finally, the assembler expands the code represented by the definition of the repeat block not just *once*, but rather it expands it *once for each actual argument*.

The **indefinite repeat prototype statement** has the form

. .IRP   *arg,⟨argument-list⟩*

where IRP stands for *Indefinite RePeat*, *arg* is *the* formal argument name, and *argument-list* consists of the actual arguments which are to replace the formal argument, separated by commas, spaces, or tabs. (The comma between the formal argument and the argument list can be replaced by a space or tab, and the paired angle brackets surrounding the argument list may be omitted. However, the prototype statement as shown is compatible with earlier macroassemblers, and from the standpoint of clarity the reader is discouraged from omitting either the comma or the angle brackets. Incidentally, the angle brackets are specific here and may *not* be replaced by other grouping symbols defined by the circumflex construction as described in Section 18.4—ˆ#...#, for example.) Thus a typical .IRP directive might be

.IRP   DUMMY,⟨1,MOV,8,R4⟩

an indefinite repeat prototype statement in which the formal argument DUMMY will be replaced successively by the actual arguments "1", "MOV", "8", and "R4".

An **indefinite repeat block** consists of a .IRP directive (indefinite repeat prototype statement), followed by some VAX assembly language constructions, followed by a **.ENDR** directive—*END R*epeat block. (.ENDM will also successfully end a repeat block, but since .ENDR is more descriptive of what is being ended, we shall use it consistently.)

When the assembler encounters a .IRP directive, it inserts *at that point* in the source program the assembly language code making up the definition of the repeat block and then replaces the formal argument with the *first* actual argument in the argument list, following all the rules for argument replacement: direct substitution, concatenation, and so on. Having expanded the repeat block, the assembler then expands it *again*, with the formal argument replaced by the *second* actual argument. Thus we now have *two* copies of the body of the repeat block definition, one after the other. In the first copy, the first actual argument was used to replace *the* formal argument; in the second copy, the replacement was by the second actual argument. This process continues until the actual argument list is exhausted, at which point the assembler has completed the expansion of the repeat block.

The name *indefinite repeat block* is clearly appropriate—the *block* of instructions making up the definition is *repeated indefinitely*; the number of repeats depends on the number of actual arguments. As a pair of simple examples of this construction, consider the repeat blocks of Figure 18.9.1. At lines 34 to 37 an indefinite repeat is defined which is to generate two longwords for each actual argument, one the argument itself, and the other being twice that argument. As we see, the assembler has expanded the repeat block as a set of 10 .LONG directives. The second example is the repeat block defined at lines 79 to 81, and the reader will find it reminiscent of the macroinstruction SAV3ARGS of Figure 18.6.1.

As with any other kind of macroinstruction, indefinite repeat arguments may require grouping (see Figure 18.4.6, for example). As before, this may be done using the paired angle brackets—⟨...⟩—as grouping symbols, even though angle brackets are used as a part of the indefinite repeat prototype statement. Other characters may be used as grouping symbols, provided that the first instance is preceded by a circumflex (ˆ). Figure 18.9.2 shows some examples of these constructions; the reader should have no difficulties following them, since they are

```
                                        .
                                        .
                        0A42    34      .IRP    X,⟨1,2,-27,34,7⟩
                        0A42    35      .LONG   X
                        0A42    36      .LONG   2*X
                        0A42    37      .ENDR
        00000001        0A42            .LONG   1
        00000002        0A46            .LONG   2*1
                        0A4A
        00000002        0A4A            .LONG   2
        00000004        0A4E            .LONG   2*2
                        0A52
        FFFFFFE5        0A52            .LONG   -27
        FFFFFFCA        0A56            .LONG   2*-27
                        0A5A
        00000022        0A5A            .LONG   34
        00000044        0A5E            .LONG   2*34
                        0A62
        00000007        0A62            .LONG   7
        0000000E        0A66            .LONG   2*7
                                        .
                                        .
                        0B94    79      .IRP    NO,⟨1,11,4⟩
                        0B94    80      PUSHL   ARG'NO
                        0B94    81      .ENDR
    00000BD2'EF   DD    0B94            PUSHL   ARG1
                        0B9A
        F462 CF   DD    0B9A            PUSHL   ARG11
                        0B9E
        FEA0 CF   DD    0B9E            PUSHL   ARG4
                                        .
                                        .
```

Figure 18.9.1

similar to examples we have already examined in detail for normally constructed macroinstructions.

Since an indefinite repeat block is not named, its definition must be included in the program each time it is needed. If this occurs with sufficient frequency to be an annoyance, we can eliminate the problem by constructing a normally formed (and thus *named*) macroinstruction whose definition simply consists of the repeat block. Then, in effect, the repeat block can be "called" simply by invoking the macroinstruction. Figure 18.9.3 gives an example of a repeat block which saves on the stack, and then clears, a register, and also adds the number of that register to a byte table pointed at by R0. The indefinite repeat is "surrounded" by the macroinstruction SAVE_AND_CLEAR; the reader should note how the formal arguments for SAVE_AND _CLEAR are passed through to the indefinite repeat construction and how the replacement by actual arguments takes place when the macroinstruction SAVE_AND_CLEAR is invoked.

We conclude this part of our discussion of indefinite repeats with a more complex example, but one which proves to be quite useful. In the program segment of Figure 18.6.3 we wrote a macroinstruction GEN_INPUT_MACROS whose purpose was to generate other macroinstructions, namely the input macroinstruc-

```
                         .
                         .
             0A04    52    .IRP    X,<INCL   R1,DECL   R1>
             0A04    53    CLRL    R1
             0A04    54    X
             0A04    55    .ENDR
     51   D4  0A04         CLRL    R1
          D6  0A06         INCL
%MACRO-E-NOTENUFOPR, Not enough operands supplied
     51   D4  0A07         CLRL    R1
             0A09         R1
%MACRO-E-UNRECSTMT, Unrecognized statement
     51   D4  0A09         CLRL    R1
          D7  0A0B         DECL
%MACRO-E-NOTENUFOPR, Not enough operands supplied
     51   D4  0A0C         CLRL    R1
             0A0E         R1
%MACRO-E-UNRECSTMT, Unrecognized statement
                         .
                         .
             0E10    97    .IRP    X,<<INCL   R1>,<DECL   R1>>
             0E10    98    CLRL    R1
             0E10    99    X
             0E10   100    .ENDR
     51   D4  0E10         CLRL    R1
     51   D6  0E12         INCL    R1
             0E14
     51   D4  0E14         CLRL    R1
     51   D7  0E16         DECL    R1
             0E18
                         .
                         .
             103A   212    .IRP    ARG,<<Cats and dogs>,^?X > Y?>
             103A   213    .ASCII  /ARG/
             103A   214    .ENDR
  73 . . 43  103A         .ASCII  /Cats and dogs/
             1047
  59 . . 58  1047         .ASCII  /X > Y/
             104C
                         .
                         .
```

Figure 18.9.2

tion $I.xx$—$I.1B$, $I.4D$, $I.2H$, and so on. Since the BYTES argument may
take on any of three values 1, 2, and 4, and since the FORMAT argument may
take on B, D, and H as values, evidently we have the potential of defining nine
different macroinstructions. To define them all would thus require nine calls to
GEN_INPUT_MACROS, but they can all be generated simply by including the
macrodefinition within a pair of nested indefinite repeat blocks. This is the technique used in Figure D.6.1 of Appendix D to generate these macroinstruction
definitions, and what follows is almost identical to those definitions. Figure 18.9.4
shows some of these calls as they are generated, but the listing has been doctored
in the following two ways. First, we have not listed all the input macroinstructions

```
                    0000    1        .MACRO   SAVE_AND_CLEAR  A,B,C
                    0000    2        .IRP     X,<A,B,C>
                    0000    3        PUSHL    R'X
                    0000    4        CLRL     R'X
                    0000    5        MOVB     #'X,(R0)+
                    0000    6        .ENDR
                    0000    7        .ENDM
                                       .
                                       .
                    02AD    84       SAVE_AND_CLEAR  3,7,4
                    02AD             .IRP     X,<3,7,4>
                    02AD             PUSHL    R'X
                    02AD             CLRL     R'X
                    02AD             MOVB     #'X,(R0)+
                    02AD             .ENDR
          53   DD   02AD             PUSHL    R3
          53   D4   02AF             CLRL     R3
     80   03   90   02B1             MOVB     #3,(R0)+
                    02B4
          57   DD   02B4             PUSHL    R7
          57   D4   02B6             CLRL     R7
     80   07   90   02B8             MOVB     #7,(R0)+
                    02BB
          54   DD   02BB             PUSHL    R4
          54   D4   02BD             CLRL     R4
     80   04   90   02BF             MOVB     #4,(R0)+
                    02C2
                                       .
                                       .
```

Figure 18.9.3

that were generated, since they add excessively to the length of the listing, without adding correspondingly to our understanding of repeat blocks. Second, we have inserted line numbers in brackets ([..]) to aid in our discussion, since the assembler does not assign line numbers to the lines of source code making up the expansion of a macroinstruction or repeat block. The input macroinstructions themselves are defined from lines [3] through [8], and we see that this definition is enclosed within an indefinite repeat (lines [2] and [9]), which in turn is enclosed within an indefinite repeat which begins at line [1] and ends at line [10]. When these repeat blocks are encountered by the assembler, the expansion takes place in the following order. The formal argument BYTES (the outer repeat block) is given its first actual argument, namely, 1. The inner repeat block is then entered, and we see the *expansion* of the outer repeat block at lines [11] through [18]. Observe that these lines contain the *definition* of the inner repeat block and, of course, the actual macrodefinition $I.'BYTES''FORMAT, but observe that the replacement of 1 for BYTES has been made—$I.1'FORMAT. Next, the inner repeat block is expanded, with the formal argument FORMAT taking on its first actual value, B. That expansion is shown at lines [19] through [24], where the macroinstruction $I.1B is defined. FORMAT then takes on its remaining values H and D, and this results in the definitions of $I.1H and $I.1D, which are not shown in the figure. Since the actual argument list of the inner definite repeat construction is now

```
[1]     0000     1     .IRP     BYTES,<1,2,4>
[2]     0000     2     .IRP     FORMAT,<B,H,D>
[3]     0000     3     .MACRO   $I.'BYTES''FORMAT        ARG
[4]     0000     4     PUSHAB   ARG
[5]     0000     5     MOVW     #'BYTES,-(SP)
[6]     0000     6     MOVW     #^A/I'FORMAT'/,-(SP)
[7]     0000     7     CALLS    #2,...$
[8]     0000     8     .ENDM
[9]     0000     9     .ENDR
[10]    0000    10     .ENDR
[11]    0000           .IRP     FORMAT,<B,H,D>
[12]    0000           .MACRO   $I.1'FORMAT        ARG
[13]    0000           PUSHAB   ARG
[14]    0000           MOVW     #1,-(SP)
[15]    0000           MOVW     #^A/I'FORMAT'/,-(SP)
[16]    0000           CALLS    #2,...$
[17]    0000           .ENDM
[18]    0000           .ENDR
[19]    0000           .MACRO   $I.1B    ARG
[20]    0000           PUSHAB   ARG
[21]    0000           MOVW     #1,-(SP)
[22]    0000           MOVW     #^A/IB/,-(SP)
[23]    0000           CALLS    #2,...$
[24]    0000           .ENDM
                       .
                       .
[25]    0000           .IRP     FORMAT,<B,H,D>
[26]    0000           .MACRO   $I.2'FORMAT        ARG
[27]    0000           PUSHAB   ARG
[28]    0000           MOVW     #2,-(SP)
[29]    0000           MOVW     #^A/I'FORMAT'/,-(SP)
[30]    0000           CALLS    #2,...$
[31]    0000           .ENDM
[32]    0000           .ENDR
[33]    0000           .MACRO   $I.2B    ARG
[34]    0000           PUSHAB   ARG
[35]    0000           MOVW     #2,-(SP)
[36]    0000           MOVW     #^A/IB/,-(SP)
[37]    0000           CALLS    #2,...$
[38]    0000           .ENDM
                       .
                       .
[39]    0000           .MACRO   $I.4D    ARG
[40]    0000           PUSHAB   ARG
[41]    0000           MOVW     #4,-(SP)
[42]    0000           MOVW     #^A/ID/,-(SP)
[43]    0000           CALLS    #2,...$
[44]    0000           .ENDM
                       .
                       .
```

Figure 18.9.4

exhausted, control is returned to the *outer* repeat block, where its formal argument BYTES is given its next value, 2. Since the inner repeat block is once again encountered (lines [25] through [32]), it is expanded another time and yields the definition of $I.2B, as shown at lines [33] to [38]. These expansions and corresponding macroinstruction definitions continue until both argument lists are exhausted. The last macroinstruction definition generated is shown at lines [39] to [44], where BYTES = 4 and FORMAT = D—the definition of $I.4D.

There is a variation on the .IRP repeat block in which the argument list is a *string of individual characters*. The format for the prototype statement of this repeat construction is

.IRPC   *arg*,⟨*argument-string*⟩

where .IRPC stands for *Indefinite RePeat with Character* argument, *arg* is *the* formal argument, and *argument-string* is a string of characters. When the repeat block is encountered, the body of the block is expanded with the first character in the argument string being used as the actual argument to replace *arg*; the block is next expanded with *arg* replaced by the second character of the string; and so on, until the characters in the string are exhausted. As with .IRP, the comma between the formal argument and the argument string may be replaced by a space or tab, and the paired angle brackets are generally not necessary to enclose the string. However, neither of these variations is recommended. As with .IRP, a repeat block controlled by .IRPC is terminated with .ENDR (or .ENDM).

```
                                    .
                                    .
                    0231    24    .IRPC    NO,⟨193⟩
                    0231    25    PUSHL    ARG'NO
                    0231    26    .ENDR
       FD AF    DD  0231          PUSHL    ARG1
                    0234
      FDC8 CF   DD  0234          PUSHL    ARG9
                    0238
  0000049A'EF    DD  0238          PUSHL    ARG3
                    023E

                                    .
                                    .
                    0281    109   .IRPC    BYTES,⟨124⟩
                    0281    110   .IRPC    FORMAT,⟨BHD⟩
                    0281    111   .MACRO   $I.'BYTES''FORMAT        ARG
                    0281    112   PUSHAB   ARG
                    0281    113   MOVW     #'BYTES,-(SP)
                    0281    114   MOVW     #^A/I'FORMAT'/,-(SP)
                    0281    115   CALLS    #2,...$
                    0281    116   .ENDM
                    0281    117   .ENDR
                    0281    118   .ENDR
                                    .
                                    .
```

Figure 18.9.5

Figure 18.9.5 illustrates the .IRPC construction with two familiar examples. The first repeat block is essentially the same as that of Figure 18.9.1 (lines 79 to 81), but observe that the present offering could *not* deal with the actual argument 11. The second block of Figure 18.9.5 is the same as that of the example of Figure 18.9.4, namely, the definitions of the input macroinstructions. (We have suppressed the actual expansions here since, as we know, they are quite lengthy.)

There is one additional repeat construction which is sometimes useful but not frequently used. The directive **.REPEAT** has the format

.REPEAT   *expression*

where *expression* is some expression that can be evaluated by the assembler as an absolute (and thus not relocation-sensitive) value. The body of the repeat block is repeated as many times as the value of *expression*. Note that there is *no* argument transmission in this case, since there is no formal argument. A repeat block initiated by .REPEAT is terminated with .ENDR (or .ENDM). One simple example is offered in Figure 18.9.6, a repeat construction which generates a number of zero bytes. Some applications and further investigations are given in the exercises.

We close this section with a final comment that pertains to the transmission of arguments in any macro-type construction. We have had occasion to construct macroinstructions which invoke other macroinstructions, or which within their definitions contain the definitions of other macroinstructions. We have seen that in some cases, arguments passed to one macroinstruction may be passed through to another. The example of Figure 18.9.7, in which the macroinstruction SPECIAL, with the formal argument ARG, invokes the macroinstruction INSTR and passes that argument to it, reveals that some care needs to be exercised when passing certain types of actual arguments. In particular, we see from the call at line 129 that even enclosing the intended argument CLRL R0 in angle brackets has not prevented an error. But enclosing this argument in *two* sets of angle

```
                          .
                          .
                          .
00000005   0000     11    VAL = 5
                          .
                          .
           0A06     83    .REPEAT 2*VAL-6
           0A06     84    .BYTE   0
           0A06     85    .ENDR
     00    0A06           .BYTE   0
           0A07
     00    0A07           .BYTE   0
           0A08
     00    0A08           .BYTE   0
           0A09
     00    0A09           .BYTE   0
           0A0A
```

Figure 18.9.6

```
                              0000    1      .MACRO   SPECIAL   ARG
                              0000    2      INSTR    ARG
                              0000    3      .ENDM
                                             .
                                             .
                              02A2    35     .MACRO   INSTR     ARG
                              02A2    36     ARG
                              02A2    37     .ENDM
                                             .
                                             .
                              03A6    129    SPECIAL  <CLRL     R0>
                              03A6           INSTR    CLRL      R0
%MACRO-E-TOOMNYARGS, Too many arguments in MACRO call
                              03A6
                       D4     03A6           CLRL
%MACRO-E-NOTENUFOPR, Not enough operands supplied
                              03A7
                                             .
                                             .
                                             .
                              07A8    211    SPECIAL  <<CLRL R0>>
                              07A8           INSTR    <CLRL R0>
                  50   D4     07A8           CLRL R0
                              07AA
                                             .
                                             .
                                             .
```

Figure 18.9.7

brackets, as in the call at line 211, seems to take care of the matter. We correctly infer from this that whenever the macroassembler encounters an argument enclosed in grouping symbols (angle brackets, or something else using the circumflex construction), it *removes* the outer set of grouping symbols. Thus in this example, the *two* nested calls resulted in *two* sets of grouping symbols being stripped from the argument, exactly as desired.

18.10 CONDITIONAL ASSEMBLIES: IMMEDIATE CONDITIONALS

The numerical input macroinstructions $I.xx, which have been generated in a variety of ways in the preceding several sections, still contain a serious deficiency which perhaps the reader has noted (see Figure 18.9.4 for the latest version of these macroinstructions). All nine macroinstructions contain the instruction

PUSHAB   ARG

regardless of the context of the macroinstruction. That is, even though $I.2H inputs *word* data into the location specified by ARG, the context of the PUSH Address instruction is *byte*. Although this may cause no problems in some cases, consider the programming segment of Figure 18.10.1, in which the argument is an autoincremented register. Presumably, R3 has been initialized in such a way that it

```
              0000    1        .IRPC   BYTES,<124>
              0000    2        .IRPC   FORMAT,<BHD>
              0000    3        .MACRO  $I.'BYTES''FORMAT   ARG
              0000    4        PUSHAB  ARG
              0000    5        MOVW    #'BYTES,-(SP)
              0000    6        MOVW    #^A/I'FORMAT'/,-(SP)
              0000    7        CALLS   #2,...$
              0000    8        .ENDM
              0000    9        .ENDR
              0000   10        .ENDR
                          .

              0A2C   172       $I.2H   (R3)+
        83  9F  0A2C           PUSHAB  (R3)+
     7E  02  B0  0A2E          MOVW    #2,-(SP)
   7E  4849 8F  B0  0A31       MOVW    #^A/IH/,-(SP)
00000000'EF  02  FB  0A36      CALLS   #2,...$
              0A3D
                          .
                          .
```

Figure 18.10.1

points at the first of a collection of words. The first time $I.2H is invoked a number, in hexadecimal format, will be read from the keyboard and placed at the word location pointed at by R3. But because of the PUSHA*B* instruction, c(R3) will be advanced *by 1*, and thus R3 will *not* be pointing at the next *word*. There is a conflict in the contexts of the *names* of the macroinstructions and the VAX instructions which comprise them, a conflict that will surely trap the unsuspecting programmer through no fault of his or her own. This must be repaired, but the question is: How?

One solution to the problem would be to rename the macroinstructions so that the formal argument BYTES, instead of taking on the values 1, 2, and 4, would take on the values B, W, and L—Byte, Word, and Longword. If this were done, the PUSHAx instruction could be written as

PUSHA'BYTES   ARG

which would generate the appropriate PUSHA instruction—PUSHAB, PUSHAW, or PUSHAL. However, this change would have additional consequences (in the procedure ...$) which would require quite a bit of repair. For this reason, we decline to take this approach. Another solution, of course, would be to define the macroinstructions three at a time—the byte-type macroinstructions, then those which input words, and finally the longword oriented macroinstructions. This would require a bit more writing, but it is a totally acceptable way of dealing with the problem.

The approach we take here is an instance of the well-known method of "programming by wishful thinking"—what we would *like* the assembler to do at this point in the definitions of these macroinstructions is to react favorably to the following "commands:"

1. If the formal parameter BYTES has the actual value "1", assemble the instruction "PUSHAB ARG" here; otherwise do nothing.

2. If the formal parameter BYTES has the actual value "2", assemble the instruction "PUSHAW ARG" here; otherwise do nothing.

3. If the formal parameter BYTES has the actual value "4", assemble the instruction "PUSHAL ARG" here; otherwise do nothing.

Thus if we are defining, say, $I.2D, BYTES will be given the actual value "2", and as a result statement 2 above will be acted upon, while 1 and 3 will be ignored, thereby generating precisely the desired PUSHAW construction. In fact, there is no reason why the assembler cannot respond to these requests; it knows the character that is being substituted for the formal argument BYTES, and it can certainly compare that character with the characters "1", "2", and "4" in succession. Hence it should come as no surprise to the reader to find that the assembler can be instructed as above; the assembly language constructions are

```
.IIF   IDN,BYTES,1,   PUSHAB   ARG
.IIF   IDN,BYTES,2,   PUSHAW   ARG
.IIF   IDN,BYTES,4,   PUSHAL   ARG
```

where .IIF stands for *Immediate IF* and IDN stands for *IDeNtical*. (The use of the word *immediate* here is in contradistinction to another type of "if" statement which is investigated later in this section; for the moment the reader should not try to assign any special meaning to it.)

```
                    0000     1    .IRPC    BYTES,<124>
                    0000     2    .IRPC    FORMAT,<BHD>
                    0000     3    .MACRO   $I.'BYTES''FORMAT   ARG
                    0000     4    .IIF     IDN, BYTES,1, PUSHAB ARG
                    0000     5    .IIF     IDN, BYTES,2, PUSHAW ARG
                    0000     6    .IIF     IDN, BYTES,4, PUSHAL ARG
                    0000     7    MOVW     #'BYTES',-(SP)
                    0000     8    MOVW     #^A/I'FORMAT'/,-(SP)
                    0000     9    CALLS    #2,...$
                    0000    10    .ENDM
                    0000    11    .ENDR
                    0000    12    .ENDR
                             .
                             .
                    0A2C   174    $I.2H    (R3)+
                    0A2C          .IIF     IDN, 2,1, PUSHAB   (R3)+
              83 3F 0A2C          .IIF     IDN, 2,2, PUSHAW   (R3)+
                    0A2E          .IIF     IDN, 2,4, PUSHAL   (R3)+
         7E   02 B0 0A2E          MOVW     #2,-(SP)
    7E 4849 8F B0 0A31          MOVW     #^A/IH/,-(SP)
00000000'EF 02 FB 0A36          CALLS    #2,...$
                    0A3D
                             .
                             .
```

Figure 18.10.2

Figure 18.10.2 shows our final (and correct) version of the nested .IRPCs that define the nine numerical input macroinstructions. Although we do not show the listing of the *definitions* of these macroinstructions because of their length, we show one *expansion* of a macro call, the same call of Figure 18.10.1. Notice that here the three .IIFs are shown, but only the second, in which "2" is identical to "2"—that is, only the .IIF which is *true*—generates any machine code.

The format of the **Immediate IF** directive is

$$\text{.IIF} \quad cond, arg(s), instruction$$

where *cond* is one of the *conditionals* described in Figure 18.10.3; *arg(s)* is an argument for the conditional or if the conditional requires two arguments, *arg(s)* consists of the two arguments, separated by a comma; and *instruction* is any (single) VAX assembly language instruction. [The comma between *cond* and *arg(s)* may sometimes be replaced by a space or tab; however, since in some cases only the comma will suffice, we have shown it as required in the description above.]

The conditionals that may be used in a .IIF construction are shown and described in Figure 18.10.3. Observe that each conditional has a *complementary* conditional. The various conditionals take one of three types of arguments: "value" (explained below), symbol, and string. We have already seen an example of a macroinstruction which compares strings (IDN and DIF), the macroinstructions of Figure 18.10.2. Thus we shall look at examples of each of the remaining types,

FIGURE 18.10.3

Cond	Meaning	Argument(s)	Assembled if:
EQ	Equal to 0	Value[a]	Value $= 0$
NE	Not equal to 0	Value[a]	Value $\neq 0$
GT	Greater than 0	Value[a]	Value > 0
LE	Less than or equal to 0	Value[a]	Value ≤ 0
LT	Less than 0	Value[a]	Value < 0
GE	Greater than or equal to 0	Value[a]	Value ≥ 0
DF	Defined	Symbol	Symbol is defined
NFD	Not defined	Symbol	Symbol is not defined
B	Blank	String	Argument is a blank string
NB	Nonblank	String	Argument is a nonblank string
IDN	Identical	String$_1$, String$_2$	String$_1$ is identical to String$_2$
DIF	Different	String$_1$, String$_2$	String$_1$ is different from String$_2$

[a] By *value* we mean any expression to which the assembler can assign a *numerical value*. Thus expressions such as ADDR, 7, START − ADDR, $\langle$START − ADDR + 2$\rangle$/2 + 14, and so on, are all values, whereas R3, AP + 4, and so on, are not.

```
                              .
                              .
             0000   22        .MACRO   SAVARGS A,B,C,D,E,F,G,H,I,J,K,L
             0000   23        .IRP     X,⟨A,B,C,D,E,F,G,H,I,J,K,L⟩
             0000   24        .IIF     NB,X, PUSHL  ARG'X
             0000   25        .ENDR
             0000   26        .ENDM
                              .
                              .
             033C   78        SAVARGS 1,2,12
             033C            .IRP     X,⟨1,2,12,,,,,,,,,⟩
             033C            .IIF     NB,X, PUSHL  ARG'X
             033C            .ENDR
FCC0 CF  DD  033C            .IIF     NB,1, PUSHL   ARG1
             0340
FCBC CF  DD  0340            .IIF     NB,2, PUSHL   ARG2
             0344
FCB8 CF  DD  0344            .IIF     NB,12, PUSHL  ARG12
             0348
             0348            .IIF     NB,, PUSHL   ARG
             0348
                              .
                              .
             044A   110       SAVARGS 11
             044A            .IRP     X,⟨11,,,,,,,,,,,⟩
             044A            .IIF     NB,X, PUSHL  ARG'X
             044A            .ENDR
FBB2 CF  DD  044A            .IIF     NB,11, PUSHL  ARG11
             044E
                              .
                              .
             047D   142       SAVARGS 1,2,3,4,5
             047D            .IRP     X,⟨1,2,3,4,5,,,,,,,⟩
             047D            .IIF     NB,X, PUSHL  ARG'X
             047D            .ENDR
FB7F CF  DD  047D            .IIF     NB,1, PUSHL   ARG1
             0481
FB7B CF  DD  0481            .IIF     NB,2, PUSHL   ARG2
             0485
FB77 CF  DD  0485            .IIF     NB,3, PUSHL   ARG3
             0489
FB73 CF  DD  0489            .IIF     NB,4, PUSHL   ARG4
             048D
FB6F CF  DD  048D            .IIF     NB,5, PUSHL   ARG5
             0491
                              .
                              .
```

Figure 18.10.4

beginning with a "nonblank" (NB) conditional directive, which deals with a *single* string. The macroinstruction SAV3ARGS defined early in the chapter saved three of the arguments ARG1, ..., ARG12 and we soon found that one of its short-comings was that it saved a *specific* three arguments. We were ultimately able to resolve that by passing arguments to a modified version of SAV3ARGS (see Figure 18.6.1). A remaining deficiency, however, is that despite the improvements we

```
00000007  0000     1        FLAG    = 7
                            .
                            .
          0042     33       .IIF    EQ, FLAG-4, INCB  DATA+2
                            .
FF7E CF  96  00C3  76       .IIF    EQ, FLAG-7, INCB  DATA+3
                            .
                            .
```

Figure 18.10.5

have made, SAV3ARGS still stacks *three* arguments, whereas it is easy to imagine environments in which we would need to save three arguments in one place and, say, seven arguments somewhere else. We clearly do not want to write an entire collection of macroinstructions to be used to save any number of arguments, and in fact we do not need to—one macroinstruction will do, and we give an example in Figure 18.10.4. The macroinstruction SAVARGS makes provision for saving up to 12 longword arguments. The formal arguments A, B, ..., L are passed through the macroinstruction to a .IRP construction, which *conditionally* pushes arguments on the stack. The condition is that the actual argument (in the .IRP directive) is *NonB*lank. When SAVARGS is invoked at line 78 with actual argument list 1,2,12, the first three PUSHL instructions are assembled. But the fourth instruction (at address 00000348) is *not* assembled, for as we see the actual argument (which is between the two consecutive commas—is an "empty" argument) *is* blank. The listing of the remaining seven conditionals, none of which will be true, is not shown, nor are the similar **unsatisfied conditionals** which are generated when the macroinstruction is invoked at lines 110 and 142.

The conditionals whose single argument is a "value" require some explanation. As stated in the footnote in Figure 18.10.3, a *value* is any expression to which the *assembler* can assign a numerical value. Thus expressions such as 9, 2*3-7, and ADDR yield numerical *values* and thus are appropriate arguments for the numerical comparison conditionals EQ, NE, GT, LE, LT, and GE, but we need to make two comments here. First, note that all the comparisons are against 0, and thus to determine, for example, if "X LT Y" we must ask if "(X − Y) LT 0." Second, "values" such as ADDR and START must be treated with much care. Consider the program segment of Figure 18.10.5, in which the symbol FLAG has been *directly assigned* the value 7. Conditionally assembled instructions are found at line 33, where FLAG is tested against 4 (the conditional found to be false and thus no code being generated), and again at line 76, where FLAG is found to equal 7 and thus the assembler has generated the code for the INCB instruction. All of this is quite straightforward and leaves little room for potential error. However, consider next the segment of Figure 18.10.6(a). The instruction at line 63 is to clear the contents of ADDR and then, at line 64, we find that the conditional INCL *is* assembled, because the condition, "EQ, ADDR", is *true*. But why does this condition test as true? Because the contents of ADDR has just been cleared at line 63? Absolutely *not*, for not only is the contents of this longword not cleared until *execution* time, but also the assembler has no knowledge of the contents of

```
    00000004  0000    1 ADDR:   .BLKL   1
                                   .
                                   .
FEF2 CF   D4  010A    63          CLRL    ADDR
FEEE CF   D6  010E    64          .IIF    EQ, ADDR, INCL   ADDR
                                   .
                                   .

                        (a)


                                   .
                                   .
    0000000A  0006    2 ADDR:   .BLKL   1
                                   .
FEF8 CF   D4  010A    64          CLRL    ADDR
             010E    65          .IIF    EQ, ADDR, INCL   ADDR
                                   .
                                   .

                        (b)
```

Figure 18.10.6

any memory locations. What the assembler knows is that the *value* of ADDR is 0, since ADDR is simple a symbolic name for the address of the location at which it was assembled, 00000000. It is this *value*, not the *contents* of ADDR, that is being tested at line 64; since ADDR = 0, the INCL instruction is assembled. These comments are verified in Figure 18.10.6(b), where ADDR has the value 6 (the value of the assembler's location counter at the time ADDR was encountered on assembly pass one). As we see, the INCL instruction at line 65 is *not* assembled, since in this case ADDR is *not* 0. These remarks may strike the reader as quite obvious, but they deal with ideas that are the source of many errors committed by the novice programmer.

Figure 18.10.7 shows another example of the same EQ construction, in which the symbolic address START is tested against the number 8. As we see, the resulting conditional tests as *true*, and thus the CLRL instruction is assembled. There is nothing peculiar about the way in which the assembler has treated this construction; but we must ask what is meant by "START = 8". The listing certainly shows that START has the value 8, as would the symbol table. But START is a *relocation sensitive* symbol, and by the time this module is linked and

```
    00000008  0000    1 BLOCK:  .BLKL   2
              0000  0008    2 START:  .WORD   ^M<>
                                   .
                                   .
    53   D4  0054    24          .IIF    EQ, START-8, CLRL  R3
                                   .
                                   .
```

Figure 18.10.7

executed, START will probably have been relocated up to some higher address, for example, 0000080C. What, then, is the "value of START"? Is it 00000008, or is it 0000080C? The assembler has answered this question based on the information it had at the time. The programmer must simply be aware of these matters to avoid potential execution time errors.

The conditionals DF and NDF—*defined* and *not defined*—take a symbol as a single argument, and they ask whether that symbol is defined or not *at the time the conditional is encountered*. The program segment of Figure 18.10.8 is quite contrived, but it does show that the assembler treats DF as meaning "defined *at this time*." When DATA is tested at line 62, it is not yet defined and no machine code is generated. But by the time the test at line 125 is encountered, DATA *is* in the assembler's symbol table, and the instruction is assembled. As a more practical example, we may point to the procedure ...$ which actually implements the input and output macroinstructions that we have used throughout the text and have discussed in this chapter. The macroinstructions, and also those portions of the procedure ...$ that implement them, have been divided into several groups of commands. One group implements the numerical output macroinstructions ($0.2D, $0.4H, etc.), and another provides character and string input ($I.STR, $I.CHR, and $I.NL). These macroinstructions and the procedure which provides for their execution are designed so that the user need not implement *all* of them. For example, if the user anticipates that there will be no need for numerical input from the keyboard, the group containing the definitions of $I.2B, $I.4D, and so on, and the code in ...$ that implements them, need not be included in the package. But now how can the procedure ...$ know whether a particular portion of code has been included to handle a certain type of request? To be specific, to manage numerical output, a module in the procedure ...$ whose entry point address is named OUTPUTN is required. If the procedure receives such a request (for example, $0.2H), it jumps to OUTPUTN *provided it is defined*. Indeed, the reader will find the following two lines of assembly language code in Figure D.6.2:

.IIF   DF, OUTPUTN, JMP   OUTPUTN
RET

which has the effect of *assembling* the JMP instruction *if* OUTPUTN has been

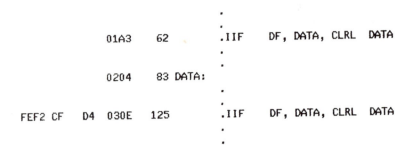

Figure 18.10.8

Macroinstructions and Conditional Assemblies   Chap. 18

defined. Thus upon *execution* the jump will take place *if* it was assembled—*if* OUTPUTN was defined at assembly time. But if *not*, the JMP is not assembled, and the RET is executed; in effect, the output request is simply ignored altogether.

18.11 CONDITIONAL ASSEMBLIES: CONDITIONALS AND SUBCONDITIONALS

Consider a program in which four registers, R0 through R3, are to be cleared IF the symbol DATA is defined. To be more precise, the assembler is to generate these four CLRL instructions if DATA is defined. This is easy enough to accomplish with the conditional constructions we have at hand, and the result is shown in the programming segment of Figure 18.11.1. The reader will detect a certain awkwardness in the programming style here, which would be far more pronounced if even more instructions were to be assembled IF DATA is DeFined. In terms of high-level languages we presently have available the construction

$$\text{IF } cond \text{ THEN } statement$$

What we are seeking is some kind of "IF...ENDIF" block found in many programming languages:

$$\text{IF } cond \text{ THEN}$$
$$statement_1$$
$$.$$
$$.$$
$$statement_n$$
$$\text{ENDIF}$$

The VAX assembler supports such a construction, and its format is the following.

$$\text{.IF } cond, arg(s)$$
$$instruction_1$$
$$.$$
$$.$$
$$instruction_n$$
$$\text{.ENDC}$$

```
                                          .
                                          .
              02AC      62 DATA:          .
                                          .
    50  D4  03AE   94    .IIF DF, DATA, CLRL  R0
    51  D4  03B0   95    .IIF DF, DATA, CLRL  R1
    52  D4  03B2   96    .IIF DF, DATA, CLRL  R2
    53  D4  03B4   97    .IIF DF, DATA, CLRL  R3
                                          .
                                          .
```

Figure 18.11.1

$$
\begin{array}{lll}
02AC & 62 & DATA:
\end{array}
$$

```
              03AE  94       .IF    DF, DATA
50   D4       03AE  95          CLRL   R0
51   D4       03B0  96          CLRL   R1
52   D4       03B2  97          CLRL   R2
53   D4       03B4  98          CLRL   R3
              03B6  99       .ENDC
```

Figure 18.11.2

The directive .IF is called the **conditional** directive (and distinguished from the *immediate* conditional directive .IIF of the preceding section). *cond* is one of the conditionals of Figure 18.10.3, with *arg(s)* also as described in that table. **.ENDC** is an assembler directive standing for *END Conditional*, and the lines of directives and instructions between .IF and .ENDC is called a **conditional block.**

The somewhat amateurish-appearing constructions of Figure 18.11.1 may now be written as the conditional block of Figure 18.11.2. Observe that we have not really conserved any writing of source lines here, but we have a *logical* construction which reads far more smoothly than our earlier version. In fact, since *any* VAX instructions may appear within a conditional block, we might be inclined to write a repeat block to generate the CLRL instructions, as shown in Figure 18.11.3. Observe that in these last two programming segments, and henceforth in those which involve conditional blocks, we have taken advantage of the fact that the VAX assembler is insensitive to spacing and have done some indenting to make even more clear the instructions that belong to various blocks.

Consider now a program in which the instructions to clear registers R0 to R3 are to be assembled IF the symbol DATA is DeFined, and otherwise—that is, IF the symbol DATA is Not DeFined—the instructions to clear R1, R3, and R5 are

```
              02AC   62 DATA:

              03AE   94    .IF   DF, DATA
              03AE   95       .IRPC  X,<0123>
              03AE   96       CLRL   R'X
              03AE   97       .ENDR
50   D4       03AE           CLRL   R0
              03B0
51   D4       03B0           CLRL   R1
              03B2
52   D4       03B2           CLRL   R2
              03B4
53   D4       03B4           CLRL   R3
              03B6
              03B6   98    .ENDC
```

Figure 18.11.3

```
                        .
                        .
        03AE    93      .IF  DF, DATA
        03AE    94           CLRL   R0
        03AE    95           CLRL   R1
        03AE    96           CLRL   R2
        03AE    97           CLRL   R3
        03AE    98      .ENDC
        03AE    99      .IF  NDF, DATA
51  D4  03AE   100           CLRL   R1
53  D4  03B0   101           CLRL   R3
55  D4  03B2   102           CLRL   R5
        03B4   103      .ENDC
                        .
                        .
```

Figure 18.11.4

to be assembled. A segment to do so is shown in Figure 18.11.4, where we assume that DATA is *not* defined. The resulting source program instructions are the obvious ones and are perfectly clear, but as before the two consecutive conditional blocks seem a bit awkward. Once again it will be helpful to investigate the constructions available in high-level programming languages. Although most of these contain some kind of IF...THEN construction, no matter how primitive, as we have already noted many also contain a block structure such as

IF *cond* THEN *statement-block* ENDIF

the construct corresponding to our conditional block. But some languages also implement the very powerful ELSE clause as a part of the IF...THEN structure:

IF *cond* THEN
statement$_1$

.

.
statement$_m$
ELSE
 statement$_{m+1}$

.

.
statement$_n$
ENDIF

The reader is doubtless aware that the code in the main IF block is executed if the *cond* is true, and that otherwise the instructions in the ELSE block are executed. The VAX macroassembler has a similar capability, but in a sense it is even more sophisticated. (The use of the comparative phrase "more sophisticated" is something of a hoax; we must keep in mind that in the case of the assembler, decisions are being made as to whether to *assemble* some code and the decisions are being made by the assembler at *assembly time*. In the case of the high-level language, the decisions are made at *execution time* about whether to *execute* some instructions,

```
                              .
                              .
              03AE    93      .IF  DF, DATA
              03AE    94              CLRL    R0
              03AE    95              CLRL    R1
              03AE    96              CLRL    R2
              03AE    97              CLRL    R3
              03AE    98          .IF_FALSE
       51 D4  03AE    99              CLRL    R1
       53 D4  03B0   100              CLRL    R3
       55 D4  03B2   101              CLRL    R5
              03B4   102      .ENDC
                              .
                              .              Figure 18.11.5
```

the decisions being made by the program code itself. Hence we are really comparing two different concepts here, no matter how similar they may appear, and thus the comparison is automatically suspect.)

The VAX assembler implements a directive, .IF_FALSE, which is known as a **subconditional directive**, and its effect is much the same as ELSE in a high-level language. Before giving a formal description, we show in Figure 18.11.5 an assembly language construction analogous to "IF...THEN...ELSE...ENDIF" which has the desired effect and tidies up the somewhat more clumsy construction of Figure 18.11.4. Notice that .IF_FALSE takes no condition or argument(s); rather, it behaves precisely like ELSE, in that it causes the assembly of instructions when the condition stated in the .IF clause is *false*.

There are two other subconditional directives, .IF_TRUE and .IF_TRUE_FALSE. These three directives are described formally below. (An abbreviated form of each directive is shown in parentheses, but we choose not to use them in our programming examples.)

A **subconditional directive** may appear only within a conditional block (.IF....ENDC) and must be one of the following.

.IF_FALSE (.IFF) The assembler is to assemble the source instructions beginning at the .IF_FALSE subconditional directive and continuing up to the next subconditional directive or to the end of the conditional block, *provided* that the conditional in the .IF directive tests as *false*.

```
                              .
                              .
              03AE    93      .IF  DF, DATA
              03AE    94              CLRL    R0
              03AE    95              CLRL    R2
              03AE    96          .IF_FALSE
       55 D4  03AE    97              CLRL    R5
              03B0    98          .IF_TRUE_FALSE
       51 D4  03B0    99              CLRL    R1
       53 D4  03B2   100              CLRL    R3
              03B4   101      .ENDC
                              .
                              .              Figure 18.11.6
```

```
    .
    .
.IF  conditional₁
    ·        ⎫ Assembled provided
    ·        ⎭ conditional₁ true
  .IF_FALSE
    ·
    ·                                              ⎫
  .IF  conditional₂                                ⎪
    ·        ⎫ Assembled provided                  ⎪
    ·        ⎭ conditional₂ true                   ⎪
    .IF_FALSE                                      ⎪
    ·        ⎫ Assembled provided                  ⎬  Assembled only if
    ·        ⎭ conditional₂ false                  ⎪  conditional₁ false
    .IF_TRUE                                       ⎪
    ·        ⎫ Assembled provided                  ⎪
    ·        ⎭ conditional₂ true                   ⎪
   .ENDC                                           ⎪
    ·                                              ⎪
    ·                                              ⎪
  .IF_TRUE                                         ⎭
    ·        ⎫ Assembled provided
    ·        ⎭ conditional₁ true
  .IF_TRUE_FALSE
    ·        ⎫ Assembled regardless of
    ·        ⎭ value of conditional₁
.ENDC
    ·
    ·
```

Figure 18.11.7

.IF_TRUE (.IFT) The assembler is to assemble the source instructions beginning at the .IF_TRUE subconditional directive and continuing up to the next subconditional directive or to the end of the conditional block, *provided* that the conditional in the .IF directive tests as *true*.

.IF_TRUE_FALSE (.IFTF) The assembler is to assemble the source instructions beginning at the .IF_TRUE_FALSE subconditional directive and continuing up to the next subconditional directive or to the end of the conditional block, *regardless* of whether the conditional in the .IF directive tests as *true* or *false*.

Thus .IF_FALSE and .IF_TRUE act as "toggles" which turn the assembly off and on, while .IF_TRUE_FALSE acts as an unconditional directive to assemble instructions. We use these new subconditionals further to simplify the logic of the segment of Figure 18.11.5, since we note that the CLRL of R1 and R3 is to be assembled under any circumstances (see Figure 18.11.6). As before, we infer that the symbol DATA has not yet been defined.

Because of the vast number of ways in which conditionals and subconditionals can be combined, it is not practicable to describe exactly how these directives behave in all possible circumstances. In Figure 18.11.7 we show one example in a diagrammatic fashion, and the reader should take special note of the fact that the inner conditional block (controlled by *conditional₂*) will not even be considered by the assembler unless the condition in the outer block (*conditional₁*) tests *false*, since the inner block is defined within a .IF_FALSE subconditional block.

18.12 THE DIRECTIVE .*MEXIT*

Sections 18.10 and 18.11 have had little to do with macroinstructions, the principal topic of this chapter, although we note that the conditionals B, NB, IDN, and DIF have not been used except in macrodefinitions and it is difficult to conceive of uses for them that are not associated with macroinstruction arguments. In general we can say that conditional assemblies are frequently employed in the definitions of macroinstructions, but their use is not restricted to that application. These directives may appear anywhere in a program, as we have seen. We return to macroinstructions in this brief section to add a "convenience" feature, the directive **.MEXIT.**

It sometimes happens that in defining a macroinstruction, we need to deal with special cases of argument values, and in some instances the most obvious thing to do in these cases is simply to terminate expansion of the macroinstruction. We can always design the logic of conditionals and subconditionals to do this for us (if it is possible at all), but these sometimes lead to confusing constructions. In many instances we would simply like to direct the assembler to stop expanding the

```
        0000    1       .MACRO  CLEAR   B
        0000    2       .IRP    X,<0,1,2,3,4,5,6,7,8,9,10,11>
        0000    3       .IIF    LT, B-X, .MEXIT
        0000    4       CLRL    R'X
        0000    5       .ENDR
        0000    6       .ENDM
                        .
                        .
        0A04    88      CLEAR   2
        0A04            .IRP    X,<0,1,2,3,4,5,6,7,8,9,10,11>
        0A04            .IIF    LT, 2-X, .MEXIT
        0A04            CLRL    R'X
        0A04            .ENDR
        0A04            .IIF    LT, 2-0, .MEXIT
   50 D4 0A04          CLRL    R0
        0A06
        0A06            .IIF    LT, 2-1, .MEXIT
   51 D4 0A06          CLRL    R1
        0A08
        0A08            .IIF    LT, 2-2, .MEXIT
   52 D4 0A08          CLRL    R2
        0A0A
        0A0A            .IIF    LT, 2-3, .MEXIT
        0A0A
                        .
                        .
```

Figure 18.12.1

```
                    0000    1        .MACRO   FACT     N
                    0000    2        .IF      LE, N-1
                    0000    3        .MEXIT
                    0000    4        .ENDC
                    0000    5        MULL     #'N,R1
                    0000    6        FACT     N-1
                    0000    7        .ENDM
                                     .
                                     .
   51   01   D0     010A    80       MOVL     #1,R1
                    010D    81       FACT     3
        00000002    010D             .IF      LE, 3-1
                    010D             .MEXIT
                    010D             .ENDC
   51   03   C4     010D             MULL     #3,R1
                    0110             FACT     3-1
        00000001    0110             .IF      LE, 3-1-1
                    0110             .MEXIT
                    0110             .ENDC
   51   02   C4     0110             MULL     #3-1,R1
                    0113             FACT     3-1-1
        00000000    0113             .IF      LE, 3-1-1-1
                    0113             .MEXIT
                    0113
                                     .
                                     .
```

Figure 18.12.2

macroinstruction.   And this is precisely what the .MEXIT directive does—it is the *M*acroexpansion *EXIT* directive.   We offer two examples of the use of .MEXIT, the first of which is quite straightforward.   Figure 18.12.1 shows the definition and subsequent call of the macroinstruction CLEAR.   Its function is to clear (CLRL) registers R0 to Rn inclusive, where n is passed as the argument to the macroinstruction.   The .IIF directive determines when, in the repeat block, all the requested CLRL instructions have been assembled, at which time it invokes the .MEXIT directive to terminate the expansion.

The second example, shown in Figure 18.12.2, is somewhat more bizarre, since in the course of its definition, the macroinstruction *invokes itself*, but observe that it does so *conditionally*.   This is an example of a recursive macroinstruction call, which terminates with .MEXIT at the appropriate time, and thus avoids putting the *assembler* into an infinite loop, a phenomenon that would otherwise happen when a macroinstruction invokes itself.   We do not claim any great merit for this macroinstruction except as an example of a use of .MEXIT and as proof that macroinstructions can successfully call themselves, although there is serious question that we would actually want to do this in practice.   The reader will find the macrodefinition reminiscent of some of the code in Chapter 9, where recursive subroutines and procedures were discussed.   We can even devise macroinstructions that call one another (similar to *coroutines*), and some examples are given in the exercises.   In the meantime, the reader should have no difficulty showing that FACT simply generates the code necessary to produce N!, factorial N.

18.13 CLOSING COMMENTS

The reader has probably noted that the program listings of this chapter, especially those of the last several sections, are excessively long. The listings of macro-expansions typically take many lines, especially if any sort of repeat construction is involved. We have seen that when conditional assemblies are listed, all the lines of source instructions are listed, whether any machine code is generated for them or not. In the case of macroinstructions, their *expansions* (but not *definitions*) can be suppressed with the directive .NOSHOW ME, and as we have already noted, this is, in fact, the default—macroexpansions have been shown only because we have included the required directive .SHOW ME. In a similar fashion, we may suppress the listing of unsatisfied conditionals—conditional statements for which no code is generated—by using the directive **.NOSHOW CND.** Compare the listings in Figure 18.13.1.

Recently developed high-level languages have been designed in such a way that *readability* is almost built in, in the sense that the requirements of the language itself force on the programmer certain practices which enhance the appearance of his or her programs. Although we do not claim that assembly language programs can reach these levels of readability, we do insist that the careful use of macroinstructions can result in dramatic improvements in this direction. As a concrete example, consider the two segments of Figure 18.13.2, in which the familiar macroinstructions $I.2D, ABS, and $0.2D are invoked in part (a). Figure 18.13.2(b) is the equivalent collection of instructions, but here the actual code required for

```
                          .
                          .
00000000  0C44   233     .IF      EQ, TEST
   50  D4  0C44   234     CLRL     R0
          0C46   235     .IF_FALSE
          0C46   236     CLRL     R1
          0C46   237     .IF_TRUE
   53  D4  0C46   238     CLRL     R3
          0C48   239     .IF_TRUE_FALSE
   54  D4  0C48   240     CLRL     R4
          0C4A   241     .ENDC
                          .
                          .
```

(a)

```
                          .
                          .
          0C44   232     .NOSHOW CND
   50  D4  0C44   234     CLRL     R0
   53  D4  0C46   238     CLRL     R3
   54  D4  0C48   240     CLRL     R4
                          .
                          .
```

(b)   **Figure 18.13.1**

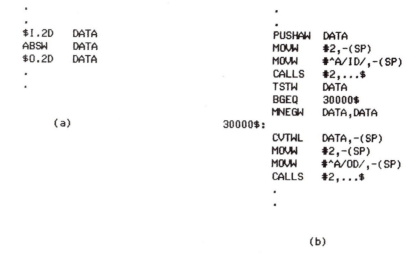

```
     .                                    .
     .                                    .
     .                                    .
$I.2D    DATA                        PUSHAW  DATA
ABSW     DATA                        MOVW    #2,-(SP)
$0.2D    DATA                        MOVW    #^A/ID/,-(SP)
     .                               CALLS   #2,...$
     .                               TSTW    DATA
                                     BGEQ    30000$
                                     MNEGW   DATA,DATA
        (a)                 30000$:

                                     CVTWL   DATA,-(SP)
                                     MOVW    #2,-(SP)
                                     MOVW    #^A/OD/,-(SP)
                                     CALLS   #2,...$
                                          .
                                          .
                                          .
```

(b)

Figure 18.13.2

these tasks is inserted into the instruction stream. We maintain that segment (a) is far more understandable than segment (b), and the reasons for this are twofold— the *names* applied to these macroinstructions are quite suggestive, and many of the *details* of the instructions are successfully *hidden*, a fact that enhances the apparent simplicity of these constructions.

In this chapter we have examined numerous features of the VAX macro-assembler. We have selected those features on the basis of maximum utility to the average programmer, but the assembler has other features, and the interested reader is directed to the appropriate source for investigating them, principally the *VAX-11 MACRO Language Reference Manual*. Although our purpose in this chapter has been to describe in detail a number of the ways in which macroinstruc-tions and conditional assemblies can be put to use, the large number of ways in which these can be written and combined clearly precludes our investigating any-thing more than a small sampling. The conscientious programmer will develop an understanding of these concepts by *doing*—by writing many program segments, with their attendant trial and error.

Finally, we began this chapter with a brief discussion of subroutines and their uses. We have seen that both subroutines and macroinstructions can be invoked to perform tasks for the user a number of times in a program module, yet by now we understand that these are really quite different concepts. The macroinstruction has the potential for a tremendous amount of flexibility in the manner in which it is called and thus in the tailor-made code that it can generate. On the negative side, calls to a macroinstruction can use up sizable amounts of main memory, one of the computing system's most limited resources, since each such call results in the instructions being coded in line. A subroutine provides far less flexibility in the way it may be called (which is normally fixed once the routine is written), but it saves space since its code appears once only. The experienced programmer will balance the flexibility of macroinstructions with the conservation of memory of subroutines and procedures and make appropriate decisions based on the total task to be accomplished.

18.14 EXERCISES

18.1.1. We observed that the subroutine of Figure 18.1.3 will not return properly, since the return address had been "buried" in the stack. Show that the subroutine of Figure 18.14.1, with the modified "return from subroutine" as shown, will stack the three arguments and then properly return.

```
              .
              .
              .
SAV3ARGS:  MOVL    (SP)+,RETURN+2
           PUSHL   ARG1
           PUSHL   ARG2
           PUSHL   ARG3
RETURN:    JMP     @#0
              .
              .
```

Figure 18.14.1

18.3.1. In Figure 18.3.6 we saw an example of a macroinstruction (SAV5ARGS) whose definition involves the invoking of another macroinstruction (SAV3ARGS). Conjecture about what would happen if a macroinstruction invoked *itself*. Consider as an example the macrodefinition

```
.MACRO   SAMPLE
CLRL     R4
SAMPLE
.ENDM
```

18.3.2. As an extension of Exercise 18.3.1, conjecture what would happen when either of the macroinstructions AMAC or BMAC shown below is invoked.

```
.MACRO   AMAC          .MACRO   BMAC
INCL     R4            INCL     R3
BMAC                   AMAC
.ENDM                  .ENDM
```

18.3.3. In Figure 18.3.7 the definition of SAV5ARGS invokes the macroinstruction SAV3ARGS, which has not yet been defined. Explain why the assembler has generated no error when it encountered the reference to the (as yet undefined) macroinstruction SAV3ARGS at line 8, and why this situation is different from that of Figure 18.3.4.

18.4.1. Figure 18.3.5 shows a macroinstruction SAV3ARGS which is defined, invoked, and then *redefined*. When SAV3ARGS is invoked again, the definition used is the latest version the assembler has seen at the time of the call. Show that, in fact, one of the assembler's *permanent symbols* can even be redefined by defining

```
.MACRO   INCL   X
ADDL     #2,X
.ENDM
```

Verify that this redefines the VAX INCL operation, by writing and assembling a program segment that first executes the instruction INCL R0, then defines INCL as above, and then again executes INCL R0. Explain why the ADDL instruction shown cannot be replaced by

```
INCL   X
INCL   X
```

18.4.2. Suppose that as in Exercise 18.4.1, we redefine the symbol HALT as follows:

```
.MACRO   HALT
$EXIT
.ENDM
```

Could we now *redefine* HALT so that it will again generate the code to "halt the processor?"

18.4.3. It would appear that once one of the assembler mnemonics is redefined as was done in Exercises 18.4.1 and 18.4.2, there is no hope of ever defining it "back to" its original "definition" in the current programming module. (Why not?) For example, we could redefine INCL *again* as, say,

```
.MACRO   INCL   X
ADDL2    #1,X
.ENDM
```

and this new definition would have the same *effect* as the VAX instruction INCL, but it would not *be* INCL. What we need to restore INCL to its original state is some way of telling the assembler to *forget* the fact that INCL was ever redefined in the first place. In fact, there is an assembler directive which does just that— it *removes* the current definition of a macroinstruction from the user's table of macroinstruction definitions. Note that we said it *removes* it, not just replaces it with something else. Verify this as follows. Continue with Exercise 18.4.1 by invoking the directive

.MDELETE   INCL

after the second instance of INCL R0, and then invoke INCL R0 one final time, paying particular attention to the machine code generated each of the three times the assembler encounters this expression. (.MDELETE stands for *Macrodefinition DELETE*, and its function is exactly as described—it *removes* a macrodefinition from the table of macroinstruction definitions. Further details may be found in the *VAX-11 MACRO Language Reference Manual*).

18.4.4. Consider the macroinstruction defined by

```
     .MACRO   DUMMY   A,B,C
C':  MNEGL    B
     DECL     A
     BRB      C
     .ENDM
```

State what the macroexpansion would be for each of the following calls.

(a) DUMMY   R1,R2,LOOP
(b) DUMMY   R1,⟨R2,R3⟩,LOOP
(c) DUMMY   R1,R2
(d) DUMMY   LOOP,⟨@(R1)+,−(R2)⟩,LOOP

18.4.5. Write a macroinstruction, named CALLSUB, which has two arguments, ARG and SUB. CALLSUB first pushes ARG onto the stack as a longword and then jumps to SUB, using a JSB instruction.

18.4.6 (a) Show, perhaps by a sample program, that the argument ˆX74A cannot be passed to a macroinstruction as it stands, but that it can be transmitted if it is enclosed in angle brackets—<ˆX74A>.

(b) How could the argument

$$Z > ˆX74A$$

be transmitted to a macroinstruction?

(c) Is ˆ;...; a legitimate pair of grouping symbols?

18.4.7 We found early in Section 18.4 that the assembler does not recognize "ARGX", for example, as an instance of the symbol X (see Figure 18.4.1). Verify, however, that the assembler *does* recognize each of the following expressions as an instance of the symbol X, and conjecture as to *why* it does so here, but not in the case of "ARGX".

(a) #X   (b) 'X   (c) X: (d) X,   (e) ,X   (f) X;

18.5.1. Determine what will happen if the argument A2 is elided when the macroinstruction ARGLIST of Figure 18.5.3 is invoked.

18.5.2. Show two different ways of invoking the macroinstruction ARGLIST of Figure 18.5.3 so that all arguments get their default values. except A1 and A2, which receive the values 1 and 2, respectively.

18.6.1 How will the macroinstruction

```
.MACRO   DUMMY  X,Y
.LONG    'X"Y'
.ENDM
```

be expanded for each of the following calls?

(a) DUMMY   ADD,R   (b) DUMMY   'ADD,R'
(c) DUMMY   ADD',R   (d) DUMMY   ADD','R

18.6.2. What will be the macroexpansion **TEST A,B** if TEST is defined by

```
.MACRO   TEST  X,Y
.LONG    'X'"Y'
.ENDM
```

What would be the result if the second argument (Y) were elided?

18.6.3. Consider the macroinstruction defined by

```
.MACRO   STRING  X,Y
.ASCII   /'X'"Y'cat/
.ENDM
```

Show how the macroinstruction will be expanded for each of the following calls.
(a) STRING John,s   (b) STRING John's   (c) STRING Chris

18.6.4 Consider the macroinstruction

```
.MACRO   SAVREG  P,Q,R
MOVL     R'P,-(SP)
MOVL     R'Q,-(SP)
MOVL     R'R,-(SP)
.ENDM
```

How will **SAVREG 1,2,3** be expanded?

18.6.5 How will **ZERO 2** be expanded, where ZERO is defined by

```
.MACRO   ZERO   V
CLRL     RV'
.ENDM
```

18.6.6. The macroinstructions SAV3ARGS of Figure 18.6.1 pushes three longword arguments onto the stack. Write a macroinstruction RESTOR3ARGS that pops three arguments from the stack. How could the macroinstruction be written so that the call **RESTOR3ARGS ARG1,ARG2,ARG3** will pop the stack into ARG3, ARG2, and ARG1, in that order? (This would then be the true companion to SAV3ARGS, since the arguments would be pushed and popped in the proper order.)

18.8.1. Consider the macroinstruction defined by

```
.MACRO   DUMMY  A,?B
MOVL     A,(B)
.ENDM
```

State how each of the following calls will be expanded.
(a) DUMMY R1,R9   (b) DUMMY (SP)+,SP   (c) DUMMY (SP)+

18.8.2. Expand the macroinstruction calls and write the symbol table for the program of Figure 18.14.2. Does the program contain any local labels?

```
        .MACRO   BIGGER  A,B,C,?D
        MOVL     R'A,R'C
        CMPL     R'A,R'B
        BGEQ     L'D
        MOVL     R'B,R'C
L'D:
        .ENDM

START:  .WORD    ^M<>

        BIGGER   1,2,3
        BIGGER   4,5,6

        .END     START            Figure 18.14.2
```

18.8.3. Use the macroinstruction ABS of Figure 18.8.3 to define three macroinstructions ABSB, ABSW, and ABSL, which replace a byte, word, or longword argument, respectively, with its absolute value.

18.8.4 Despite the fact that the VAX has a very large and comprehensive instruction set, there are still a few instructions which are not available and which, from time to time, are needed. One can usually program around these "missing" operations, although such programming is frequently awkward. Two of these missing operations are ROTB and ROTW—*ROT*ate *B*yte and *ROT*ate Word. We wish to construct macroinstructions under these names which will have the obvious effects—rotate a byte or word a specified number of bits, right or left, and put the result in a specified byte or word. As a rather modest beginning in this direction, consider the macroinstruction ROLB of Figure 18.14.3. Verify that ROLB will rotate the byte contents of X one bit to the left (counterclockwise) and put the result in Y. Explain why the stack is used as a location for the shifted longword instead of, say, a register. Show also that *any* source argument will do, and that *almost any* destination argument Y will also do; however, explain why Y may not be a stack reference such as −(SP). Using Figure 18.14.3 as a model, write a macroinstruction RORB that rotates a byte one bit to the right.

```
0000    1        .MACRO  ROLB    X,Y,?L
0000    2        MOVZBL  X,-(SP)
0000    3        ASHL    #1,(SP),(SP)
0000    4        BITL    #^X100,(SP)
0000    5        BEQL    L
0000    6        BISL    #1,(SP)
0000    7 L:     MOVB    (SP)+,Y
0000    8        ADDL    #3,SP
0000    9        .ENDM
```
                                                    Figure 18.14.3

18.8.5. Show that the problem with the destination argument in the macroinstruction of Exercise 18.8.4 can be eliminated as shown in Figure 18.14.4. (The principal change here is at lines 7 and 8, where the management of the stack is handled somewhat differently. We have also eliminated the need for a local label by employing the "dot" construction, standing for the *location counter* (see Section B.7 of Appendix B). Using the changes suggested by Figure 18.14.4, rewrite the macroinstruction RORB of Exercise 18.8.4.

```
0000    1        .MACRO  ROLB    X,Y
0000    2        MOVZBL  X,-(SP)
0000    3        ASHL    #1,(SP),(SP)
0000    4        BITL    #^X100,(SP)
0000    5        BEQL    .+4
0000    6        BISL    #1,(SP)
0000    7        TSTL    (SP)+
0000    8        MOVB    -4(SP),Y
0000    9        .ENDM
```
                                                    Figure 18.14.4

18.8.6. The macroinstructions ROLB and RORB of Exercise 18.8.5 can be modified to obtain *word* rotate macroinstructions RORW and ROLW. However, the differences between the byte and word forms are so minor that we suggest the writing of a single macroinstruction, say, LROTATE, which takes *three* arguments—the source A and destination B locations, together with the SIZE—a "B" or "W" to signal a "byte" or "word" left rotate. The actual rotation macroinstructions can then simply invoke LROTATE with appropriate arguments (see Figure 18.14.5).

```
.MACRO   ROLB     X,Y                    .MACRO   RORB     X,Y
LROTATE X,Y,B                            RROTATE X,Y,B
.ENDM                                    .ENDM


.MACRO   ROLW     X,Y                    .MACRO   RORW     X,Y
LROTATE X,Y,W                            RROTATE X,Y,W
.ENDM                                    .ENDM

.MACRO   LROTATE A,B,SIZE                .MACRO   RROTATE A,B,SIZE
   .                                        .
   .                                        .
   .                                        .
.ENDM                                    .ENDM
```

Figure 18.14.5

Write the definitions of the macroinstructions LROTATE and its right-rotate companion, RROTATE.

18.9.1. Would an indefinite repeat block of the form

$$.IRP \quad X,\langle W,X,Y.Z\rangle$$

cause a conflict between the two different uses of the symbol X?

18.9.2. Explain why the repeat block at lines 24 to 26 in Figure 18.9.5 could not be used to save ARG7, ARG12, and ARG9.

18.9.3. Write a repeat block using .REPEAT, .IRP, or .IRPC which will generate 12 consecutive words, the first containing the number 1, the second the number 2, and so on, the last containing the number 12. Can this be done using all three of these directives?

18.9.4 In partial answer to Exercise 18.9.3, show that

```
VAL = 1
.REPEAT      12
.WORD        VAL
VAL = VAL   + 1
.ENDR
```

will generate the desired words. In an analogous fashion construct a repeat block that generates 26 words, each of which contains in its high-order byte the ASCII code for a blank and in its low-order byte the ASCII code for the consecutive lowercase alphabetic characters.

18.9.5. Show what text will be created when the macroinstruction AMAC, defined by

```
.MACRO   AMAC   X
BMAC     X
.ENDM
.MACRO   BMAC   Y
CMAC     Y
.ENDM
.MACRO   CMAC   Z
.ASCII   /Z/
.ENDM
```

is invoked as follows:

    (a) AMAC Cats   (b) AMAC ⟨Cats⟩

    (c) AMAC Cats & Dogs   (d) AMAC ⟨Cats & Dogs⟩

    (e) AMAC ⟨⟨Cats & Dogs⟩⟩   (f) AMAC ⟨⟨⟨Cats & Dogs⟩⟩⟩

18.9.6. Modify the macroinstructions LROTATE and RROTATE of Exercise 18.8.6 in such a way that ROLB, ROLW, RORB, and RORW can pass a *rotate count* as an argument, just as the VAX operation ROTL does—

$$\text{ROLx} \quad count.br,src.rx,dest.wx \qquad (x = \text{B or W})$$

for example. There are a number of problems here. Since the left or right shift ASHL needs to be repeated a number of times, the obvious construction might be a .REPEAT block. However, the assembler may be unable to calculate the repeat count. (Why?) Thus the "counting" will have to take place at execution time, in a loop of some sort. But the loop may *not* be controlled by the contents of a register. (Why not?) Instead, put the rotate count on top of the stack.

18.9.7. Complete the task begun in Exercise 18.8.4 by writing the macroinstructions ROTB and ROTW, each with three arguments consisting of the rotate count, source, and destination, and which rotate left for positive counts and right for negative counts. A single macroinstruction ROTATE should be at the heart of the process, with the macroinstructions ROTB and ROTW invoking it with appropriate arguments.

18.9.8. How will the repeat block

$$\begin{array}{ll} .\text{IRPC} & X,\langle 1,2,3\rangle \\ \text{PUSHL} & R'X \\ .\text{ENDR} & \end{array}$$

be expanded?

18.10.1. In the macroinstruction of Figure 18.10.2, explain why line 4, for example, could or could not be rewritten as

$$.\text{IIF} \quad \text{EQ, BYTES-1, PUSHAB ARG}$$

18.10.2. Let MARK be a symbol defined by the direct assignment statement MARK = 7. Explain which, if any, of the instructions below will be assembled, and why.

  (a) .IIF IDN, MARK,7, ⟨instruction⟩

  (b) .IIF EQ,   MARK-7, ⟨instruction⟩

  (c) .IIF DIF, MARK,7, ⟨instruction⟩

  (d) .IIF NE,   MARK-7, ⟨instruction⟩

18.10.3. Each of the conditionals EQ, GT, LT, DF, B, and IDN of Figure 18.10.3 has a complementary conditional: NE, LE, GE, NDF, NB, and DIF. Show that none of the complementary conditionals is actually *required*—that they are included for programmer convenience—by verifying that

$$.\text{IIF} \quad compl\text{-}cond, \quad arg(s), \quad \langle instructions\rangle$$

can always be replaced by

$$.IIF \quad cond, \quad arg(s), \quad BRB \quad NEXT$$
$$\langle instruction \rangle$$
NEXT:

where *compl-cond* is the complement of the conditional *cond*.

18.10.4. Explain why the .IRP directive in Figure 18.10.4 could not be replaced by a .IRPC directive.

18.10.5. In Exercise 18.9.6 rotate byte and word macroinstructions are to be written, the direction of rotation depending on the *sign* of one of the arguments. Explain why a .IIF construction using a LT or GT conditional would *not* be appropriate for this purpose.

18.11.1. Use the result of Exercise 18.10.3 to improve the appearance of the program segment of Figure 18.11.1.

18.11.2. Tell what instructions are assembled by the following conditional block, for each of the four possible combinations of the symbols SYM1 and SYM2 being definded or undefinded.

```
.IF   DF  SYM1
BGEQ  NEXT
.IF_FALSE
.IF   NDF  SYM2
BLEQ  NEXT
.IF_FALSE
INCL  R0
.ENDC
.IF_TRUE_FALSE
DECL  R0
.ENDC
```

18.11.3. Using only conditionals (and not *sub*conditionals), write one (or more) conditional block(s) which assembles instructions based on the values of two symbols VAL1 and VAL2, as follows:

CLRL	R3	is assembled if VAL1 = 6;
CLRL	R4	is assembled if VAL1 = 6 and VAL2 $\neq$ 6;
INCL	R0	is assembled if VAL1 $\neq$ 6 and VAL2 $\neq$ 6;
PUSHL	R2	is assembled if VAL1 = 6 and VAL2 = 6;
MOVW	#5,R4	is assembled if VAL1 $\neq$ 6 and VAL2 = 6.

18.11.4. Repeat Exercise 18.11.3 using subconditionals.

18.12.1. Consider the macroinstruction SAVREG defined by

```
.MACRO  SAVREG  P,Q,S,T,U,V
.IRP    X,⟨P,Q,S,T, U,V⟩
.IIF    B, X, .MEXIT
PUSHL   R'X
.ENDR
.ENDM
```

which will save the contents of *up to* 6 registers on the stack. Why cannot the formal argument list A,B,C,D,E,F be used here? Why cannot the formal argument R be used?

18.12.2. Show what will be assembled as a result of the call to the macroinstruction AMAC at line 86 of Figure 18.14.6.

```
0000     1     .MACRO   AMAC     X,Y,Z
0000     2     BMAC     Y,Z
0000     3     .ENDM
0000     4     .MACRO   BMAC     S,T
0000     5     .IF      B, S
0000     6     .MEXIT
0000     7     .IF_FALSE
0000     8     MOVL     R'S,-(SP)
0000     9     .IF      NB, T
0000    10     MOVL     R'T,-(SP)
0000    11     .ENDC
0000    12     AMAC     S,T
0000    13     .ENDC
0000    14     .ENDM
                        .
                        .
022A    86     AMAC     1,2,3
                        .
                        .
```

Figure 18.14.6

18.12.3. Write a macroinstruction that will print a two-dimensional array of any dimensions (rows and columns), containing bytes, words, or longwords, in any format—binary, hexadecimal, or decimal. Thus a typical call might be

$$\text{PRINT\_ARRAY} \quad \text{MATRIX},\#4,\#9,B,D}$$

and would be taken as a request to print the array named *MATRIX*, which is *4* by *9* and consists of *B*ytes, in *D*ecimal format.

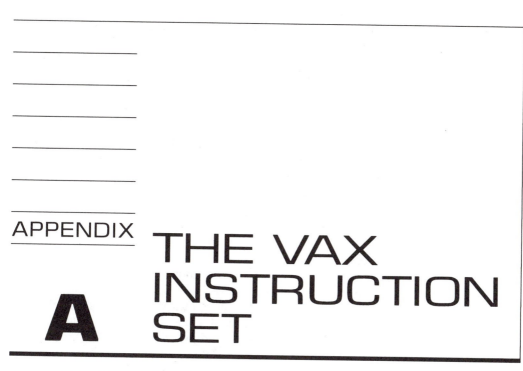

THE VAX INSTRUCTION SET

A.1 OPERAND DESCRIPTORS

An **operand descriptor** is a string of characters consisting of three components:

$$\langle name \rangle.\langle access\ type \rangle\langle datatype\ context \rangle$$

The three components and their possible values are as follows.

(a) name

The *name* component of a descriptor is any word or abbreviation which is descriptive of the operand involved. Names such as *src* ("source"), *dest* ("destination"), *pos* ("position"), and so on, are used to give some indication as to the significance of the operand.

(b) access type

The *access type* component of a descriptor can take on a number of possible values.

 r   **read-only.** The operand is a structure (byte, word, and so on, depending on the operation's context) whose location is specified by any general register or program counter addressing mode. The operand is read by the processor, but is not written by it.

w **written-only.** The operand is a structure (byte, word, and so on, depending on the operation's context) whose location is specified by any addressing mode *except* 0, 1, 2, or 3 (short literal) or program counter mode 8 (immediate). The operand is written by the processor, but is not read by it.

m **modified.** The operand is a structure (byte, word, and so on, depending on the operation's context) whose location is specified by any addressing mode *except* 0, 1, 2, or 3 (short literal) or program counter mode 8 (immediate). The operand is read by the processor, and it *may* be modified and its new value written back to its location.

b **branch displacement.** There is no structure reference. Rather, the operand is a program counter displacement, whose size is determined by the operation's context, and whose value is sign extended to a longword upon execution.

a **address access.** The operand is the *address* of a structure (byte, word, and so on, depending on the operation's context). The operand may be specified by any addressing mode *except* 0, 1, 2, 3 (short literal); general register mode 5 (register); and program counter mode 8 (immediate). Regardless of the operation's context, the operand is always a longword (since it is an address). The context of the address calculation is determined by the operation's context.

v **bit field.** The operand is one of the following.

1. The *address* of a structure (byte, word, and so on, depending on the operation's context). The operand may be specified by any addressing mode *except* 0, 1, 2, 3 (short literal); general register mode 5 (register); and program counter mode 8 (immediate). Regardless of the operation's context, the operand is always a longword (since it is an address). The context of the address calculation is determined by the operation's context.

2. The contents of a register, the operand being specified by a general register mode 5 construction—R*n*. The operand is the contents of R*n*, or of R[$n+1$]'R[n].

(c) datatype context

The *datatype context* component of the descriptor specifies the operation's context and is used to determine side effects, to calculate addresses, and to determine the factor by which register contents are multiplied in index mode instruction. The possible datatype descriptors are the following.

b byte
w word

l	longword
q	quadword
o	octaword
x	datatype of the first (or only) operand specified by the operation
y	datatype of the second operand specified by the operation

A.2 NOTATION

$\leftarrow$	is given the value
$\{\ldots\}$	$=1$, if $\ldots$ is TRUE; $=0$, if $\ldots$ is FALSE
$-(SP) \leftarrow$	is pushed onto the stack
$\leftarrow (SP)+$	is popped off the stack
$+$	addition
$-$	subtraction, or unary minus
$*$	multiplication
$/$	division
$**$	exponentiation
$c(\ldots)$	contents of $\ldots$
SEXT$(\ldots)$	the value of $\ldots$, sign extended to a longer structure
ZEXT$(\ldots)$	the value of $\ldots$, zero extended to a longer structure
$m:n$	the bit field of a structure, consisting of bits m, $m-1$, $m-2$, $\ldots$, $n+1$, n
$x\langle n \rangle$	bit n of the structure x
$x\langle m:n \rangle$	bits m:n of the structure x
$a[b]$	the address a indexed by the value b
MAX(x,y)	the maximum of the numbers x and y
MIN(x,y)	the minimum of the numbers x and y
EQL	equal to, signed or unsigned
GEQ	greater than or equal to, signed
GEQU	greater than or equal to, unsigned
GTR	greater than, signed
GTRU	greater than, unsigned
LEQ	less than or equal to, signed
LEQU	less than or equal to, unsigned
LSS	less than, signed
LSSU	less than, unsigned
NEQL	not equal to, signed or unsigned

A.3 THE *VAX* INSTRUCTION SET IN MNEMONIC ORDER*

The following pages list the VAX operations, operation codes, assembler formats, descriptions, exceptions, the effects on the condition codes and other side effects.

The types of *exceptions* (errors) that may be detected upon execution of the operations are for the most part quite straightforward and are described in the text proper—integer overflow, floating point overflow and underflow, and so on. The one exception that is rather catch-all in nature and thus is more elusive of specific description is the **reserved operand** exception, and it normally refers to an *improper use* of an operand or to an *improperly formed* operand. A simple example is

$$\text{BICPSW} \quad \#\text{`X2A4}$$

which will generate a reserved operand exception since for this instruction the mask word—`X2A4—cannot have a nonzero high-order byte. Although the descriptions and comments that follow do not explicitly state the potential cause of a reserved operand exception, the reader should have little difficulty determining it in specific cases.

Finally, a few operations, primarily those which are quite special-purpose or which require exceptional privileges and are thus useful principally in an operating system environment, are not listed here. These may be found in the Digital Equipment Corporation *VAX Architecture Handbook*.

ACB   *Add Compare and Branch*

Format	ACBx *limit.rx,add.rx,index.mx,disp.bw*
Operation	*index* ← *index* + *add*; if ((*add* GEQ 0) AND (*index* LEQ *limit*)) OR ((*add* LSS 0) AND (*index* GEQ *limit*)) then PC ← c(PC) + SEXT(*disp*)
Condition codes	N ← {*index* LSS 0} Z ← {*index* EQL 0} V ← {integer or floating-point overflow} C ← C

Operation codes		
9D	ACBB	Add Compare and Branch Byte
3D	ACBW	Add Compare and Branch Word
F1	ACBL	Add Compare and Branch Longword
4F	ACBF	Add Compare and Branch F_floating
6F	ACBD	Add Compare and Branch D_floating
4FFD	ACBG	Add Compare and Branch G_floating
6FFD	ACBH	Add Compare and Branch H_floating

*The material of this section is adapted, with permission, from *VAX Architecture Handbook*, copyright Digital Equipment Corporation 1983. All rights reserved.

Description	The addend operation *add* is added to, and the sum replaces, the index operand *index*, and the result is compared to the limit operand *limit*. If *add* GEQ 0 and *index* LEQ *limit*, or if *add* LSS 0 and *index* GEQ *limit*, the displacement operand *disp* is sign extended and added to c(PC); otherwise, no branch takes place.
Exceptions	Integer overflow Floating-point overflow Floating-point underflow Reserved operand
Comment	ACB implements the high-level language FOR construction.

ADD   *ADD* operands

Format	ADDx2 *add.rx,sum.mx*	(2-operand)
	ADDx3 *add1.rx,add2.rx,sum.wx*	(3-operand)

Operation	$sum \leftarrow sum + add$	(2-operand)
	$sum \leftarrow add1 + add2$	(3-operand)

Condition codes	N ← {*sum* LSS 0} Z ← {*sum* EQL 0} V ← {integer or floating overflow} C ← {carry out of most-significant bit} (integer) C ← 0 (floating-point)

Operation codes	80	ADDB2	ADD Byte, 2-operand
	81	ADDB3	ADD Byte, 3-operand
	A0	ADDW2	ADD Word, 2-operand
	A1	ADDW3	ADD Word, 3-operand
	C0	ADDL2	ADD Longword, 2-operand
	C1	ADDL3	ADD Longword, 3-operand
	40	ADDF2	ADD F_floating, 2-operand
	41	ADDF3	ADD F_floating, 3-operand
	60	ADDD2	ADD D_floating, 2-operand
	61	ADDD3	ADD D_floating, 3-operand
	40FD	ADDG2	ADD G_floating, 2-operand
	41FD	ADDG3	ADD G_floating, 3-operand
	60FD	ADDH2	ADD H_floating, 2-operand
	61FD	ADDH3	ADD H_floating, 3-operand

Description	In its 2-operand form, the addend operand *add* is added to the sum operand *sum* and the result replaces *sum*. In its 3-operand form, the addend operand *add1* is added to the addend operand *add2*, and the result replaces the sum operand *sum*.
Exceptions	Integer overflow Floating-point overflow Floating-point underflow Reserved operand
Comment	Floating-point sums are rounded.

ADDP   *ADD* Packed decimal strings

Format

ADDP4 *addlen.rw,addaddr.ab,*   (4-operand)
          sumlen.rw,sumaddr.ab

ADDP6 *add1len.rw,add1addr.ab,*   (6-operand)
          add2len.rw,add2addr.ab,
          sumlen.rw,sumaddr.ab

Operation

sumstr ← sumstr + addstr   (4-operand)

where *sumstr* is the packed decimal string defined by the length and address operands *sumlen* and *sumaddr*, and *addstr* is the string defined by *addlen* and *addaddr*

sumstr ← add1str + add2str   (6-operand)

where *sumstr* is the packed decimal string defined by the length and address operands *sumlen* and *sumaddr*, and *addKstr* is the string defined by *addKlen* and *addKaddr* (*K* = 1,2)

Condition codes

N ← {*sum* LSS 0}
Z ← {*sum* EQL 0}
V ← {decimal overflow}
C ← 0

Operation codes

20 ADDP4   ADD Packed 4-operand
21 ADDP6   ADD Packed 6-operand

Description

For ADDP4, the string specified by the addend length *addlen* and address *addaddr* operands is added to the string specified by the sum length *sumlen* and address *sumaddr* operands, the result replacing the later string.

For ADDP6, the strings specified by the addend lengths, *add1len* and *add2len*, and addresses, *add1addr* and *add2addr*, are added and the result is stored in the string specified by the length *sumlen* and address *sumaddr* operands.

Exception

Decimal overflow
Reserved operand

Side effects

Upon execution of ADDP4:

R0 ← 0
R1 ← address of the byte containing the most-significant digit of the addend string
R2 ← 0
R3 ← address of the byte containing the most-significant digit of the sum string

Upon execution of ADDP6:

R0 ← 0
R1 ← address of the byte containing the most-significant digit of the addend1 string
R2 ← 0
R3 ← address of the byte containing the most-significant digit of the addend2 string
R4 ← 0
R5 ← address of the byte containing the most-significant digit of the sum string

Comment

The sum string, condition codes, and the contents of R0 to R3 (or R0 to R5 in the case of ADDP6) are unpredictable if the sum string overlaps any addend string, or if any string contains an invalid 4-bit decimal code.

ADWC   ADd With Carry

Format	ADWC *add.rl,sum.ml*
Operation	*sum ← sum + add* + c(C)
Condition codes	N ← {*sum* LSS 0} Z ← {*sum* EQL 0} V ← {integer overflow} C ← {carry out of most-significant bit}
Operation code	D8 ADWC ADd With Carry
Description	The addend operand *add* and the contents of the carry bit C (either 0 or 1) are added to the sum operand *sum*, the result replacing the sum operand. The two additions are performed simultaneously.
Exception	Integer overflow
Comment	ADWC implements multiple-precision additions and increments.

AOB   Add One and Branch

Format	AOBccc *limit.rl,index.ml,disp.bb*

Operation	*index ← index* + 1; (AOBLSS)
	if (*index* LSS *limit*) then
	PC ← c(PC) + SEXT(*disp*)
	index ← index + 1; (AOBLEQ)
	if (*index* LEQ *limit*) then
	PC ← c(PC) + SEXT(*disp*)

Condition codes	N ← {*index* LSS 0} Z ← {*index* EQL 0} V ← {integer overflow} C ← C
Operation codes	F2 AOBLSS Add One and Branch if LeSS than F3 AOBLEQ Add One and Branch if Less than or EQual
Description	One is added to the *index* operand, the sum replacing that operand. The result is compared to the *limit* operand. If the comparison is LSS (for AOBLSS) or LEQ (for AOBLEQ), the sign-extended displacement *disp* is added to c(PC) and a branch occurs; otherwise no branch is taken.
Exception	Integer overflow

ASH   Arithmetic SHift

Format	ASHx *count.rb,src.rx,dest.wx*
Operation	*dest ← src*, shifted *count* bits
Condition codes	N ← {*dest* LSS 0} Z ← {*dest* EQL 0}

$V \leftarrow$ {integer overflow}
$C \leftarrow 0$

Operation codes	78	ASHL	Arithmetic SHift Longword
	79	ASHQ	Arithmetic SHift Quadword

Description The source operand *src* is shifted *count* bits, positive counts representing left shifts and negative counts representing right shifts. On left shifts, 0s replace the vacated bits. On right shifts, the high-order bit is replicated in the vacated bits. An integer overflow occurs on a left shift if a bit is shifted into the high-order bit which differs from the high-order bit of the *src* operand.

Exception Integer overflow

Comments If the *count* operand is GTR 32 (for ASHL) or GTR 64 (for ASHQ), the *dest* operand is replaced with 0. If the *count* operand is LEQ −31 (for ASHL) or LEQ −63 (for ASHQ), the *dest* operand is filled with copies of the high-order bit of the *src* operand.

If a register Rn is specified as an operand for ASHQ, the operand is the concatenation $R[n+1]'R[n]$.

ASHP Arithmetic *SH*ift and round *P*acked decimal string

Format ASHP *count.rb,srclen.rw,srcaddr.ab,*
round.rb,destlen.rw,destaddr.ab

Operation $deststr \leftarrow [srcstr + (round\langle 3:0\rangle)*(10**(-count-1))] *(10**count)$
where *deststr* is the packed decimal string defined by the length and address operands *destlen* and *destaddr*, and *srcstr* is the string defined by *srclen* and *srcaddr*

Condition codes $N \leftarrow$ {*deststr* LSS 0}
$Z \leftarrow$ {*deststr* EQL 0}
$V \leftarrow$ {decimal overflow}
$C \leftarrow 0$

Operation code	F8	ASHP	Arithmetic SHift Packed decimal

Description The string specified by *srclen* and *srcaddr* is multiplied by the power of 10 specified by the *count* operand, and the scaled result is put in the string specified by *destlen* and *destaddr*. When the *count* operand is negative (division by a power of 10), the low-order 4 bits of the *round* operand are used for rounding the result.

Exceptions Decimal overflow
Reserved operand

Side effects Upon execution of ASHP:
$R0 \leftarrow 0$
$R1 \leftarrow$ address of the byte containing the most-significant digit of the source string
$R2 \leftarrow 0$
$R3 \leftarrow$ address of the byte containing the most-significant digit of the destination string

Comments	The destination string, R0 to R3, and the condition codes are unpredictable if: the source and destination strings overlap; the source string contains an invalid 4-bit packed decimal code; or the *round* operand is not in the range 0 to 9. The *round* operand has no effect if the *count* operand is positive.

B *Branch conditionally*

Format	Bcc *disp.bb*
Operation	If condition (cc) tested is TRUE then PC ← c(PC) + SEXT(*disp*)
Condition codes	N ← N Z ← Z V ← V C ← C

Operation codes			
12	BNEQ	Branch on Not EQual, signed (Z EQL 0)
12	BNEQU	Branch on Not EQual, Unsigned (Z EQL 0)
13	BEQL	Branch on EQual, signed (Z EQL 1)
13	BEQLU	Branch on EQual, Unsigned (Z EQL 1)
14	BGTR	Branch on GreaTeR than, signed ((N OR Z) EQL 0)
15	BLEQ	Branch on Less than or EQual, signed ((N OR Z) EQL 1)
18	BGEQ	Branch on Greater than or EQual, signed (N EQL 0)
19	BLSS	Branch on LeSS than, signed (N EQL 1)
1A	BGTRU	Branch on GreaTeR than, Unsigned ((C OR Z) EQL 0)
1B	BLEQU	Branch on Less than or EQual, Unsigned ((C OR Z) EQL 1)
1C	BVC	Branch on oVerflow Clear (V EQL 0)
1D	BVS	Branch on oVerflow Set (V EQL 1)
1E	BGEQU	Branch on Greater than or EQual, Unsigned (C EQL 0)
1E	BCC	Branch on Carry Clear (C EQL 0)
1F	BLSSU	Branch on LeSS than, Unsigned (C EQL 1)
1F	BCS	Branch on Carry Set (C EQL 1)

Description	If the condition tested is TRUE, the displacement byte is sign extended to a longword and added to c(PC).
Exceptions	None

BB *Branch on Bit*

Format	BBc *pos.rl,base.vb,disp.bb*
Operation	if *bit* EQL 1 then PC ← c(PC) + SEXT(*disp*) (BBS, BBSS, BBSC)

if *bit* EQL 0 then
PC ← c(PC) + SEXT(*disp*)

bit ← 1
bit ← 0

where *bit* is the one-bit field determined by *pos* and *base*

Condition codes   N ← N
Z ← Z
V ← V
C ← C

Operation codes   E0   BBS   Branch on Bit Set
E1   BBC   Branch on Bit Clear
E2   BBSS   Branch on Bit Set and Set
E3   BBCS   Branch on Bit Clear and Set
E4   BBSC   Branch on Bit Set and Clear
E5   BBCC   Branch on Bit Clear and Clear

Description   The 1-bit field (*bit*) determined by the base address *base* and position *pos* is tested. If it is in the state specified by the instruction, the displacement *disp* is sign extended to a longword and added to c(PC); otherwise, no branch takes place.
The specified bit is set or cleared in the case of BBSS, BBCS and BBSC, BBCC, respectively, *regardless* of whether or not the branch takes place.

Exception   Reserved operand

Comment   If *base* is a register, *pos* must be in the range 0 to 31.

BIC   *BIt Clear*

Format   BICx2   *mask.rx,dest.mx*   (2-operand)
BICx3   *mask.rx,src.rx,dest.wx*   (3-operand)

Operation   *dest* ← *dest* AND (NOT *mask*)   (2-operand)
dest ← *src* AND (NOT *mask*)   (3-operand)

Condition codes   N ← {*dest* LSS 0}
Z ← {*dest* EQL 0}
V ← 0
C ← C

Operation codes   8A   BICB2   BIt Clear Byte, 2-operand
8B   BICB3   BIt Clear Byte, 3-operand
AA   BICW2   BIt Clear Word, 2-operand
AB   BICW3   BIt Clear Word, 3-operand
CA   BICL2   BIt Clear Longword, 2-operand
CB   BICL3   BIt Clear Longword, 3-operand

Description   The one's complement of the *mask* operand is ANDed with the *dest* operand (2-operand form) or *src* operand (3-operand form). The result replaces the *dest* operand.

Exceptions   None

BICPSW   *BIt Clear Processor Status Word*

Format BICPSW *mask.rw*

Operation PSW ← c(PSW) AND (NOT *mask*)

Condition codes N ← N AND (NOT *mask*⟨3⟩)
Z ← Z AND (NOT *mask*⟨2⟩)
V ← V AND (NOT *mask*⟨1⟩)
C ← C AND (NOT *mask*⟨0⟩)

Operation code B9 BICPSW   BIt Clear PSW

Description The Processor Status Word is ANDed with the one's complement of the *mask* operand; the result replaces the PSW.

Exception Reserved operand

Comment Bits 15:8 of the *mask* operand must be zero.

BIS   *BIt Set*

Format BISx2 *mask.rx,dest.mx*   (2-operand)
BISx3 *mask.rx,src.rx,dest.wx*   (3-operand)

Operation *dest* ← *dest* OR *mask*   (2-operand)
dest ← *src* OR *mask*   (3-operand)

Condition codes N ← {*dest* LSS 0}
Z ← {*dest* EQL 0}
V ← 0
C ← C

Operation codes
88 BISB2 BIt Set Byte, 2-operand
89 BISB3 BIt Set Byte, 3-operand
A8 BISW2 BIt Set Word, 2-operand
A9 BISW3 BIt Set Word, 3-operand
C8 BISL2 BIt Set Longword, 2-operand
C9 BISL3 BIt Set Longword, 3-operand

Description The *mask* operand is ORed with the *dest* operand (2-operand form) or *src* operand (3-operand form). The result replaces the *dest* operand.

Exceptions None

BISPSW   *BIt Set Processor Status Word*

Format BISPSW *mask.rw*

Operation PSW ← c(PSW) OR *mask*

Condition codes N ← N OR *mask*⟨3⟩
Z ← Z OR *mask*⟨2⟩
V ← V OR *mask*⟨1⟩
C ← C OR *mask*⟨0⟩

Operation code	B8 BISPSW BIt Set PSW
Description	The Processor Status Word is ORed with the *mask* operand; the result replaces the PSW.
Exception	Reserved operand
Comment	Bits 15:8 of the *mask* operand must be zero.

BIT   *BIt Test*

Format	BITx *mask.rx,src.rx*
Operation	*src* AND *mask*
Condition codes	N ← {(*src* AND *mask*) LSS 0} Z ← {(*src* AND *mask*) EQL 0} V ← 0 C ← C
Operation codes	93 BITB BIt Test Byte B3 BITW BIt Test Word D3 BITL BIt Test Longword
Description	The *src* and *mask* operands are ANDed, and the condition codes N and Z are set according to the result. Neither operand is affected.
Exceptions	None

BLB   *Branch on Low Bit*

Format	BLBc *src.rl,disp.bb*
Operation	PC ← c(PC) + SEXT(*disp*) if *src*⟨0⟩ EQL 1 (BLBS) PC ← c(PC) + SEXT(*disp*) if *src*⟨0⟩ EQL 0 (BLBC)
Condition codes	N ← N Z ← Z V ← V C ← C
Operation codes	E8 BLBS Branch on Low Bit Set E9 BLBC Branch on Low Bit Clear
Description	Bit 0 of the *src* operand is tested. The displacement operand *disp* is sign extended to a longword and added to c(PC) if the tested bit corresponds to the specified condition.
Exceptions	None

BR   *BRanch*

Format	BRx *disp.bx*
Operation	PC ← c(PC) + SEXT(*disp*)

Condition codes	N ← N
	Z ← Z
	V ← V
	C ← C

Operation codes	11	BRB	BRanch with Byte displacement
	31	BRW	BRanch with Word displacement

Description   The displacement byte or word *disp* is sign extended to a longword and added to c(PC).

Exceptions   None

BSB   *Branch to SuBroutine*

Format   BSBx   *disp.bx*

Operation
$$-(SP) \leftarrow c(PC);$$
$$PC \leftarrow c(PC) + SEXT(disp)$$

Condition codes	N ← N
	Z ← Z
	V ← V
	C ← C

Operation codes	10	BSBB	Branch to SuBroutine with Byte displacement
	30	BSBW	Branch to SuBroutine with Word displacement

Description   The contents of the program counter is pushed onto the stack; the byte or word displacement *disp* is then sign extended to a longword and added to c(PC).

Exceptions   None

CALLG   *CALL* procedure with *General* argument list

Format   CALLG   *arglist.ab,dest.ab*

Operation
temp ← c(SP);
align the stack pointer;
save registers specified by entry mask word;
save PC, FP, and AP;
enable traps;
set new values of AP and FP;
PC ← *dest* + 2.

Condition codes	N ← 0
	Z ← 0
	V ← 0
	C ← 0

Operation code	FA	CALLG	CALL procedure with General argument list

Description	c(SP) is saved in a temporary longword, *temp*. Bits 0:1 of SP are replaced by 0s, to align SP on a longword boundary. The contents of the registers corresponding to bits 11:0 of the procedure entry mask word are pushed onto the stack, together with the contents of PC, FP, and AP. A longword is created on the stack, containing the following data:

bits 31:30 ← *temp*⟨1:0⟩
bits 29:28 ← 0
bits 27:16 ← entry mask⟨11:0⟩
bits 15:5 ← PSW bits 15:5
bits 4:0   ← 0

A longword containing 0 is pushed on the stack, and FP is replaced by c(SP). AP is replaced by the *arglist* operand. Integer and decimal overflow trap enables are set according to bits 14 and 15 of the procedure entry mask word. (Bits 13:12 of the entry mask word must be 0.) PC is given the value *dest* + 2.

Exception   Reserved operand

CALLS   *CALL* procedure with *Stacked* argument list

Format   CALLS   *argcnt.rl,dest.ab*

Operation
push *argcnt* on stack;
temp ← c(SP);
align the stack pointer;
save registers specified by entry mask word;
save PC, FP, and AP;
enable traps;
set new values of AP and FP;
PC ← *dest* + 2.

Condition codes
N ← 0
Z ← 0
V ← 0
C ← 0

Operation code   FB   CALLS   CALL procedure with Stacked
                                    argument list

Description   The argument count *argcnt* is pushed onto the stack. c(SP) is saved in a temporary longword, *temp*. Bits 0:1 of SP are replaced by 0s, to align SP on a longword boundary. The contents of the registers corresponding to bits 11:0 of the procedure entry mask word are pushed onto the stack, together with the contents of PC, FP, and AP. A longword is created on the stack, containing the following data:

bits 31:30 ← *temp*⟨1:0⟩
bit 29   ← 1
bit 28   ← 0
bits 27:16 ← entry mask⟨11:0⟩
bits 15:5 ← PSW bits 15:5
bits 4:0   ← 0

A longword containing 0 is pushed on the stack, and FP is replaced by c(SP). AP is replaced by *temp*. Integer and decimal overflow trap enables are set according to bits 14 and 15 of the procedure entry mask word. (Bits 13:12 of the entry mask word must be 0.) PC is given the value *dest* + 2.

Exception   Reserved operand

CLR   *CLeaR*

Format	CLRx *dest.wx*
Operation	*dest* ← 0
Condition codes	N ← 0 Z ← 1 V ← 0 C ← C

Operation codes

94	CLRB	CLeaR Byte
B4	CLRW	CLeaR Word
D4	CLRL	CLeaR Longword
D4	CLRF	CLeaR F_floating
7C	CLRQ	CLeaR Quadword
7C	CLRD	CLeaR D_floating
7C	CLRG	CLeaR G_floating
7CFD	CLRO	CLeaR Octaword
7CFD	CLRH	CLeaR H_floating

Description   The destination operand *dest* is given the value 0.

Exception   Reserved operand

CMP   *CoMPare* numerical quantities

Format	CMPx *src1.rx,src2.rx*
Operation	*src1* − *src2*
Condition codes	N ← {*src1* LSS *src2*} Z ← {*src1* EQL *src2*} V ← 0 C ← {*src1* LSSU *src2*} (integer) C ← 0 (floating-point)

Operation codes

91	CMPB	CoMPare Byte
B1	CMPW	CoMPare Word
D1	CMPL	CoMPare Longword
51	CMPF	CoMPare F_floating
71	CMPD	CoMPare D_floating
51FD	CMPG	CoMPare G_floating
71FD	CMPH	CoMPare H_floating

Description   The operand *src2* is subtracted from the operand *src1*, and the condition codes are set accordingly. Neither operand is affected.

Exceptions   None (integer)
Reserved operand (floating-point)

CMPC   *CoMPare Character strings*

Format

CMPC3   *len.rw,src1addr.ab,src2addr.ab*   (3-operand)
CMPC5   *src1len.rw,src1addr.ab,fill.rb*   (5-operand)
        src2len.rw,src2addr.ab

Operation

$i \leftarrow 1$;
$i \leftarrow i+1$ while $((str1[i]$ EQL $str2[i])$ AND $(i$ LEQ LEN$))$
where $strK[i]$ is the ith byte of $strK$ ($K = 1,2$).
In the 3-operand form, LEN $= len$ and $strK$ is the byte array defined by len and
$srcKaddr$.
In the 5-operand form, LEN $= $ MAX($src1len,src2len$), and
$strK[i] = i$th byte of the array defined by $srcKlen$
          and $srcKaddr$ if i LEQ $srcKlen$
         $= fill$ if i GTR $srcKlen$

Condition codes

N $\leftarrow \{str1[$LAST$]$ LSS $str2[$LAST$]\}$
Z $\leftarrow \{str1[$LAST$]$ EQL $str2[$LAST$]\}$
V $\leftarrow 0$
C $\leftarrow \{str1[$LAST$]$ LSSU $str2[$LAST$]\}$
    where LAST $=$ index of last bytes compared

Operation codes

29   CMPC3   CoMPare Character strings, 3-operand
2D   CMPC5   CoMPare Character strings, 5-operand

Description

In the 3-operand form, the bytes of the first character array, defined by the *len* and *src1addr* operands, are compared with those of the second array, defined by the *len* and *src2addr* operands. The comparison continues until unequal bytes are detected, or until all bytes have been compared. The condition codes are set according to the last comparison made.

In the 5-operand form, the bytes of the first character array, defined by the *src1len* and *src1addr* operands, are compared with those of the second array, defined by the *src2len* and *src2addr* operands. The comparison continues until unequal bytes are detected, or until all bytes in the longer string have been compared. If the strings are of unequal length, the comparison continues beyond the length of the shorter string, the character *fill* being used as a substitute character for the shorter string. The condition codes are set according to the last comparison made.

Exceptions

None

Side effects

Upon execution of CMPC3:
R0 $\leftarrow$ number of bytes remaining in *str1*, including the byte that caused the comparisons to terminate; if the strings are identical, R0 is given the value 0
R1 $\leftarrow$ address of byte in *str1* at which the comparisons terminated; if the strings are identical, R1 is given the value *src1addr* + SEXT(*len*)
R2 $\leftarrow 0$
R3 $\leftarrow$ address of byte in *str2* at which the comparisons terminated; if the strings are identical, R3 is given the value *src2addr* + SEXT(*len*)
Upon execution of CMPC5:
R0 $\leftarrow$ number of bytes remaining in *str1*, including the byte that caused the

comparisons to terminate; if the strings are of equal length and identical, or if *str1* is identical to a substring of *str2*, then R0 is given the value 0

R1 ← address of byte in *str1* at which the comparisons terminated; if *str1* is identical to a substring of *str2*, then R1 is given the value *src1addr* + SEXT(*src1len*)

R2 ← number of bytes remaining in *str2*, including the byte that caused the comparisons to terminate; if the strings are of equal length and identical, or if *str2* is identical to a substring of *str1*, then R2 is given the value 0

R3 ← address of byte in *str2* at which the comparisons terminated; if *str2* is identical to a substring of *str1*, then R3 is given the value *src2addr* + SEXT(*src2len*)

Comment   If both strings are of length 0, Z is set and N, V, and C are cleared.

CMPP   *CoMPare Packed decimal strings*

Format

CMPP3	*len.rw,src1addr.ab,src2addr.ab*	(3-operand)
CMPP4	*src1len.rw,src1addr.ab,*	(4-operand)
	src2len.rw,src2addr.ab	

Operation   *str1 − str2*

where *strK* is the packed decimal string defined by the base address *srcKaddr* and the length operand, *len* or *srcKlen* (*K* = 1,2)

Condition codes   N ← {*str1* LSS *str2*}
Z ← {*str1* EQL *str2*}
V ← 0
C ← 0

Operation codes

| 35 | CMPP3 | CoMPare Packed decimal, 3-operand |
| 37 | CMPP4 | CoMPare Packed decimal, 4-operand |

Description   The packed decimal string defined by the base address *src2addr* and the length operand (*len* for CMPP3, *src2len* for CMPP4) is packed-decimal subtracted from the packed decimal string defined by the base address *src1addr* and the length operand (*len* for CMPP3, *src2len* for CMPP4), and the condition codes are set according to the result.

Exceptions   Reserved operand

Side effects   Upon execution of CMPP3 or CMPP4:
R0 ← 0
R1 ← address of the byte containing the most-significant digit of *str1*
R2 ← 0
R3 ← address of the byte containing the most-significant digit of *str2*

Comment   The condition codes and the contents of R0 to R3 are unpredictable if the source strings overlap, or if either string contains an invalid 4-bit decimal code.

CMPV, CMPZV   *CoMPare Variable bit field to integer*

Format

| CMPV | *pos.rl,size.rb,base.vb,src.rl* |
| CMPZV | *pos.rl,size.rb,base.vb,src.rl* |

Operation	temp − src, where:

temp − src, where:

temp ← 0, if size EQL 0; else
temp ← SEXT(field)   (CMPV)
temp ← ZEXT(field)   (CMPZV)
where field = variable-length bit field determined by the pos, size, and base operands

Condition codes N ← {temp LSS src}
Z ← {temp EQL src}
V ← 0
C ← {temp LSSU src}

Operation codes

EC	CMPV	CoMPare sign extended Variable bit field
ED	CMPZV	CoMPare Zero extended Variable bit field

Description The variable-length bit field specified by the pos, size, and base operands is (sign or zero) extended to a 32-bit field temp and compared with the src operand, and the condition codes are set accordingly. None of the operands is affected.

Exception Reserved operand

Comments The size operand must be LEQ 32.

If the base operand is a register and size GTR 0, the pos operand must be in the range 0 to 31.

CVT   ConVerT datatypes

Format CVTxy   src.rx,dest.wy

Operation dest ← src, converted to dest datatype

Condition codes N ← {dest LSS 0}
Z ← {dest EQL 0}
V ← {integer overflow} (integer)
V ← {src datatype cannot be represented in
      dest datatype} (floating)
C ← 0

Operation codes

99	CVTBW	ConVerT Byte to Word
98	CVTBL	ConVerT Byte to Longword
4C	CVTBF	ConVerT Byte to F_floating
6C	CVTBD	ConVerT Byte to D_floating
4CFD	CVTBG	ConVerT Byte to G_floating
6CFD	CVTBH	ConVerT Byte to H_floating
33	CVTWB	ConVerT Word to Byte
32	CVTWL	ConVerT Word to Longword
4D	CVTWF	ConVerT Word to F_floating
6D	CVTWD	ConVerT Word to D_floating
4DFD	CVTWG	ConVerT Word to G_floating
6DFD	CVTWH	ConVerT Word to H_floating
F6	CVTLB	ConVerT Longword to Byte
F7	CVTLW	ConVerT Longword to Word
4E	CVTLF	ConVerT Longword to F_floating

6E	CVTLD	ConVerT Longword to D_floating
4EFD	CVTLG	ConVerT Longword to G_floating
6EFD	CVTLH	ConVerT Longword to H_floating
48	CVTFB	ConVerT F_floating to Byte
49	CVTFW	ConVerT F_floating to Word
4A	CVTFL	ConVerT F_floating to Longword
4B	CVTRFL	ConVerT, Rounded, F_floating to Longword
56	CVTFD	ConVerT F_floating to D_floating
99FD	CVTFG	ConVerT F_floating to G_floating
98FD	CVTFH	ConVerT F_floating to H_floating
68	CVTDB	ConVerT D_floating to Byte
69	CVTDW	ConVerT D_floating to Word
6A	CVTDL	ConVerT D_floating to Longword
6B	CVTRDL	ConVerT, Rounded, D_floating to Longword
76	CVTDF	ConVerT D_floating to F_floating
32FD	CVTDH	ConVerT D_floating to H_floating
48FD	CVTGB	ConVerT G_floating to Byte
49FD	CVTGW	ConVerT G_floating to Word
4AFD	CVTGL	ConVerT G_floating to Longword
4BFD	CVTRGL	ConVerT, Rounded, G_floating to Longword
33FD	CVTGF	ConVerT G_floating to F_floating
56FD	CVTGH	ConVerT G_floating to H_floating
68FD	CVTHB	ConVerT H_floating to Byte
69FD	CVTHW	ConVerT H_floating to Word
6AFD	CVTHL	ConVerT H_floating to Longword
6BFD	CVTRHL	ConVerT, Rounded, H_floating to Longword
F6FD	CVTHF	ConVerT H_floating to F_floating
F7FD	CVTHD	ConVerT H_floating to D_floating
76FD	CVTHG	ConVerT H_floating to G_floating

Description

The source operand *src* is converted to the datatype of the destination operand *dest*. For integer conversion, a shorter datatype is converted to a longer datatype by sign extension, and a longer datatype is converted to a shorter datatype by truncation of the higher-order bits. Floating-point conversion is **exact**, **rounded**, or **truncated**, according to the following table.

CVTBF	exact		CVTFL	truncated
CVTBD	exact		CVTRFL	rounded
CVTBG	exact		CVTFD	exact
CVTBH	exact		CVTFG	exact
			CVTFH	exact
CVTWF	exact			
CVTWD	exact		CVTDB	truncated
CVTWG	exact		CVTDW	truncated
CVTWH	exact		CVTDL	truncated
			CVTRDL	rounded
CVTLF	rounded		CVTDF	rounded
CVTLD	exact		CVTDH	exact
CVTLG	exact			
CVTLH	exact		CVTGB	truncated
CVTFB	truncated		CVTGW	truncated
CVTFW	truncated		CVTGL	truncated

CVTRGL	rounded		CVTHL	truncated
CVTGF	rounded		CVTRHL	rounded
CVTGH	exact		CVTHF	rounded
			CVTHD	rounded
CVTHB	truncated		CVTHG	rounded
CVTHW	truncated			

Exceptions Integer overflow
Floating-point overflow
Floating-point underflow
Reserved operand

Comment Integer overflow occurs only when the destination operand *dest* is of integer type, and then only when the bits truncated from the *src* operand do not all agree with the high-order bit of the *dest* operand.

CVTLP *ConVerT Longword to Packed decimal string*

Format CVTLP *src.rl,destlen.rw,destaddr.ab*

Operation *deststr* ← *src*, converted to packed decimal
where *deststr* is the packed decimal string defined by the length operand *destlen* and base address *destaddr*

Condition codes N ← {*deststr* LSS 0}
Z ← {*deststr* EQL 0}
V ← {decimal overflow}
C ← 0

Operation code F9 CVTLP ConVerT Longword to Packed decimal

Description The source longword *src* is converted to a packed decimal string and stored in the destination string defined by *destlen* and *destaddr*.

Exceptions Decimal overflow
Reserved operand

Side effects Upon execution of CVTLP:
R0 ← 0
R1 ← 0
R2 ← 0
R3 ← address of the byte containing the most-significant digit of the destination string

Comment If the source and destination operands overlap, the resulting destination string will be correctly formed.

CVTPL *ConVerT Packed decimal string to Longword*

Format CVTPL *srclen.rw,srcaddr.ab,dest.wl*

Operation *dest* ← *srcstr*, converted to a longword
where *srcstr* is the packed decimal string defined by the length operand *srclen* and base address *srcaddr*

Condition codes	N ← {dest LSS 0}
	Z ← {dest EQL 0}
	V ← {integer overflow}
	C ← 0

Operation code	36 CVTPL ConVerT Packed decimal to Longword

Description The source string defined by the *srclen* and *srcaddr* operands is converted to a longword and stored in the destination longword *dest*.

Exceptions Integer overflow
Reserved operand

Side effects Upon execution of CVTPL:
R0 ← 0
R1 ← address of the byte containing the most-significant digit of the source string
R2 ← 0
R3 ← 0

Comments If the source and destination operands overlap, the resulting destination longword will be correctly formed.

Any of R0 to R3 may be used as the destination, since the side effects noted above occur prior to the storing of the converted longword.

The condition codes, registers R0 to R3, and the destination longword are unpredictable if the source string contains an invalid 4-bit decimal code.

CVTPS   ConVerT Packed decimal to leading Separate numeric

Format CVTPS   *srclen.rw,srcaddr.ab,*
    destlen.rw,destaddr.ab

Operation *deststr ← srcstr*, converted to a leading separate numeric string
where *deststr* is the leading separate numeric string defined by *destlen* and *destaddr*, and *srcstr* is the packed decimal string defined by *srclen* and *srcaddr*

Condition codes	N ← {srcstr LSS 0}
	Z ← {srcstr EQL 0}
	V ← {decimal overflow}
	C ← 0

Operation code	08 CVTPS ConVerT Packed decimal string to leading Separate numeric string

Description The source packed decimal string defined by *srclen* and *srcaddr* is converted to a leading separate numeric string, the result replacing the string defined by *destlen* and *destaddr*.

Exceptions Decimal overflow
Reserved operand

Side effects Upon execution of CVTPS:
R0 ← 0
R1 ← address of the byte containing the most-significant digit of the source string
R2 ← 0

R3 ← address of the byte in the destination string which contains the sign character

Comments   If the source and destination strings overlap, or if the source string contains an invalid 4-bit decimal code, the condition codes, destination string, and the contents of R0 to R3 are unpredictable.

If the converted string represents −0, and if no decimal overflow occurred, the leading separate numeric string is converted to +0.

CVTPT   *ConVerT Packed decimal to Trailing numeric*

Format   CVTPT   *srclen.rw,srcaddr.ab,tableaddr.ab,*
                            destlen.rw,destaddr.ab

Operation   *deststr* ← *srcstr*, converted to a trailing numeric string

where *deststr* is the trailing numeric string defined by *destlen* and *destaddr*, and *srcstr* is the packed decimal string defined by *srclen* and *srcaddr*

Condition codes N ← {*srcstr* LSS 0}
                     Z ← {*srcstr* EQL 0}
                     V ← {decimal overflow}
                     C ← 0

Operation code   24   CVTPT   ConVerT Packed decimal to
                                    Trailing numeric string

Description   The packed decimal string *srcstr* is converted to trailing numeric form and replaces the string *deststr*.

The unsigned contents of the highest-addressed byte *hibyte* of *srcstr*, which contains the least-significant digit and the sign nibble of *srcstr*, is used as an index into a 256-byte table defined by the *tableaddr* operand. The contents of *tableaddr*[c(*hibyte*)] is used as the least-significant byte of *deststr*. The remaining nibbles of *srcstr* are converted to their ASCII representations and stored in *deststr*.

Exceptions   Decimal overflow
                    Reserved operand

Side effects   Upon execution of CVTPT:
                    R0 ← 0
                    R1 ← address of the byte containing the most-significant digit of the source string
                    R2 ← 0
                    R3 ← address of most-significant digit of the destination string

Comments   If the source and destination strings overlap, or if the source string contains an invalid 4-bit decimal code, then the condition codes, destination string, and the contents of R0 to R3 are unpredictable.

Decimal overflow occurs if the destination string is too short to contain the converted source string.

CVTSP ConVerT leading Separate numeric to Packed decimal

Format	CVTSP *srclen.rw,srcaddr.ab,* *destlen.rw,destaddr.ab*
Operation	*deststr* ← *srcstr*, converted to a packed decimal string where *deststr* is the packed decimal string defined by *destlen* and *destaddr*, and *srcstr* is the leading separate numeric string defined by *srclen* and *srcaddr*
Condition codes	N ← {*deststr* LSS 0} Z ← {*deststr* EQL 0} V ← {decimal overflow} C ← 0
Operation code	09 CVTSP ConVerT leading Separate numeric to Packed decimal string
Description	The source leading separate numeric string defined by *srclen* and *srcaddr* is converted to a packed decimal string, the result replacing the string defined by *destlen* and *destaddr*.
Exceptions	Decimal overflow Reserved operand
Side effects	Upon execution of CVTSP: R0 ← 0 R1 ← address of the sign byte of the source string R2 ← 0 R3 ← address of the byte containing the most-significant digit of the destination string
Comments	The condition codes, destination string, and contents of R0 to R3 are unpredictable if the source and destination strings overlap; the length of either source or destination string is not within the range 0 to 31; or the source string contains a byte other than an ASCII 0 through ASCII 9 in its numeric bytes, or an ASCII plus sign, minus sign, or space character in its sign byte.

CVTTP ConVerT Trailing numeric to Packed decimal string

Format	CVTTP *srclen.rw,srcaddr.ab,tableaddr.ab,* *destlen.rw,destaddr.ab*
Operation	*deststr* ← *srcstr*, converted to a packed decimal string where *deststr* is the packed decimal string defined by *destlen* and *destaddr*, and *srcstr* is the trailing numeric string defined by *srclen* and *srcaddr*
Condition codes	N ← {*deststr* LSS 0} Z ← {*deststr* EQL 0} V ← {decimal overflow} C ← 0
Operation code	26 CVTTP ConVerT Trailing numeric to Packed decimal string

Description	The source trailing numeric string defined by *srclen* and *srcaddr* is converted to a packed decimal string, the result replacing the string defined by *destlen* and *destaddr*.
	The trailing (highest-addressed) byte of *srcstr* is used as an unsigned index to a 256-byte table whose address is *tableaddr*. The contents of this table entry replaces the highest-addressed byte of *deststr* (the low-order digit and sign nibble). The remaining digits in *deststr* are replaced by the low-order nibbles of the bytes of *srcstr*.
Exceptions	Decimal overflow
	Reserved operand
Side effects	Upon execution of CVTTP:
	$R0 \leftarrow 0$
	$R1 \leftarrow$ address of the most-significant digit of the source string
	$R2 \leftarrow 0$
	$R3 \leftarrow$ address of the byte containing the most-significant digit of the destination string
Comments	The condition codes, destination string, and contents of R0 to R3 are unpredictable if the source and destination strings overlap; the length of either source or destination string is not within the range 0 to 31; or the source string contains a byte other than an ASCII 0 through ASCII 9 in its numeric bytes, or the table translation of the least significant digit yields an invalid 4-bit decimal code or sign code.
	If the conversion produces -0 (without overflow), the resulting string is replaced by $+0$.
	If *srclen* is 0, *deststr* is set to 0 and no table translation takes place.

DEC   *DEC*rement operand

Format	DECx *dest.mx*
Operation	$dest \leftarrow dest - 1$
Condition codes	$N \leftarrow \{dest \text{ LSS } 0\}$
	$Z \leftarrow \{dest \text{ EQL } 0\}$
	$V \leftarrow \{\text{integer overflow}\}$
	$C \leftarrow \{\text{borrow from most-significant bit}\}$
Operation codes	97 DECB DECrement Byte
	B7 DECW DECrement Word
	D7 DECL DECrement Longword
Description	The number 1 is subtracted from the operand, the result replacing the operand.
Exception	Integer overflow
Comment	Integer overflow occurs only if the largest negative number is decremented.

DIV   *DIV*ide operands

Format	DIVx2 *divr.rx,quot.mx*	(2-operand)
	DIVx3 *divr.rx,divd.rx,quot.wx*	(3-operand)

Operation	$quot \leftarrow quot / divr$		(2-operand)
	$quot \leftarrow divd / divr$		(3-operand)

Condition codes
N ← {*quot* LSS 0}
Z ← {*quot* EQL 0}
V ← {integer or floating overflow}
    OR {*divr* EQL 0}
C ← 0

Operation codes

86	DIVB2	DIVide Byte, 2-operand
87	DIVB3	DIVide Byte, 3-operand
A6	DIVW2	DIVide Word, 2-operand
A7	DIVW3	DIVide Word, 3-operand
C6	DIVL2	DIVide Longword, 2-operand
C7	DIVL3	DIVide Longword, 3-operand
46	DIVF2	DIVide F_floating, 2-operand
47	DIVF3	DIVide F_floating, 3-operand
66	DIVD2	DIVide D_floating, 2-operand
67	DIVD3	DIVide D_floating, 3-operand
46FD	DIVG2	DIVide G_floating, 2-operand
47FD	DIVG3	DIVide G_floating, 3-operand
66FD	DIVH2	DIVide H_floating, 2-operand
67FD	DIVH3	DIVide H_floating, 3-operand

Description

In the 2-operand form, the quotient operand *quot* is divided by the divisor operand *divr*, and the result replaces the quotient operand.

In the 3-operand form, the dividend operand *divd* is divided by the divisor operand *divr*, and the result replaces the quotient operand *quot*.

Exceptions

Integer overflow
Divide-by-zero
Floating-point overflow
Floating-point underflow
Reserved operand

Comments

Integer division is performed so that the remainder is of the same sign as the dividend (*quot* or *divd*).

Integer overflow occurs only when the largest negative number is divided by −1.

In the 2-operand form, divide-by-zero does not affect the quotient operand. In the 3-operand form, the quotient operand is replaced by the dividend operand upon divide-by-zero.

DIVP   *DIVide Packed decimal strings*

Format

DIVP   *divrlen.rw,divraddr.rw,*
          divdlen.rw,divdaddr.ab,
          quotlen.rw,quotaddr.ab

Operation

$quotstr \leftarrow divdstr / divrstr$

where *quotstr* is the packed decimal string defined by *quotlen* and *quotaddr*, *divdstr* is the packed decimal string defined by *divdlen* and *divdaddr*, and *divrstr* is the packed decimal string defined by *divrlen* and *divraddr*

Condition codes	$N \leftarrow \{quotstr \text{ LSS } 0\}$
	$Z \leftarrow \{quotstr \text{ EQL } 0\}$
	$V \leftarrow \{decimal \ overflow\}$
	$C \leftarrow 0$
Operation code	27 DIVP DIVide Packed decimal strings
Description	The packed decimal dividend string defined by the length and base address operands *divdlen* and *divdaddr* is divided by the packed decimal divisor string defined by the length and base address operands *divrlen* and *divraddr*. The result replaces the packed decimal quotient string defined by the length and base address operands *quotlen* and *quotaddr*.
Exceptions	Decimal overflow
	Divide-by-zero
	Reserved operand
Side effects	Upon execution of DIVP:
	$R0 \leftarrow 0$
	$R1 \leftarrow$ address of the byte containing the most-significant digit of the divisor string
	$R2 \leftarrow 0$
	$R3 \leftarrow$ address of the byte containing the most-significant digit of the dividend string
	$R4 \leftarrow 0$
	$R5 \leftarrow$ address of the byte containing the most-significant digit of the quotient string
Comments	The quotient string, the condition codes, and the contents of R0 to R5 are unpredictable if the quotient string overlaps either the divisor or dividend string, or if either string contains an invalid four-digit decimal code.
	The absolute value of the (lost) remainder is LSS absolute value of the divisor.
	The instruction DIVP may use 16 bytes of stack space as a scratch stack area [although c(SP) is ultimately restored to its original value]. Thus upon completion of execution of DIVP, the contents of the bytes with addresses $c(SP) - 1$ to $c(SP) - 16$ are unpredictable.

EDIV   *Extended DIVide*

Format	EDIV *divr.rl,divd.rq,quot.wl,rem.wl*
Operation	$quot \leftarrow divd \ / \ divr$
	$rem \leftarrow \text{REM}(divd,divr)$
	where REM(*divd,divr*) is the remainder upon dividing *divd* by *divr*
Condition codes	$N \leftarrow \{quot \text{ LSS } 0\}$
	$Z \leftarrow \{quot \text{ EQL } 0\}$
	$V \leftarrow \{integer \ overflow\} \text{ OR } \{divr \text{ EQL } 0\}$
	$C \leftarrow 0$
Operation code	7B EDIV Extended DIVide
Description	The dividend operand *divd* is divided by the divisor operand *divr*; the quotient replaces the quotient operand *quot* and the remainder replaces the remainder operand *rem*.

Exceptions	Integer overflow Divide-by-zero
Comments	The remainder has the same sign as the dividend. If the divisor operand is 0, *quot* is replaced by *divd*⟨31:0⟩ and *rem* is given the value 0.

EMUL   *Extended MULtiply*

Format	EMUL *multr.rl,multd.rl,add.rl,prod.qw*
Operation	$prod \leftarrow (multr * multd) + \text{SEXT}(add)$
Condition codes	$N \leftarrow \{prod \text{ LSS } 0\}$ $Z \leftarrow \{prod \text{ EQL } 0\}$ $V \leftarrow 0$ $C \leftarrow 0$
Operation code	7A EMUL Extended *MUL*tiply
Description	The multiplier operand *multr* is multiplied by the multiplicand operand *multd*. The product operand *prod* is given the value of this product plus the addend operand *add*, sign extended to a quadword.
Exceptions	None

EXTV, EXTZV   *EXTract Variable bit field*

Format	EXTV *pos.rl,size.rb,base.vb,dest.wl* EXTZV *pos.rl,size.rb,base.vb,dest.wl*	(EXTV) (EXTZV)
Operation	*dest* ← 0, if *size* EQL 0; else *dest* ← SEXT(*field*) *dest* ← ZEXT(*field*) where *field* is the variable-length bit field determined by the *pos*, *size*, and *base* operands	(EXTV) (EXTZV)
Condition codes	$N \leftarrow \{dest \text{ LSS } 0\}$ $Z \leftarrow \{dest \text{ EQL } 0\}$ $V \leftarrow 0$ $C \leftarrow 0$	

Operation codes	EE EXTV EXTract sign extended Variable
	              bit field
	EF EXTZV EXTract Zero extended Variable
	              bit field	

Description	The variable-length bit field defined by the position, size, and base address operands *pos*, *size*, and *base* is extracted and converted to a longword, which is written to the destination operand *dest*. The conversion is by sign extension for EXTV and by zero extension for EXTZV.	
Exception	Reserved operand	
Comments	The *size* operand must be in the range 0 to 32. If the *base* operand is a register and the *size* operand is greater than 0, the *pos* operand cannot exceed 31.	

FF   Find First bit in variable bit field

Format	FFc *pos.rl,size.rb,base.vb,find.wl*
Operation	*find* ← position in *field* of first bit Set (FFS) or Clear (FFC) where *field* is the variable-length bit field defined by *pos*, *size*, and *base*
Condition codes	N ← 0 Z ← {specified bit not found} V ← 0 C ← 0
Operation codes	EA FFS Find First Set bit EB FFC Find First Clear bit
Description	The field specified by the position, size, and base address operands *pos*, *size*, and *base* is scanned, starting at bit 0, for the first (lowest-position) bit having the specified state. If the bit is found, the *find* operand is set to the bit's position within the field and the PSW Z bit is cleared. If the bit is not found, the *find* operand is set to the position one bit to the left of the field, and the PSW Z bit is set. If the *size* operand is 0, *find* is replaced by *pos* and the PSW Z bit is set.
Exception	Reserved operand
Comments	The *size* operand must be in the range 0 to 32. If the *base* operand is a register and the *size* operand is greater than 0, the *pos* operand cannot exceed 31.

HALT   HALT the processor

Format	HALT
Operation	Halt the processor
Condition codes	N ← N Z ← Z V ← V C ← C
Operation code	00 HALT HALT the processor
Description	The processor enters a HALT state, and instruction fetch and execution ceases.
Exception	Privileged instruction
Comment	HALT is a privileged instruction which can only be executed in kernel mode.

INC   INCrement operand

Format	INCx *dest.mx*
Operation	*dest* ← *dest* + 1
Condition codes	N ← {*dest* LSS 0} Z ← {*dest* EQL 0}

$$V \leftarrow \{\text{integer overflow}\}$$
$$C \leftarrow \{\text{carry out of most-significant bit}\}$$

Operation codes	96	INCB	INCrement Byte
	B6	INCW	INCrement Word
	D6	INCL	INCrement Longword

Description The number 1 is added to the operand, the result replacing the operand.

Exception Integer overflow

Comment Integer overflow occurs only if the largest positive number is incremented.

INDEX   calculate array *INDEX*

Format INDEX *sub.rl,low.rl,high.rl,*
             size.rl,index.rl,calcindex.wl

Operation *calcindex* $\leftarrow$ (*index* + *sub*) $*$ *size*
                if *low* LEQ *sub* LEQ *high*
                else **subscript range trap** occurs.

Condition codes
$$N \leftarrow \{calcindex \text{ LSS } 0\}$$
$$Z \leftarrow \{calcindex \text{ EQL } 0\}$$
$$V \leftarrow 0$$
$$C \leftarrow 0$$

Operation code 0A INDEX   calculate array INDEX

Description The index operand *index* is added to the subscript operand *sub* and the result is multiplied by the size operand *size*. The product replaces the calculated index operand *calcindex*. If the value of the specified subscript is not in the range of low to high subscripts (*low* to *high*), a subscript range exception occurs.

Exception Subscript range

Comment The INDEX instruction is useful for the calculation of the offset from an array address of a particular array element, when specified by its subscript or subscripts.

INSQUE   *INS*ert entry into *QUE*ue

Format INSQUE *entry.ab,pred.ab*

Operation
$$c(entry) \leftarrow c(pred);$$
$$c(entry+4) \leftarrow pred;$$
$$c(c(pred)+4) \leftarrow entry;$$
$$c(pred) \leftarrow entry.$$

Condition codes
$$N \leftarrow \{c(entry) \text{ LSS } c(entry+4)\}$$
$$Z \leftarrow \{c(entry) \text{ EQL } c(entry+4)\}$$
$$V \leftarrow 0$$
$$C \leftarrow \{c(entry) \text{ LSSU } c(entry+4)\}$$

Operation code 0E INSQUE   INSert entry into QUEue

Description	The new entry whose address is *entry* is inserted in the queue logically following the entry whose address is *pred*. If *entry* is the first queue entry beyond the header entry, the PSW Z-bit is set.
Exceptions	None
Comments	Prior to the start of execution of INSQUE, all memory references are verified for permitted access. If the user has access to these locations, execution of INSQUE begins and goes to completion. (In this way, a memory management exception cannot leave the queue in a partially altered state.)
	INSQUE is a noninterruptible instruction.

INSV   *INS*ert integer in *V*ariable bit field

Format	INSV *src.rl,pos.rl,size.rb,base.vb*
Operation	*field* ← *src*⟨(*size* − 1):0⟩
	where *field* is the variable-length bit field defined by *pos*, *size*, and *base*
Condition codes	N ← N
	Z ← Z
	V ← V
	C ← C
Operation code	F0 INSV INSert integer in Variable bit field
Description	The field defined by the position, size, and base address operands *pos*, *size*, and *base* is replaced by the low-order *size* bits of the source longword *src*.
Exception	Reserved operand
Comments	If the *size* operand is 0, no action is taken by the operation.
	The *size* operand must be in the range 0 to 32.
	If the *base* operand is a register and the *size* operand is greater than 0, the *pos* operand cannot exceed 31.

JMP   *Ju*MP

Format ·	JMP *dest.ab*
Operation	PC ← *dest*
Condition codes	N ← N
	Z ← Z
	V ← V
	C ← C
Operation code	17 JMP JuMP to destination
Description	The program counter contents is replaced by the destination operand *dest*.
Exceptions	None

JSB   Jump to SuBroutine

Format	JSB *dest.ab*
Operation	$-(SP) \leftarrow c(PC);$ $PC \leftarrow dest$
Condition codes	$N \leftarrow N$ $Z \leftarrow Z$ $V \leftarrow V$ $C \leftarrow C$
Operation code	16 JSB Jump to SuBroutine
Description	The contents of the program counter is pushed onto the stack; the program counter contents is replaced by the destination operand *dest*.
Exceptions	None

LOCC   LOCate Character

Format	LOCC *char.rb,len.rw,addr.ab*
Operation	Scan *str* for the first instance of the byte *char* and set c(R0), c(R1), and the condition codes accordingly where *str* is the byte string whose beginning address is *addr* and whose length in bytes is *len*
Condition codes	$N \leftarrow 0$ $Z \leftarrow \{c(R0) \; EQL \; 0\}$ $V \leftarrow 0$ $C \leftarrow 0$
Operation code	3A LOCC LOCate Character
Description	The byte string whose beginning address is *addr* is compared, byte by byte, with the byte whose value is *char*, up to and including *len* bytes. If the specified character is located, the PSW Z-bit is cleared; otherwise, the Z-bit is set.
Exceptions	None
Side effects	R0 ← number of bytes which remain in the string, including the byte at which the specified byte was located; if the byte was not located, R0 is set to 0 R1 ← address in the string of the located byte; if the byte was not located, R1 is set to *addr* + SEXT(*len*)
Comment	The PSW Z-bit is cleared if *len* EQL 0.

MATCHC   MATCH Character string

Format	MATCHC *objlen.rw,objaddr.ab,srclen.rw,srcaddr.ab*
Operation	Search character string *srcstr* for the first occurrence of the substring *objstr* where *srcstr* is the string defined by *srclen* and *srcaddr*, and *objstr* is the string defined by *objlen* and *objaddr*

Condition codes	$N \leftarrow 0$
	$Z \leftarrow \{c(R0) \text{ EQL } 0\}$
	$V \leftarrow 0$
	$C \leftarrow 0$

Operation code	39 MATCHC MATCH Character string
Description	The source string defined by the length and address operands *srclen* and *srcaddr* is searched, beginning at address *srcaddr* and continuing up to address *srcaddr* + *srclen* − 1 for the first occurrence of the object string defined by the length and address operands *objlen* and *objaddr*. If the substring is found, the PSW Z-bit is set; otherwise, Z is cleared.
Exceptions	None
Side effects	R0 ← 0 if a match occurred; otherwise, R0 is set equal to the number of bytes in *objstr*
	R1 ← the address *objaddr* + SEXT(*objlen*) if a match occurred; otherwise, R1 is set equal to *objaddr*
	R2 ← number of bytes remaining in *srcstr* after the match, if the substring was found; otherwise, R2 is given the value 0
	R3 ← the address which is one byte beyond the last byte matched, if the substring was found; otherwise, R3 is given the value *srcadr* + SEXT(*srclen*)
Comments	If the object string has length 0, the Z-bit is set.
	If the source string has zero length and the object string has positive length, the Z-bit is cleared.

MCOM   *Move COMplemented*

Format	MCOMx *src.rx,dest.wx*
Operation	*dest* ← NOT *src*
Condition codes	$N \leftarrow \{dest \text{ LSS } 0\}$
	$Z \leftarrow \{dest \text{ EQL } 0\}$
	$V \leftarrow 0$
	$C \leftarrow 0$
Operation codes	92 MCOMB Move COMplemented Byte
	B2 MCOMW Move COMplemented Word
	D2 MCOML Move COMplemented Longword
Description	The ones-complement of the source operand *src* is moved to the destination operand *dest*.
Exceptions	None

MNEG   *Move NEGated*

Format	MNEGx *src.rx,dest.wx*
Operation	*dest* ← − *src*
Condition codes	$N \leftarrow \{dest \text{ LSS } 0\}$
	$Z \leftarrow \{dest \text{ EQL } 0\}$

V ← {integer overflow} (integer)
V ← 0 (floating)
C ← 0

Operation codes	8E	MNEGB	Move NEGated Byte
	AE	MNEGW	Move NEGated Word
	CE	MNEGL	Move NEGated Longword
	52	MNEGF	Move NEGated F_floating
	72	MNEGD	Move NEGated D_floating
	52FD	MNEGG	Move NEGated G_floating
	72FD	MNEGH	Move NEGated H_floating

Description   The negative of the source operand *src* is moved to the destination operand *dest*.

Exceptions   Integer overflow
Reserved operand

Comments   Integer overflow occurs only when the source operand is the largest negative number.

MOV   *MOV*e numerical quantities

Format   MOVx   *src.rx,dest.w*

Operation   *dest ← src*

Condition codes   N ← {*dest* LSS 0}
Z ← {*dest* EQL 0}
V ← 0
C ← C

Operation codes	90	MOVB	MOVe Byte
	B0	MOVW	MOVe Word
	D0	MOVL	MOVe Longword
	7D	MOVQ	MOVe Quadword
	7DFD	MOVO	MOVe Octaword
	50	MOVF	MOVe F_floating
	70	MOVD	MOVe D_floating
	50FD	MOVG	MOVe G_floating
	70FD	MOVH	MOVe H_floating

Description   The destination operand *dest* is replaced by the source operand *src*.

Exceptions   None (integer)
Reserved operand (floating point)

MOVA   *MOV*e Address

Format   MOVAx   *src.ax,dest.wl*

Operation   *dest ← src*

Condition codes   N ← {*dest* LSS 0}
Z ← {*dest* EQL 0}

$$V \leftarrow 0$$
$$C \leftarrow C$$

Operation codes	9E	MOVAB	MOVe Address Byte
	3E	MOVAW	MOVe Address Word
	DE	MOVAL	MOVe Address Longword
	DE	MOVAF	MOVe Address F_floating
	7E	MOVAQ	MOVe Address Quadword
	7E	MOVAD	MOVe Address D_floating
	7E	MOVAG	MOVe Address G_floating
	7EFD	MOVAO	MOVe Address Octaword
	7EFD	MOVAH	MOVe Address H_floating

Description   The destination operand *dest* is replaced by the source operand *src*.   (Note that the source operand is an address.)

Exceptions   None

MOVC   *MOV*e Character string

Format

MOVC3	*len.rw,srcaddr.ab,destaddr.ab*	(3-operand)
MOVC5	*srclen.rw,srcaddr.ab,fill.rb,*	(5-operand)
	destlen.rw,destaddr.ab	

Operation

deststr ← *srcstr*   (3-operand)

where *deststr* is the string defined by *len* and *destaddr*,
and *srcstr* is the string defined by *len* and *srcaddr*

deststr ← bytes 1 to *destlen* of   (5-operand)
    srcstr if *destlen* LEQ *srclen*
deststr ← bytes 1 to *srclen* of *srcstr* plus
    destlen − *srclen* copies of the *fill*
    character, if *destlen* GTR *srclen*

where *deststr* is the string defined by *destlen* and *destaddr*, and *srcstr* is the string defined by *srclen* and *srcaddr*

Condition codes

N ← 0	(3-operand)
Z ← 1	
V ← 0	
C ← 0	
N ← {*srclen* LSS *destlen*}	(5-operand)
Z ← {*srclen* EQL *destlen*}	
V ← 0	
C ← {*srclen* LSSU *destlen*}	

Operation codes

28	MOVC3	MOVe Character string, 3-operand
2C	MOVC5	MOVe Character string, 5-operand

Description   In the 3-operand form, the source string defined by the length and base address operands *len* and *srcaddr* is moved to the destination string defined by the length and base address operands *len* and *destaddr*.

In the 5-operand form, the source string defined by the length and base address operands *srclen* and *srcaddr* is moved to the destination string defined by the length and base address operands *destlen* and *destaddr*, as follows:

If the source string is longer than or the same length as the destination string, the destination string is filled with the first *destlen* bytes of the source string.

If the source string is shorter than the destination string, the source string is moved to the first *srclen* bytes of the destination string, the remaining bytes being replaced by the fill character *fill*.

Exceptions	None
Side effects	Upon execution of MOVC3:

$R0 \leftarrow 0$
$R1 \leftarrow$ address *srcaddr* + SEXT(*len*)
$R2 \leftarrow 0$
$R3 \leftarrow$ address *destaddr* + SEXT(*len*)
$R4 \leftarrow 0$
$R5 \leftarrow 0$

Upon execution of MOVC5:

$R0 \leftarrow$ number of bytes in the source string not moved
$R1 \leftarrow$ address of the first byte beyond the last byte in the source string that was moved to the destination string
$R2 \leftarrow 0$
$R3 \leftarrow$ address *destaddr* + SEXT(*destlen*)
$R4 \leftarrow 0$
$R5 \leftarrow 0$

Comments   MOVC3 may be used to move a block of memory of length *len* bytes from one location to another.

MOVC5 may be used to fill a block of memory with a constant byte by setting *fill* equal to the value of the byte, and by setting *srclen* equal to 0. (In this case, *srcaddr* may be any address.)

MOVP   *MOVe Packed decimal string*

Format	MOVP *len.rw,srcaddr.ab,destaddr.ab*
Operation	*deststr ← srcstr*

where *deststr* is the packed decimal string defined by length *len* and base address *destaddr*, and *srcstr* is the packed decimal string defined by length *len* and base address *srcaddr*

Condition codes	$N \leftarrow \{deststr \text{ LSS } 0\}$
	$Z \leftarrow \{deststr \text{ EQL } 0\}$
	$V \leftarrow 0$
	$C \leftarrow C$
Operation code	34 MOVP MOVe Packed decimal string
Description	The bytes of the source string, defined by the length and base address operands *len* and *srcaddr*, are moved to the destination string, defined by the length and base address operands *len* and *destaddr*. (Note that *len*/2 bytes are moved.)
Exceptions	Reserved operand
Side effects	Upon execution of MOVP:

$R0 \leftarrow 0$
$R1 \leftarrow$ address of the byte containing the most-significant digit of the source string
$R2 \leftarrow 0$

R3 ← address of the byte containing the most-significant digit of the destination string

Comments   The condition codes, the contents of R0 to R3, and the destination string are unpredictable if the source and destination strings overlap, or if the source string contains an invalid 4-bit decimal code.

If the source string equals −0, the destination string is set to +0, and the PSW N- and Z-bits are cleared and set, respectively.

MOVPSL   *MOVe Processor Status Longword*

Format   MOVPSL   *dest.wl*

Operation   *dest* ← c(PSL)

Condition codes   N ← N
Z ← Z
V ← V
C ← C

Operation code   DC   MOVPSL   MOVe Processor Status Longword

Description   The longword destination operand *dest* is replaced by the contents of the Processor Status Longword.

Exceptions   None

MOVTC   *MOVe Translated Characters*

Format   MOVTC   *srclen.rw,srcaddr.ab,fill.rb,*
tableaddr.ab,destlen.rw,destaddr.ab

Operation   *deststr* ← translated bytes 1 to *destlen* of *srcstr* if *destlen* LEQ *srclen*
deststr ← translated bytes 1 to *srclen* of *srcstr* plus (*destlen* − *srclen*) copies of the *fill* character, if *destlen* GTR *srclen*

where *deststr* is the string defined by *destlen* and *destaddr*, and *srcstr* is the string defined by *srclen* and *srcaddr*

Condition codes   N ← {*srclen* LSS *destlen*}
Z ← {*srclen* EQL *destlen*}
V ← 0
C ← {*srclen* LSSU *destlen*}

Operation code   2E   MOVTC   MOVe Translated Characters

Description   A character in the source string is translated by using its byte value as an index into the 256-byte table whose address is *tableaddr*, the corresponding entry in the table being the translated value of the byte.   The source string defined by the length and base address operands *srclen* and *srcaddr* is translated and moved to the destination string defined by the length and base address operands *destlen* and *destaddr*, as follows:

1. If the source string is longer than or the same length as the destination string, the destination string is filled with the translations of the first *destlen* bytes of the source string.

2. If the source string is shorter than the destination string, the translated bytes of the source string are moved to the first *srclen* bytes of the destination string, the remaining bytes being replaced by the fill character *fill*.

Exceptions   None

Side effects   Upon execution of MOVTC:

R0 ← number of bytes in the source string not translated and moved
R1 ← address of the first byte beyond the last byte in the source string that was translated and moved to the destination string
R2 ← 0
R3 ← address *tableaddr*
R4 ← 0
R5 ← address *destaddr* + SEXT(*destlen*)

Comments   The source and destination strings may overlap without affecting the contents of the destination string.

The source string and the translation table may not overlap.

MOVTUC   *MOVe Translated Until escape Character*

Format   MOVTUC   *srclen.rw,srcaddr.ab,escape.rb,*
                        tableaddr.ab,destlen.rw,destaddr.ab

Operation   *deststr*[i] ← translated *srcstr*[i] while (i LEQ MIN(*srclen*,*destlen*))
                    AND ((translated *srcstr*[i]) NEQL *escape*)

where *deststr* is the string defined by *destlen* and *destaddr*, and *srcstr* is the string defined by *srclen* and *srcaddr*

Condition codes   N ← {*srclen* LSS *destlen*}
Z ← {*srclen* EQL *destlen*}
V ← {translation terminated by *escape* character}
C ← {*srclen* LSSU *destlen*}

Operation code   2F   MOVTUC   MOVe Translated Until escape
                                      Character

Description   A character in the source string is translated by using its byte values as an index into the 256-byte table whose address is *tableaddr*, the corresponding entry in the table being the translated value of the byte. The source string defined by the length and base address operands *srclen* and *srcaddr* is translated and moved to the destination string defined by the length and base address operands *destlen* and *destaddr*, until:

1. the source string or destination string is exhausted; or
2. the translated character is equal to the escape character *escape*, in which case the PSW V-bit is set

Exceptions   None

Side effects   Upon execution of MOVTUC:

R0 ← number of bytes in the source string not translated and moved, including the byte which caused the escape
R1 ← address of the byte in the source string which resulted in exhaustion of the destination string or termination by escape; otherwise, R1 is given the value *srcaddr* + SEXT(*srclen*)
R2 ← 0

R3 ← address *tableaddr*

R4 ← number of bytes remaining in the destination string

R5 ← address of the byte in the destination string that would have received the escape character, or the value *destaddr* + SEXT(*srclen*) if the source string was exhausted; otherwise, R5 is given the value *destaddr* + SEXT(*destlen*)

Comments The source and destination strings may overlap without affecting the contents of the destination string only if the source and destination strings have identical base addresses.

The source string and the translation table may not overlap.

MOVZ   *MOVe Zero* extended numerical quantities

Format MOVZxy   *src.rx,dest.wy*

Operation *dest* ← ZEXT(*src*)

Condition codes
$N \leftarrow 0$
$Z \leftarrow \{dest \text{ EQL } 0\}$
$V \leftarrow 0$
$C \leftarrow C$

Operation codes
9B	MOVZBW	MOVe Zero extended Byte to Word
9A	MOVZBL	MOVe Zero extended Byte to Longword
3C	MOVZWL	MOVe Zero extended Word to Longword

Description The source operand byte or word *src* is moved to the low-order byte or word of the destination operand *dest*. The remaining high-order bits of *dest* are replaced with 0s.

Exceptions None

Comment MOVZ converts an unsigned integer to a numerically equal unsigned integer of larger datatype.

MUL   *MUL*tiply operands

Format
MULx2   *multr.rx,prod.mx*   (2-operand)
MULx3   *multr.rx,multd.rx,prod.wx*   (3-operand)

Operation
prod ← *prod* * *multr*   (2-operand)
prod ← *multr* * *multd*   (3-operand)

Condition codes
$N \leftarrow \{prod \text{ LSS } 0\}$
$Z \leftarrow \{prod \text{ EQL } 0\}$
$V \leftarrow \{integer\ overflow\}$ (integer)
$V \leftarrow \{floating\ overflow\}$ (floating)
$C \leftarrow 0$

Operation codes
84	MULB2	MULtiply Byte, 2-operand
85	MULB3	MULtiply Byte, 3-operand
A4	MULW2	MULtiply Word, 2-operand
A5	MULW3	MULtiply Word, 3-operand
C4	MULL2	MULtiply Longword, 2-operand

C5	MULL3	MULtiply Longword, 3-operand
44	MULF2	MULtiply F_floating, 2-operand
45	MULF3	MULtiply F_floating, 3-operand
64	MULD2	MULtiply D_floating, 2-operand
65	MULD3	MULtiply D_floating, 3-operand
44FD	MULG2	MULtiply G_floating, 2-operand
45FD	MULG3	MULtiply G_floating, 3-operand
64FD	MULH2	MULtiply H_floating, 2-operand
65FD	MULH3	MULtiply H_floating, 3-operand

Description

In the 2-operand form, the multiplier operand *multr* is multiplied by the product operand *prod* and the result replaces the product operand.

In the 3-operand form, the multiplier operand *multr* is multiplied by the multiplicand operand *multd* and the result replaces the product operand *prod*.

Exceptions

Integer overflow
Floating-point overflow
Floating-point underflow
Reserved operand

Comments

For the floating-point operations, the product is rounded.

Integer overflow occurs if the upper half of the double-length product is different from the extension of the sign bit of the lower half of the product.

MULP   *MUL*tiply Packed decimal strings

Format

MULP   *multrlen.rw,multraddr.rw,*
multdlen.rw,multdaddr.ab,
prodlen.rw,prodaddr.ab

Operation

*prodstr ← multdstr * multrstr*

where *prodstr* is the packed decimal string defined by *prodlen* and *prodaddr*, *multdstr* is the packed decimal string defined by *multdlen* and *multdaddr*, and *multrstr* is the packed decimal string defined by *multrlen* and *multraddr*

Condition codes

N ← {*prodstr* LSS 0}
Z ← {*prodstr* EQL 0}
V ← {decimal overflow}
C ← 0

Operation code

25   MULP   MULtiply Packed decimal strings

Description

The packed decimal multiplicand string defined by the length and base address operands *multdlen* and *multdaddr* is multiplied by the packed decimal multiplier string defined by the length and base address operands *multrlen* and *multraddr*. The result replaces the packed decimal product string defined by the length and base address operands *prodlen* and *prodaddr*.

Exceptions

Decimal overflow
Reserved operand

Side effects

Upon execution of MULP:
R0 ← 0
R1 ← address of the byte containing the most-significant digit of the multiplier string

R2 ← 0

R3 ← address of the byte containing the most-significant digit of the multiplicand string

R4 ← 0

R5 ← address of the byte containing the most-significant digit of the product string

Comment   The product string, the condition codes, and the contents of R0 to R5 are unpredictable if the product string overlaps either the multiplier or multiplicand string, or if either string contains an invalid four-digit decimal code.

NOP   *No OPeration*

Format	NOP
Operation	None
Condition codes	N ← N
	Z ← Z
	V ← V
	C ← C
Operation code	01 NOP No OPeration
Description	NOP results in no operation being performed. However, it does require a complete fetch and execution cycle.
Exceptions	None

POPR   *POP Registers*

Format	POPR *mask.rw*
Operation	R[i] ← (SP)+ while (i LEQ 14) AND (*mask⟨i⟩* EQL 1).
Condition codes	N ← N
	Z ← Z
	V ← V
	C ← C
Operation code	BA POPR POP Registers
Description	The mask word *mask* is scanned from bit 0 up to bit 14. For each bit which is on, the longword on top of the stack is popped into the corresponding general register. Bit 15 is unused.
Exceptions	None

PUSHA   *PUSH Address*

Format	PUSHA *src.ax*
Operation	−(SP) ← *src*

Condition codes	N ← {*src* LSS 0}
	Z ← {*src* EQL 0}
	V ← 0
	C ← C

Operation codes	9F	PUSHAB	PUSH Address Byte
	3F	PUSHAW	PUSH Address Word
	DF	PUSHAL	PUSH Address Longword
	7F	PUSHAQ	PUSH Address Quadword
	7FFD	PUSHAO	PUSH Address Octaword
	DF	PUSHAF	PUSH Address F_floating
	7F	PUSHAD	PUSH Address D_floating
	7F	PUSHAG	PUSH Address G_floating
	7FFD	PUSHAH	PUSH Address H_floating

Description   The source operand *src* is pushed onto the stack. (Note that the source operand is a longword address regardless of the operation context.)

Exceptions   None

PUSHL   *PUSH Longword on the stack*

Format   PUSHL   *src.rl*

Operation $-(SP) \leftarrow src$

Condition codes	N ← {*src* LSS 0}
	Z ← {*src* EQL 0}
	V ← 0
	C ← C

Operation code   DD   PUSHL   PUSH Longword on the stack

Description   The longword operand *src* is pushed onto the stack.

Exceptions   None

PUSHR   *PUSH Registers*

Format   PUSHR   *mask.rw*

Operation $-(SP) \leftarrow c(R[i])$ while (*i* LEQ 14) AND (*mask*⟨*i*⟩ EQL 1).

Condition codes	N ← N
	Z ← Z
	V ← V
	C ← C

Operation code   BB   PUSHR   PUSH Registers

Description   The mask word *mask* is scanned from bit 14 down to bit 0. For each bit which is on, the contents of the corresponding general register is pushed onto the stack. Bit 15 is unused.

Exceptions   None

REI   *Return from Exception or Interrupt*

Format   REI

Operation

$savedPC \leftarrow (SP)+;$
$savedPSL \leftarrow (SP)+;$
if PSL$\langle 26 \rangle$ EQL 1 then ISP $\leftarrow$ SP
else CMSP $\leftarrow$ SP;
if PSL$\langle 30 \rangle$ EQL 1 then $savedPSL\langle 30 \rangle \leftarrow 1;$
PC $\leftarrow$ c($savedPC$);
PSL $\leftarrow$ c($savedPSL$);
if PSL$\langle 26 \rangle$ EQL 0 then SP $\leftarrow$ CMSP;
if PSL$\langle 26 \rangle$ EQL 0 then
    if PSL$\langle 25:24 \rangle$ GEQU AST-level then request IPL2 interrupt.
A reserved operand fault occurs if any of the following conditions is true:
    $savedPSL\langle 25:24 \rangle$ LSSU PSL$\langle 31 \rangle$;
    ($savedPSL\langle 26 \rangle$ EQL 1) AND (PSL$\langle 26 \rangle$ EQL 0);
    ($savedPSL\langle 26 \rangle$ EQL 1) AND ($savedPSL\langle 25:24 \rangle$ NEQ 0);
    ($savedPSL\langle 26 \rangle$ EQL 1) AND
      ($savedPSL\langle 20:16 \rangle$ EQL 0);
    ($savedPSL\langle 20:16 \rangle$ GTRU 0) AND
      ($savedPSL\langle 25:24 \rangle$ NEQ 0);
    $savedPSL\langle 23:22 \rangle$ LSSU $savedPSL\langle 25:24 \rangle$;
    $savedPSL\langle 20:16 \rangle$ GTRU PSL$\langle 20:16 \rangle$;
    $savedPSL\langle 29:28 \rangle$ NEQ 0;
    $savedPSL\langle 21 \rangle$ NEQ 0;
    $savedPSL\langle 15:8 \rangle$ NEQ 0.

Condition codes

N $\leftarrow savedPSL\langle 3 \rangle$
Z $\leftarrow savedPSL\langle 2 \rangle$
V $\leftarrow savedPSL\langle 1 \rangle$
C $\leftarrow savedPSL\langle 0 \rangle$

Operation code   02   REI   Return from Exception or Interrupt

Description

The stack is popped into two temporary longwords, *savedPC* and *savedPSL*.
The bits of *savedPSL* are checked for validity. The current stack pointer is
saved, and a new stack pointer is assigned based on the current interrupt stack
flag and current mode bits (bits 26 and 25:24, respectively). A check is made
for any pending Asynchronous System Traps (ASTs). Finally, the saved PC
and PSW are restored, so that execution resumes at the point of exception or
interruption.

Exception   Reserved operand

Comment

The description of REI given above is quite complex and detailed, and it refers
to concepts not explained in the text. To the programmer who wishes to use
REI simply to "Return from Exception" in a condition handler, REI can be
thought of as taking the actions:
PC $\leftarrow$ (SP)+
PSL $\leftarrow$ (SP)+

REMQUE   *REMove entry from QUEue*

Format

REMQUE   *entry.ab,addr.ab*

Operation

c(c(*entry* + 4)) ← c(*entry*);
c(c(*entry*) + 4) ← c(*entry* + 4);
addr ← *entry*.

Condition codes

N ← {c(*entry*) LSS c(*entry* + 4)}
Z ← {c(*entry*) EQL c(*entry* + 4)}
V ← {*entry* EQL c(*entry* + 4)}
C ← {c(*entry*) LSSU c(*entry* + 4)}

Operation code

0F   REMQUE   REMove entry from QUEue

Description

The queue entry whose address is *entry* is removed from the queue, and its address is saved in the address operand *addr*. If the queue was empty, the PSW V-bit is set; otherwise, it is cleared. If the queue is empty after removal of the specified entry, the PSW Z-bit is set, and it is cleared otherwise.

Exceptions

None

Comments

Prior to the start of execution of REMQUE, all memory references are verified for permitted access. If the user has access to these locations, execution of REMQUE begins and goes to completion. (In this way, a memory management exception cannot leave the queue in a partially altered state.)
REMQUE is a noninterruptible instruction.

RET   *RETurn from called procedure*

Format

RET

Operation

SP ← c(FP);
temp ← (SP) + ;
restore contents of AP, FP, and PC;
restore contents of general registers;
restore stack pointer (drop SP alignment);
if CALLS, remove argument list;
restore c(PSW).

Condition codes

N ← *temp*⟨3⟩
Z ← *temp*⟨2⟩
V ← *temp*⟨1⟩
C ← *temp*⟨0⟩

Operation code

04   RET   RETurn from called procedure

Description

After SP is restored from FP, the top of the stack is popped into a longword, *temp*. The saved values of AP, FP, and PC are popped from the stack. *temp*⟨27:16⟩ is used as a register mask for the restoration of general register contents from the stack. The stack pointer's original value is restored by replacing SP⟨1:0⟩ with *temp*⟨31:30⟩. If *temp*⟨29⟩ EQL 1 (that is, if the procedure was invoked with CALLS), the argument list is removed from the stack by popping the longword argument count from the stack, multiplying the unsigned low-order byte of this longword by 4, and adding the result to c(SP).

Exception	Reserved operand
Comment	RET is used to return from procedures invoked with CALLG and CALLS.

ROTL   *ROTate Longword*

Format	ROTL *count.rb,src.rl,dest.wl*
Operation	*dest* ← *src*, rotated *count* bits
Condition codes	N ← {*dest* LSS 0} Z ← {*dest* EQL 0} V ← 0 C ← C
Operation code	9C ROTL ROTate Longword
Description	The longword source operand *src* is rotated logically the number of bits specified by the count operand *count*. If *count* is positive, the rotation is to the left (counterclockwise); if *count* is negative, the rotation is to the right (clockwise). The destination operand *dest* receives the rotated longword; the source operand is unaffected.
Exceptions	None

RSB   *Return from SuBroutine*

Format	RSB
Operation	PC ← (SP)+
Condition codes	N ← N Z ← Z V ← V C ← C
Operation code	05 RSB Return from SuBroutine
Description	The longword on top of the stack is popped into the program counter.
Exceptions	None
Comment	RSB is used to return from subroutines invoked with BSBB, BSBW, and JSB.

SBWC   *SuBtract With Carry*

Format	SBWC *subtr.rl,diff.ml*
Operation	*diff* ← *diff* − *subtr* − c(C)

Condition codes	$N \leftarrow \{diff\ \text{LSS}\ 0\}$
	$Z \leftarrow \{diff\ \text{EQL}\ 0\}$
	$V \leftarrow \{\text{integer overflow}\}$
	$C \leftarrow \{\text{borrow from most-significant bit}\}$
Operation code	D9 SBWC SuBtract With Carry
Description	The subtrahend operand *subtr* and the PSW C-bit are subtracted from the difference operand *diff*, the result replacing *diff*. The two subtractions are performed simultaneously.
Exception	Integer overflow
Comment	SBWC implements multiple-precision subtractions and decrements.

SCANC   *SCAN* Character string

Format	SCANC *len.rw,addr.ab,tableaddr.ab,mask.rb*
Operation	Scan the bytes of *str* until
	((translated byte) AND *mask*) NEQL 0
	where *str* is the string defined by length *len* and base address *addr*
Condition codes	$N \leftarrow 0$
	$Z \leftarrow \{c(R0)\ \text{EQL}\ 0\}$
	$V \leftarrow 0$
	$C \leftarrow 0$
Operation code	2A SCANC SCAN Character string
Description	A character in the string is translated by using its byte value as an index into the 256-byte table whose address is *tableaddr*, the corresponding entry in the table being the translated value of the byte. The character string defined by the length and base address operands *len* and *addr* is translated, byte by byte, until the translated byte, ANDed with the mask byte *mask*, is nonzero.
Exceptions	None
Side effects	Upon execution of SCANC:
	R0 ← number of bytes remaining in the string, including the byte which resulted in the nonzero ANDing with the mask byte
	R1 ← address of the byte in *str* which produced a nonzero AND with the mask byte; or if no such byte is found in the string, R1 is given the value *addr* + SEXT(*len*)
	R2 ← 0
	R3 ← address *addr*
Comment	If *len* EQL 0, the PSW Z-bit is set.

SKPC   *SKiP* Character

Format	SKPC *char.rb,len.rw,addr.ab*
Operation	Scan *str* for the first instance of a byte different from the byte *char*, and set c(R0), c(R1), and the condition codes accordingly

where *str* is the byte string whose beginning address is *addr* and whose length in bytes is *len*

Condition codes	$N \leftarrow 0$ $Z \leftarrow \{c(R0) \text{ EQL } 0\}$ $V \leftarrow 0$ $C \leftarrow 0$
Operation code	3B SKPC SKiP Character
Description	The byte string whose beginning address is *addr* is compared, byte by byte, with the byte whose value is *char*, up to and including *len* bytes. If a byte different from the specified character is located, the PSW Z-bit is cleared; otherwise, the Z-bit is set.
Exceptions	None
Side effects	Upon execution of SKPC: $R0 \leftarrow$ number of bytes which remain in the string, including the byte at which a difference from the specified byte was detected; if no such byte is located, R0 is set to 0 $R1 \leftarrow$ address in the string at which the first byte different from the specified byte *char* was located; if none such is located, R1 is set to *addr* + SEXT(*len*)
Comment	The PSW Z-bit is cleared if *len* EQL 0.

SOB   *Subtract One and Branch*

Format	SOBccc *index.ml,disp.bb*

Operation	$index \leftarrow index - 1;$ (SOBGEQ)
	if (*index* GEQ 0) then
	$PC \leftarrow c(PC) + \text{SEXT}(disp);$
	
	$index \leftarrow index - 1;$ (SOBGTR)
	if (*index* GTR 0) then
	$PC \leftarrow c(PC) + \text{SEXT}(disp).$

Condition codes	$N \leftarrow \{index \text{ LSS } 0\}$ $Z \leftarrow \{index \text{ EQL } 0\}$ $V \leftarrow \{\text{integer overflow}\}$ $C \leftarrow C$

Operation codes	F4 SOBGEQ Subtract One and Branch if Greater
	                     than or EQual
	F5 SOBGTR Subtract One and Branch if GreaTeR
	                     than

Description	The number 1 is subtracted from the index operand *index*. If the result is GEQ 0 (for SOBGEQ) or GTR 0 (for SOBGTR), the displacement operand *disp* is sign extended to a longword and added to c(PC); otherwise, no branch is taken.
Exception	Integer overflow
Comment	Integer overflow occurs only in the case that *index* is the largest negative integer.

SPANC   *SPAN* Character string

Format

SPANC   *len.rw,addr.ab,tableaddr.ab,mask.rb*

Operation

Scan the bytes of *str* until
((translated byte) AND *mask*) EQL 0
where *str* is the string defined by length *len* and base address *addr*

Condition codes

$N \leftarrow 0$
$Z \leftarrow \{c(R0) \text{ EQL } 0\}$
$V \leftarrow 0$
$C \leftarrow 0$

Operation code

2B   SPANC   SPAN Character string

Description

A character in the string is translated by using its byte value as an index into the 256-byte table whose address is *tableaddr*, the corresponding entry in the table being the translated value of the byte. The character string defined by the length and base address operands *len* and *addr* is translated, byte by byte, until the translated byte, ANDed with the mask byte *mask*, is zero.

Exceptions

None

Side effects

Upon execution of SPANC:

$R0 \leftarrow$ number of bytes remaining in the string, including the byte which resulted in the zero ANDing with the mask byte
$R1 \leftarrow$ address of the byte in *str* which produced a zero AND with the mask byte; or if no such byte is found in the string, R1 is given the value *addr* + SEXT(*len*)
$R2 \leftarrow 0$
$R3 \leftarrow$ address *addr*

Comment

If *len* EQL 0, the PSW Z-bit is set.

SUB   *SUBtract operands*

Format

SUBx2 *sub.rx,diff.mx*		(2-operand)
SUBx3 *sub.rx,min.rx,diff.wx*		(3-operand)

Operation

diff $\leftarrow$ *diff* − *sub*	(2-operand)
diff $\leftarrow$ *min* − *sub*	(3-operand)

Condition codes

$N \leftarrow \{diff \text{ LSS } 0\}$
$Z \leftarrow \{diff \text{ EQL } 0\}$
$V \leftarrow \{\text{integer or floating overflow}\}$
$C \leftarrow \{\text{borrow from most-significant bit}\}$ (integer)
$C \leftarrow 0$ (floating point)

Operation codes

82	SUBB2	SUBtract Byte, 2-operand
83	SUBB3	SUBtract Byte, 3-operand
A2	SUBW2	SUBtract Word, 2-operand
A3	SUBW3	SUBtract Word, 3-operand
C2	SUBL2	SUBtract Longword, 2-operand

C3	SUBL3	SUBtract Longword, 3-operand
42	SUBF2	SUBtract F_floating, 2-operand
43	SUBF3	SUBtract F_floating, 3-operand
62	SUBD2	SUBtract D_floating, 2-operand
63	SUBD3	SUBtract D_floating, 3-operand
42FD	SUBG2	SUBtract G_floating, 2-operand
43FD	SUBG3	SUBtract G_floating, 3-operand
62FD	SUBH2	SUBtract H_floating, 2-operand
63FD	SUBH3	SUBtract H_floating, 3-operand

Description

In its 2-operand form, the subtrahend operand *sub* is subtracted from the difference operand *diff* and the result replaces *diff*.

In its 3-operand form, the subtrahend operand *sub* is subtracted from the minuend operand *min*, and the result replaces the difference operand *diff*.

Exceptions

Integer overflow
Floating-point overflow
Floating-point underflow
Reserved operand

Comment

Floating-point sums are rounded.

SUBP   *SUBtract Packed decimal strings*

Format

SUBP4   *sublen.rw,subaddr.ab,*   (4-operand)
                    difflen.rw,diffaddr.ab

SUBP6   *sublen.rw,subaddr.ab,*   (6-operand)
                    minlen.rw,minaddr.ab,
                    difflen.rw,diffaddr.ab

Operation

$diff \leftarrow diff - sub$ (4-operand)
$diff \leftarrow min - sub$ (6-operand)

Condition codes

$N \leftarrow \{diff \text{ LSS } 0\}$
$Z \leftarrow \{diff \text{ EQL } 0\}$
$V \leftarrow \{\text{decimal overflow}\}$
$C \leftarrow 0$

Operation codes

| 22 | SUBP4 | SUBtract Packed 4-operand |
| 23 | SUBP6 | SUBtract Packed 6-operand |

Description

For SUBP4, the string specified by the subtrahend length *sublen* and address *subaddr* operands is subtracted from the string specified by the difference length *difflen* and address *diffaddr* operands, the result replacing the later string.

For SUBP6, the string specified by the subtrahend length *sublen* and address *subaddr* is subtracted from the string specified by the minuend length *minlen* and address *minaddr*, and the result is stored in the string specified by the difference length *difflen* and address *diffaddr* operands.

Exceptions

Decimal overflow
Reserved operand

Side effects

Upon execution of SUBP4:
$R0 \leftarrow 0$

R1 ← address of the byte containing the most-significant digit of the subtrahend string

R2 ← 0

R3 ← address of the byte containing the most-significant digit of the difference string

Upon execution of SUBP6:

R0 ← 0

R1 ← address of the byte containing the most-significant digit of the subtrahend string

R2 ← 0

R3 ← address of the byte containing the most-significant digit of the minuend string

R4 ← 0

R5 ← address of the byte containing the most-significant digit of the difference string

Comment   The difference string, condition codes, and the contents of R0 to R3 (or R0 to R5 in the case of SUBP6) are unpredictable if the difference string overlaps the minuend or subtrahend string, or if any string contains an invalid 4-bit decimal code.

TST   *TeST* operand

Format   TSTx   *src.rx*

Operation   *src* − 0

Condition codes   N ← {*src* LSS 0}
Z ← {*src* EQL 0}
V ← 0
C ← 0

Operation codes

95	TSTB	TeST Byte
B5	TSTW	TeST Word
D5	TSTL	TeST Longword
53	TSTF	TeST F_floating
73	TSTD	TeST D_floating
53FD	TSTG	TeST G_floating
73FD	TSTH	TeST H_floating

Description   The condition codes are set according to the contents of the source operand *src*.

Exceptions   None (integer)
Reserved operand (floating point)

XOR   *eXclusive OR*

Format   XORx2   *mask.rx,dest.mx*   (2-operand)
XORx3   *mask.rx,src.rx,dest.wx*   (3-operand)

Operation   *dest* ← *dest* XOR *mask*   (2-operand)
dest ← *src* XOR *mask*   (3-operand)

Condition codes	$N \leftarrow \{dest \text{ LSS } 0\}$
	$Z \leftarrow \{dest \text{ EQL } 0\}$
	$V \leftarrow 0$
	$C \leftarrow C$

Operation codes	8C	XORB2	eXclusive OR Byte, 2-operand
	8D	XORB3	eXclusive OR Byte, 3-operand
	AC	XORW2	eXclusive OR Word, 2-operand
	AD	XORW3	eXclusive OR Word, 3-operand
	CC	XORL2	eXclusive OR Longword, 2-operand
	CD	XORL3	eXclusive OR Longword, 3-operand

Description In the 2-operand form, the destination and mask operands *dest* and *mask* are EXCLUSIVE-ORed, the result replacing the destination operand.

In the 3-operand form, the source and mask operands *src* and *mask* are EXCLUSIVE-ORed, the result replacing the destination operand *dest*.

Exceptions None

A.4 THE *VAX* INSTRUCTION SET IN OPERATION CODE ORDER

Listed below are the operation codes and mnemonics for the VAX operations. Those shown in parentheses are not described in Section A.3; their descriptions may be found in the Digital Equipment Corporation *VAX Architecture Handbook*. Operation codes not listed represent **reversed instructions**.

Opcode	Mnemonic	Opcode	Mnemonic	Opcode	Mnemonic
00	HALT	17	JMP	2E	MOVTC
01	NOP	18	BGEQ	2F	MOVTUC
02	REI	19	BLSS	30	BSBW
(03	BPT)	1A	BGTRU	31	BRW
04	RET	1B	BLEQU	32	CVTWL
05	RSB	1C	BVC	33	CVTWB
(06	LDPCTX)	1D	BVS	34	MOVP
(07	SVPCTX)	1E	BGEQU	35	CMPP3
08	CVTPS	IF	BLSSU	36	CVTPL
09	CVTSP	20	ADDP4	37	CMPP4
0A	INDEX	21	ADDP6	(38	EDITPC)
(0B	CRC)	22	SUBP4	39	MATCHC
(0C	PROBER)	23	SUBP6	3A	LOCC
(0D	PROBEW)	24	CVTPT	3B	SKPC
0E	INSQUE	25	MULP	3C	MOVZWL
0F	REMQUE	26	CVTTP	3D	ACBW
10	BSBB	27	DIVP	3E	MOVAW
11	BRB	28	MOVC3	3F	PUSHAW
12	BNEQ	29	CMPC3	40	ADDF2
13	BEQL	2A	SCANC	41	ADDF3
14	BGTR	2B	SPANC	42	SUBF2
15	BLEQ	2C	MOVC5	43	SUBF3
16	JSB	2D	CMPC5	44	MULF2

Opcode	Mnemonic	Opcode	Mnemonic	Opcode	Mnemonic
45	MULF3				
46	DIVF2	79	ASHQ	AD	XORW3
47	DIVF3	7A	EMUL	AE	MNEGW
48	CVTFB	7B	EDIV	(AF	CASEW)
49	CVTFW	7C	CLRQ	B0	MOVW
4A	CVTFL	7D	MOVQ	B1	CMPW
4B	CVTRFL	7E	MOVAQ	B2	MCOMW
4C	CVTBF	7F	PUSHAQ	B3	BITW
4D	CVTWF	80	ADDB2	B4	CLRW
4E	CVTLF	81	ADDB3	B5	TSTW
4F	ACBF	82	SUBB2	B6	INCW
50	MOVF	83	SUBB3	B7	DECW
51	CMPF	84	MULB2	B8	BISPSW
52	MNEGF	85	MULB3	B9	BICPSW
53	TSTF	86	DIVB2	BA	POPR
(54	EMODF)	87	DIVB3	BB	PUSHR
(55	POLYF)	88	BISB2	(BC	CHMK)
56	CVTFD	89	BISB3	(BD	CHME)
		8A	BICB2	(BE	CHMS)
(58	ADAWI)	8B	BICB3	(BF	CHMU)
		8C	XORB2	C0	ADDL2
		8D	XORB3	C1	ADDL3
		8E	MNEGB	C2	SUBL2
(5C	INSQHI)	(8F	CASEB)	C3	SUBL3
(5D	INSQTI)	90	MOVB	C4	MULL2
(5E	REMQHI)	91	CMPB	C5	MULL3
(5F	REMQTI)	92	MCOMB	C6	DIVL2
		93	BITB	C7	DIVL3
60	ADDD2	94	CLRB	C8	BISL2
61	ADDD3	95	TSTB	C9	BISL3
62	SUBD2	96	INCB	CA	BICL2
63	SUBD3	97	DECB	CB	BICL3
64	MULD2	98	CVTBL	CC	XORL2
65	MULD3	99	CVTBW	CD	XORL3
66	DIVD2	9A	MOVZBL	CE	MNEGL
67	DIVD3	9B	MOVZBW	(CF	CASEL)
68	CVTDB	9C	ROTL	D0	MOVL
69	CVTDW	9D	ACBB	D1	CMPL
6A	CVTDL	9E	MOVAB	D2	MCOML
6B	CVTRDL	9F	PUSHAB	D3	BITL
6C	CVTBD	A0	ADDW2	D4	CLRL
6D	CVTWD	A1	ADDW3	D5	TSTL
6E	CVTLD	A2	SUBW2	D6	INCL
6F	ACBD	A3	SUBW3	D7	DECL
70	MOVD	A4	MULW2	D8	ADWC
71	CMPD	A5	MULW3	D9	SBWC
72	MNEGD	A6	DIVW2	(DA	MTPR)
73	TSTD	A7	DIVW3	(DB	MFPR)
74	EMODD	A8	BISW2	DC	MOVPSL
(75	POLYD)	A9	BISW3	DD	PUSHL
76	CVTDF	AA	BICW2	DE	MOVAL
		AB	BICW3	DF	PUSHAL
78	ASHL	AC	XORW2		

Opcode	Mnemonic	Opcode	Mnemonic	Opcode	Mnemonic
E0	BBS	45FD	MULG3		
E1	BBC	46FD	DIVG2		
E2	BBSS	47FD	DIVG3	7CFD	CLRO
E3	BBCS	48FD	CVTGB	7DFD	MOVO
E4	BBSC	49FD	CVTGW	7EFD	MOVAO
E5	BBCC	4AFD	CVTGL	7FFD	PUSHAO
(E6	BBSSI)	4BFD	CVTRGL		
(E7	BBCCI)	4CFD	CVTBG		
E8	BLBS	4DFD	CVTWG		
E9	BLBC	4EFD	CVTLG		
EA	FFS	4FFD	ACBG		
EB	FFC	50FD	MOVG		
EC	CMPV	51FD	CMPG		
ED	CMPZV	52FD	MNEGG		
EE	EXTV	53FD	TSTG	98FD	CVTFH
EF	EXTZV	(54FD	EMODG)	99FD	CVTFG
F0	INSV	(55FD	POLYG)		
F1	ACBL	56FD	CVTGH		
F2	AOBLSS				
F3	AOBLEQ				
F4	SOBGEQ				
F5	SOBGTR				
F6	CVTLB				
F7	CVTLW				
F8	ASHP	60FD	ADDH2		
F9	CVTLP	61FD	ADDH3	F6FD	CVTHF
FA	CALLG	62FD	SUBH2	F7FD	CVTHD
FB	CALLS	63FD	SUBH3		
(FC	XFC)	64FD	MULH2		
		65FD	MULH3		
		66FD	DIVH2		
32FD	CVTDH	67FD	DIVH3		
33FD	CVTGF	68FD	CVTHB		
		69FD	CVTHW		
		6AFD	CVTHL		
		6BFD	CVTRHL		
		6CFD	CVTBH		
		6DFD	CVTWH		
		6EFD	CVTLH		
		6FFD	ACBH		
		70FD	MOVH		
		71FD	CMPH		
		72FD	MNEGH		
		73FD	TSTH		
		(74FD	EMODH)		
40FD	ADDG2	(75FD	POLYH)		
41FD	ADDG3	76FD	CVTHG		
42FD	SUBG2				
43FD	SUBG3				
44FD	MULG2			(FDFF	BUGL)
				(FEFF	BUGW)

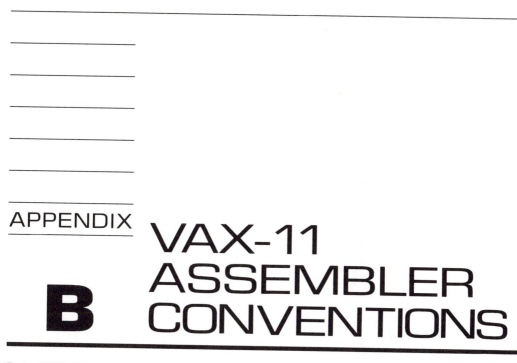

VAX-11 ASSEMBLER CONVENTIONS

B

B.1 INTRODUCTION

This appendix summaries the VAX-11 assembler conventions that pertain to the text. Those assembler capabilities and conventions which are not referenced here may be found in the Digital Equipment Corporation *VAX-11 MACRO Language Reference Manual*.

B.2 THE *VAX* CHARACTER SET

The characters recognized by the VAX assembler are listed in Appendix C and are essentially those found on an ASCII-coded computer terminal.

B.3 SPECIAL CHARACTERS

The characters in the general character set that are of special significance to the VAX assembler are summarized in Figure B.3.1. Several of these are discussed in subsequent sections in this appendix.

FIGURE B.3.1

Symbol	Assembler interpretation
Space	Separator between instruction fields or macro arguments
Tab	Separator between instruction fields or macro arguments
,	(comma) Separator between operands in instruction operand field, or between macro arguments
.	(period) Location counter symbol, decimal point, or symbol name character
:	(colon) Symbolic label terminator
::	(double colon) Symbolic label terminator that specifies the symbol as global
=	(equal sign) Direct assignment of a value to a symbol, or macro keyword argument symbol
= =	(double equal sign) Direct assignment of a value to a symbol that specifies the symbol as global
#	(number sign) Immediate expression symbol
@	(commercial-at) Deferred addressing symbol, or arithmetic shift operator
;	(semicolon) Start-of-comment symbol
(. . .)	(parentheses) Deferred register addressing mode indicator
⟨...⟩	(angle brackets) Grouping symbols, or enclosing symbols for embedded numerical argument in a .ASCIx directive
[...]	(square brackets) Index mode register symbol, or repeat count indicator
+	(plus sign) Addition symbol, post-autoincrement mode symbol, or unary plus symbol
−	(minus sign) Subtraction symbol, pre-autodecrement mode symbol, unary minus symbol, or line continuation indicator
*	(asterisk) Multiplication symbol
/	(slash) Division symbol
^	(circumflex) Unary operator symbol
'	(apostrophe) Macro argument concatenation symbol
?	(question mark) Automatically created local label symbol in macro argument
&	(ampersand) Logical AND operator
!	(exclamation mark) Logical OR operator
\	(backslash) Logical EXCLUSIVE-OR operator

B.4 SOURCE STATEMENT FORMAT

Each line of source code input to the assembler is of the form

$$label:\quad op\quad opnd_1, \ldots, opnd_n\quad ;comment$$

The source line components have the following properties.

label If a label is included in a line of source code, it must be the first entry on the line, and it must be followed by a colon or double colon. More than one label may be placed on a line, provided that they precede any other source statement component, thus

LABL1: LABL2: LABL3: LABL4:

in which case all labels are assigned the same value.

op   *op* is an assembler operation mnemonic, or an assembler directive mnemonic, or the name of a macroinstruction.

opnd$_k$ This field contains 0 or more operation operands or assembler directive arguments, separated by commas, or macroinstruction arguments, separated by commas, spaces, or tab characters.

comment   Any part of a line (including the entire line) which is preceded by a semicolon is taken as a comment, and except for being reproduced on the program listing, it is ignored by the assembler. (The single exception is a semicolon occurring within ASCII code generation delimiters, in which cases the symbol is taken as a literal semicolon.)

All components of the source line are optional, except that if an operand is present, an operation or directive mnemonic must be included also.

B.5 SYMBOLS

Symbols are of two types, *permanent symbols* and *user-defined symbols*. The permanent symbols consist of the VAX assembler operation mnemonics, register symbols, and the assembler directives. All other symbols are user defined.

The valid characteristics that may be used in a symbol are

A–Z	the alphabetic characters
0–9	the numerical characters
$	the dollar-sign character
.	the period character
_	the underscore character

A symbol consists of one or more such characters, but must not contain more than 31 characters. The first character of a symbol may *not* be numerical. (The sole exceptions are the *local labels*, in which *all* characters must be numerical, and must be followed by a dollar-sign character.)

A symbol may begin with the period character (.); however, it may *not* consist solely of a period.

With the exception of the name of a macroinstruction, a user-defined symbol is assigned a value either by appearing as a label, in which case it is given the current value of the location counter, or by appearing on the left-hand side of a direct assignment statement. A symbol may be assigned a value by direct assignment (=) more than once, its value at any time being the last value assigned to it. A symbol may *not* appear as a label more than once, nor may it be given a value by appearing as a label *and* by direct assignment. (A user-defined symbol may also be defined by means of the .OPDEF directive. See the *VAX-11 MACRO Language Reference Manual*.)

B.6 NUMBERS

Numbers, either integer, floating point, or packed decimal, are assumed to be in *decimal* radix. The number system base may be altered for an individual number by use of the unary operator, ˆ (see Section B.8).

B.7 THE LOCATION COUNTER

Throughout the assembly process, the assembler maintains a **location counter**, whose value is the address of the *first byte* of the operand currently under assembly. The location counter may be referenced by the period (.) symbol. For example, the assignment statement

$$. = . + n$$

will advance the location counter by n and hence is equivalent to the preferred construction

$$.BLKB \quad n$$

Since the assembler maintains the value of the location counter as the address of the *first* byte of an *operand* throughout that operand's assembly, the location counter does not quite coincide with the value of the program counter *upon execution* of the instruction. For example, the destination of the MOVL instruction

$$0C \; AF \; 52 \; D0 \quad 0226 \quad MOVL \quad R2,. + 14$$

will be the longword at 00000236 = 00000228 + 0000000E.

Although constructions such as

$$BNEQ \quad . + 6$$

to skip around *five* bytes, are valid, they must be used with much care. Subsequent program modifications can alter the desired displacement ($. + 6$ might have to be changed to $. + 9$, for instance), and the appropriate modifications in the displacement might easily be overlooked. Since errors of this nature are frequently quite difficult to locate, such constructions are discouraged.

B.8 THE UNARY OPERATOR, CIRCUMFLEX (ˆ)

The circumflex is combined with another symbol and is used in a variety of ways, which are summarized in Figure B.8.1. We expand briefly on two of these.

The ASCII generation operator, ˆA, may be used to generate the ASCII codes for up to 16 characters, depending on the context of the operation or as-

FIGURE B.8.1

Operator	Operation
ˆB	Specifies that the number immediately following is in *B*inary radix (base 2)
ˆD	Specifies that the number immediately following is in *D*ecimal radix (base 10, the default)
ˆX	Specifies that the number immediately following is in he*X*adecimal radix (base 16)
ˆO	Specifies that the number immediately following is in *O*ctal radix (base 8)
ˆA	Generates an ASCII string, consisting of the codes for the characters immediately following between matching delimiters
ˆC	Generates the ones-complement of the value immediately following
ˆF	Specifies that the number immediately following is in floating-point format
ˆM	Register and/or trap mask word specifier

sembler directive. The format of the operator is

$$ˆA/character\ string/$$

where the slash (/) is used as a delimiter for the string of characters. (Any printing character will serve as the delimiting character.) Figure B.8.2 shows some valid constructions using this operator, and the code generated. Observe that if the number of bytes generated by ˆA is smaller than the size of the receiving field, the assembler fills excess high-order bytes with ASCII NULs (00). If the size of the receiving field is smaller than the number of bytes generated by ˆA, a "data truncation" error results.

The ones-complement operator, ˆC, may be used to generate the ones-complement of the value immediately following. Figure B.8.3 shows some examples of valid constructions and the code generated.

```
                                    4241        .WORD    ^A/AB/

                          00000000 00004241     .QUAD    ^A/AB/

     504F4E4D 4C4B4A49 48474645 44434241        .OCTA    ^A/ABCDEFGHIJKLMNOP/

               54     00434241 8F    D0          MOVL     #^A/ABC/,R4

                      41 8F     80    91          CMPB     (R0)+,#^A/A/
```
Figure B.8.2

```
                    FF7E              .WORD    ^C129

                    D808DFB2          .LONG    ^C^X27F7204D

          80     D8 8F      91         CMPB     #^C^X27,(R0)+

                                      A = 127
          54     FF80 8F     3C        MOVZWL   #^CA,R4
```
Figure B.8.3

B.9 THE CONTINUATION SYMBOL, HYPHEN (-)

A line of source code may be continued onto a second line if the last character (not including comments) on the first line is followed by a hyphen (-). For example, the assembler will treat the lines

```
MOVAL   BUFFER + 8, -     ;Use R10 as pointer
        R10               ;   to data buffer
```

as if they were written as the single line

```
MOVAL   BUFFER + 8,R10    ;Use R10 as pointer to data buffer
```

Line continuation can occur at any point, but user-defined and permanent symbols should not be bisected by the hyphen. The continuation symbol cannot be used to divide a comment over two lines. Thus

```
        ;The current line consists-
         exclusively of a comment
```

should be written as

```
        ;The current line consists
        ;   exclusively of a comment
```

B.10 THE REPEAT COUNT SYMBOL, [...]

A value that enters into a storage allocation directive may be *repeated* any number of times by enclosing the repeat count in square brackets. For example,

```
.WORD   ^X6F4[3]
```

is equivalent to

```
.WORD   ^X^6F4,^X6F4,^X6F4
```

The repeat count may also be an expression. For example, the construction

```
NUM = 27
.BYTE   67[3*NUM/2]
```

will generate 40 bytes, each containing the (decimal) number 67.

B.11 THE ARITHMETIC SHIFT OPERATOR, COMMERCIAL-AT (@)

The arithmetic shift operator @*n* is used as a *suffix* to any expression whose value is known to the assembler. Its effect is to shift the value left or right *n* bits, in the same fashion as the operation ASHL. Positive values of *n* yield left shifts, the vacated bits being replaced by 0s; right shifts replicate the sign bit of the structure. But in shifting to the right, the structure is always interpreted as a *longword*. That is, a byte or word is *zero extended* to a longword, then shifted right (consequently with 0s being replicated in the high-order bit of the longword), and then truncated back down to a byte or word. Thus for bytes and words, the high-order bit is *not* replicated on right shifts. Figure B.11.1 shows some examples and their values, as generated by the assembler.

		0938		.WORD	^X127@3
		16		.BYTE	^B10110010@-3
		0007C000		.LONG	124@12
				A = -4	
	54	01	90	MOVB	#^X10@A,R4
54	80	8F	90	MOVB	#^X10@-A/2,R4
		003F9570		.LONG	^X7F2AC+2@3
		1560		.WORD	^X2AC@4/2
		0AB0		.WORD	^X2AC@<4/2>

Figure B.11.1

B.12 THE LOGICAL OPERATORS *AND* (&), *OR* (!), AND *EXCLUSIVE-OR* (\)

The symbols &, !, and \ will cause the assembler to generate the logical AND, OR, and EXCLUSIVE-OR of values, as illustrated by the examples of Figure B.12.1.

		70FFAC2B		.LONG	^X12A403 ! ^X70FF282A
		82		.BYTE	^B10110010 & ^B11001011
73	8F	70	91	CMPB	-(R0),#^X33 ! ^A/C/
		42E6		.WORD	^XF27A \ ^XB09C

Figure B.12.1

B.13 ASSEMBLER DIRECTIVES

Figure B.13.1 is a summary of the more commonly used assembler directives. Most of these are discussed in detail in Section 8.9. Those which are not, and a few directives which are not listed here, may be found either elsewhere in the text or in the *VAX-11 MACRO Language Reference Manual*.

FIGURE B.13.1

Directive	Argument(s)	Operation
.ADDRESS	adr1, adr2, ...	Generates successive longwords containing the specified addresses
.ALIGN	Keyword	Aligns the assembler's location counter on the natural boundary of the next structure specified by the "keyword," where keyword = BYTE, WORD, LONG, QUAD
.ASCII	String	Generates a block of bytes consisting of the ASCII codes for the characters in the string (enclosed in delimiters)
.ASCIC	String	Same as .ASCII, except the block is preceded by a byte containing the character count
.ASCIZ	String	Same as .ASCII, except that the block is followed by a NUL byte
.BLKA	Expression	Reserves storage for longword addresses
.BLKB	Expression	Reserves storage for byte data
.BLKD	Expression	Reserves storage for double-precision (quadword) floating-point data
.BLKF	Expression	Reserves storage for single-precision (longword) floating-point data
.BLKG	Expression	Reserves storage for G_floating data
.BLKH	Expression	Reserves storage for H_floating data
.BLKL	Expression	Reserves storage for longword data
.BLKO	Expression	Reserves storage for octaword data
.BLKQ	Expression	Reserves storage for quadword data
.BLKW	Expression	Reserves storage for word data
.BYTE	exp1, exp2, ...	Generates successive bytes containing the values of the specified expressions
.D_FLOATING	lit1, lit2, ...	Generates successive double-precision (quadword) floating-point constants containing the values of the specified literal numbers
.DISABLE	arg	Disable a function (arg) previously enabled with the .ENABLE directive
.DOUBLE	lit1, lit2, ...	Same as .D_FLOATING
.ENABLE	arg	Enable the assembler function specified by the argument
.END	[Symbol]	Indicates end of source program; if a symbol is specified as an argument, its value is taken as the module's transfer address
.ENTRY	Symbol, exp	Defines the symbol as the module entry point and declares it to be global; a register/trap entry mask word is created from the expression
.EVEN		Aligns location counter on even address
.EXTERNAL	sym1, sym2, ...	Declares sym1, sym2, ... as external

Directive	Argument(s)	Operation
.F_FLOATING	lit1, lit2, ...	Generates successive single-precision (longword) floating-point constants containing the values of the specified literal numbers
.FLOAT	lit1, lit2, ...	Same as .F_FLOATING
.G_FLOATING	lit1, lit2, ...	Generates successive G_floating constants (quadword) containing the values of the specified literal numbers
.H_FLOATING	lit1, lit2, ...	Generates successive H_floating constants (octaword) containing the values of the specified literal numbers
.IF	cond, arg(s)	Begins a conditional block
.IF_FALSE		Begins an "if-false" subconditional block; appears only within a conditional block
.IF_TRUE		Begins an "if-true" subconditional block; appears only within a conditional block
.IF_TRUE_FALSE		Begins an "if-true-or-false" subconditional block; appears only within a conditional block
.IIF	cond, arg(s), statement	Signifies immediate conditional assembly directive
.LIST	arg1, arg2, ...	Same as .SHOW
.LONG	exp1, exp2, ...	Generates successive longwords containing the values of the specified expressions
.MDELETE	arg	Remove a macroinstruction (arg) from the table of macrodefinitions
.NLIST	arg1, arg2, ...	Same as .NOSHOW
.NOSHOW	arg1, arg2, ...	Disable assembler listing control options (see .SHOW for argument values)
.OCTA	exp1, exp2, ...	Generates successive octawords containing the values of the specified expressions
.ODD		Aligns location counter on odd address
.PACKED	string	Generates packed decimal data, two digits per byte, from the specified decimal string
.PAGE		Forces a new assembler listing page
.PSECT	name, [arg(s)]	Defines a named program section, with attributes
.QUAD	exp1, exp2, ...	Generates successive quadwords containing the values of the specified expressions
.SHOW	arg1, arg2, ...	Enable assembler listing control options according to the following arguments (.NOSHOW is complementary directive)
		CND List unsatisfied conditionals (default is SHOW)
		ME List macro, repeat block expansions (default is NOSHOW)
		MEB List macro, repeat block expansions that generate binary code (default is NOSHOW)
		MC List macro, repeat block calls (default is SHOW)
		MD List macro, repeat block definitions (default is SHOW)
.SUBTITLE	String	The string is placed in the assembly listing table of contents and is printed as the second line of listing on the current and subsequent pages
.TITLE	Name, comment	The name string is the title assigned to the module; the name and comment string are printed at the top of each page of listing

FIGURE B.13.1

Directive	Argument(s)	Operation
.WORD	exp1, exp2, ...	Generates successive words containing the values of the specified expressions

Notes:		
	adr	32-bit address
	arg	Argument
	comment	= string
	cond	Conditional
	exp, expression	Any expression whose relocation insensitive value can be calculated by the assembler
	keyword	One of the values BYTE, WORD, LONG, QUAD
	lit	A literal constant
	name	= string
	string	Any collection of ASCII characters
	sym, symbol	A symbol, whose value is assigned as the location counter or through direct assignment
	[...]	Indicates optional argument

B.14 ASSEMBLY TIME ERRORS

The VAX assembler detects a wide variety of assembly time errors. The more common errors, together with a brief description of the cause, are listed in Figure B.14.1. The remaining errors may be found in the Digital Equipment Corporation *VAX-11 MACRO User's Guide.*

Each error message is in the form

$$\%\text{MACRO-}l\text{-}code, \textit{text}$$

where *l* is the severity level (E = error, W = warning) and *code* is an abbreviation of the error message *text*. For example,

%MACRO-E-NOTENUFOPR, Not enough operands supplied

In Figure B.14.1 we list only the text of the message.

FIGURE B.14.1

Message	Meaning
Address list syntax error	One or more addresses in a .ADDRESS directive is invalid
ASCII string too long	The string in a .ASCIC directive contains more than 255 characters
Assignment syntax error	A direct assignment statement contains a syntax error
Bad format for .ENTRY statement	A .ENTRY directive contains no entry point or entry mask

Message	Meaning
Block directive syntax error	Syntax error in conditional or repeat block
Block expression not absolute	The expression which determines the amount of storage to be set aside by a .BLKx directive is not absolute
Branch destination out of range	Destination displacement not in the range -128 to $+127$
Data list syntax error	Syntax error in a data generation directive (.LONG, .QUAD, etc.)
Data truncation error	Receiving field is too small to hold specified data
Directive syntax error	Syntax error in an assembler directive
Division-by-zero	An expression resulted in division by zero
Entry mask not absolute	A program or procedure entry mask expression is not an absolute number
Floating point syntax error	Syntax error in a floating-point constant
Illegal ASCII argument	A .ASCIx expression does not have matching delimiters
Illegal branch destination	A branch destination is not an address
Illegal character	A character is illegal in the context in which it is used
Illegal character in decimal string	A decimal string contains a character other than a digit from 0 to 9, or a leading plus or minus sign
Illegal expression	Unmatched angle brackets, or invalid use of a unary operator
Illegal mode	Addressing mode is invalid
Illegal register number	A register was not in the range R0 to R12, or was not AP, FP, SP, or PC
Invalid index register	The register used for indexing was PC or was used in the calculation of the base address in an invalid mode
Missing .END statement	The assembler encountered the end of the source file without seeing .END
Multiple definition of label	The same label is defined more than once in the same module
Not enough operands supplied	An operation requires more operands than were supplied
Not a legal listing option	An option for the .SHOW or .NOSHOW directive is illegal
Operand syntax error	An operand has invalid syntax in the specified context
Packed decimal string too long	The .PACKED directive string may not exceed 31 characters
Register operand syntax error	Syntax error in addressing mode
Repeat count not absolute	The value of the repeat count in a data generation directive is not an absolute number
Reserved bits set in entry mask	Bits 12 and/or 13 in entry mask word are set
Symbol declared external	A symbol which was previously declared to be external is used as a label or in a direct assignment statement

Message	Meaning
Symbol exceeds 31 characters	Symbols may be no longer than 31 characters
Symbol is defined in module	A symbol already defined in the module is declared external
Symbol out of phase	The values of a symbol on pass 1 and pass 2 do not agree
This mode may not be indexed	Register, immediate, and literal modes may not be indexed
This register may not be used here	The program counter may not be used in certain addressing modes
Too many operands for instruction	An operation requires fewer operands than were supplied
Undefined symbol	A symbol which is not defined in the module, nor declared as external, is referenced
Undefined transfer address	The transfer address in the .END directive is not defined, or is external
Unrecognized statement	The assembler was unable to locate the operation in the permanent or user-defined symbol table
Unterminated argument	Missing delimiter in string argument

TABLE OF ASCII CODES

C

The table on the following page shows the 7-bit ASCII codes for the VAX character set, in their hexadecimal and decimal representations. Those between (decimal) 0 and 32 are usually referred to as *nonprinting characters*, and we have assigned the customary names to them. Of these, some will be familiar to the reader (for example, NUL, BACKSPACE, CARR. RET. and SPACE), whereas others, introduced in the early days of computing and influenced to a large extent by the first real computer terminal—the Teletypewriter—will not (SOH = Start-Of-Header, SI = Shift-In, RS = Record-Separator, and so on).

Hex	Dec	Character	Hex	Dec	Character	Hex	Dec	Character
00	0	NUL	2B	43	+	56	86	V
01	1	SOH	2C	44	,	57	87	W
02	2	STX	2D	45	-	58	88	X
03	3	EXT	2E	46	.	59	89	Y
04	4	EOT	2F	47	/	5A	90	Z
05	5	ENQ	30	48	0	5B	91	[
06	6	ACK	31	49	1	5C	92	\
07	7	BEL	32	50	2	5D	93	]
08	8	BACKSPACE	33	51	3	5E	94	^
09	9	HORIZ. TAB	34	52	4	5F	95	_
0A	10	LINE FEED	35	53	5	60	96	`
0B	11	VERT. TAB	36	54	6	61	97	a
0C	12	FORM FEED	37	55	7	62	98	b
0D	13	CARR. RET.	38	56	8	63	99	c
0E	14	SO	39	57	9	64	100	d
0F	15	SI	3A	58	:	65	101	e
10	16	DLE	3B	59	;	66	102	f
11	17	DC1	3C	60	⟨	67	103	g
12	18	DC2	3D	61	=	68	104	h
13	19	DC3	3E	62	⟩	69	105	i
14	20	DC4	3F	63	?	6A	106	j
15	21	NAK	40	64	@	6B	107	k
16	22	SYN	41	65	A	6C	108	l
17	23	ETB	42	66	B	6D	109	m
18	24	CAN	43	67	C	6E	110	n
19	25	EM	44	68	D	6F	111	o
1A	26	SUB	45	69	E	70	112	p
1B	27	ESC	46	70	F	71	113	q
1C	28	FS	47	71	G	72	114	r
1D	29	GS	48	72	H	73	115	s
1E	30	RS	49	73	I	74	116	t
1F	31	US	4A	74	J	75	117	u
20	32	SPACE	4B	75	K	76	118	v
21	33	!	4C	76	L	77	119	w
22	34	"	4D	77	M	78	120	x
23	35	#	4E	78	N	79	121	y
24	36	$	4F	79	O	7A	122	z
25	37	%	50	80	P	7B	123	{
26	38	&	51	81	Q	7C	124		
27	39	'	52	82	R	7D	125	}
28	40	(	53	83	S	7E	126	~
29	41	)	54	84	T	7F	127	DELETE
2A	42	*	55	85	U			

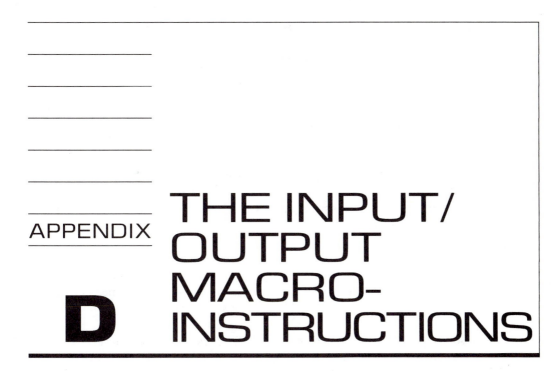

THE INPUT/ OUTPUT MACRO- INSTRUCTIONS

D

D.1 INTRODUCTION

Input to and output from the sample programs in the text are accomplished by *macroinstructions*, which are sequences of standard VAX assembly language instructions packaged under a specific *name*. When a source program that invokes these macroinstructions is assembled, only the name of the macroinstruction is listed, since by default the assembler does not *list* the individual instructions that make up a macroinstruction (although, of course, it *does assemble*—translate to machine code—those instructions). See Chapter 18 for the details of the formation of macroinstructions.

Input and output are essential to meaningful programming. Yet the actual programming involved in "driving" the devices that provide this programmer-computer intercommunication, together with the data conversions required to input and output numbers in various formats, are tasks of sufficient complexity that it would be unreasonable to expect that the novice programmer could manage them. Thus these macroinstructions are supplied to provide terminal input and output without any knowledge about the device itself.

Even though the format of *numerical* data output by the macroinstructions is *fixed*, nonetheless the programmer has some control over the appearance of printed output, as we shall see. Input—either character or numerical—is somewhat more *free-format*.

D.2 BASIC CHARACTER OUTPUT MACROINSTRUCTIONS

There are two basic macroinstructions which provide the user with the capability of printing single characters or strings of characters. There is one that simply generates a ⟨carriage-return/line-feed⟩ combination (called a "New Line"), and a macroinstruction to terminate program execution and return control to the VAX operating system is also supplied. These are described in detail below.

$EXIT The macroinstruction $EXIT, which has no arguments, terminates program execution and returns control of the computer to the VAX operating system.

$O.CHR The macroinstruction $O.CHR sends a *single* character to the terminal. Its format is

$$\text{\$O.CHR} \quad char.rb$$

The character whose ASCII code is the contents of the byte specified by the operand is printed.

$O.STR The macroinstruction $O.STR sends a string of characters to the terminal, where a **character string** is defined to be a collection of contiguous bytes, each containing the ASCII code for some character, and ending in a ⟨NUL⟩ byte. (A ⟨NUL⟩ byte is a byte containing the number 0.) The format of $O.STR is

$$\text{\$O.STR} \quad straddr.ab$$

where *straddr* is the address of the first byte of a character string, obtainable from any address access operand.

$O.NL The macroinstruction $O.NL generates a **new line** on the terminal (that is, the characters "carriage-return" and "line-feed"). $O.NL takes no arguments.

For example, the command

$$\text{\$O.CHR} \quad \text{\#\textasciicircum A/t/}$$

will result in the printing of the single character *t*, as will

$$\text{\$O.CHR} \quad R8$$

assuming that the low-order byte of R8 contains the number ˆX74, the ASCII code for a lower case *t*. In a similar fashion, if R8 contains the *address* 000020FC, and if c(000020FC) = ˆX51, then any of

$$\$O.CHR \quad ˆX20FC$$
$$\$O.CHR \quad (R8)$$
$$\$O.CHR \quad (R8)+$$

will generate the character *Q*. Notice that in the last case, the contents of R8 will be incremented *by 1* to 000020FD.

If TEXT is the symbolic address of the first of a contiguous collection of bytes containing the ASCII codes for the characters "This is a string of characters ⟨NUL⟩", and if c(R4) = TEXT, then either of the commands

$$\$O.STR \quad TEXT$$

or

$$\$O.STR \quad (R4)$$

will generate on the terminal the message:

This is a string of characters

(Observe that a character string, as defined above, is exactly the construction that is generated by the .ASCIZ directive; thus the generation of text messages within a program to be output to the terminal by $O.STR is an especially easy task.)

Neither $O.CHR nor $O.STR generates a "new line" at the completion of printing. Thus when the text string in the last example is printed, the result will be

This is a string of characters_

where the underscore symbol (_) is used here to denote the position of the terminal cursor or printhead. This can be a convenient feature, since it allows for the printing of partial lines, the building up of print lines in a piecemeal fashion, and the printing of input "prompts" without returning the cursor or printhead. The macroinstruction $O.NL forces a "new line" and thus to print the message above and return the cursor to the left margin:

This is a string of characters

we would use

$$\$O.STR \quad TEXT$$
$$\$O.NL$$

D.3 CHARACTER AND CHARACTER STRING INPUT MACROINSTRUCTIONS

Before we describe the actions of the character and string input macroinstructions, it is essential that the reader understand what happens to characters typed at the keyboard. When a string of characters (some or all of which may be interpreted by the user as "numbers") is entered at the keyboard, followed by RETURN, the input/output routine places those characters in a **keyboard buffer**, a 132-byte block of storage, and it then sets a **keyboard buffer pointer** at the first character in the buffer. When the user issues an **input request** by invoking an input macroinstruction, the software checks to see if the keyboard buffer pointer is pointing to a character in the buffer, or if it is at the end of the buffer. If there are still characters in the buffer, the routine honors the request from the current keyboard buffer. However, if the buffer pointer is at the *end* of the buffer (which is interpreted as a *buffer empty* condition), the macroinstruction displays a colon (:) to **prompt** the user for input. In this case characters are accepted from the keyboard and placed in the keyboard buffer up to the RETURN character, the keyboard buffer pointer is reset to the beginning of the buffer, and the user's input request is *then* honored. One of the implications of this buffered scheme is that if upon receiving the prompt (:) to put characters in the buffer, the user actually types *more* than is needed to satisfy the current request, then when the routine receives the *next* input request, it will *not* prompt the user, but rather fulfill this second request from the (not yet empty) keyboard buffer.

With this understanding of just what happens to an input line, we can now easily describe the two macroinstructions that implement character and string input.

$I.CHR The macroinstruction $I.CHR accepts a *single* character from the keyboard buffer, for which it prompts (:) if the buffer is currently empty. The format of the macroinstruction is

$$\text{\$I.CHR} \quad chraddr.ab$$

where *chraddr* is the address of the byte, obtainable from any address access operand, in which the character is to be placed.

$I.STR The macroinstruction $I.STR places the entire contents of the current keyboard buffer, from the buffer pointer to the *end* of the keyboard buffer, in the block of contiguous bytes beginning at a specified address in the user's program space and appends a ⟨NUL⟩ to this string of characters. If the keyboard buffer is currently empty, the input prompt (:) is displayed. The format of $I.STR is

$$\text{\$I.STR} \quad straddr.ab$$

where *straddr* is the address of the first byte of a character string, obtainable from any address access operand. The buffer characters are placed in the user's block of storage, followed by a ⟨NUL⟩ (= ˆX00).

Observe that one of the consequences of $I.STR is that it *clears* the keyboard buffer, since the entire buffer, from the current pointer position to the end of the buffer, is always transmitted to the user's block of storage. Notice also that since $I.STR appends a ⟨NUL⟩ to the end of the string, a string input to the user's program by $I.STR is completely compatible with strings generated by the .ASCIZ directive. Finally, it is clear that it is the user's responsibility to ensure that the specified block of storage to which the string will be transferred is sufficiently large to hold the input string and its terminating ⟨NUL⟩.

As an example, suppose that the keyboard buffer is currently empty and that the user issues the request

$$\text{\$I.CHR} \quad \text{CHAR1}$$

The routine will print its prompt (:) since the buffer is empty. Assume that the user responds to the prompt by entering the characters

$$\text{Made in U.S.A. ⟨RETURN⟩}$$

Then the code for the character *M* will be placed in the byte whose address is CHAR1. If the next two requests are

$$\text{\$I.CHR} \quad \text{CHAR2}$$

and

$$\text{\$I.STR} \quad \text{TEXT}$$

then CHAR2 will contain the ASCII code for the character *a* and TEXT through TEXT + 12 will contain the codes for the characters

$$\text{de in U.S.A. ⟨NUL⟩}$$

The final "input" macroinstruction simply clears the keyboard buffer.

$I.NL The macroinstruction $I.NL sets the keyboard buffer pointer to the end of the buffer, thus effectively clearing the buffer. Any characters that were in the buffer at the time are lost.

D.4 NUMERICAL OUTPUT MACROINSTRUCTIONS

There are nine macroinstructions which provide for the output of numerical data for three datatypes—integer bytes, words, and longwords—in three different formats—binary, hexadecimal, and decimal. The numerical output macroinstructions are of the form

$$\$O.\langle bytes\rangle\langle format\rangle$$

where $\langle bytes\rangle$ = 1, 2, or 4, and $\langle format\rangle$ = B, H, or D. $\langle bytes\rangle$ represents the number of bytes in the datatype, and $\langle format\rangle$ determines whether the number is to be shown in its binary (B), hexadecimal (H), or decimal (D) representation. Thus the nine macroinstructions are:

$O.1B	$O.2B	$O.4B
$O.1H	$O.2H	$O.4H
$O.1D	$O.2D	$O.4D

$O.*bf*   *O*utput the specified number of *b*ytes in the specified *f*ormat.   The format of the macroinstructions is

$$\$O.\langle bytes\rangle\ \langle format\rangle\quad num.rx$$

where *num* is any operand specifier.   The datatype *x* is *b* (byte), *w* (word), or *l* (longword), depending on the particular macroinstruction.

The actual printing of numerical output on the terminal is done in a uniform way, regardless of the format (binary, hexadecimal, or decimal), as follows.   Any of the macroinstructions prints a single number, without generating a "new line," and each number is always preceded by two blank or space characters.   This is for the purpose of separation when more than one number is printed on a single line.   In the case of binary and hexadecimal output, leading zeros are *always* printed and thus, for example, binary bytes, words, and longwords always occupy 8, 16, and 32 print positions, respectively, while in hexadecimal the printing of these numbers takes up 2, 4, and 8 print positions, each in addition to the two leading blanks.   In decimal, the field in which the number is printed is always exactly large enough to accommodate any number of that datatype, together with a possible minus sign; that is, numbers printed in decimal are regarded as *signed*.   Leading zeros are replaced with spaces, and the minus sign, if present, is printed immediately preceding the leftmost digit.   Thus in decimal, a byte requires 4 print positions, a word requires 6, and a longword takes 11.   As with the other formats, these print positions are in addition to the two leading blanks.   For example, if the byte containing ˆB00101011, the word containing -652 and the longword containing ˆX7FE255A9 were printed on the same line (in the formats indicated), that print line would appear as

$$\not{b}\not{b}00101011\not{b}\not{b}\not{b}\not{b}\text{-}652\not{b}\not{b}7\text{FE}255\text{A}9$$

where the symbol $\not{b}$ represents a "blank" or "space" character.   If desired, of course, additional spacing between numbers can be provided by printing character strings containing appropriately many space characters.   (The reader familiar with the concepts from Chapter 18 could easily define a macroinstruction such as

$$\text{\$O.SP} \quad \text{ARG}$$

using

$$\text{\$O.CHR} \quad \text{\#\^A//}$$

to generate ARG spaces.)

D.5 NUMERICAL INPUT MACROINSTRUCTIONS

There are nine numerical input macroinstructions which correspond in datatype and format to the numerical output macroinstructions. They are

$I.1B	$I.2B	$I.4B
$I.1H	$1.2H	$I.4H
$I.1D	$1.2D	$I.4D

$I · *bf* *I*nput the specified number of *b*ytes in the specified *f*ormat. The format of the macroinstructions is

$$\text{\$I.}\langle\text{bytes}\rangle \ \langle\text{format}\rangle \quad \textit{numaddr.ax}$$

where *numaddr* is any address obtainable from an address access operand. The datatype *x* is *b* (byte), *w* (word), or *l* (longword), depending on the particular macroinstruction.

As was the case with the character and string input macroinstructions, it is essential that we understand just which characters in the keyboard buffer will be "read" when a numerical input request is issued. This depends on the *format* in which the input is requested, but the general rule is the following: When numerical input is requested, the characters beginning with the current buffer pointer position—but ignoring *leading* spaces and tabs—will be read and converted to integers until the end of the buffer is reached *or* a character is encountered which is not valid in the requested format. A few examples will clarify this concept.

Let the current input buffer be

$$\underline{1}011375$$

where we use the underscore character (_) to indicate the position of the buffer pointer. If the request

$$\text{\$I.4D} \quad \text{NUMBER}$$

is issued, the decimal number 1011375 will be placed in the longword whose address is NUMBER, and the buffer pointer will be at the end of the buffer:

$$1011375\_$$

On the other hand, if the request were

$$\text{\$I.4B \quad NUMBER}$$

instead, the number (in binary format)

$$00000000000000000000000000001011$$

will be placed in NUMBER, and the buffer will be

$$1011\underline{3}75$$

the numerical conversion of characters to binary terminating when the "3" is encountered, since this is *not* a valid character in binary format. What will happen if, at this point, another *binary* input request is issued? The answer is that the value returned will be 0, since the buffer pointer is currently *at* the invalid (in binary) character "3" and thus *no* character conversion takes place.

As a final example of things of which the user must be aware, consider again the buffer

$$\underline{1}011375$$

and the input request

$$\text{\$I.1D \quad NUMBER}$$

Notice that here we are requesting decimal input to a *byte*, and the "number" in the keyboard buffer is far larger than that which will fit in an individual byte. What happens is exactly what is described above: the buffer is scanned until a nondecimal character or end of buffer is encountered. The resulting number— or more precisely, its *low-order bits*—are placed in the byte specified by the address NUMBER. In this case, then, the *high-order* bits are simply *lost*, and the input request results in the numer −81 being placed in the *byte* whose address is NUMBER; the *integer overflow* is *not* detected. Thus we see that no input request can ever generate an error per se, but if the user does not take some care with the requests and their responses, unpredictable data (and consequently answers) can be the result.

We close this section with two additional comments. First, when more than one number value is entered into the keyboard buffer at one time, good practice dictates that they be separated by one or more spaces or tabs. Thus if the input line is

$$123\,\cancel{b}\,\cancel{b}\,\cancel{b}\,\cancel{b}56$$

and two input requests are issued, the number 123 will be put in the address specified by the first request, the conversion of characters terminating when the first blank after the "3" is encountered, and 56 will be put in the location specified by the next request, since the four leading blanks are ignored. Second, when entering characters to satisfy an input request in *hexadecimal* format, the hexadecimal characters A...F *must* be entered in *uppercase*. A response such as

172d3

to such a request will result in the number ^X172, since the conversion of characters will have stopped when the *d* was encountered—this lowercase letter is not considered to be a valid hexadecimal character.

D.6 IMPLEMENTATION OF THE MACROINSTRUCTIONS

The actual implementation of the macroinstructions described in this appendix requires the text creation of the definitions themselves (Figure D.6.1) and the source code for the routines to execute them, as shown in Figure D.6.2. However, not all definitions and source code need to be implemented. Both the definitions and assembly code are divided into modules, each of which implements *some* of the features that have been discussed here. For example, if simple character and string output are sufficient for one's needs, only the "base module" of macro-definitions and the "base module" of source code need be created. Adding module 1 of Figures D.6.1 and D.6.2 will implement the numerical output macroinstructions. Modules 2 and 3 yield character and string input, and numerical input, respectively. Thus the user can implement only those modules which are required, rather than having to create definitions and source code for functions that will perhaps never be used. With this goal in mind, the definitions and routines have been written in such a way as to minimize the amount of text that must be created (and, in fact, this is one of the reasons that the numerical input macroinstructions were written as they were—incapable of generating any errors—to eliminate the code required for error checking.) In any event, the documentation within the listings of Figures D.6.1 and D.6.2 should be sufficient to act as a guide to tailoring a set of macroinstruction definitions and source code to fulfill a particular user's needs.

While the macroinstruction definitions of Figure D.6.1 can be incorporated into a macroinstruction library, they are in fact intended to be used simply as a "prologue" file to user programs, being *pre*concatenated onto the user's source program. Thus if the file of macroinstruction definitions is named, say, MACDEF. MAR, then a command such as

MACRO/LIST = TT: MACDEF + USERFILE/OBJECT

(shown here as a standard DCL command) will suffice to predefine the macroinstructions and thus to create an object file USERFILE.OBJ, which can then be linked to the object file created from the code of Figure D.6.2. (This accounts for the presence of the .NOSHOW and .SHOW directives at the beginning and end of Figure D.6.1, which suppress the listings of macrodefinitions.)

```
.NOSHOW

.EXTERNAL ...$

;-----------------------------------------------;
;                                               ;
;              B A S E   M O D U L E            ;
;              - - - -   - - - - -              ;
;                                               ;
;    Defines the basic macroinstructions:       ;
;                                               ;
;    $EXIT          Return control to VMS monitor ;
;    $0.CHR         Print a single character    ;
;    $0.STR         Print a string of characters ;
;    $0.NL          Generate "New line" (<CR/LF>) ;
;                                               ;
;-----------------------------------------------;

.MACRO   $EXIT
MOVZWL   #^A/MN/,-(SP)
CALLS    #1,...$
.ENDM    $EXIT

.MACRO   $0.CHR   ARG
MOVZBL   ARG,-(SP)
MOVZWL   #^A/OR/,-(SP)
CALLS    #2,...$
.ENDM    $0.CHR
```

Figure D.6.1

```
        .MACRO   $O.STR   ARG
        PUSHAB   ARG
        MOVZWL   #^A/OS/,-(SP)
        CALLS    #2,...$
        .ENDM    $O.STR

        .MACRO   $O.NL
        MOVZWL   #^A/OL/,-(SP)
        CALLS    #1,...$
        .ENDM    $O.NL
```

```
;--------------------------------------------------;
;                                                  ;
;              M O D U L E    1                     ;
;              - - - - - -    -                     ;
;                                                  ;
;   Defines the output macroinstructions:          ;
;                                                  ;
;              $O.<byte><format>                    ;
;                                                  ;
;   where <byte> is the number of bytes in the     ;
;   data type to be printed (<byte> = 1, 2, 4)     ;
;   and <format> = B (binary), H (hexadecimal)     ;
;   or D (decimal):                                ;
;                                                  ;
;      $O.1B          $O.1H          $O.1D          ;
;      $O.2B          $O.2H          $O.2D          ;
;      $O.4B          $O.4H          $O.4D          ;
;                                                  ;
;--------------------------------------------------;
```

```
.IRPC    BYTES,<124>
.IRPC    FORMAT,<BHD>
.MACRO   $O.'BYTES''FORMAT       ARG
.IIF     IDN      BYTES,1,       CVTBL   ARG,-(SP)
.IIF     IDN      BYTES,2,       CVTWL   ARG,-(SP)
.IIF     IDN      BYTES,4,       MOVL    ARG,-(SP)
MOVW     #BYTES,-(SP)
MOVW     #^A/O'FORMAT'/,-(SP)
CALLS    #2,...$
.ENDM    $O.'BYTES''FORMAT
.ENDR
.ENDR
```

```
;--------------------------------------------------;
;                                                  ;
;              M O D U L E    2                     ;
;              - - - - - -    -                     ;
;                                                  ;
;   Defines the basic input macroinstructions:     ;
;                                                  ;
;   $I.CHR          Input a single character       ;
;   $I.STR          Input a string of characters   ;
;   $I.NL           Clear current input buffer      ;
;                                                  ;
;--------------------------------------------------;
```

Figure D.6.1   (continued)

```
.MACRO   $I.CHR   ARG
PUSHAB   ARG
MOVZWL   #^A/IR/,-(SP)
CALLS    #2,...$
.ENDM    $I.CHR

.MACRO   $I.STR   ARG
PUSHAB   ARG
MOVZWL   #^A/IS/,-(SP)
CALLS    #2,...$
.ENDM    $I.STR

.MACRO   $I.NL
MOVZWL   #^A/IL/,-(SP)
CALLS    #1,...$
.ENDM    $I.NL
```

```
;---------------------------------------------;
;                                             ;
;              M O D U L E   3                ;
;              - - - - - -   -                ;
;                                             ;
;                                             ;
;    Defines the input macroinstructions:     ;
;                                             ;
;              $I.<byte><format>              ;
;                                             ;
;    where <byte> is the number of bytes in the ;
;    data type to be input (<byte> = 1, 2, 4) ;
;    and <format> = B (binary), H (hexadecimal) ;
;    or D (decimal):                          ;
;                                             ;
;      $I.1B         $I.1H         $I.1D       ;
;      $I.2B         $I.2H         $I.2D       ;
;      $I.4B         $I.4H         $I.4D       ;
;                                             ;
;---------------------------------------------;
```

```
.IRPC    BYTES,<124>
.IRPC    FORMAT,<BHD>
.MACRO   $I.'BYTES''FORMAT      ARG
.IIF     IDN     BYTES,1,       PUSHAB ARG
.IIF     IDN     BYTES,2,       PUSHAW ARG
.IIF     IDN     BYTES,4,       PUSHAL ARG
MOVW     #BYTES,-(SP)
MOVW     #^A/I'FORMAT'/,-(SP)
CALLS    #2,...$
.ENDM    $I.'BYTES''FORMAT
.ENDR
.ENDR

.SHOW
```

Figure D.6.1 (continued)

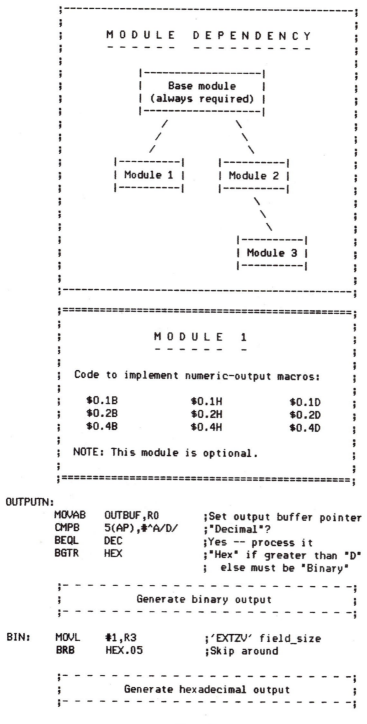

```
;-----------------------------------------------------;
;                                                     ;
;        M O D U L E   D E P E N D E N C Y            ;
;        - - - - - -   - - - - - - - - - -            ;
;                                                     ;
;              |------------------|                   ;
;              |    Base module   |                   ;
;              | (always required)|                   ;
;              |------------------|                   ;
;                    /       \                         ;
;                   /         \                        ;
;                  /           \                       ;
;         |----------|     |----------|                ;
;         | Module 1 |     | Module 2 |                ;
;         |----------|     |----------|                ;
;                              \                       ;
;                               \                      ;
;                                \                     ;
;                            |----------|              ;
;                            | Module 3 |              ;
;                            |----------|              ;
;                                                     ;
;-----------------------------------------------------;
```

```
;=====================================================;
;                                                     ;
;              M O D U L E   1                         ;
;              - - - - - -   -                         ;
;                                                     ;
; Code to implement numeric-output macros:            ;
;                                                     ;
;     $0.1B          $0.1H          $0.1D             ;
;     $0.2B          $0.2H          $0.2D             ;
;     $0.4B          $0.4H          $0.4D             ;
;                                                     ;
; NOTE: This module is optional.                      ;
;                                                     ;
;=====================================================;
```

```
OUTPUTN:
        MOVAB    OUTBUF,R0        ;Set output buffer pointer
        CMPB     5(AP),#^A/D/     ;"Decimal"?
        BEQL     DEC              ;Yes -- process it
        BGTR     HEX              ;"Hex" if greater than "D"
                                  ; else must be "Binary"

;- - - - - - - - - - - - - - - - - - - - - - - - - -;
;              Generate binary output               ;
;- - - - - - - - - - - - - - - - - - - - - - - - - -;

BIN:    MOVL     #1,R3            ;'EXTZV' field_size
        BRB      HEX.05           ;Skip around

;- - - - - - - - - - - - - - - - - - - - - - - - - -;
;              Generate hexadecimal output          ;
;- - - - - - - - - - - - - - - - - - - - - - - - - -;
```

Figure D.6.2

```
HEX:      MOVL     #4,R3            ;'EXTZV' field_size
HEX.05:   MNEGL    R3,R4            ;'ACBL' incr. = - <field_size>
          MOVZWL   6(AP),R2         ;Get no. bytes from stack,
          ASHL     #3,R2,R2         ;  multiply by 8
          ADDL     R4,R2            ;  and subtract field_size
                                    ;  to get field position in R2
          MOVW     #^A/  /,(R0)+    ;Pad buffer with 2 blanks

100$:     EXTZV    R2,R3,8(AP),R1   ;Extract some no. of bits from
                                    ;  number to be converted
          MOVB     DIGIT[R1],(R0)+  ;Put ASCII digit in buffer
          ACBL     #0,R4,R2,100$    ;Adjust field position and
                                    ;  branch back if nonnegative
          CLRB     (R0)             ;Else put <NUL> in buffer
          BRW      COMOUT           ;  and print it

;- - - - - - - - - - - - - - - - - - - - - - - -;
;              Generate decimal output           ;
;- - - - - - - - - - - - - - - - - - - - - - - -;

DEC:      ADDL     #6,R0            ;Adjust buffer pointer for byte
          CMPW     6(AP),#2         ;Is there a word on the stack?
          BLSS     120$             ;No -- byte -- skip around
          BEQL     110$             ;Word -- skip to add 2
          ADDL     #5,R0            ;Long-word -- add 5 more
110$:     ADDL     #2,R0            ;Add 2 more to buffer pointer
120$:     CLRB     (R0)             ;Put a <NUL> at end of buffer
          CLRL     R3               ;High-order 32 bits of dividend
          MOVL     8(AP),R2         ;Low-order 32 bits of dividend
                                    ;  (= number to be converted)
          BGEQ     130$             ;Skip if nonnegative
          MNEGL    R2,R2            ;  else make positive
          INCB     SIGN             ;  and set "sign" flag
130$:     EDIV     #10,R2,R2,R4     ;Divide -- remainder in R4
          ADDB3    #^A/0/,R4,-(R0)  ;Convert number to ASCII
          TSTL     R2               ;Dividend still nonzero?
          BNEQ     130$             ;Yes -- divide again
          TSTB     SIGN             ;Number originally negative?
          BEQL     140$             ;No -- skip around
          MOVB     #^A/-/,-(R0)     ;  else put minus-sign in buffer
140$:     MOVB     #^A/ /,-(R0)     ;Put ASCII blank in buffer
          CMPL     R0,#OUTBUF       ;At beginning of buffer?
          BGTRU    140$             ;No -- put in another blank

;- - - - - - - - - - - - - - - - - - - - - - - - - - -;
;          Common routine for numeric output           ;
;- - - - - - - - - - - - - - - - - - - - - - - - - - -;

COMOUT:   MOVAB    OUTBUF,R2        ;Set up buffer pointer
          JMP      OUTST            ;  and jump to print routine
```

Figure D.6.2 (continued)

```
;===================================================;
;                                                   ;
;                  M O D U L E   2                  ;
;                  - - - - - -   -                  ;
;                                                   ;
;   Code to implement character-input macros:       ;
;                                                   ;
;   $I.CHR        Input single character            ;
;   $I.STR        Input string of characters        ;
;   $I.NL         Clear input buffer                ;
;                                                   ;
;   NOTE: This module is optional, but REQUIRED     ;
;         if Module 3 is to be implemented.         ;
;                                                   ;
;===================================================;

INPUTC: CMPB    5(AP),#^A/R/    ;Single-character request?
        BLSS    INLIN          ;No -- "clear buffer"
        BGTR    INSTR          ;No -- "input string"


;- - - - - - - - - - - - - - - - - - - - - - - - -;
;             Input a single character             ;
;- - - - - - - - - - - - - - - - - - - - - - - - -;

INCHR:  BSBB    GETCHR         ;Get a nonnull character
        MOVB    R5,@8(AP)      ;  and put in caller's byte
        INCL    BUFPTR         ;Adjust buffer pointer
        RET                    ;  and return to caller

;- - - - - - - - - - - - - - - - - - - - - - - - -;
;           Input a string of characters           ;
;- - - - - - - - - - - - - - - - - - - - - - - - -;

INSTR:  MOVL    8(AP),R4       ;Get caller's buffer address
        BSBB    GETCHR         ;  and get nonnull character
200$:   MOVB    R5,(R4)+       ;Put in caller's buffer
        BNEQ    220$           ;Get another char if nonnull
        RET                    ;  else return
220$:   INCL    BUFPTR         ;Adjust buffer pointer,
        BSBB    GETCH          ;  get a character
        BRB     200$           ;  and put in buffer


;- - - - - - - - - - - - - - - - - - - - - - - - -;
;                Clear input buffer                ;
;- - - - - - - - - - - - - - - - - - - - - - - - -;

INLIN:  MOVAB   ENDBUF,BUFPTR  ;Reset buffer pointer
        RET                    ;  and return


;- - - - - - - - - - - - - - - - - - - - - - - - -;
;   Get a character from input buffer (but do      ;
;            NOT adjust buffer pointer)            ;
;- - - - - - - - - - - - - - - - - - - - - - - - -;

GETCHR: TSTB    @BUFPTR        ;Pointing at <NUL>?
        BEQL    GETC.5         ;Yes -- get another buffer
```

Figure D.6.2   (continued)

```
GETCH:  MOVZBL  @BUFPTR,R5        ;Put character in R5
        RSB                       ;  and return to internal caller
GETC.5: MOVAB   INBUF,BUFPTR      ;Set pointer to beginning
        CLRB    INBUF             ;  and start it with a <NUL>
        MOVAB   PROMPT,R2         ;Set print line pointer
        JSB     OUTS              ;  and send prompt
        MOVAB   INBUF,IORAB-
                +RAB$L_UBF        ;Set buffer address and
        MOVW    #132,IORAB-
                +RAB$W_USZ        ;  buffer size in RAB
        $GET    RAB=IORAB         ;Get a line from keyboard
        MOVZWL  IORAB-
                +RAB$W_RSZ,R0     ;Get input line length
        CLRB    INBUF(R0)         ;  and end string with a <NUL>
        BRB     GETCHR            ;Go look for first character
```

```
;=================================================;
;                                                 ;
;                M O D U L E   3                  ;
;                - - - - - -   -                  ;
;                                                 ;
;   Code to implement numeric-input macros:       ;
;                                                 ;
;     $I.1B          $I.1H          $I.1D         ;
;     $I.2B          $I.2H          $I.2D         ;
;     $I.4B          $I.4H          $I.4D         ;
;                                                 ;
;   NOTE: This module is optional.                ;
;                                                 ;
;=================================================;
```

```
INPUTN: CLRL    R3                ;Converted integer goes here
        MOVL    #10,R4            ;Assume decimal
        CMPB    5(AP),#^A/D/      ;Assumption correct?
        BEQL    320$              ;Yes -- skip around
        BGTR    300$              ;  else handle hexadecimal
        MOVL    #2,R4             ;Set up for binary
        BRB     320$              ;  and skip around
300$:   MOVL    #16,R4            ;Set up for hexadecimal
320$:   JSB     GETCHR            ;Get first character
        CMPB    R5,#^A/ /         ;"Space" or "tab"?
        BGTR    340$              ;No -- skip around
        INCL    BUFPTR            ;Increment pointer,
        BRB     320$              ;  and get next character
340$:   CMPB    R5,#^A/+/         ;"Plus-sign"?
        BEQL    INP.30            ;Yes -- ignore it
        CMPB    R5,#^A/-/         ;"Minus-sign"?
        BNEQ    INP.40            ;No -- process character
        INCB    SIGN              ;  else set "sign" flag
INP.30: INCL    BUFPTR            ;Increment pointer
        JSB     GETCH             ;  and get a character
INP.40: LOCC    R5,R4,DIGIT       ;Locate character in string
        BEQL    INP.80            ;Done if not found
        SUBL    #DIGIT,R1         ;  else make numeric
        MULL    R4,R3             ;Multiply number by base
```

Figure D.6.2 (continued)

```
        ADDL    R1,R3            ;  and add this digit
        BRB     INP.30           ;Process next character
INP.80: TSTB    SIGN             ;"Sign" flag set?
        BEQL    360$             ;No -- skip around
        MNEGL   R3,R3            ;  else negate result
360$:   CMPW    6(AP),#2         ;"Word" data?
        BLSS    370$             ;No -- "byte"
        BGTR    380$             ;No -- "longword"
        MOVW    R3,@8(AP)        ;Move word to caller's word
        RET                      ;  and return
370$:   MOVB    R3,@8(AP)        ;Move byte to caller's byte
        RET                      ;  and return
380$:   MOVL    R3,@8(AP)        ;Move longword to caller's
        RET                      ;  longword and return
```

```
;=================================================;
;                                                 ;
;              B A S E   M O D U L E              ;
;              - - - -   - - - - - -              ;
;                                                 ;
; Code to implement character-output macros:      ;
;                                                 ;
; $EXIT          Return control to VMS monitor    ;
; $O.CHR         Print a single character         ;
; $O.STR         Print a string of characters     ;
; $O.NL          Generate "New line" <CR/LF>       ;
;                                                 ;
; NOTE: This module is REQUIRED for the           ;
;       implementation of ANY of the I/O          ;
;       macros.                                   ;
;                                                 ;
;       This module contains ALL buffers,         ;
;       pointers, flags, strings and FAB/RAB      ;
;       blocks required by ANY module.            ;
;                                                 ;
;=================================================;
```

```
...$::  .WORD   ^M<R0,R1,R2,R3,R4,R5>

;- - - - - - - - - - - - - - - - - - - - - - - - -;
;              Initialize terminal channels        ;
;- - - - - - - - - - - - - - - - - - - - - - - - -;

        TSTB    INIT             ;Already initialized?
        BNEQ    10$              ;Yes -- skip
        INCB    INIT             ;  else set flag,
        $CREATE FAB=IOFAB        ;  create block
        $CONNECT RAB=IORAB       ;  and connect to record block

10$:    CLRB    SIGN             ;Clear "sign" flag
        CMPB    4(AP),#^A/M/     ;"Exit"?
        BLSS    IN               ;No -- input request
        BGTR    OUT              ;No -- output request
```

Figure D.6.2 (continued)

```
;- - - - - - - - - - - - - - - - - - - - - - -;
;                Handle "$EXIT" macro           ;
;- - - - - - - - - - - - - - - - - - - - - - -;

        $CLOSE  FAB=IOFAB          ;Close devices
        $EXIT_S                    ;Exit (let system clean stack)

;- - - - - - - - - - - - - - - - - - - - - - -;
;                Handle input request           ;
;- - - - - - - - - - - - - - - - - - - - - - -;

IN:     CMPB    5(AP),#^A/L/       ;Character-input request?
        BGEQ    INBAS              ;Yes -- skip around

;- - - - - - - - - - - - - - - - - - - - - - -;
;       Handle numeric- (INPUTN) and character- ;
;              (INPUTC) input macros            ;
;- - - - - - - - - - - - - - - - - - - - - - -;

        .IIF    DF      INPUTN, JMP    INPUTN
                                   ;Do input IF routines included
        RET                        ; else ignore this request

INBAS:
        .IIF    DF      INPUTC, JMP    INPUTC
                                   ;Do input IF routines included
        RET                        ; else ignore this request

;- - - - - - - - - - - - - - - - - - - - - - -;
;       Handle numeric- (OUTPUTN) and character-;
;         (OUTPUTC) output macroinstructions    ;
;- - - - - - - - - - - - - - - - - - - - - - -;

OUT:    CMPB    5(AP),#^A/L/       ;Character-output request?
        BGEQ    OUTPUTC            ;Yes -- skip around
        .IIF    DF      OUTPUTN, JMP    OUTPUTN
                                   ;Do output IF routines included
        RET                        ; else ignore this request

OUTPUTC:
        CMPB    5(AP),#^A/R/       ;Single-character output?
        BLSS    OUTLIN             ;No -- "New line"
        BGTR    OUTSTR             ;No -- "String"

;- - - - - - - - - - - - - - - - - - - - - - -;
;              Output a single character        ;
;- - - - - - - - - - - - - - - - - - - - - - -;

OUTCHR: MOVAL   8(AP),R2           ;Put address of char in R2
        BSBB    PRINT              ; and go transmit it
        RET                        ;Return to calling program

;- - - - - - - - - - - - - - - - - - - - - - -;
;                Output a new-line              ;
;- - - - - - - - - - - - - - - - - - - - - - -;
```

Figure D.6.2 (continued)

```
OUTLIN: MOVAB    NULINE,R2          ;Set buffer pointer
        BRB      OUTST              ;  and send <CR/LF>

;- - - - - - - - - - - - - - - - - - - - - - - - - - -;
;          Output a string ending in a <NUL>          ;
;- - - - - - - - - - - - - - - - - - - - - - - - - - -;

OUTSTR: MOVL     8(AP),R2           ;Addr. of 1st byte of string in R2
OUTST:  BSBB     OUTS               ;Send string to terminal
        RET                         ;  and return to caller

OUTS:   TSTB     (R2)               ;String terminator <NUL>?
        BNEQ     30$                ;No -- print it
        RSB                         ;  else return to internal caller
30$:    BSBB     PRINT              ;  else transmit character
        BRB      OUTS               ;  and go test next character

;- - - - - - - - - - - - - - - - - - - - - - - - - - -;
;      Transmit a single character to terminal        ;
;- - - - - - - - - - - - - - - - - - - - - - - - - - -;

PRINT:  MOVAB    (R2)+,IORAB-
                 +RAB$L_RBF         ;Set up address and
        MOVW     #1,IORAB-
                 +RAB$W_RSZ         ;  byte count
        $PUT     RAB=IORAB          ;Put out a character
        RSB                         ;  and return

;- - - - - - - - - - - - - - - - - - - - - - - - - - -;
;          Strings, flags and buffers                 ;
;- - - - - - - - - - - - - - - - - - - - - - - - - - -;

DIGIT:  .ASCII   /0123456789ABCDEF/
                                    ;Binary, hex and decimal digits
NULINE: .BYTE    13,10,0            ;<CR><LF><NUL>
PROMPT: .ASCIZ   /: /               ;Input request prompt
SIGN:   .BLKB    1                  ;"Sign" flag
INIT:   .BYTE    0                  ;"Device initialized" flag

OUTBUF: .BLKB    35                 ;Output buffer
INBUF:  .BLKB    132                ;Input buffer
ENDBUF: .BYTE    0                  ;  followed by a <NUL>
BUFPTR: .ADDRESS ENDBUF             ;Input buffer pointer --
                                    ;  initialized to end of buffer

;- - - - - - - - - - - - - - - - - - - - - - - - - - -;
;          FILE and RECORD ACCESS BLOCKS              ;
;- - - - - - - - - - - - - - - - - - - - - - - - - - -;

        .PSECT   IOBLOCKS,LONG

IOFAB:  $FAB     FNM=<SYS$COMMAND>,MRS=132
IORAB:  $RAB     FAB=IOFAB

        .END
```

Figure D.6.2   (continued)

D.7 FLOATING-POINT INPUT AND OUTPUT

The macroinstructions in this appendix make no provision for the input and output of floating-point numbers, in their various formats. The programming for the manipulation of such data is more tedious than difficult, but at best it uses up quite a bit of source code. For the user who wishes to implement floating-point input and output, and who has a FORTRAN compiler available, we offer below two modules which allow for input and output of numbers of type F_floating. They are distinguished far more by their expediency than by their elegance or educational value.

$I.F Input the specified F_floating number. The format of the macroinstruction is

$$\text{\$I.F} \quad numaddr.al$$

where *numaddr* is any address obtainable from an address access operand. Because $I.F uses FORTRAN formatting (and in particular F80.0 format), only one number at a time may be entered in response to the input prompt character (:). However, that number may be entered in any form whatsoever, since the placement of the decimal point in the input will override the FORTRAN format specification. If no decimal point is entered, the number is taken as the F_floating version of the corresponding integer.

$O.F Output the specified F_floating number. The format of the macroinstruction is

$$\text{\$O.F} \quad num.rl \, , \, width.rl, \, decpla.rl$$

where *num* is the number to be printed, *width* is the number of print positions the number is to occupy (including the decimal point and a possible minus sign), and *decpla* is the number of decimal places to be printed. If either or both of *width* and/or *decpla* is elided, they are given the default values 12 and 3, respectively. As with the other output macroinstructions, $O.F does not generate a "new line" after printing. (Specifically, all FORTRAN carriage control is suppressed.)

$I.F and $O.F are compatible with the other macroinstructions described previously. They may be implemented by including the macroinstruction definitions shown in Figure D.7.1 as a prologue to user source files, and then linking in the FORTRAN subroutine shown in Figure D.7.2.

```
        .NOSHOW

        .EXTERNAL      FL_O,FL_I        ;FORTRAN I/O routines


        ;----------------------------------------------------------;
        ;                                                          ;
        ; F L O A T I N G   P O I N T   I N P U T / O U T P U T ;
        ; - - - - - - - -   - - - - -   - - - - -   - - - - - - ;
        ;                                                          ;
        ; Defines the macroinstructions:                          ;
        ;                                                          ;
        ;    $O.F     Output floating point numbers               ;
        ;    $I.F     Input floating point numbers                ;
        ;                                                          ;
        ; Input and output data is of type F_floating only        ;
        ;                                                          ;
        ;----------------------------------------------------------;

        .MACRO  $O.F   VALUE,WIDTH,DECPLA,?VL,?WD,?DC,?DONE

        MOVF   VALUE,VL          ;Store value to be printed

                                 ;Store field-width and number-of-
                                 ;  decimal-places, if not elided
        .IIF   NB    ,WIDTH,  MOVL   WIDTH,WD
        .IIF   NB    ,DECPLA, MOVL   DECPLA,DC

        PUSHAL DC                ;Stack 'decimal-places' address,
        PUSHAL WD                ;  'width' address
        PUSHAL VL                ;  and 'value' address
        CALLS  #3,FL_O           ;Invoke FORTRAN output routine
        BRB    DONE              ;  and skip around temporary storage

VL:     .BLKL  1
WD:     .LONG  12                ;Default field-width and number-of-
DC:     .LONG  3                 ;  decimal-places (if elided at
                                 ;  time of macroinstruction call)

DONE:
        .ENDM                    ;End of macroinstruction '$O.F'

        .MACRO $I.F   VALUE

        PUSHAL VALUE             ;Stack 'value' address
        CALLS  #1,FL_I           ;Invoke FORTRAN input routine
        .ENDM                    ;End of macroinstruction '$I.F'

        .SHOW
```

Figure D.7.1

```
*         ;-----------------------------------------------------------;
*         ;                                                           ;
*         ;         F O R T R A N   I / O   R O U T I N E S           ;
*         ;         - - - - - - -   - - -   - - - - - - - -           ;
*         ;                                                           ;
*         ;   Invoked from I/O macroinstructions $I.F and $O.F        ;
*         ;                                                           ;
*         ;-----------------------------------------------------------;
          SUBROUTINE FL_O(VALUE,WIDTH,DECPLA)
          INTEGER*4 WIDTH,DECPLA
          REAL*4 VALUE

          OPEN(UNIT=2,FILE='SYS$OUTPUT',STATUS='SCRATCH',
      -         CARRIAGECONTROL='NONE')
          WRITE(2,60)VALUE
60        FORMAT(F<WIDTH>.<DECPLA>)
          GOTO 100

          ENTRY FL_I(VALUE)
          OPEN(UNIT=2,FILE='SYS$COMMAND',STATUS='SCRATCH',
      -         CARRIAGECONTROL='NONE')
          WRITE(2,70)
70        FORMAT(': ')
          READ(2,80)VALUE
80        FORMAT(BN,F80.0)

100       CLOSE (2)
          RETURN

          END
```

Figure D.7.2

SOLUTIONS TO SELECTED EXERCISES

E

2.5.2.   **(a)** 1101111_2 **(c)** 233_6 **(e)** 11011111_2
       (g) 1122220_3 **(i)** 13_5

2.5.3.   **(b)** 1100101_2 **(c)** 1000000_2 **(e)** 1111111_2
       (g) 11111111111_2 **(h)** 100000000000_2

2.5.4.   **(a)** 5_{10} **(c)** 32_{10} **(d)** 31_{10} **(f)** 227_{10}

2.5.5.   **(b)** 65_{16} **(c)** 40_{16} **(d)** $3F_{16}$ **(f)** $3FF_{16}$

2.5.6.   **(a)** 5_{16} **(c)** 20_{16} **(d)** $1F_{16}$ **(f)** $E3_{16}$

2.5.7.   **(c)** 1110100000000_2 **(d)** 1000011111111_2
       (g) 1010101011100_2 **(h)** 10101_2

2.5.8.   **(a)** 2606_{10} **(b)** 4353_{10} **(d)** 4351_{10}
       (f) 8191_{10} **(h)** 21_{10}

2.5.9.   **(a)** 1025_8 **(b)** $3E6_{16}$ **(e)** AD_{16}
       (g) $162A8_{16}$ **(h)** 416_{12}

2.5.10.   **(a)** $1 \cdot 16^2 + 10 \cdot 16^1 + 4 \cdot 16^0 + 3 \cdot 16^{-1} + 13 \cdot 16^{-2}$
       (b) $3A.4_{16}$

2.7.1.   255; 4,095; 65,535; 16,777,215; 4,294,967,295

2.7.2. $\underbrace{111\ldots111}_{n \text{ copies}} = (\underbrace{111\ldots111}_{n \text{ copies}} + 1) - 1 = \underbrace{1000\ldots000}_{n \text{ copies}} - 1 = 2^n - 1$

2.8.2.   **(a)** 1100 (9 + 3 = 12)   **(c)** 0011 (13 + 6 = 3)
       (e) 0000 (1 + 15 = 0)

2.8.4.   **(a)** 0110 (9 − 3 = 6)   **(c)** 0111 (13 − 6 = 7)
       (e) ?101 (6 − 9 = ?)

| | | 2.9.1. | (b) 0001 [+6 + (+3) = +1] | (c) 0101 [−0 + (+5) = +5] |

2.9.1. (b) 0001 [+6 + (+3) = +1]   (c) 0101 [−0 + (+5) = +5]
         (d) 0001 [−3 − (−4) = +1]   (f) 0101 [+5 − (−0) = +5]
         (i) 1000 [−0 − (+0) = −0]

2.9.3. (a) 0010   (c) 0000   (e) 0101

2.9.4. (a) −2   (c) −0   (e) −5

2.9.5. The sign bit (bit 3) is changed if and only if there is a carry out of bit 2.

2.9.6. Ones-complement addition will be correct if and only if (a) no carry, into or out of bit 3, occurs; or (b) both carries, into and out of bit 3, occur.

2.9.7. The definition is incompatible if a carry out of bit 3 occurs; otherwise, it is the same as the definition of unsigned 4-bit addition.

2.9.9. (a) 1000 (incorrect; carry into bit 3)
         (c) 1101 (correct)
         (e) 1110 (correct)
         (g) 0010 (correct)
         (i) 1010 (correct)

2.10.1. (a) 0011   (c) 0001   (d) 0000

2.10.3.

	Result	Bit 3 carry		Result correct?	
		Out of	Into	Unsigned	Signed
(a)	1000	No	Yes	Yes	No
(c)	1010	Yes	Yes	Yes	Yes
(f)	1001	No	Yes	No	No
(g)	1010	No	No	Yes	Yes
(h)	1010	Yes	Yes	Yes	Yes

2.10.5. The sign bit (bit 3) is changed if and only if there is a carry into bit 3.

2.10.6. Since a carry out of bit 3 occurs, the sign will be preserved if and only if a carry into bit 3 also occurs.

3.1.1. (a) BUT is equivalent to AND.
         (c) IF...THEN is equivalent to IMPLIES (Exercise 3.1.6).

3.1.3. $p \cdot q = (p' + q')'$

3.1.5. $((p' + q) \cdot p)' + q = (p' \cdot p + q \cdot p)' + q$
         $= (0 + q \cdot p)' + q = (q \cdot p)' + q$
         $= q' + p' + q = (q' + q) + p' = 1 + p' = 1$

3.4.2. (b) The logical statement corresponding to the circuit is $((A' + B)A)' + B$. Let $A = p$ and $B = q$, and use the result of Exercise 3.1.5.

3.4.3. $((A' + B)A)'B = (A'A + BA)'B = (0 + BA)'B$
         $= (B' + A')B = B'B + A'B = 0 + A'B = A'B$

3.5.3. The output is the twos-complement of the input.   ? = 0 if and only if a carry out of bit 3 occurs during the twos-complementing.

4.1.1. (a) 177; −79   (c) 255; −1   (d) 109; +109

4.1.2. (a) 00100101   (b) 11011011   (d) 10000001
         (e) 01111111   (h) 11111111   (j) 11000001

4.1.3. (a) 01001110; 01001111   (c) 00000000; 00000001

4.1.4.

	Result	Bit 3 carry Out of	Bit 3 carry Into	C	V	Result correct? Unsigned	Result correct? Signed
(a)	00000010	Yes	Yes	1	0	No	Yes
(d)	10001111	No	Yes	1	1	No	No
(e)	11111111	No	No	0	0	Yes	Yes

4.2.1.   **(a)** 3112   **(b)** 0022   **(e)** 0123

4.2.2.   **(a)** 10110001   **(d)** 11111111

4.2.3.   **(a)** D6   **(b)** 0A   **(d)** FF   **(f)** E4

4.2.4.   **(a)** 11111010   **(c)** 10001010   **(d)** 01111111

4.2.5.   **(a)** 05; 06   **(c)** 80; 81   **(e)** FF; 00

4.2.6.

	Result	Bit 3 carry Out of	Bit 3 carry Into	C	V	Result correct? Unsigned	Result correct? Signed
(a)	63	Yes	Yes	1	0	No	Yes
(b)	25	Yes	Yes	0	0	Yes	Yes
(e)	EE	No	Yes	1	1	No	No

4.4.1.   **(b)** 0000; 0001   **(c)** 5919; 591A

4.4.2.   **(a)** 00000D0F; 00000D10   **(d)** 7FFFFFFF; 80000000

4.4.5.

	Result	Bit 3 carry Out of	Bit 3 carry Into	C	V	Result correct? Unsigned	Result correct? Signed
(a)	076696F1	Yes	Yes	1	0	No	Yes
(b)	8E4DBA44	No	No	1	0	No	Yes
(d)	00000000	Yes	Yes	0	0	Yes	Yes

4.5.2.   An overflow occurs (that is, V = 1) when the byte is incremented; it does not when the word is incremented.

4.5.4.   Add the two low-order longwords, and note if a carry out of bit 31 occurs. Add the two high-order longwords; then increment this last sum by 1 *if* the previously noted carry did occur.

5.8.1.   **(a)** 00000024   **(b)** FFFFFF84   **(e)** 0000009A
(f) FFFF9207

5.8.2.   **(a)** 0000B303   **(c)** 0000B259   **(e)** 0000B2D7
(f) 0000B2D9   **(h)** 0000B2D5

5.8.3.   **(b)** 0000B2D2   **(d)** 0000B2DA   **(g)** 000032DA
(h) 000132D9

5.8.4.

	(a)	(b)	(d)
	31	11	31
	0084	E9	9F89
	(f)	(h)	(i)
	Out of	11	31
	range	FC	8F60

5.9.1. (a) 14   (c) 14   (e) 14
        09   9B   00

5.10.1. 7; 1; will HALT after 65536 or fewer iterations, because of the 16-bit number system wraparound.

7.4.1. (a) MOVL   R3,R4   (c) MOVW   R3,R4
          c(R4) = 0020406A   c(R4) = 0000406A

         (e) MOVW   R3,(R4)   (f) MOVL   (R4)+,R3
          c(00000208) = 1043406A   c(R3) = 104327E5
                                                   c(R4) = 0000020C

         (h) MOVL   @(R3)+,R4   (i) MOVW   B^2(R3),W^4(R4)
          c(R3) = 0020406E   c(0000020C) = 00030000
          c(R4) = 0EF41043

         (k) MOVW   −(R3),R4   (m) MOVL   @W^−4(R3),R4
          c(R3) = 00204068   c(R4) = 1072A5A6
          c(R4) = 00000003

         (n) MOVB   ^X20406A(R5),(R4)+   (q) MOVB   R3,(R4)[R5]
          c(R4) = 00000209   c(00000208) = 106A27E5
          c(00000208) = 10432700

         (r) MOVW   (R4)[R5],(R3)   (t) MOVL   B^−4(R4)[R5],R3
          c(0020406A) = 00000EF4   c(R3) = 00030EF4

         (u) MOVB   @B^−4(R3)[R5],(R4)[R5]
          c(00000208) = 107227E5

7.4.3. Moves c(R2) to R3, c(R1) to R2.

7.4.4. (a) MOVL   R6,R9   (c) MOVB   R9,R0
          59   56   D0   50   59   90

         (e) MOVB   1(R9),R6   (f) MOVW   @(R6),R9
          56   01   A9   90   59   00   B6   B0

         (h) MOVB   @(R6),(R9)   (j) MOVW   1(R9),(R6)[R0]
          69   00   B6   90   66   40   01   A9   B0

7.6.1. (a) 00001082   (c) 00001049
         (d) 0000114A   (f) c(00001084) + 00000054
         (h) c(0000104A)

7.6.3. MOVL   #5,R2 will assemble as: 52 05 D0;
         MOVL   #−5,R2 will assemble as: 52 FFFFFFFB 8F D0.

7.6.4. None.

7.6.5. MOVB   @ARRAY[R2],R3 moves c(c(c(ARRAY))+c(R2)) to R3.
         MOVB   @ARRAY(R2),R3 moves c(c(ARRAY+c(R2))) to R3.

7.6.8. ^X42 is too large to be generated as a short literal. (Note also that short literal mode cannot be indexed.)

7.6.10. The assembler has no way of knowing the contents of the longword (whose contents is the operand address).

7.6.11. Either construction is valid.

8.3.1. For example,

       LOOP: MOVL   R0,(R1)+   or   LOOP: MOVL   R0,(R1)+
                 ADDL   #2,R0   TSTW   (R0)+

[where the only purpose of the TSTW is to add 2 to c(R0)].

8.3.2.   **(a)** MOVZBL   R3,R4   **(c)** CVTWL   R3,R4

           (e) MOVZWL   R3,R3   **(g)** MOVB   R4,R3

8.5.1.   **(a)** None.

           (b) In the first case, the destination address is c(R2); in the second case, it is c(R2) + 4.

8.5.2.   **(a)** 120   **(b)** -74 **(c)** 94

8.5.3.   There has been a *carry* out of the high-order bit of the byte result. This cannot be detected directly by means of the condition codes. However, one possible way to catch the error is as follows. Zero extend A and B to *words* and then use

$$\text{MULW3} \quad \text{A,B,C}$$

Now check the high-order byte of the result, C. If it is nonzero, a carry out of the high-order bit of the product occurred.

8.5.4.   ^X80

8.5.5.   **(a)** Quotient = 0001; remainder = 0025

           (c) Quotient = 0002; remainder = 01C8

           (e) Quotient = FFFF; remainder = C327

8.5.6.   None, except for possible effects on the condition codes.

8.5.7.

```
ADDL   OCTA1,OCTA2
ADWC   OCTA1+4,OCTA2+4
ADWC   OCTA1+8,OCTA2+8
ADWC   OCTA1+12,OCTA2+12
```

8.5.8.

```
MOVL   QUAD2+4,QUAD3+4
ADDL3  QUAD1,QUAD2,QUAD3
ADWC   QUAD1+4,QUAD3+4
```

8.5.11.

```
INCL   QUAD
ADWC   #0,QUAD+4
```

8.6.1.   **(a)**

```
BICL   #^X01004808,R5
BISL   #^X00202504,R5
```

8.6.2.   The ASCII code for a digit between 0 and 9 consists of 0011 in the high-order nibble and the digit itself in the low-order nibble.

8.6.4.

```
BICL   #^XFFFF0000,R6
BICL   #^X0000FFFF,R10
BISL   R10,R6
```

8.6.6.

```
MOVZxy   A,B
```

can be written as

```
BICy   #-1,B
BISx   A,B
```

8.6.8. Exchanges the contents of R1 and R2.

8.6.11. ROTL #16,R*n*,R*n*

8.6.12.

```
INPUT:   .BLKL   1               ;Number input here

START:   .WORD   0               ;Program entry point
         $I.4H   INPUT           ;Get 32-bit number
         CLRL    R0              ;Clear bit counter
         MOVL    #32,R1          ;  and set loop counter
LOOP:    BLBC    INPUT,ROTATE    ;Skip if low bit clear
         INCL    R0              ;  else increment bit counter
ROTATE:  ROTL    #1,INPUT,INPUT  ;Rotate left 1 bit
         DECL    R1              ;  and decrement loop counter
         BNEQ    LOOP            ;Branch to LOOP if more bits
         $0.4D   R0              ;  else print bit count
         $0.NL                   ;  (and "new line")
         $EXIT                   ;  and EXIT

         .END    START
```

8.6.14. A number is *even* or *odd* if, and only if, its low-order bit is *clear* or *set*, respectively.

8.6.15. (a) Bit 4 of 0094AC5C
      (b) Bit 0 of 00000A14
      (c) Bit 2 of 0094ACE6

8.7.1. (a) 6   (b) 3

8.7.2. (a) 15   (b) 5

8.7.3. (a) Eventually, c(R4) is decremented (by TSTW) to $+32767$, which is not less than 51.
      (b) Eventually, c(R7) will be incremented to the largest negative integer, and the loop will terminate at that point.

8.7.6. LOOP is out of range of the *byte* displacement generated by SOBGTR. SOBGTR can be replaced by ACB, which generates a *word* displacement. Another repair is to place the following construction at, say, 0380.

```
029A  LOOP:            .

0380              BRB      BTSTRAP+2
0382  BTSTRAP:    BRB      LOOP
0384                       .

0427              SOBGTR   R7,BTSTRAP
```

8.10.1. (a)

```
                  CLRL     R5
        SEARCH:   BBCS     R5,MAP,FOUND
                  AOBLSS   #24,R5,SEARCH
        ERROR:
                           .

        FOUND:
```

8.10.4. Suppose that the longword in question is called X. If $X = 0$, then it does *not* satisfy the stated condition. Thus suppose that $X \neq 0$. The stated condition is true if, and only if,

$$X = X \text{ AND } -X$$

(Why?)

8.10.6. (a)

```
NUM:     .BLKB    1                      ;8-bit unsigned number
NUMW:    .BLKW    1                      ;16-bit work area
START:   .WORD    0                      ;Program entry point
         ;
         $I.1H    NUM                    ;Get 8-bit number
         MOVZBW   NUM,NUMW               ;  and convert to word
         CLRL     R1                     ;Clear index
DIVIDE:  DIVW3    POW10[R1],NUMW,R0      ;Divide by power of 10,
         BISB     #^X30,R0               ;  make it ASCII code
         MOVB     R0,CODE[R1]            ;  and put in string
         BICB     #^X30,R0               ;Restore quotient,
         MULW     POW10[R1],R0           ;  multiply by power of 10
         SUBW     R0,NUMW                ;  and get remainder
         AOBLEQ   #2,R1,DIVIDE           ;Do next power of 10
         $0.STR   CODE                   ;Done -- print string
         $0.NL                           ;  (and "new line")
         $EXIT                           ;  and EXIT
         ;
CODE:    .BLKB    3                      ;ASCII code goes here
         .BYTE    0                      ;(For printing purposes)
POW10:   .WORD    100,10,1               ;1st 3 powers of 10
         ;
         .END     START
```

9.1.1.

```
         CLRL     R5                     ;Initialize array index
LOOP1:   MOVL     #6,R4                  ;Set column counter
LOOP2:   $0.2D    ARRAY[R5]              ;Print array entry
         AOBLEQ   #35,R5,CONTIN          ;  and adjust index
         $EXIT                           ;EXIT if all entries printed
CONTIN:  SOBGTR   R4,LOOP2               ;  else print 6 entries
         $0.NL                           ;Then print a "new line"
         BRB      LOOP1                  ;  and print next line
```

9.2.1. As it stands, the

$$\text{MOVL} \quad \text{R8,PC}$$

instruction will return to the

$$\text{JMP} \quad \text{PRINT}$$

instruction. What is required is that, prior to "returning," the number of bytes occupied by the

$$JMP \quad PRINT$$

instruction must be added to c(R8).

9.2.2. (R8) is *not* a valid addressing mode for BRB or BRW.

9.2.3. Some register other than R6 would then have to be used to hold the array address.

9.3.2.

```
        MOVAW   ARRAY,R6        ;Put ARRAY address in R6
        MOVL    #N,R4           ;  and array size in R4
        MOVAB   NEXT,R8         ;Put return address in R8
        JMP     PRINT           ;  and jump to PRINT
NEXT:   <next instruction>
        .
        .
        .
PRINT:  MOVL    R4,R5           ;Copy size for column count
LOOP1:  MOVL    R5,R7           ;Set column counter
LOOP2:  $O.2D   (R6)+           ;Print a row entry
        SOBGTR  R7,LOOP2        ;Print next row entry
        $O.NL                   ;  else generate "new line"
        SOBGTR  R4,LOOP1        ;Reset column counter and
                                ;  print next row
                                ;  else done printing array

        JMP     (R8)            ;Resume "mainline" execution
                                ;  (return address in R8)
```

9.4.2.

```
        BGEQ    = ^X13          ;Code for 'BGEQ'
        BLEQ    = ^X15          ;Code for 'BLEQ'

MIN:    MOVB    #BLEQ,BRANCH    ;Insert 'BLEQ' code in
                                ;  branch instruction
        BRB     BEGIN           ;  and skip around entry point

MAX:    MOVB    #BGEQ,BRANCH    ;Insert 'BGEQ' code in
                                ;  branch instruction

BEGIN:  MOVL    R1,R0           ;Copy 1st number and
        CMPL    R0,R2           ;  compare against 2nd number
BRANCH: BRB     RETURN          ;Return if R0 was correctly set
                                ;  (NOTE! BRB replaced by BGEQ
                                ;  or BLEQ, at entry point MAX
                                ;  or MIN)

        MOVL    R2,R0           ;Replace R0 if not correctly set

RETURN: JMP     (R8)            ;Return to calling routine
```

9.4.3. Control will return to location XCHNG in the subroutine SORT, rather than to the calling routine.

9.5.2.

```
MAX1:    .BLKL   1              ;Return address goes here
         MOVAL   @MAX1,R1       ;Get return address
         MOVL    (R1)+,R0       ;  and put 1st number in R0
         CMPL    R0,(R1)        ;Compare 1st number with 2nd
         BGEQ    RETURN         ;  and return if larger
         MOVL    (R1),R0        ;Else replace R0 with 2nd number
RETURN:  ADDL    #8,MAX1        ;Adjust return address to take two
                                ;  longwords into account
         JMP     @MAX1          ;Return
```

9.6.1.

```
PUSH_STACK:   SUBL   #4,STKPTR
              MOVL   ???,@STKPTR

POP_STACK:    MOVL   @STKPTR,???
              ADDL   #4,STKPTR
```

9.6.2. If $c(R6) = $ BLOCK, the stack is full;
if $c(R6) = $ BLOCK $+ 400$, the stack is empty.

9.6.3. (a) 100   (b) 100   (c) 100
(d) The R10 stack is empty if $c(R10) = $ BLOCK;
the R11 stack is empty if $c(R11) = $ BLOCK $+ 400$.
(e) Either stack is full if $c(R10) = c(R11)$.

9.6.4. (a) $c(R3) = $ EF930482
$c(R4) = $ 000026A7
$c(R5) = $ AF004CC4
(c) $c(R3) = $ 00000482
$c(R4) = $ FFFFEF93
$c(R5) = $ 000026A7
(e) $c(R3) = $ FFFFFF82
$c(R4) = $ A7EF9304
$c(R5) = $ 00000026

9.7.1. (R7) is *not* a valid addressing mode for BSBB or BSBW.

9.7.3. SUBR can access ARG by referring to 4(SP). Prior to returning, SUBR can execute

```
MOVL   (SP)+,(SP)
```

to overlay ARG with the proper return address.

9.7.4. To jump to the subroutine, use

```
JSB   @4(SP)
```

To clear the stack:

```
MOVL   (SP)+,4(SP)
TSTL   (SP)+
RSB
```

9.7.6. **(a)** If the return address is copied into, say, R4 with

$$\text{MOVL} \quad (\text{SP}),\text{R4}$$

then the address of the longword containing ARGK can be referenced as

$$\langle 4*K - 2 \rangle(\text{R4})$$

(c) The address of the BRB instruction is on the top of the stack when SUBR is entered; the second byte of that instruction is four times the number of arguments.

9.8.1. **(a)** 0094   **(b)** 2607   **(c)** 0094   **(d)** 0000

9.8.2. **(a)** Push the longword whose address is in R8 on the stack, and increment c(R8) by 4.

(c) Push the address of the word whose address is in the longword whose address is in R8 onto the stack, and increment c(R8) by 4.

(e) Decrement c(R8) by 2, and then push the address of the word whose address is in R8 onto the stack.

9.9.3. Each longword argument might be preceded by a (longword) code, say 0 or 1, to indicate whether the argument is an address or a value.

10.3.3. The main module would be loaded at 00000874.

10.4.1. **(a)**   16
00000000′
The PC displacement to EXSUB, as calculated by the linker, is added to 00000000, the sum replacing the longword 00000000′.

(c)   16
FFFFFFFC′
The PC displacement to EXSUB, as calculated by the linker, is added to FFFFFFFC (-4), the sum replacing the longword FFFFFFFC′.

(g)   16
0000′
The PC displacement to EXSUB, as calculated by the linker, is truncated to a word and added to 0000, the sum replacing the word 0000′.

10.4.4. **(a)** PLA(MOD1) = 00000200;
PLA(MOD2) = 0000020E

(b) 00000204

(e) 00708F27

10.5.2.

```
                    .EXTERNAL  DAYS
                    ;
        MONTH:      .BLKB      1
                    ;
        START:      .WORD      ^M<>
                    $I.1D      MONTH
                    MOVZBL     MONTH,R0
                    $0.1D      DAYS-1[R0]
                    $EXIT
                    .END       START
```

11.4.1. No user program, or any component of it, can be located by the linker at 00000000.

11.4.2. Exception handling is active *only if* the Frame Pointer is pointing at a nonzero address.

11.4.4. (a) 0, since no exception handling has been established by the routine ERROR.

(c) Frame Pointer of the routine executing at the time the exception occurred. (This is the routine EVAL.)

(f) The Frame Pointer of the routine (EVAL) which established this routine (ERROR) as a condition handler.

(j) The PC at the time of the mainline's call to EVAL—the return-from-EVAL program counter.

11.6.1. The exception *is* resignalled, but since the mainline is the *current* condition handler establisher, the resignaling causes a search for a *lower*-level handler—in this case the default handler established by the operating system. (The keys here are the FP of the current establisher—the mainline—and the *depth argument*.)

11.6.2. The second sequence resets PC to the exception PC. REI pops the stack into the PC and PSL and thus has the effect of the first sequence. However, there are differences; for example, the second sequence does *not* restore the contents of R0 and R1.

12.4.2. $.00001_2 = .03125_{10}$ and $111.1_2 = 7.5_{10}$

12.4.3. There is none.

12.4.6. Exponent overflows can then be detected with a BITB instruction, followed by a conditional branch of the form BGEQ or BLSS.

12.4.7. For example, 01111000 will test as being *larger* than 00111000, even though these are the FPF-1 representations of $.01_2 = .25_{10}$ and $100.0_2 = 4.0_{10}$, respectively.

12.7.1. (a) 0 110 1001 + 0 101 0001 = 0 111 0000
(d) 0 101 1000 + 1 100 1110 = 0 100 0010

12.7.2. (a) 0 110 1001 + 0 101 0001 = 0 111 0001
(d) 0 101 1000 + 1 100 1110 = 0 100 0010

12.9.1. (a) 00004148;
00000000 00004148;
00000000 00004029;
00000000 00000000 00000000 90004002

12.9.2. (a) -1.25 (c) 9,646,899,200

12.12.2. (a) 72.0   (b) 1.875   (d) 26.0

12.12.3. (a) ˆX17; 3.75   (c) ˆX27; 15.0   (e) ˆX00; 0.5

13.2.1. (a) 34 37 32 31 20   (b) 34 37 32 31 2D

13.2.2. (a) 100249   (b) -7000

13.3.1. (a) 34 37 32 31   (b) 74 37 32 31

13.3.2. (a) 100249   (b) -7004

13.3.3. (a) 44 37 32 31   (b) 4D 37 32 31

13.3.4. (a) 100249   (b) -7008

13.4.1. (a) 4C 27 01   (b) 4D 27 01

13.4.2. (a) 0030274   (b) -274

13.5.1. (a) 1C 38 42 07   (b) 1C 38 42 07 00
(c) Decimal overflow

14.1.1.

```
INSTR:   .WORD   ^M<R1>            ;Save c(R1)
         MOVAB   @8(AP),R1         ;Get input string address
GETCHR:  $I.CHR  (R1)+             ;Get characters as long as
         SOBGTR  4(AP),GETCHR      ; character count > 0
         RET                       ;Return
```

14.2.4. The CMPC instructions may be used for comparing collections of bytes of any kind, not simply those representing ASCII coded characters. If the bytes are interpreted by the user as being *unsigned* 8-bit numbers, the carry indicator, in conjunction with the other condition codes, will yield useful information.

14.3.6. "What hath God wrought?"

15.2.1. (a) 1111100   (c) 1111100
        (d) 00010   (f) 110010001000110101011

15.2.2. (a) B = QUAD, P = 21, S = 6; B = QUAD + 3, P = -3, S = 6
        (e) B = QUAD + 7, P = 1, S = 6; B = QUAD, P = 57, S = 6

15.3.1.

```
                    .
                    .
                    .
             MOVL    #31,R9
LOOP:        EXTZV   R9,#1,R2,R3
             $O.CHR  TABLE[R3]
             ACBL    #0,#-1,R9,LOOP
                    .
                    .
TABLE:       .ASCII  /01/
```

15.3.3. (a) 00000017   (c) 00000001
        (d) FFFFFC2F   (e) 00000821

15.3.5. (a) Branch is not executed.
        (c) Branch is not executed.
        (h) Branch is executed.

15.3.6. (a) AA7F   (c) A9BF

15.3.7. (a) $c(R5)$ = 00000001; $c(Z)$ = 0
        (c) $c(R5)$ = 00000007; $c(Z)$ = 0
        (e) $c(R5)$ = 0000000F; $c(Z)$ = 1

16.1.2.

```
INDEX:    .WORD   ^M<>            ;Save no registers
          MOVAL   @8(AP),R0       ;Get list address
          BRB     LOOPEND         ;Start by decrementing index
LOOP:     MOVAL   @(R0),R0        ;Get pointer to next entry
          BNEQ    LOOPEND         ;Actual entry if pointer nonNIL
          BISB    4(FP)           ; else set user's C-bit
          RET                     ; and return
LOOPEND:  SOBGTR  4(AP),LOOP      ;Decrement index and check entry
          RET                     ;Return -- R0 points at entry
```

16.1.3. **(a)** No programming module, and thus no list entry, will be located by the linker at 00000000.

(b) No, for in this case NIL will be *relocated* by the linker to a nonzero value.

16.2.2. The required level of deferment is one greater than what can be achieved directly. RET will clean the stack.

17.1.1. Evaluates the polynomial $1 \cdot x^4 - 2 \cdot x^3 + 4 \cdot x^2 + 6$.

17.5.4. Any memory block in an overlaid program section which is *not* of the same length in two modules that reference it must appear at the end of the section in order to maintain the proper sizes and positions of the other memory blocks in the program section.

17.5.6. The additional 3 bytes result from the linker's use of longword alignment.

17.5.7. No, since BYTE is the default attribute.

18.4.4. **(b)**

```
        LOOP:  MNEGL  R2,R3     (d) :  MNEGL  R2
               DECL   R1               DECL   R1
               BRB    LOOP             BRB
```

18.5.1. .LONG, without an argument, will be treated as if it were

$$\text{.LONG} \quad 0.$$

18.5.2. ARGLIST A1=1,A2=2; ARGLIST 1,2

18.6.2. .LONG A'B; .LONG A'

18.6.3. **(a)** John's cat   **(c)** Chris' cat

18.8.2. BIGGER 1,2,3 expands as

```
                    MOVL   R1,R3
                    CMPL   R1,R2
                    BGEQ   L30000$
                    MOVL   R2,R3
          L30000$:
```

There are no local labels.

18.9.1. No.

18.9.2. The "12" in "ARG12" would be treated by .IRPC as *two* arguments, "1" and "2".

18.9.5. **(a)** Cats

(d) The error message "Too many arguments in MACRO call"

(f) Cats & Dogs

18.10.5. In general, the *assembler* will not be able to determine the value or sign of the argument that represents the rotate count.

18.12.1. The "B" in

$$\text{.IIF} \quad \text{B, X, .MEXIT}$$

will be replaced by the actual argument. In a similar fashion, the "R" in

$$\text{PUSH} \quad \text{R'X}$$

will be replaced by the actual argument.

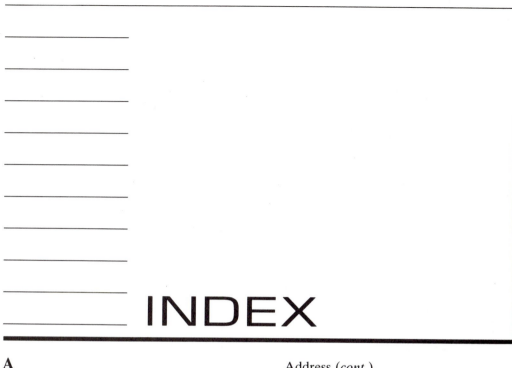

INDEX

A

Absolute mode, 182
ACB, 228
Access mode (*See* Mode)
Access type, 198, 571
   address, 198, 572
   branch displacement, 198, 572
   modified, 198, 572
   read-only, 198, 571
   variable bit field, 198, 572
   written-only, 198, 572
Access violation, 359
Actual argument, 514
Actual parameter, 514
ADD, 206
Adder, 50
   full, 50
   half, 49
ADDP4, 419
ADDP6, 419
.ADDRESS, 230
Address, 59, 72
   assembly load, 344

Address (*cont.*)
   base, 224
   byte, 59, 60
   load, 122
   longword, 61, 73
   octaword, 62
   physical load, 344
   quadword, 62
   return, 248
   start, 139, 233, 341, 346, 353
   symbolic, 123
   transfer, 139, 233, 341, 346, 353
   word, 61, 73
Address access type, 198, 572
Address alignment, 72
Address boundary, 72
Addressing
   indirect, 153
Addressing mode (*See also* Mode)
   program counter, 175
Addressing scheme, 59
   ambiguity of, 63
ADWC, 213
ALA (*See* Assembly Load Address)

.ALIGN, 494
Alignment attribute, 494
Alignment
  address, 72
Allocation map, 501
ALU (*See* Arithmetic-Logic Unit)
AND, 39, 216
AND-gate, 46–7
AOBLEQ, 227
AOBLSS, 227
AP (*See* Argument Pointer)
Argument, 253, 288
  actual, 514
  concatenation of, 523–24
  default, 520
  elided, 520
  formal, 514, 522
  keyword, 523
  macroinstruction, 513
Argument list, 294, 297, 326
  general, 294, 303, 326
  stacked, 297, 303, 326
  standard, 326
Argument pointer, 294, 298, 300, 303, 306
Argument table, 288–89
Argument transmission, 253, 288
  by address, 297, 326
  by name, 297, 326
  by reference, 297, 326
  by value, 297, 326
Arithmetic exception, 366
Arithmetic shift operator (@), 629
Arithmetic-logic unit, 5
.ASCIC, 231
.ASCII, 231
ASCII code, 65
.ASCIZ, 231
ASH, 218
ASHP, 419
Assembler, 134
  one-pass, 194 (*Exercise 7.6.12*)
Assembler directive, 139, 230, 630
Assembly
  conditional, 545, 553
  program, 127
Assembly language program, 127

Assembly load address, 129, 342, 344
Assignment
  direct, 318
Attributes
  program section, 492–93, 497
Autodecrement mode, 158
Autoincrement deferred mode, 160
Autoincrement mode, 155
Automatically generated local label, 535

B

B, 548
Backward link, 475
Backward pointer, 475
Base, 13
Base address, 224, 447
BBC, 223
BBCC, 223
BBCS, 223
BBS, 223
BBSC, 223
BBSS, 223
BCD (*See* Binary-Coded Decimal)
Biased exponent, 386, 398
BIC, 215
BICPSW, 218
Bidirectional linked list, 475
Binary point, 378
Binary representation system, 15
Binary-coded decimal, 412
BIS, 214
BISPSW, 218
Bistable device, 10
BIT, 222
Bit, 18
  Carry (*See* Carry bit)
  exponent, 380
  guard, 391
  hidden, 387, 398
  high-order, 18
  least-significant, 18, 56
  low-order, 18
  magnitude, 380
  most-significant, 18, 56
  Negative (*See* Negative bit)

Bit (*cont.*)
  Overflow (*See* Overflow bit)
  sign, 21
  trace, 306
  Zero (*See* Zero bit)
Bit field (*See* Variable bit field)
Bit offset, 447
Bit operation, 214
Bitmap, 456
. BLANK ., 491
BLBC, 222
BLBS, 222
.BLKB, 232
.BLKD, 401
.BLKF, 401
.BLKG, 401
.BLKH, 401
.BLKL, 232
.BLKO, 232
.BLKQ, 232
.BLKW, 232
Boolean algebra, 40
Boolean relations, 41
Borrow, 20
Boundary, 72
  address, 72
  natural, 73
Branch, 85, 89
  conditional, 91–92, 205–6
  unconditional, 91, 205
Branch displacement access type, 198, 572
Branch instruction, 85
BRB, 205
BRW, 205
BSBB, 284
BSBW, 284
Bubble sort, 244 (*Exercise 8.10.2*), 318
Buffer
  instruction, 83
Bus, 2, 5
  address, 5, 72
  control, 5, 72
  data, 5
.BYTE, 125, 233
Byte, 56
  high-order, 61

Byte (*cont.*)
  low-order, 61
  mode, 150
  NUL, 426
Byte address, 59–60
BYTE attribute (program section), 495

C

C (*See* Carry Indicator)
Call, 248, 507
CALL frame, 305, 307–9, 364–65
CALLG, 303–6, 309, 312
CALLS, 303, 310–11, 313
Capacitor, 9
Carry, 19, 28–29
  half-byte, 425 (*Exercise 13.6.1*)
Carry bit, 31, 51, 213–14
Carry indicator, 31
Central processing unit, 2, 4, 30
Channel, 75
Character, 65, 623, 635
  nonprinting, 635
  special, 65, 623
Character datatype, 64
Character set, 623
Character string, 65, 291, 426
  address of, 426
  length of, 426
Chopping (*See* Truncation)
Circuit
  parallel, 43
  series, 43
  switching, 42
Circular list, 479
CLR, 208
CMP, 229
CMPC3, 429
CMPC5, 430
CMPP3, 419
CMPP4, 419
CMPV, 452
CMPZV, 452
Code
  ASCII, 65

COMMON, 502
Communication device, 4
Complementary conditional, 548
Complementary routines, 259
Compound statement, 38
Computer, 1, 76
CON, 497
Concatenated registers, 151
Concatenation of arguments, 523–24
Condition codes, 30, 31, 91–92, 306
Condition handler, 361, 363, 365
Conditional
  complementary, 548
  immediate, 548
  unsatisfied, 550
Conditional assembly, 545, 553–54
Conditional block, 554
Conditional branch, 91–92, 205–6
Conjunction, 39
Connective, 38
Console terminal, 84
Continuation
  source line, 627
Control unit, 5
Coroutines, 259
Coupled inverter latch, 52
CPU (*See* Central Processing Unit)
CVT, 203
CVTLP, 416
CVTPL, 415
CVTPS, 417
CVTPT, 417
CVTSP, 417
CVTTP, 417–18
Cypher, 443 (*Exercise 14.3.6*)

D

Data, 7
Datatype, 63, 66
  character, 64
Datatype context, 63, 197, 199, 572
  operand descriptor, 199
Datatype descriptor access type, 198
DEC, 209

Decimal Adjust instruction, 425 (*Exercise 13.6.1*)
Decimal overflow, 308, 416
Decimal overflow trap, 416
Decimal representation system, 14, 59
Decode, 443 (*Exercise 14.3.6.*)
Decoder, 5
Default argument value, 520
Delimiter, 231
  string, 231
Dense list, 463
Depth argument, 362
Depth pointer, 372
Descriptor
  operand, 197, 571
Destination, 99, 119
Destructive read, 10–11
Device
  bistable, 10
  communication, 4
  peripheral, 2–4
  semiconductor, 11
  solid-state, 11
  storage (*See* Storage device)
DF, 552, 548
DIF, 548, 548
Direct assignment, 318
Directive
  assembler, 139, 230, 630
.DISABLE, 530–31
Disjunction, 39
Dispatcher
  exception, 361, 363
Displacement
  program counter, 87, 88
Displacement deferred mode, 168
Displacement mode, 163
DIV, 211
Divide-by-0, 359
DIVP, 419
.DOUBLE, 401
Double-byte (*See* Word)
Double-precision, 213–14
Double-word, 61
Dumpty, H., 301
DV (*See* Decimal oVerflow)

.D_FLOATING, 401
D_floating, 398–99
D_floating representation, 399

E

EDIV, 212
Electromagnet, 45
Elided argument, 520
EMUL, 210
.ENABLE, 530–31
Encode, 443 (*Exercise 14.3.6*)
.END, 139, 233, 341
.ENDC, 554
.ENDM, 508, 527, 544
.ENDR, 538, 544
.ENTRY, 144–45, 233, 305, 350
Entry point, 144, 248
   program, 144
   subroutine, 248
EQ, 548, 550
Equivalent statements, 41
Escape character, 437
Exception, 360–61, 367
   arithmetic, 366
   resignaled, 372
Exception dispatcher, 361, 363
Exception handler, 361, 363, 365, 369
   catch-all, 372
   default, 372
Exception service routine, 361
Excess-n, 386, 398
Exchange sort, 244 (*Exercise 8.10.2*)
EXCLUSIVE-OR, 39, 217
EXCLUSIVE-OR-gate, 47–48
Execution, 82
$EXIT, 139, 638
Expansion of macroinstruction, 507, 509
Exponent, 380, 398
   biased, 386, 398
Exponent bits, 380
.EXTERNAL, 340, 349
External reference, 347
External reference table, 347
External symbol, 142, 340

Externally defined symbol, 340
Extraction operators, 450
EXTV, 450
EXTZV, 450

F

Factorial, 270–71
False, 37–38
Fault, 360
Fetch, 78, 82–83
FFC, 454
FFS, 454
Fill character, 429–30, 436
Fixed-point number system, 376
Flip-flop, 55 (*Exercise 3.5.4*)
.FLOAT, 401
Floating-point input macroinstruction, 656
Floating-point output macroinstruction, 656
Floating underflow, 308
Floating-Point Format-1, 382
Floating-Point Format-2, 387
Floating-point number representation, 377, 381
   normalized, 387
Floating-point number system, 377, 381
Floating-point
   overflow, 402
   precision, 390
   range, 390
   rounding, 392
   truncation, 391
   underflow, 395, 402
   zero, 389
Forced immediate mode, 180
Formal argument, 514, 522
Formal parameter, 514
Forward link, 475
Forward pointer, 475
Forward reference, 109, 512
FP (*See* Frame Pointer)
FPF-1 (*See* Floating-Point Format-1)
FPF-2 (*See* Floating-Point Format-2)
Fraction, 398

Frame, 75
Frame (*See* CALL frame)
Frame pointer, 307–8, 362
FU (*See* Floating Underflow)
Full adder, 50
Function, 326
Function procedure, 326
.F_FLOATING, 401
F_floating, 398–99
F_floating representation, 399

G

Gate, 46–47
  AND, 46–47
  EXCLUSIVE-OR, 47–48
  NAND, 54 (*Exercise 3.4.6*)
  NOR, 54 (*Exercise 3.4.5*)
  NOT (*See* Inverter)
  OR, 46–47
GE, 548
General argument list, 294, 303, 326
.GLOBAL, 349
Global, 349
Global symbol, 349
Global symbol table, 349
GT, 548
Guard bits, 391
.G_FLOATING, 401
G_floating, 398, 400
G_floating representation, 400

H

Half-adder, 49
Half-byte, 61
Half-byte carry, 425 (*Exercise 13.6.1*)
HALT, 230
Hardware stack, 281
Head (of a list), 479
Header (in a linked list), 467
Hexadecimal representation system, 14,
  58–59
Hidden bit, 387, 398
High-order bit, 18
High-order byte, 61

Hollerith code, 442 (*Exercise 14.3.1*)
.H_FLOATING, 401
H_floating, 398, 400
H_floating representation, 400

I

$I.\langle bytes\rangle\langle format\rangle$, 643
$I.CHR, 640
$I.F, 656
$I.NL, 641
$I.STR, 640
IDN, 547–48
.IFF (*See* .IF_FALSE)
.IFT (*See* .IF_TRUE)
.IFTF (*See* .IF_TRUE_FALSE)
.IF_FALSE, 556
.IF_TRUE, 556–57
.IF_TRUE_FALSE, 556–57
.IIF, 547–48
Immediate conditional, 548
Immediate IF, 548
Immediate mode, 180
  forced, 180
IMPLIES, 53 (*Exercise 3.1.6.*)
INC, 208
Indefinite repeat block, 537–38, 543
Index, 226, 463
  list, 482
Index mode, 170
Indexed list, 482
Indirect addressing, 153
Information, 7
  stored, 8
Input macroinstruction, 640–41, 643
  floating-point, 656
Input prompt, 640
INSQUE, 477–78
Instruction, 70–71, 148
  reserved, 359
  stored, 76
Instruction buffer, 83
Instruction execution, 82–83
Instruction fetch, 78
INSV, 453
Integer overflow, 308, 359, 416

Inverter, 47
Invoke, 248, 507
.IRP, 537, 543
.IRPC, 543
Iterative routine, 328
IV (*See* Integer oVerflow)

J

JMP, 205
JSB, 283
Jump, 85, 89
Jump-to-subroutine, 283

K

Keyword argument, 523

L

Label, 124
   local, 528
Last-in/first-out, 270, 276
Latch, 52, 55 (*Exercise 3.5.4.*)
LE, 548
Leading separate numeric string, 408
   address of, 409
   length of, 409
Least-significant bit, 18, 56
LIFO (*See* Last-In/First-Out)
Linear list, 460
Link, 463
   backward, 475
   forward, 475
Linkage, 339
   fast, 327
   subroutine, 327
Linked list, 463
   bidirectional, 475
Linker, 352, 490–91, 501
Linker map, 501
List, 460, 482–83
   circular, 479
   dense, 463
   indexed, 482
   linear, 460

List(*cont.*)
   linked, 463
   multilinked, 483
List index, 482
Literal
   short, 137–38
Load address, 122
   assembly, 129, 342
   physical, 342
Load map, 501
Loader, 342
Loader-editor, 346
Loader-editor-linker, 352
Local block (*See* Local label block)
Local label, 528
   automatically generated, 535
Local label block, 528, 530
Local storage area, 322, 327
Local variable, 327
Location, 72
Location assignment counter (*See* Location counter)
Location counter, 129, 489, 626
LOCC, 431
Logic of statements, 38
Logical AND operator (&), 629
Logical EXCLUSIVE-OR operator ($\setminus$), 629
Logical operation, 38
Logical OR operator (!), 629
.LONG, 125, 233
LONG attribute (program section), 495
Longword, 61
Longword address, 61, 73
Loop, 225–28
Low-order bit, 18
Low-order byte, 61
LT, 548

M

Machine language program, 93, 105
.MACRO, 508
Macro (*See* Macroinstruction)
Macroassembler, 134

Macroinstruction, 138, 507
  expansion of, 507, 509
  floating-point input, 656
  floating-point output, 656
  input, 640, 643
  output, 638, 641
Macroinstruction argument, 513
Macroinstruction definition, 507
Macroinstruction prototype statement, 514
Magnetic core, 10
Magnitude, 21, 378, 380, 398
Magnitude bits, 21, 380
.MAIN., 234
Main store (*See* Memory)
Map
  allocation, 501
  linker, 501
Mask, 142, 144, 287, 304, 306, 439
MATCHC, 432
MCOM, 213
.MDELETE. 563 (*Exercise 18.4.3*)
Mechanism array, 362
Memory, 2–3, 17
  accessing, 72
  human, 8
  random access, 73
Memory address (*See* Address)
Memory cell, 11–12, 17
Memory location (*See* Location)
Memory unit, 12, 17, 56
.MEXIT, 558
MNEG, 212
Mnemonic, 119
Mode, 150, 189
  absolute, 182
  autodecrement, 158
  autoincrement, 155
  autoincrement deferred, 160
  displacement, 163
  displacement deferred, 168
  immediate, 180
  index, 170
  register, 152
  register deferred, 153
  relative, 184

Mode (*cont.*)
  relative deferred, 187
  short literal, 173–74, 402–3
Mode byte, 150
Modified access type, 198, 572
Modifier
  logical, 40
Module, 339
Most-significant bit, 18, 56
MOV, 200
MOVA, 200
MOVC3, 428
MOVC5, 428
MOVP, 419
MOVTC, 436
MOVTUC, 437
MOVZ, 202
MUL, 209
MULP, 419
Multilinked list, 483

N

N (*See* Negative indicator)
NAND-gate, 54 (*Exercise 3.4.6*)
Natural address boundary, 73
NB, 548
NDF, 548, 552
NE, 548
Negative bit, 30
Negative indicator, 30
Nested subroutine call, 258, 314–15
Nibble, 61
NIL pointer, 464
Noise, 7
Nonprinting character, 635
NOP, 230
NOR-gate, 54 (*Exercise 3.4.5*)
Normalization, 387
Normalized floating-point representation, 387
.NOSHOW, 510, 560
.NOSHOW CND, 560
.NOSHOW ME, 510
NOT, 40

NOT-gate (*See* Inverter)
NOWRT, 493
NUL byte, 426
Number, 12
Number representation, 13, 57
  binary, 15
  decimal, 14, 59
  floating-point, 377, 381
  hexadecimal, 14, 58–59
  octal, 58
  ones-complement, 23
  sign-magnitude, 21, 381
  sign-magnitude floating-point, 381
  twos-complement, 28
Number representation system
  base of, 13
Number system, 18–20
  fixed-point, 376
  floating-point, 377, 381
  signed, 20
  unsigned, 22
Numeric string, 408
  leading separate, 408
  packed decimal, 413
  trailing, 411

O

$O.1H, 138
$O.⟨*bytes*⟩⟨*format*⟩, 642
$O.CHR, 638
$O.F, 656
$O.NL, 138, 638
$O.STR, 638
Object file, 135, 338, 351, 354–55
Object program, 135
.OCTA, 234
Octal representation system, 58
Octaword, 62
Octaword address, 62
One-pass assembler, 194 (*Exercise 7.6.12*)
Ones-complement, 23
Operand, 71, 78–80, 83, 148
  reserved, 359, 574

Operand access mode (*See* Mode)
Operand descriptor, 197, 571
Operand descriptor datatype context, 199
Operand specifier, 81, 149–51
Operating system, 135
Operation, 70–71, 148
  logical, 38
Operator
  arithmetic shift (@), 629
  logical AND (&), 629
  logical EXCLUSIVE-OR (\), 629
  logical OR (!), 629
  unary, 626–27
OR, 39, 216
OR-gate, 46–47
Output macroinstruction, 638
  floating-point, 656
Overflow, 383
  decimal, 308, 416
  floating-point, 402
  integer, 308, 359, 416
  stack, 281
Overflow bit, 31, 51
Overflow indicator, 31
Overpunch numeric format, 411
OVR, 497, 502

P

.PACKED, 419
Packed decimal numeric string, 413
  address of, 413
  length of, 413
PAGE attribute (program section), 495
Paper tape, 75
Parallel circuit, 43
Parameter, 253, 288
  actual, 514
  formal, 514
PC (*See* Program Counter)
Peripheral device, 2–4
Permanent symbol, 625
Physical load address, 342, 344
PLA (*See* Physical Load Address)

Pointer, 276, 463
  argument, 294, 298, 300, 303, 306
  backward, 475
  depth, 372
  forward, 475
  frame, 307
  NIL, 464
  stack, 276
"points at", 77, 99
Pop, 276
POPR, 287
Position independent, 134, 186, 355
Precision
  floating-point, 390
Predecessor, 276
  stack, 276
Predecessor (in a linked list), 463, 475
Primary storage, 3
Procedure, 326
  function, 326
Processor (*See* Central processing unit)
Processor status, 5, 91
Processor status longword, 91, 97
Processor status word, 91–92, 97, 306
Program, 75
  assembly language, 127
  machine language, 93, 105
  object, 135
  source, 135
Program assembly, 127
Program counter, 78, 98
Program counter addressing mode, 175
Program counter displacement, 87–88
Program entry mask word, 136, 142, 144, 308
Program entry point, 144
Program section, 486
Program section attributes, 492–93, 497
Program section name, 486, 495
Prompt
  input, 640
Prototype statement, 514
.PSECT, 486, 493, 531
PSL (*See* Processor Status Longword)
PSW (*See* Processor Status Word)
Public register, 77

Push, 276
PUSHA, 286
PUSHL, 286
PUSHR, 287

Q

.QUAD, 234
QUAD attribute (program section), 495
Quadword, 62
Quadword address, 62
Queue, 479

R

RAM (*See* Random Access Memory)
Random access memory, 73
Range
  floating-point, 390
Read, 10
  destructive, 10–11
Read signal, 72
Read-only access type, 198, 571
Reciprocal routines, 259
Recursion, 270, 327
Recursive routine, 327
Register, 4, 77, 97–99
  concatenated, 151
  private, 4
  processor, 77
  public, 4, 77, 98
Register deferred mode, 153
Register mode, 152
REI, 370
Relative deferred mode, 187
Relative mode, 184
Relay, 45
Relocation, 134, 344, 355
  program, 134
Relocation sensitive, 134, 186, 343–44, 551
Relocation table, 346
REMQUE, 477–78
.REPEAT, 544
Repeat block, 537, 543
  indefinite, 537–38, 543

Repeat count, 627
Reserved instruction, 359
Reserved operand, 359, 416, 574
Resignaled exception, 362, 372
RET, 307–9, 311, 314
Return address, 248
Rotate, 221
ROTL, 221
Rounding
  floating-point, 392
Routine, 248
  complementary, 259
  exception service, 361
  iterative, 328
  reciprocal, 259
  recursive, 327
RSB, 283

S

SBWC, 214
Scaling, 383
Scaling factor, 378
SCANC, 438
Scientific notation, 378
Selection sort, 244 (*Exercise 8.10.3*)
Series circuit, 43
Shift, 218–20
Short literal, 137–38, 173–74, 402–3
Short literal mode, 173–74, 402–3
.SHOW, 510
.SHOW ME, 510
Side effect, 156
Sign bit, 21
Sign extend, 86, 203
Sign magnitude number representation, 381
Sign-magnitude, 21
Sign-magnitude floating-point number representation, 381
Signal
  read, 72
Signal array, 361
Signal name, 361, 366
Signed number system, 20

SKPC, 432
SOBGEQ, 226
SOBGTR, 226
Sort, 244 (*Exercise 8.10.2*)
Source, 99, 119
Source file, 135, 338
Source line continuation, 627
Source program, 135
SP (*See* Stack Pointer)
SPA (*See* Stack Pointer Alignment)
SPANC, 439
Special character, 65, 623
SS$_ARTRES, 366
SS$_CONTINUE, 370
SS$_RESIGNAL, 371
Stack, 274–77
  hardware, 281
Stack alignment block, 305
Stack area, 277, 308
Stack cleanup, 300–301, 312
Stack cleanup by RET, 312
Stack entry, 276
Stack overflow, 281
Stack pointer, 276, 281
Stack pointer alignment, 306, 310
Stack underflow, 281
Stacked argument list, 297, 303, 326
Standard argument list, 326
Start address, 139, 233, 341, 346
Statement, 37–38
  compound, 38
Status
  processor, 5, 91
Storage (*See* Memory)
Storage device, 9
  bulk, 4
  primary, 3
  secondary, 4
Stored instruction, 76
String, 65, 291
  character, 65, 291, 426
String delimiter, 231
SUB, 207
Subconditional, 556
SUBP4, 419
SUBP6, 419

Subroutine, 248
  call, 248
  invoke, 248
  nested, 258, 314–15
  recursive, 270
  transmitting arguments to, 253, 288
Subroutine entry mask word, 304, 306
Subroutine entry point, 248
Subroutine linkage, 327
Subroutine return, 248, 274, 283
Subscript, 463
Successor, 276
  stack, 276
Successor (in a linked list), 463, 475
Switch, 42
  closed, 42
  open, 42
Switch value, 42
Switching circuit, 42
Symbol
  external, 142, 340
  global, 349
  permanent, 625
  user-defined, 625
Symbol table, 129, 141
Symbolic address, 123
System Control Block, 361

T

Table
  argument, 288–89
  external reference, 347
  global symbol, 349
  relocation, 346
  symbol, 129, 141
  translation, 418, 435–39
  truth, 39
Tail (of a list), 479
Tape channel, 75
Tape frame, 75
Tape
  paper, 75
Terminal, 4
  console, 84

Terminal list entry, 464
.TITLE, 234
Trace bit, 306
Trailing numeric string, 411
  address of, 412
  length of, 412
Transfer address, 139, 233, 341, 346, 353
Translation table, 418, 435–39
Transmit
  by address, 297, 326
  by name, 297, 326
  by reference, 297, 326
  by value, 297, 326
Trap, 360–61
  decimal overflow, 416
Trap enable flags, 91, 142
Trap sequence, 361
True, 37–38
Truncation, 203
  floating-point, 391
Truth table, 39
Truth value, 38
TST, 230
Twos-complement, 26–27

U

Unary operator, 626–27
Unconditional branch, 91, 205
Underflow, 395
  floating-point, 308, 395, 402
  stack, 281
Unsatisfied conditional, 550
Unsigned number system, 22
User-defined symbol, 625

V

V (*See* oVerflow indicator)
Value
  switch, 42
  truth, 38
Variable bit field, 224

Variable bit field access type, 198
Variable length bit field, 447
  base address of, 447
  length of, 447
  position in, 447
  size of, 447
VAX-11, 1

W

.WORD, 125, 234
Word, 18, 61
Word address, 61, 73
WORD attribute (program section), 495
Write, 10

Written-only access type, 198, 572
WRT, 493

X

XOR, 217

Z

Z (*See* Zero indicator)
Zero
  floating-point, 389
Zero bit, 31
Zero extend, 202
Zero indicator, 31
Zoned numeric format, 411